New Critical Approaches to
the Short Stories of
Ernest Hemingway

D1604159

Michael Reynolds — Critical Essays — In our Time

New Critical Approaches to

the Short Stories of

ERNEST HEMINGWAY

Edited by Jackson J. Benson

With an Overview Essay by Paul Smith
and a Comprehensive Checklist to the Criticism, 1975–1990

Duke University Press   *Durham and London 1990*

For Charles M. Oliver
editor of the *Hemingway Review,* whose vision
and tireless effort have raised the standards of
Hemingway scholarship and provided the information
and tools which have benefited us all

Contents

●

II Story Technique and Themes

III Story Interpretations

IV An Overview of the Criticism

V A Comprehensive Checklist of Hemingway Short Fiction Criticism, Explication, and Commentary, 1975–1989

*Essay written for this volume

Acknowledgments

The publication of this volume has been made possible by the generosity of the authors of the essays, and I am grateful to them and to the editors and publishers of the publications in which many of these essays originally appeared for their permissions. I have a particular debt of gratitude to Paul Smith who not only wrote the fine survey of criticism which is the centerpiece of this collection, but who also made many suggestions regarding the contents and reviewed the checklist in great detail. Finally, I would like to thank Anne Hunsinger and JoAnne Zebroski, fine teachers, writers, and researchers in their own right, for their years of work in assembling, arranging, and editing the extensive checklist at the end of this volume—heroines both.

Introduction

●

This volume is an all-new sequel to a previous collection, *The Short Stories of Ernest Hemingway: Critical Essays*, which was published in 1975. While a few of the essays here were originally published in the late 1970s, most were published in the 1980s and many in the last few years. In the first volume the "Comprehensive Checklist" (which broke new ground by listing the criticism by story) attempted to include all of the short story criticism, in English, from the beginning through the first part of 1975. The checklist at the end of this volume attempts to list all of the short story criticism from and including 1975 (not previously listed) up to early 1990. In doing so the checklist becomes the first comprehensive bibliography of Hemingway secondary materials published since Audre Hanneman published her *Supplement to Ernest Hemingway: A Comprehensive Bibliography* in 1975.

In my introduction I spoke of the checklist in the first volume as "a monster which has haunted and nearly overcome its creator." With this new compilation, the monster became nearly unmanageable, as I and several assistants over three years struggled with a body of Hemingway short story criticism that had grown enormous. All of the articles published in all the years prior to 1975 are roughly equal in number to those published in the decade following, and the output in the last decade is nearly double that of the preceding decade. The process of selecting the essays for this volume involved reading, evaluating, and segregating by type and topic nearly four hundred essays, published as articles or in books, from which we have been able to publish twenty-eight (plus five written just for this collection and the overview essay). Obviously, for reasons of space and distribution of topic a good many excellent essays had to be omitted.

There are a number of reasons for the immense growth of Hemingway short story criticism. Most important, I think, has been the recognition in recent years that, despite the continued popularity of several of his novels, the short stories are Hemingway's great contribution to our literature. In addition, the antagonism inspired by the Hemingway public persona, which had turned many academics and critics against his work, has gradually, nearly three decades after his death in 1961, dissipated. Indeed, the change in the author's standing has been dramatic, although it has come so gradually over the last two decades that few have stood back and commented on it.

Those of us who have written about the author for many years, however, can feel a definite shift in the atmosphere. A good number of bright young scholars are devoting some or all of their attention to Hemingway research, many more women have become involved, and several older, well-established scholars are coming back or turning to Hemingway studies for the first time. Clearly, it is no longer an embarrassment in intellectual circles to be identified as someone who has written about Hemingway, and suddenly those who write about him no longer feel the need to be as defensive of their subject as they once were.

Beyond the elevation of Hemingway's status and the new talent this has attracted, there are other reasons why the short story criticism has not only expanded, but improved in quality from what in the mid-1970s appeared to be a criticism that was becoming sterile, ingrown, and repetitious. Perhaps the most important of these has been the availability, in the mid-1970s, of the Hemingway papers, first in temporary quarters and then at the Kennedy library. In addition, the process has no doubt been enriched by the publication of the *Selected Letters* in 1981, the previously unpublished "On the Art of the Short Story" (first published in the *Paris Review* and now reprinted in this volume) also in 1981, and, in more recent years, a series of new biographies and the posthumous publication of *Garden of Eden*. One stimulus has followed another in adding to our knowledge or altering our perspective of the man and his work.

The present volume is not only more substantial than the previous one, but its organizational pattern (which has since been imitated by other anthologists) has had to be altered to fit changes in the critical climate. The relatively recent concern with "theory" has turned our attention to methodology, the differences between critical approaches, and the philosophical underpinnings of critical processes. While the illumination of the short stories has been the primary criterion in my choice of essays, I thought it might be helpful to student and scholar, in order to respond to this concern, to display at the outset a wide variety of critical approaches, grouped together.

This section of the book contains some approaches which, like the semiotic analysis of Robert Scholes, reflect the strict application of a theory with a specific name; others, like the essay by William Braasch Watson, were given names by me to reflect the dominant approach as I perceived it. The essay by Nina Baym does not set out to apply a specific feminist theory to "The Short Happy Life of Francis Macomber," but it obviously applies, as many essays in recent years have, a generalized, feminist perspective to the material. Unfortunately, not every approach one might desire is represented in the section, since there are no essays on the short stories using some types of theory, such as phenomenology or deconstruction.

Lying, as I have thought of it, halfway between critical approaches and interpretative essays on individual stories are those essays grouped under Section II which focus on techniques and themes, rather than particular stories, and which discuss ideas that can be applied to several stories or the stories as a whole. New critical approaches have been joined in recent years by what can only be viewed as a wave of revisionism, and several of the essays in this section reflect this in rebutting traditional assumptions and turning to new possibilities. For example, the essay by Kenneth Lynn questions certain long-accepted tenets of Hemingway criticism, as set forth by such early commentators as Malcolm Cowley and Philip Young, and proposes a different sort of inner landscape for the writer as reflected in his work.

Indeed, with the new biographies by Michael Reynolds, Jeffrey Meyers, Peter Griffin, and Kenneth Lynn and with the textual research of such scholars as Paul Smith and Susan Beegel (both concentrating on the short story), a host of questions about the author and his work that once seemed settled have been opened up again, so that the atmosphere for discussion is freer and the opportunities for research more fertile than they have been for decades. All of a sudden, as Frederick Crews said recently, Hemingway criticism is fun once again.

The purpose of this volume remains largely the same as the first: "To bring together out of [the] welter of material many of the best essays on the stories, while trying to maintain the widest possible range of commentary." My hope is that this book will serve not so much as a collection of definitive commentaries, as a series of provocations, springboards to further discussion, while at the same time marking the way to the possibilities of new research. Again, as I said in my introduction, "Here, I would hope, we have some indication of what we have and do not have, of what we know and what we do not know." I would only add that there is much indication here also of what we thought we knew but now will have to wonder and think about further.

In two essays on the state of Hemingway criticism, one in 1975 and the other in 1988, I pointed out that one of the persistent problems has been repetition, since so many critics have written while largely unaware of what has already been said. This problem has become in recent years even more acute in response to the explosion of material—even the most well-intentioned scholar must have some difficulty in finding and reading everything he should read as background to his criticism. This is the main justification for our checklist, for confronting the monster. Call it a civic duty. Or putting deeds where one's mouth is.

Jackson J. Benson
San Diego State University

The Art of the Short Story

Ernest Hemingway

●

In March 1959 Ernest Hemingway's publisher Charles Scribner, Jr., suggested putting together a student's edition of Hemingway short stories. He listed the twelve stories which were most in demand for anthologies but thought that the collection could include Hemingway's favorites and that Hemingway could write a preface for classroom use. Hemingway responded favorably. He would write the preface in the form of a lecture on the art of the short story.

Hemingway worked on the preface at La Consula, the home of Bill and Annie Davis in Malaga. He was in Spain that summer to follow the mano a mano competition between the brother-in-law bullfighters, Dominguín and Ordóñez. Hemingway traveled with his friend, Antonio Ordóñez, and wrote about this rivalry in "The Dangerous Summer," a three-part article which appeared in Life.

The first draft of the preface was written in May, and Hemingway completed the piece during the respite after Ordóñez was gored on May 30th. His wife, Mary, typed the draft, and, as she wrote in her book How It Was, she did not entirely approve of it. She wrote her husband a note suggesting rewrites and cuts to remove some of what she felt was its boastful, smug, and malicious tone. But Hemingway made only minor changes.

Hemingway sent the introduction to Charles Scribner and proposed changing the book to a collection for the general public. Scribner agreed to the change. However, he diplomatically suggested not printing the preface as it stood but rather using only the relevant comments as introductory remarks to the individual stories. Scribner felt that the preface, written as a lecture for college students, would not be accepted by a reading audience which might well "misinterpret it as condescension." [Scribner to E. H. June 24, 1959.]

The idea of the book was dropped.

Hemingway wrote the preface as if it were an extemporaneous oral presentation before a class on the methods of short story writing. It is similar to a transcript of an informal talk. Judging it against literary standards or using it to assess Hemingway's literary capabilities would elevate it beyond this level and would be inappropriate. Both Hemingway's wife and his publisher were against its publica-

tion, and in the end Hemingway agreed. It appears here because of its content.
Hemingway relates the circumstances under which he wrote the short stories; he
gives opinions on other writers, critics, and on his own works; he expresses views
on the art of the short story.

The essay is published unedited except for some spelling corrections. A
holograph manuscript, two typescripts, and an addendum, written for other
possible selections for the book, are in the Hemingway Collection at the John F.
Kennedy Library.*

Gertrude Stein who was sometimes very wise said to me on one of her
wise days, "Remember, Hemingway, that remarks are not literature."
The following remarks are not intended to be nor do they pretend to be
literature. They are meant to be instructive, irritating and informative. No
writer should be asked to write solemnly about what he has written.
Truthfully, yes. Solemnly, no. Should we begin in the form of a lecture
designed to counteract the many lectures you will have heard on the art of
the short story?

Many people have a compulsion to write. There is no law against it and
doing it makes them happy while they do it and presumably relieves
them. Given editors who will remove the worst of their emissions, supply
them with spelling and syntax and help them shape their thoughts and
their beliefs, some compulsive writers attain a temporary fame. But when
shit, or *merde*—a word which teacher will explain—is cut out of a book,
the odor of it always remains perceptible to anyone with sufficient
olfactory sensibility.

The compulsive writer would be advised not to attempt the short story.
Should he make the attempt, he might well suffer the fate of the
compulsive architect, which is as lonely an end as that of the compulsive
bassoon player. Let us not waste our time considering the sad and lonely
ends of these unfortunate creatures, gentlemen. Let us continue the
exercise.

Are there any questions? Have you mastered the art of the short story?
Have I been helpful? Or have I not made myself clear? I hope so.

Gentlemen, I will be frank with you. The masters of the short story
come to no good end. You query this? You cite me Maugham? Longevity,
gentlemen, is not an end. It is a prolongation. I cannot say fie upon it,
since I have never fied on anything yet. Shuck if off, Jack. Don't fie on it.

Should we abandon rhetoric and realize at the same time that what is

---

*This introduction is reprinted from the *Paris Review* 79 (1981), where "The Art of the Short
Story" was first published.

the most authentic hipster talk of today is the twenty-three skidoo of to-morrow? We should? What intelligent young people you are and what a privilege it is to be with you. Do I hear a request for authentic ballroom bananas? I do? Gentlemen, we have them for you in bunches.

Actually, as writers put it when they do not know how to begin a sentence, there is very little to say about writing short stories unless you are a professional explainer. If you can do it, you don't have to explain it. If you can not do it, no explanation will ever help.

A few things I have found to be true. If you leave out important things or events that you know about, the story is strengthened. If you leave or skip something because you do not know it, the story will be worthless. The test of any story is how very good the stuff is that you, not your editors, omit. A story in this book called "Big Two-Hearted River" is about a boy coming home beat to the wide from a war. Beat to the wide was an earlier and possibly more severe form of beat, since those who had it were unable to comment on this condition and could not suffer that it be mentioned in their presence. So the war, all mention of the war, anything about the war, is omitted. The river was the Fox River, by Seney, Michigan, not the Big Two-Hearted. The change of name was made purposely, not from ignorance nor carelessness but because Big Two-Hearted River is poetry, and because there were many Indians in the story, just as the war was in the story, and none of the Indians nor the war appeared. As you see, it is very simple and easy to explain.

In a story called "A Sea Change," everything is left out. I had seen the couple in the Bar Basque in St.-Jean-de-Luz and I knew the story too too well, which is the squared root of well, and use any well you like except mine. So I left the story out. But it is all there. It is not visible but it is there.

It is very hard to talk about your work since it implies arrogance or pride. I have tried to get rid of arrogance and replace it with humility and I do all right at that sometimes, but without pride I would not wish to continue to live nor to write and I publish nothing of which I am not proud. You can take that any way you like, Jack. I might not take it myself. But maybe we're built different.

Another story is "Fifty Grand." This story originally started like this:

"'How did you handle Benny so easy, Jack?' Soldier asked him.

"'Benny's an awful smart boxer,' Jack said. 'All the time he's in there, he's thinking. All the time he's thinking, I was hitting him.'"

I told this story to Scott Fitzgerald in Paris before I wrote "Fifty Grand" trying to explain to him how a truly great boxer like Jack Britton func-tioned. I wrote the story opening with that incident and when it was finished I was happy about it and showed it to Scott. He said he liked the story very much and spoke about it in so fulsome a manner that I was embarrassed. Then he said, "There is only one thing wrong with it, Ernest, and I tell you this as your friend. You have to cut out that old chestnut about Britton and Leonard."

At that time my humility was in such ascendance that I thought he must have heard the remark before or that Britton must have said it to someone else. It was not until I had published the story, from which I had removed that lovely revelation of the metaphysics of boxing that Fitzgerald in the way his mind was functioning that year so that he called an historic statement an "old chestnut" because he had heard it once and only once from a friend, that I realized how dangerous that attractive virtue, humility, can be. So do not be too humble, gentlemen. Be humble after but not during the action. They will all con you, gentlemen. But sometimes it is not intentional. Sometimes they simply do not know. This is the saddest state of writers and the one you will most frequently encounter. If there are no questions, let us press on.

My loyal and devoted friend Fitzgerald, who was truly more interested in my own career at this point than in his own, sent me to *Scribner's* with the story. It had already been turned down by Ray Long of *Cosmopolitan Magazine* because it had no love interest. That was okay with me since I eliminated any love interest and there were, purposely, no women in it except for two broads. Enter two broads as in Shakespeare, and they go out of the story. This is unlike what you will hear from your instructors, that if a broad comes into a story in the first paragraph, she must reappear later to justify her original presence. This is untrue, gentlemen. You may dispense with her, just as in life. It is also untrue that if a gun hangs on the wall when you open up the story, it must be fired by page fourteen. The chances are, gentlemen, that if it hangs upon the wall, it will not even shoot. If there are no questions, shall we press on? Yes, the unfireable gun may be a symbol. That is true. But with a good enough writer, the chances are some jerk just hung it there to look at. Gentlemen, you can't be sure. Maybe he is queer for guns, or maybe an interior decorator put it there. Or both.

So with pressure by Max Perkins on the editor, *Scribner's Magazine* agreed to publish the story and pay me two hundred and fifty dollars, if I would cut it to a length where it would not have to be continued into the back of the book. They call magazines books. There is significance in this but we will not go into it. They are not books, even if they put them in stiff covers. You have to watch this, gentlemen. Anyway, I explained without heat nor hope, seeing the built-in stupidity of the editor of the magazine and his intransigence, that I had already cut the story myself and that the only way it could be shortened by five hundred words and make sense was to amputate the first five hundred. I had often done that myself with stories and it improved them. It would not have improved this story but I thought that was their ass not mine. I would put it back together in a book. They read differently in a book anyway. You will learn about this.

No, gentlemen, they would not cut the first five hundred words. They gave it instead to a very intelligent young assistant editor who assured me he could cut it with no difficulty. That was just what he did on his first attempt, and any place he took words out, the story no longer made sense. It had been cut for keeps when I wrote it, and afterwards at Scott's request I'd even cut out the metaphysics which, ordinarily, I leave in. So they quit on it finally and eventually, I understand, Edward Weeks got Ellery Sedgwick to publish it in the *Atlantic Monthly*. Then everyone wanted me to write fight stories and I did not write any more fight stories because I tried to write only one story on anything, if I got what I was after, because Life is very short if you like it and I knew that even then. There are other things to write about and other people who write very good fight stories. I recommend to you "The Professional" by W. C. Heinz.

Yes, the confidently cutting young editor became a big man on *Reader's Digest*. Or didn't he? I'll have to check that. So you see, gentlemen, you never know and what you win in Boston you lose in Chicago. That's symbolism, gentlemen, and you can run a saliva test on it. That is how we now detect symbolism in our group and so far it gives fairly satisfactory results. Not complete, mind you. But we are getting in to see our way through. Incidentally, within a short time *Scribner's Magazine* was running a contest for long short stories that broke back into the back of the book, and paying many times two hundred and fifty dollars to the winners.

Now since I have answered your perceptive questions, let us take up another story.

This story is called "The Light of the World." I could have called it "Behold I Stand at the Door and Knock" or some other stained-glass window title, but I did not think of it and actually "The Light of the World" is better. It is about many things and you would be ill-advised to think it is a simple tale. It is really, no matter what you hear, a love letter to a whore named Alice who at the time of the story would have dressed out at around two hundred and ten pounds. Maybe more. And the point of it is that nobody, and that goes for you, Jack, knows how we were then from how we are now. This is worse on women than on us, until you look into the mirror yourself some day instead of looking at women all the time, and in writing the story I was trying to do something about it. But there are very few basic things you can do anything about. So I do what the French call *constater*. Look that up. That is what you have to learn to do, and you ought to learn French anyway if you are going to understand short stories, and there is nothing rougher than to do it all the way. It is hardest to do about women and you must not worry when they say there are no such women as those you wrote about. That only means your women aren't like their women. You ever see any of their women, Jack? I have a couple of times and you would be appalled and I know you don't appall easy.

What I learned constructive about women, not just ethics like never blame them if they pox you because somebody poxed them and lots of times they don't even know they have it—that's in the first reader for squares—is, no matter *how* they get, always think of them the way they were on the best day they ever had in their lives. That's about all you can do about it and that is what I was trying for in the story.

Now there is another story called "The Short Happy Life of Francis Macomber." Jack, I get a bang even yet from just writing the titles. That's why you write, no matter what they tell you. I'm glad to be with somebody I know now and those feecking students have gone. They haven't? Okay. Glad to have them with us. It is in you that our hope is. That's the stuff to feed the troops. Students, at ease.

This is a simple story in a way, because the woman, who I knew very well in real life but then invented out of, to make the woman for this story, is a bitch for the full course and doesn't change. You'll probably never meet the type because you haven't got the money. I haven't either but I get around. Now this woman doesn't change. She has been better, but she will never be any better anymore. I invented her complete with handles from the worst bitch I knew (then) and when I first knew her she'd been lovely. Not my dish, not my pigeon, not my cup of tea, but lovely for what she was and I was her all of the above which is whatever you make of it. This is as close as I can put it and keep it clean. This information is what you call the background of a story. You throw it all away and invent from what you know. I should have said that sooner. That's all there is to writing. That, a perfect ear—call it selective—absolute pitch, the devotion to your work and respect for it that a priest of God has for his, and then have the guts of a burglar, no conscience except to writing, and you're in, gentlemen. It's easy. Anybody can write if he is cut out for it and applies himself. Never give it a thought. Just have those few requisites. I mean the way you have to write now to handle the way now is now. There was a time when it was nicer, much nicer and all that has been well written by nicer people. They are all dead and so are their times, but they handled them very well. Those times are over and writing like that won't help you now.

But to return to this story. The woman called Margot Macomber is no good to anybody now except for trouble. You can bang her but that's about all. The man is a nice jerk. I knew him very well in real life, so invent him too from everything I know. So he is just how he really was, only he is invented. The White Hunter is my best friend and he does not care what I write as long as it is readable, so I don't invent him at all. I just disguise him for family and business reasons, and to keep him out of trouble with the Game Department. He is the furthest thing from a square since they invented the circle, so I just have to take care of him with an adequate disguise and he is as proud as though we both wrote it, which actually you always do in anything if you go back far enough. So it is a secret between us. That's all there is to that story except maybe the lion when he is hit and I am thinking inside of him really, not faked. I can think inside of a lion, really. It's hard to believe and it is perfectly okay with me if you don't believe it. Perfectly. Plenty of people have used it since, though, and one boy used it quite well, making only one mistake. Making any mistake kills you. This mistake killed him and quite soon everything he wrote was a mistake. You have to watch yourself, Jack, every minute, and the more talented you are the more you have to watch these mistakes because you will be in faster company. A writer who is not going all the way up can make all the mistakes he wants. None of it matters. He doesn't matter. The people who like him don't matter either. They could drop dead. It wouldn't make any difference. It's too bad. As soon as you read one page by anyone you can tell whether it matters or not. This is sad and you hate to do it. I don't want to be the one that tells them. So don't make any mistakes. You see how easy it is? Just go right in there and be a writer.

That about handles that story. Any questions? No, I don't know whether she shot him on purpose any more than you do. I could find out if I asked myself because I invented it and I could go right on inventing. But you have to know where to stop. That is what makes a short story. Makes it short at least. The only hint I could give you is that it is my belief that the incidence of husbands shot accidentally by wives who are bitches and really work at it is very low. Should we continue?

If you are interested in how you get the idea for a story, this is how it was with "The Snows of Kilimanjaro." They have you ticketed and always try to make it that you are someone who can only write about theirself. I am using in this lecture the spoken language, which varies. It is one of the ways to write, so you might as well follow it and maybe you will learn something. Anyone who can write can write spoken, pedantic, inexorably dull, or pure English prose, just as slot machines can be set for straight, percentage, give-away or stealing. No one who can write spoken ever starves except at the start. The others you can eat irregularly on. But any good writer can do them all. This is spoken, approved for over fourteen I hope. Thank you.

Anyway we came home from Africa, which is a place you stay until the money runs out or you get smacked, one year and at quarantine I said to the ship news reporters when somebody asked me what my projects were that I was going to work and when I had some more money go back to Africa. The different wars killed off that project and it took nineteen years to get back. Well it was in the papers and a really nice and really fine and really rich woman invited me to tea and we had a few drinks as well and she had read in the papers about this project, and why should I have to wait to go back for any lack of money? She and my wife and I could go to Africa any time and money was only something to be used intelligently for the best enjoyment of good people and so forth. It was a sincere and fine and good offer and I liked her very much and I turned down the offer.

So I get down to Key West and I start to think what would happen to a character like me whose defects I know, if I had accepted that offer. So I start to invent and I make myself a guy who would do what I invent. I know about the dying part because I had been through all that. Not just once. I got it early, in the middle and later. So I invent how someone I know who cannot sue me—that is me—would turn out, and put into one short story things you would use in, say, four novels if you were careful and not a spender. I throw everything I had been saving into the story and spend it all. I really throw it away, if you know what I mean. I am not gambling with it. Or maybe I am. Who knows? Real gamblers don't gamble. At least you think they don't gamble. They gamble, Jack, don't worry. So I make up the man and the woman as well as I can and I put all the true stuff in and with all the load, the most load any short story ever carried, it still takes off and it flies. This makes me very happy. So I thought that and the Macomber story are as good short stories as I can write for a while, so I lose interest and take up other forms of writing.

Any questions? The leopard? He is part of the metaphysics. I did not hire out to explain that nor a lot of other things. I know, but I am under no obligation to tell you. Put it down to *omertá*. Look that word up. I dislike explainers, apologists, stoolies, pimps. No writer should be any one of those for his own work. This is just a little background, Jack, that won't do either of us any harm. You see the point, don't you? If not it is too bad.

That doesn't mean you shouldn't explain for, apologize for or pimp or tout for some other writer. I have done it and the best luck I had was doing it for Faulkner. When they didn't know him in Europe, I told them all how he was the best we had and so forth and I over-humbled with him plenty and built him up about as high as he could go because he never had a break then and he was good then. So now whenever he has a few shots, he'll tell students what's wrong with me or tell Japanese or anybody they send him to, to build up our local product. I get tired of this but I figure what the hell he's had a few shots and maybe he even believes it. So you asked me just now what I think about him, as everybody does and I always stall, so I say you know how good he is. Right. You ought to. What is wrong is he cons himself sometimes pretty bad. That may just be the sauce. But for quite a while when he hits the sauce toward the end of a book, it shows bad. He gets tired and he goes on and on, and that sauce writing is really hard on who has to read it. I mean if they care about writing. I thought maybe it would help if I read it using the sauce myself, but it wasn't any help. Maybe it would have helped if I was fourteen. But I was only fourteen one year and then I would have been too busy. So that's what I think about Faulkner. You ask that I sum it up from the standpoint of a professional. Very good writer. Cons himself now. Too much sauce. But he wrote a really fine story called "The Bear" and I would be glad to put it in this book for your pleasure and delight, if I had written it. But you can't write them all, Jack.

It would be simpler and more fun to talk about other writers and what is good and what is wrong with them, as I saw when you asked me about Faulkner. He's easy to handle because he talks so much for a supposed silent man. Never talk, Jack, if you are a writer, unless you have the guy write it down and have you go over it. Otherwise, they get it wrong. That's what you think until they play a tape back at you. Then you know how silly it sounds. You're a writer aren't you? Okay, shut up and write. What was that question?

Did I really write three stories in one day in Madrid, the way it said in that interview in *The Paris Review* and *Horizon*? Yes sir. I was hotter than a—let's skip it, gentlemen. I was laden with uninhibited energy. Or should we say this energy was canalized into my work. Such states are compounded by the brisk air of the Guadarramas (Jack, was it cold) the highly seasoned bacalao vizcaíno (dried cod fish, Jack) a certain vague loneliness (I was in love and the girl was in Bologna and I couldn't sleep anyway, so why not write.) So I wrote.

"The stories you mention I wrote in one day in Madrid on May 16 when it snowed out the San Isidro bullfights. First I wrote 'The Killers' which I'd tried to write before and failed. Then after lunch I got in bed to keep warm and wrote 'Today is Friday.' I had so much juice I thought maybe I was going crazy and I had about six other stories to write. So I got dressed and walked to Fornos, the old bull fighter's cafe, and drank coffee and then came back and wrote 'Ten Indians.' This made me very sad and I drank some brandy and went to sleep. I'd forgotten to eat and one of the waiters brought me up some bacalao and a small steak and fried potatoes and a bottle of Valdepeñas.

"The woman who ran the Pension was always worried that I did not eat enough and she had sent the waiter. I remember sitting up in bed and eating, and drink the Valdepeñas. The waiter said he would bring up another bottle. He said the Señora wanted to know if I was going to write all night. I said no, I thought I would lay off for a while. Why don't you try to write just one more, the waiter asked. I'm only supposed to write one, I said. Nonsense, he said. You could write six. I'll try tomorrow, I said. Try it tonight, he said. What do you think the old woman sent the food up for?

"I'm tired, I told him. Nonsense, he said (the word was not nonsense). You tired after three miserable little stories. Translate me one.

"Leave me alone, I said. How am I going to write it if you don't leave me alone. So I sat up in bed and drank the Valdepeñas and thought what a hell of a writer I was if the first story was as good as I'd hoped."

I have used the same words in answering that the excellent Plimpton elicited from me in order to avoid error or repetition. If there are no more questions, should we continue?

It is very bad for writers to be hit on the head too much. Sometimes you lose months when you should have and perhaps would have worked well but sometimes a long time after the memory of the sensory distortions of these woundings will produce a story which, while not justifying the temporary cerebral damage, will palliate it. "A Way You'll Never Be" was written at Key West, Florida, some fifteen years after the damage it depicts, both to a man, a village and a countryside, had occurred. No questions? I understand. I understand completely. However, do not be alarmed. We are not going to call for a moment of silence. Nor for the man in the white suit. Nor for the net. Now gentlemen, and I notice a sprinkling of ladies who have drifted in attracted I hope by the sprinkling of applause. Thank you. Just *what* stories do you yourselves care for? I must not impose on you exclusively those that find favor with their author. Do *you* too care for any of them?

You like "The Killers"? So good of you. And why? Because it had Burt Lancaster and Ava Gardner in it? Excellent. Now we are getting somewhere. It is always a pleasure to remember Miss Gardner as she was then. No, I never met Mr. Lancaster. I can't tell you what he is really like but everyone says he is terrific. The background of that story is that I had a lawyer who had cancer and he wanted cash rather than any long term stuff. You can see his point I hope. So when he was offered a share in the picture for me and less cash, he took the more cash. It turned out badly for us both. He died eventually and I retained only an academic interest in the picture. But the company lets me run it off free when I want to see Miss Gardner and hear the shooting. It is a good picture and the only good picture ever made of a story of mine. One of the reasons for that is that John Huston wrote the script. Yes I know him. Is everything true about him that they say? No. But the best things are. Isn't that interesting.

You mean background about the story not the picture? That's not very sporting, young lady. Didn't you see the class was enjoying itself finally? Besides it has a sordid background. I hesitate to bring it in, on account of there is no statute of limitations on what it deals with. Gene Tunney, who is a man of wide culture, once asked me, "Ernest, wasn't that Andre Anderson in 'The Killers'?" I told it was and that the town was Summit, Illinois, not Summit, N.J. We left it at that. I thought about that story a long long time before I invented it, and I had to be as far away as Madrid before I invented it properly. That story probably had more left out of it than anything I ever wrote. More even than when I left the war out of "Big Two-Hearted River." I left out all Chicago, which is hard to do in 2951 words.

Another time I was leaving out good was in "A Clean Well-Lighted Place." There I really had luck. I left out everything. That is about as far as you can go, so I stood on that one and haven't drawn to that since.

I trust you follow me, gentlemen. As I said at the start, there is nothing to writing short stories once you get the knack of it.

A story I can beat, and I promise you I will, is "The Undefeated." But I leave it in to show you the difference between when you leave it all in and when you take it out. The stories where you leave it all in do not re-read like the ones where you leave it out. They understand easier, but when you have read them once or twice you can't re-read them. I could give you examples in everybody who writes, but writers have enough enemies without doing it to each other. All really good writers know exactly what is wrong in all other good writers. There are no perfect writers unless they write just a very little bit and then stand on it. But writers have no business fingering another writer to outsiders while he is alive. After a writer is dead and doesn't have to work any more, anything goes. A son of a bitch alive is a son of a bitch dead. I am not talking about rows between writers. They are okay and can be comic. If someone puts a thumb in your eye, you don't protest. You thumb him back. He fouls you, you foul him back. That teaches people to keep it clean. What I mean is, you shouldn't give it to another writer, I mean really give it to him. I know you shouldn't do it because I did it once to Sherwood Anderson. I did it because I was righteous, which is the worst thing you can be, and I thought he was going to pot the way he was writing and that I could kid him out of it by showing him how awful it was. So I wrote *The Torrents of Spring.* It was cruel to do, and it didn't do any good, and he just wrote worse and worse. What the hell business of mine was it if he wanted to write badly? None. But then I was righteous and more loyal to writing than to my friend. I would have shot anybody then, not kill them, just shoot them a little, if I thought it would straighten them up and make them write right. Now I know that there is nothing you can do about any writer ever. The seeds of their destruction are in them from the start, and the thing to do about writers is get along with them if you see them, and try not to see them. All except a very few, and all of them except a couple are dead. Like I said, once they're dead anything goes as long as it's true.

I'm sorry I threw at Anderson. It was cruel and I was a son of a bitch to do it. The only thing I can say is that I was as cruel to myself then. But that is no excuse. He was a friend of mine, but that was no excuse for doing it to him. Any questions? Ask me that some other time.

This brings us to another story, "My Old Man." The background of this was all the time we spent at the races at San Siro when I used to be in hospital in Milan in 1918, and the time put in at the tracks in Paris when we really worked at it. Handicapping I mean. Some people say that this story is derived from a story about harness racing by Sherwood Anderson called "I'm a Fool." I do not believe this. My theory is that it is derived from a jockey I knew very well and a number of horses I knew, one of which I was in love with. I invented the boy in my story and I think the boy in Sherwood's story was himself. If you read both stories you can form your own opinion. Whatever it is, it is all right with me. The best things Sherwood wrote are in two books, *Winesburg, Ohio* and *The Triumph of the Egg.* You should read them both. Before you know too much about things, they are better. The best thing about Sherwood was he was the kind of guy at the start his name made you think of Sherwood Forest, while in Bob Sherwood the name only made you think of a playwright.

Any other stories you find in this book are in because I liked them. If you like them too I will be pleased. Thank you very much. It has been nice to be with you.

June 1959
La Consula
Churriana
Malaga, Spain

Critical
Approaches

The Unifying Consciousness of a Divided Conscience: Nick Adams as Author of *In Our Time*

Debra A. Moddelmog

●

(Composite Novel?)

In the lengthy passage that was Hemingway's original ending to "Big Two-Hearted River," Nick Adams, having caught "one good trout" (*NAS*, 213), rests and reflects on many things, particularly his writing.[1] For readers of *In Our Time*, who have arrived with "Big Two-Hearted River" at the book's final story, this interior monologue (had Hemingway kept it) would have revealed some interesting facts, but none more so than that Nick has written two of the stories we have just read: "Indian Camp" and "My Old Man." Indeed, in the final scene of this ending, Nick heads back to camp "holding something in his head" (*NAS*, 220) and is apparently preparing to write "Big Two-Hearted River" itself. But lest we misunderstand these stories, Nick also explains his method of composition: "Nick in the stories was never himself. He made him up. Of course he'd never seen an Indian woman having a baby. That was what made it good. Nobody knew that. He'd seen a woman have a baby on the road to Karagatch and tried to help her. That was the way it was" (*NAS*, 217–18).

Most critics who discuss this rejected conclusion generally assume that Hemingway lost control of his art here, identified too closely with Nick, and began writing autobiography rather than fiction.[2] In fact, both Hemingway's critics and biographers quote from this monologue as if Hemingway, not Nick, were the speaker.[3] Even when a critic, like Robert Gibb, takes Hemingway at his word, he concludes that we need not worry finally about distinguishing between Nick and Hemingway. Whether a story has been written by "Hemingway the writer who wrote in the character of Nick Adams" or by "Nick Adams the writer who, by existing, shaped the idea of a man and his cosmos" matters not, according to Gibb: "Remembrance goes both ways."[4]

Remembrance may go both ways, but Gibb is finally wrong to suggest that our understanding of a story remains the same regardless of whom we see as its author. Obviously, all words lead back to Hemingway, and I would not wish to suggest that in stories of *In Our Time* he is introducing the kinds of author-character confusions we have come to expect from many postmodern writers. However, as I hope to show, there are some good reasons for seeing Nick as the implied author of *In Our Time*, and doing so resolves many confusions about the book's unity, structure, vision, and significance. Moreover, such an approach casts new light on Nick Adams as a character separate from yet also an extension of Hemingway.

In his book-length study of Nick, Joseph Flora states, "No one would argue that 'Big Two-Hearted River' would gain from the inclusion of Nick's several memories and theories of writing."[5] I want to make clear from the start that I wholeheartedly agree with this statement. From the moment Nick arrives at Seney he does everything in his power to hold back his thoughts, yet in the nine pages that Hemingway finally rejected, Nick suddenly begins thinking and does so calmly and contentedly. This ending would have reduced the story's tension and given us a very different Nick Adams. That Hemingway realized this indicates how clear a vision he had formed of what he wanted to accomplish in his fiction. His letter to Robert McAlmon—written in mid-November 1924, about three months after he finished "Big Two-Hearted River" and two months after he had arranged and submitted *In Our Time* for publication—provides the fullest explanation of his reasoning: "I have decided that all that mental conversation in the long fishing story is the shit and have cut it all out. The last nine pages. The story was interrupted you know just when I was going good and I could never get back into it and finish it. I got a hell of a shock when I realized how bad it was and that shocked me back into the river again and I've finished it off the way it ought to have been all along. Just the straight fishing."[6] In brief, Hemingway recognized that "all that mental conversation" jarred asthetically with the rest of his story and actually contradicted its point.[7] Wisely, he cut.

But just because Hemingway saved "Big Two-Hearted River" by removing Nick's monologue does not mean that we, like a jury commanded to disregard a witness's last remark, should automatically ignore all we learn here. Certainly critics are right that Hemingway comes close to crossing the boundary between fiction and experience in these pages, but that is a line he almost always approaches in his Nick Adams stories. As Flora notes, "Although Nick is not Hemingway, he reflects more of Hemingway than any other Hemingway hero,"[8] and Philip Young observes that Nick has "much in common" with his creator and was, for Hemingway, "a special kind of mask."[9] Significantly, Hemingway's letter to McAlmon disloses that he revised his conclusion because he was worried about the artistic integrity of his story, not about his artistic persona.

Ironically, it is actually *because* Hemingway was so close to Nick and yet not Nick that he was able to conceive of surrendering authorship to Nick without destroying the illusion of his fictional world. Of course, when he wrote "Big Two-Hearted River," Hemingway had already written almost every story in *In Our Time* (only "The Battler" and "On the Quai at Smyrna" came later), and so obviously he did not plan from the time he composed these stories to attribute any of them to Nick. However, Nick shared so much of Hemingway's personality and experience that turning him into the author of the stories ex post facto required very little work. All Hemingway had to do was supply Nick with the relevant background, specifically a writing career and some postwar history. This he was doing in the nine pages he eventually cut out. And, as I indicated above, Hemingway actually gave Nick the background needed to be considered author of all of *In Our Time*, not just of the two stories he specifically mentions, "My Old Man" and "Indian Camp."

The evidence leading to this deduction begins with a sentence quoted earlier in which Nick tells us: "Nick in the stories was never himself." The use of the plural "stories" is significant. Because Nick is not in "My Old Man," he apparently has written other stories about himself besides "Indian Camp." This hypothesis is supported by Nick's references in this lengthy monologue to people and places that play a part in other Nick Adams stories. For example, Nick thinks about fishing at Hortons Creek (*NAS*, 216), the scene of the breakup with Marjorie in "The End of Something," and he remembers "drinking with Bill's old man" (*NAS*, 215) which calls to mind "The Three-Day Blow." He also mentions his wife, Helen, a figure whose existence we learn of in "Cross-Country Snow." Finally, Nick states that his family has misunderstood his stories, believing that they were all recountings of his experience (*NAS*, 217). One implication of this statement is that his relatives have been reading fiction in which Nick appears as a central character and have presumed that the other characters are themselves; the most likely candidate to provoke this reaction would be "The Doctor and the Doctor's Wife."

But Nick's memories of people and places are not limited to those which materialize in stories about himself. Many of his allusions also recall non-Nick narratives of *In Our Time*. For instance, the woman giving birth on the road to Karagatch, the encounter from which Nick indicates that "Indian Camp" derives, is presented without change in chapter 2. Nick also states that too much talking had made the war unreal (*NAS*, 217), an attitude shared by Harold Krebs in "Soldier's Home." The matador Maera figures prominently in Nick's thoughts (e.g., "Maera was the greatest man he'd ever known," *NAS*, 216), as he does in chapters 13 and 14 of *In Our Time*. Nick even confesses that "His whole inner life had been bullfights all one year" (*NAS*, 216), an obsession that could explain why six of the fifteen chapters deal with that subject. All of these connections between Nick's memories reviewed during his fishing trip to upper Michigan and the narratives of *In Our Time* support the premise that this original conclusion supplied the personal history necessary to see Nick as the author of this book.

To repeat what I said earlier, we need not assume that Nick lost all of this past when we lost this ending. In fact, a key sentence in the version of "Big Two-Hearted River" that was finally published implies that this background did not disappear forever but simply moved, so to speak, underground. Soon after Nick starts hiking away from Seney and toward the river, he discovers that "He felt he had left everything behind, the need for thinking, the need to write, other needs" (*IOT*, 134).[10] Exactly why Nick feels so relieved to leave behind these three needs becomes clear when we see *In Our Time* as the product of his experiences and imagination. Although obviously we cannot pin down the precise date when Nick wrote any particular story in *In Our Time*—excluding perhaps "Big Two-Hearted River"—we can, I think, safely infer that he composed most of the book after World War I. Not only do most of the stories describe events of this war or shortly thereafter (the Greco-Turkish War, American couples visiting Europe, soldiers returning to the States), but also Nick admits that "He always worked best when Helen was unwell" (*NAS*, 218), a condition that definitely arises after the war. By roughly dating the composition of these stories, we are able to connect them to that stage in Nick's life immediately following World War I, and they can, therefore, help us to understand the Nick Adams we meet in "Big Two-Hearted River."

In approaching the stories of *In Our Time* as if Nick were their author, we discover that it will, indeed, be easier to trace through them Nick's recent psychological history than his actual history. Because Nick has told us that he was never himself in his stories and because we lack the biographical evidence (letters, memoirs, interviews) that usually fill the gap between an author's life and his fiction, we are left wondering where we might find the real Nick Adams. The fact that Nick's family has taken his fiction for autobiography suggests that, like Hemingway, Nick was drawing heavily from life when he wrote his stories.[11] Still, we will have to guess, for the most part, at what Nick actually experienced, at "the way it was" (*NAS*, 218). But since our main interest is Nick's psyche, we need not worry too much about our inability to sort reality from imagination. By looking for repeated patterns and by studying the subjects that Nick chooses to develop as well as his manner of presenting those subjects, we should uncover those fixations of his imagination that reveal his basic outlook on life.

Having established the parameters of our investigation, we find new fascination in one fact about Nick's history that we *do* know: "he'd never seen an Indian woman having a baby. . . . He'd seen a woman have a baby on the road to Karagatch and tried to help her." This confession about the source of "Indian Camp" indicates, first of all, that the woman Nick attempted to help has affected him deeply. As I have already noted, Nick reports this encounter directly in chapter 2 of *In Our Time,* a description which ends with the comment "Scared sick looking at it" (21). Apparently neither version alone was enough to purge Nick of this memory, and the question is why he is so preoccupied with it.

Part of the answer could lie in the transformations Nick makes when turning the experience into fiction. Not only does he concentrate on the pain and suffering of childbirth, but he also changes the witness of the delivery from an adult immersed in war and evacuation to a child involved with family life and night-time adventures. Such a transference is psychologically symbolic. It implies, first, that the older Nick views his meeting with the woman on the road to Karagatch as an initiation of the innocent. By projecting himself as a young boy present at a difficult childbirth, Nick suggests that he feels victimized by the exigencies of the adult world ("It was an awful mess to put you through," his father says— *IOT,* 18) and also reveals a lingering inability to accept suffering and dying ("[C]an't you give her something to make her stop screaming?" "Do ladies always have such a hard time having babies?" "Do many men kill themselves?" "Is dying hard?"—*IOT,* 16, 19). A strong degree of self-pity thus permeates the story, especially its final scene where the young Nick questions the all-knowing father. However, Nick also attacks that self-indulgence with self-irony by ending his story with the child's denial of his own mortality, a denial that he, a war veteran and writer, now knows to be a lie.

But "Indian Camp" discloses more about Nick than just the fact that he feels victimized and confused by life. It also reveals his despair, possibly even his guilt, over being unable to ease the suffering of the woman on the road to Karagatch. In describing the source of his story, Nick tells us that he "tried" to help this woman, a qualifier which implies failure. He reproduces that sense of helplessness and frustration in the person of the Indian father who commits suicide because he "couldn't stand things"

(*IOT*, 19). But he also places the suffering Indian mother in the professional hands of Dr. Adams, who *does* stop her pain and delivers her child. Nick thereby completes in his imagination what he failed to do in reality. Fiction serves as wish fulfillment by enabling Nick to control a world that seems to deny all attempts at such control.

Feelings of horror and frustration, and a desire not to enter the complex realm of adulthood help to explain why Nick has built two separate narratives out of his meeting with the woman in Asia Minor. But, in fact, this focus on pain and suffering—both experienced and observed, physical and mental—countered by a wish to escape or deny that vision actually forms a pattern found throughout the stories of *In Our Time*, especially those in which Nick is a central character. In "The Doctor and the Doctor's Wife" we are witnesses to the marriage of incompetence and insularity and find that its sole issue is incompatibility. The young Nick responds to the friction of his parents' relationship and the myopia of his mother by ignoring the latter's summons for that of black squirrels. In "The End of Something" and "The Three-Day Blow," Nick discovers for himself the agony of relationships and reacts to that pain, first, by retreating from all companionship, even that of his friend Bill, and then by retreating from the home, the conventional domain of woman, to the woods where "the Marge business was no longer so tragic. It was not even very important. The wind blew everything like that away" (*IOT*, 49). Nick learns in "The Battler" about the cruelty of society and the viciousness of insanity, a lesson which ends, once again, in confused escape. And, finally, in chapter 6, the violence of war so shatters Nick's spine and peace of mind that he vows to make "a separate peace," to desert not only the battlefield but also the patriotism that led him to that destructive arena.

A quick glance at the six non-Nick stories which follow chapter 6—our last look at Nick until he reappears in "Cross-Country Snow"—is enough to confirm the paradigm. In fact, although the flight from pain is not depicted as regularly in these stories, the vision they present is so similar to that found in the Nick narratives that we can have no doubt that their author is the same. In "A Very Short Story" a soldier who wants to marry his girlfriend-nurse "to make it so they could not lose it" (*IOT*, 65) does lose "it." The woman jilts him, and he subsequently loses his health when he contracts gonorrhea from a salesgirl in the backseat of a cab. Harold Krebs, the soldier come home, loses touch with the reality of World War I and his own identity: by lying he "lost everything" (*IOT*, 70). The revolutionist, failing to comprehend the political reality of the world, is captured by the Swiss and loses his freedom; the narrator of his story has already lost his own political idealism. And the couples in "Mr. and Mrs. Elliot," "Cat in the Rain," and "Out of Season" all dramatize loss of understanding, communication, and love; in place of these things they substitute reading, a cat, writing reams of poetry, a lesbian affair, fishing.

This consistency of vision found throughout the stories we have examined so far suggests that Nick has a fairly inflexible, troubled way of seeing the world. No matter what or whom he writes about, he tends to view life as a losing proposition. Gertrude Stein's "You are all a lost generation" describes *In Our Time* as aptly as it describes *The Sun Also Rises* in this sense: Nick seems to believe that the things most worth having and caring about—life, love, ideals, companions, peace, freedom—will be lost sooner or later, and he is not sure how to cope with this assurance, except through irony, bitterness, and, sometimes, wishful thinking. Although we cannot determine definitely when such a belief was formed, the most likely candidate to have precipitated this change is, of course, Nick's involvement in two wars—WWI and the Greco-Turkish war of 1922—which brought him face to face with many kinds of losses, especially of life and ideals. As I have already discussed, Nick was so shaken by his encounter with the pregnant woman on the road to Karagatch, an encounter that certainly included violent pain and possibly death, that he created two stories out of it. The several other narratives of *In Our Time* depicting the violence and senselessness of war ("On the Quai at Smyrna" and chapters 3, 4, 5, and 7) emphasize Nick's obsession with these matters.

And as if we needed further evidence, the bullfighting chapters (9–14) reinforce the extent and nature of Nick's fixation. Nick, we recall, has declared that "His whole inner life had been bullfights all one year," and thus he implies that these narratives represent his inner experience as much as his actual experience. In general, these six chapters repeat themes and images found in the earlier war chapters: men and animals being maimed and killed, cowardice, fear, rare stoicism in the face of death, even rarer triumphs over the enemy, be it man or beast. However, the most interesting chapter in terms of Nick's mental state is the last one in which Nick "kills off" his friend, the matador Maera, a man who, as Nick's monologue makes clear, is still living. By projecting Maera's death, Nick seems to be preparing himself for the inevitable, the loss of another comrade like Rinaldi whose situation in chapter 6 closely resembles Maera's: both men lie face down, silent, still, unable to defend themselves, waiting for stretchers to carry them off the field.

In "Big Two-Hearted River" we find another hint at how much Nick is bothered by losing friends when he thinks about Hopkins, a memory associated with bitterness and one he is glad exhaustion prevents him from contemplating further. Hopkins seems to have disappeared suddenly from Nick's circle of comrades—either because of death or wealth—for "They never saw Hopkins again," despite plans for a fishing trip the next summer (*IOT*, 141). As Nick says in the excised conclusion to "Big Two-Hearted River"—in a statement that refers to artists but seems to have more general applications—"They died and that was the hell of it. They worked all their lives and then got old and died" (*NAS*, 219). In sum, part of what brought Nick to the Big Two-Hearted River is the same thing that brought him to writing: a need to come to terms with all the loss he has experienced in the last few years and, equally important, the loss he has come to expect.

That Nick takes his trip to upper Michigan to restore both his mind and his spirit debilitated by war has, of course, been the accepted reading of "Big Two-Hearted River" ever since critics began to assess the story formally.[12] Hence, my analysis so far has primarily enabled me to clarify the state of Nick's mind, the memories which are troubling him. However, an important question regarding Nick's trip which has never been satisfactorily settled is why he waits so long after the war to take it. Many readers of *In Our Time* have assumed that its Nick stories are arranged chronologically so that the Nick who appears in "Cross-Country Snow," the husband and soon-to-be father, is slightly younger than the Nick who appears in "Big Two-Hearted River." But if this chronology is correct, then we somehow have to explain why Nick, who seems healthy in "Cross-Country Snow," could suddenly become so unstable that he must take off to the Michigan woods to escape "the need for thinking, the need to write, other needs."

In 1972, Philip Young resolved Nick's apparent about-face by reversing the order of these two stories in *The Nick Adams Stories*. "Big Two-Hearted River" takes place, he asserted, immediately after World War I; "Cross-Country Snow" follows, displaying the success of Nick's recuperative journey to the river.[13] Yet Hemingway's original conclusion to "Big Two-Hearted River" disputes this rearrangement, for in it Nick mentions Helen and discusses the reactions his friends have had to his marriage. Obviously, when Hemingway wrote this story he saw Nick as a married man, someone who had been back from the war for some time. But even without this external evidence, we should still, I think, date "Big Two-Hearted River" several years after the war. Support for this proposal lies in the stories that Nick has written, especially in those that come after chapter 6 describing Nick's wounding.

The non-Nick stories that follow this chapter might seem, simply by virtue of their point of view, to be based less on Nick's actual experience and more on his imagination than those narratives in which his namesake plays a central role. However, without biographical evidence we cannot prove this. Given some of the parallels between Nick's ideas stated in the excised "Big Two-Hearted River" monologue and those presented in the non-Nick stories, it appears that Nick is still drawing heavily from his life. To repeat an earlier example, Nick claims that the war was made unreal by too much talking, an assertion that sounds very similar to Harold Krebs's discovery that "to be listened to at all he had to lie, and after he had done this twice he, too, had a reaction against the war and against talking about it" (*IOT*, 69).

Why Nick should choose to present some of his experiences through the medium of his alter ego and other experiences through varying viewpoints could have to do, therefore, with his sensitivity to certain subjects. In other words, Nick might romanticize a protagonist named after himself yet be willing to describe his most painful, embarrassing, and passionate experiences when safely shielded—from both his readers and himself—behind a more opaque persona. Young maintains that this is the approach Hemingway took in his writing: "he tended to smuggle certain things away in his fiction; if they were compromising or shameful and he wanted to get rid of them he chose masks much less transparent than Nick's."[14] In a classic psychoanalytic paradox, the closer the matter is to Nick the writer, the further away Nick the character is likely to be. The non-Nick stories can thus hold the key to Nick's innermost secrets and fears.

The area of chronology provides the first clue that the non-Nick stories reflect those anxieties that trouble Nick most deeply. As we have seen, the first half of *In Our Time* traces the growth of Nick's alter ego from a young boy to a young man, almost qualifying it as a bildungsroman. However, throughout the rest of the stories, except for "My Old Man," the age of the male protagonist remains steady, from late teens to mid twenties, or approximately Nick's age at the time he wrote these narratives. And while an age correspondence between the male characters in the non-Nick stories and Nick himself does not definitely prove that the former are fictional alter egos, it does seem more than just a coincidence that Nick has written so many stories about men who are basically his age or a bit younger.

Moreover, these men share more with Nick than simply his age. Excluding the narrator of "The Revolutionist" (whose story may or may not be founded in Nick's history), all of these men are pictured in situations which we know—from the discarded conclusion to "Big Two-

Hearted River''—that Nick himself has recently experienced, specifically, returning from the war and getting married. Once again, we cannot be sure how directly Nick has drawn from his own life in creating these stories, and so the more general patterns and attitudes are what most concern us.

In the two stories about recovering soldiers, "A Very Short Story" and "Soldier's Home," the protagonists attempt to engage in normal civilian life, yet find this participation difficult. The anonymous soldier's plans for such a life are foiled when Luz jilts him; Harold Krebs is simply repulsed by the hypocrisy of postwar America and its middle-class life-style. However, both men react, rather than act, and consequently lose the chance to control their own destinies. The soldier rebounds from Luz into the arms of a nameless salesgirl who gives him not love but gonorrhea. Krebs surrenders to his family's demands to lie and to get a job and thereby contributes to the hypocrisy he detests. These stories thus show us men who are greatly confused about their futures after returning from the war.

Significantly, the problems that the soldier and Krebs have adjusting to life after the war center as much on women as on making the transition from a military to a civilian lifestyle. The soldier had been ready to change his life radically upon returning to America. He was going to give up both alcohol and his friends; all he wanted was to get a job and get married. He blames Luz for destroying that dream. Krebs "would have liked to have a girl" (*IOT*, 71), but he dreads the consequences, that is, the complications involved in close relationships. The difficulties that these two men have with women prepares us for the three non-Nick stories preceding "Cross-Country Snow," the so-called marriage group of *In Our Time*. In these stories—"Mr. and Mrs. Elliot," "Cat in the Rain," and "Out of Season"—we observe the disintegration of three marriages. And although each relationship is falling apart for its own reason, the disintegration always hinges on an awareness of the disparity between the ideal and the real.

This awareness is revealed directly in "Mr. and Mrs. Elliot," for both partners had kept themselves "pure" but were equally disappointed on their wedding night. The physical insufficiency of their lovemaking is more than just sexual frustration. Despite their efforts, they cannot conceive what they most desire: a child. In "Cat in the Rain" and "Out of Season," the general cause of the couples' discontent is more subtly conveyed, but a key phrase indicates that, once again, it comes down to unfulfilled expectations. The wife in the former story compares herself to the cat outside her hotel window when she declares, first, that "It isn't *any fun* to be a poor kitty out in the rain" and, then, that "If I can't have long hair or *any fun,* I can have a cat" (*IOT* 93, 94; my emphasis). Like the cat in the rain, she feels shut out, unwanted, unnoticed, unloved; she and her husband do not make each other happy anymore. In "Out of Season" the husband voices a similar sentiment when he sends his wife back to the hotel with: "It's a rotten day and we aren't going to have *any fun,* anyway" (*IOT,* 101; my emphasis). The concentration in both stories on a lack of fun recalls Nick's reason for breaking up with Marjorie in "The End of Something": "It isn't fun any more" (*IOT,* 34). "Isn't love any fun?" Marjorie asks. "No," Nick answers, and so might the couples in "Mr. and Mrs. Elliot," "Cat in the Rain," and "Out of Season."

Thus, the marriage group, "A Very Short Story," and "Soldier's Home" present us with a series of portraits of failed love and/or overall dissatisfaction with male-female relationships. Such a consistently unflattering picture of love calls into question the state of Nick's own marriage. In the dropped ending to "Big Two-Hearted River," Nick says that when he married Helen he lost all his old friends "because he admitted by marrying that something was more important than the fishing" (*NAS,* 214). Although this sounds like a positive statement about his marriage, Nick contradicts himself when he says that he loved his fishing days "more than anything" and admits that he has nightmares about missing a fishing season: "It made him feel sick in the dream, as though he had been in jail" (*NAS,* 215).

Nick makes one other seemingly positive remark about marriage in this monologue when he says that he remembers the horror he once had of marriage: "It was funny. Probably it was because he had always been with older people, nonmarrying people" (*NAS,* 215). But even this confession does not indicate Nick's true feelings; marriage might not be a horror, but it also might not be a piece of cake. In "Cross-Country Snow" Nick's alter ego is similarly ambiguous. When George says—about life in general, including marriage, parenthood, responsibility—"It's hell, isn't it?" Nick responds, "No. Not exactly" (*IOT,* 111). Not exactly? Why not "Definitely not"?

In fact, the most important thing we learn about Helen may be that she's never about. In "Cross-Country Snow" Nick and George ski the mountains of Switzerland without Helen. In "Big Two-Hearted River" Nick takes his fishing trip alone. This habitual absence of Helen combined with the attitude toward relationships revealed in Nick's stories suggests that Nick's marriage is one of those "other needs" which has motivated his journey to the Michigan woods in "Big Two-Hearted River." A later Nick Adams Story, "Now I Lay Me," shows Nick and his orderly, John, discussing the advantages of marriage. Although Nick doesn't instantly agree with John that marriage "would fix up everything" (*NAS,* 134), he promises to think about it. Significantly, the patterns implied by and within *In Our Time* indicate that Nick has married soon after his return from Europe, but has since discovered that far from healing everything, as John guaranteed, marriage actually aggravated his pain. Nick's feelings about Helen thus make up the darker depths of the swamp he must one day fish.[15]

In Our Time reveals one final other need which has possibly sent Nick to the river and which seems to be among those darker depths of his own mental swamp: the duties of fatherhood. As I have noted, Nick was greatly upset by his meeting with the pregnant woman on the road to Karagatch, and the horror of that scene is, of course, enough to explain Nick's preoccupation with it. But, in fact, the several other references to pregnancy and children in the book indicate that this preoccupation has expanded into a generalization. The British narrator of "On the Quai at Smyrna" cannot forget the Greek women who were having babies, particularly those who refused to give up their dead babies. They were the worst, he declares (*IOT,* 11). Mr. and Mrs. Elliot try, without success, to have a child, even though Mrs. Elliot obviously finds sex with her husband distasteful or painful—or both. In "Cross-Country Snow" Nick assumes the German waitress is unhappy because she is pregnant but unmarried. Nowhere in *In Our Time* are the joys of pregnancy and young children described. Whenever mentioned, children and having babies are associated with suffering, unhappiness, an end of freedom and innocence, even death. As Jackson J. Benson puts it, "we are brought back again and again to pain, mutilation and death in connection with birth, sex, and the female."[16]

A likely source of this association for Nick was his encounter with the woman in Asia Minor, but given this view, he would certainly face the prospect of fatherhood with great trepidation. "Cross-Country Snow" exhibits that fear both directly and obliquely. Nick tells George that he is glad *now* about Helen's pregnancy, a distinction which points to his initial displeasure. However, the lie of that assertion is shown in his reaction to the pregnant waitress: he fails to notice her condition immediately and wonders why. The psychological answer is that to do so would mean allowing the reality of his married life to interfere with the happiness of his skiing excursion. Once again, in writing about himself, Nick reveals a desire to avoid those adult responsibilities which inhibit freedom and complicate life. To have a child means one can no longer be a child.

Neither "Big Two-Hearted River" nor its original conclusion contains any explicit evidence that Nick is or is about to become a father. Yet if we see these various references to children as representative of Nick's feelings about fatherhood and if we assume that "Cross-Country Snow" is based in Nick's experience, then perhaps the lack of evidence itself is important. In other words, through his silence Nick could be revealing just how painful the whole matter of children has become; he does not even trust himself to think or talk about it. Thus, his impending or actual fatherhood is the most recent need that urged Nick's trip to the Michigan woods, even the one that may have directly motivated it. Interestingly, "Big Two-Hearted River" is immediately preceded by "My Old Man." Although this story depicts a strong father-son relationship, the positive image is offset by the story's conclusion with the father dead and the son feeling assaulted by life's realities. The characters form a composite of Nick, who seems near to a spiritual death, burdened by anxieties that include his memories of war, married life, and fatherhood. He thus turns to the one great pleasure which has never failed him, the one activity he knows will allow him to escape the world that is too much with him: fishing.

This explanation of Nick's actions in "Big Two-Hearted River" may make him sound much like the character he writes about who shares his name: constantly running away from suffering and responsibility. And Nick definitely possesses that desire; his fiction shows that he wishes there were some kind of escape hatch, a way out, a way back to a more carefree, careless time. However, we must be careful not to confuse Nick the writer with Nick the character. And here is where approaching *In Our Time* as if Nick were its author begins to change our understanding of both the book and Nick Adams. In "Fathers and Sons," a later Nick Adams story—both in terms of when it was written and when it takes place— Nick announces, "If he wrote it he could get rid of it. He had gotten rid of many things by writing them" (*NAS*, 237). Although this confession is anachronistic in reference to my present study, writing often serves as catharsis. If we view Nick's work as partly an act of exorcism, then we can assume that the Nick who has written a story is one step further on the road to health than the Nick who writes the story and two steps ahead of the Nick who is described in the story.

But we should not be overly generous in formulating this assumption, for the patterns I have found throughout *In Our Time* indicate that Nick also has not been able to heal himself in the space of one or two tales. In fact, what begins as an act of purging can end as an act of control, an attempt to contain the emotions that are playing havoc with one's insides. The repetitions of loss, suffering, violence, and general unhappiness in Nick's fiction suggest that his recent experiences have dug so deeply into his psyche that he must continually bring them out, look them in the face, and thereby convince himself that by controlling them, they are not controlling him. And even though Nick has yet to admit to others—and possibly even to himself—that he fears such things as marriage and fatherhood, his fiction reveals that at some level he recognizes these anxieties. Such awareness is the first step toward conquering his fears.

The escape that he typically shows his namesake seeking is, therefore, not a real option for Nick the writer. Nick's fiction is his greatest effort to face life and himself. In fact, had Hemingway kept the original ending to "Big Two-Hearted River," we would have had a much clearer picture of the artist as hero. In the last scene of this conclusion, Nick returns to camp to write a story which will describe the country like Cézanne had painted it, a story very similar to the one we have just read. Lest we underestimate the significance of that enterprise—and with Nick's announcement that he writes because "It was really more fun than anything" (*NAS*, 218) it would be easy to do so—we should remember that writing is not only one of those needs from which Nick was seeking relief, but it is also an activity that will undoubtedly engage him in another need he had hoped to escape: thinking. To put this another way, in the act of writing Nick will *have* to fish that symbolic mental swamp, an effort which, in the final version of "Big Two-Hearted River," he is not quite ready to make. Of course, just how honestly and fully Nick will confront what troubles him (especially those "other needs" which are so new and sensitive that he cannot even name them, as if to do so would be to admit their reality and his own limitations) is another matter and one we cannot gauge since it occurs outside the pages and time period of *In Our Time*. The book is a record of how Nick has been and is, not how he will be.

At this record of Nick's recent mental history, *In Our Time* should thus be seen as a novel, not merely a collection of short stories. D. H. Lawrence, one of the book's first reviewers, came close to making this assessment when he called *In Our Time* a "fragmentary novel," and Young once proposed that it was "nearly a novel" about Nick.[17] However, as I have argued, although Nick's mind is fragmented, confused to pieces by his accelerated entry into adulthood, *In Our Time* is not at all fragmentary. It is a complete work, unified by the consciousness of Nick Adams as he attempts to come to terms through his fiction with his involvement in World War I and, more recently, with the problems of marriage and his fear of fatherhood. Furthermore, reading the book from this perspective removes our focus from Hemingway's biographical sources, a focus which has too often caused critics to juggle the sequence of the stories in an attempt to make their chronology match the order of events in Hemingway's life or to state simply that *In Our Time* lacks structural unity. To the contrary, the stories are ordered precisely to reflect the actual history and the pyschological state of Nick Adams. As F. Scott Fitzgerald suggested in 1926, *In Our Time* does not pretend to be about one man, but it is.[18]

Finally, though, we do come back to Hemingway. For while this analysis of *In Our Time* has separated Nick Adams' history from Hemingway's in ways that are important to our understanding of the book, it has also revealed that Nick's inner life is similar to that of his creator in areas that readers have often failed to notice. First of all, although two of Hemingway's most recent biographers, Jeffrey Meyers and Kenneth Lynn, challenge earlier conclusions about the effects of Hemingway's participation in World War I on his psyche, there can be no doubt that at some level he was significantly affected.[19] Both point out that Hemingway was obsessed by the fear of loss; as Lynn puts it, Hemingway always sank into a depression "whenever he lost anything, whether good or bad."[20] It seems possible that this obsession grew out of his experiences in the war, or at least increased after that time. Second, and just as important, Meyers and Lynn both show that Hemingway was afraid that marriage and fatherhood would change his life drastically, and for the worse. According to Meyers, "he was too emotionally immature (despite his wide experience) to accept domestic and paternal responsibility."[21] Thus we can claim for Hemingway what we have claimed for Nick, that, as Lynn argues, "Uncertain to the point of fear about himself, he was compelled to write stories in which he endeavored to cope with the disorder of his inner world by creating fictional equivalents for it."[22]

Yet it is Hemingway's initial inclination to turn over his stories to Nick that gives us our most fascinating look into his psyche. Besides the possibility that Hemingway recognized that making Nick the author of his stories would help unify *In Our Time*, we can also infer that by this plan he could add another layer of insulation between himself and the truths contained in his stories. Apparently the distance provided by a fictional persona was not enough room for a man whose greatest fiction was rapidly becoming the lies he passed off to friends, relatives, critics, and himself as the truth about his life.[23] Hence, in his original conclusion to "Big Two-Hearted River," Hemingway was engaging Nick Adams in the new capacity of author to run interference for him, to block out what he had disclosed about himself to himself (and others) in the writing of his fiction.

However, despite Hemingway's desire, which increased as he got older, to deny that he was troubled, immature, or anything less than a courageous man, *In Our Time* suggests—as it does for Nick—that finally he could not deceive himself. Norman Mailer once said that "It may even be that the final judgment on [Hemingway's] work may come to the notion that what he failed to do was tragic, but what he accomplished was heroic, for it is possible he carried a weight of anxiety within him from day to day which would have suffocated any man smaller than himself."[24] Hemingway's public image still persists as that of a brave man constantly proving himself in battles with both men and animals. *In Our Time* reveals, through the unifying consciousness of Nick Adams, a more substantial kind of bravery, for it indicates that the greatest opponent he wrestled with was himself.

Decoding Papa: "A Very Short Story" As Work and Text

Robert Scholes

●

The semiotic study of a literary text is not wholly unlike traditional interpretation or rhetorical analysis, nor is it meant to replace these other modes of response to literary works. But the semiotic critic situates the text somewhat differently, privileges different dimensions of the text, and uses a critical methodology adapted to the semiotic enterprise. Most interpretive methods privilege the "meaning" of the text. Hermeneutic critics seek authorial or intentional meaning; the New Critics seek the ambiguities of "textual" meaning; the "reader response" critics allow readers to make meaning. With respect to meaning the semiotic critic is situated differently. Such a critic looks for the generic or discursive structures that enable and constrain meaning.

Under semiotic inspection neither the author nor the reader is free to make meaning. Regardless of their lives as individuals, as author and reader they are traversed by codes that enable their communicative adventures at the cost of setting limits to the messages they can exchange. A literary text, then, is not simply a set of words, but (as Roland Barthes demonstrated in *S/Z*, though not necessarily in just that way) a network of codes that enables the marks on the page to be read as a text of a particular sort.

In decoding narrative texts, the semiotic method is based on two simple but powerful analytical tools: the distinction between story and discourse on the one hand and that between text and events on the other. The distinction between story and discourse is grounded in a linguistic

Because of the author's restrictions against reprinting "A Very Short Story" as a whole in any work other than a volume made up exclusively of his own work, the full text of the story has not been included here. The reader is requested to consult the text of "A Very Short Story" in Hemingway's *In Our Time* or *The Short Stories of Ernest Hemingway*, New York: Charles Scribner's Sons (The Scribner Library), before reading this essay. My apologies for the inconvenience.

observation by Emile Benveniste to the effect that some languages (notably French and Greek) have a special tense of the verb used for the narration of past events. (See "The Correlations of Tense in the French Verb," chapter 19 of *Problems in General Linguistics*. See also Seymour Chatman, *Story and Discourse*.) This tense, the aorist or *passé simple*, emphasizes the relationship between the utterance and the situation the utterance refers to, between the narration and the events narrated. This is par excellence the mode of written transcriptions of events: *histoire* or "story." Benveniste contrasts this with the mode of *discours* or "discourse," in which the present contact between speaker and listener is emphasized. Discourse is rhetorical and related to oral persuasion. Story is referential and related to written documentation. Discourse is now; story is then. Story speaks of he and she; discourse is a matter of you and me, I and thou.

In any fictional text, then, we can discern certain features that are of the story: reports on actions, mentions of times and places, and the like. We can also find elements that are of the discourse: evaluations, reflections, language that suggests an authorial or at least narratorial presence who is addressing a reader or narratee with a persuasive aim in mind. When we are told that someone "smiled cruelly," we can detect more of story in the verb and more of discourse in the adverb. Some fictional texts, those of D. H. Lawrence for example, are highly discursive. To read a Lawrence story is to enter into a personal relationship with someone who resembles the writer of Lawrence's private correspondence. In contrast, Hemingway often seems to have made a strong effort to eliminate discourse altogether—an effort that is apparent in "A Very Short Story."

The distinction between story and discourse is closely related to another with which it is sometimes confused, and that is the distinction between the *récit* and *diégésis* of a narrative. In this case we are meant to distinguish between the whole text of a narration as a text on the one hand and the events narrated as events on the other. We can take over the Greek term, diegesis, for the system of characters and events and simply anglicize the other term as recital, or just refer to the "text" when we mean the words and the "diegesis" for what they encourage us to create as a fiction.

The text itself may be analyzed into components of story and discourse, but it may also be considered in relation to the diegesis. One of the primary qualities of those texts we understand as fiction is that they generate a diegetic order that has an astonishing independence from its text. To put it simply, once a story is told it can be recreated in a recognizable way by a totally new set of words—in another language, for instance—or in another medium altogether. The implications of this for analysis are profound. Let us explore some of them.

A fictional diegesis draws its nourishment not simply from the words of its text but from its immediate culture and its literary tradition. The magical words "once upon a time" in English set in motion a machine of considerable momentum which can hardly be turned off without the equally magical "they lived happily ever after" or some near equivalent. The diegetic processes of "realistic" narrative are no less insistent. "A Very Short Story," by its location in Hemingway's larger text (*In Our Time*) and a few key words (Padua, carried, searchlights, duty, operating, front, armistice), allows us to supply the crucial notions of military hospital, nurse, soldier, and World War I that the diegesis requires.

This process is so crucial that we should perhaps stop and explore its implications. The words on the page are not the story. The text is not the diegesis. The story is constructed by the reader from the words on the page by an inferential process—a skill that can be developed. The reader's role is in a sense creative—without it no story exists—but it is also constrained by rules of inference that set limits to the legitimacy of the reader's constructions. Any interpretive dispute may be properly brought back to the "words on the page," of course, but these words never speak their own meaning. The essence of writing, as opposed to speech, is that the reader speaks the written words, the words that the writer has abandoned. A keen sense of this situation motivates the various sorts of "envoi" that writers supplied for their books in the early days of printing. They felt that their books were mute and would be spoken by others.

In reading a narrative, then, we translate a text into a diegesis according to the codes we have internalized. This is simply the narrative version of the normal reading process. As E. D. Hirsch has recently reminded us (in the *Philosophy of Composition* [Chicago, 1977], 122–23), for almost a century research in reading (Binet and Henri in 1894, Fillenbaum in 1966, Sachs in 1967, Johnson-Laird in 1970, Levelt and Kampen in 1975, and Brewer in 1975—specific citations can be found in Hirsch) has shown us that memory stores not the words of texts but their concepts, not the signifiers but the signifieds. When we read a narrative text, then, we process it as a diegesis. If we retell the story, it will be in our own words. To the extent that the distinction between poetry and fiction is a useful one, it is based on the notion of poetry as monumental, fixed in the words of the text and therefore untranslatable; while fiction has proved highly translatable because its essence is not in its language but in its diegetic structure. As fiction approaches the condition of poetry, its precise words become more important; as poetry moves toward narrative, its specific language decreases in importance.

In reading fiction, then, we actually translate from the text to a diegesis, substituting narrative units (characters, scenes, events, and so on) for verbal units (nouns, adjectives, phrases, clauses, etc.). And we perform other changes as well. We organize the material we receive so as to make it memorable, which means that we systematize it as much as possible. In the diegetic system we construct, time flows at a uniform rate; events occur in chronological order; people and places have the qualities expected of them—unless the text specifies otherwise. A writer may relocate the Eiffel Tower to Chicago, but unless we are told this we will assume that a scene below that tower takes place in Paris—a Paris equipped with all the other items accorded it in our cultural paradigm.

Places and other entities with recognizable proper names (Napoleon, Waterloo, Broadway) enter the diegesis coded by culture. The events reported in a narrative text, however, will be stored in accordance with a syntactic code based on a chronological structure. The text may present the events that compose a story in any order, plunging in medias res or following through from beginning to end, but the diegesis always seeks to arrange them in chronological sequence. The text may expand a minute into pages or cram years into a single sentence for its own ends, but the minutes and years remain minutes and years of diegetic time all the same. In short, the text may discuss what it chooses, but once a diegesis is set in motion no text can ever completely control it. "How many children had Lady Macbeth?" is not simply the query of a naive interpreter but the expression of a normal diegetic impulse. Where authors and texts delight in equivocation, the reader needs certainty and closure to complete the diegetic processing of textual materials. From this conflict of interests comes a tension that many modern writers exploit.

The semiotician takes the reader's diegetic impulse and establishes it as a principle of structuration. The logic of diegetic structure provides a norm, a benchmark for the study of textual strategies, enabling us to explore the dialogue between text and diegesis, looking for points of stress, where the text changes its ways in order to control the diegetic material for its own ends. The keys to both affect and intention may be found at these points. Does the text return obsessively to one episode of diegetic history? Does it disturb diegetic order to tell about something important to its own discursive ends? Does it omit something that diegetic inertia deems important? Does it change its viewpoint on diegetic events? Does it conceal things? Does it force evaluations through the rhetoric of its discourse? The calm inertia of diegetic process, moved by the weight of culture and tradition and the needs of memory itself, offers a stable background for the mapping of textual strategies. And our most aesthetically ambitious texts will be those that find it most necessary to put their own stamp on the diegetic process.

Hemingway's "A Very Short Story" presents itself as exceptionally reticent. The familiar Hemingway style, which Gérard Genette has called "behaviorist," seems to efface itself, to offer us a pure diegesis. Boy meets girl—a "cute meet," as they used to say in Hollywood—they fall in love, become lovers, plan to marry, but the vicissitudes of war separate them, and finally forces that are too strong for them bring about their defeat. This is the story, is it not: a quasi-naturalistic slice of life that begins almost like a fairy tale ("Once upon a time in another country . . .")—and ends with the negation of the fairy-tale formula ("and they lived unhappily ever after")—a negation that proclaims the text's realistic or naturalistic status? But there is already a tension here, between the open form of the slice of life and the neat closure of the fairy tale, which emerges most clearly if we compare the progress of diegetic time with the movement of the text. We can do this in a crude way by mapping the hours, days, and weeks of diegetic time against the paragraphs of the text. The slowest paragraphs are the first: one night; and the third: one trip to the Duomo. The fastest are the fourth: his time at the front; the sixth: Luz's time in Pordenone; and the seventh or last: which carries Luz to the point of infinity with the word "never." The narrative thus increases its speed throughout and achieves its effect of culmination by the use of the infinite terms in the last paragraph. The text might easily have contented itself with recounting the fact that the major did not marry Luz in the spring, but it feels obliged to add "or any other time," just as it is obliged to use the word "never" in the next sentence. Something punitive is going on here as the discourse seems to be revenging itself upon the character. Why?

Before trying to answer that question, we would do well to consider some other features of the text/diegesis relationship. From the first paragraph on it is noticeable that one of the two main characters in the diegesis has a name in the text while the other is always referred to by a pronoun. Why should this be? The answer emerges when we correlate this detail with other features of the text/diegesis relationship. The text, as we have observed, is reticent, as if it, too, does not want to "blab about anything during the silly, talky time." But it is more reticent about some things than others. In the first paragraph the male character is introduced in the first sentence. Luz appears in the fifth. When she sits on the bed, we are told "she was cool and fresh in the hot night." Why this information about her temperature? She is the nurse, after all, and he the patient. In fact it is not important about how she feels at all, but about how she appears to him. The text is completely reticent about how he feels himself, though the implication is that he finds her coolness attractive. How he seems to her or how she feels about him are not considered relevant. This is a selective reticence. Our vision is subjectively with him (as the personal pronoun implies), while Luz is seen more objectively (as the proper name implies). The final implication of paragraph one is that they make love right then and there. But the reticent text makes the reader responsible for closing that little gap in the diegesis.

This matter of the point of view taken by the text can be established more clearly with the use of a sort of litmus test developed by Roland Barthes. If we rewrite the text substituting the first-person pronoun for the third, we can tell whether or not we are dealing with what Barthes calls a "personal system," a covert, first-person narration (see "Introduction to the Structural Analysis of Narratives," in *Image-Music-Text*, 112). In the case of "A Very Short Story," where we have two third-person characters of apparently equal consequence, we must rewrite the story twice to find out what we need to know. Actually, the issue is settled conclusively after the first two paragraphs, which are all I will present here:

The first two paragraphs of "A Very Short Story" rewritten—"he" transposed to "I":

> One hot evening in Padua they carried me up onto the roof and I could look out over the top of the town. There were chimney swifts in the sky. After a while it got dark and the searchlights came out. The others went down and took the bottle with them. Luz and I could hear them below on the balcony. Luz sat on the bed. She was cool and fresh in the hot night.
>
> Luz stayed on night duty for three months. They were glad to let her. When they operated on me she prepared me for the operating table; and we had a joke about friend or enema. I went under the anaesthetic holding tight on to myself so I would not blab about anything during the silly, talky time. After I got on crutches I used to take the temperatures so Luz would not have to get up from the bed. There were only a few patients, and they all knew about it. They all

liked Luz. As I walked back along the halls I thought of Luz in my bed.

The same paragraphs—"Luz" transposed to "I":

> One hot evening in Padua they carried him up onto the roof and he could look out over the top of the town. There were chimney swifts in the sky. After a while it got dark and the searchlights came out. The others went down and took the bottles with them. He and I could hear them below on the balcony. I sat on the bed. I was cool and fresh in the hot night.
>
> I stayed on night duty for three months. They were glad to let me. When they operated on him I prepared him for the operating table; and we had a joke about friend or enema. He went under the anaesthetic holding tight on to himself so he would not blab about anything during the silly, talky time. After he got on crutches he used to take the temperatures so I would not have to get up from the bed. There were only a few patients, and they all knew about it. They all liked me. As he walked back along the halls he thought of me in his bed.

"He" transposes to "I" perfectly, but "Luz" does not. In the second rewriting the first person itself enters the discourse with a shocking abruptness, since the earlier sentences seem to have been from the male patient's point of view. The stress becomes greater in the last sentence of the first paragraph, which has been constructed to indicate how she appeared to him, not how she seemed to herself. But the last two sentences of the second paragraph in the second rewriting are even more ludicrous, with the first-person narrator informing us of how well liked she was and finally describing his thoughts about her. In this rewriting there is simply too great a tension between the angle of vision and the person of the voice. The discourse loses its coherence. But the first rewriting is completely coherent because in it voice and vision coincide. It is really his narrative all the way. The third-person narration of the original text is a disguise, a mask of pseudo-objectivity worn by the text for its own rhetorical purposes.

The discourse of this text, as I have suggested, is marked by its reticence, but this reticence of the text is contrasted with a certain amount of talkativeness in the diegesis. He, of course, doesn't want to "blab," but *they* want "every one to know about" their relationship. Implication: *she* is the one who wants the news spread. There is absolutely no direct discourse in the text, but there are two paragraphs devoted to letters and one to recounting a quarrel. Here, too, we find reticence juxtaposed to talkativeness. Luz writes many letters to him while he is at the front. But the text does not say whether he wrote any to her. Hers are clearly repetitive and hyperbolic. The style of the discourse becomes unusually paratactic—even for Hemingway—whenever her letters are presented. "They were all about the hospital, *and how* much she loved him *and how* it was impossible to get along without him *and how* terrible it was missing him at night" (my italics). The repetitive "hows," the hyperbolic "impossible" and "terrible," and all the "ands" suggest an unfortunate prose style even without direct quotation. Above all, they indicate an ominous lack of reticence.

The quarrel is not represented in the text, but the "agreement" that causes it is summarized for us, at least in part. It takes the form of a series of conditions that *he* must fulfill in order to be rewarded with Luz's hand in marriage. Curiously, the conditions are represented not only as things it is "understood" that he will and will not do but also as things he wants and does not want to do. He does not "want to see his friends or any one in the States. Only to get a job and be married." It is not difficult to imagine a man being willing to avoid his friends, to work, and to stay sober to please a woman, but it is hard to imagine any human being who does not *"want* to see his friends or *anyone."* Not *want* to? Not *anyone*? The text seems to be reporting on the diegesis in a most curious way here. This is not simply reticence but irony. There is a strong implication that he is being coerced, pushed too far, even having his masculinity abused. If there are any conditions laid upon Luz, we do not hear of them.

Finally, the final letter arrives. In reporting it the text clearly allows Luz's prose to shine through once again, complete with repetition of the horrible phrase about the "boy and girl" quality of their relationship and the splendidly hyperbolic cacophony of "expected, absolutely unexpectedly." Her behavior belies her words. Her true awfulness, amply suggested earlier by the reticent text, blazes forth here as her hideous discourse perfectly complements her treacherous behavior.

But how did *he* behave while she was discovering the glories of Latin love? *Nihil dixit.* The text maintains what we can now clearly see as a specifically manly reticence. Did he drink? Did he see his friends? Or anyone? Did he want to? We know not. We do know, however, of his vehicular indiscretion in Lincoln Park and its result. The text is too generous and manly to say so, of course, but we know that this, too, is Luz's fault. She wounded him in the heart and, "a short time after" this salesgirl got him in an even more vital place. The discourse leaves them both unhappy, but it clearly makes Luz the agent of the unhappiness.

And what does it make him? Why, the patient, of course. He is always being carried about, given enemas, operated on, sent to the front, sent home, not wanting anything, reading letters. He is wounded at the beginning and wounded at the end. The all-American victim: polite, reticent, and just waiting for an accident to happen to him. Who is to blame if his accidents keep taking the form of women? Who indeed? Whose discourse is this, whose story, whose diegesis, whose world? It is Papa's, of course, for Hemingway taught a whole generation of male readers to prepare for a world where men may be your friends but women are surely the enema.

The story quite literally leaves its protagonist wounded in his sex by contact with a woman. From the bed in Padua to the back seat in Lincoln Park our hero is carried from wound to wound. We never hear the accents of his voice or the intonations of his prose. We do not have to. The text speaks for him. Its voice is his. And its reticence is his as well. In this connection we should look once again at a passage in the second paragraph: "they had a joke about friend or enema. He went under the anaesthetic holding tight on to himself so he would not. . . ." Up to this point in the second sentence we are not aware that there has been a change of topic from that which closed the earlier sentence. The language of oral retentiveness coincides neatly with that of anal retentiveness. Logorrhea and diarrhea are equally embarrassing. Enemas are enemies and to "blab about anything during the silly, talky time" (to finish the sentence) would be as bad as to discharge matter freely from the opposite end of the alimentary canal. As Hemingway put it on another occasion: "If you talk about it, you lose it."

The point of this discussion is that the text reveals the principle behind its reticent prose style through an impartial and equal distress at the idea of excessive discharge of either verbal or fecal matter. It is an anal retentive style, then, in a surprisingly literal way. And through this style the text presents us with a lesson about women. Luz first gives our retentive hero a literal enema and then she metaphorically emasculates him by making him renounce alcohol, friends, and all the pleasures of life. The salesgirl from the loop merely administers the literal coup de grace to his already figuratively damaged sexuality.

Having come this far with a semiotic analysis, we can begin to distinguish it more precisely from New Critical exegesis. In doing so we must begin by admitting that the two approaches share a certain number of interpretive gestures. We must also recognize that no two semiotic analyses or New Critical exegeses are likely to be identical. The major differences in the two critical approaches can be traced to their different conceptions of the object of study: for New Criticism, the work; for semiotics, the text. As a work, "A Very Short Story" must be seen as complete, unified, shaped into an aesthetic object, a verbal icon. The pedagogical implications of this are important.

The student interpreting "A Very Short Story" as a "work" is put into an interesting position. Like many of Hemingway's early stories, this one presents a male character favorably and a female unfavorably. In fact, it strongly implies favorable things about masculinity and unfavorable things about feminity. It does this, as our semiotic analysis has shown, by mapping certain traits on to a value structure. The good, loyal, reticent male character is supported by the discourse, through its covert first-person perspective and the complicity of its style with those values. The bad, treacherous, talkative female is cast out. Even the carefully established point of view is violated in the last paragraph so that the narrator can track Luz through eternity and assure us that she never married her major "in the spring, or any other time." But for the most part Hemingway's control over his text is so great that the anger at the root of the story is transformed into what we may take as the cool, lapidary prose of the pure, impersonal artist.

And there definitely is an anger behind this story, to which we shall soon turn our attention. For the moment we must follow a bit further the situation of the student faced with this story in the form of a "work" to be interpreted. The concept of "the student" is one of those transcendental abstractions that we accept for convenience's sake and often come to regret. We can begin to break it down by reminding ourselves that students come in at least two genders. Actual students read this story in different ways. Most male students sympathize with the protagonist and are very critical of Luz—as, indeed, the discourse asks them to be. Many female students try to read the story as sympathetic to Luz, blaming events on the "weakness" of the young man or the state of the world. This is a possible interpretation, but it is not well supported by the text. Thus the female student must either "misread" the work (that is, she must offer the more weakly supported of two interpretations) or accept one more blow to her self-esteem as a woman. Faced with this story in a competitive classroom, women are put at a disadvantage. They are, in fact, in a double bind.

By New Critical standards the narrator is impersonal and reliable. The words on the page are all we have, and they tell us of a garrulous, faithless woman who was unworthy of the love of a loyal young man. But semiotic analysis has already suggested alternatives to this view. Seen as a text that presents a diegesis, this story is far from complete. There are gaps in the diegesis, reticences in the text, and highly manipulative use of covert first-person narrative. There are signs of anger and vengefulness in the text, too, that suggest not an omniscient impersonal author but a partial, flawed human being—like the rest of us—behind the words on the page.

As a text, this story refers to other texts: to the fairy tale it is so definitely not, to other stories of betrayal (like *Troilus and Criseyde*, in which the Greek Diomedes plays the part of the Italian major), and to the other stories that surrounded it in Hemingway's *In Our Time*. But it also must be seen as a text among a particular set of other texts by Hemingway that present very similar diegetic material. These are, in chronological order, a manuscript called "Personal" (Young and Mann, *The Hemingway Manuscripts* [University Park, Penn., 1969], 11C), "chapter 10" in *in our time* (Paris, 1924), and various drafts of a novel that was finally published as *A Farewell to Arms* in 1929. All of these texts generate diegesis centered on a nurse in an Italian hospital. From Hemingway's letters and various other texts, including reports of interviews with the principals, yet another diegesis can be generated. In this one a nineteen-year-old American Red Cross worker named Ernest Hemingway meets a Red Cross nurse named Agnes Hannah von Kurowsky, a twenty-six-year-old American woman, at a hospital in Milan, and falls in love with her. She calls him Kid and he calls her Mrs. Kid. When she volunteers for service in Florence during an influenza outbreak, he writes her many letters. ("He wrote to her daily, sometimes twice a day. She answered as often as her duties would allow." Carlos Baker, *Ernest Hemingway* [New York, 1980], 71.) They continue to correspond when she moves to Treviso near Padua to help out during another epidemic. He travels around in Italy, but his wounds prevent him from returning to the front. He sees Agnes a few more times before leaving Italy for the States.

He describes one of these visits in a letter to his friend, Bill Smith:

> But listen what kind of a girl I have: Lately I've been hitting it up— about 18 martinis a day and 4 days ago I left the hospital and hopped camions 200 miles up to the Front A.W.O.L. to visit some pals. Ossifers in the R.G.A. British outside of Padova. Their batteries are en repose. They gave me a wonderful time and we used the staff car and I rode to the hounds on the Colonels charger. Leg and all.
>
> But Bill to continue. We went in the staff car up to TREVISO where the missus [Agnes von Kurowsky] is in a Field Hospital. She had heard about my hitting the alcohol and did she lecture me? She did not.
>
> She said, "Kid we're going to be partners. So if you are going to

drink I am too. Just the same amount." And she'd gotten some damn whiskey and poured some of the raw stuff out and she'd never had a drink of anything before except wine and I know what she thinks of booze. And William that brought me up shortly. Bill this is some girl and I thank God I got crucked so I met her. Damn it I really honestly can't see what the devil she can see in the brutal Stein but by some very lucky astigmatism she loves me Bill. So I'm going to hit the States and start working for the Firm. Ag says we can have a wonderful time being poor together and having been poor alone for some years and always more or less happy I think it can be managed.

So now all I have to do is hit the minimum living wage for two and lay up enough for six weeks or so up North and call on you for service as a best man. Why man I've only got about 50 more years to live and I don't want to waste any of them and every minute that I'm away from that Kid is wasted. (Carlos Baker, ed., *Ernest Hemingway, Selected Letters 1917–1961*, New York, 1981, 20)

When Ernest leaves Italy from Genoa in January 1919, the romance is still sexually unconsummated (according to Agnes von Kurowsky herself and the best judgment of Michael Reynolds, who reports this in *Hemingway's First War* [Princeton, 1976] and Carlos Baker, who discusses these events in *Ernest Hemingway, A Life Story* [New York, 1969].) Hemingway in fact goes home believing that when he gets established in a job that will support two people, Agnes will return and marry him. What she believed at that time cannot be determined.

At home Ernest saw many of his friends and partied a good deal. After one of these parties in his parents' home the unconscious bodies of two friends were stumbled over by Ernest and his older sister as they closed up the house. They agreed that the "Italian celebrations had gone too far." He still did not have a regular job when a letter from Agnes arrived in March 1919. This is the way his sister Marcelline describes the event:

For days Ernie had been watching the mails. He was irritable and on edge with the waiting. Then the letter came. After he read it he went to bed and was actually ill. We didn't know what was the matter with Ernie at first. He did not respond to medical treatment, and he ran a temperature. Dad was worried about him. I went up to Ernie's room to see if I could be of any help to him. Ernie thrust the letter toward me.

"Read it," he said from the depths of his grief. "No. I'll tell you." Then he turned to the wall. He was physically sick for several days but he did not mention the letter again.

Ag, Ernie told me, was not coming to America. She was going to marry an Italian major instead.

In time Ernest felt better. He got out among his friends again. (Marcelline Hemingway, *At the Hemingways*, Boston, 1962, 188)

By the end of April Ernest had recovered sufficiently to jest about his situation in a letter to an old Red Cross buddy: "I am a free man! That includes them all up to and including Agnes. My Gawd man you didn't think I was going to marry and settle down did you?" (Baker, *Selected Letters*, 24). But before that he had written to another nurse from Italy, Elsie MacDonald, "telling her the news and adding that when Agnes disembarked in New York on her way home, he hoped that she would stumble on the dock and knock out all her front teeth" (Baker, *Ernest Hemingway*, 81).

In June he received another letter from Agnes, in which she told him that her Italian lieutenant's (his actual rank) aristocratic family had forbidden the marriage, so she would be coming home unmarried after all. Ernest did not answer this letter but wrote a buddy from the ambulance unit about it:

Had a very sad letter from Ag from Rome yesterday. She has fallen out with her Major. She is in a hell of a way mentally and says I should feel revenged for what she did to me. Poor damned kid. I'm sorry as hell for her. But there's nothing I can do. I loved her once and then she gypped me. And I don't blame her. But I set out to cauterize out her memory and I burnt it out with a course of booze and other women and now it's gone. (Baker, *Selected Letters*, 25)

This diegesis we are constructing from various texts is not yet finished. It goes on for some time. After Ernest marries a woman about the same age as Agnes and moves to Paris, living mostly off her income, he writes a friendly letter to Agnes and receives a friendly response in December 1922: "You know there has always been a little bitterness over the way our comradeship ended. . . . Anyhow I always knew that it would turn out right in the end, and that you would realize it was the best way, as I'm positive you must believe, now that you have Hadley" (Baker, *Ernest Hemingway*, 136). A few months later he writes a sketch for a collection of vignettes that will be published in 1924 as *in our time*. Sometime before the final version is delivered to the Three Mountains Press in Paris (the date of composition is not known), he had begun a draft called "Personal." A pencil copy exists among the Hemingway papers. In Philip Young and Charles Mann's catalog of the manuscripts it is described as beginning with the words "One hot evening in Milan they carried me up onto the roof" (*The Hemingway Manuscripts*, item 11C). For the published volume this sketch was rewritten in the third person. It appeared as "chapter 10" in *in our time*, and it was virtually identical to what we know as "A Very Short Story," but the nurse is called "Ag" instead of Luz in this version, and the hospital is located in Milan instead of Padua. In short this text gives us a diegesis closer to the one we can construct for Ernest Hemingway himself from the letters and other documents than does the later version. When the American publication of *In Our Time* was arranged, the little vignettes of the original *in our time* were used to separate the longer stories in the new volume and two of the original set were promoted to the status of stories. In this way the tenth vignette became "A Very Short Story," and Ag became Luz, Milan became Padua, and The Fair became a Loop department store. The changes were made, Hemingway said, to avoid possible libel suits: "Ag is libelous, short for Agnes," he wrote to Maxwell Perkins (discussing the 1938 publication of his collected stories—see Baker, *Selected Letters*, 469).

Brooding still over this episode, Hemingway began a novel called "Along With Youth," in which Nick Adams, the hero, was to be followed in his adventures as an ambulance driver "to a love affair with a nurse named Agnes" (Baker, *Ernest Hemingway*, 191). This manuscript stopped at page 27, with Nick still on a troop transport headed for Europe. But Hemingway continued to brood over this episode of his youth until he finally transformed Agnes into Catherine Barkley and laid her to rest in *A Farewell to Arms*.

Many texts, many diegeses. What can we say about them? First of all, it is clear that we are not dealing with an impersonal artist constructing aesthetic wholes here, but with a dogged human being trying to produce texts that will pass as works, drawing upon one of the most painful events of his life for his material. As interpreters what are we to make of the shift from Milan to Padua for the location of our diegesis, since nothing else is changed? Every Italian city has a duomo. The name Padua or Milan is there to generate with its apparent specificity "the effect of the real" as Roland Barthes calls it, though the precise city is not important. The fictional diegesis has a tidiness, of course, that actuality rarely assumes and a sexuality that extends well beyond the events from which it derives. The need to add carnality to an affair that really was a "boy and girl" romance is especially notable now. Those words of Luz about the "boy and girl affair" are absurd when written by someone who had waited in bed while her crippled lover did her hospital work for her. As the words of Agnes von Kurowsky—which they may or may not actually be—they could be simply accurate.

We can also note that in life the Kid did not go back to the front; she did, in effect, by volunteering to help with an epidemic. And he wrote her at least as often as she wrote him. At one point five of his letters reached her in the same batch (Baker, *Ernest Hemingway*, 71). The gonorrhea, of course, which shocked Ernest's father so deeply that he mailed his copies of *in our time* back to the publisher, saying he "would not tolerate such filth in his house" (*At the Hemingways*, 219), was apparently an invention. About "friend or enema" we can only speculate.

The text produced by Hemingway responds to a double motivation. It wants to be art, to be a work that is complete in itself. But it also wants to rewrite life, to make its surrogate protagonist more triumphant as a lover, more active as a soldier, and more deeply victimized as a man than was the author himself.

Where does this leave the critic, the teacher, the student of literary texts? I hope it leaves them suspicious and flexible. I chose this Hemingway text for discussion because it *is* a very short story and it had interested me since I first read it as an undergraduate. I began to study it not knowing what I would find. I did the analysis first, then the scholarship. My work is not done. My own text is incomplete. So be it. My purpose, too, is perhaps unachieved, but lest it be misinterpreted as well, let me restate it here.

I do not wish to suggest that we jettison the critical ingenuity we have learned from the New Critics. Certainly I will not give up my own. But I do wish to suggest that we approach fictions as texts traversed by codes rather than as formal artifacts. A semiotic approach, it seems to me, allows critic, teacher, student, and reader more scope for thought, more freedom and more responsibility, than a merely exegetical one. This Hemingway text is neither the greatest story ever told nor a horrible example. It is, in miniature, a model of all fictions—better than the man who made it because he worked hard to make it that way, but still flawed, still a communication to be tested and weighed, not an icon to be worshiped. For all forms of idolatry, whether of gods, men, or literary works, teach us finally the worst of all lessons: to bend the knee and bow the head, when what we must do instead is examine everything before us freely and fearlessly, so as to produce with our own critical labor things better than ourselves.

Hemingway's "After the Storm": A Lacanian Reading

Ben Stoltzfus

●

"After the Storm" is ostensibly a "true story" told to Ernest Hemingway in 1928 by Eddie "Bra" Saunders, a Key West charter-boat captain, about a conch-fisherman's account of the sinking off the Florida Keys, in the late summer of 1919, of a Spanish steamer, the *Valbanera*. The genesis of the story has been fully documented by Susan Beegel in her book *Hemingway's Craft of Omission: Four Manuscript Examples*, in a chapter entitled "Just Skillful Reporting? Fact and Fiction in 'After the Storm'" (69–88). For the most part, however, commentators have paid little attention to the story, and there are no Freudian or Lacanian readings of it.

The story begins on the waterfront with a fight between two men: the narrator and his assailant. The aggressor is choking the narrator, but the latter manages to free himself by slashing the other man with a knife. In the mistaken belief that he has killed his opponent, the narrator-fugitive hides out and with his skiff tries to salvage what he can from a sunken ship that has gone down in the storm. The man dives repeatedly, first with a wrench, then with a grapple, in a vain attempt to break the porthole of a cabin in which he sees a woman with flowing hair and rings on her fingers. Meanwhile, sea birds are feeding on pieces of flesh that rise to the surface from a hole in the ship's hull. Unable to salvage anything, the narrator returns to shore where he is informed that the man with whom he had fought is not dead. The storm resumes, and the narrator describes how and why the ship sank. When he returns again to the sunken vessel, he discovers that she has been cleaned out by the Greeks. The narrator, the ship, and the place itself have no names. Mango Key, Sou'west Key, and Eastern Harbor are identified, but they may be useful only to sailors familiar with the region. For the general reader, since the Florida Keys are not referred to, these names are vague enough to be almost anywhere.

This deliberate vagueness gives the story a special aura that belies its realism. Moreover, "It wasn't about anything" is the narrator's first utterance, and he goes on from there to describe events that are, at best, ambiguous. He thinks he has killed a man, but he has not. He tries to salvage something from the sunken ship, but he can't. When he finally does return to the wreck, it is too late. The narrator is misinformed, ill-equipped, and frustrated. Nothing works, he has nothing, and he is left with nothing. The reader, like the narrator, is left with a pervasive feeling of emptiness and failure. The real tragedy is and should have been the sinking of the ship at sea and the loss of all life on board, but this event is anterior to the ones being described and is not the center of narrative focus. The narrator describes the sinking in two pages only, as a flashback at the end of the story. Nonetheless, the storm and the sinking grow in importance as the title of the story and the "nothing" of the opening sentence begin to cast their lengthening shadows across descriptions of events that, on the surface, seem clear and uncomplicated. But the original clarity, like the water in which the narrator-diver swims, becomes progressively opaque.

What is going on? Are we seeing only one eighth of the iceberg? Should we try to account for the seven-eighths which, like the sunken ship, are below the surface? Is there an unverbalized metaphorical level that *is* about something? Can we perform a salvage operation on the story that will give us the riches that the Greeks retrieved but were beyond the grasp or ken of the narrator? Can we "grapple" with the discourse in order to "wrench" meaning from a narrative in which these two words are used primarily as nouns? Fortunately, Jacques Lacan's work serves as the basis for a theory of narration within the context of an unconscious discourse that provides insight and answers to these questions. A Lacanian reading of "After the Storm" reveals a weave of metaphors whose meaning is veiled and whose connotations are repressed.

According to Lacan every narrative ("After the Storm" is no exception), like Oedipus in search of his history and destiny, manifests *desire*. In order to understand what the function of desire is, we need to look briefly at the structure of the Oedipus complex. As Sigmund Freud and Lacan define it, it is a blockage of a need that demands satisfaction. In addition to the blocked and repressed desire for the mother, it postulates two fantasized or imaginary visions of death. One is the father's death (imaginary murder), and the other is the subject's death (imaginary castration). The Oedipus complex is eventually resolved through the child's identification with the father, and this constitutes his superego. According to Lacan, the resolution is made possible by means of the introjection of the father's Name, the *non/nom du père*, which embodies the Law of incest prohibition and which, in time, also constitutes a portion of the child's unconscious. The father's No and Name is the first linguistic sign and symbol, and it coincides with the repression of sexuality, the beginnings of language, and the emergence of identity. The father's Name displaces the desire for the mother, in effect incorporating the child's assumption of his own death as a condition for his renunciation. This replacement of desire is the symbolic castration and death of the self that is repressed, thereby constituting the unconscious.

This triangulation is a critical moment for the child at a time when s/he accedes to language, confronts the Imaginary in the mirror, during the so-called mirror phase, and sees this self as Other. This misrecognition of self is due to the mediating presence of the mother (desire) and the interference of the father (prohibition). The ego is constituted as a fiction of sliding surfaces composed of the Imaginary (self), the Symbolic (father), and the Real. Although Lacanians have some difficulty defining the Real, discourse or storytelling (like neurosis) is a metaphorical substitute for blocked desire. Whatever the Real may be, narration is the manifestation of a primordial self that has been displaced and decentered. Thus, the father's Name, in addition to all subsequent signs and symbols, forms a chain of linguistic substitutions (metaphorical and metonymical) that are the signs and symptoms of the child's renunciation.

Lacan's analysis of narration begins with language and proceeds to rediscover the "discourse of the Other" that is embedded in speech which, in "After the Storm," is the narrative. The blockage of desire, along with its corollary, repression, produce a neurosis whose narrative symptoms are metaphorical. In the production of narrative (the sailor's story of his fight, the hiding out, and the salvage), unconscious content is condensed as metaphor and displaced as metonymy. These discoveries prompted Lacan to say that "the unconscious is structured as a language." The narrative process embodies the same characteristics of Freud's dream-work, only differently. It remains for the literary critic to determine how the manifest discourse veils the latent meaning, that is, how the signifiers resolve simultaneously into manifest signifieds and latent referents. If the dream is the iconic, although masked, mirror of the unconscious, fiction is its linguistic reflector. Lacan's focus thus enables us to understand, as Robert Con Davis phrases it in his "Introduction" to *Lacan and Narration: The Psychoanalytic Difference in Narrative Theory*, "how language in literary texts is constituted, buoyed up, permeated, and decentered by the unconscious" (848).

If we accept the premise that the unconscious is structured as a language, then all speech (every text) contains repressed material that manifests a never-ending dialog with the Other—that fictitious self made up of the melding of the Imaginary and the Symbolic. The symbolic is the Law, the father (*le non/nom du père*), eventually all *doxa*. The Imaginary is that displaced self that has to come to terms with the postponement of satisfaction, the repression of desire, the nurturing of discontent, in short, the maturation and acculturation that civilized adults claim to value. In this context "After the Storm," like every narrative, is the melding of language and the unconscious.

Moreover, Freud's interpretation of dreams enabled Lacan to show that the operations of the unconscious, encompassing the extremes of pictographic and linguistic analyses, are themselves a linguistic process. Like the iconic nature of dreams, language and narration have a manifest and a latent content. In dreams condensation and displacement disguise the content of the unconscious in the same way that metaphor and metonymy veil the pulsive forces of the subject's (author's) desire whenever s/he uses language.

Let us next apply Lacan's theory to Hemingway's "After the Storm." If the summary at the beginning of this essay gives the story's manifest content, then the fight, the choking, the storm, the sea, the sunken vessel, the wrench, the grapple, and the fragmented bodies inside the wreck must all have latent value and metaphorical meaning. If so, they become the displaced and condensed images of the author's unconscious. On the manifest level the events describe an adventure of action and would-be plunder, but on the latent level they reveal impotence, death, and desire.

If we accept Lacan's premise that every narrative is a manifestation of the unconscious, then the metaphorical symptoms of its discourse reveal the workings of desire. In a post-Freudian era the author's conscious manipulation of Freudian symbols may disrupt this process, and so, inevitably, the question arises, did Hemingway consciously imbue his text(s) with Freudian symbols or not? Although his work after 1950, particularly *The Garden of Eden*, suggests a Freudian connection, I agree with Gerry Brenner who, in *Concealments in Hemingway's Works*, states that although "Hemingway was fixated upon his father," he "seems unconscious of how extensively father-son dynamics empowered his writing" (17). This would also apply to Hemingway's relationship with his mother. In any case the repressive forces of the Law that come into play during the "mirror phase" of the child's development relate to the incest taboo in society at large, whether the father is present or not, whether he is dominant or submissive, and it is the mother, by virtue of this societal taboo, who distances herself from the child. It would be simplistic to assume that in Hemingway's case the repressive forces of the "mirror phase" were not at work or that the father-mother roles were reversed as a result of his father's diffidence or his mother's dominance and abrasiveness, of which Hemingway was fully conscious.

Although it is probable that Hemingway did read Freud sometime before he died, there is no evidence that I can find to suggest that Hemingway had read him before 1932, when he was writing "After the Storm." Although "After the Storm" belongs to the mature period of his short story writing ("Fathers and Sons," "The Gambler, the Nun, and the Radio," "God Rest you Merry, Gentlemen"), when almost everything in Hemingway's craft was conscious and controlled, evidence for the deliberate use of Freud is lacking. Even if he had read Freud, he would have concealed his symbols. In the December 13, 1954, issue of *Time* magazine he compares the writing process to putting raisins in bread: "No good book has ever been written that has in it symbols arrived at beforehand and stuck in. That kind of symbol sticks out like raisins in raisin bread. Raisin bread is all right, but plain bread is better" (72). Even if these symbolic omissions are deliberate, and there is no reason to think that they are since Michael S. Reynold's inventory of Hemingway's reading between 1910 and 1940 does not list any of Freud's works, the omissions function as unknowns. They are concealed the way the discourse of the unconscious is concealed. It is this concealment, whether conscious or not, that gives "After the Storm" its strange dreamlike aura. The manifest content belies the latent content.

It is perhaps worth noting that nonpsychoanalytic explorations of Hemingway's works can also point toward suppressed sexuality, the nada, the winner-take-nothing syndrome, and the failure of love. It should, therefore, be good news to everybody that a Lacanian exploration of metaphor and the metaphoric process of veiling confirms conclusions reached by other means. Perhaps it is useful that a Lacanian reading, which claims to be more "scientific" in its approach to the creative process, should support readings that tend to be intuitive and impressionistic.

Lacan's discourse of the Other thus makes it possible to list a series of equivalencies that structure the story's conscious and unconscious levels. The storm that sank the ship, the fight, and the choking are metaphors for the primal scene. Like Oedipus killing his father, Laius, on the road to Corinth, over "nothing" (a simple dispute over the right of way), the narrator's desire to kill his assailant over "nothing" is the symptom of anger and hostility directed at the Law. "What the hell you want to choke me for?" says the narrator, adding, "I'd have killed him" (372). The imagined death of the assailant precipitates the narrator's guilt and his hiding from the authorities. It corresponds to the repression that occurs when the Law prohibits the child's desire for the mother. The narrator's attempt to get at the woman floating in the ship that "looked a mile long under the water" (374) is the sign of this prohibition and the symptom of desire. The narrator's failure to pry the woman away from the ship, even in death, confirms the overriding Law of the Phallus. Failure is synonymous with castration and the perceived death of the self.

In this story almost every detail reveals a latent meaning. Moreover, because discourse veils the presence of the Other, that is, repressed desire, "innocent" nouns, references, and utterances take on special significance. The sea on which the narrator is sailing is alternately "as white as a lye barrel" and as "white as chalk" (372–73). The homonymous connotations of the nouns "lye" and "chalk" easily refer to the deception and the veiling that are inherent in every narrative. Fiction is a lie that somehow manages to write the truth on the surface of the sea where, metaphorically speaking, the conscious and unconscious worlds come together.

For Lacan the act of writing posits the enticement of textuality, thereby acknowledging, unconsciously, the child's "wound" and alienation. To produce a text, whatever its conscious modes and operations, is also to relive the process by which an affective charge—a cathexis—is released from its generating poles. The writer, and eventually the reader, directs this charge, imbuing it with the Reality that both produces and attracts it. Fiction (fantasy) thus has the power to link the conscious and unconscious systems. The writer's need to repeat, rather than simply remember, repressed material illustrates the need to reproduce and work through painful events from the past as if they were present. Writing, like psychoanalysis, repeats the discontent of what never took place during that "time-event" referred to as the primal scene. The so-called fantasy of desire, incest, castration, death, and repression reenact not what took place, but what did not. Nonetheless, it is this scene that is replayed and reenacted on the stage of discourse as the metaphorical actors put on their veils and perform their masked ritual.

After the fight and "after the storm" are therefore synonymous. The storm is a metaphor of shipwreck, actual as well as psychological. Not only is the title a metaphor for tragedy and trauma, the story itself is a metaphor of repression, death, and desire: a death of the self, a death wish against the father (the Law), and desire for the mother. Lacan maintains that in the aftermath of the splitting of the self during the so-called "mirror phase," misrecognition of one's identity is inevitable. "You couldn't recognize the shore" (373), says the narrator in describing the storm's aftermath. He is in his skiff on the white water looking toward a shoreline that is beyond recognition. It is as though Hemingway were giving us an objective correlative of cleavage: "There was a big channel blown right out through the middle of the beach. Trees and all blown out and a channel cut through and all the water white as chalk and everything on it; branches and whole trees and dead birds" (373). Psychologically it is a landscape of devastation in which the subject feels dead but is not dead because "inside the keys were all the pelicans in the world and all kinds of birds flying" (373). For narrative purposes, and in order to carry the full weight of double impact, realistic descriptions and inner states of mind are fused: the visible and the invisible overlap. The story describes a "real" hurricane and "real" events, but they are also the pretext for the unveiling of a portrait of the unconscious that confirms Lacanian theory with uncanny precision.

The law of the hurricane is death to birds on the high seas, but "they must have gone inside there [the keys, that is, the unconscious—"the key" to the narrative] when they knew it was coming" (373). We all carry within us the emotional storm of the primal scene when the child's desire is proscribed by the Law of the father: the choking episode may be read as the father's prohibition while the wrecked shoreline is the image of the subject's symbolic death. The mother-infant unit that constituted the child's sense of wholeness is split by the Phallus (the storm) during the mirror phase. The big channel down the middle of the shore—a shore that was once whole—is the visual equivalent of the repression that cleaves the self and produces the Other. Hemingway's short story, like the workings of the unconscious mind, functions simultaneously on a realistic level of descriptive detail and on a symbolic level of covert desire. The narrator may be out to salvage what he can from the wrecked ship of the self, but in the glaucous depths of his unconscious lurk the images of failure.

Pieces of flesh float to the surface from a hole in the hull of the sunken liner "way down below near the bottom" (374). These pieces are like dream images that appear when the so-called censor is asleep and the opening between our conscious and unconscious worlds permits an exchange between the two. Consciousness is above the surface where the birds feed on the pieces that float into view. But "you couldn't tell what they were" (374). You have to go below the surface to find out, and even then insight is not immediate. Although, at first, with the aid of the water glass, the narrator can "see everything sharp and clear" (374), it is not until later that he finds out that all the crew and passengers were dismembered by the exploding boilers when the water rushed in.

The sunken liner plays a double and ambivalent role. On the one hand it is the Phallus that is "a mile long" (374) and "as big as the whole world" (373), and on the other it is a "she." The narrator drifts over "her" (373), and when he uses the heavy grapple in order to try to break the porthole, he "slides along the curved side of her" and has to let go lest he drown (375). The liner is thus the combined symbol of the father-mother unit that excludes the child. His "head felt cracked open" (375) from the depth and the exertion. The narrator rests in his skiff and his nose stops bleeding and he looks up into the sky where he sees "a million birds" (375). In spite of the birds that died in the storm, many have survived, and so has he, but he is bleeding and he was choked, and he feels guilty even though he has killed no one.

One last time the narrator tries to break the porthole with the wrench lashed to a grains pole, but it is too light and too small and slips off and sinks into the quicksand below (376). "I couldn't get into her" (374) says the narrator in words whose sexual connotations are unmistakable. His instrument is not up to the task. Either the wrench is too small or the grapple is too heavy. His tools are inadequate. He is impotent. However, the reader can grapple with the text and wrench meaning from it, metaphorically, using the narrator's tools, provided s/he uses the water glass in order to decipher the letters of the ship's name—letters that lie below the surface. Although the narrator-diver stands on them to buoy himself, he does not and cannot recognize "the letter of the unconscious," Lacan's euphemism for desire and the discourse of the Other. "I stood on the bow of the liner with my bare feet on the letters of her name and my head just out" (375). The narrator's feet are in touch with the letter(s) of the unconscious, even as he tries repeatedly but without success to break the porthole in order to get the rings from the woman's fingers.

The name of the ship is "the letter of the unconscious," and this is the name that embodies Lacan's system. His system gives us the tools with which to get at the latent meaning (and into the ship) that is embedded in quicksand and that only the Greeks could plunder. They blew "her open and cleaned her out. . . . She carried gold and they got it all. They stripped her clean" (376). The very vagueness of the epithet "Greek" allows us to write Oedipus on the ship's prow because Oedipus symbolizes the conditions that are present during "the storm," when we run aground on the father's Law and into the quicksand of desire. "Oedipus" in Greek means swollen foot, and it is the narrator's feet that are standing on the ship's name.

In the last two pages of "After the Storm" (376–78), Hemingway's narrator provides plausible realistic details with which to explain the ship's sinking. He describes her grounding and the treacherous effects of the quicksand. We learn that whatever is rising to the surface from a hole in the vessel was caused by exploding boilers. Except for an allusion to the captain and his mate who may or may not have been together on the bridge when they died, these details add little to the psychological impact of the narrative that precedes it. They function as a denouement, whereas the "meat" of the story, so to speak, is to be found in the latent meaning of the fight, the choking, the attempted salvage, and the letters of the ship's name.

In French the word *dénouement* can mean the undoing of a knot. *Noeud* is the word for "knot" but, as Jane Gallop points out in her book *Reading Lacan* (156), *noeud* is also a crude term for "penis." Since all discourse veils the Phallus, the real denouement in "After the Storm" depends on the reader's willingness to use the water glass in order to produce meaning by going beneath the surface of appearances. The primal scene produces an emotional knot that must be untangled if we are to lead productive lives. Writing fiction is a process of untangling the knot. As a collaborator in the process the reader must engage in a recreative endeavor in order to break the porthole (metaphorically speaking) to get at the woman (again metaphorically speaking). Since the narrator is unable to break the porthole and gain access to the woman, he cannot experience the bliss (*jouissance*) of incest, although he is happy that he has at least cracked the glass.

"It is natural," says Lacan, "that everything would fall on Oedipus, since Oedipus embodies the central knot of speech" (S-II, 269). If writers write because they have to, then a discourse that dramatizes the exteriorization of desire goes to the very heart of language. It is a discourse within which the author reassembles the fragments of the self and projects them onto the mirror of fiction where we, in turn, recognize the author's metaphorical image of himself as the image of the Other. Although fiction is a mirror that distorts, it is, nonetheless, a mirror of the self. But this image, like the glass of the porthole, will forever remain cracked. This discourse of the self, which is always a discourse of desire, seeks to retrieve the lost object, be it breast or mother. Because language manifests the presence of the mother tongue, writing, in recovering an absence, tends to be incestuous. Because the narrator's actions are directed toward retrieving the lost "mother," "After the Storm" asks to be read as a metaphor of desire.

Freud talks of dreams being structured as a rebus, and Lacan applies the same principle to fiction. The gold is there for us to retrieve provided that we use the water glass as a window onto the unconscious. The glass reveals the mother, the father, and the child all knotted together with the discursive weave. A Lacanian reading of the narrator's repressed images reveals the story's latent content that comes into focus as metonymical structure and metaphorical discourse. Like the narrator, we the readers are also buoyed up by the letters of the ship's name. The difference, once we discern her origin, is in what we do with the knowledge.

Structuralism and Interpretation:
Ernest Hemingway's "Cat in the Rain"

Oddvar Holmesland

●

The question raised in this essay is whether modern structuralist theories offer a valuable model for critical reading of texts. Structuralism is not a new critical method which discovers or assigns meanings. Structuralism seeks to define the conditions of meaning. It is based on the recognition that actions and objects only make sense with respect to a set of institutional conventions. Culture is seen to consist of a set of symbolic systems, and the meaning of language depends on a whole system of constitutive rules. The study of literature must accordingly be an attempt to explain how these systems work and what conventions make literature possible.

A related question is to what extent analysis of narrative structure, in turn, aids interpretation of theme, or whether it merely imposes abstract academic clichés on the representation of reality. The conclusion arrived at here is that applied structuralism offers genuine guidance to settle interpretative problems. However, the principles by which different structuralist methodologies operate may produce contradictory answers. It follows that analytic theory is far from attaining the status of science. The balancing of contradictory methodologies must ultimately be guided by sound subjective judgment in relation to individual texts.

Ernest Hemingway's short story, "Cat in the Rain," has been selected for examination for several reasons. It contains ambiguities which demonstrate the validity, but also the variability, of a structuralist approach. Moreover, another critic, David Lodge, has already applied the relevant methodologies to a critical reading of this text, which will serve as useful background to interpretation.[1] Finally, Hemingway's story condenses the component parts of the novel into greater prominence, which facilitates a lucid analysis of structure and narrative techniques. Every detail of conversation and description carries significance for the understanding of the whole.

A realistic text like "Cat in the Rain" requires a special angle of analysis to match its characteristics. The story is realistic in that it centers on the dramatization of a problem in human relationships, located to a particular time and place, and purports to reveal some truth about the situation. A convincing realistic plot depends on the creation of *vraisemblance*, a semblance of reality, through the right combination of signs. This objective involves interaction of two planes: the author must reproduce actuality as accurately as possible by way of descriptions and plausible conversations; but creation of thematic meaning requires at the same time that language used to record reality must also have a denotative or connotative form counterpointed to actuality, in order to act as commentary on life. Since the text of "Cat in the Rain" becomes the grid through which we experience reality, meaning derives from the tension between our conceptualized recognition of natural life and its modification by the rhetorical technique.

This interaction coincides with the distinction between "fabula" and "sjuzet" (or story and discourse) defined by the Russian formalists.[2] The former is the neutral, matter-of-fact continuum of connected events corresponding with our innate or culturally conditioned tendency to apprehend objects and events in a chronological and spatial relation. The latter has to do with the way in which a story is narrated and possibly modified by stylistic devices according to the author's private evaluations. Different aspects of the story may be accentuated through shifting points of view or perspectives, contrasts, repetition, distortion of durational time, gaps in logic, etc.

The fabula of "Cat in the Rain" runs as follows: A young American couple is presented alone in a hotel room looking out on an empty square. From the hotel window the wife sees a cat crouching under a rain-dripping garden table. She declares that she will go down and fetch the "poor kitty." The husband, lying on the bed reading, offers to do it but does not rise. As she opens the door, she sees a man in a rubber cape crossing the empty square in the rain. The maid then comes and holds a protective umbrella over her, but when she gets to the table, she discovers that the cat is gone. On her returning to her room, George only briefly diverts his eyes from the book. When she resumes her position at the window and restlessly expresses her many wants, including a cat, he tells her to shut up and find something to read. There suddenly is a knock at the door, and the maid appears with a big tortoise-shell cat for the wife.

Hemingway's characteristic method of creating sjuzet on "a new theory that you could omit anything if you knew that you omitted, and the omitted part would strengthen the story and make people feel something more than they understood."[3] Omission of units in the logical chain mystifies the reader, inviting a greater imaginative involvement in the life presented. But his synthesizing efforts will be frustrated in seeking to deduce the meaning along a traditional narrative line of complication and denouement. Meaning will instead have to be inferred from the total form in which the ending constitutes only one of the many indices. The final return of the cat, for example, does not confirm the resolution of conflict because we do not know how the characters are going to react. To identify this interpretative problem, it is useful to adopt the terminology of J. A. Greimas.[4] All narrative, he stipulates, centers on the transfer of an object or value from one "actant" to another. The functions of actants in a story are those of Subject or Object, Sender or Receiver, Helper or Opponent. Greimas distinguishes between different performative tasks in which the actants are involved. The pattern of "Cat in the Rain" is disjunctional since it deals with the disappearance and return of a cat (object) to the American wife (subject).

The ambiguity of the ending, Lodge suggests, hinges on the mystery of the tortoise-shell cat's identity. We do not know whether it is the "kitty" the wife spotted outside and so do not know whether she will be pleased to get it. The fact that it is only seen from the husband's perspective accounts for this ambiguity: George did not stir from the bed to look out of the window at the cat his wife wanted and consequently has no possibility of knowing whether the two are identical. Accordingly, he perceives the tortoise-shell cat as "a" cat and not with the definite article as a sign of recognition. Conversely, "a" cat seen from the wife's point of view would have clarified that it is a different cat.

Greimas points out how ambiguous disjunctional endings may be by opposing "departure" to "incognito arrival," "arrival" to "return" (since we do not know whether the tortoise-shell cat is the one that disappeared, we do not know whether the ending means arrival or return), and "negative return" to "positive return."[5] Confirmation of the common identity of the cats would have opened certain interpretative possibilities, while excluding others. If the wife's desire for the cat were viewed as compensatory for lack of marital fulfillment (as indeed most critics see it), the ending might thus have served as an ironic crack at the husband's lack of deference for his wife. If the big tortoise-shell animal is definitely not the kitty she wants, the irony might turn against her unrealistic longings and irrational discontent.

It is doubtful whether the enigma of the cat's identity can be solved, considering the wealth of contradictory indices. The critic needs different criteria for explicating Hemingway's method. There is at the heart of the story not simply the mystery of what will happen after the story ends. The notion of resolution implied in Greimas's definition of the disjunctional plot cannot embrace all levels of significance: the wife wants a cat and after some difficulties, gets a cat. One needs to find out more about what kind of plot this really is. Its action is definitely not strictly linear; the revelation of a state of mind and a state of affairs is an equally essential part. Analysis of the "symbolic systems" may clarify how much the comprehension of a state of mind depends on the retroactive illumination of the ending.

The cat initiates and sustains the main action of the story. Though its full meaning cannot be paraphrased, its function as a symbol around which the whole story centers may be analyzed. An understanding of what symbolic level the cat pertains to provides vital insight about the appropriate symbolic level at which to read the entire plot. The climactic condensation of story and cat symbolism in the final scene significantly reduces the number of possible interpretations. Here is the situation acted out: previous to the final incident the wife's pleading request for a cat is broken off by the author's snapshot of the state of affairs. From the angle of a disengaged observer, he pictures the scene in a few terse sentences: "George was not listening. He was reading his book. His wife looked out of the window where the light had come on in the square." It is at this moment the perspective shifts again to add a poignant finale: "Someone knocked at the door. 'Avanti,' George said. He looked up from his book. In the doorway stood the maid. She held a big tortoise-shell cat pressed tight against her and swung down against her body." It takes some openness of mind to perceive the poetic force of this coda. The suddenness and unexpectedness of the cat's appearance in the doorway makes it loom with Imagist immediacy. This big animal is "pressed tight against her [the maid] and swung down against her body." Its heavy, animal sensuality is unmistakable. Seen against the background of marital triteness and the quest for a cat to compensate needs, it looms as a metaphor of the wife's deeper, unfulfilled desires. This link is rooted in the structuralist concept of binary oppositions. Opposition here means an intuitive logical operation by which the presence of one term or image inevitably generates its opposite in our mind. It is impossible, in this context, to conceive of the provocative sensuality of the cat without sensing its contrast. Hemingway's technique of omitting parts of the narrative does not make ambiguity normative. He is more than anything else the master of calculated implications. This implied opposition significantly evokes the kernel state of affairs.

If the big cat is conceived of as a poetic metaphor, its identity becomes irrelevant. The wife gives evidence to this point. As a matter of fact, she does not necessarily require "the" cat; she repeatedly declares: "I want a cat." This detail is crucial not only because it signals that any specimen of cat may do, but also because it raises the object of quest from a metonymic to a metaphoric stature. This distinction pertains to Roman Jakobson's definition of the poetic function of language as "the projection of the principle of equivalence from the axis of selection into the axis of combination."[6]

In verbal communication we select certain units from a store of possible equivalents and combine them into larger or more complex entities. The relation between the selected segments and their equivalents is one of lexical or syntactic similarity (the metaphoric principle). Combination of units into larger ones presupposes a common code of meaning for communicative purposes. How expressions and their meanings may be combined depends on social conventions, based on a codified contiguity between expression and content. The metonymic principle thus builds on association of part and whole, and contiguity of time, space, and cause and effect. The distinction between poetic and practical language can hence be characterized as a difference between similarity and contiguity in the relation between expression and content. Poetic combination is governed by similarity and does not subserve the codified contiguity. It may be apprehended as a series of open systems containing meaning instead of only referring to meaning. The metaphoric principle of equivalence thus creates a sense of immediacy between the expression or image and the content, stressing the symbolic significance of the unit.

Determination of the big cat's identity is consequently only important at the metonymic narrative level. It would provide the resolution required for seeing the story as a coherent pattern of cause and effect. By a metonymic reading the kitty might be viewed as part of a whole range of other things the girl desires to gratify some private need: "And I want to eat at a table with my own silver and I want candles. And I want it to be spring and I want to brush my hair out in front of a mirror and I want a kitty and I want some new clothes." Carlos Baker bases his interpretation on the principle of contiguity when assuming the cats to be identical and that it "somehow stands in [the wife's] mind for comfortable bourgeois domesticity."[7] His notion of a resolved plot is not shared by John V. Hagopian who applies a different version of metonymic reading: "the sum total of the wants that do reach consciousness amounts to motherhood, a home with a family, an end to the strictly companionate marriage with George."[8] To this sum of maternal desiderata, Hagopian adds the "kitty, now an obvious symbol for a child." According to this reading, the ending is deeply ironic, for "the girl is willing to settle for a child-surrogate, but the big tortoise-shell cat obviously cannot serve that purpose." To use different terms, he finds the story ironic because only a little "kitty" fits into the metonymic group of contiguities he defines, with an innocent little baby as its center.

The problem about these interpretations is that the girl's purpose is not that concretely identifiable. There is no definite verification in the text for drawing the kitty/tortoise-shell cat or tortoise-shell cat/baby equivalence along the metaphoric axis. The final scene evokes a symbolic reverberation but does not refer directly to another concrete object.

What the climactic ending primarily does is to reinforce the metaphoric significance of the central action in the story—the quest for a cat. When the big cat appears in the doorway, the visual immediacy creates a stark antithesis between the cat's symbolic vitality and the state of the couple. Meaning becomes all the clearer by the final shift of perspective to that of the husband's. Previous to the shift, George, supine on the bed, reading, has been reprimanding his young wife for her restless longings, which he finds irrational and cannot gratify for some reason. The cat's sudden intrusion upon their separateness and lack of communication (this connection established through contiguity of time) thus acts as a smack in the face for George and his point of view. Whether there is, at the same time, an ironic hint of the wife's immature disposition, which may equally separate them from fulfillment, remains more uncertain. The fact that her perspective is dominant throughout the bulk of the story, however, indicates authorial sympathy, making this last possibility less likely.

The preceding interaction of metonymy and metaphor identifies the kernel conflict in the story. Consequently, the climactic "resolution" provides the most reliable point of departure for applying a structuralist analysis. Without a recognition of its significance, the clues for analysis and interpretation are insufficient. These conditions do not imply reservations about the great value of utilizing structuralist theories for critical readings of texts like this one. Structuralism can no doubt uncover meanings that would otherwise evade critical consideration. In fact, the procedure which disclosed the central conflict of "Cat in the Rain" was precisely grounded on the structuralist notion of meaning as the product of binary oppositions. With the oppositions indicated, the disparate surface manifestations of the text may be traced down to a deep structure of values bearing on the opposition of "desire for Life/denial of Life." A theoretical framework for this approach is offered by Greimas, neatly summarized by Lodge: "All concepts are semantically defined by a binary relationship with their opposites (e.g. Life/Death) or negatives (e.g. Life/

Non-Life) yielding the basic semiotic model A:B::-A-B (e.g. Life:Death :: Non-Life:Non-Death), so that all narrative can be seen as the transformation into actants and actions of a thematic four-term homology.''9

Greimas's model offers valuable guidance in analyzing the second dominant motif of the story: rain. Furthermore, it clarifies the critical procedures of two contradictory views. Hagopian presents one reading: "As she [the wife] looks out into the wet empty square, she sees a man in a rubber cape crossing to the cafe in the rain. The rubber cape is protection from rain, and rain is a fundamental necessity for fertility, and fertility is precisely what is lacking in the American wife's marriage.''10 Hagopian makes an elaborate network of symbolic explanations to derive a coherent meaning from the various elements. The rubber cape, by some subconscious projection of the wife's preoccupations, becomes a symbol of contraception. She is allegedly childless and therefore wants a kitty to cuddle as compensation. In effect, such a reading combines the fertility associated with the rain and the "public garden," the "big palms and green benches." As signaled by her awareness of the man with the rubber cape, the wife's marriage to George is a contraceptive against fertility. One might argue that the possibility of such a connection is strengthened by the fact that the hotel proprietor brings her an umbrella for protection against the rain.

A very different analysis is provided by Lodge, who applies a model of binary oppositions to counter Hagopian's interpretation: "Now rain *can* symbolize fertility, when defined by opposition to drought. In this story, however (and incidentally, throughout Hemingway's work), it is opposed to 'good weather' and symbolizes the loss of pleasure and joy, the onset of discomfort and ennui.''11

One critic regards the rain as a positive force, the other takes it to be negative. Lodge views the situation both inside and outside as belonging to one single group of metonymies. The incidents in the hotel room and the various wet objects outside function as part of a whole, a dominant oppressive atmosphere. The rain/good weather model naturally conditions the interpretation of the cat's role. It loses its credibility as child-surrogate, since the symbolic properties of the metaphors are reduced. All that may be stated with certainty is that the different objects are integral facets of a total atmosphere. To Lodge, then, atmosphere is merely presentational and suggestive, with no differentiated meaning implied, and as such explains why the ending would be ambiguous.

Since the analytic methodology makes possible some interpretations while excluding others, the methodology has to be based on the kernel oppositions in the text. Jonathan Culler accounts for the "general models, which we apply unconsciously in the process of reading." Postulating Greimas's four-term homology as the basic structure of plot, he suggests that:

> what the reader is looking for in a plot is a passage from one state to another—a passage to which he can assign thematic value. . . . First of all, the incidents of the plot must be organized into two groups and these groups must be named in such a way that they represent either an opposition (problem and solution, refusal and acceptance or vice versa) or a logical development (cause and effect, situation and result). Secondly, each of these groups can in turn be organized either as a series of actions with a common unifying factor which serves as name for the series, or as a dialectical movement in which incidents are related as contraries and named either by a temporary synthesis or by a transcendent term which covers both members of a contrast. [12]

The division of "Cat in the Rain" into a rain/good weather opposition does not build on "incidents of the plot" as outlined above. Good weather, only briefly mentioned, remains an abstract concept of no dramatic consequence in an economical and condensed narrative like this. The essential balance between these two contraries is too unequal to signify a major conflict. The only two references to good weather in the text will do as examples of this point. The description of the monument in the garden, "It was made of bronze and glistened in the rain," does not identify any thematically significant opposition, as Lodge suggests. All it does is to imply that the monument looks different when it is not raining. Nor does the following passage identify thematic distinctions. "In the good weather there was always an artist with his easel. Artists liked the way the palms grew and the bright colours of the hotels facing the gardens and the sea." This is a gay picture of bright reflected colors, but it bears no thematic opposition to the same scenery in rain, for the table in the garden is also "bright green in the rain," light-reflecting like the "glistening" bronze statue. Similarly, there is no one single valid inter-pretation of the following picture: "The sea broke in a long line in the rain and slipped back down the beach to come up and break again in a long line in the rain." It is by no means certain that it primarily signifies, as says Lodge, "Excess of wetness. Monotony. Ennui." It may just as well represent the rhythmic elemental pulsations toward which the wife is oriented, made even more elemental by the fact that all the tourists and artists and motor cars have disappeared, leaving nature to itself.

Meaning depends on what symbolic level this is to be read at. The repeated remarks to the wife about rain as an unpleasant element indirectly refer to more pleasant associations of good weather. However, subjective attitudes of individual characters may not express the author's message. His intent may rather be to focus on some characters' estrangement from pulsating nature and their lack of vital perceptivity. Lodge means to analyze the conditions for meaning but in doing so pays insufficient attention to different levels of the text. He establishes a dominant rain/good weather antithesis on uncertain grounds, thereby excluding far more relevant structural and thematic oppositions. Attempting to reconcile his model with the text, moreover, he invokes an interpretative meaning which narrows the symbolic richness.

With any decisive temporal opposition between rain and good weather diminished, a spatial division becomes all the more obvious: the dryness inside the hotel and the objects associated with the rain outside. In the spatial perspective drought attains different connotations from the comfort associated with good weather. Between the two worlds stands another important motif: the window. Its transparency does not merely enhance the marital ennui within through the aggravating atmosphere of endless rain without; it points to central thematic oppositions. An indication of this is provided by the fact that the window is by no means a metaphor-free image but to a high degree an acknowledged metaphoric cultural stereotype. T. S. Eliot's famous essay, "Tradition and the Individual Talent," stresses the dependence of literary works on conventions, for a work of art does not imitate experience but previous works of art. Section one (named "The Window") of Virginia Woolf's *To the Lighthouse* depicts Mrs. Ramsay by her drawing-room window, contemplating life's "myriad impressions" and gazing at the lighthouse which prevents her from finding a harmonizing balance by its symbolic remoteness. In Emily Brontë's *Wuthering Heights* the window designates the boundary between two opposed realms of existence. To Catherine Earnshaw, after her marriage to Edgar Linton, the window marks separation by cultural constrictions from a fuller engagement with natural life. She implores Nelly, the housekeeper:

> "Open the window again wide, fasten it open! Quick, why don't you move?"
>
> "Because I won't give you your death of cold," I answered.
>
> "You won't give me a chance of life, you mean," she said.[13]

The window organizes the elements into binary oppositions bearing on either life or death. When Catherine, reconciled with the natural elements by her corporeal death, seeks Heathcliff, she can only scratch on the pane but cannot get in, whereas Heathcliff, forcing the window open, cannot get out into the night to join her spirit. When he dies, Nelly Dean notices the window swinging open. It suggests, at one level, a breaking-through of a separating medium between isolated individualism and a vital natural harmony.

In "Cat in the Rain" the image of the wife, ensconced behind her hotel window, yearning for a more pulsating reality, suggests a mythical reading. "Cat in the Rain" may be said to be equivalent with the quest myth which, according to Northrop Frye, has "as its final cause the resolution of the antithesis . . . the realizing of a world in which the inner desire and the outward circumstance coincide. This is the same goal, of course, that the attempt to combine human and natural power in ritual has."[14] Within this myth perspective in which the protagonist's quest is principally directed toward fulfillment, structuralist theories offer invaluable guidance in systematizing archetypal images. The central window motif, as a divider between worlds, plays a crucial role in the mythical scheme. Inside is the isolated heroine whom Frye associates with the tragic vision; outside is a garden of life. Contradictory images occur as well, however. In the garden is the kitty, which naturally belongs in the comic world of gentle, domesticated animals, whereas the big tortoise-shell cat is harder to label. Furthermore, the sea, in traditional myth, is usually a sinister element (as opposed to the river), but there are no such connotations here. There finally is mention of the passage from light to dark in the story, not merely a reminder of cyclic inevitability or monotony, but of life's polarizations. Recognition of the metaphoric richness of the outside world allows for a double meaning in nature. Perhaps the wife, in the final analysis, feels most attracted to the dynamic quality of life's contradictory possibilities.

The central metaphor of the wife's quest is the cat which, initially, eludes her and is mystically lost. As she again returns to her place at the window, darkness enhances the sense of mysticism surrounding the animal. Her needs are suddenly answered by the unexpected delivery of a cat. In mythical terms its vigorous sensuality emphasizes her subconscious wishes and its significance as a messenger transcending boundaries between worlds. Hermes, the boundary-crosser in Greek mythology, whose images are ithyphallic, is the god of fertility, closely connected with deities of vegetation. As the patron of travelers, he may, as cat, mediate between the garden and the hotel, for he is, among other things, the god of doorways. Doorways are salient in the story. The wife stands hesitant in the doorway of the hotel before venturing out into the rain, and the doorway of the hotel room frames the cat's climactic entry.

As the messenger of the gods, Hermes crosses thresholds to attend to the needs of the recently born, but also to those of the dying.[15] And the couple may be dying spiritually and in need of the services of some phallic herm.

The possibility of a mythical reading only strengthens what already seems clear: the structural opposition is between drought and rain. It seems equally implicit that the two poles are metaphors of spiritual equivalents, the incentive of the quest being natural fertility. The author embeds persuasive clues to confirm the underlying conflict of attitudes among the characters. The repeated warnings, as the wife goes out to find the cat, that she must be careful not to get wet, are not fortuitous. "Don't get wet," George says, not looking up from his book. "It is very bad weather," the maid warns her when reaching the vestibule. "You must not get wet," the maid reminds her opening an umbrella behind her. And the American wife knows, "Of course, the hotel-keeper had sent her." A little later she repeats her warning, " 'Come, Signora,' she said. 'We must get back inside. You will be wet.' "

These exchanges convey subtle indices of the functions of the different characters. In reference to Greimas, the wife is subject of the story, the cat is object. George is the opponent, but so is also the hotel-keeper indirectly, and the maid enacts the role as his helper. The two men attempt to shield the wife from the rain (they even decide to avoid the rain themselves), and the maid is acting out the hotel-keeper's orders. It is equally significant that the third male in the story is trying to protect himself from the rain by wearing a rubber cape. In fact, this figure is the first one she sees after opening the door to go out. The sight is again a reminder that "It was raining harder" and that she must be careful. When the American wife agrees to retreat inside on account that she will be wet, she mutters, "I suppose so." The scene represents the compliance of a young wife dominated by conventional male expectations. It may further be argued that the hotel-keeper's deference to his client has little to do with interest in her as a woman. The fact that he always sends the maid to execute his services indicates the professional attitude behind his attentiveness.

The pattern, however, is more complex. There is the wife/(little) girl, kitty/large cat opposition. The moment the wife discovers that the creature has disappeared, she is no longer described as "the American wife" but becomes "the American girl." It may be that her disappointment causes regression to an immature obstinacy. Or it may rather be that, at a symbolic level, her femininity suffers when her quest for the cat fails. There are many indications that the kitty and the cat are symbolic opposites; that the little kitty, in need of shelter, pertains to her more regressive self, whereas the big cat reflects her desire for a more natural femininity. Their symbolic opposition may further signal her anxious ambivalence. In the first part of the story, she says she wants a kitty; at the end she insists she wants a cat; and a large cat is what she finally gets and probably has been wanting all the time.

A central male/female opposition supports the previous reading. The wife yearns for long hair and disapproves of the short hair she shares with her husband. He, however, remarks that he likes it the way it is. The fact that he tells her "You look pretty darn nice," might suggest his responsiveness to her attractions after all. In this context, however, his male instincts fail to convince. His attention and approval concern her hair "clipped close like a boy's," a hint that he is a stranger to her real feminine distinctness. The woman in her needs to expand: to grow longer hair, to have a larger cat, to commune with a more inclusive natural world.

The wife's natural instinctual self-assertion is tamed by domestication. As she retreats inside, "something felt very small and tight inside the girl." This is a contracting, inhibited feeling, a similar reaction of failed communion experienced by the Italian maid in relation to the American wife a few sentences previously: "When she talked English the maid's face tightened." Both girls act in accordance with civil patterns which are no true expression of their feminine natures. The maid's opening the umbrella behind the wife happens with the almost comical automatism of a shadow always there to serve the guests. The wife is entrapped in conventional clichés and perceives the cat, not as in any way a vigorous challenge, but an innocent little female creature like herself: "The cat was trying to make herself so compact that she would not be dripped on."

Subconsciously, however, the wife's desire for the cat stems from a discontented restlessness: "I don't know why I wanted it so much. I wanted that poor kitty." It may have had to do with finding consolation in her self-pity. Her problem is that her insulated existence removes her from pulsating nature. Her craving is to break through the windowpane of abstracted observation to vital involvement and fulfillment of her female energies. In her vague, confused manner, she says, "I want to pull my hair back tight and smooth and make a big knot at the back that I can *feel*" (emphasis added). Since the story is largely told from her point of view, moreover, only that which attracts her attention is described, an important factor. Hagopian notes how the narrator repeats seven times "She liked" as she passes the hotel-keeper, the intensity of the repetitions reflecting the force of her need to *feel*. They are phrases succeeded with even greater insistence by sixteen repetitions of "I wanted" and "I want." As evidenced by her emotional intensity, her many desiderata—

including the kitty, silver, candles, spring—are really sublimations of a deeper instinctual female urge. When the cat she finally gets is not a harmless little kitty but a vigorous furry animal, the irony consequently seems to turn partly on her self-deception.

Reading the story as a spatial opposition between natural fertility and its contrast incorporates the parts of the plot into a coherent design. The very opening line signals the main theme of estrangement. "There were only two Americans stopping at the hotel. They did not know any of the people they passed on the stairs on their way to and from their room." This sense of cultural and social segregation and confinement in one room identifies the interaction of actants. The author repeatedly refers to "the American wife" or "the American girl" as a symptom of her isolation from the Italian hotel staff and other nationalities. Subserving the Italian proprietor's commands, the maid's role in bringing the cat to the wife is accordingly inconsequential. But it is not inconsequential that she is pictured with the "cat pressed tight against her and swung down against her body." The image of instinctual intimacy between the maid and the animal at this moment allies her with the wife through their shared sensuality. The scene suggests the transcendence of cultural boundaries, and by the shift of perspective, the exclusion of George, an opponent for his lack of responsiveness to his wife's femininity.

As a possible herald transcending boundaries, the cat's natural element is outside. Its association with rain is implied in the title of the story. When the wife catches sight of it for the first time, it is "under one of the dripping green tables" in the garden. Though the table is the property of the hotel, it is wet like nature and has the same color as vegetation. The image suggests the integration of culture and nature. What she seeks in the cat is symbolically present in its temporary habitat, "washed bright green in the rain," reflecting the fertility associated with the rain and park and palm trees. In terms of a spatial opposition, the green table at which the wife halts is significantly positioned directly "under their window," thus deepening the reference to the faded greenness inside.

The wife's instinctual needs cannot be gratified through vicarious compensation, as indicated by the kitty's disappearance. Nor can they be expressed by her verbal realizations, but only through the quest for and mystical disappearance of the cat and values associated with it. In the same context it is significant that the escaped kitty reappears in a different apparition at the very moment she cries, "I want a cat now."

In keeping with the structural reading laid out, the meaning of the cat cannot be defined more explicitly than as a metaphor for the wife's instinctual desire for a vital openness to life. Hagopian's precise identification of it as "an obvious symbol for a child" is consequently not reliable. All that can be said is that it reflects her need to experience emotional fertility and is not attached to a definable object. Nor does the text allow for the correlation of the man in the rubber cape (as a symbol of contraception) and the wife's frustration with her husband because he is unable to give her the child she wants. As Lodge points out, there is no evidence of her being childless. Perhaps the author is in fact portraying a woman who is already pregnant? "Something felt very small and tight inside the girl. The padrone made her feel very small and at the same time really important. She had a momentary feeling of being of supreme importance."

Ambiguity notwithstanding, the author is deliberately drawing attention to the question of pregnancy or lack of pregnancy. It is, in the same context, an implied probability that the man in the rubber cape is symbolically protecting himself against nature, especially in view of the conspicuously many times the wife is warned against the rain. The cape is parallel to the umbrella, but whereas the man is protecting himself, the wife is being protected—another indication of the male/female opposition in the story. Though any specific correlation between symbol and symbolized object or person is beyond verification, the wealth of indices strongly point to conflicting experiences concerning fertility, be it emotional or biological.

"Cat in the Rain" is basically a metonymic realistic story. There is an implied notion of vraisemblance which assumes a correlation between text and reality. The story aims to expose some human problem, and the referential function of the text appears to subordinate the expressiveness of an artistic form. It again presupposes an interdependence between expression and meaning. Hemingway's technique consists precisely in creating a metonymic pattern of contiguous parts which, through its vraisemblance, encourages the reader to explain its message. By his method of omitting logical links, however, he manages to complicate interpretation while inspiring the reader's imaginative involvement to solve the enigma. For the same reason he avoids using what W. B. Yeats calls "intellectual symbols"; they do not possess a specific denotative meaning. Rather, they function as indices creating resonances of import through implication. Temporal and spatial contiguities, compositional contrasts, and foregrounding of certain elements through selection and repetition produce significance. Import is thereby produced beyond the words, in the gap to be filled in by the synthesizing imagination.

Structuralist theories provide valuable criteria for systematizing the conditions of meaning. As in the case of the tortoise-shell cat, analysis elucidates how meaning emanates from the interaction of metaphor and context. The outside world expresses the contradictory forces that incite and give direction to the wife's quest. It is a quest with no concretely definable end, but a quest for a more fulfilling process of Being. The tortoise-shell cat, with its animal sensuality, ultimately serves as a metaphor for the dynamic sensuality required to reconcile nature to man's desire.

"That Always Absent Something Else": "A Natural History of the Dead" and Its Discarded Coda

Susan F. Beegel

●

"A Natural History of the Dead" begins as graphic satire, with an autobiographical account of civilian and military corpses Hemingway observed during World War I's Austro-Italian conflict. The story then shifts to an equally grim fictional account of a wounded lieutenant's hysterical response to war's human refuse and concludes as a dressing station's doctor orders the raving officer restrained. In the earliest extant version of "A Natural History of the Dead," however, the short piece continues, returning to the satirical mode with which it began. This coda, again autobiographical, describes Hemingway's encounter with an Italian sergeant robbing Austrian corpses on the battlefield.

"A Natural History of the Dead" was originally published as chapter 12 of *Death in the Afternoon* and, together with the aforementioned additional ending, first appears in the bullfight book's intermediate typescript.[1] With the exception of the four-page coda, affixed to "A Natural History of the Dead" just after the final sentence "'Hold him very tight,'" which ends the published text, this version differs only slightly from the published work.[2] Apparently Hemingway added the coda as an afterthought, later rejecting the material before *Death in the Afternoon* was set in galley proofs.[3]

Writing to Maxwell Perkins in 1940, Hemingway confessed that "My temptation is always to write too much. I keep it under control so as not to cut out crap and rewrite. Guys who think they are geniuses because they have never learned to say no to a typewriter are a common phenomenon."[4] The discarded coda to "A Natural History of the Dead" is one example of Hemingway's tendency to write too much and of his self-disciplined control of that tendency. It represents material that Hemingway labored to create, yet chose to omit from finished work in order that his published writing might have more "dignity of movement" (*DIA*, 192). Nevertheless, study of the discarded coda can enhance a reader's appreciation of "A Natural History of the Dead" by revealing the craft of omission Hemingway exercised to achieve his final published product.

Before looking at the coda, it is necessary to examine its context—"A Natural History of the Dead"—the more so as there is no widely accepted interpretation of the work to rely upon. By present calculation fewer than thirty among thousands of pages of Hemingway criticism have been devoted to "A Natural History of the Dead."[5] Nor is the bulk of the existing work interpretative. For example, John Portz and John A. Yunck, the two critics who have written at greatest length about the work, confine themselves to explication of Hemingway's somewhat arcane allusions.[6]

One reason for critical neglect of "A Natural History of the Dead" may be its curious double identity, which defies generic classification. First published as a chapter in a book-length work of nonfiction and later as a short story, half satirical essay and half fiction, "A Natural History of the Dead" shifts in midstream from first-person exposition to third-person narration. Yunck in particular dislikes this combination of genres and objects to Hemingway's using a short story as "a vehicle for miscellaneous criticism."[7] Nevertheless, by including "A Natural History of the Dead" with only minor revision in *Winner Take Nothing*, his 1933 anthology of short fiction, Hemingway himself suggests that the work can be read as a coherent whole in isolation from *Death in the Afternoon*.[8]

The published version of "A Natural History of the Dead" begins by satirizing four natural historians of the eighteenth and nineteenth centuries: W. H. Hudson, the Reverend Gilbert White, Bishop Stanley, and Mungo Park (*DIA*, 133–34).[9] To Hemingway these naturalists, two of them clergymen, were notable for their efforts to elucidate the presence of God in nature. With the exception of Hudson, they had all published their natural histories well before Charles Darwin's *Origin of Species* appeared in 1859 and had little difficulty in reconciling the observable facts of nature with their faith in the unseen truths of divine creation. Hemingway paraphrases a characteristic passage from Mungo Park's *Travels in the Interior Districts of Africa* (1799) treating the reflections of the explorer, when perishing in the desert, on "a small moss-flower of extraordinary beauty": "'Though the whole plant,' says he, 'was no longer than one of my fingers, I could not contemplate the delicate conformation of its roots, leaves and capsules without admiration. Can that Being who planted, watered and brought to perfection, in this obscure part of the world a thing which appears of so small importance, look with unconcern upon the situation of creatures formed after his own image. Surely not. Reflections like these would not allow me to despair'" (*DIA*, 134).[10]

Reared in the post-Darwinian world, Hemingway nevertheless (or perhaps necessarily) received childhood instruction on the compatibility of science and religion and on the divine creation revealed in nature. His father, Dr. Clarence Hemingway, was an inventive physician who designed special forceps for spinal laminectomies, fashioned artificial ears and chins for deformed children, and proposed advanced theories of infant nutrition.[11] An avid amateur naturalist, Dr. Hemingway organized Ernest's eighth grade class into a club named for the famous naturalist Louis Agassiz and took the children for weekly nature walks in the woods along the Des Plaines River.[12] At the same time, Dr. Hemingway was an unbending pillar of Oak Park's Third Congregational Church, where he taught a Sunday school class for young men.[13] Apparently Clarence Hemingway had no difficulty reconciling his scientific vocation and avocation with his religious faith and instructed his own and the neighborhood's children accordingly. His oldest daughter, Marcelline, recalled that

> Daddy always made a point of explaining to us that though God created the world in seven days, according to the Bible, and we were not to doubt that statement, nobody had ever explained how long a day was. He also told us that the men who wrote the Bible explained natural history the best they could, but that now through research we knew much more about how things must have been made thousands of years ago. He told us that our new knowledge only added to the truths we learned in Sunday school.[14]

Ironically, the skills of observation Dr. Hemingway taught his son on nature walks helped achieve Ernest's ultimate disillusionment with God. The boy, who had learned to look among the branches of trees for hidden birds' nests and beneath the underbrush for wild hepaticas and mayflowers,[15] as a young man turned his sharpened eyesight on the fragmented bodies of women workers killed in a munitions factory explosion outside Milan, on corpses abandoned to swell in the Italian sun after the Austrian offensive of June 1918, and on mules and horses left broken-legged to drown during the Greek evacuation of Smyrna. While Clarence Hemingway hoped that the observant habits of a natural historian would increase his son's reverence for divine creation, those same habits, applied to the refuse of war rather than dogtooth violets, achieved a far different result.

World War I exploded Hemingway's childhood religious training. While Christianity depends upon a belief in life everlasting and constitutes a codified and systematic denial of death, Sigmund Freud accurately predicted that the war would render all those it touched unable to ignore death's reality: "Death can no longer be denied; we are forced to believe in him. People really are dying, and not now one by one, but many thousands at a time, often ten thousand in a single day. Nor is it any longer an accident."[16] A Christian belief in immortality was no longer possible to Hemingway after he observed the sights, sounds, and smells of death on the Italian front. While as a child under his father's protection Hemingway may have felt, like Nick Adams in "Indian Camp," "quite sure that he would never die" (*SS*, 95), an Austrian *Minenwerfer* soon gave him a private lesson in personal mortality.[17] Through "research" on the battlefield, Hemingway had gained a knowledge of death incompatible with the "truths" he had learned in Sunday school.

The opening satire of "A Natural History of the Dead" depends upon the ironic tension between the spiritual beliefs and positivist methods of the antique natural historians Hemingway imitates. He poses Bishop Stanley's confidently rhetorical religious question ("With a disposition to wonder and adore in like manner . . . can any branch of Natural History be studied without increasing that faith, love and hope which we also, every one of us, need in our journey through the wilderness of life?" [*DIA*, 134]) and sets up a shattering answer by embarking on a study of the natural history of the dead. Parodying the expository prose of early naturalists, Hemingway catalogs aspects of the dead as a natural historian would catalog the characteristics of a plant or animal species:

> Until the dead are buried they change somewhat in appearance each day. The color change in Caucasian races is from white to yellow, to yellow-green, to black. If left long enough in the heat, the flesh comes to resemble coal-tar, especially where it has been broken or torn, and it has quite a visible tar-like iridescence. The dead grow larger each day until sometimes they grow too big for their uniforms, filling these until they seem blown tight enough to burst. The individual members may increase in girth to an unbelievable extent and faces fill as tight and as globular as balloons. (*DIA*, 137)

Naturalistic observation of the dead does not give Hemingway "any such thoughts as Mungo Park about those formed in His own image" (*DIA*, 138).

Hemingway does not name exactly what he fails to find upon observing the dead. Avoiding abstract words like "God," "soul," "immortality," "everlasting life," Hemingway says only that he has found no evidence of "that always absent something else" Mungo Park and others claim to have seen in nature (*DIA*, 139). Instead of finding "something," he has found nothing, an absence of God in nature, an absence of life in death, an absence of divine concern for human suffering. In "A Natural History of the Dead," through a pseudoscientific study of corpses decaying on an Italian battlefield, Hemingway provides positivistic proof of an absence at the heart of the universe.

At first, Hemingway tells us, "I blamed it on the war" because "I'd never seen a natural death, so-called" (*DIA*, 139). He purports to be confused by the semantic distinction that suggests that death from disease is somehow more "natural" than death by violence. Like "the persevering traveller, Mungo Park," he still believes "that always absent something else," invisible on the battlefield, may nevertheless shine through a "natural death." This illusory hope evaporates when he witnesses a death from Spanish influenza: "In this you drown in mucus, choking, and how you know the patient's dead is; at the end he shits the bed full" (*DIA*, 139).[18] The narrator learns only that a "natural death, so-called" is no more natural, and no less degrading, than "unnatural" death in war.

Here Hemingway widens the satirical scope of "A Natural History of the Dead" to include Humanist literary critics Irving Babbitt, Paul Elmer More, and Seward Collins, as well as early natural historians.[19] The Humanist school insisted on the duality of man and nature and felt that human experience was essentially ethical. In their view literature should avoid graphic depiction of man's natural functions, including death and sex, unless able to relate those functions to man's ethical experience. In "A Natural History of the Dead," Hemingway challenges the Humanist school to prove the duality of man and nature by dying and reproducing decorously themselves, by demonstrating personal immunity to natural processes:

> So now I want to see the death of any self-called Humanist because a persevering traveller like Mungo Park or me lives on and maybe yet will live to see the actual death of members of this literary sect and watch the noble exits that they make. In my musings as a naturalist it has occurred to me that while decorum is an excellent thing some must be indecorous if the race is to be carried on since the position prescribed for procreation is indecorous, highly indecorous, and it occurred to me that perhaps that is what these people are, or were; the children of decorous cohabitation. But regardless of how they started I hope to see the finish of quite a few, and speculate how worms will try that long preserved sterility; with their quaint pamphlets gone to bust, and into footnotes all their lust. (*DIA*, 139)[20]

Hemingway's rather vicious satire of Humanist literary critics is actually a counterattack, a response to reviews of *A Farewell to Arms* published in *The Bookman*, a Humanist magazine edited by Seward Collins. The most offensive of these reviews, Robert Herrick's "What Is Dirt?," roundly applauded the Boston Watch and Ward Society's decision to ban *A Farewell to Arms*[21] and deemed its love passages no more significant "than what goes on in a brothel, hardly more than the copulation of animals."[22] A *Bookman* editorial by Collins deplored the "extreme license" permitted to war books and, in particular, bemoaned the strong language Hemingway used to describe the retreat from Caporetto.[23] Such language, Collins effetely reminded readers, "isn't realism, it's paprika."[24]

Irving Babbitt and Paul Elmer More, the founders of the "New Humanism," belonged to Hemingway's parents' generation.[25] Robert Herrick, when he calls *A Farewell to Arms* "mere garbage," and Seward Collins, when he calls the novel "disgusting," speak from prewar literary values not far divorced from Dr. and Mrs. Hemingway's moral values.[26] Clarence Hemingway declared that he would not tolerate "such filth" as *in our time* in his home and that he "would rather see Ernest dead than writing about such seamy subjects," while Grace Hemingway wrote her son that *The Sun Also Rises* was one of "the filthiest books of the year."[27] Promulgated briefly in the 1920s by men approaching their sixties, literary Humanism, like Hemingway's parents' outrage, was in part the reaction of an older generation whose most deeply held assumptions were being challenged by a new generation. It was the reaction of the last Victorians to the Lost Generation, defined by Gertrude Stein as "all of you young people who served in the war" (*MF*, 29).

That same war, which permanently severed young Hemingway from his parents' religious values, also severed him from the values of literary Humanism. While Humanism admitted that "all human activities are the rightful property of the creative artist from the lowest to the highest," it also insisted that the artist "endow them with some larger significance, a meaning," "something of larger import than the facts themselves."[28] In *A Farewell to Arms*, that target of passionate Humanist attack, Hemingway had tacitly declared that World War I had made "Humanistic" art obsolete. While literary Humanists still mentally resided in the prewar world where, according to Paul Fussell, "everyone knew what Glory was and what Honor meant,"[29] the war had taught Hemingway that "the things that were glorious had no glory and the sacrifices were like the stockyards at Chicago if nothing were done with the meat except to bury it" (*FTA*, 185). He set out to replace the "New Humanism" with a new literary naturalism dealing exclusively in "the facts themselves," never attempting to diminish their inherent significance by assigning them abstract meaning.

For Hemingway true obscenity resided not in graphic descriptions of sex or death, but in attempts to deny with comfortable abstractions the harsh realities of mechanized slaughter. "A Natural History of the Dead" is both a defense and a demonstration of one well-known sentence from *A Farewell to Arms:* "Abstract words such as glory, honor, courage or hallow were obscene beside the concrete names of roads, the names of rivers, the numbers of regiments, and the dates" (*FTA*, 185). In the short story's satirical section, Hemingway sets up a pseudoscientific experiment to prove his point to those Humanist critics who upheld the novel's suppression. Borrowing from early naturalists, he places such abstract words as "faith, love, and hope" beside concrete nouns denoting places (Smyrna, Milan, Pocol, Caporetto, Udine), roads (mountain roads, poplar-shaded roads), regiments (Bavarian Alpenkorps), and dates (June 1918) (*DIA*, 134–40). Going to the heart of the conflict between literary Humanism and his own naturalism, Hemingway juxtaposes Victorian abstractions about "those formed in His own image" against concretions describing the dead: "the heat, the flies, the indicative positions of the bodies in the grass" (*DIA*, 138).

Twice in the opening satire of "A Natural History of the Dead" Hemingway demonstrates the obscenity of abstraction by using rather clichéd figurative language to describe the dead and then interpreting his own figures literally. One might call these "exploding figures," designed by the author to self-destruct and reveal their deviation not only from the standard significance of words, but also from reality itself. The technique contributes to the black comedy in "A Natural History of the Dead":

> *Figure:* "The numbers of broken-legged mules and horses drowning in the shallow water called for a Goya to depict them."
> *Explosion:* "Although, speaking literally, one can hardly say that they called for a Goya since there has only been one Goya, long dead, and it is extremely doubtful if these animals, were they able to call, would call for pictorial representation of their plight but, more likely, would, if they were articulate, call for someone to alleviate their condition." (*DIA*, 135)
>
> *Figure:* ". . . this general died in a trench dug in the snow, high in the mountains, wearing an Alpini hat with an eagle feather in it and a hole in front you couldn't put your little finger in and a hole in back you could put your fist in . . ."

Explosion: "if it were a small fist and you wanted to put it there."
(*DIA,* 140)[30]

Far more graphic, and hence far more obscene by Humanist standards,
than *A Farewell to Arms,* "A Natural History of the Dead" makes deliberate
use of shock tactics like "exploding figures" to convert readers to literary
naturalism. Robert Coates might be referring to "A Natural History of the
Dead" when, in a favorable review of *Death in the Afternoon,* he observes
that "death in wartime . . . still preoccupies [Hemingway], and he
cannot find words strong enough in his determination to make you, too,
feel the horror of it."[31] Indeed, Hemingway defended both his use of
obscenity and "A Natural History of the Dead" in terms that echo
Coates's. Writing to Everett R. Perry, a Los Angeles librarian who had
"tactfully asked [Hemingway] what he thought was gained by using
certain plain words in *Death in the Afternoon,*"[32] the author explained that
he used occasional obscenities "as I used 'A Natural History of the
Dead.'"[33] The purpose of obscenity, and by extension of "A Natural
History of the Dead," was "to give calculated and what seems to me
necessary shock," "to make the person reading feel it has happened to
them."[34]

With its ironic contrasts and graphic descriptions, "A Natural History
of the Dead" assaults Humanism's failure to assign "some larger significance" to the facts of war. The "New Humanism" is irresponsible
precisely because its literature is so far removed from these realities.
Indeed, Hemingway emphasizes this point by apologizing for mentioning Humanist critics in what purports to be a natural history of the dead
and by hinting at how little literary criticism has ever meant to the young
men who die in wars: "While it is perhaps legitimate to deal with these
self-designated citizens [Humanists] in a natural history of the
dead . . . yet it is unfair to the other dead, who were not dead in their
youth of choice, who owned no magazines, many of whom had doubtless
never even read a review, that one has seen in the hot weather with a half-
pint of maggots working where their mouths have been" (*DIA,* 140).

Hemingway felt that the modern writer's chief responsibility to those
who had died in the war was to accurately depict their condition. As the
satirical portion of "A Natural History of the Dead" draws to a close,
Hemingway carries his attack from natural historians and Humanist
critics to authors of escapist war fiction. He cites Charles Yale Harrison's
Generals Die in Bed as an example of inaccurate treatment of war.[35]
Hemingway explodes Harrison's glib title with the already cited description of entrance and exit wounds in an unnamed general's skull and with

an account of General Von Behr's death as he led the Bavarian Alpenkorps into the Udine. "The titles of all such books," Hemingway
observes drily, "should be *Generals Usually Die in Bed*, if we are to have any
accuracy in such things" (*DIA*, 140).

 Here the Old Lady interrupts to inquire "When does the story start?"
(*DIA*, 140). Thus prompted, the author leaves his discussion of accurate
war fiction for fiction itself, setting out to show, rather than tell, how it
should be done.

 The story concerns a mortally wounded soldier who, unconscious but
still alive, has been left to die in a tomblike cave full of corpses:

> In the mountains, too, sometimes, the snow fell on the dead outside
> the dressing station on the side that was protected by the mountain
> from any shelling. They carried them into a cave that had been dug
> into the mountainside before the earth froze. It was in this cave that a
> man whose head was broken as a flower pot may be broken,
> although it was all held together by membranes and a skillfully
> applied bandage now soaked and hardened, with the structure of the
> brain disturbed by a piece of broken steel in it, lay a day, a night, and
> a day. (*DIA*, 141)

According to Hemingway's taxonomy of the dead developed in the
earlier satire, the soldier may be classified with "the dead" who "die like
cats, a skull broken in and iron in the brain, they lie alive two days like cats
that crawl into the coal bin with a bullet in the brain and will not die until
you cut their heads off" (*DIA*, 138–39).

 Yet the fictive portion of "A Natural History of the Dead" does more
than merely illustrate Hemingway's previous assertion that "most men
die like animals, not men" (*DIA*, 139). Instead, its chief concern is the
impact of this fact upon the living. The dying man is oblivious, but his
presence among the dead disturbs the stretcher-bearers, who want to
take him out and place him with the badly wounded, set aside elsewhere
to await death. Still more distressed by the dying man's situation is a
wounded lieutenant, who demands that the dressing station's doctor kill
the shattered soldier with an overdose of morphine. A firm and unemo-
tional adherent to the system of triage, the doctor refuses to let the
stretcher-bearers waste their effort ("'If you take him out of there you will
just have to put him back in'") or to squander valuable morphine on an
obviously terminal case ("'Do you think that is the only use I have for
morphine? Would you like me to have to operate without morphine?'"
[*DIA*, 141–42]). The stretcher-bearers want to remove the dying soldier
from the cave because they don't like to hear him breathing "'in there

with the dead'" (*DIA*, 141). The doctor correctly diagnoses this reaction as fear—"'Are you afraid of him, then?'" (*DIA*, 141). As a writer, Hemingway strove always to "see exactly what the action was that gave you the emotion."[36] In "A Natural History of the Dead," the action that frightens the stretcher-bearers is the breathing of a man alive but dying in a cave of corpses. Their fear, however, is not of the dying man himself, but of their own mortality. The sound of his breath in the cave of dead reminds them that they too are alive but must die, are already irrevocably consigned to the tomb. They want the dying man removed from the cave and placed with the badly wounded so they need not confront the equation of living and dead implied by his presence among corpses.

The wounded lieutenant's identification with the man in the cave is even more extreme than the stretcher-bearers': "'I will shoot the poor fellow,' the artillery officer said. 'I am a humane man. I will not let him suffer'" (*DIA*, 142). The lieutenant's desire to euthanize the dying soldier is irrational. The man is unconscious and cannot suffer. He feels neither the pain of his wound nor the horror of his situation. Instead, it is the lieutenant who is suffering—from the pain of his own wound, but especially from the horror of his own mortality. He has projected that suffering onto the unconscious soldier. The lieutenant's desire to end the dying man's wholly imaginary misery by shooting him may represent a suicidal impulse on his own behalf, an impulse not uncommon among shellshock victims and familiar to Hemingway.[37] Indeed, the lieutenant's subsequent hysteria and abortive attempt to shoot the implacable doctor suggest that he is suffering from some form of battle neurosis.

The argument about what to do with the dying soldier escalates. The lieutenant lacks the moral conviction to shoot the man himself, although the doctor dares him to go ahead and "assume the responsibility." Nevertheless, like Job seeking an explanation for the evil in the universe,[38] the lieutenant continues to plague the doctor with questions: "'Why don't you care for him then? Why don't you send him down on the cable railway?'" (*DIA*, 142). The doctor, like Job's God, does not answer questions, but poses some of his own, invoking his superior authority: "'Who are you to ask me questions? Are you my superior officer? Are you in command of this dressing post? Do me the courtesy to answer'" (*DIA*, 142–43).[39]

The lieutenant, of course, cannot answer except with an obscene litany of frustration: "'Fuck yourself. Fuck your mother. Fuck your sister'" (*DIA*, 142–43). He stands up and walks menacingly toward the doctor, who attempts to quell the lieutenant's rising hysteria by tossing a saucer of iodine in his face. Enraged, the blinded man fumbles for his pistol and tries to shoot the doctor. In a later portion of *Death in the Afternoon*, Hemingway wrote that "when a man is in rebellion against death he has pleasure in taking to himself one of the God-like attributes, that of giving it" (*DIA*, 233). In "A Natural History of the Dead" the lieutenant rebels simultaneously against death and the doctor by attempting to kill the latter, who easily overwhelms and disarms him, ordering the hysterical officer forcibly restrained so that his eyes can be rinsed and his wound treated.

At this juncture the man in the cave vindicates the doctor and justifies his presence among the dead by dying. "'See, my poor lieutenant?'" says the doctor. "'We dispute about nothing. In time of war we dispute about nothing'" (*DIA*, 144). The doctor's statement is triply ironic. He and the lieutenant have been arguing about nothing—a moot point of no practical importance—and nothing—the terrifying emptiness of death. The lieutenant cannot "see" anything—the doctor has blinded him with iodine—but the lieutenant *can* see "nothing," and that vision of emptiness causes him to scream—"'Ayee! Ayee!'"—in mental and physical anguish.

The concluding story of "A Natural History of the Dead" can be read as an artist fable, a fable that dramatizes the artist's responsibility to use "calculated and . . . necessary shock" to make the reader experience the horror of death. Like the ideal artist of the opening satire, the doctor is a man hardened by painful sights. His eyes, red and swollen with tear gas, suggest that fact. He is not afraid to look at death; he carries a flashlight into the cave to examine the soldier dying among corpses. The doctor cannot alleviate the soldier's condition, but he can depict it. His visit with the flashlight not only would make "a good etching for Goya," but also illuminates the contents of the sepulcher-cave for the doctor's audience of stretcher-bearers.[40]

However, the wounded lieutenant is afraid to confront death so squarely. Although he proclaims himself "a humane man," his self-proclaimed humanitarianism, like that of the satire's Humanist critics, is compounded of inexperience and cowardice. He has not seen the dying man, but nevertheless wants the doctor-artist to censor death's reality for him by killing or removing the unconscious soldier. Terrified rather than hardened by painful sights, the lieutenant has no claim to any experience that would allow him to criticize the doctor. Rather, the lieutenant may have counterfeited experience in order to avoid it—the doctor likens him to the many men who have rubbed onions in their eyes to simulate the effects of tear gas and obtain removal from the front line. When the doctor-artist tosses iodine in the lieutenant-critic's face, he has not merely administered a shock to quell his hysteria, but has forcibly imbued his frightened and hostile audience with his own vision. Finally, the doctor has given his red and swollen eyes to the lieutenant, has blinded him with iodine, and taught him to see nothing.

The concluding fiction dramatizes the opening satire's assertion that no one can assign "some larger significance, a meaning . . . something of larger import than the facts themselves" to the experience of death.[41] The war and the doctor have forced the wounded lieutenant to confront the absence of "something else" for the first time. "A Natural History of the Dead" climaxes at the moment when the lieutenant recognizes the nothingness beyond life and concludes as, unable to cope with his new knowledge, he begins to scream and must be forcibly restrained. Fulfilling Hemingway's insistence that literature must depict war with unflinching realism, the final story of "A Natural History of the Dead" treats war's psychological disasters as graphically as the satirical essay treats war's physical refuse.

The doctor speaks the final published words of "A Natural History of the Dead": " 'Hold him tight. He is in much pain. Hold him very tight' " (*DIA*, 144). The lines reflect the doctor's understanding of the lieutenant's physical and psychic injuries and include the doctor among Hemingway's "code heroes," men who, in Arthur Waldhorn's words, "[know] what the [lieutenant] must learn, that holding tight is almost all a man can salvage."[42]

The discarded coda to "A Natural History of the Dead" commences immediately after the doctor's final speech and is important for several reasons. It illuminates the published version by extending and even expounding on its imagery. It provides an additional ending to the work. It exemplifies the type of material Hemingway chose to omit from his writing, and it contains an undoubtedly autobiographical vignette about his experiences with Austrian war dead on the lower Piave. Portions of the discarded coda are here reproduced in print for the first time and provide a glimpse of "the underwater part" of "A Natural History of the Dead":[43]

Aside from the uniformity of their sex, the seeming unwillingness of many of them to die, even though unconscious and fatally wounded and the consequent nervous effect on the surviving members of their species, which is of course the point of the just related anecdote, another aspect of the dead, in a way related to the matter of their progressive changes in appearance, was the fact that the dead rarely retained any precious or semi-precious metals in their composition.

The coda's opening sentence is a bit of literary splicing; its first four dependent clauses refer back to, and even echo, the language of earlier portions of the published story.[44] So obvious are the echoes that even if the coda were discovered in a trunk, say, rather than the carefully cataloged Hemingway Collection, it could be identified as a fragment of "A Natural History of the Dead." Such summarizing of material already discussed is monotonous and ought to be unnecessary to help the reader follow something as short as "A Natural History of the Dead." But the need to splice implies that the rope has previously been severed, and the coda clearly represents an attempt to extend the interrupted satire.

While "A Natural History of the Dead" begins by satirizing eighteenth- and nineteenth-century natural historians to prove the absence of God in nature and nature's indifference to human suffering, Hemingway's satiric conceit—the pseudoscientific exposition—cannot sustain the weight of his emotion. When Hemingway comes to the impact of the dying on the living, he has reached the limits of satire. "A Natural History of the Dead" neatly meets Northrop Frye's definition of irony as satire that breaks down under the oppressive reality of its content.[45] The jargon of early Victorian taxonomy cannot express the trauma death causes the living. Hemingway breaks from satirical exposition into fiction as naturally as an excited man struggling in a foreign tongue breaks into his native language. The coda attempts to mend this severance by returning the reader—after the fiction of the doctor, the lieutenant, and the dying soldier—to more satirical exposition, more cataloging of aspects of the dead.

Besides endeavoring to return the reader to earlier material and thereby mend the broken illusion of a scientific narrative, the first sentence also contains a capsule interpretation of the dying soldier fiction. According to the coda, the anecdote's "point" is "the seeming unwillingness of many of them [the dead] to die, even though unconscious and fatally wounded and the consequent nervous effect on the surviving members of their [the dead's] species." This interpretation of the fiction is only superficially pat. Hemingway's complex pronoun reference in this sentence suggests that it is the dead who are unwilling to die, and the surviving members of the dead who are made uncomfortable by this unwillingness. Here a master stylist deliberately violates the conventions of English usage to give a startling significance to the deceitfully straightforward "which is *of course* [my italics] the point of the just related anecdote." Just as the sound of the dying man's breathing reminds the stretcher-bearers of their own mortality, Hemingway's pronoun reference here reminds his readers of their kinship with those corpses swelling and changing color in the sun.

The heavily subordinated opening sentence finally concludes by introducing a new subject for discussion: "the fact that the dead rarely retained any precious or semi-precious metals in their composition." In yet another effort to splice this tail to the story's body, Hemingway tells the reader that the new subject is related "in a way" to an old subject, the dead's progressive changes in appearance. However, having introduced a new subject, Hemingway does not move on. He returns instead to old themes:

> Someone has observed our bodies are made from dust and return to dust and while this does not entirely agree with my own observation which has led me to the conclusion that our bodies are originally made from the elements contained in semen, a pleasantly viscous [sic] liquid with an odor rather like that of a freshly caught barracuda, and have a tendency, if unembalmed after death, not to return to anything at all but rather to enter on a putrescance [sic] which, while highly attractive to the various carrion beetles and larvae of certain common insects, is moist rather than dry. But I would not care from my limited observations to dispute the possibility of an ultimate return to dust, granted the death of all the beetles and flies, and the possibility of a prolonged period of drought.

Here Hemingway jabs at the phony neatness of the official Christian birth and death sketched in Ecclesiastes—"All go unto one place; all are of the dust, and all turn to dust again"—and from his naturalist's stance points out that we are made from semen and subject to damp rot.[46] This portion of the coda recalls Hemingway's earlier attack on the piety of Humanist critics, an attack that also emphasizes the indignities of sex and death and the vanity of denying them.

After breaking from satirical exposition into narrative and then, in the coda, using repetition to return "A Natural History of the Dead" to satirical exposition, Hemingway breaks into narrative once again with the following sentence: "This is, however, beside the point of the absence of precious or semi-precious metals in the dead which was first drawn to my attention late on a July afternoon in the summer of 1918[47] when I was on the road from Fossalta di Piave[48] to a place called Monastir, not to be confused with, Monastir in Serbia, on a bicycle to see some friends." This time the narrative seems deliberately autobiographical rather than fictive. Hemingway tells the tale in the first person and inserts it into a book-length work of nonfiction also told in the first person. Surely coupling these facts with the wide publicity already given his war heroism and wounding, Hemingway could not have expected his readers to mistake for anyone else's the following experiences along the Piave River:

> In the end of June on the lower Piave the grain is ripe and now in early July it was past the time when it should have been cut but there was no one there to cut it and, as I went along the road, I was thinking of this, noting how little actual damage the standing grain had sustained even though it had been fought through in the Italian advance to the river bank and thinking how, when boys, we had been pursued, caught and chastized by farmers for going through a field of standing grain just before harvest and yet here were fields of grain through which a battle had been fought and the grain only down in a few clumps and in single patches that marked the position of the dead and there were no farmers here to harvest it although the fighting had been over for some time and I was sure it was now too late to harvest the grain that year even if there had been no question of unexploded hand grenades and shells. It would shell out of the heads from overripeness. So as I went along, pushing the bicycle, since this road was too badly broken up to make riding pleasant, even though the fields this far back from the river were little marked, I noticed how the trees had been marked and splintered occasionally by machine gun fire and wondered when I would be back in the mountains and what would they be doing in Schio that night.[49]

This stream-of-consciousness account, more than a digression, is a successful effort to establish the story's credentials and to make the reader experience the story through the narrator's earlier self. The multiplicity of detail, painstakingly described, give the scene its compelling reality. As the young man pushes his bicycle by the Piave, the current of his stream-of-conciousness sweeps the reader up and along, and the reader experiences in the present a story told in the past tense. By reconstructing the scene and his youthful thought processes in some detail, Hemingway, and the reader with him, relive rather than remember death on a July afternoon near Fossalta di Piave.

The encounter with death begins when the coda's protagonist smells chloride of lime. However, he is still so innocent of horror that the smell of quicklime as yet only provokes a boyhood memory of reading in the family outhouse, rather, if the comparison is not too outré, as the smell of madeleines dipped in lime-scented tea returns Marcel Proust to the Sunday afternoons of his childhood in Combray:

I had one great ambition; to go swimming at the Lido[50] in war time and this now seemed steadily more difficult of attainment and I was going along the road which was now quite wide, riding the bicycle, since the shell holes here this far back from the river were large and easily avoided, looking at the road and enjoying the shade and not thinking at all when I smelled Chloride of Lime which in spite of all latrines, made me remember digging a deep pit in the sandy loam of Michigan to move the old outhouse[51] where I had sat in high seated, unwindowed dimness, reading Montgomery Ward catalogues and sometimes the bound volumes of the St. Nicholas magazine for the years 1885 to 1896.[52] These last were forbidden to be taken there but you took the chance, of being caught when you went for this best reading time of all, and the smell of lime was when the good, smooth-seated weather-[?] backhouse was pushed over on its side and moved, the pit filled in, another dug and the house set up again. It was in the shade of two big hemlock trees and in the family, we called it Hemlock Park and now the smell of lime brought back the path smooth on the brown hemlock needle loam, the weathered boards of the fence and the pile of fire logs beside the gate and behind the fence the hemlock woods with fallen trees rotted dry on the ground.

The present reality of war intrudes on this memory as, from his bicycle, the young man spots "a burial squad filling a long pit which had water in the bottom" and "in a moment" is "glad of what smell of lime there had been."

The imagery of this particular sequence, while it has a natural un-premeditated air, emphasizes yet once more a theme developed earlier in the narrative—the simultaneous decomposition of human bodies and human faith. Obviously this passage is meant to answer Bishop Stanley's earlier question "Can no branch of Natural History be studied without increasing that faith, love, and hope which we, every one of us, need in our journey through the wilderness of life?" (*DIA*, 134). The coda to "A Natural History of the Dead" necessarily destroys that faith, love, and hope by reminding the reader that man's destiny is no more than the destiny of excrement.

When the outhouse revery is coupled with the wheat field sequence that precedes it, the discarded coda begins to develop yet another theme: the abandonment of childish beliefs and literature's responsibility to foster that abandonment. The boy scolded and punished by farmers "for going through a field of standing grain just before harvest" learns, to his surprise, that men may fight and die in a field of wheat without doing it substantial harm. The grain is "only down in a few clumps and in single patches that marked the position of the dead." The farmers who should harvest the grain and the soldiers who fought in it are vanished or dead, and the young man learns that human life is more ephemeral than ripe wheat. The child who sneaked *St. Nicholas* magazine into a Michigan outhouse to read in lime-scented solitude learns that there are other uses for lime and other purposes for literature. Like the published story, this portion of the coda suggests that Hemingway's perceived purpose in "A Natural History of the Dead" was to correct the romantic boys' story attitude toward war with accurate, brutally realistic reporting.

For the coda's protagonist, the narrator of "A Natural History of the Dead" as a young man, this process of education begins as he dismounts his bicycle, retreats to windward of the pit and its malodorous contents, and "observe[s]" the burial squad closely, "as a naturalist." He soon learns the reason for the "absence of precious or semi-precious metals" in the dead:

> the notable thing about this burial was that the sergeant in charge pried open the mouths of the dead, which had been brought from the field and carried to the pit, when these mouths were not already wide and investigated the condition of their teeth. I got off the bicycle to windward of the pit and observed. The sergeant had taken no notice of me, he was evidently working against time, and I watched him pry out a filling with a trench knife, then use a piece of pipe to break out other filled teeth entirely, putting them in a German gas mask tin to be worked over later. When he saw me he stopped, then tried a grin to see if it would go off on a between men of the world basis, then when I turned away he said, "They're Austrians. They're all Austrians."
>
> I said nothing and remounted the bicycle to ride on but I looked back and saw him after watching me roll away, turn and go back, to work with the remaining dead.

Confronted with the sergeant knocking gold teeth from corpses and with the sergeant's tentative grin, to see if it would go off on "a between men of the world basis," the young Red Cross corpsman must reassess his Oak Park idealism.[53] "In those days my conscience was very active," the older and wiser narrator recalls, and his younger self thinks about the incident for a long time that evening, endeavoring to decide whether to report the sergeant. Finally, after lengthy questioning and some complex moral equations, he realizes that if the sergeant is robbing the dead for personal gain, the war is robbing the dead for public gain, and that the

Oak Park notion of patriotic and morally upright behavior is purest hypocrisy. Having understood that the sergeant's actions, albeit illegal, are nevertheless consistent with the morality of the public and its war machine, the corpsman cannot report him for punishment. By deciding not to report the sergeant, the corpsman has decided not to participate in the war machine's hypocrisy. Like Nick Adams in *In Our Time*, he has made "a separate peace" (*SS*, 139). The ending of the sequence paraphrased in the preceding paragraph is psychologically revealing. The middle-aged narrator admits that as a young man he "did not state the problem so clearly and simply" as he has stated it in this story, thirteen years after the fact. Rather he "lay awake and thought awhile" about what he "had seen" and whether he should "do anything." Hemingway then says that "thinking about whether I should do anything was soon over," but the implication of the parallel structure (and of this detailed recollection thirteen years later) is that thinking about what he had seen was not soon over. This early experience of death and man's inhumanity was more bewildering to a teenager lying awake in wartime Italy than to an adult rationalizing in peacetime America. It might be one of the nightmare recollections that made Hemingway an insomniac for years after the war and that keep Nick Adams awake in "Now I Lay Me."

The coda's narrator next denies that he is much impressed by "so called" horrors, but then contradicts himself by going on to describe two of the "greatest horrors" (no "so called" this time) he can recall.

> And as for thinking about what I had seen; I have never been much impressed by horrors so called, due perhaps to a great curiosity which forces me to look at them closely whereupon the horror is difficult of persistence [sic] and the greatest horrors I can recall are, first a child being lifted with his legs dangling oddly after being run over by a bus on the stone road between Grau and Valencia54 and an old man in Madrid struck by a motor car and fallen from his bicycle, his bicycle broken and twisted, his glasses broken and dust and dirt in the places where skin had been scoured from his face, his hands and his knees. I suppose I must have turned away from both of these since I remember them with no element of the grotesqueness that replaces horror when the object or occurrence is closely observed.

Although the narrator says that had he carefully observed these incidents, a sense of grotesquerie would have replaced the sense of horror, he again contradicts himself. Would a man who had averted his gaze from such scenes have such flawless recollection of their details? Indeed, the narrator is not certain he turned away; he only says "I *suppose* [my emphasis] I must have turned away." These incidents are horrific to the narrator, and to the reader as well, precisely because they have been closely observed and described.

The passage never resolves these internal contradictions. In it Hemingway seems to be wondering aloud to himself why his memories of violence persist so clearly, some with and some without an attendant sensation of horror. He seems to want to deny that he is impressed by horror, yet his entire literary output belies him, and the impressions of horror crowd onto the pages even as he denies them. The passage seems to be a moment of spontaneous and ultimately unresolved self-analysis.

The final paragraph of the coda provides an alternative ending to "A Natural History of the Dead":

> Now, as I write, years after everything is over, I think this is perhaps, enough about the dead. There is no need to continue and write an accurate observation on a friend dead, a dead lover or a dead parent since a writer can deal at length with these in fiction rather than in natural history, an ill enough paid branch of writing, Is [sic] it not so, Hudson? So perhaps the inspiration from the moss flower of extraordinary beauty is to be derived not from the dead themselves, too big for their uniforms in the heat, but from the contemplation of the sergeant at work on them. Let us learn from observing the industrious sergeant, let us take inspiration from the sergeants [sic] researches, who knows how profitable the dead may be if we live long enough? Who knows how much gold may be extracted from them? Ah, Mungo Park, You [sic] should have seen the dead. You should have seen them Bishop. All of you naturalists should have seen the dead. You should have seen them.

By cynically equating his own profession with the corpse-robber's, the narrator further underscores the hypocrisy that would have been involved in his reporting the sergeant. Writing about the dead, Hemingway acknowledges, is profitable, but more profitable when the treatment is fiction, a romanticized vision of war, than when it is natural history, an unflinching stare at the realities of violent death. The authors of books like *Generals Die in Bed*, the passage implies, profit by stealing the dignity of truth from the dead, as surely as the sergeant profits by bashing out their gold-filled teeth.[55]

This unpublished ending to "A Natural History of the Dead" is a "bookend" conclusion. It closes the story by returning it to its opening question ("let us therefore see what inspiration we can derive from the dead" [*DIA*, 134]) and answering it ironically. The coda's ending returns the reader to Mungo Park's rhetorical question ("Can that Being who planted, watered, and brought to perfection, in this obscure part of the world, a thing which appears of so small importance, look with unconcern upon the situation and sufferings of creatures formed after His own image?" [*DIA*, 134]) and answers by suggesting that God does not exist and mankind is without compassion. The corpses swelling in the sun cannot have been formed in a divine image and suggest the absence of God in nature, while the industrious sergeant at work on them demonstrates that man himself can not only look with "unconcern upon the situation and suffering" of his fellows, but even profit from their tragedies.

The coda's ending is neater and more direct than the published ending, yet it has its own poetic quality, and it does nudge the reader to an interpretation of the story he is left to infer with more difficulty from the doctor's "'Hold him very tight.'" Its last four sentences are lyrical with repetition and call individuals like Mungo Park and Bishop Stanley, who saw divinity in nature, severely to account: "Ah, Mungo Park, you should have seen the dead. You should have seen them, Bishop. All of you naturalists should have seen the dead. You should have seen them." It echoes the words of the doctor, his eyes red and swollen with tear gas: "'What about these eyes?' He pointed the forceps at them. 'How would you like these?'" (*DIA*, 144). And as it echoes the doctor, the coda's lines express the overall purpose of "A Natural History of the Dead"—to give the reader Hemingway's scorched and scorching vision. It asks the reader to look realistically at war and death and to abandon all romantic notions of them. It figuratively flings a saucer of iodine into the eyes of its readers; it gives them an agonizing vision of nothing; it assaults their placid moral assumptions.

By contrast, the published ending defies closure. The doctor's "'Hold him tight. He is in much pain. Hold him very tight'" opens the story by refusing to interpret it. The reader is left to speculate about the physical and mental anguish afflicting the lieutenant, about the doctor's motives for blinding him, about this story's relationship to the satiric exposition that preceded it.[56] The published ending relies on the "theory of omission": Hemingway assumes (and assumes safely) that he has written his tale truly enough to give his readers a feeling for these things as truly as if he had stated them.

The coda of "A Natural History of the Dead" exemplifies some of Hemingway's characteristic traits and thematic interests, but it could have been omitted for one, several, or all of a number of reasons. In some places it is repetitive, anticlimactic, overly digressive, and even embarrassingly narcissistic. The opening sentence, with its many repetitions, is a clumsy and monotonous patch job. To return, as the coda returns to satirical exposition from fiction, is to treat the story of the dying soldier as a digression from the main purpose of "A Natural History of the Dead," rather than the final, and most climactic, expression of that purpose. To return to satirical exposition only to ponder the already pondered indignities of sex and death, and then to break again into narrative, is simply disruptive. To dwell, particularly in the first person, on the horrors and unresolved conflicts of one's youth is at least self-indulgent. Finally, to end with a "the wheel has come full circle" conclusion that interprets the story for the reader is to destroy the story's frightening and resonant ambiguities.

That Hemingway omitted the coda is doubtless a tribute to his literary judgment and self-discipline. With his "theory of omission," Hemingway was too shrewd a writer to spoil a story's drama by revealing the backstage machinery of personal experience that generated the fiction. Yet finally, the coda's worth lies precisely in the glimpse it gives of its author's life. "Late on a July afternoon in the summer of 1918," Ernest Hemingway was nineteen years old and just days away from his wounding. As Philip Young has demonstrated, the trauma of that wounding is responsible certainly for the content, and perhaps for the very existence, of Hemingway's fiction.[57]

The coda, which shows the ground being paved for the enormity of Hemingway's trauma, reinforces Young's view. Working in the battlefields of the Piave, the adolescent Hemingway, still physically unscarred, observed the dying and the dead and learned that dying in war, however heroic, could also be agonizing; that death for one's country, however *dulce et decorum*, was also pointless. He learned too that death was final, that decay was unavoidable, loathsome, and ignominious. In this little sequence on the Piave, the reader sees young Hemingway's preparation for the wounding that exploded him into manhood, if not into maturity. Life in the ambulance corps was rubbing his young nose in death's most gruesome realities, stripping him of childish beliefs. When an Austrian *Minenwerfer* brought him suddenly and horribly to an adult recognition of his own mortality, his head had already been filled with Bosch-like images of death, his psyche already emptied of the patriotic and religious faith that might have prevented those images from permanently occupying his imagination.

In *Beyond the Pleasure Principle* Sigmund Freud seeks an explanation for the terrifying and recurrent battle dreams of veterans and finds one in an observation of children at play:

> the unpleasurable nature of an experience does not always unsuit it for play. If the doctor looks down a child's throat or carries out some small operation on him, we may be sure that these frightening experiences will be the subject of the next game; but we must not in that connection overlook the fact that there is a yield of pleasure from another source. As the child passes over from the passivity of the experience, to the activity of the game, he hands on the disagreeable experience to one of his playmates and in this way revenges himself on a substitute.[58]

Freud goes on to argue that children do this because through imaginative repetition of a traumatic experience "they can master a powerful impression far more thoroughly than they could by merely experiencing it passively," and he adds that the recurring nightmares of soldiers may serve a similar function.[59] Freud further draws an analogy between such play and "the artistic imitation carried out by adults," which, when the art is tragedy, does not spare the audience "the most painful experiences."[60] Like the child assuming the role of doctor and "operating" on a playmate, the tragic artist becomes the controlling agent of trauma, rather than its passive victim.

Certainly "A Natural History of the Dead," which Hemingway confessed was designed "to give calculated and . . . necessary shock" and "to make the person reading feel it has happened to them" is tragic art springing from the impulse Freud describes—an author's desire to inflict his own "most painful experiences" on an audience.[61] Read in the light of *Beyond the Pleasure Principle,* the discarded coda reveals the origin of the story's cruelly graphic author in the innocent and soon-to-be-wounded Lieutenant Hemingway, revulsed by the sights and smells of the battlefield and terrified by the absence at the heart of the universe they imply.

In addition, the authorial experience exposed in the coda is clearly the source of the published story's artist fable. The doctor-artist of "A Natural History of the Dead" scorches the eyes of the hysterical lieutenant not only as painfully as his own have been scorched, but also as remorselessly as the Hemingway-artist of "A Natural History of the Dead" masters his own horrifying experience of war by inflicting it on his readers. Knowledge of the coda helps readers to locate both the doctor's and Hemingway's half-sadistic creative impulse in the fictive lieutenant's (and Lieutenant Hemingway's) terror of death's emptiness.

By omitting the coda to "A Natural History of the Dead," Hemingway rendered the short story a more compelling fiction and disguised its autobiographical sources. Yet the preservation of the discarded four pages allows readers to penetrate beneath the iceberg of "A Natural History of the Dead" and to see the submerged experience that gives the published story the authentic ring of horror.

Reflection vs. Daydream: Two Types of the Implied Reader in Hemingway's Fiction

Hubert Zapf

●

The role of the reader in Hemingway's works had attracted the attention of critics even before the rise of modern reception theory made such attention part of a more or less established methodology of literary scholarship. The strange emotional intensity of his fiction vis-à-vis the objective, decidedly nonemotional quality of his style pointed to a paradoxical tension in his writing which could be resolved only by interpolating what was in effect the dimension of an "implied reader" in the texts, whose "involuntary subjective response" was recognized as an essential part of the author's literary technique.[1] The most conspicuous elements of this technique were the use of emotional understatement; the extreme reduction of language, style, and fictional world; and the deliberate strategy of leaving out relevant information, that is, of providing blanks in the textual surface that have an appellative function, calling upon the reader's activity to supply the missing context.[2] Hemingway himself described his technique metaphorically in the famous comparison of his writing with the movement of an iceberg, of which only the smallest part is visible on the surface.[3] Beneath the delusively factual surface of realistic description and objective report there was recognized, especially after the reconsideration of Hemingway as a symbolist and even expressionist writer, a deep structure of potential significance which required the intense imaginative participation of the reader in the constitution of the text.[4] This deep structure presented, in the language of reception theory, an implicit dimension of indeterminacy which allowed for a great variety of symbolic, ironic, emotional, or reflective realizations of the text.

However, the iceberg metaphor and similar concepts for describing the specific mode of communication between text and reader in Hemingway designate only one aspect of the implied reader in his fiction. This aspect could be called "vertical," as it considers the texts primarily from the vertical tension expressed in the spatial metaphor of surface vs. depth. The other equally important aspect is the "horizontal" aspect of the text as a temporal process in which the expectations of the reader are built up, modified, fulfilled, or disappointed in successive steps in the course of the text. Little attention has been paid in criticism to the psychodynamic structure of this process, although it is highly operative in producing the strong emotional effect that Hemingway's works, perhaps because of their carefully controlled surface realism, communicate to the reader.

These two aspects of reception (the vertical aspect of the implied reader as defined by the indeterminacy of a suggested deep structure of the text and the horizontal aspect of the implied reader as defined by the process of experience inscribed into the text) represent *two different types* of appellative structure in Hemingway's fiction. The first appeals to the reader's sense of discovery and cognitive coherence, to his ability to detect, connect, and interpret implicit, ambiguous, or incomplete textual information. It therefore involves a predominantly mental, reflective activity of the reader. The second type appeals to the reader's sense of empathy with significant human fate, building upon the psychic tension of expectation vs. result, desire vs. reality, hope vs. disappointment. It involves a predominantly emotional, psychological activity. The first reception type is essentially spatial and circular, the second essentially temporal and linear. The one is characterized by the structural simultaneity of opposing elements of meaning, the other by the dramatized succession of opposing phases of psychodynamic development. The one leads to reflective distance, the other to emotional identification. In many texts, of course, these types occur in mixed form and with varying emphasis. But they nevertheless can be distinguished as two contrasting, ideal-typical variants of the implied reader in Hemingway which mark the range of possible responses evoked by his works.

Type I will be exemplified here by *The Sun Also Rises* and "Big Two-Hearted River." Type II will be exemplified by some of the best known works of Hemingway's middle and late periods of composition—"The Short Happy Life of Francis Macomber," "The Snows of Kilimanjaro," *A Farewell to Arms,* and *The Old Man and the Sea.*

Before going to concrete textual analyses, however, it seems useful to determine on a theoretical level what is meant here by the vertical and the horizontal axes of Hemingway's texts and how they are related to "reflection" and "daydream" as predominant reader-responses. For clarification of these concepts it is helpful to consult two of the most influential theories of reader-response, Wolfgang Iser's phenomenological reception theory and the psychological theory of Sigmund Freud.

Iser, who introduced the implied reader as a critical category, defined it not in the sense of a concrete, historical reader but as the characteristic *activity* of reading as it is generated by and inscribed into what he calls the "appellative structure" of literary texts.[5] How is this structure conceived in Iser's theory? A guiding assumption of his reception aesthetics, which has become widely popular in recent criticism, is the idea of the indeterminacy of the literary text. The text presents itself to the reader not as a finished whole but only in the form of "schematized views,"[6] It consists only of reduced, incomplete outlines and "component parts" of an imaginary world which must be completed and put together in the reader's mind to be fully realized.[7] Because literature is a highly indirect, nonreferential mode of speech, there results a constant tension between the explicit statements on the textual surface and the implicit connotations, symbolic cross-references, ironic undercurrents which, though not directly formulated, make up the truly "literary" quality of the discourse. Literary communication is thus defined by the tension between what is stated and what is left out, between what is formulated and what is left unformulated in the actual text. And it is particularly the dimension of the unformulated that decisively stimulates the reader's activity. "Thus by reading," as Iser states, "we uncover the unformulated part of the text, and this very indeterminacy is the force that drives us to work out a configurative meaning while at the same time giving us the necessary degree of freedom to do so."[8]

It can be seen here that the underlying concept of literature in this theory is essentially a concept of negativity. Literature is defined by what it is, says, and does *not* say, by techniques and strategies that negate the reader's expectations of coherence and consistency. It becomes a medium that distances the reader from immediate experience, that subliminally counteracts his tendency of illusion-building and emotional identification. It defamiliarizes the familiar and thus irritates any affirmative views of man and the world.

What kind of receptive activity does this model imply? In the final analysis it turns literature into a medium of *reflection*. The typical activities of Iser's implied reader remind one of an aesthetical version of the reflective consciousness which philosophy distinguishes from the naive consciousness and its "natural attitude" toward reality.[9] In the act of reflection the subjective consciousness "turns back" upon itself, distancing itself from immediate experience and questioning all apparent certainties and determinacies of the everyday world. By radically suspending habitual values and "prejudgments,"[10] the reflecting consciousness becomes aware of its own constitutive role in the structuring and interpretation of the "objective" world. One need only replace the "world" by the "text" to see that Iser's implied reader, in a similar way, is conceived as an all-pervading critical consciousness which explicates itself in progressive acts of (self-) reflection. Indeed, the very negativity that Iser attributes to literature, as well as the emancipatory effect that this negativity assumes in the sense of an increased self-awareness and thus self-realization of the reader's subjectivity, corresponds to the most distinctive features of reflection as it has been defined in philosophy. According to Walter Schulz, "It is the interest and intention of all reflection to negate the given as the substantial, to suspend its objective validity, and to incorporate it into one's own subjectivity."[11]

Sigmund Freud's theory of reading is quite different from Iser's. Indeed, one could say that Freud emphasizes precisely those aspects of the reading activity that are neglected in Iser's reception aesthetics. To Freud the reading of fictional literature is not an act of hermeneutic (self-) reflection but like the enactment of a symbolic *daydream*.[12] Reading—like writing—is the fictive realization of a wish-fulfilling fantasy, which to Freud is the primary motive and content of all daydreams. "Wish-fulfillment" should not be understood here in any fixed, narrow sense— such as referring only to sexual fantasies or to a regressive reenactment of primal childhood scenes—but in the sense of a basic anthropological desire for idealization, for the imaginative correction of a deficient reality, which manifests itself in many different forms.[13] The scenarios of fictional daydreams can range from more simple forms of heroic self-aggrandizement and of all sorts of erotic, professional, and other success fantasies to more elevated fantasies of moral greatness and humane self-realization.

Instead of Iser's emphasis on the negativity of literature, then, Freud's emphasis is on its "positivity"—in a thematic as well as in a structural sense. What induces the reader's reaction is not what is "left out" or remains indeterminate but what is "put in" and is determined by the immanent logic of the world of the text as the author has symbolically projected it. Literature here is not primarily a means of criticizing or negating existing systems of sociocultural reality but an imaginative counterworld which offers a possible escape from or alternative to reality. The act of reading is not conceived as the cognitive enactment of a highly mediated, secondary form of experience but as the emotional enactment of an immediate, lifelike form of primary experience. Instead of the self-reflective detachment of the reader from the narrated world, Freud postulates the reader's psychological involvement in it.

Although at first sight these two models appear to be contradictory, they should nonetheless be seen as complementary. Instead of universal concepts which can be applied to all texts indifferently, they should be viewed as specific, analytical concepts which describe two different dimensions of the act of reading and, correspondingly, two kinds of appellative structure in literature. The response-patterns of reflection and daydream should not be considered primarily as projections of the reader's subjectivity but as inherent possibilities of fictional texts.[14] They gain hermeneutic value only if they are viewed as dimensions of the *implied* reader, that is, of the dynamics of response as it is inscribed within the structure of the narrative itself.

As stated, these theoretical models can serve to illuminate two characteristic types of reader-appeal in Hemingway's works. In which sense, then, can the first type be called vertical, the second horizontal? The two types refer to two fundamental aspects of narrative composition, and they specifically emphasize one of these aspects in the communication between text and reader: the aspect of the text as a *system* of potential meaning and the aspect of the text as a *process* of potential experience. In the first case we tend to get a vertical effect in that the explicitly formulated surface of the narrative must be constantly related to the unformulated implications of the narrative to figure out its "deeper" meaning and significance. What happens on the level of narrated events is no more important than what these events signify, how they are to be interpreted and related to other elements and layers of the text. If, as in Hemingway's *The Sun Also Rises*, we have an almost pathological distance from, and indifference of the narrator toward, the narrated world, and if this world is furthermore presented as a world of stasis and futility where human action loses any meaningful direction and teleological purpose, the focus of the reader's attention is all the more turned away ("re-flected") from the reported facts toward an inner, subjective world beneath the external surface world of appearances. Of course, this reflective activity is in itself a temporal process. In reading we cannot but react to one sentence after another, following the lines of the written text. But what matters here is that the reading process in the reflective response pattern is not simply defined by the progress of fictional events but also by the gradual accumulation of interpretive data about these events. Reflection essentially occurs in a timeless mental space, because by its very nature of "turning back" upon itself it breaks up the objective flux of time and suspends the laws of temporal linearity and irreversibility, making past and present simultaneous in the potentially infinite space of subjective thought.

This is different in Type II of the implied reader. In the daydream pattern of response the reader, instead of being confronted with his own interpretive subjectivity, is drawn into the imaginative world of the text. His psyche is brought to experience the fictitious world under the simulated conditions of "real life." He is not primarily led to question the premises of this world but to follow the immanent logic of the developing narrative. What this means is that above all he is psychically subject to the temporal process of the fiction, to the changes and the promising or disappointing turns of events on the horizontal axis of the text. The reader is not put in a reflective position "above" the narrative (in an indeterminate mental space where each step is potentially reversible) but is implicated in its horizontal unfolding in time, which is inscribed in successively determined, irreversible steps into the narrative sequence of the text. In Hemingway's "Macomber," for example, the reading process is characterized not by the static wasteland effect of sterility and monotonous repetition but by sharp changes of mood and highly emotionalized climaxes of the narrative. The story dramatizes the daydream of Macomber's rise from utter humiliation to heroic self-affirmation. This daydream is gradually built up in the reader's expectation, is almost miraculously fulfilled in the course of the text, and is destroyed in the shock of Macomber's unexpected death at the end of the story.

The following analysis of selected texts demonstrates the validity of this distinction between two types of the implied reader in Hemingway; and it examines the way in which they help to shape the narrative composition of his works.

In *The Sun Also Rises*, which will serve here as chief example of Type I of appellative structure, the reader experiences the world as from a painfully insurmountable distance. He is informed early in the book of Jake Barnes's impotence which, as the physical manifestation of his psychic war trauma, becomes a more general metaphor for his inability to participate fully in the life that is going on around him. Jake's paralysis is like a silent center of indifference, an ever-present principle of negativity which inhabits all potentially positive and meaningful experiences in the novel and taints them with the same color of a controlled but extreme disillusionment. The surface of the text is above all characterized by Jake's desperate attempt at composure and self-control and at rigorously suppressing all signs of his wounded subjectivity. In his obsession with objectivity, he restricts his narrative largely to a neutral, almost monotonous registration of external facts, actions, and dialogues. The inner world of his subjectivity, however, which is responsible for this reduced perspective, is almost entirely excluded from the explicit text. It thus forms a kind of central indeterminacy in the novel which undermines the apparent determinateness of the textual surface as an element of constant irritation and uncertainty and puts the reader at a skeptical distance to the narrated world. As Jake Barnes mistrusts "all simple people, especially when their stories hold together,"[15] the reader is led to mistrust the facade of controlled matter-of-factness and naturalistic certainty that the narrator strives to establish. No real change, no development is possible in such a constellation, neither in the external world, whose activities appear as a pointless *circulus vitiosus* in the light of Jake's disillusioned subjectivity, nor in Jake's subjectivity itself, which is imprisoned, as in a gloomy inner exile, in its paralysis. The expectation of the reader of such change and the psychodynamic potential of the temporal-horizontal tension it would create is therefore neutralized early in the novel, and what is left is a reflective, vertical tension between different levels of meaning and reality that are interrelated in a sort of negative coexistence, simultaneously defining and denying each other.

Only at some points in the novel does Jake's suppressed subjectivity come to the surface, creating short moments of intensity that interrupt the overall sense of objective control and frustrated emotion—for example, when in chapter 4 he lies awake in bed at night thinking of Brett and, as the strain of his depression is getting too strong, starts to cry (31); or when in chapter 17 he goes up to the hotel room of Robert Cohn—who has had a psychic breakdown—and remembers a blow on his head which he suffered when playing football in his youth. This experience is a parallel to his later war wound, as well as to the desperate situation of his weaker alter ego, Robert Cohn (192ff.). But these are only short moments in the book, signals from the deep structure of the text which do not really shape or substantially change the reading experience. They are flashlights illuminating an internal reality which is largely concealed beneath the surface of external events and which appears as a deep-rooted feeling of self-alienation and of a traumatic division from life that goes back to Jake's earliest confrontations with the world. As the incident with Cohn is placed in the context of the bullfights in Pamplona, this psychic division from life is specifically emphasized, because the scenes of unbroken vitality at the fiesta seem strangely removed from the two isolated American expatriates, whose incommunicable emptiness and "impotence" stand in sharp contrast to the communicative celebration of life, and death, surrounding them.

Even the bullfights, which are seen by some critics as an authentic alternative to the world of social frustration and as a "climax of the entire novel,"[16] are undercut in their immediate effect by the distance and alienation implied in the novel's narrative perspective. It is certainly true that the bullfighting scenes create moments of great intensity in the novel, which transmit some sense of Jake's enthusiasm as an aficionado (who has projected what is left of his vital emotions into the bullfighting myth) to the reader. But they do not add up to an actualized *process* of experience for the reader, because the short moments of a ritualized coherence of life that they convey are sharply juxtaposed with the much longer scenes of the totally deritualized and incoherent life of the foreign group of bourgeois bohemians who, including Jake, seem strangely eccentric and out of place in the quasi-mythic world of the fiesta. The bullfights represent an idealized mythical counterworld, which we are allowed to glimpse, but which only increases our awareness of the fragmentation and disorientation of life in the real, modern world of the main characters—and of the reader. This is mirrored in the narrative focus which, with Jake Barnes, shows a contradictory tendency throughout the fiesta to move away from the center of the action to which it is simultaneously attracted, to seek some sort of mythic identity with the community of the fiesta, and yet compulsively to withdraw into an isolated outsider-position. Although Jake admires Romero as the natural man of action and archetypical bullfighter, he remains at an impersonal distance from him. It is rather that he finds Romero fascinating as an example of that original beauty and vitality of life from which he himself is forever separated. And it may in a sense be true, as has often been maintained, that Hemingway expounds his own principle of art in his description of Romero's art of bullfighting (167ff.). But that is only one, idealized side of his art, of which the other side is the irredeemable "break" between self and reality, consciousness and life, which through Jake's perspective determines the structure of the novel—and of the way in which Hemingway presents the fiesta.

As Paul Goodman has shown in an analysis of the bullfighting scenes, this is also true from a linguistic viewpoint. Through the "passive style" of descriptive objectivity, "the persons are held at arm's length, [and] there is no way to get inside them or identify with them"; indeed, "the effect . . . is like the Brechtian 'alienation,' which Hemingway achieves more consistently than Brecht."[17] In other words the text calls not for the identification of the reader but embodies a specific *resistance* to such identification. Hemingway's alienation effect, however, differs from Brecht's in that this resistance is not transformed into an epic meta-discourse with the audience—and thus dissolved into rational understanding—but points to a deeper structure of textual meaning which requires continuous interpretation of the presented reality without offering any finished version of that reality.

A similar "break" in the textual surface can be observed in the fishing episode at Burguete. As the scene is a particularly illuminating example of Hemingway's technique of reader-guidance in the novel, it should be looked at in some detail. Like the bullfights, the fishing prima facie suggests a meaningful alternative, a return from the spiritual wasteland of modern society to natural life, and thus promises a potential emotional change or even climax for the reader. Yet again a closer look reveals that this potential is not used but is in fact deliberately *counteracted* by the way in which the episode is related. The fishing excursion is the first real contact with nature that Jake and his friend Bill establish after their long travel from Paris and from the anonymous jungle of the city that it symbolizes. But other than Bill, who is full of eager ambition and wades deep into the stream to catch particularly great fish, Jake—and with him the focus of the reader's attention—again remains curiously detached from the fishing, avoiding any immediate involvement in the experience. He sits on a dam above the falls where the water "was deep" (99) and gets through with his fishing in a very economical, almost mechanical way, catching six identical trout in a row at the easiest place of the stream: "While I had him on [the first trout] several trout had jumped at the falls. As soon as I baited up and dropped in again I hooked another and brought him in the same way. In a little while I had six. They were all about the same size. I laid them out side by side, all their heads pointing the same way, and looked at them" (119).

With this Jake's fishing adventure is about over. Clearly, the effect here is anticlimactic, emphasizing not the dynamic element of action and experience but the static or, rather, circular element of recurrence of the same—note the conspicuous repetition of the word "same" in reference to Jake's activities, as well as to the "result" of these activities (the trout). This is even sharper brought to light in view of Bill's unreserved engagement in the fishing and of the far more impressive success of his efforts: "Bill sat down, opened up his bag, laid a big trout on the grass. He took out three more, each one a little bigger than the last, and laid them side by side in the shade from the tree. His face was sweaty and happy" (120). Bill has indeed had an experience, and the excited ambition and "climax" of his adventure are not only mirrored in his face but, in a nice bit of ironic imagery, in the increasingly bigger size of his trout. Yet again, the energy and adventure of active life which Bill's fishing symbolizes are distinctly removed from the novel's narrative center. His experience happens in absentia; it is not accessible to the reader as a subjective process but only as the "dead," objectified result of that process. This detachment from concrete experience is underlined by the fact that while Bill, outside the novel's narrative focus, is engaged in fishing, Jake has withdrawn under a tree to read. What he is reading is a story "about a man who had been frozen in the Alps and fallen into a glacier and disappeared, and his bride was going to wait twenty-four years exactly for his body to come out on the moraine, while her true love waited too, and they were still waiting when Bill came up" (120). This strange story of a love-relationship which contains the impossibility of its own realization, and which indicates a more general stalemate of human feelings and, indeed, of life itself, is an ironic-reflective comment on Jake's situation in the book. It emphasizes his unrealized, self-negating relationship to Brett Ashley, with which he continues to be preoccupied even in this pastoral scene (see the ensuing dialogue with Bill, 103–4), signifying once more his psychic alienation from active life and experience.

From the analysis of these key passages in the book, the implied reader in *The Sun Also Rises* clearly emerges as an example of Type I of the reader-appeal in Hemingway distinguished above. The emotive potential of fictional wish fulfillment is a priori neutralized here, because all potentially life-affirming experiences are undermined by the implicit negativity of the narrator's consciousness which distances the reader from any immediate involvement in the fictional world. The tension created in the reader's mind is thus not primarily dynamic but static, not primarily processual but simultaneous. Rather than an emotional tension between distinct and alternating phases of reception, it is a reflective tension between surface vs. deep structure, external vs. internal reality, explicit vs. implicit text.

A variation of this type of reader-appeal is represented by the story "Big Two-Hearted River." Placed at the end of *In Our Time*, it is significantly reduced in external action and conflict. All that happens is Nick's journey to a river in the country, his stay there overnight, and his trout fishing on the next day. At the same time, however, there are symbolic and linguistic signals in the formulated text which, in the sense of the iceberg theory, point to a constitutive dimension of the unformulated, to deeper and more problematical levels of meaning beneath the uneventful and apparently unproblematical surface of the explicit text. Examples of such signals are the interchapters with their horrifying scenes of death and violence that are placed before Part I and between the two parts like electrifying psycho-shocks; the wasteland motif of the burnt town at the beginning; the nervous control and intensity of Nick's activities, in which every detail seems to gain disproportionate importance; his overreaction to "deeper" areas of reality, as in the "shock" he suffers when he steps into the stream to fish[18] or in the characterization of the fishing of the swamp as a "tragic adventure";[19] the symbol of the swamp itself, which is an objective correlative of the unexplored depths of Nick's psyche. Nick's behavior thus appears as a compulsive attempt to remain on a safe, unproblematical surface of life and to avoid, for the time being, any conscious confrontation with the experiences which lie behind him, but which, as these signals show, in fact form a constituent part of his present situation. This discrepancy between the formulated and the unformulated dimensions of the text, between the manifest pastoral idyl of a man's ritual regeneration in nature and the latent crisis of his psyche which, in his overidentification with this idyllic pattern, he tries to suppress, creates a constant tension in the reader's mind, provoking him to reflect on those problematical, subconscious implications that Nick, like Jake Barnes, tries to exclude from consciousness and communication. Nick's effort to certify and (over-) determine the reality of his experience, by clinging to simplistic rituals and sensory details, on a level of unproblematical, "natural" action produces a paradoxical result, causing instead an irritating feeling of uncertainty and indeterminacy which all the more activates the reflective skepticism of the reader. The more Nick suppresses reflection, the more the reader is forced into it. Nick's psyche, like Jake's, marks a central indeterminacy of the text, a "black box" of the actions in the story which, at the same time that it motivates these actions, constantly threatens to undermine the attempt at a new life. Other examples of this type of reader-appeal are Hemingway's "static stories" such as "Mr. and Mrs. Elliot," "Cat in the Rain," "A Clean, Well-Lighted Place," "Hills Like White Elephants"—in all of which a similar effect of emotional deadlock and reflective distance is created.

A model example of the second type of the implied reader in Hemingway is "The Short Happy Life of Francis Macomber," but "The Snows of Kilimanjaro" or novels like *A Farewell to Arms* and *The Old Man and the Sea* are also distinctively shaped in their appellative structure by this type. As has been said, the second type, in contrast to the first, is very much defined by the horizontal aspect of reception, by the dynamic process of experience inscribed into the text. The two sides of affective reader-appeal—the daydream of an imaginative fulfillment of life and the shock of witnessing the destruction of that daydream—which are fused and mutually neutralized in Type I in favor of reflection, are separated in Type II and projected into a temporal sequence of distinct and successive phases of reception. The psychodramatic potential of this tension is fully released and pushed to the extreme here, involving the reader in a fictional experience characterized by sharp changes and contrasting climaxes of his emotional participation in the text. Indeed, the characteristic pattern of Type II quite distinctly follows the model of a daydream, which is developed as an idealizing counterfantasy out of the experience of a negative reality, is—sometimes almost miraculously—fulfilled in the course of the text and is inevitably destroyed in its clash with the reality from which it has tried to emancipate itself.[20]

This pattern can be seen in an analysis of "The Short Happy Life of Francis Macomber," one of the author's major stories, where it occurs in an almost ideal-typical form. Basically, the story can be divided into three parts, which correspond to different yet interrelated phases of reception.

(1) The situation at the beginning is one of utter humiliation for Macomber, who has behaved like a coward at a lion hunt and is now the subject of contempt among the hunting company. Because his cowardice is the implicit center of attention to which the other characters—Wilson, the guide, and Margot Macomber—react, the reader is involuntarily placed in Macomber's position and is made to feel, indirectly but all the more painfully, his frustration and isolation.[21] This feeling is enforced and at the same time charged with an aggressive undertone by Margaret's behavior, who demonstrates her disdain of her husband to a degree that she provokes not only Wilson's but the reader's sharp antipathy (16ff.). However, there are already some first signals in the text that direct the hopeful attention of the reader to the buffalo-hunt of the following day, which is repeatedly mentioned in the dialogue and is associated with the intense but diametrically opposed expectations of the couple. To Margaret it means the promise of another defeat for her husband and thus of another triumph for herself: "You don't know how I look forward to tomorrow" (16). To Macomber it represents the desperate hope of rehabilitating himself: "Maybe I can fix it up on buffalo" (15), and "I would like to clear away this lion business" (17). Clearly, the reader is with Macomber here, although the vague hope of a reaffirmation of his virtually annihilated self that is evoked here may still seem rather unrealistic at this point. This is especially true as there follows, first of all, a further intensification of Macomber's feeling of (self-) humiliation and a retrospective exploration of the reasons for his crisis within his own subjectivity. As he lies awake at night, he becomes aware of the extreme shame and the "cold, hollow fear" (20) which entirely dominate and paralyze his psyche. In a reconstruction of the events of the preceding day, his act of cowardice is retraced in its successive steps and is communicated to the reader in all the nightmarish intensity it gains through Macomber's fear-ridden perspective. It is retold as a process of inevitable failure which results from his lifelong fear of death and which culminates in the scene

when he runs away in panic as the wounded lion charges: "they had just moved into the grass when Macomber heard the blood-choked coughing grunt, and saw the swishing rush in the grass. The next thing he knew he was running; running wildly in the open, running toward the stream" (25). This is the first, *negative* climax in the reading process which is inscribed into the story. Though rendered retrospectively, it is brought alive through scenic dramatization and is thus conveyed to the reader not as a finished event of the past but as a concrete emotional experience, which is actualized in his consciousness as a determining part of the present situation. And when afterward Margaret, who has been absent from the tent during Macomber's painful recollections, returns from Wilson's tent, provocatively admitting her adultery, this appears as an act of final humiliation which makes Macomber's defeat complete. At the same time, however, it psychologically prepares the reader for the dramatic change of emotion that takes place in the second part of the story.

(2) For on the morning of the next day, Macomber's mood is conspicuously altered. The negation of his whole personality has been pushed to a point where his self-destructive despair has been transformed into a feeling of violent aggression, which finds its first object in Wilson. "At breakfast they were all three at the table before daylight and Francis Macomber found that, of all the many men that he had hated, he hated Robert Wilson the most" (28). Macomber is in an explosive mood, in which he throws off all restrictions of social appearances. All at once, anything can be expected of him, as his paralyzed, fear-ridden state of crisis has turned into an irresistible impulse to action: "'Going shooting?' he [Wilson] asked. 'Yes,' said Macomber, standing up. 'Yes'" (30). The reader's identification increases as Macomber more and more seems to fill the heroic role of fearless self-affirmation that has been built up as a counterfantasy to his preceding crisis in the reader's expectation. Indeed, the nightmare of cowardice and fear, which dominates the first part of the story, is transformed in the second part into a trancelike triumph of self-assertion, in which Macomber, as the reader's fictional second self, feels a "drunken elation," a moment of supreme happiness: "In his life he had never felt so good" (33). From the reader's point of view, then, the hope of Macomber's rehabilitation which is raised *ex negativo* in the first part is fulfilled in the second part in the form of a wish-fulfilling daydream which, as the *positive* climax of the implied reader-response, forms a symmetrical counterpart to the negativity of the preceding experience.

(3) All the more shocking to the reader is the sudden, new turn of

events shortly afterward when Macomber, boldly confronting the wounded buffalo, is shot in the head by his wife:

> he shot again at the wide nostrils and saw the horns jolt again and fragments fly, and he did not see Wilson now and, aiming carefully, shot again with the buffalo's huge bulk almost on him and his rifle almost level with the coming head, nose out, and he could see the little wicked eyes and the head started to lower, and he felt a sudden white-hot, blinding flash explode inside his head and that was all he ever felt. (39)

As the narrative focus is entirely on Macomber, the shot hits the reader, metaphorically speaking, as if "from behind," disillusioning, like a *vis a tergo*, the euphoric fantasy of his heroic daydream. With this unexpected anticlimax, the reader is left in shock and bewilderment and is forcefully lead back to a problematical reality from which his heroic daydream has promised to take him away. Mrs. Macomber's (accidental?) shot creates a central indeterminacy in the story that retrospectively invalidates the attempt of determining modern human reality in terms of direct, physical action which Macomber—like Wilson before him—has undertaken. Her shot thus becomes the pivotal point in the text, whose interpretation largely decides about the interpretation of the story as a whole. It forces the reader to reflect on the fictional experience he has gone through and possibly to recognize the problematical implications, the narrowness and one-sidedness of that experience.[22]

This is roughly the psychodramatic pattern inscribed into the activity of the implied reader in "Macomber," and this pattern is to a considerable extent responsible for the high degree of emotional involvement which the story provokes and which is reflected in the particularly passionate critical controversies it has set off. The reader's reaction to the story is characterized by extreme contrasts and sharp changes of emotional mood. His participation in the text is not, as in Type I, primarily evoked by structural-reflective ambiguity but by the immediacy of a psychic experience which only *afterward*, after Mrs. Macomber's shot has wakened him from his fictional daydream, is subject to the retrospective and, potentially, (self-) critical reflection of the reader. Instead of the static effect of simultaneous, largely unchanging, mutually obstructing emotions as in Type I, we have here the dynamic effect of a process of sharply alternating, mutually intensifying emotions which are transmitted through the temporal sequence of contrasting climaxes marked by the wish-fulfilling daydream vs. the shock of disillusioning reality.

This pattern recurs more frequently in Hemingway than one would think, especially since he is a writer often labeled a naturalist and a clinical realist. In it an element of hope and affirmation of life manifests itself, as well as a high degree of sensibility for the resistance that this hope encounters in the modern world. In fact a closer look reveals that some of the author's major works follow this or a similar model. Thus in "The Snows of Kilimanjaro" Harry's hopeless situation is transformed near the end of the story into the dream of his miraculous rescue by an airplane. To the reader, as to Harry, this waking dream, which at first is presented quite realistically and which only later, during the flight to the top of the mountain, becomes recognizable as a mere fantasy, quite explicitly resembles the structure of a wish-fulfilling daydream. And as in "Macomber"—though in a temporally much more condensed form—the daydream is developed out of a desperate death-in-life situation, dramatizing in the reader's psyche the rise of the wounded hero to symbolic self-fulfillment, before he is forced to witness his destruction in the shocklike clash with the disillusioning forces of reality (Harry is discovered to be dead on his cot by his wife). *A Farewell to Arms* also draws on the appellative potential of the daydream structure. Here it is the dream of peace and love that is evoked as a counterfantasy to the experience of war. It begins to materialize in Henry's relationship to Catherine in the first part of the novel, is built up further in his desertion and his idea of a "separate peace," and is fulfilled in an idealized way in the symbiotic union of the two lovers in the Utopian sphere of the Swiss mountains, before it is all the more mercilessly destroyed with Catherine's death at the end of the book. A paradigmatic example of the structure is *The Old Man and the Sea*. From the very beginning the reader's expectation is directed, by the exceptionally luckless situation of the old man (he "was now definitely and finally *salao*")[23] and by his wish for an all the more triumphant compensation for his humiliating lack of success, toward the Great Fish.[24] With Santiago's sailing out to sea, and with the increasing size of the fish he encounters, this expectation if further intensified finds its first climax in the actual appearance of the Great Fish, whose gigantic size borders on the fantastic, and is after a long, fierce struggle, marvelously fulfilled in the eventual defeat of the Fish. And again the reader is made to feel all the more painfully the relentless disillusionment which follows, on the way back to the harbor, with the attacks of the sharks, against whose ever-growing number the old man is powerless and who finally have left only the skeleton of the fish when he reaches home. Quite clearly, the reader's participation in the novel is shaped by the daydream pattern, which is employed here, as in other texts, to increase the psychic intensity of the fictional experience and to activate the life-affirming tendencies in the reader's consciousness in order to make him even more acutely aware of—and, possibly, also better able to cope with—the disillusioning facts of reality.

As has been said, there are of course overlappings between the two types of implied reader here distinguished. The vertical tension between surface and depth, between the formulated and the unformulated dimension of the text, is also part of the reader-appeal in "Macomber" or *The Old Man and the Sea;* and there is the indication of a horizontal tension, of an at least symbolic development of the hero, in *The Sun Also Rises* and in "Big Two-Hearted River."[25] But what matters here is that one or the other of these aspects more or less clearly dominates in the texts, giving the role of the reader a distinctly different character. They represent the two basic forms of appellative structure in Hemingway that mark the endpoints of a whole range of possible combinations and variations. At the same time, they illustrate different phases in the literary development of the author in that Type I more frequently occurs in his earlier work and Type II in his middle and later work. All that can be done here is to indicate the main characteristics of these two types and to demonstrate their realization in a few selected works. A much more extensive and systematic study of the reader-appeal of Hemingway's fictions would be necessary to arrive at a more differentiated typology, involving the careful analysis and comparison of many more texts.

"Actually, I Felt Sorry For the Lion"

Nina Baym

●

Feminist literary critics are not responsible for the view that Ernest Hemingway's work is deeply antiwoman in its values. On the contrary, in making this familiar case feminists have perhaps too quickly accepted the main approach of standard Hemingway criticism. Their innovation is to view this "fact" about the author as a defect rather than something to praise. In espousing the cause of a manhood displayed through male bonding and attained by participation in blood sports, the argument goes, Hemingway's fiction casts all but the most passive, submissive, and silent women as corrupting or destructive. Only when women accept their "place" as a lower order of being than men, rightly assigned the functions of waiting on them when they are around and waiting for them when they are elsewhere, do they win authorial approval. Women can only be men's helpers, never their allies. Men who think of women as human beings like themselves are fools.

This long-lived and monolithic approach has been modified in recent years. We see now that stories like "Cat in the Rain" or "Hills Like White Elephants" present a woman's point of view and attribute her plight—and there is always a plight—to a combination of male self-involvement and self-aggrandizement, a combination of which the text is aware and to which it is not sympathetic.[1] "The Short Happy Life of Francis Macomber," however, seems resistant to interpretive revision along these lines because it has been absolutely central in the standard interpretation of Hemingway and his work.

Margot Macomber and Brett Ashley in *The Sun Also Rises* are the two outstanding examples of Hemingway's "bitch women." Brett, with her irresistible combination of sexual allure and sexual appetite, creates competition, hence disharmony and antagonism, among men who would otherwise be friends. Her wiles undermine the hard-boiled facade with which men should respond to social chaos and the indifference of the universe. As for Margot, she commits adultery virtually under her husband's nose and then kills him at the very moment when his belated entrance into manhood (through blood sport and male bonding) threatens her dominance. It is not surprising that a feminist short story anthology has featured it, through four editions, as a leading example of the "bitch" stereotype.[2]

There is no point in trying to reinterpret the story merely to make it and its author acceptable in changed times. Indeed, if Hemingway really "was" machismo in this story (if not in all his work), it would be unethical to present him differently. Yet, there have also been critics who argue that Margot Macomber did not shoot to kill.[3] And if she did not shoot to kill, then she shot to save her husband, and the vision of Margot Macomber as a "bitch" misrepresents her. I agree with this revisionist approach, and I would add that it is not merely the character who is misrepresented; it is the story itself—its dynamics and its techniques. Hence, the misrepresentation is not only of its author's "message," but also of his craft. Yet I think it less important to rehabilitate "The Short Happy Life of Francis Macomber" on behalf of its author than on behalf of its readers, who, when unconstrained by interpretations that enforce a single, correct, reading of the story, turn out to be responsive to its play of narrative voices and points of view, as well as to the twists of its plot.

If one takes the process of interpretation as advancing a correct reading and dismissing alternate interpretations as error, "The Short Happy Life of Francis Macomber" might be read as an ironic commentary on such activity. It begins by marking out a variety of speaking subject positions and then tells a story in which all but one are silenced. Although the language of "The Short Happy Life of Francis Macomber" belongs mainly to its narrator, the story is focused through five "points of view" including an omniscient though taciturn narrator; Robert Wilson, the white hunter; Francis Macomber, his employer; Margot Macomber, the wife of Francis; and a lion's.[4] Of these the lion's is especially important (and has been critically neglected), and the lion's story evolves as a story embedded within the story of Francis Macomber.[5]

If we were to arrange events in "The Short Happy Life of Francis Macomber" chronologically, the story would begin with the voice of the lion: "It had started the night before when he had wakened and heard the lion roaring somewhere up along the river" (110).[6] Chronology is manipulated in the story so that the lion takes almost half of the narrative space to die, and when the group returns to camp after killing him (on the eighteenth page of a thirty-four-page story), the narrator self-reflexively marks the moment as a closure: "That was the story of the lion" (120). The dead lion continues to exert his presence in the story, and his point of view, through which we have seen much of the hunt and slaughter, is transferred to Margot Macomber. She registers Macomber's cowardice, Wilson's brutality, and the interdependence of the two as epitomized in the lion's fate. She also recognizes that the animals in the wild are not true adversaries or antagonists, because they are so massively overpowered by the men's technology—their guns, their cars. The safari as she sees it is a sham, its participants hypocrites. Wilson, who makes his living by manipulating the appearances of mortal danger for the titillation of his clients, is anxious to suppress her point of view, and he appears to succeed at the story's close.

Though he does succeed in the story's plotline, that he does not prevail in the minds of readers we may surmise from the anxiety with which male authorities once felt bound to continue his work. Another Wilson, name of Edmund, set the tone by praising the "Short Happy Life" as "a terrific fable of the impossible civilized woman who despises the civilized man for his failure in initiative and nerve and then jealously tries to break him down as soon as he begins to exhibit any." And later in his career the increasingly self-protective and publicity-seeking author himself adopted this interpretation, telling an interviewer in 1953—seventeen years after the story was published—that "Francis' wife hates him because he's a coward. . . . But when he gets his guts back, she fears him so much she has to kill him—shoots him in the back of the head."[7]

Of course Margot Macomber shoots and kills her husband; of that there is no doubt. But no careful and unprejudiced reader should doubt that she did so accidentally. Here is the relevant passage, in which a buffalo charges at Macomber and Wilson:

> Wilson had ducked to one side to get in a shoulder shot. Macomber had stood solid and shot for the nose, shooting a touch high each time and hitting the heavy horns, splintering and chipping them like hitting a slate roof, and Mrs. Macomber, in the car, had shot at the buffalo with the 6.5 Mannlicher as it seemed about to gore Macomber and had hit her husband about two inches up and a little to one side of the base of his skull. (135)

No reader of any persuasion has ever doubted that Wilson did, indeed, duck aside for a shoulder shot; or that Macomber did, indeed, stand tall and shoot high; and no conceivable textual argument allows us to declare one, and only one, portion of the otherwise impeccable report unreliable. Equally nonsensical is the idea that a homicidal Margot had any *need* to shoot her husband at this moment. As John Howell and Charles Lawler put it, "if she had wanted her husband dead, the bull seemed about to do that job for her."[8] Of course Margot Macomber might be thoroughly stupid. But we have even Robert Wilson's word on this subject: "She had a very perfect oval face, so perfect that you expected her to be stupid. But she wasn't stupid, Wilson thought, no, not stupid" (107).

In brief, Margot Macomber's bad press stems from the critics' desire to identify what they take to be Wilson's ethical code with the valves of the story itself, a desire in pursuit of which they must turn the faceted narration of "The Short Happy Life of Francis Macomber" into a monologue. Carlos Baker in *Hemingway: The Writer as Artist* provides a paradigm instance of the assertion that the core of values in the story resides in Wilson, so that to read the story as his vehicle is to align oneself properly with Hemingway's moral intention:

> Easily the most unscrupulous of Hemingway's fictional females, Margot Macomber covets her husband's money but values even more her power over him. To Wilson, the Macombers' paid white hunter, who is drawn very reluctantly into the emotional mess of a wrecked marriage, Margot exemplifies most of the American wives he has met in the course of his professional life. Although his perspectives are limited to the international sporting set, the indictment is severe. These women, he reflects, are "the hardest in the world; the hardest, the cruelest, the most predatory, and the most attractive, and their men have softened or gone to pieces nervously as they have hardened."[9]

In Baker's handling Wilson's subjective and self-serving indictment of Margot and other women like her becomes an objective description that the reader should accept as true. For Wilson, in Baker's account, is the yardstick figure, a fine characterization, the man free of woman and of fear, the standard of manhood toward which Macomber rises.[10]

Kenneth Lynn's *Hemingway* is not the first study to call Wilson a brute, but it makes clearer than any earlier criticism Wilson's motive for the accusation of murder by which he silences Margot at the conclusion of "The Short Happy Life of Francis Macomber."[11] His purpose is to blackmail her into keeping quiet about the illegal car chase that preceded the buffalo kill. For in the excitement of the hunt Wilson has allowed a pursuit to take place by automobile, and Margot has recognized that this breaks the rules under which safaris are supposed to be conducted:

> "I didn't know you were allowed to shoot them from cars though."
> "No one shot from cars," said Wilson coldly.
> "I mean chase them from cars."

"Wouldn't ordinarily," Wilson said. "Seemed sporting enough to me though while we were doing it. . . . Wouldn't mention it to any one though. It's illegal if that's what you mean." . . .

"What would happen if they heard about it in Nairobi?"

"I'd lose my license for one thing. . . . I'd be out of business." (128–29)

There is, however, even more going on here. Wilson's recorded behavior puts in question not only his adherence to the laws of the hunt as the fraternity of white hunters has devised them. It shows that he is not nearly so skillful a hunter as he makes himself out to be—a point to which I will return. And it shows that making a coward into a brave man crucially involves, to Wilson's perhaps rationalizing mind, the very motorcar whose use is illegal. Whether the use of the motorcar seemed sporting or not at the time becomes less important than that such use helped Wilson turn Macomber into a man. "Beggar had probably been afraid all his life. Don't know what started it. But over now. Hadn't had time to be afraid with the buff. That and being angry too. Motor car too. Motor cars made it familiar. Be a damn fire eater now." (132)

In fact Wilson deploys more than one questionable tactic to help Macomber overcome his fear. He also deploys a gun so powerful that he himself calls it a "cannon."[12] And with this canon Wilson in effect kills every single animal that is killed in the story—although his killings are not done cleanly or well by any means. To demonstrate this point we will have to look closely at some passages in the text.

Consider first the buffalo hunt whose action comprises the last third of the story. (In Aristotelian fashion we may divide the story's action thus: beginning—the botched killing of the lion; middle—the repercussions of that killing on the party of three; end—the restorative killing of the buffalo.) Macomber downs one of three bulls, and Wilson tells him that he has succeeded in killing it. But Wilson is mistaken. His mistake, which the skillful hunter he is supposed to be would not have made, lulls all members of the group into a false sense of security that later allows the wounded but far from dead bull to make an unexpected charge and thus to become the indirect cause of Macomber's death. This bull is ultimately killed, after Macomber is dead, by Wilson.

After downing the first bull, Macomber shoots at the second. He hits the animal but does not drop him with the first shot, and then he misses with the second. Wilson shoots next and downs the animal for Macomber to finish off later. Both hunters at first miss the third bull, who runs away, but a second illegal car chase gives them a new opportunity. Macomber fires at the bull five times—*five!*—with no effect on the animal. "Then Wilson shot, the roar deafening him, and he [Macomber] could see the bull stagger" (127). That is, this bull too is downed by Wilson for Macomber to make a technical kill. Putting aside the first animal, then, we see that in the other two cases the bull is crippled by Wilson for his client to kill, but in no ethical deployment of language can one say that Macomber killed either of them. And, to iterate, neither did he kill the first one.

Wilson killed them all. Wilson is a "white hunter," a professional organizer and guide of private safaris. He "hunted for a certain clientele," and has no hesitation in accepting the standards of that clientele "as long as they were hiring him" (125). Since from time to time the women on these outings make sexual advances, he carries "a double size cot on safari to accommodate any windfalls he might receive" (125). If money has corrupted both Margot Macomber and Francis Macomber, it has equally corrupted Wilson, who lives off them and their kind by catering to their illusions—the men's that they are brave, the women's that they are attractive. The phrase "hunted for" may be taken to have double reference—Wilson has hunted on behalf of his clients, and he has also hunted them, that is, they have been his prey.

According to his interior monologue, Wilson accepts the standards of his clients "in all except the shooting." "He had his own standards about the killing and they could live up to them or get some one else to hunt them" (125). These standards, as we see, include chasing buffaloes illegally and shooting them with megaguns so that the client can kill them without danger to himself. The illusion above all to which Wilson caters— the illusion that he in large measure creates—is that the safari is a dangerous exposure to wild animals and that real bravery is demonstrated by killing them. Margot sees through the illusion. "'It seemed very unfair to me,' Margot said, 'chasing those big helpless things in a motor car'" (129).

With this view of Wilson as eliciting from his (male) clients the simulacrum of courage, and thus leaving them safely in possession of their illusions, we may now consider the killing of the lion, which is funneled to the reader through Francis Macomber's perceptions as follows:

He heard the *ca-ra-wong!* of Wilson's big rifle, and again in a second crashing *carawong!* and turning saw the lion, horrible-looking now, with half his head seeming to be gone, crawling toward Wilson in the edge of the tall grass while the red-faced man worked the bolt on the short ugly rifle and aimed carefully as another blasting *carawong!* came from the muzzle, and the crawling, heavy, yellow bulk of the lion stiffened and the huge, mutilated head slid forward. (119)

The lion, as segments of action represented from an interesting combination of lion's and narrator's point of view have made clear, is already virtually dead: "sick with the wound through his full belly, and weakening with the wound through his lungs that brought a thin foamy red to his mouth each time he breathed. His flanks were wet and hot and flies were on the little opening the solid bullets had made in his tawny hide, and his big yellow eyes, narrowed with hate, looked straight ahead, only blinking when the pain came as he breathed, and his claws dug in the soft baked earth. All of him, pain, sickness, hatred and all of his remaining strength, was tightening into an absolute concentration for a rush" (118). There is nothing in the story that equals the physical immediacy and power of this description, and it is, indeed, surprising that in the published criticism only Howell and Lawler identify the lion as the standard of true bravery in the story.[13] At any rate, Wilson fires three shots into this animal's head and face. Margot, sitting in the car, has "been able to see the whole thing"—both Macomber's cowardly flight *and* Wilson's killing (119). That these two acts are parts of a whole to her we realize when we recall her comment, recorded earlier, at lunch to Wilson: "I want *so* to see you perform again. You were lovely this morning. That is if blowing things' heads off is lovely" (108).

Now, if we move forward again to Margot Macomber who is sitting in the car during the buffalo chase, we see her in process of seeing that "there was no change in Wilson. She saw Wilson as she had seen him the day before when she had first realized what his great talent was. But she saw the change in Francis Macomber now" (132). What was it that Margot, the day before, had realized Wilson's "great talent" to be? It was his talent for "blowing things' heads off." We might surmise that Margot sees in her husband the process of transformation into a man like Wilson. "You're both talking rot," said Margot. "Just because you've chased some helpless animals in a motor car you talk like heroes," she says, including both of them in her assessment (132).

If it is true that Macomber is becoming another Wilson, and that Margot is aware of it, then her attempt to save her husband from the buffalo at just that moment becomes a quixotic act that may even be called heroic. Certainly her interests coincide with those of the animals, not with men of Wilson's sort. That in shooting to save her husband from the buffalo she has acted against her own interests is made clear by the story's trick ending, and of course it is a trick, in the tradition of Guy de Maupassant, when the intended act backfires—one might say literally backfires—in every respect.

Before the incident with the lion, Margot Macomber has not been hostile to hunting: "'You'll kill him marvelously,' she said, 'I know you will. I'm awfully anxious to see it'" (112). She comes to hate hunting when she sees what it consists of. She sees that Macomber, with Wilson and his gun behind him, is never in any real danger. And she sees that what is a matter of life and death for the animal becomes a wasteful war game for men. The story quietly endorses her judgment by giving the lion himself the last word on his wounding and death:

> That was the story of the lion. Macomber did not know how the lion had felt before he started his rush, nor during it when the unbeliev-able smash of the .505 with a muzzle velocity of two tons had hit him in the mouth, nor what kept him coming after that, when the second ripping crash had smashed his hind quarters and he had come crawling on toward the crashing, blasting thing that had destroyed him. Wilson knew something about it and only expressed it by saying, "damned fine lion." (120)

Macomber knew nothing about the lion; Wilson knew something, but a good deal less than he thought; Margot knows almost everything. But Margot does not recognize, it seems safe to say, that she too, in relation to these men, is in the situation of the lion—imaged as dangerous, but in fact helpless. I am not saying that Margot "should" have let the buffalo kill her husband, nor do we know what would have happened if she had held her fire. Strictly speaking, we cannot even speculate on this matter since these are not real events and since they are narrated to the end of this conclusion and no other. The point is that whatever she does, Margot is as "buffaloed" as the buffalo. She has an illusion of power which she exercises in occasional infidelities to her husband, but such exercises rather than freeing her deliver her from the power of one man to the power of another. Yet when she acts for her husband instead of against him, she is no better off.

I offer this approach to "The Short Happy Life of Francis Macomber" on behalf of its readers, not its author. Classroom observation has shown me that students who are not constrained by the need to anchor an interpretation of the story to known (or supposedly known) facts about Hemingway's life or to reigning interpretation do indeed see the story as a larger, albeit confusing, structure in which Wilson occupies only a point.[14] "Does Margot Macomber kill her husband?" a teacher asks.

"Wilson *thinks* she does" is the cagey answer. But is Wilson right, the teacher pursues. "It says"—it, not Hemingway—"that she shot *at* the buffalo," the students respond. The teacher's attempts to define Wilson's values as the moral center of the story elicit scattered counterevidence of his inconsistencies. Nobody much *likes* Wilson. "Well," the teacher concedes, "it's true that intentionally or not, Hemingway at times does undercut his point—whom *can* you like in this story?" Silence. Then, a woman student speaks up:

"Actually, I felt sorry for the lion."

This is going too far. The teacher responds, too quickly to have reflected on what he's heard: "Now you sound like Margot."

Here, then, a male in authority silences a woman by, in effect, assuming Wilson's voice and casting her in the role of Margot; if we are not sure whom to care for in the story, it is at least sure that we may not care for *her*. The story's plot is reenacted, in a nonfatal but deeply political fashion, right in the classroom. This woman in resisting the interpretation of the story that allows Wilson to bully us was not resisting or misreading the story so much as she was remaining sensitive to the many voices that spoke in it. The teacher's ire reflects the discomfort of the enfranchised when the silenced *really* talk.

But the lion, and Margot, do have voices in "The Short Happy Life of Francis Macomber" and whatever Hemingway himself came eventually to say about the story, the attentive reader should hear them. Otherwise, reading "The Short Happy Life of Francis Macomber" becomes an episode of forced indoctrination into a dominant male ethos whose hypocrisies and inconsistencies the story presents for our consideration.

"Old Man at the Bridge": The Making of a Short Story

William Braasch Watson

●

Writing a Story Instead of a Dispatch

When Ernest Hemingway returned to Spain for the third time at the beginning of April 1938 to cover the Spanish Civil War for the North American Newspaper Alliance (NANA), he was not, in all likelihood, expecting to do much writing other than his newspaper work and a biweekly article for a new political magazine called *Ken*. The reason would have been obvious to any newspaperman. The Rebel forces under General Francisco Franco had broken through the Republican lines on the Aragonese front in the second week of March, and by the end of the month, when Hemingway arrived in Spain, they were threatening to split the Republican zone in two and to bring the civil war to a rapid end. The front lines were changing dramatically almost every day, requiring that correspondents like Hemingway get as close to the action as they could and file their dispatches as quickly as possible. Hemingway may not have been the professional correspondent that Herbert Matthews of the *New York Times* or Henry Buckley of the *London Daily Telegraph* were, but he took his responsibilities seriously and worked hard at his job. He was also experienced enough to know that he would be kept too busy to write any fiction.

And yet that is what he wanted most to be doing. The previous February, shortly after getting back to Key West from his second visit to the war, Hemingway had written Maxwell Perkins, his editor at Scribner's, that he wanted to stay home and write some stories, even though the war was still so close to him that writing about it was difficult.[1] Plans were already under way to bring out a new collection of his short stories in the fall, and he was hoping to add a few more before the book went to press later that summer.[2] But the war in Spain disrupted his plans, just as it had in the fall of 1936 when he was trying to finish *To Have and Have Not*.

When the news from Spain in the second week of March revealed the extent of the Rebel breakthrough in the Republican lines, in a matter of days Hemingway decided that he could no longer stay home writing stories. "I feel like a bloody shit to be here in Key West when I should be in Aragon or in Madrid," he wrote Perkins on March 15. Two days later, as soon as he could clean up his affairs at home, he left Key West, and the day after that he sailed from New York on the *Ile de France* with a briefcase full of the stories he was planning to include in the new collection. He arrived in Paris on March 24, made a quick trip to the Spanish border to see if he could get into the Rebel side, and somehow found time to go over the stories while waiting for Martha Gellhorn to join him.[3] On March 30 he took the night train to Perpignan with Vincent Sheean and young Jim Lardner, where they picked up a car for the trip into Spain.[4] They arrived in Barcelona in the evening of March 31, and the next day Hemingway set off with Herbert Matthews to visit the Aragon front.[5]

Throughout the last two weeks of March the military situation of the Republican forces had been growing steadily worse as the Rebels pressed their drive to the Mediterranean. By April 1 the Rebels had virtually achieved their objective and, perhaps even more threatening, large numbers of the Republican forces, including elements of the International Brigades, were in retreat toward Catalunya. Hemingway's first task was to make his way to Gandesa, where many of the remaining forces of the International Brigades were said to be concentrated, but when he and Matthews tried to reach the Brigades, they were brought to a halt on the road outside Falset by a continuous stream of fleeing peasants with their carts and animals and by retreating soldiers who told them that Gandesa had just fallen to the Rebels. The rear guard, they said, was trying to hold the bridge at Mora de Ebro nearby. Unable to get any closer, the next day Hemingway and Matthews turned back to Barcelona, where Hemingway filed his first dispatch describing the flight of these refugees and soldiers.[6]

The next four weeks would become the most intensive stretch of reporting Hemingway was to do during the entire war. The first dispatch of April 3 was followed by two others on April 4 and 5, and there was another burst of four dispatches in little over a week in the middle of the month as the Rebel forces finally broke through to the Mediterranean at Vinaroz on April 15. The Republican zone was cut in two, and the conquest of Catalunya now seemed imminent. The Rebels began bombing Tortosa, the first major town on the coastal road to Barcelona, while Hemingway reconnoitered the banks of the Ebro River as they prepared their assault. By the end of April he had sent off nine dispatches, more than twice the number he had filed in any previous month of the war, and he wrote three more in the first ten days of May, one of which he chose not to send.[7]

It had been a month of exhausting work. Most correspondents covering the battles along the Aragon front were based in Barcelona. To get
their dispatches out the same day required some six hours of hard driving to the front lines just beyond the Ebro and another six hours back
again, a drive often slowed by the flood of refugees from the war zone or
interrupted by the bombing and strafing of Rebel aircraft. Hemingway also knew from the difficulties he had encountered on his first two
trips to the war that delays at the censorship office or in the telephone
lines out of Spain would probably confront him once he was back in
Barcelona and that to make his deadlines he would have to write his
pieces quickly and without time for reflection or polishing. There was a
stretch, beginning on April 13, when he was making the trip from
Barcelona down to the Ebro and back almost every day and filing reports
every other day.

It was also dangerous work. Italian and German aircraft operated at
will behind the lines, bombing and strafing the roads leading into and out
of Tortosa without fear of encountering Republican aircraft or effective
antiaircraft fire. Correspondents driving up and down these roads could
never know when their own cars would become targets or when they
would get trapped in a line of stalled tanks and trucks. Nor could they
know where or when the Rebels might break through the Republican
defenses, possibly cutting off their return to Barcelona. And when they
got closer to watch the movement of the opposing infantry, there was
always the danger of a sniper's bullet or a random artillery shell finding its
victim.

On Easter Sunday, April 17, in the midst of this intensive period of
reporting and just as he was about to cross the Ebro and enter its Delta in
search of the advancing Rebel forces, Hemingway saw an old man sitting
beside the pontoon bridge at Amposta. When he returned to the bridge
an hour or two later, the old man was still there. Although Hemingway
had not been able to locate the enemy forces, he knew they were not far
away, and he had seen enough fighting and had run enough risks himself
in the last two weeks to know that the old man could not stay there long.
He apparently stopped to talk with the old man and to take in the scene of
the fleeing refugees crossing the pontoon bridge, for he made a set of
notes recording his impressions of the scene and some of the details of his
conversation with the old man.[8]

1

Grey sky—deserted road where formerly streams of trucks—glum
faces on Tarragona road—The colour of retreat is grey.

Rain—Battalion of prisoners with picks and shovels ["guarded by" scratched out] marched in column of fours—guarded by carabineros—yellow belts—

herds of sheep and goats—Peasants retreating with umbrellas—camp under the olive trees breaking up—carts taking to the road again.

2

Old man with steel spectacles—sitting by the dusty road—scattered with corn from a coop of chickens tied to back of a cart—dog on a chain under the cart—bucket dangling behind—/3 [inserted] women [changed from "woman"] /one [inserted] with 2 folded blankets on her head—another holding 3 live chickens—a boy with a basket—third woman riding a mule packed

3

Old man had left San Carlos—he stayed behind [with "4" scratched out] to take care of ["4" scratched out] 2 goats /3 cats [inserted]—4 pair of pigeons—But the captain said the artillery were coming—he was 68 [scratched out]—72—Had to leave them finally ["They wi" changed to] The cats will be all right—But who will feed the pigeons—had walked 12 kilometers—since day light—

These notes from the Amposta bridge are much like the notes he had been taking all along. To help him meet deadlines, Hemingway had developed the practice, common to journalists then, of jotting down his observations on pieces of paper folded into quarters. These observation notes provided most of the material for the dispatches he would file later that night or the next day.[9]

Whatever the differences in details, the field notes for the story and the dispatches he filed during the months of April and May are made up of quick impressions grouped around a set of images or a single, direct experience. The practiced observer is at work, searching the landscape for a visual image or a key notion that will help focus the imagination and give the writer the control he needs over his material. Telegraphic reminders of things mostly seen, seldom heard, the notes were only meant to jog the memory into releasing enough details for that night's or the next day's article. "Pink of almond blossoms," "camped by road like gypsies," "soldiers . . . holding their rifles by the muzzles," the notes for his April 3 dispatch on the flight of refugees from the Ebro valley recorded. The notes seldom contained reflections on what was happening, although occasionally some of them caught a moment's reflection on the beauty of what he saw. "The bright blue of the Mediterranean turned milky by the yellow flood of the Ebro" began the notes of April 5,[10] and there were other lyrical moments in other notes scattered among the staccato impressions.[11]

Because the notes he made at the Amposta bridge are similar in form to the notes for his news dispatches of this period, it looks as though Hemingway originally intended the notes for "Old Man at the Bridge" to end up as another dispatch. Even the circumstances of the story's composition and the form by which it was sent out of Spain make it look like another dispatch. We know, because of the Barcelona censor's stamp on Hemingway's copy of the cable, that the story went out at 11:10 on the night of April 17, the same day he encountered the old man at the Amposta bridge. He must have written it in a great rush, for he was twelve hours that day on the road and probably had no more than four or five hours after he got back to Barcelona in which to write.[12] It was only 800 words long, and Hemingway sent it out, not by mail, as he did his other stories, but by cable, the way he did his news dispatches. In almost every respect, therefore, the story of the old man at the Amposta bridge looks like another dispatch.[13]

But something happened that day to change his mind about the material he had gathered, for instead of sending the cable to NANA, he sent it to *Ken* magazine. The immediate reason was a deadline. Before he returned to Spain, Hemingway had contracted with Arnold Gingrich, the editor of *Ken* as well as the editor of *Esquire*, to write a biweekly article for this new antifascist and anticommunist magazine. For a variety of reasons, not the least of which was financial, Hemingway had been scrupulous about meeting his first deadlines. His last article for *Ken* had been sent from Paris at the end of March, and now, in mid-April, he knew another one was due.[14]

What he had seen that day could be turned into something other than a news story. He must have realized, moreover, that a news story about an old man, a refugee, would have differed little in the eyes of the NANA editors from the report on refugees he had already filed at the beginning of the month. He had earlier discovered, much to his annoyance, that NANA would balk at releasing material of his that seemed to them repetitious or un-newsworthy. He would use the material for a short story, he decided, and beat the *Ken* deadline.

We know from his own testimony that writing a story, although it usually took days or weeks rather than hours, could sometimes go quickly. "I can't write a story like a piece," he told Arnold Gingrich later that year. "The story takes charge of itself very quickly."[15] Apparently it had been the figure of the old man sitting beside the bridge worrying about his animals that had taken charge of Hemingway's imagination by the time he got back to Barcelona. His confidence in his ability to get the story down quickly, his knowledge that Gingrich was waiting for another piece and would accept virtually anything he wrote, his need for the money *Ken* magazine would pay him, and most of all his intuitive sense that the old man sitting beside the Amposta bridge represented much of what he had seen of the war these last two weeks led him to write a story instead of another news dispatch.[16]

After setting the scene with a brief description of the fleeing refugees and explaining that the narrator had come to that place in order to locate the advancing enemy, Hemingway builds the rest of his story around "an old man with steel rimmed spectacles and very dusty clothes" seated by the side of the road. The narrator stops to ask the old man where he is from and finds out that he had been taking care of animals in a nearby town. He does not look like a shepherd, so the narrator questions him further. It turns out the animals are a cat, some pigeons, and two goats. The old man is now worried about what will happen to them.

All the while this conversation is taking place the narrator is scanning the horizon and listening for the first signs of contact with the approaching enemy. He realizes the old man cannot stay there and urges him to move on up the road where he can catch a ride on a truck, but the old man is tired, and when he finds out the trucks are headed for Barcelona, he realizes he cannot accept the offer. "'I know no one in that direction,' he said, 'but thank you very much. Thank you again very much.'" His world, we suddenly understand, scarcely extends beyond his village of San Carlos.

The narrator, a man who seems to know his way in the world, is momentarily stymied. They talk again about the animals, and the narrator tries to reassure the old man.

> "Why they'll probably come through it all right."
> "You think so?"
> "Why not," I said, watching the far bank where now there were no carts.

The old man, wanting to be agreeable with the helpful stranger, reassures himself that the cat can take care of itself, and the narrator, encouraged by this touch of hope, helps the old man to see that because he has left the dove cage unlocked, the pigeons will fly away when the artillery starts firing. "'Yes, certainly they'll fly. But the others. It's better not to think about the others,' he said," knowing that the animals are the only family he has and are all that he can think about. The narrator tries once more to get the old man moving.

> "If you are rested I would go," I urged. "Get up and try to walk now."
> "Thank you," he said and got to his feet, swayed from side to side and then sat down backwards in the dust.

The story ends abruptly as the narrator moves off, leaving the old man to his unspoken fate.

Hemingway must have known that, however brief it was, he had written a powerful story. He soon found out that others thought so too. The next day Gingrich cabled him: "Marvellous piece. Feel that these short punches have done more good for Loyalist cause than volumes ordinary reporting, judging by terrific response received."[17] Gingrich's praise was not forgotten when Hemingway returned to the United States, for shortly after he got back he wrote Max Perkins that he wanted to include "Old Man at the Bridge" in the new collection of his short stories. "I enclose that story I cabled to *Ken* the day we evacuated Amposta. It would make a story for the book I think—An Old Man at a Bridge. What do you think?"[18] Perkins agreed, and the title of the book was promptly changed from the First Forty-eight to the First Forty-nine Stories.

When *The Fifth Column and the First Forty-nine Stories* was published later that fall, Edmund Wilson reviewed it in The *Nation* along with "The Spanish War," a collection of Hemingway's civil war dispatches reprinted by *Fact*.[19] Although Wilson generally praised the stories, especially the four most recent ones (including "Old Man at the Bridge"), he was critical of the play and thought the dispatches, where Hemingway was "always diverting attention to his own narrow escapes from danger," were inept.

The review provoked an angry reply from Hemingway, too angry in fact to send.[20] Before his anger took over, however, Hemingway explained to Wilson that the news dispatches had been reprinted "behind my back and without my knowledge." "I am not ashamed of the dispatches," he went on. "All are true. But I do not go in for reprinting journalism." "Old Man at the Bridge" was another matter, he told Wilson.

> The odd thing, and what I thought might interest you, was that the story of the old man at the pontoon bridge at Amposta was

written and sent out by cable the same night we lost the Amposta bridge-head. The difference was that it was for a magazine so I could write a story about the old man and not a news dispatch.

Transforming Facts into Fiction

The fact that Hemingway ended up with a short story instead of a news dispatch may have been an accident of timing and circumstance, but it proves to be an unusually revealing accident, for it provides a unique insight into the nature of his talent for writing short stories. Thanks to his field notes and drafts, we can watch from beginning to end the process of creation and see in detail how he transformed his experiences and observations into a work of art. In seeing how differently, moreover, he used his field notes to write his dispatches on the one hand and this short story on the other, we can begin to appreciate why Hemingway insisted, with Wilson and with everyone else, that his fiction was not to be confused with his journalism.

In writing his NANA dispatch of April 3 on the flight of the refugees, Hemingway depended heavily on his field notes for almost all of his observations.[21] Sometimes a dozen words in the notes are expanded into several paragraphs. "Planes—the ditch—the olive trees—Reus—the bombing—clouds of dust—brown dust"—these fragments become a three paragraph account of how Hemingway and his driver had to dive into a ditch when an airplane flew low over their car on its way to bombing the town of Reus up ahead, one of those scrapes with danger that Wilson found so inept. At other times he hardly expands on the notes at all. "Old women—crying driving the carts—8 children behind one cart—2 goats tied-behind—one sheep—cooking pots—mattresses—sewing machines—bags of grain for the mules—4 goats—mattresses wrapped in matting"—all end up as the substance of a single paragraph.

That was how the day started but no one yet alive can say how it will end. For soon we began passing carts loaded with refugees. An old woman was driving one, crying and sobbing while she swung a whip. She was the only woman I saw crying all day. There were eight children following another cart and one little boy pushed on the wheel as they came up a difficult grade. Bedding, sewing machines, blankets, cooking utensils, mattresses wrapped in mats, and sacks of grain for the horses and mules were piled in the carts and goats and sheep were tethered to the tailboards. There was no panic. They were just plodding along.

Altogether Hemingway made use of almost two-thirds of the images he had put down in his notes while traveling up and down the Falset road, and if he did not include an observation in the dispatch, it was usually because something quite like it had already been noted. In effect virtually every fresh observation in the notes ended up in his dispatch.

There is one episode in the dispatch, however, that hardly received a mention in the notes but becomes, or looks as though Hemingway wanted it to become, a story in its own right. "Babies born on road," he jotted down in the notes. In the dispatch he describes a woman riding on a mule piled high with bedding and holding her newborn baby. For a moment it seems as though this scene of the mother and her baby would break out of the constraints of the article and become a story on its own. There is even some dialogue between the husband and the correspondent, but the correspondent is riding in a car, and they are going in opposite directions—the correspondent heading into the war to gather more material for his article, the father fleeing from it with his family and possessions. And so the article cuts the story off and picks up another scene from the panorama of fleeing refugees. Toward the end of the dispatch Hemingway returns to the baby and its mother, now covered with dust after two days on the road, and uses them as an image of the weariness the refugees were now suffering. Despite the narrative power of this vignette, neither it nor any of the other vignettes he recorded are allowed to develop on their own terms.

The dispatch restricts itself to the visual details of a vast, colorful scene. There is no sustained focus of attention, no time, really, to understand what is going on. As a result, we have no way of knowing what these refugees, or even Hemingway for that matter, are thinking and feeling, and thus we have no way of sharing the meaning of their experiences. We can only imagine what is happening to them from the condition they are in, and even this is not always a reliable guide. "Many of the people seemed cheerful," Hemingway noted at one point. In the end there are so many of them and the correspondent is so committed to describing as accurately as he can the whole of the changing panorama around him that this dispatch, although a perfectly straightforward, well-observed account of the tragic and sometimes dramatic sights of war, fails nonetheless to achieve the clarity and intensity of a good story.

If the inquiry into the emotions of people is constrained by the need to be comprehensive and inclusive—to provide, that is, good coverage—and as a result the fleeing refugees and soldiers become objects whose lives we cannot fully comprehend rather than subjects with whom we can engage our imaginations, part of the reason is the persona that the writer of news stories must assume. That persona is the dispassionate observer. Although Hemingway was expected to write "color stuff" and sometimes included himself in the dispatch because, as he explained to Wilson, "if you are paid to get shot at and write about it you are supposed to mention the shooting," in the bulk of his reporting he is not involved.[22] This dispatch, like most of his others of this period, is a dispassionate accounting with little of the self-consciousness that intruded upon his Greco-Turkish war reports of the 1920s.[23] The effect of the dispatch on the reader depends on the cumulative weight of its details and not on the involvement of the observer with the subject.

The story of the old man at the bridge, on the other hand, seeks to achieve a different emotional response. Whereas the dispatch does not give itself time to enlarge the meaning of any single event, the story builds almost wholly upon a single encounter. Through the conversation between the old man and the narrator, Hemingway carefully exposes the sense of loss and confusion that is about to overwhelm the old man and, by extension, the other refugees being driven from their homes by the war.

In transforming his notes from the Amposta bridge into a story, Hemingway made much more selective use of his notes than he did in writing the dispatch.[24] In fact, except for a brief description of the grey, overcast sky that appeared at the head of the notes and that Hemingway used to good effect at the end of the story, everything else in the notes that did not pertain to the old man at the bridge was suppressed. The rain, the herds of sheep and goats, the battalion of prisoners with picks and shovels, the dog on a chain under a cart, and the woman with two folded blankets on her head, these and other images of the fleeing refugees near the Amposta bridge, images that had been the staple of the dispatch from the Falset road, were now discarded.

The story does begin with visual details much like those that described the flight of the refugees, but none of these details comes from the field notes. They serve, moreover, a different purpose from what they did in the dispatch. Although Hemingway sets the scene for his story by describing how the soldiers and refugees with their carts were struggling to get across the pontoon bridge and up the steep bank on the other side of the river, his main purpose in describing these frantic efforts is not, as it would have been in the dispatch, to present another dramatic event, but to contrast this activity with the immobility of the old man. "But the old man," he wrote at the end of the first paragraph, "sat there without moving. He was too tired to go any farther."

After explaining that the narrator of the story is there because he is trying "to find out to what point the enemy had advanced," Hemingway from this point on focuses the story on the old man and on the narrator's changing relationship with him. In doing so, Hemingway uses every image and idea he had jotted down about the old man in his notes, altering some of them slightly in order to clarify and dramatize the old man's predicament.[25] There were three cats in his notes, for instance, but only one in the story. The old man was seventy-two in the notes, but seventy-six in the story. He was worried about the pigeons in the notes; it is the goats he cannot bear to think about in the story. Otherwise the story hardly elaborates at all on the descriptive facts of the old man, Including the fact that he had walked twelve kilometers that day from San Carlos de la Rápita in the lower Ebro Delta to get to the closest river crossing at Amposta.[26] In this literal sense we can say that this is a "true" report. Like so much of his fiction, no matter how much of it is made up, the story remains faithful to the observed realities on which it is based.

If the notes reflect the central drama of the old man, it is because Hemingway the observer, Hemingway the correspondent who had been driving back and forth on these roads for more than two weeks witnessing the plight of these refugees, now saw in the old man and his story the whole of their uprooting. Some other refugee's story would have served him just as well, but it was the old man's concern for his animals that caught Hemingway's attention. What dignifies the old man and makes him more than just another casualty of war is his selflessness, his worries about his animals, his reluctance to leave them behind, and his uncomplaining acceptance of his own fate. These give him dignity and purpose. He is no longer simply a victim of war; he is a courageous and defeated human being struggling to survive and to keep alive his last hopes.

And yet the awful inappropriateness of his worries, so small and ineffective when measured against the destructive forces that are about to overtake him, lend pathos to his single-mindedness. The pathos and dignity of the old man make the story what it is, and the detail Hemingway devoted to this old man in his field notes suggests that he must have recognized it right away.

By contrast, it was Hemingway's own broader sense of the danger confronting them both that provides the underlying structure of the story, for the narrator knows, in a way the old man does not yet seem to comprehend, that unless the old man moves on he will probably be killed or captured. The tension in this finely wrought miniature comes from their talking about something else—what will happen to the old man's animals.

His sensitivity to the plight of the old man is heightened by his awareness of his own dilemma, for in the end he had to leave the old man to his fate by the side of the road. Hemingway must have been acutely aware of the difference between himself, the correspondent who could come and go as he pleased and in the end could leave it all behind, and the old man whose age and whose love for his animals and his native town bound him to the earth he had just walked over. The difference between them is beautifully and sensitively portrayed in the gentleness with which the narrator questions the old man and encourages him to move on. They are together for only a moment, for that is all this war would allow them, but it is enough for us to see and understand the underlying compassion that brought them together and the terrible forces that will now drive them apart.

Hemingway's ability to achieve these powerful effects in such a brief compass depended, of course, on more than his own particular sensitivity. It also required an ability to write convincing dialogue. It required a sense of structure so that the story is pulled taut at the beginning and held tight until the end. It required an eye for credible detail and an experienced sense of the surrounding realities. These are the skills of a seasoned writer, skills acquired over a lifetime of disciplined craftsmanship. In Spain, under the pressure of repeated deadlines and conflicting obligations, Hemingway managed to use these skills with stunning economy and precision. In a few hours, certainly in no more than four or five, he had made the old man at the Amposta bridge into an enduring witness to the Spanish Civil War, to the tragedy, in fact, that engulfs all human beings caught up in the disasters of war.

The ending, however, remains perplexing. Just as we are caught up in the old man's struggle, the story comes to a sudden end. The narrator finally persuades the old man that he must move on. The old man gets up only to fall back again into the dust at the side of the road. There is a terrible moment of stillness in the story as the narrator has to decide what he will do—stay and help the old man and run the risk of getting caught or killed himself or leave the old man to fend for himself.[27] After paragraphs of intimate dialogue the story suddenly shifts to an objective, impersonal perspective. The lack of sentiment at the end and the coldness with which the narrator makes his decision cloak the emotions and the confusion we can imagine he must have felt.

There was nothing to do about him. It was Easter Sunday and the Fascists were advancing toward the Ebro. It was a gray overcast day with a low ceiling so their planes were not up. That and the fact that cats know how to look after themselves was all the good luck that old man would ever have.

The Boundary between Fiction and Fact

Nothing else Hemingway wrote on the Spanish Civil War captured as flawlessly and accurately the depths of the tragedy that was then engulfing Spain. It is also, in its way, a perfect short story. It has a fully developed character, a powerful drama whose resolution we fearfully anticipate, and a point of view that seems wholly natural and realistic. It is tight and coherent and nothing seems lacking, and yet much of its power comes from a veiled danger we can feel but never quite see. It may not stand, to be sure, in the same rank as Hemingway's greatest short stories—"Indian Camp," "Big Two-Hearted River," and some others— but in the small scale on which it is etched it is a minor masterpiece, a finely shaped portrait of a moment central to the experience of the Spanish Civil War, indeed of all wars in which ordinary people are innocent victims.

Hemingway was correct to insist that his imaginative writing should not be confused with his journalism. Even though "Old Man at the Bridge" and the dispatch on the refugees fleeing the war along the Ebro River deal with the same subject and are composed from the same kind of raw note materials, they are recognizably different in tone and style and emotional impact. However modest its scale, "Old Man at the Bridge" clearly transcends the direct record of these same experiences contained in his dispatch.

What, then, makes the difference? Why was this "short punch," as Arnold Gingrich called it, so much more compelling, more instructive, and in the end more memorable than "volumes of ordinary reporting?" Why do the story and the dispatch evoke such different responses from the reader?

The details in the dispatch add up and by their cumulative weight make sense as a whole, but they do not grow together to create a single, dominant feeling the way the details in the story do. In the story we become imaginatively involved in the old man's plight and in the narrator's dilemma in a way we never have time for in the passing tide of refugees described in the dispatch. We may remember fragmented episodes from the stream of refugees whose lives we observed but never fully understood, but who will forget this old man at the bridge, worried about his animals and too old and tired to walk away from the path of war?

The transformation of an event, an idea, or some experience in life into a work of art is a complex and largely mysterious process. We seldom have a chance to witness it in any detail, and even more rarely do we have a chance to observe a work of art gain form and meaning from beginning to end. The rough field notes Hemingway jotted down in Spain are but a small hoarding of his creative life, but in bringing them back with him to Key West he has given us a unique opportunity to see how his talent transformed his encounter with an old man at the Amposta bridge into a fine short story.

Although we can never know precisely how the imagination of Hemingway transformed the observed details of this event into a transcendent work of art, we can begin to see in the transforming power of his imagination why it was that he guarded so carefully his reputation as a craftsman of fiction and why, when a good critic like Edmund Wilson seemed to blur the sacred boundaries between his stories and his newspaper writing, he was outraged.

Some writers, such as Orwell or Koestler or Naipul, move with equal power and grace from one form of writing to another and give equal weight to their powers of observation in whatever form they may write. Hemingway too could master a subject and give an authoritative account of it, as many of his best newspaper and magazine articles and his books on bullfighting and big game hunting demonstrate. But for all their excellence they do not represent his fullest creative powers nor do they draw upon the deepest sources of his imagination. "Old Man at the Bridge," modest as it is in scale, does draw upon those sources and fully displays those powers in a way that none of his factual reporting ever could.

The boundary Hemingway drew between his fiction and his reporting was not, therefore, an arbitrary line, but a way of defining who he chose to be as a writer. In distinguishing his fiction from his reporting, Hemingway was insisting on something essential to his artistic imagination and to the art of his short stories. Throughout his career he zealously guarded this sense of himself as a writer of fiction, and as "Old Man at the Bridge" demonstrates, even in the midst of a war that demanded virtually all of his attention and energy he was still first and foremost a writer of fiction.

Perhaps for this reason the story seems to have had a special meaning for him, for it was the only story from the Spanish Civil War period that he chose to include in the definitive collection of his short stories. Even in later years, when he could have revised the collection and added stories he had written later, "Old Man at the Bridge" remained the last to be included.

Story
Technique
and Themes

Hemingway's Apprentice Fiction: 1919–1921

Paul Smith

●

In the three years between Ernest Hemingway's triumphant return from Italy in January 1919 and his departure for Paris in December 1921, he lived in Chicago for less than a year—a year-and-a-half if you count his intermittent residence in Oak Park, but Oak Park was never meant to count as Chicago. The better half of those years was spent in and around Petoskey and Toronto, for there he wrote the best of both his unpublished and published work, like the "Cross Roads" sketches and his *Toronto Star Weekly* articles. In Chicago, however, he labored at grub-street stuff for the *Cooperative Commonwealth*, most of it now in oblivion, and in his time off he wrote poetry, much of it in a style he later called "erectile."[1]

When he remembered the fall of 1919, he recalled shoveling gravel for the county to pay his rent in Petoskey and writing

> stories which I sent to the Saturday Evening Post. The Saturday Evening Post did not buy them nor did any other magazine and I doubt if worse stories were ever written. . . . I was always known in Petoskey as Ernie Hemingway who wrote for the Saturday Evening Post due to the courtesy of my landlady's son, who described my occupation to the reporter for the Petoskey paper. . . . After Christmas when I was still writing for the Saturday Evening Post and had $20 left of my savings, I was promised a job at the pump factory . . . and was looking forward to laying off writing for the magazines for a time. (item 820)[2]

The manuscripts of these stories, for which the pump factory offered some relief, are among a group of some thirteen he wrote between 1919 and 1921, including a few written in the fall of 1918 or on the way home from Italy.[3] His first stake in a gamble at writing, these manuscripts range from submitted stories to one-page unfinished sketches. The first was written on Red Cross stationery in November 1918, and the last is the earliest version of "Up in Michigan" from the fall of 1921. Although this number of manuscripts is irreducible to final categories, out of that welter of exploratory writing three emergent styles may be identified. Here I will give each a place-name and cite the first and last sentences of manuscripts that are typical of each.

First, the "Chicago" style and an example from "The Mercenaries," written in late 1919:

If you are honestly curious about pearl fishing conditions in the Marquesas, the possibility of employment on the projected Trans Gobi Desert Railway, or the potentialities of any of the hot tamale republics, go to the Cafe Cambrinus on Wabash Avenue in Chicago.

"Aw, say, Napoleon!" broke in Graves, embarrassedly, "Let's change that to 'Vive la doughnut!'"4
[The reference to the "doughnut"—earlier in the story, "Peruvian doughnuts"—is apparently a slang phrase for a simple task, "a piece of cake."]

Secondly, the "Italian" style and an example from a 1918 sketch, "Nick lay in bed . . ." (item 604):

Nick lay in bed in the hospital while from outside came the hysterical roar of the crowd milling through the streets.

'I had a rendezvous with Death'—but Death broke the date and now it's all over. God double-crossed me."

And third, the "Michigan" style and an example from one of the sketches from "Cross Roads"—again from late 1919:

Old Man Hurd has a face that looks indecent.

So after a while she married him, and she told my mother, "The awful part about it was that he looked then just like he looks now."5

Consider first the example of the Chicago style. The narrator is an intermediary; he stands between his audience and the unfamiliar scene and characters he observes, but he has the credentials of a trusted listener. He is an inside witness, the reporter with a tip or a password (in "The Woppian Way"); he has passed the test in the "famous camel-needle's eye gymkhana of entering" the Café Cambrinus (in "The Mercenaries"). So his diction mingles the periphrastic and the colloquial: circumlocutions to delight his audience and display his worldliness along with the language of the streets that admits him to Chicago's nether-world.

This style suggests a convenient stance from which Hemingway could write for Oak Park—if not for its churches, then for its literary clubs and English teachers—about characters and scenes he had witnessed in Chicago—if not in the bars on Wabash Avenue and Kid Howard's boxing ring, then in the pages of the *Chicago Tribune* and the ring he set up in his mother's music room.[6]

The stock characters are all there, from the tough detective with his contempt for squealers to the hired gun with a fatal weakness for Italian opera. The latter, Hand-of-God Evans from "The Ash Heels Tendon" is a revealing figure: he is a cold-eyed killer whose sobriquet, Hand-of-God, italicizes an indifferent and inevitable fate—pure "Chicago"—but his flaw testifies not only to the cliché of the Italian sentiment for Caruso but also to Hemingway's dutiful attendance at the Chicago Opera, for which his mother provided season tickets.

Hemingway did not invent this style; however much it suited his situation, he found it ready-to-wear in his reading of Ring Lardner and Rudyard Kipling, as critics from Charles Fenton to Michael Reynolds have shown. Nor was it a postwar style. Hemingway had adopted it in his school stories like "A Matter of Colour"; and as a reporter for his school paper he was by-lined as Ring Lardner Junior. In his senior year he wrote a story that predicted some of these postwar Chicago fictions. Drawn from an address to the Hanna Club by A. F. Hammesfahr (December 1916), this tale, narrated by "Ham," tells of a regiment massacred by Philippine natives after the soldiers had been warned by the older veterans; it ends with a bloody vengeance wreaked on the natives by the commanding officer, now in Leavenworth (item 859). A grisly legend with a familiar Hanna Club moral, "Listen to your elders," it predicts Hemingway's use of a narrator in the role of the privileged reporter retelling the tale of an old hand.

There are seven of these Chicago sketches and stories. The first is a story written on *Giuseppe Verdi* stationery in early January 1919. "The galleria in Milan . . ." (item 416) is a framed narrative of a poker game with a deck of six kings and six aces in which the narrator, with two of each, folds early as the stakes rise between two players who hold the rest. It has Lardner's language, an O. Henry switch, and something of Kipling;[7] and with its younger narrator of the frame insisting on hearing one story and being told another, it also draws on Mark Twain's "The Jumping Frog of Calaveras County." Like "The Mercenaries" it begins with a triplet of dropped place-names with a Prohibition joke: "The galleria in Milan is a combination of the Rue de la Paix, Fifth Avenue, and South State Street before the reformation—not Martin Luther's but Martin Burney's. In it you can get anything from the best hors d'oeuvres in Europe to a bronze bust of President Wilson."

The second is a fragment of a longer sketch written in April 1919, "The lights of the line . . ." (item 550). A brief dialogue among some officers celebrating Christmas as they ride in a carriage outside La Scala, it might be passed over were it not for its nervous wit: "Be comfortable . . . old cock. . . . In the language of the pale-face, 'heap big war in Europe over.' You fought to make the world safe for democrats," and so on. There is also an early indication of Hemingway's predilection for a British dialect, one that infected even Frederic Henry's speech ten years later,[8] but it is the strained jesting in this passage that will assume more meaning later.

The three central manuscripts of the Chicago group are "The Woppian Way," "The Mercenaries," and "The Ash Heels Tendon," the first begun in the summer of 1919 and, like the other two, completed in the fall or early winter. "The Woppian Way," or "The Passing of Pickles McCarty," begins with the narrator-reporter's recollections of Pickles as "a ham-and-egger, pork-and-beaner . . . in short a bum box-fighter," good enough only for preliminaries (item 843), and joins it with Pickles' own story of finding his true main bout on the Austro-Italian front with the Arditi. He is met as he is about to join D'Annunzio's "band of irregulars" attempting to free the besieged city of Fiume in the fall of 1919,[9] and he treats the reporter to a bloody account of an Arditi attack on Asalone. In "The Mercenaries" Rinaldi Rinaldo similarly tells of listening to a tale told by Perry Graves of an amorous night with the wife of an Italian war hero that ends with a point-blank duel with the husband the morning after. The story takes a plot from Byron's *Don Juan* and ends it with a Western shoot-out. "The Ash Heels Tendon," the only one of the three without a second narrator, ends with the last gunfight between Jack Farrel and Hand-of-God Evans; the tough detective knows the killer's fatal flaw—play Leoncavallo and any true son of Italy will take his hands from his guns to applaud.

Two features of these stories are remarkable. First, two of them use a narrator reporting another's first-person narrative, a strategy for distancing the reporter from the story in order both to make the tacit claim of objectivity and to assume an immunity to questions of the story's truth. It is no coincidence, of course, that both of these inside narratives are versions of anecdotes Hemingway had passed off on Chink Dorman-

Smith. The first is that he had been the victim of an Italian woman's sexual voracity and never made it to Taormina, where his days and nights with Jim Gamble were somewhat more delicate; the other is that he had been "wounded leading Arditi troops on Mount Grappa."[10] Each story then is simultaneously a claim and a disclaimer for the veracity of the war stories Hemingway collected, like battlefield souvenirs, after his own brief and accidental engagement in the conflict.

The second feature to note here is that two of the narratives depend upon something of a joke, an ironic twist, or a clever trick for their resolutions. Certainly Hemingway had this device at hand in the fiction of Ring Lardner and O. Henry, and his choice of the strategy may signify nothing more than a young writer's desperation to publish in the narrative ways that seem to work. But, when this device recurs in the Italian stories and sketches, it assumes a significance beyond the explanation of ordinary literary influence.

The list of manuscripts in the Chicago style ends in an anticlimax of the sentimental and dubious in 1921. "The Current" mixes pugilistic gore with popular romance: Stuyvesant Byng, a wealthy and philandering sportsman, must convince his beloved, Dorothy Hadley, that he is worthy of her love by becoming not just a runner-up but a champion in some sport. Since she would not accept fly-fishing and "there won't be any polo to speak of for a year,"[11] he trains for and wins the middleweight boxing title and, of course, Dorothy. Although he is inspired by the steady current of his love, he wins with a trick, staggering with his gloves down after a long count and then decking his apish opponent.[12] The last, to which Griffin has given the title "Portrait of the Idealist in Love," needs only a note to relieve it of the heavy burden of biography it has been made to bear. There is enough evidence in the typescript (item 270 A) to argue that, although the brief introduction and conclusion are Hemingway's, the long, maudlin, and lofty vacuities of the idealist's letter are not Hemingway's but were hastily copied and framed as a private joke and then set aside.[13]

Although there are fewer Italian manuscripts—two stories and two sketches—they have about them an aura from the backlighting of *A Farewell to Arms* and the later war stories; in that light we may risk seeing more than was there at first, but it is a risk worth taking for the serious reading of these early works.

The first sketch, "Nick lay in bed . . ." (item 604), was written soon after the Armistice in November 1918. The narrator describes Nick Grainger lying wounded in a hospital and talking with a nurse. As they listen to the sounds of the Armistice celebration, Nick is reminded of

Halloween, and the nurse wonders what it is like now on Broadway. When Nick asks if she is a New Yorker, she admits she is from Fort Wayne; then he, too, confesses to the cosmopolitan strategy: "Sure, I've used that stuff too." That bit of confessional dialogue in which the Midwesterners agree to shed their pretensions looks ahead to the early conversations between Frederic Henry and Catherine Barkley.[14]

When she leaves with a parting smile, Nick takes two objects from his bedside table: a bottle of bichloride of mercury, which he hides when the nurse returns, and his war medal with its citation, which he reads to himself. Each of them, the bichloride and the citation, is a deadly antiseptic. That he hides the bichloride suggests an impulse to suicide, but it could heal his physical wounds. So, too, the citation was meant as a sort of rhetorical curative for a wound that brought him close, but not to some ultimate glory.[15] At the sketch's end Nick folds the citation and thinks to himself, "that counterfeit dollar represents my legs and that tin cross is my left arm. 'I had a rendezvous with Death'—but Death broke the date and now it is all over. God double-crossed me." That counterfeit dollar, the citation, is later inflated to a "ten thousand lira note" when Colonel Cantwell ritually buries his wound and its honors with "merde, money, and blood" in *Across the River and Into the Trees*.[16]

But Nick's embittered recollection of Alan Seeger's "I Have a Rendezvous with Death" is more instructive. The poem contrasts the "hushed awakenings" of a night of love with his date with death "at some disputed barricade" and conjoins the pledge to love with one to death: "And I to my pledged word am true / I shall not fail my rendezvous." I suspect that the poet was more important to Hemingway than his poem. Seeger, Harvard class of 1910, resident of Greenwich Village and Paris, and a true mercenary with the Foreign Legion, wrote his famous poem and died in France when Hemingway was trying out for the junior varsity. The poet not only predicted and kept his appointment with death, and that heroically, but he also won literary fame with one very remarkable poem. How could he fail to represent the perfected image of the soldier-artist? Hemingway's quotation of the emblematic line with his own ironic tag, "Death broke the date," is more than a deflation of romantic rhetoric; it is a tacit admission of patriotic shame for not having given the last full measure, of whatever.

Somewhere, I suspect, there is a connection between this moment in the sketch and Hemingway's celebration of McCarty's suicidal attack with the Arditi, Perry Graves's swaggering into a duel, and even Stuyvesant Byng's bloody bout for love. A romantic and unfulfilled death wish pervades these early manuscripts. The wounded Nick never drinks the healing poison hidden in his bed, but the shame at having been stood up by death lingers on, however muted, in the embarrassment later characters, like Frederic Henry, feel at serving on a "picturesque front."[17] There is a resonant meaning in the change of tenses from "I *have*" to "I *had* a rendezvous with Death"; and the mocking tag suggests a common but serious note of the romantic, perhaps a little less than "half in love with easeful Death," blaming it all on a double-crossing destiny.

Sometime in the winter of 1919–1920, Hemingway drew again on the device of the ironic twist for the war story "The Visiting Team" (items 670 A, B). In this tale an adolescent jest turns deadly, and the picturesque front is shattered into realism.[18] The story begins with a denial of the plot Hemingway may have had in mind for his earlier sketch, "Nick lay in bed . . .": "Red Smith lay on a cot, no go on, this is no hospital story. There is no soft-eyed, gentle-voiced nurse, who might have stepped out of the Winter Garden chorus, no romantic young Second Lieutenant romantically wounded through the shoulder. There is not even a Captain with a Croix de Guerre pinned to his pillow, both eyes bandaged while his gruff but tender-hearted Irish orderly—but back to Red who lay on a cot."

There is none of that here, but Hemingway would draw on these stereotypes a decade later. To go on, Red Smith's perceptions inform the story; he gazes at the barrage balloons over the Austrian lines and imagines the mountain ranges as the magnified edges of razor blades while his friend Tommy sees them as "something out of the Follies"; but together they devise a practical joke for the arrival of some new recruits—from Harvard, of course. When they arrive, these veterans of a picturesque front tell the newcomers of nightly bombardments, mustard gas, and shell shock. During the night they imitate it all with pistol shots, burst light bulbs, and chloride of lime, and then the joke explodes in their hands with a real attack. Red is called out to drive an ambulance, is wounded, and is brought back to die. His death mingles predictions of *A Farewell to Arms* ("only the good die young"), echoes of Kipling ("and so passed wonderingly a gentleman unafraid"), and a recognition of the fatal boyishness implied in the title, "The Visiting Team."[19] The story ends with a question: having overheard the American's sporting term for the Austrians, an Italian surgeon, covered with the blood of the ironic prankster, asks "Who are these Viseeting Teem?" The answer the story demands is: they are the enemy, they mean to kill you, and nothing from the playing fields of Eton or Oak Park can change that.[20]

The last of the Italian stories is one of the most extraordinary of Hemingway's early manuscripts. An untitled typescript, "He had known he wouldn't get up . . ." (item 445) is a sampler of his various styles from his school fiction to the chapters of *In Our Time*. It begins with an exhausted British soldier named Orpen defending a bridge against attacking German troops. As he lies in the weeds, a "German cyclist rode slowly onto the bridge. He crossed and then dismounted. He stood uneasily and looked around. A rifle tapped just once. [The] man fell and crawled and flopped about grotesquely like a spider with a leg torn off. He reached the parapet of the bridge, tried to pull himself up with his hands and then slipped to the ground. The front wheel of his bicycle was still turning. The man was dead before it stopped turning." This is close to the perception of ironic incongruity that informs the chapters of *In Our Time*; but not close enough, for Hemingway has yet to discover that that perception will do and that he need not go on, as he does, with "A life was gone. The machine went on. You pressed a trigger. Someone died."

As the Germans advance, Orpen hears gunfire; a "machine-gun went tac-tac-tac like a typewriter," and the image recalls another he used in 1921 in "Mitrailliatrice":

> Ugly short infantry of the mind
> Advancing over difficult terrain,
> Make this Corona
> Their mitrailleuse.[21]

Although Orpen is no writer, the analogy between warfare and the creation of art might well occur to him, for he is a pianist and composer. When he imagines machine-gun drill, he thinks, "Remove the clips! Insert the pans! Keep mind on business at hand! On the other hand—left hand or right hand? Left hand, bass. Right hand, treble. Fingers to skip over keys." With this the narrative introduces its second motif: the artist as soldier, the creator as killer, the young celebrant of life mired in death—a common theme in the poetry of World War I.

The reverie of Orpen's early career as a talented composer is broken when he is buried in a shell-burst. Imagining that he is still defending the bridge, he hears the opening cello chords of the second movement of Beethoven's Seventh, and the final element of this already surprising narrative is introduced. He finds himself translated into Valhalla where a score of heroes of history and legend play at the game of war. He is welcomed, appropriately, by Horatius and introduced to everyone from Eric the Red and Tamerlane to Davey Crockett and Custer. After Lord Nelson explains the rules of the game and they resume play, Hemingway's imagination runs amok until Orpen, now in the spirit of things, runs his bayonet into General George Washington's groin, and the Father of Our Country exclaims, "Oh, good thrust, . . . I forgot you were

British.''[22] Orpen then wanders off to a peaceful setting very much like home and meets his mother, who tells him he is a hero for defending the bridge and has entered Heaven. Then he comes to, of course, and finds himself being attended by a surgeon taking shrapnel from his chest and a comforting nurse reassuring him that he does not have to return to Valhalla—or even Heaven.

However ill-conceived and typical of his exuberant school fictions this story may be, the bittersweet image of the soldier-artist who endures a heroic death and still lives on to create and that more promising image of the dead cyclist and the still turning bicycle wheel both call for our serious attention.

The two Michigan manuscripts, "Cross Roads: An Anthology" (items 347, 348) and the earliest version of "Up in Michigan" (item 800), offer a certain symmetry to Hemingway's Chicago years, standing like parentheses around most of his writing of this time. "Cross Roads" was begun in the fall of 1919 (preceded only by the early Italian sketches and a version of "The Woppian Way"); the first version of "Up in Michigan" was hastily typed in the fall of 1921 in anticipation of the move to Paris with Sherwood Anderson's letter of introduction to Gertrude Stein hanging over him. Together these manuscripts mark with their style and subjects Hemingway's first tentative exploration of what was to become his only native literary territory.

In the fall of 1919 he very deliberately set out, with the uneven collaboration of his friend William Smith, to imitate the sketches of E. W. Howe's "An Anthology of Another Town" appearing in the *Saturday Evening Post*. But once burnt with rejections, he dropped the project for two years and picked at the worn fringes of tough and delicate sentimentality in stories like "The Ash Heels Tendon" and "The Current." Either Hemingway wrote better than he knew in the "Cross Roads" sketches, or knowing how well he could write, but with his eye still on the main chance of publishing, he set them aside. The sentimental notion that Hemingway was driven weeping to Walloon and to the discovery of his style by the soul-searing knowledge that Agnes von Kurowsky had jilted him ignores the facts of the matter.[23]

A less dramatic review of the fall and winter of 1919 argues that Howe, a minor and derivative writer himself, set Hemingway some simple and salutary lessons. And the first was to be brief: like most of Howe's, Hemingway's sketches run from a paragraph to little more than a page, while his other Chicago manuscripts are stylistically prolix and the narratives inflate brief anecdotes in the tall-tale tradition.

Howe's narrative voice and attitude would have been familiar to

Hemingway and appropriate for his subjects—the "Bayites," as he called them. His experience as one of the summer people from Oak Park among the villagers and farmers of Horton Bay and Petoskey might well have encouraged that narrative stance, both a part of and apart from his subject. Throughout his correspondence with Bill Smith and others there is a two-stranded thread of supercilious affection for these naive natives.

The voice in these sketches is that of a local storyteller speaking in the idiom of the country and with local loyalties. If the irony of the sketch turns back upon the Bay villagers, the narrator rarely disassociates himself from the town. After Ed Paige went six rounds against Stanley Ketchell, "most everyone has forgotten all about it and quite a few say they'll never believe Ed really did it"; and when Bob White tells of his experiences in the war, the "people out at the Bay don't think much of France or of the Marines either, for that matter, now that Bob's back with the news right direct."[24] As we hear or, as it sometimes seems, overhear these twice-told tales of the General Store, it is assumed that we know these people and neither need nor deserve any other explanation or pointed moral than the one that is there in the story.

The narrative pattern in these sketches is like the one Hemingway found in Howe's anthology. They take their titles from a character's name; the opening sentence includes that name and offers some apparently innocent but teasing fact—"Pauline Snow was the only beautiful girl we ever had out at the Bay"; then a brief dramatic narrative; and a conclusion, often ending with a remark by one of the characters or the laconic narrator—Pauline Snow is seduced, talked about, and then sent to a correction home, and her seducer, "Art [Simons] was away for awhile, and then came back and married one of the Jenkins girls."

Two years later in the fall of 1921 Hemingway returned to the structure and style of these sketches, particularly to the one of Pauline Snow, when he hurriedly drafted the first version of "Up in Michigan." The similarities between the brief sketch and longer story are necessarily few, but they are strong. Pauline has Liz Coates's innocence; her parents are dead, Liz's are never mentioned; Art Simons has some of Jim Gilmore's physical characteristics, especially his hands; the sexual act implied in the sketch is realized in the story; and Pauline's ostracism was a possible consequence that Liz worries about in a rejected conclusion of the early version of "Up in Michigan."

The first typescript (item 800) of the story begins with a canceled introduction similar to those in the "Cross Roads" sketches: "Wesley Dilworth got the dimple in his chin from his mother. Her name had been Liz Buell. Jim Dilworth married her when he came to Horton's Bay from

Canada." A related typescript (item 801) includes a variant ending in which Liz returns from the dock to worry through the night: "Liz was frightened and sick when she got up to her room. She put on one of her unwell pads because she was afraid of blood getting on the sheets. She felt ashamed and sick and cried and prayed until she fell asleep. She woke up frightened and stiff and aching. . . . 'What if I have a baby?' she thought. . . . She thought about having a baby until it was morning."

The parenthetical beginning-and-ending was finally rejected months later in Paris. But had Hemingway retained it, the story would have had the frame typical of the "Cross Roads" sketches, beginning with the provocatively innocent reference to Wesley Dilworth's dimple and ending with Liz's worrisome question, "What if I have a baby?" The answer to her question would have been there in the story's first sentence: Wesley Dilworth, dimple and all.[25]

Hemingway knew that this or any other version would not have amused the editors of the popular magazines; he was, I think, for the first time writing for himself. An unusual manuscript for that reason, it may be unique for another. If Hemingway's account in *A Moveable Feast* of the loss of his manuscripts is true—and some wonder if it is—then this typescript is the only Chicago story for which there is tangible evidence that it was packed for Paris in the late months of 1921.

That single typescript says, finally, a good deal about the value he placed on the rest of the manuscripts he left boxed in Chicago: simply that they exist, oddly enough, is proof of his early and harsh judgment. And that you can hold this typescript of "Up in Michigan" in your hand somehow makes unsubstantial all the other "lost" manuscripts, the sometime existence of which depends on a love letter, a remark passed on, or a late memory answering the needs of Hemingway, those who knew him then, or the biographers who wish to know him now.

Throughout the fragmentary remains of Hemingway's Chicago years—the manuscripts, the letters, and the memoirs—there are some bitter and urgent notes: first he wanted to publish, then he wanted Hadley, and finally he wanted out. His best work was appearing in the *Toronto Star Weekly*, while in Chicago he was hacking for the *Cooperative Commonwealth*. However much Hadley liked his poetry, no one this side of Paris would print it; and for every submitted story he had at least one rejection slip.

To end this review of the manuscripts from Hemingway's Chicago years one looks for some representative anecdote, and it is there, where it should be, in one of his stories set outside of Chicago, "The Killers." Its manuscript reflects the cold winter of 1919, for its rejected beginning opens in Petoskey. I will take that story of Nick Adams's initiation as an analogue of Hemingway's. At the end, what Nick realizes is that for some people, like his friend George, an inevitable and "awful thing" can be dismissed with a popular explanation: "He must have got mixed up in something in Chicago, . . . [and] that's what they kill them for." But Nick Adams, and before him Ernest Hemingway, decided, "I'm going to get out of this town."[26]

The Troubled Fisherman

Kenneth S. Lynn

●

The longest of the fishing trips he took in the summer of 1919 was into the woods in the upper peninsula of Michigan near the town of Seney, about fifteen miles south of Lake Superior. In seven days of casting in the Big Fox and Little Fox rivers, Ernest and two friends, Al Walker and Jock Pentecost, caught about two hundred trout. One of the fish pulled in by Jock was fifteen and a half inches long, but it was Ernest who almost landed what would have been the prize catch. "I lost one on the Little Fox below an old dam," he wrote to Howie Jenkins, "that was the biggest trout I've ever seen. I was up in some old timbers and it was a case of horse out. I got about half of him out of wasser and my hook broke at the shank!"[1] He did, however, gather in the materials for a notable piece of fiction.

In the fish story he had just finished writing, he told Gertrude Stein and Alice B. Toklas on August 15, 1924, he had been "trying to do the country like Cézanne and having a hell of a time and sometimes getting it a little bit. It is about 100 pages long and nothing happens and the country is swell. I made it all up, so I see it all and part of it comes out the way it ought to, it is swell about the fish, but isn't writing a hard job though?"[2] His sense that the story was swell about the fish was not mistaken. ("He watched them holding themselves with their noses into the current, many trout in deep, fast moving water, slightly distorted as he watched far down through the glassy convex surface of the pool, its surface pushing and swelling smooth against the resistance of the log-driven piles of the bridge.")[3] Nor was he speaking idly when he suggested that his recreations of landscape were like a series of pictures by Cézanne. ("Ahead of him, as far as he could see, was the pine plain. The burned country stopped off at the left with the range of hills. On ahead islands of dark pine trees rose out of the plain. Far off to the left was the line of the river.")[4] In two respects, that is to say, his letter furnished the Misses Stein and Toklas with an accurate sense of what he had accomplished. But interestingly enough, he made no mention of the most difficult of all the objectives he had been seeking to attain in "Big Two-Hearted River": to endow a story in which "nothing happens" with an inner drama of terrific intensity.

As the solitary Nick Adams leaves the train station at Seney and walks across a "burned-over country" toward "the far blue hills that marked the Lake Superior height of land,"[5] he feels a wonderful sense of release. "He felt he had left everything behind, the need for thinking, the need to write, other needs. It was all back of him."[6] Toward the end of the day he pitches his tent and crawls inside, noting with pleasure how "homelike" the space seems. At last, he thinks, "he was settled. Nothing could touch him. It was a good place to camp. He was there, in the good place. He was in his home where he had made it."[7]

From this point forward the story abounds in details of how splendid the fishing is and of what a good time Nick is having. Nevertheless, dark thoughts of some sort are lurking on the margins of his consciousness. While he is finishing his supper the first night, he suddenly becomes aware that his mind is "starting to work," but because he is tired he is able to "choke it."[8] The next day his happiness is again interrupted. An arduous battle with the biggest trout he has ever seen ends with the trout's escape, and as Nick is reeling in his line he feels "a little sick, as though it would be better to sit down."[9] To avoid the possibility of a second defeat in one day, he thereupon modifies his plans. Instead of plunging into the armpit-deep water of a swamp overshadowed by big trees, where he might hook big trout in places impossible to land them, he decides to postpone the adventure. "There were plenty of days coming when he could fish the swamp," he says to himself, as the story ends.[10]

What are the "other needs" Nick feels he has put behind him as he heads off toward the river? Why does he more than once refer to his tent as his home, and why does he feel so pleased to be in it? Why is it that failure to kill the big fish makes him feel sick? With the exception of "The Battler," "Big Two-Hearted River" raises more tantalizing questions than any other Hemingway story.

Plausible answers to these questions may be found by placing the story in its biographical context. Ernest spent the summer of 1919 thinking and writing. He also spent it in bitter contention with his mother. The following summer the ill will between the two of them exploded into open warfare when she expelled him from Windemere within days of his twenty-first birthday and presented him as he was leaving with a letter that was indisputably the masterpiece of her epistolary career. Consequently, by the time he wrote the story about his fishing trip to Seney he was not only burdened by upsetting memories of the first summer after the war, but by even more upsetting memories of the second. Perhaps, then, the "other needs" Nick feels he has put behind him include a need to please his mother, while his talk of his tent as his home may represent a reaction to being thrown out of his parents' summer cottage. Perhaps, too, the burned-over country and the grasshoppers that have turned black from living in it constitute tacit reminders to him of his mother's penchant for burning things. And finally, the activity of his mind that keeps threatening to overwhelm his contentment could be rage.

The angler on the bank of the Big Two-Hearted River is clearly a man with a divided heart—but the precise nature of the division is never identified. "In the swamp the banks were bare, the big cedars came together overhead, the sun did not come through, except in patches; in the fast deep water, in the half light, the fishing would be tragic."[11] The words apply well to the fisherman's efforts to shun the murky depths of his troubled inner life. First and last, Nick remains an enigma.

But to many readers in the twenties, Nick was not an enigma. For these people assumed that the key to Nick's secret was the fact that his creator was the archetypal representative of a war-scarred "lost generation." Ultimately, this assumption crept into formal assessments of the story. The experience that has given Nick "a touch of panic," Edmund Wilson announced in "Ernest Hemingway: Bourdon Gauge of Morale" (1939), is "the wholesale shattering of human beings in which he has taken part."[12] Leading up to and away from this statement, "Bourdon Gauge" contains some wonderfully appreciative comments about the stifled pangs and undruggable disquiet that lurk beneath the most innocent surfaces in Hemingway's stories. In the case of "Big Two-Hearted River," however, Wilson felt a need to specify the malaise underlying it, and in doing so he could only think that it had to do with World War I. He cited no textual evidence in support of this diagnosis for the simple reason that there was none. Not a single reference to war appears in the story, and it is highly doubtful, furthermore, judging by what can be observed of Nick's behavior, that panic is the feeling that he is fending off. Nor does battlefield trauma bear any discernible relation to those vague "other needs" that he feels he has put behind him or to his strong expressions of contentment with his "homelike" tent.

Half a decade after "Bourdon Gauge," Wilson's interpretation was reinforced by Malcolm Cowley's introduction to the Viking *Portable Hemingway* (1944). To Hemingway this essay could not have come as a surprise. For in *Exile's Return* (1934) Cowley had already proclaimed that the young American writers born in the years around 1900 were a lost generation, inasmuch as the war had shattered their relationship with the country of their boyhood and they had become attached to no other. That Hemingway felt precisely the way he himself did about the war was one of Cowley's cardinal beliefs, and he delighted in drawing other parallels between their lives. The equivalent for him of Hemingway's Michigan was Cambria County, Pennsylvania, on the western slope of the Alleghenies, where he had spent his boyhood summers fishing and shooting and walking in the woods, and his equivalent of Oak Park was a residential section of Pittsburgh, where his father practiced medicine, just like Dr. Hemingway. When America entered World War I, Cowley had wanted to join an ambulance corps in France, but because the demand for drivers had slackened by the time he got to Paris, he ended up driving a camion for the French military transport—which in his retrospective view was not all that different from driving a Red Cross truck in Italy. So closely did he identify himself with Hemingway that in his *Portable Hemingway* introduction he erroneously asserted that the novelist had been born in 1898, the year of his own birth. Hemingway's awareness of Cowley's habit of superimposing his own life on his was made explicit by him more than once. Thus, in a letter to Harvey Breit of the *New York Times* five years before his death, he sardonically observed that "Malcolm thot I was like him because my father was a Dr. and I went to Michigan when I was 2 weeks old where they had Hemlock trees."[13] That Cowley would someday go on from the lost-generation argument of *Exile's Return* to a lost-generation interpretation of "Big Two-Hearted River" must have seemed to him like an inevitable development.

In the *Portable Hemingway* Cowley argued, not so much by direct statement as by artful implication, that Hemingway's fisherman, like Hemingway himself, was a war veteran who was trying to block out fear-ridden recollections of being wounded. Proof of Nick's state of mind was not to be found in the story, to be sure, but that didn't bother Cowley. Hemingway's stories "are most of them continued," he said, by which he meant that the emotions underlying "Big Two-Hearted River" could be understood in the light of the emotions expressed in "Now I Lay Me," written three years later.[14] Since the hero of the latter story is an American lieutenant in war-time Italy who is afraid to close his eyes at night, "Now I Lay Me" has the effect, said Cowley, of giving readers "a somewhat different attitude toward the earlier story" and of drawing attention to something that "we probably missed at first reading; that there are shadows in the background and that part of the story takes place in an inner world."[15]

In stressing an emotional consistency between "Big Two-Hearted River" and "Now I Lay Me," Cowley neglected to point out that the most emotional moment in the latter story is set in the hero's childhood and involves a confrontation between his parents. Nevertheless, Cowley's endorsement of the war-trauma argument soon became an inspiration to other critics, most notably to an impressionable young man named Philip Young, who "ported a *Portable Hemingway* halfway across Europe during World War II."[16] In 1952 Young projected the admiration he felt for the Cowley introduction, amplified by his own reactions to war, into a book that proclaimed that the wound suffered by Hemingway in 1918 had so deeply affected him that he had spent his whole life as a writer composing variations on the story of the psychically crippled "sick man" in "Big Two-Hearted River."[17] Ten years later Mark Schorer spoke for what was now a critical cliché when he characterized Hemingway as the lifelong victim of the events that had befallen him at Fossalta di Piave. "Nothing more important than this wounding was ever to happen to him," Schorer sweepingly declared.[18]

Thus, the war-wound interpretation of the story was established not by textual evidence, but by what the critics knew about the author's life— or rather, by what they thought they knew about his life. And after he was dead, they eagerly seized on his posthumously published comment in *A Moveable Feast* that "Big Two-Hearted River" was about "coming back from the war but there was no mention of the war in it" as clinching proof that they were right.[19] They would have been better advised to wonder if a master manipulator was not making fools of them from beyond the grave, as he so often had in life.

For a quarter of a century after the story was published, Hemingway kept his own counsel about it. But in the aftermath of World War II he made a number of statements in which he related it to World War I. In all likelihood, though, these revelations reflected latter-day events. The late forties marked the beginning of the end for Hemingway. Fantasies of suicide thronged his mind, intermingled with fears of insanity, and his friend Buck Lanham saw him writing in the morning with a drink in his hand. For years he had been given to saying that the first war had cost him a lot of sleep, but he had usually been careful to couple such confessions with manly assertions that he had finally put insomnia behind him and was once again in wonderful shape. The breathtaking tragedy that took form in the late forties exposed the hollowness of that boast. All too keenly aware of his problems and yet adamantly opposed to seeking professional help in understanding them, he more than ever felt the need of a heroic explanation for his life. In an effort to account for his imperiled sense of himself, as well as to preserve his macho reputation, he turned once more to Fossalta.

Thus, in a letter dated August 25, 1948, he informed Malcolm Cowley that he could now see that in the first war he had been hurt very badly in body, mind, and spirit and also morally, that "Big Two-Hearted River" was about a man who was home from the war, and that he, the author, was still hurt in that story. The real truth about himself, he assured Cowley, was that in the war "I was hurt bad all the way through and I was really spooked at the end."[20] And in another letter a few years later to the *New York Times*'s Charles Poore, he again characterized "Big Two-Hearted River" as "a story about a boy who has come back from the war. The war is never mentioned though as far as I can remember. This may be one of the things that helps it."[21] Private communications, however, were merely warm-ups for the gloss he offered the public at large in *A Moveable Feast*.

The book was written between 1957 and 1961, during which time the author's long debate with himself about self-destruction was moving inexorably toward violent resolution, despite his terrifying belief that suicide was a cowardly, unmanly act. In the wake of his death his enemies in the critical world took the same line toward it, as he had feared they would. To these commentators his life had ended with a whimper, not a bang. After 1930 he just didn't have it any more, Dwight Macdonald fairly gloated in the pages of *Encounter* in January 1962, and by the summer of 1961—the critic savagely continued—the position was outflanked, the lion couldn't be stopped, the sword wouldn't go into the bull's neck, the great fish was breaking the line, it was the fifteenth round and the champ looked bad, and the only way out was to destroy himself.

Even a Hemingway fan like Norman Mailer felt moved to confess in a troubled essay in *Esquire* entitled "The Big Bite" that his suicide had been "the most difficult death in America since [Franklin] Roosevelt's."[22] What made it difficult for Mailer was that in taking his life Hemingway had seemed to call into question all that he had represented. Consistently, he had presented himself as the champion of whatever endeavor he had undertaken; consistently, he had proclaimed that the great thing was to last and get your work done. How could such a life be reconciled with such a death?

Mailer's ultimate answer to this question was that "It is not likely that Hemingway was a brave man who sought danger for the sake of the sensations it provided him. What is more likely the truth of his own odyssey is that he struggled with his cowardice and against a secret lust to suicide all his life, that his inner landscape was a nightmare, and he spent his nights wrestling with the gods. It may even be that the final judgment on his work may come to the notion that what he failed to do was tragic, but what he accomplished was heroic, for it is possible that he carried a weight of anxiety with him which would have suffocated any man smaller than himself."[23]

As a hypothesis, Mailer's comment was marvelously suggestive and ought to have inspired searching examinations of the dynamics of Hemingway's early life. But it did not. Old habits of mind prevailed. Fossalta had been the break-point in a gallant hero's history. By seeming to imply in *A Moveable Feast* that "Big Two-Hearted River" was about a man who was doing his best to defend himself against memories of a dirty war, Hemingway himself helped to buttress that assumption.

From "Sepi Jingan" to "The Mother of a Queen": Hemingway's Three Epistemologic Formulas for Short Fiction

Gerry Brenner

●

Of the very young Ernest Hemingway, Kenneth Lynn writes,

> The willingness with which the little boy played the part of his sister's sister was more than matched . . . by the vehemency with which he fought it. Even minor frustrations of his will to be a boy could cause him to slap his mother, and one day he symbolically shot her. She called him her Dutch dolly, as was her wont, but this time the feminine epithet triggered an outburst of sexual rage. "I am not a Dutch dolly, I Pawnee Bill. Bang, I shoot Fweetee [Sweetie, Ernest's early name for his mother]." . . . That his mother was delighted to hear him say he was Pawnee Bill was typical of the baffling inconsistency of her behavior. Could it be that she really wanted him to be a boy after all? By sometimes dressing him in pants and a shirt, she tantalized him into thinking so. To a lesser degree, Marcelline was similarly confused by the sexual signals emanating from her mother. For if Grace gave her "twins" identical tea sets, she also bought them identical air rifles.[1]

Although Lynn melodramatizes the young boy's "sexual rage," he cogently observes Grace Hemingway's inconsistent behavior, her mixed gender signals, and the confusion with which she early saddled her children. She got help, of course, from her husband. Clarence's behavior also confused the children, plagued as it was by a long history of "a nervous condition," chronic depression and paranoia.[2] Between them the two parents wrought in their famous son confusions about his identity, his perceptions, and his understanding of the world he inhabited. Little wonder, then, that confusion resonates at the center of all his fiction, informing the puzzles that so beset him, and that he, in turn, exercised with imagination and creativity. Less wonder that Hemingway would repeatedly exercise that confusion—a common term for what an epistemologic philosopher would study as a problem in knowledge. Least wonder that repetitive exercising of confusion led to habitual routines, to a few epistemologic formulas, that facilitated his creation of flawed and flawless stories.

Hemingway's fixation on epistemologic puzzles and his discovery of the rudiments of a formula to which he would repeatedly return occur at least as early as his 1916 story for the Oak Park High School *Tabula*, "Sepi Jingan."³ An unidentified boy records his encounter with Billy Tabeshaw, who tells him about being saved by his dog, Sepi Jingan, from certain death at the hands of a pike-pole-wielding murderer, Paul Black Bird. Paul, a "bad Indian" who could drink all day and get crazy but never drunk, had killed Billy's cousin, a game warden. Although the sheriff failed to track Paul down, Billy succeeded. But Paul spotted his tracker, blindsided him with a blow to the head, and when Billy came to, stood grinning at him, pike-pole in hand, prodding and taunting, "cussing and pricking" Billy. While Paul toyed with his prey, Sepi crawled toward him and "'[s]uddenly sprang like a shaggy thunderbolt,'" catching Paul's throat in his "'long, wolf jaws.'" Billy boasts of making "'a very neat job'" of Paul's death. He put Paul on the railroad tracks so that the "'Pere Marquette Resort Limited removed all the traces.'" That caused people to conclude wrongly that Paul had lain down on the tracks in a drunken stupor.

A small epistemological puzzle precipitates Billy's telling his story to the narrator. In the story's frame Billy lets his dog bolt out of Hauley's store with a three-pound string of sausages. He pays for the sausages without reprimanding the dog. Billy's Jack London–like indebtedness to Sepi for having saved his life, of course, solves that small puzzle. But as Hemingway would continue to do in more sophisticated ways later, here too he characteristically complicates the story. He adds other problems to invite discovery of stories within the dog-rescues-man story. Hemingway sublimates his childhood anger at being called "Dutch dolly" instead of "Pawnee Bill" by telling a story of the human penchant for labeling, for assigning names that, while serving as a form of epistemologic shorthand, nevertheless violate accuracy, complexity, truth, and knowledge. When Sepi flees from the store with the sausage, the clerk calls him "robber," ignorant of Sepi's lifesaving action and his private label as "hero" in Billy's and, presumably by story's end, in the narrator's eyes. Likewise, since Paul's mutilated body was found on or after the fourth of July along the railroad tracks, the narrator expresses the communal verdict that Paul was "a drunk who fell asleep on the tracks," a label uninformed by the events that allegedly occurred. More, Hemingway lets readers conclude both that Sepi was the "avenging hero," his jaws having dealt Paul's death blow, and that Billy was an "innocent bystander." But unknown is whether Sepi's jaws were lethal or whether Billy had a hand in the revenge killing of Paul—whether Billy is a "murderer."

Hemingway's probing of oversimplified labels is reflected in Billy's authoritarian judgments on tobaccos. The odors from six brands merit his censure: Velvet (like red hot pepper), Prince Albert (like cornsilk), Stag (like dried apricots), Honest Scrap (like burnt rubber hose), Giant, and Tuxedo. Only Peerless suits his taste. But Hemingway's narrator does not share Billy's taste, for Billy exhorts him, in the story's penultimate line, "'You take my advice and stay off that "Tuxedo"—"Peerless" is the only tobacco.'" Hemingway's narrator may also not share Billy's self-portrayal as shrewd justice-fighter. For at the end of Billy's story the narrator refuses comment or response. To Billy's invitation to respond, asking "'Funny, ain't it?'" the narrator offers nothing. Nor does he respond to Billy's advice on smoking Peerless. Nor does he bid goodbye when Billy says, "'Come on, Sepi.'" The narrator's silence may signal yet another epistemologic puzzle, one that hinges on discovering yet another story within the story, the narrator's response to Billy's story. Does the narrator's silence signify his contempt for Billy's self-aggrandizement or scorn for what he may have decided is a tall tale that Billy has concocted in order to wow impressionable young boys? Or is the narrator so overawed by Billy's story, so convinced of its veracity, so impressed with the secret story Billy has shared with him that he is rendered speechless? Or is the narrator staggered by the burden of now knowing who was responsible for Paul's death, a knowledge that he must now guard, lest his spilling it to others cause problems for Billy?

How to read the narrator of "Sepi Jingan" poses an epistemologic puzzle characteristic of much of Hemingway's fiction. The invitation to assign a label to him—gullible or contemptuous narrator, Dutch dolly or Pawnee Bill—is the recurrent invitation to naive readers of Hemingway's fiction: to resolve confusions, to minimize complexities, to shortchange truth, and to grasp at some certitude that will pass for knowledge. Yet the element fundamental to his short fiction, the alchemical ingredient that so frequently transmutes the materials of his art, is a confusion that bespeaks Hemingway's epistemologic concerns. Whether he would call them by that highfalutin name or not, the heightened emotion and marked ambivalencies nurtured by his mother and father's mixed signals and inconsistent behaviors provided Hemingway with the key to successful formulas for writing fiction that presumably works on the principle of an iceberg. Definitions of his three formulas and brief discussions of stories that fall under each may lead readers to better appreciate a revisionist reading of Hemingway's long-neglected masterpiece, "The Mother of a Queen."

Admittedly, a number of Hemingway's stories, even vintage Hemingway, depend primarily upon irony for their effects, stories like "Up in Michigan," "The Capitol of the World," "Mr. and Mrs. Elliot," "The Three-Day Blow," and "Soldier's Home." But while irony is invariably an ingredient in his stories, a larger number of them depend primarily upon one or more of Hemingway's three epistemologic formulas: textual perplexity, lexical riddle, and extratextual reversal.

Textual perplexity is best seen in the Nick Adams on-the-road stories. Whether Nick eats a meal at the hobo camp of "The Battler," sits in Henry's lunchroom and stands in Ole's bedroom of "The Killers," or feels the tremors of huge Alice's laughter and tears on the train-station bench in "The Light of the World," Hemingway puts him into situations abuzz with perplexity. These stories, among which "Sepi Jingan" might be numbered, repeatedly poke a character into circumstances ripe for his initiation. But the circumstances so overwhelm him with mixed signals that he is struck speechless or regresses to some comforting nostrum that ill deals with the confusions at hand. The perplexing behavior of the boxers in all three stories—Ad, Ole, and Stan or Steve Ketchel—have Hemingway upping the ante with each story. Ad's change from friend to foe over the matter of getting his hands on Nick's knife gives Nick a sudden introduction to the world of a "crazy," a punchy pug. But Ad's reversal is small stuff compared to the dizzying information Bugs tells about Ad's background and relationship with his sister/wife/manager. The incongruity of Bugs's maternal protection of Ad, requiring as it does the thump of his blackjack, does little to allay Nick's perplexity. Similarly the often-remarked mismatchings in "The Killer" find Hemingway at his formula, creating discrepancies between lunchroom name and operator, boardinghouse owner and manager, clock hands and actual time, ordered plates and taken plates. But the story's major discrepancy hinges upon Nick's perplexity at discovering that Ole Anderson, a man who has made his living as a fighter, will simply no longer fight.

"Light of the World" is the extreme version of textual perplexity. Not only is there perplexity over which whore Steve Ketchel loved, over which Ketchel the women debate, over which "god" their worship parodies, over which light the story refers to (the whores' red, the cook's white, or believers' religious). But Hemingway also laces the story with the perplexities that accrue to his use of an extensive assortment of slang terms: dinge, mossback, C and M, stagged, interfere, sixty-nine, and the like.4

To this short list of textual-perplexity stories I would add "On the Quai at Smyrna," "Out of Season," "A Pursuit Race," "An Alpine Idyll," "Homage to Switzerland," "Indian Camp," "Ten Indians," "Now I Lay me," "A Way You'll Never Be," and "A Clean Well-Lighted Place." In all of these stories Hemingway confounds readers and seems resolved to puzzle them with riddles. Do the textual confusions in the dramatic monologue of "Quai" reflect a crazed or coherent narrator and point of view? Do the marital discord, town indifference, or dersision toward Peduzzi and the confusion over "daughter" and "doctor" in "Season" have any bearing on some action Peduzzi may take?5 Are the drug-induced lunacies about wolf, horses, eagles, and sheets by "Sliding Billy," the bicycle racer in "Pursuit," the stuff of synecdoche or of insignificant cameo? Are the innkeeper's and sexton's accounts of the peasant's treatment of his wife in "Idyll" matter for morality or an alpine-high tall tale played on outsiders? Do the geographical dislocations in "Homage" present three different men or only one?6 Does the silence between Uncle George and the Indian husband of "Camp" expose the pair as gratuitous props or reveal an intimate relationship between them, the Indian woman, and the newborn infant?7 Do the textual innuendoes between the Garners and the verbal evasions of Nick's father in "Ten Indians" mean to suggest that the father failed to spend a national holiday with his son because he was sexually interested in that tenth Indian? Do the repetitions and rememberings of the no-longer insomniac of "Lay Me" portray a recovered or a still psychically scarred battle victim, one whose equation of his war-wounding and the front-yard burnings of his youth explains his fear of marriage? In "Never Be" has the mentally recuperative Nick—who flips from reconstructing battlefield logistics to stream-of-consciousness maunderings to grasshopper lecturing— actually been ordered to visit the front lines to boost troop morale?8 And do the confusions of attributing dialogue to different waiters in "Well-Lighted Place" signal that we misread the story if we view it nihilistically, decoyed by its parodic nada prayers to miss its minimal but positive philosophic message?

My condensations of the above textual-perplexity stories will understandably lead some readers to conclude that I deal from an old deck of ambiguities. But I mean for the shorthand condensations to suggest that the stories' perplexities are more extensive than I can begin to indicate here. Indeed, as the criticism on the stories attests, imbedded in them are mystifications that mislead readers into misreadings, riddles that require readers to unravel what they read. And by creating such perplexity-encoded stories, Hemingway teases engaged readers into replicating the process that he—as Dutch dolly, Pawnee Bill, and other assigned or self-assigned monikers—went through to decipher the perplexities that confronted him.

Hemingway's second epistemologic formula is the lexical riddle, visible in stories like "Hills Like White Elephants," "The Sea Change," and "A Simple Enquiry." These pivot upon a lexical crux, the unarticulated or ambiguous words abortion, lesbian, and corrupt. Hemingway's strategy here is to have readers so stew over the missing or ambiguous term that once they discover it or its meaning, they will feel they have solved the story and can mosey on along to the next one. But we long ago learned that the mystery of Jig's operation, the lexical riddle in "Hills," is a red herring; it distracts us from the significant decisions of whether to sympathize with Jig and scorn her insistent American man or to sympathize with him and feel disgust for her stubbornness and sarcasm.[9] Similarly, upon discovering that the "girl" of "The Sea Change" is lesbian, we may understand Phil's wrath and feel the story solved. But tucked beneath the lexical riddle is, on one hand, Hemingway's sensitively sympathetic portrayal of a young woman who has just discovered her lesbianism and who is quite uncertain of how it will affect her future, and, on the other, his scornful portrayal of Phil's incivility toward her and his defensive bluster and bravado before the barman.[10] Once we realize that the major who questions his orderly in "A Simple Enquiry" does so to determine whether the orderly is a homosexual, it is an easy step to reconstruct the evidence to prove the major a homosexual too. But lexical riddles extend beyond just the word "corrupt" and invite a semiotic analysis to unravel the story's complexities.[11]

To this short list of lexical-riddle stories add "Big Two-Hearted River," "In Another Country," "Cat in the Rain," "Wine of Wyoming," "God Rest You Merry, Gentlemen," "A Day's Wait," "Today is Friday," and "A Canary for One," which I take up with in reverse order. The lexical riddles in the last two are pushovers. The nearly missing word in "Canary" is "divorce," in "Friday" the name of the man who "was pretty good in there today." "Gentlemen" and "Day's Wait" hinge on two boys' lexical mistakes, the older boy's notion that castration of his penis will cure his "awful lust," the younger's that temperatures are registered only in centigrade. In "Wine" the thin lexical riddle is a slogan between which and Prohibition lies the explanation for the Fontans' deep disillusionment: that America is the "home of the free." And underlying the behavior of the American wife in "Cat" is the easy-to-come-by lexical crux, "maternal instincts": her wish for the cat in the rain is a substitute for the domestic maternity she longs for.

A more complex lexical riddle is at work in "In Another Country," for the narrator is preoccupied with his differences from "hawks," who scorn his medals because he has not been combat wounded, and a martinet major, who scorns his conversation because he fails to speak grammatically. At the core of his preoccupation, however, is his puzzlement over the concept of bravery. He is certain that the bravery of the hawks is meritorious, for it is duly recognized with medals. But he also admires the major's bravery in continuing with the nonsensical therapy and with living on in the face of his young wife's sudden death. But whether the major himself signifies bravery is problematic; he may as readily signify a resentful survivor who displays peevishness and the pathos of failing to act on his belief of therapeutic futility. And the narrator's fixation on this major as the centerpiece of a tale of recuperation may signify the narrator's retrospective scorn for an allegedly brave man. As well may it signify the narrator's self-pitying insinuation of why he has failed to become brave: a poor role model in the authoritarian major.

Perhaps the best of the lexical-riddle stories is "Big Two-Hearted River," pivoting as its psychological ramifications do on two words, "khaki" and "tragic." When the narrator informs us that Nick tucks his sandwiches into a khaki, not a mufti, shirtpocket, he suddenly opens a seam in the controlled discipline of Nick's fishing trip, letting up peep through the curtain just behind the story and glimpse the backstage scene of war—where khaki was not de rigueur until World War I—and the image of Nick in military uniform. And when Nick oddly regards fishing the swamp "tragic," a word too heavy for an ordinary fisherman's outing, then it is all but certain that Nick's term signals some deep fear of experience. He dreads that some seemingly minor event—such as a snagged line or a hooked trout tangled in roots or grass—will trigger a loss of control that will so shatter his fragile, recuperating psyche as to allow the experience to tragically unman him.[12]

Hemingway's third epistemologic formula is extratextual reversal, most visible in "Fifty Grand," "After the Storm," and "My Old Man." In these stories Hemingway sets into action a character whose occupation or easily labeled role calls up cultural expectations of stereotypical behavior, ones Hemingway partly honors (to keep the stereotype intact) but primarily subverts (to violate the typecasting label and to render freshly the individual behind the stereotype). And by invoking those stereotyped labels Hemingway also welcomes the moral prejudgments that conventionally accompany them so as to maneuver his textual materials and subvert those judgments. (These techniques are "extratextual" because they rely upon mental predispositions, cultural codes, and ideologies that readers bring to a text before they even begin to read it.)[13] In "Fifty Grand," for instance, Hemingway honors stereotypical expectations in characterizing his boxer: Jack Brennan is a hard-training, tough-talking champ who shows his fighting instincts when he realizes he's been set up to win a fixed fight that he knows he should lose. But onto the label of "tough boxer" Hemingway attaches traits not common to the label: tight-fisted with his money, Jack is a worried family man, moody and brooding, unliked by those he works with, save the story's narrator. And Jack is a thinker, rapidly calculating whether to allow the foul punch that will let him win his last fight but cause him to forfeit the money he stands to gain by losing.[14] At story's end Hemingway pinpoints the extratextual reversal by invoking a stock reaction to Jack's conduct: moral contempt for returning the low blow that secures his bet against himself. Yet this reaction overlooks Hemingway's craft in weaving the fabric of the story to reverse that judgment and find Jack morally commendable. His foul, that is, restores professional integrity to the sport he has given his best years to, ensures that a rigged fight will be spoiled, and sees that financial justice is done to his betrayers.

"After the Storm" seems to portray little more than a waterfront tough. The unnamed first-person narrator is a barroom brawler, briber, and amoral opportunist insensitive to human calamity. He registers greed, not compassion, toward the woman trapped and dead inside a sunken liner, for he remarks only her floating hair and the rings on one of her hands. But in the last segment of the story Hemingway subverts the stereotype. His narrator uses one-fourth of the story's length in an unexpected display of imagination, compassion, and empathy for the liner's captain, a man who must have been taken completely by surprise by the liner's sudden grounding and sinking in quicksand.[15] As in these two stories, in "My Old Man" Hemingway invites us to view his jockey stereotypically: a weight-conscious, horse racing addict who so thrives on the shady world of the gambling racetrack that he thinks nothing of raising his son in its midst. And Hemingway invites us also to label the jockey a crook, for his son overhears two disgruntled bettors slur his father as one. But as I have explained elsewhere, the text fails to support such a label and challenges us to read over the son's shoulder. By doing so we must reverse our judgment and recognize his jockey father as a man of integrity, an ethical maverick who has set out to dismantle the fixed racing world by buying and riding his own mount, thereby guaranteeing the uncertainty of a race's outcome.[16]

To this short list of textual-reversal stories I would add "The Revolutionist," "The Undefeated," "Old Man at the Bridge," and "The Short
Happy Life of Francis Macomber." In the first of these the discrepancy
between the story's title, which automatically evokes the stereotype of a
credo-spouting firebrand, and its character—a shy, naive, art and nature
lover—makes for a pure but unsuccessful example of this formula. Not so
with the other three stories. "The Undefeated" appears to focus on the
ineptitude of a has-been torero, best illustrated by his Chaplinesque
efforts to kill his first bull, his sword springing up and bending from
repeated attempts to dispatch the bull. But it is the animal's anatomy that
thwarts Manuel's otherwise superb faena. The bull's nearly impenetrable
hump deprives Manuel of the finish that would reestablish him as a torero
of exceptional artistry. Gored, his act of sitting upright on the operating
table when his friend Zurito teasingly threatens to cut off his pigtail asks
us to disdain him as pathetically vainglorious. But it also asks us to
reverse our verdict, to respect him as justifiably proud of his professional
standards and conduct, as someone who, even when seriously gored,
will jeopardize his recovery rather than permit a slight against his
professionalism. In "Old Man at the Bridge" an aged man will retreat no
farther toward Barcelona to escape the fascist army's offensive. Hemingway lets us identify the man as a pathetic quitter who warrants our scorn
for failing to take heart on this story's day of all days, Easter Sunday. But
extratextual reversal calls for a view of him as a man of dignity, philosophically rejecting a life bereft of others to care for. Similarly the story
welcomes identification of its other character, the reconnaisance officer.
He talks with the old man but abandons him sitting in the dust, nudging
us to brand him an inhumane professional, unwilling to neglect duty long
enough to help this aged brother. But a reversed reading finds him a
humane benefactor who displays consummate respect: he checks the
vulgar impulse to meddle in the old man's rendezvous with death.

In perhaps Hemingway's most label-laden story, "The Short Happy
Life of Francis Macomber," extratextual reversal seems strongly at work,
even though Hemingway may have intended otherwise.[17] As the one-
hundred-plus items of criticism and scholarship on the story testify, the
problem of fitting accurate labels to the story's trio, especially its alleged
bitch, is most vexing.[18] Not the least of the problems is construing Margot
Macomber's act of adultery. Immoral and sinful by matrimonial and
religious precepts, it is nevertheless *the* provocative action that propels
Francis's behavior from "boyhood" to "manhood" during the events of
the single day that constitutes his short, happy life. And both because her
adultery takes that impelling position in the sequence of Francis's alleged

maturation and because, as Wilson admits, "What's in [Margot's] heart God knows," her adultery can be regarded as morally commendable. After all, "in her heart" she may have committed the act with the design in mind that it would result as it did, triggering Francis's anger and the more assertive behavior that he evinces even before the activity which completes his transformation, the buffalo hunt.

But the success of "Short Happy Life" is not solely attributable to Hemingway's use of extratextual reversal. The story also relies on a variant of textual perplexity. Rather than perplex his readers with the verbal confusions of his earlier stories, here Hemingway does it by skillfully disjointing the story's narrative sequence with flashbacks and its point of view with shifts among the characters' perspectives (excepting, of course, Margot's). Impeding a reader's full grasp of the story's ethical issues, Hemingway once again underscores the epistemologic problems in a story. He uses similar strategies in other stories with overlapping formulas, as in, for example, "The Snows of Kilimanjaro" (with its flashbacks and dream flashforward) and "A Natural History of the Dead" (with its juxtaposition of mock essay and superb vignette). But the story that best shows Hemingway using all three epistemological formulas is his long-neglected masterpiece, "The Mother of a Queen."

By constructing a dramatic monologue in "The Mother of a Queen," Hemingway imbeds textual perplexity in the discourse of the story's narrator, Roger. Given his intention to denigrate Paco's character, Roger makes himself vulnerable to the charge of unreliability, sowing skepticism in the reader toward his facts and impressions. For instance, was Paco responsible for having so poorly packed the six new fighting suits he bought in Spain that four were ruined by seawater? Or does the fault lie with someone else? Is Paco a profligate who freely spends money when women are around so as to fool them and others into thinking him a man? And is such behavior without effect on those who know much about him? Likewise, does Paco give his desperate townsman fifty pesos, posing as benefactor, as "the big, generous matador with a fellow townsman?"[19] Or is this, too, Roger's version, his impression? Roger's unreliable textual authority is clearest in his boasting that he is better than Paco in everything. While it may be true that Roger is a better driver of Paco's car than Paco is, surely his "everything" cannot include bullfighting. Such an overgeneralization must give a reader pause, may even cause a reader to wonder if it is fact that Paco was unable even to read and write.

Another textual perplexity dwells in Roger's preoccupation with business, a word that recurs frequently in the four-page story. While Roger faults Paco for not taking care of the business of burying his mother in a permanent plot and for not managing his cash box and paying his debts, there is question of just what kind of business manager Roger is. Paco instructs him to get from the cash box fifty pesos and to give them to the townsman, indicating that Roger has the key to the box. But what kind of a business manager can Roger be if he has the key and access to the over 600 pesos he claims Paco owes him? Just what is his business with Paco if he refuses to take what's rightfully his, having paid bills on Paco's house out of his own pocket while Paco was on his trip to Spain? Moreover, what is Roger's business in telling this small tale of character assassination? His narrative indicates that the event he tells of happened at least two years before his telling: after he left Paco, he remarks that he had not spoken to Paco "until this year." But Roger's excessive detail and obsessive need to so totally disparage Paco reveals his biographical snippet to be reaction formation. His business, that is, is to conceal his attraction to Paco and, thereby, to deny his own latent homosexuality. The durability of his grudge against Paco and the heat with which he tells it to his listener indicate the feelings of a rejected would-be lover who still winces from memory of his failure to win the affection of a desired object. Were there no such "sexual" injury, Roger could tell the story quite briefly in general details.

Roger's identity as latent homosexual opens the door on the lexical riddles in the story. His use of "queen" and "sweetheart" to label Paco a homosexual, of course, poses problems for readers unfamiliar with the slang terms, for little in the story shows Paco's behavior as exclusively homosexual. Nevertheless, Roger's derisive indictment of Paco appears to have its root in Paco's sexual deviation, which partly explains why Roger expresses such hostility toward Paco. But that hostility points as well to the other lexical riddle in the story, "mother." Given Roger's attention to Paco's disrespect for his dead mother, the mother of the story's title seems to refer to Paco's mother. But it refers equally to Roger, whose behavior throughout the story resembles some angry and domineering mother.[20] He nags Paco about sending the money to give his mother a permanent burial. Much as though Paco's inaction disrespects Roger more than Paco's mother, Roger gets upset when Paco fails to see the matter and berates him, asking Paco to identify the kind of blood he has, indignantly declaring that he wishes Paco not to speak to him. He keeps close count of Paco's finances, tallying up Paco's earnings, as some grasping mother might ride herd over a child's savings account. And Roger, like a stay-at-home mother, whines that while Paco was off "playing" in Spain, she stayed home and paid the house bills, "'and you didn't send any money while you were gone and I paid over six hundred pesos in my own money and now I need it and you can pay me.'" Paco's gravest wrong in fussbudget Roger's eyes may be his neglect of those seven new fighting suits he had made in Spain. So poorly had he packed them that on the return trip saltwater ruined four of them. Naughty boy, to be so careless of his clothing! That Roger equates himself with mothers is revealed in his insult to Paco, allegedly telling him to his face in the presence of others, that he never had a mother—according to Roger the most insulting thing to tell another Spaniard. By reproaching a wayward male who neglects to properly respect a mother's values, Roger reveals that his outrage at Paco is fueled by Paco's having treated him as an unvalued mother.[21]

Paco's violation of Mother Roger's values leads to the story's dominant epistemologic formula, extratextual reversal. By making Paco a matador, Hemingway assigns him a most flagrantly labeled role, one that in his canon calls up predictable cultural expectations of stereotyped behavior: valor artist, man who lives his life all the way up, emblem of a culture's deepest traditions, exemplar of machismo, and so on. But none of this matador's actions or statements bear upon that conventional role. Anathema to it, Paco exhibits neither the pride nor domination that a story about a bullfighter would seem to call for; nor does the story highlight Paco in the ring where his abilities might radiate forth, as do Manuel's in "The Undefeated." By adding to the mixed signal of an unprepossessing matador the label of homosexual, Hemingway creates a character with a thoroughly mixed pair of roles, a fundamental clashing of stereotypical responses. We may incline to see Paco conforming to a homosexual stereotype because of Roger's coloring of the facts and impressions he gives. But Paco's behavior and statements are not those that exclusively characterize him as a stereotypically limp-wristed, speech-affected gay— not, say, the Robert Prentiss of *The Sun Also Rises*. Indeed, when Roger offers to take care of the payment of Paco's mother's grave after Paco had received a second notice, Paco commands Roger to stay out of his business, that it is his business and that he will take care of it. And when Johnny-one-note Roger harps again on Paco's lack of filial respect, Paco emphasizes that he is quite happy with what has become of his mother, that Roger is incapable of understanding his happiness. A fundamental difference of values, it seems clear.

At the end of the story Paco shows goodwill toward Roger, offering his hand in friendship and stating that he has learned from people of Roger's bad-mouthing him, of "unjust things" Roger spreads. To Roger, of course, such civility is unheard of and must reveal Paco's thorough perversion. For that statement and Paco's failure to respond manfully to Roger's insult—that Paco never had a mother—are proof in Roger's mind that Paco is a queer: "There's a queen for you. You can't touch them. Nothing, nothing can touch them. They spend money on themselves or for vanity, but they never pay. Try to get one to pay."

The oddity of Roger's conclusions surely remark discrepancies in his labeling Paco a queen. After all, the resistance to being "touched," the motives for spending money, as well as the failure to pay a debt—these have little to do with being a homosexual. While Roger believes that Paco's behavior issues from his identity as a homosexual, his belief hides behind bluster, as indicated by his reccurrent question about the kind of blood that flows in someone like Paco. Roger, of course, can ask such a question, one that finds Paco an epistemologic puzzle. But rather than accept the uncertainty and complexity of Paco's identity, he takes shelter in cheap labels.

Undergirding Roger's willful need to freeze Paco's character in a stereotype are three labels by which Roger invokes moral censure of Paco, labels that further show Hemingway's use of extratextual reversal: maternal reverence, financial responsibility, and manly pride. Roger gets exercised over Paco's failure to pay the fee necessary to bury his mother permanently. And when Paco's failure results in the mother getting dumped into the common boneheap, Roger is morally outraged. Indeed, this is morally reprehensible, an act of gigantic filial disrespect. Or so it is if one is convention-bound and honors community and cultural norms. But if Paco is a homosexual, his deviation from sexual norms should measure other behaviors as well. Hemingway's formula challenges readers to understand Paco when he tells Roger of his happiness over his mother's being turned out of her private grave, declaring that she is dearer to him now that her body has been put in a "public boneyard." He was saddened by thoughts of her being buried in a single place: "'Now she is all about me in the air, like the birds and the flowers. Now she will always be with me.'" Paco's statements, echoing Wordworth's Lucy poem, suggest that his maternal reverence outstrips conventional and routine forms of it, and suggest that he is a pantheist, someone with truly a different "kind of blood" in him than that which sloshes through Roger's veins. Paco seems to know his "business" in this matter, even though it differs significantly from the clichéd views of busybody Roger.

Paco also views money and financial responsibility differently than Roger. To Roger a man must pay debts, must not spend money around women as a pretense of manliness, and must not play the bigshot with down-and-out townsmen. But Paco heeds not these cultural norms. He has his reasons for not paying the debts that Roger alleges Paco owes him. But most, Roger fails to view Paco's act of doling out fifty pesos to a townsman as anything other than a strutting, self-aggrandizing gesture. Roger assigns to Paco the egoistic motive that would actuate Roger, little understanding that Paco's act arguably has a genuine Samaritan impulse within it. Indeed, it is not just that the "paesano" needs money, but that he needs it to return home and attend his very ill mother. Significantly, then, to Paco's fraternal feelings are wed his filial feelings for a fellow man whose "distress" centers on regard for his mother.

Finally, Roger is justifiably perplexed by Paco's failure to carry himself with sufficient manly pride to defend his honor when assailed by an antagonistic enemy. When Roger insults Paco, Roger expects at least some fight or swapping of insults. Again, Roger is the moral and behavioral norm, the man who expects conventional behavior, predictable reaction. But unlike the grudge-carrying Roger, Paco is a pacifist, a man of equable civility and politeness, despite Roger's goading and slanderous remarks. And while Roger would have us share his moral censure of Paco for such "womanishness," the story invites a moral reversal that finds favor in Paco's behavior, standards, and ethic—if not in his courage to be open about his homosexuality, as well.

Roger's story of Paco is intensely personal. But it is also representative, for it symbolizes the human tendency to shrink a complex person into a tidy term, to shortchange the diversity of what a person *does* in favor of labeling what a person *is*—in the eyes of the labeler. Paco transcends the label of what he is in Roger's eyes—a queen—partly because of the epistemologic formulas upon which the story is structured. They lead a reader to ask the searching questions that any epistemologic philosopher would ask of Roger's story: how do we know what we know, and how do we know that what we know is true? When we ask those questions of other Hemingway characters and stories, we find that that they too transcend their assigned labels, are truly knowable as complex and contradictory entities that tenaciously resist quick and easy identification. They resemble their author, who fought early and late against labelers, be they his mother, whose female epithet so angered him, or his early biographical critics, whose reductionist theories bewildered and vexed him.[22]

To call Hemingway a formula writer may offend his enthusiasts, agreeing, as it seems to, with Faulkner's conclusion: "He learned early in life a method by which he could do his work, he has never varied from that method, it suited him well, he handled it well."[23] But to call an author a formula writer need not consign him to the ranks of potboiler, harlequin-romance, and pulp-fiction hacks. All writers rely upon formulas that, like cooks' recipes, enable them to turn out a piece of work with some expedition and to control the quality of the product. Foolish would be writers who, discovering a formula that allows expression of their vision, promptly discard it against the time a fresh formula or another original inspiration arrived. That Hemingway came up with three formulas, overlapped them, added them to his already strong sense of irony, and crafted them with an acclaimed and imitated style bespeaks a higher level of formula writing than customarily accrues to the epithet. And surely the strong resemblance among his stories' formulas runs deeper than pre-occupations with frequent themes or techniques: with code heroes and a pared-down style, with machismo and understatement, with His-panic values and polysyndeton, with tutor-tyro characters and true sen-tences.

To be attuned to the epistemologic formulas in Hemingway's short fiction may not help readers either better recognize its synecdochic and symbolic resonance or better cleave to the generalizing particulars that elevate seemingly insignificant matters into enlarged philosophic issues aesthetically clothed. But it may help readers avoid mistreating a story as Kenneth Lynn does "The Sea Change." In it, he writes, "a tale largely made up of cutting exchanges in a Paris cafe between a man and a woman who are breaking up because the woman has taken another woman as her lover, the dialogue has some of the pace and desperate energy of the talk in 'Hills Like White Elephants,' but the setting is incomparably less memorable."[24] Such a reading blithely sails past the epistemologic prob-lem of how people, in a common public setting with at least one onlooker, deal with new information. The young woman's problem is how to conduct herself with her present sexual partner when she has just discovered something radically unsettling and exciting about herself, when she has just acquired new knowledge of her sexual identity and realizes that it requires forsaking one relationship and set of values for another. The man's problem is equally grave, for he is unable to come to terms with such knowledge of his sexual partner, tries to browbeat her with morally censorious terms, releases her sarcastically, and then swag-gers before the barman, desperately trying to save face by ironically claiming, "'You see in me quite a different man.'"

But Lynn's dismissal of the story is certainly forgivable. After all, all readers are lucky if they misread only a couple of handfuls of Heming-way's stories, those puzzles that seem readily solvable, those icebergs whose small peaks point one direction, whose enormous bases point quite another. And whether puzzle or iceberg, readers are hindered both by what Hemingway admittedly omitted and by the epistemologic smokescreen within which, without admitting it, he shrouded artful stories.

Nada and the Clean, Well-Lighted Place: The Unity of Hemingway's Short Fiction

Steven K. Hoffman

●

One of his most frequently discussed tales, "A Clean, Well-Lighted Place" is justly regarded as one of the stylistic masterpieces of Ernest Hemingway's distinguished career in short fiction. Not only does it represent Hemingway at his understated, laconic best, but, according to Carlos Baker, "It shows once again that remarkable union of the naturalistic and the symbolic which is possibly his central triumph in the realm of practical aesthetics."[1] In a mere five pages, almost entirely in dialogue and interior monologue, the tale renders a complex series of interactions between three characters in a Spanish café just prior to and immediately after closing: a stoic old waiter, a brash young waiter, and a wealthy but suicidal old man given to excessive drink.

Aside from its well-documented stylistic achievement, what has drawn the most critical attention is Hemingway's detailed consideration of the concept of *nada*. Although the old waiter is the only one to articulate the fact, all three figures actually confront nothingness in the course of the tale. This is no minor absence in their lives. Especially "for the old waiter," Carlos Baker notes, "the word *nothing* (or *nada*) contains huge actuality. The great skill in the story is the development, through the most carefully controlled understatement, of the young waiter's mere *nothing* into the old waiter's Something—a Something called Nothing which is so huge, terrible, overbearing, inevitable and omnipresent that once experienced, it can never be forgotten."[2] Because the terrifying "Something called Nothing" looms so very large, and since "A Clean, Well-Lighted Place" appeared in a 1933 collection in which even "winners" take "nothing," critics have generally come to see the piece as a nihilistic low point in Hemingway's career, a moment of profound despair both for the characters and the author.[3]

If this standard position does have a certain validity, it also tends to overlook two crucial points about the story. First is its relation to the rest of Hemingway's highly unified short story canon. In the same way that two of the three characters in "A Clean, Well-Lighted Place" meet *nada* without voicing the fact, all of the major short story characters also experience it in one of its multiple guises. Thus "A Clean, Well-Lighted Place," a rather late story written in 1933, is something of a summary statement on this recurrent theme; the tale brings to direct expression the central crisis of those that precede it—including the most celebrated of the Nick Adams stories—and looks forward to its resolution in the master-pieces that come later, "The Short Happy Life of Francis Macomber" (1936) and "The Snows of Kilimanjaro" (1936).

Second, because *nada* appears to dominate "A Clean, Well-Lighted Place," it has been easy to miss the fact that the story is not about *nada* per se but the various available human responses to it.[4] As a literary artist, Hemingway was generally less concerned with speculative metaphysics than with modes of practical conduct within certain a priori conditions. The ways in which the character triad in "A Clean, Well-Lighted Place" respond to *nada* summarize the character responses throughout the canon. The fact that only one, the old waiter, directly voices his experience and manages to deal successfully with nothingness is also indicative of a general trend. Those few Hemingway characters who continue to function even at the razor's edge do so in the manner of this heroic figure—by establishing for themselves a clean, well-lighted place from which to withstand the enveloping darkness. For these reasons, "A Clean, Well-Lighted Place" must be termed the thematic as well as the stylistic climax of Hemingway's career in short fiction.

Although the difficulty of attributing certain individual statements in the tale creates some ambiguity on the subject, it is clear that the young waiter's use of the term *nada* to convey a personal lack of a definable commodity (*no thing*) is much too narrowly conceived. In his crucial meditation at the end, the old waiter makes it quite clear that *nada* is not an individual state but one with grave universal implications: "It was a nothing that he knew too well. It was *all* a nothing and a man was nothing too" [my italics].[5] According to William Barrett, the *nada*-shadowed realm of "A Clean, Well-Lighted Place" is no less than a microcosm of the existential universe as defined by Martin Heidegger and the existentialist philosophers who came before and after him, principally Kierkegaard and Sartre.[6] Barrett's position finds internal support in the old waiter's celebrated parody prayer: "Our nada who art in nada, nada be thy name thy kingdom nada thy will be nada in nada as it is in nada. Give us this nada our daily nada and nada us our nada as we nada our nadas and nada us not into nada but deliver us from nada; pues nada" (383). The character's deft substitution of the word *nada* for all the key nouns (entities) and verbs (actions) in the Paternoster suggests the concept's truly metaphysical stature. Obviously, *nada* is to connote a series of significant absences: the lack of a viable transcendent source of power and authority; a correlative lack of external physical or spiritual sustenance; the total lack of moral justification for action (in the broadest perspective, the essential meaninglessness of *any* action); and finally, the impossibility of deliverance from this situation.7

The impact of *nada*, however, extends beyond its theological implications. Rather, in the Heideggerian sense ("das Nicht"), it is an umbrella term that subsumes all of the irrational, unforseeable, existential forces that tend to infringe upon the human self, to make a "nothing." It is the absolute power of chance and circumstance to negate individual free will and the entropic tendency toward ontological disorder that perpetually looms over man's tenuous personal sense of order. But the most fearsome face of *nada*, and clear proof of man's radical contingency, is death—present here in the old man's wife's death and his own attempted suicide. Understandably, the old waiter's emotional response to this composite threat is mixed. It "was not fear or dread" (383), which would imply a specific object to be feared, but a pervasive uneasiness, an existential anxiety that, according to Heidegger, arises when one becomes fully aware of the precarious status of his very being.8

That the shadow of *nada* looms behind much of Hemingway's fiction has not gone entirely unnoticed. Nathan Scott's conclusions on this issue serve as a useful summary of critical opinion: "Now it is blackness beyond a clean, well-lighted place—this 'nothing full of nothing' that betrays 'confidence'; that murders sleep, that makes the having of plenty of money a fact of no consequence at all—it is this blackness, ten times black, that constitutes the basic metaphysical situation in Hemingway's fiction and that makes the human enterprise something very much like huddling about a campfire beyond which looms the unchartable wilderness, the great Nada."9 The problem with this position is that it tends to locate *nada* somewhere outside of the action, never directly operative within it. It is, to William Barrett, "the presence that had circulated, *unnamed* and *unconfronted*, throughout much of [Hemingway's] earlier writing" [my italics].10

The clearest indication of *nada*'s direct presence in the short stories is to be found in the characters' frequent brushes with death, notably the characteristic modern forms of unexpected, unmerited, and very often mechanical death that both Frederick J. Hoffman and R. P. Warren consider so crucial in Hemingway.11 Naturally, these instances are the climactic moments in some of the best known tales: the interchapters from *In Our Times*, "Indian Camp," "The Killers," "The Capital of the World," and "The Snows of Kilimanjaro." But death or the imminent threat of death need not be literally present to signal an encounter with *nada*. What Philip Young and others have called Nick Adams's "initiation" to life's trials is actually his initiation to *nada*.[12] In "The End of Something" and "The Three Day Blow" Nick must cope with the precariousness of love in a precarious universe; in "The Battler," with the world's underlying irrationality and potential for violence; in "Cross-Country Snow," with the power of external circumstance to circumscribe individual initiative. In several important stories involving the period in Nick's chronology after the critical "wound," *nada*, as the ultimate unmanageability of life, appears as a concrete image. In "Big Two-Hearted River" it is both the burnt-out countryside and the forbidding swamp; in "Now I Lay Me," the night; in "A Way You'll Never Be," a "long yellow house" (evidently the site of the wound).

Other imagistic references to *nada* appear in the non–Nick Adams tales. In "The Undefeated" it is the bull, a particularly apt concrete manifestation of active malevolence in the universe, also suggested by the lion and buffalo in "The Short Happy Life of Francis Macomber." These particular images, however, are potentially misleading because *nada* does not usually appear so actively and personally combative. An example to the contrary may be found in "The Gambler, the Nun, and the Radio" where *nada* is the distinctly impersonal and paralyzing banality of life in an isolated hospital, as well as the constant "risk" of a gambler's uncertain profession. Regardless of its specific incarnation, *nada* is always a dark presence which upsets individual equilibrium and threatens to overwhelm the self. And, as Jackson Benson has pointed out, "A threat to selfhood is the ultimate horror that the irrational forces of the world can accomplish."[13] In that each story in the canon turns on the way in which particular characters respond to the inevitable confrontation with *nada*, the nature of that response is particularly important. The only effective way to approach the Void is to develop a very special mode of being, the concrete manifestation of which is the clean, well-lighted place.

Again, it is the old waiter who speaks most directly of the need for a physical bastion against the all-encompassing night: "It is the light of course but it is necessary that the place be clean and pleasant. You do not want music. Certainly you do not want music. Nor can you stand before a bar with dignity" (382). In direct contrast to the dirty, noisy *bodega* to which he repairs after closing and all the "bad" places that appear in Hemingway's fiction, the pleasant café at which the old waiter works possesses all of these essential attributes: light, cleanness, and the opportunity for some form of dignity. Perhaps the most direct antithesis of this legitimate clean, well-lighted place is not even in this particular story but in one of its companion pieces in *Winner Take Nothing,* the infernal bar in "The Light of the World" (1933). Here, light does little more than illuminate the absence of the other qualities, the lack of which moves one of the characters to ask pointedly, "'What the hell kind of place is this?'" (385). Thus, in an inversion of the typical procedure in Hemingway, Nick and his companion are impelled outside where it is "good and dark" (385).

Evidently, well-lighted places in Hemingway do not always meet the other requirements of the clean, well-lighted place. Moreover, since the café in "A Clean, Well-Lighted Place" must eventually close, even the legitimate haven has distinct limitations. These facts should be enough to alert us to the possibility that tangible physical location is not sufficient to combat the darkness. The clean, well-lighted place is not actually a "place" at all; rather, it is a metaphor for an attitude toward the self and its existential context, a psychological perspective which, like the café itself with its fabricated conveniences and electric light, is man-made, artificial. The "cleanliness" of the metaphor connotes a personal sense of order, however artificial and temporary, carved out within the larger chaos of the universe, a firm hold on the self with which one can meet any contingency. By "light" Hemingway refers to a special kind of vision, the clear-sightedness and absolute lack of illusion necessary to look into the darkness and thereby come to grips with the *nada* which is everywhere. At the same time, vision must also be directed at the self so as to assure *its* cleanness. With cleanness and light, then, physical locale is irrelevant. Whoever manages to internalize these qualities carries the clean, well-lighted place with him, even into the very teeth of the darkness. The degree to which the Hemingway character can develop and maintain this perspective determines his success (or lack thereof) in dealing with the Void.

The man who does achieve the clean, well-lighted place is truly an existential hero, both in the Kierkegaardian and Heideggerian senses of the term. In the former he is content to live with his angst and, because there is no other choice, content to be in doubt about ultimate causes. Nevertheless, he is able to meet the varied and often threatening circumstances of day-to-day living, secure in the knowledge that he will always "become" and never "be." In the latter he can face the unpleasant realities of his own being and the situation into which he has been "thrown" and can accept with composure the inevitability of his death. In both instances he is an "authentic" man.[14]

Two of the main characters in "A Clean, Well-Lighted Place," as well as a host of analogous figures in other tales, fail to develop this attitude either for lack of "light" (the young waiter) or for lack of "cleanness" (the old man). As is evidenced by his inability to grasp the full impact of his partner's use of the word *nothing*, the egotistic young waiter has not even grasped the fact of *nada*—has not *seen* clearly—and therefore can hardly deal with it. "To him," comments Joseph Gabriel, "*nada* can only signify a personal physical privation. *Nothing* refers simply to the absence of those objects capable of providing material satisfaction. And by extension he applies the term to all behavior which does not grant the sufficiency of things."[15] Unable to see that the old man's wealth is a woefully inadequate bulwark against the Void, he is, in his ignorance, contemptuous both of the man and his predicament. Perhaps as a direct outgrowth of this lack of light, the young waiter also violates the principle of cleanness by sloppily pouring his customer's desperately needed brandy over the sides of the glass. Thus, he easily loses himself in a fool's paradise of blindness and illusion. Still young, secure in his job, and, as he boasts, "'I'm not lonely. I have a wife waiting in bed for me,'" (380), he is "all confidence": as such, a particularly patent example to the old waiter of those who "lived in it [*nada*] and never felt it" (383).

Yet, in the course of the story, even this naif has an unsettling glimpse of the fundamental uncertainty of existence and its direct impact on his own situation. What else can account for his sharply defensive reaction to the old waiter's joke? [Old Waiter]: "'And you? You have no fear of going home before your usual hour?'" [Young Waiter]: "'Are you trying to insult me?'" [Old Waiter]: "'No, hombre, only to make a joke'" (382). The youth's subsequent grandiose claims to security notwithstanding, the force with which he objects to the merest possibility of marital infidelity clearly underscores the shaky foundations of his "confidence." This bogus self-assurance does not emanate from a mature awareness of himself and his world, but is based on the most transitory of conditions: youth, present employment, sexual prowess, and the assumed loyalty of his wife. The young waiter depends for his very being on factors over which he has no control, leaving him particularly vulnerable, in the case of marital uncertainty, to what Warren Bennett calls the "love wound," a common form of deprivation in Hemingway.[16] But because he is essentially devoid of light or insight, he is not cognizant of the significance of his testy reply; his vision is so clouded by putative "confidence" that he fails to see through the ephemeral to the underlying darkness in his own life. Consequently, he cannot even begin to reconstruct his existence upon a more substantial basis.

Hemingway must have reveled in such naifs, aflame with so obviously compromised bravado, for he created many of them. Perhaps the most notable is Paco, the would-be bullfighter of "The Capital of the World" (1936), who even in the face of his own death is "full of illusions." For many of these characters, moreover, blindness is not a natural state but a willed escape from *nada*. Conscious flight from reality is particularly prevalent in the early stages of the "education" of Nick Adams. In "Indian Camp" (1924), for instance, one of the first segments in the Adams chronology, Nick has a youthful encounter with *nada* both as the incontrovertible fact of death (the Indian husband's suicide) and as human frailty, the intrinsic vulnerability of mankind to various species of physical and psychic suffering (the Indian woman's protracted and painful labor). The pattern of avoidance set when he refuses to witness the Caesarean section climaxes in his more significant refusal to recognize the inevitability of death itself at the end. Lulled by the deceptive calm of his present circumstances—a purely fortuitous and temporary clean, well-lighted place—he maintains an internal darkness by retreating into willed ignorance:

> They were seated in the boat, Nick in the stern, his father rowing. The sun was coming up over the hills. A bass jumped, making a circle in the water. Nick trailed his hand in the water. It felt warm in the sharp chill of the morning.
>
> In the early morning on the lake sitting in the stern of the boat with his father rowing, he felt quite sure that he would never die. (95)

In another early story, "The Killers" (1927), the somewhat older Nick is again faced with harsh reality, but his reaction to it has not appreciably altered. Again, death (the Swede's) is the primary manifestation of the Void. But here the manner of its coming is also particularly important as a signature of *nada*. As represented by the black-clad henchmen who invade the café—another inadequate place of refuge—*nada* is totally impersonal; in the words of one of the killers, " 'He [the Swede] never had a chance to do anything to us. He never even seen us' " (283). Moreover, *nada* displays its tendency to disrupt without warning any established external order, and, ironically, is visited upon its victims not without a certain macabre humor. Naturally, as Nick learns from the intended victim, its effects are totally irremediable. Thus, in spite of their suggestive black clothing, the killers do not represent forces of evil unleashed in an otherwise good world, as so many critics have claimed; rather, they stand for the wholly amoral, wholly irrational, wholly random operation of the universe, which, because it so clearly works to the detriment of the individual, is *perceived* to be malevolent and evil.

In spite of the clearly educational nature of his experience, Nick once again refuses initiation. Only now his unreasoned compulsion to escape is more pronounced than that of his younger counterpart. Deluded into thinking that this is the kind of localized danger that can be avoided by a mere change in venue, Nick vows not only physical flight (" 'I'm going to get out of this town' ") but psychological flight as well: " 'I can't stand to think about him waiting in the room and knowing he's going to get it. It's too damned awful' " (289). Both versions of Nick Adams, then, are "young waiter" figures because they neither will allow themselves to look directly at the fearsome face of *nada* nor recognize its direct applicability to their own insecure lives.

That such an attitude is ultimately insupportable is exemplified by a third early tale, "Cross-Country Snow" (1925). Here, yet another Nick employs a physically demanding activity, skiing, as an escape from yet another incarnation of *nada*, entrapping circumstance. This appearance of the Void is also ironic in that the specific circumstance involved is the life-enhancing pregnancy of Nick's wife. Nevertheless, its impact on the character is much the same as before in that it serves to severely circumscribe independent initiative, even to the point of substituting an externally imposed identity—in this case, fatherhood—on the true self.[17] Once again misled by the temporary security of the "good place," this Nick also attempts to escape the inescapable and, at the height of his self-delusion, is moved to raise his pursuit of physical release to the level of absolute value: " 'We've got to [ski again]. . . . It [life] isn't worth while if you can't' " (188).

The ski slope, however, offers only apparent protection from *nada*, for even in his joyous adventure, Nick encounters its own form or hidden danger: "Then a patch of soft snow, left in a hollow by the wind, spilled him and he went over and over in a clashing of skis, feeling like a shot rabbit" (183). Unlike the others, this story ends with clarified vision, and Nick does come to terms with the inevitable external demands upon him. Finally, he is no longer able to pretend that the pleasures of the ski slopes—themselves, not always unmixed—are anything more than temporary, in no way definitive of human existence or even a long-lived accommodation to it. Thus, in response to his companion's suggested pact to repeat their present idyll, Nick must realistically counter, " 'There isn't any good in promising' " (188).

In his relationship to *nada*, the old man of "A Clean, Well-Lighted Place" is cast as the polar opposite of the young waiter. Said to be eighty years old, virtually deaf, and recently widowed, he is "in despair" in spite of his reputed wealth and has attempted suicide shortly before the story begins. Unlike the young waiter, he has the light of unclouded vision because he has clearly seen the destructive effects of time and circumstance on love and the self and directly witnessed *nada* in its death mask. But unlike the old waiter, he has not been able to sustain a satisfactory mode of being in the face of these discoveries. He therefore seeks escape from his knowledge either through the bottle or the total denial of life in suicide. Undoubtedly, the old man senses the importance of the clean, well-lighted place, but to him it is very literally a "place" and thereby no more helpful in combating *nada* than Nick's ski slope. That it is inadequate is suggested imagistically at the outset; darkness has indeed invaded this character's "place," for he sits "in the shadows the leaves of the trees made against the electric light" (379).

What seems to offer the old man the little balance he possesses, and thus helps keep him alive, is a modicum of internal cleanness and self-possession, his dignity or style. Of course, this is an issue of great import in Hemingway in that an ordered personal style is one of the few sources of value in an otherwise meaningless universe. The old waiter draws attention to this pitiful figure's style when he rebukes the young waiter for callously characterizing the old man as "'a nasty old thing'": "'This old man is clean. He drinks without spilling. Even now, drunk'" (381). But even this vestige of grace has been compromised over time. While the old man leaves the café "with dignity," he is "walking unsteadily" (381).

The product of a series of encounters with *nada*, the old man's despair is mirrored in two Nick Adams stories on the period immediately following the critical war wound. In "Now I Lay Me" (1927) the emotional dislocation stemming from his brush with death is continued in an almost psychotic dread of the night and sleep. *Nada* is imaged both as the night itself and, as Carlos Baker has suggested, by the disturbing and seemingly ceaseless munching of silkworms, just out of sight but most assuredly not out of Nick's disturbed mind. Paradoxically, the protagonist's abject terror in the face of potential selflessness—permanent in death; temporary in sleep—has resulted in a severe dissociation of the self. Using Paul Tillich's descriptive terminology from *The Courage to Be*, one can say that he is burdened by "pathological" anxiety: a condition of drastically reduced self-affirmation, a flight from nonbeing that entails a corresponding flight from being itself:[18] "I myself did not want to sleep because I had been living for a long time with the knowledge that if I ever shut my eyes in the dark and let myself go, my soul would go out of my body. I had been that way for a long time, ever since I had been blown up at night and felt it go out of me and go off and then come back" (363).

Awakened to the fact of his own death, Nick experiences angst so strongly that he is virtually paralyzed. Unwilling to sleep in the dark and not yet able to develop an internal light and cleanness to cope with his trauma, he depends entirely on external sources of illumination: "If I could have a light I was not afraid to sleep" (363). In the absence of this light, however, he attempts to pull back from the awareness of *nada* by reliving the happier times of his youth, a period of cleanness and assured order. But the search for a good "place" in the past is ultimately fruitless; his memories of favorite trout streams tend to blur in his mind and inevitably lead him to unpleasant reminiscences of his father's ruined collection of arrowheads and zoological specimens, a chaotic heap of fragments that merely mirrors his present internal maelstrom.

In "A Way You'll Never Be" (1933) Nick's dissociation has not been remedied and is suggested initially by the postbattle debris with which the story opens. Plagued by a recurring dream of "a low house painted yellow with willows all around it and a low stable and there was a canal, and he had been there a thousand times and never seen it, but there it was every night as plain as the hill, only it frightened him" (408), he is close to an old man's despair. He now intuits something of the significance of the vision: "That house meant more than anything and every night he had it [the dream]. That was what he needed" (408). But he is still too trau-matized by the experience there to examine it more closely and can only ramble on in self-defense about the "American locust," another familiar item from his childhood. In his present condition Nick is an oddly appropriate choice for the absurd mission on which he has been sent, to display his American uniform in order to build morale among the Italian troops. At the moment his "self," like the entire American presence in the region, is solely the uniform; the clothes are as dimly suggestive of a more substantial identity as they are of the substantial military support they are designed to promise. For the present, though, this barely adequate package for his violently disturbed inner terrain is Nick's only semblance of the clean, well-lighted place. Still insufficiently initiated into the dangerous world in which he is doomed to live, he desperately clutches at any buffer that will hold *nada* in abeyance.

The other side of Hemingway's "old man" figure is epitomized by Manuel Garcia, the aging bullfighter of "The Undefeated" (1925). After numerous brushes with death in the bullring, he too depends for his very being on style. Garcia's style has also eroded, leaving him defenseless against the bull, Harold Kaplan's "beast of *nada.*"[19] Banished from the brightly lit afternoon bouts, he now performs in the shadowy nocturnals for a "second string critic" and with bulls that "'the veterinaries won't pass in the daytime'" (237). The performance itself is merely "acceptable" if not "vulgar." Largely as a result of his diminished capabilities, he is seriously (and perhaps mortally) wounded and at the conclusion is left with only his *coletta,* as is the old man his shred of dignity. With these all-important manifestations of internal cleanness sullied, the fates of both are equally uncertain: Manuel's on the operating table and the old man's in the enveloping night.

Of all Hemingway's short story characters, however, the one who most fully recapitulates the "old man" typology is Mr. Frazer of "The Gambler, the Nun, and the Radio" (1933). Confined to a backcountry hospital as a result of a riding accident, Frazer too experiences *nada*, "the Nothingness that underlies pain, failure, and disillusionment alike,"[20] in the form of his own incapacity and that of the broken men who share his predicament. He also experiences banality, one of the less overtly disturbing but nonetheless ominous visages of *nada*, in the form of the numbing routine of this claustrophobic, but clean and well-lighted place. If Frazer has an old man's clear perspective on nothingness, he is no better able to achieve the cleanness of character necessary to cope with it. As is suggested by Hemingway's first title for the story, "Give Us a Prescription, Doctor," Frazer too seeks external anodynes for his *nada*—induced pain. His compulsion to monitor random radio broadcasts and so imaginatively transport himself from his present circumstances is analogous to the old man's drinking because each involves a flight from, rather than a confrontation with, reality. His very choice of songs—"Little White Lies" and "Sing Something Simple"—serves to underscore the escapism of this pastime.

In the end, however, neither escape succeeds. The old man remains in despair, and Frazer is given to periodic fits of uncontrollable weeping. In the same way that the former cannot entirely banish the specter of loneliness and death from his consciousness, neither can Frazer, nor any man, completely cloud his view of *nada* with the various "opiums" at his disposal. The very consideration of the question of release leads Frazer through the opium haze to the terrible truth that lies beneath:

> Religion is the opium of the people. . . . Yes, and music is the opium of the people. . . . And now economics is the opium of the people; along with patriotism the opium of the people in Italy and Germany. . . . But drink was a sovereign opium of the people, oh,

an excellent opium. Although some prefer the radio, another opium of the people, a cheap one he had just been using. . . . What was the real, the actual opium of the people? . . . What was it? Of course; bread was the opium of the people. . . . [Only] Revolution, Mr. Frazer thought, is no opium. Revolution is a catharsis; an ecstasy which can only be prolonged by tyranny. The opiums are for before and for after. He was thinking well, a little too well. (485–87)

The old waiter definitely stands apart from the other two characters in "A Clean, Well-Lighted Place." If the running controversy over dialogue attribution has thrown some doubt on whether he or his young partner first learns of the old man's attempted suicide, it has done nothing to contradict earlier assumptions on which of the two is more sensitive to the reasons for it. It is evident throughout that the old waiter's insight into the word *nothing* he so frequently uses is much broader. He recognizes from the first that the old man's despair is not a reaction to a material lack but to a basic metaphysical principle. Thus, he is unable to delude himself into a bogus "confidence." When he responds to the youth's boasting with " 'You have everything' " (382), he is clearly being ironic; the latter indeed has "everything," *except* a firm hold on the "nothing" which underlies "everything." They are "of two different kinds" (382) because the old waiter knows the ability to withstand the dark "is not only a question of youth and confidence although those things are very beautiful" (382). In spite of their superficial beauty, both the transitory condition of youth and the illusory confidence that so often goes with it are clearly inadequate tools with which to combat the darkness.

There is a closer connection with the old man, however, initially because the news of his attempted suicide begins the old waiter's formal consideration of the reasons for it. In this sense, at the beginning of the tale, the old waiter is a representation of Earl Rovit's "tyro" and Philip Young's "Hemingway Hero" (as opposed to the "tutor" and "code hero") in that he is in the process of learning about the dark underside of life. But while the old man's plight is a necessary goad for the old waiter's musings on his own situation, the latter certainly outstrips his "mentor" in the lengths to which he pushes his speculations on *nada*: "What did [the old waiter] fear? It was not fear or dread. It was a nothing that he knew too well. It was all a nothing and a man was nothing too. It was only that and light was all it needed and a certain cleanness and order. Some lived in it and never felt it but he knew it all was nada y pues nada y nada y pues nada" (382–83).

Like the old man, then, the old waiter sees clearly, in fact more clearly, the fearsome nothing, but he reacts far differently to his discovery. Instead of lapsing into despair or escaping into drunkenness, this character displays true metaphysical courage in raising the concept of *nada* to a central article in his overtly existentialist creed, climaxing with his mock prayer of adoration, "Hail nothing full of nothing, nothing is with thee" (383). Perhaps even more importantly, he refuses to limit himself to abstract speculation but willingly embraces the impact of universal nothingness on his own person. Thus, in response to the barman's question, "'What's yours?'" he demonstrates the ironic sense of humor that typifies him throughout by unflinchingly answering, "'Nada'" (383). No other statement in the tale so clearly designates the old waiter as the central figure of Hemingway's 1933 collection: he is the "winner" who truly takes "nothing" as his only possible reward.

If his stoic courage in the shadow of the Void differentiates the old waiter from the old man, so does his method for dealing with it. Again, the old waiter provides some grounds for confusing the two modes of existence when he insists upon the importance of a purely physical haven: "'I am one of those who like to stay late at the cafe. . . . With all those who do not want to go to bed. With all those who need a light for the night'" (382). Yet, he does more than merely accept the dubious protection of an already established "place"; he is, in fact, the keeper of the "clean, well-lighted place," the one who maintains both its cleanness and its light. To cite Cleanth Brooks on this subject, "The order and light are supplied by *him*. They do *not* reflect an inherent, though concealed, order in the universe. What little meaning there is in the world is imposed upon that world by man."[21] Given the stark contrast between his café and the distinctly unclean and ill-lighted bar he frequents after work, his almost ritualistic efforts to furnish and consistently maintain these essential qualities are definitely not representative of those around him. Finally, the old waiter's clean, well-lighted place is distinctly portable— transcending "place" altogether—because it is so thoroughly internalized. He carries it in the form of equanimity and dignity to the shabby *bodega*, and he carries it home as well.

Thus, it is the old waiter, a man who can see clearly the darkness surrounding him yet so order his life that he can endure this awareness, who most fully attains the attitude symbolized by the clean, well-lighted place. In the society presented by this tale, and in the Hemingway canon as a whole, he is indeed *"otro loco mas"* when set against a standard of sanity epitomized by an egotistical partner, unfeeling barmen, lustful soldiers, and suicidal old men. Both realist and survivor, epitome of "grace under pressure," he is by the end of the tale an exceptional man and very much a representation of the highest level of heroism in Hemingway's fictional world, whether it be denoted by Young's "code hero" or Rovit's "tutor." Even his insomnia, which he regards as a common trait ("Many must have it"), is a mark of his extraordinary character: his vision is too clear, his sense of self too firm, to allow him the ease of insensate slumber. One need only compare this insomnia with Nick Adams' pathological fear of sleep in "Now I Lay Me" to appreciate the qualitative difference between the old waiter and other men.

Some of Hemingway's most important tales also contain characters who either presage an achievement of or actually attain the old waiter's clean, well-lighted place. A notable early example is the Nick Adams of "Big Two-Hearted River" (1925). Again, the confrontation with *nada* is critical here, but the appearance of *nada* is more artfully veiled than in other tales. There are hints of the Void in the description of the burned-over countryside at the beginning, in Nick's vision of the trout "tightened facing up into the current" (210) shortly thereafter, and in the methodical series of tasks that comprise the central action of the story. As Malcolm Cowley first suggested and Sheridan Baker has since amplified, the ritualistic series connotes a desperate attempt to hold off something "he had left behind" (210); in Philip Young's reading the "something" is the memory of the traumatic war wound that so discomfits other versions of Nick in "Now I Lay Me" and "A Way You'll Never Be."[22] But *nada* is most overtly suggested by the forbidding swamp: "Nick did not want to go in there now. . . . In the swamp the banks were bare, the big cedars came together overhead, the sun did not come through, except in patches; in the fast deep water, in the half light, the fishing would be tragic" (231). Aside from the old waiter's prayer, this is Hemingway's most detailed characterization of *nada*: it too is dark; its depth is ungauged but considerable; and, with its swiftly moving current and bare banks, it is most assuredly inhospitable to man.

As the "patches" of sunlight suggest, though, the *nada*/swamp can be discerned and therefore analyzed by human vision. And by the end of the story Nick seems to have gained the light necessary to see into the Void—at the very least, to realize that he can never truly leave it behind him. Yet Nick still lacks the inner cleanness to delve further into *nada*; he is still too dependent on a distinct physical locale as a buffer zone. As he says early on, "He was there, in the good place" (215). But the very ritualistic behavior that alerted Cowley to the possibility of a mind not right also suggests progress toward an internalized order. Like the trout's in the potentially destructive current, this discipline could hold Nick steady in the dangerous eddies of life and so enable him eventually to enter the swamp. Thus, while the tale ends with a temporary withdrawal from direct confrontation, Nick strikes a positive note when he says, "There were plenty of days coming when he could fish the swamp" (232).

Two characters in the late short stories actually do "fish" the swamp of *nada*, the sportsman Macomber in "The Short Happy Life of Francis Macomber" (1936) and the writer Harry of "The Snows of Kilimanjaro" (1936). The two men approach the clean, well-lighted place from different directions, however: Macomber from an old man's despair and Harry from a young waiter's naive faith in transitory material security. For Macomber, the master of "court games" and darling of drawing rooms, it is necessary to leave the protective enclosures of the rich to meet his *nada* in the African tall grass in the figure of the wounded lion, an epitome of pure destructive force: "All of him [the lion], pain, sickness, hatred and all of his remaining strength, was tightening into an absolute concentration for a rush" (19). The brush with externally conceived *nada* triggers Macomber's cowardly flight, but more importantly leads him to an appreciation of his own inner emptiness, a Sartrian version of nothingness, as well as a Sartrian nausea at his inauthenticity. Granted, Macomber responds to the threat with fear, but it is also more than fear, "a cold slimy hollow in all the emptiness where once his confidence had been and it made him feel sick" (11). Thus Macomber comes face to face with the fact that *nada* need not destroy the physical being to make man a "nothing"; man *is* a nothing unless and until he makes himself "something."

The black despair that follows his initiation to *nada* without and within is not Macomber's final stage. Through the ministrations of the hunter Wilson and the familiar, secure place (the jeep), he undergoes a significant and almost miraculous change at the buffalo hunt. As Wilson describes it, "Beggar had probably been afraid all his life. Don't know what started it. But over now. Hadn't had time to be afraid with the buff. That and being angry too. Motor car too. Motor cars made it familiar. Be a damn fire eater now" (33). The jeep is indeed useful as a means for facing *nada* analogous to the old waiter's café and Nick Adams' peaceful campsite, but Macomber's real "place" is distinctly internal. Again, Wilson furnishes the analysis: "Fear gone like an operation. *Something else grew in its place.* Main thing a man had. Made him into a man [italics mine]" (33). Macomber's real achievement, then, is the creation of an ordered "something" to fill the inner void. It not only prepares him for the buffalo hunt but enables him to see clearly, as if for the first time, his inauthentic condition, not the least important facet of which has been his sacrifice of personal identity to an unfulfilling marriage and social expectation. With his "place" securely inside him, he can face with dignity and courage another brush with *nada* in the "island of bushy trees" (35), a hostile testing ground certainly reminiscent of Nick's swamp.

In "Snows of Kilimanjaro," Harry too has multiple confrontations with *nada*, the first of which is with the ultimate manifestation of the Void, death: "It came with a rush; not as a rush of water nor of wind; but of a sudden evil-smelling emptiness" (64). As we learn later, this appearance certainly fits Carlos Baker's oxymoronic designation for *nada* as the "nothing that is something," for "It had no shape, any more. It simply occupied space" (74). The immediate effect of the experience is to lead Harry to an appreciation of the underlying absurdity of an existence that could be doomed by such a trivial injury—a small scratch which becomes gangrenous for lack of proper medication. With this awareness of his radical contingency, the protagonist can defuse death of its terror: "Since the gangrene started in his right leg he had no pain and with the pain the horror had gone and all he felt now was a great tiredness and anger that this was the end of it. . . . For years it had obsessed him; but now it meant nothing in itself" (54).

Like Macomber's, Harry's brush with imminent death also awakens him to a second face of *nada*, the inner nothing caused by his failure to preserve artistic integrity, his very self, against the lures of the inconsequential: material comfort, financial security, hedonistic pleasure. Every bit as much as Macomber, this most autobiographical of Hemingway's short story characters suffers a hollowness at the very core. Therefore, the basic thrust of the tale is Harry's effort to cleanse and reorder his life through a pointed self-criticism. Gradually he manages to "work the fat off his soul" (60) by jettisoning the excess baggage of a young waiter's facile confidence in the material and replaces it with something more substantial, a pledge to take up his writing once more. Again, the process is facilitated by his being situated in a tangible clean, well-lighted place: "This was a pleasant camp under big trees against a hill, with good water, and close by, a nearly dry water hole where sand grouse flighted in the mornings" (53). But again, the important "place" is actually within. According to Gloria Dussinger, Harry's difficult rite of purification leads, as it should, to a reclamation of his own identity: "Harry is left with his naked self, the irreducible *I am* that defies chaos."[23] Though the climactic dream flight from the plain is decidedly ambiguous, it does seem to vouchsafe Harry's success at this endeavor, for the author allows him imaginative entry into the cleanest and best lighted of all the places in the short story canon: "great, high, and unbelievably white in the sun, was the square top of Kilimanjaro. And then he knew that there was where he was going" (76).

Although Harry and Macomber both achieve the clean, well-lighted place, their premature deaths deprive them of the opportunity to bring additional value to their lives, as the old waiter most assuredly does. Having controlled his own life through the implementation of a clean, well-lighted place, he fulfills the remaining provisions of Eliot's "Waste Land" credo by sympathizing with the plight of others and aiding them in their own pursuits of this all important attitude. In so doing he becomes an existential hero in Martin Buber's particular sense of the term, a champion of the "I-Thou" relationship. His "style" is essentially compassion, the willingness to treat others as valid, subjective "Thous" rather than depersonalized "Its."[24] This facet of his personality is implicit as early as his expression of sympathy for the pleasure-seeking soldier who risks curfew violation. As he himself comments on the risks involved, " 'What does it matter if he gets what he's after?' " (379). But his capacity for true compassion is made most explicit near the end, particularly in his admission, " 'Each night I am reluctant to close up because there may be some one who needs the café' " (382).

The ability to extend outward to others from a firmly established self is once again in direct contrast to the narrow, selfish pride of the young waiter, who is unmoved by the needs of the old man and sees love as a matter of blind loyalty (verging on bondage) and physical gratification. This inclination is made all too clear by his insensitive comment on the old widower's plight: " 'A wife would be no good to him now' " (381). The old waiter's attitude is also contrasted to that of the old man, who is so absorbed by his own misery that he is barely cognizant of others. This admirable figure passes beyond Rovit's "tyro" stage to that of "tutor" when he humorously, but pointedly, attempts to instruct the youth on the evanescence of "confidence" and the latter's serious misuse of love (e.g., by the joke). Moreover, he tries to provide the morose old man with some basis upon which to reconstruct his shattered life by rendering to this wretched figure the respect and sympathy he so desperately needs. Thus, in Buber's sense as in Heidegger's, Kierkegaard's, and Sartre's, the old waiter "authenticates" his life by fulfilling his responsibilities both to himself and to others.

The picador Zurito in "The Undefeated," the dignified major in "Another Country" (1927), and the guide Wilson of "The Short Happy Life of Francis Macomber" all transcend the limits of self-sufficiency by sympathizing with and proferring aid to those who most need it. But the character who most closely approximates the old waiter's multifaceted heroism is Cayetano Ruiz, the luckless gambler of "The Gambler, the Nun, and the Radio," a story whose three main characters (Ruiz, Frazer, Sister Cecilia) form a triadic grouping analogous to the hero, victim, and naif of "A Clean, Well-Lighted Place."[25]

That the gambler does attain the exemplary attitude is implicit in William Barrett's summary characterization of him: "Cayetano is the absurd hero who carries on his code, even if it is only the code of a cheap gambler, defiantly and gracefully against the Void."[26] Cayetano, of course, earns his heroism in that he too encounters the death mask of *nada*. Like Harry's, his wound comes totally without warning and, given the rather unreliable aim of his assailant, almost totally by accident. Yet even before this crisis, the perspicacious gambler with eyes "alive as a hawk's" (468) has undoubtedly sensed its presence in the form of chance and the ever-present risk of his chosen profession. In spite of the fact that his work takes him into places that are anything but clean and well-lighted, he has so internalized the "place" that he can calmly face external hostility and internal suffering with honor and exemplary courage. Consequently, he refuses to inform on his assailant and also refuses opiates to dull the physical pain that serves as metaphor for the meta-physical pain *nada* induces.

But Ruiz is far more than Barrett's "cheap," albeit heroic, gambler because he strives to communicate his insights on life to others. Indirect proof of his compassion is to be found both in his embarrassment over the offensive odor of his peritonitis and in his considerate silence even in periods of terrible pain. Direct evidence is available in the conversations with Frazer. Here Ruiz incisively analyzes the untreatable ills of the human condition—the absurd irony, the prevalence of accident and risk, and, most of all, the difficulty of maintaining a self amidst the vagaries of fortune that have driven his auditor to tears. Like the old waiter, he is quite capable of humbling himself, denigrating his own considerable courage, in order to provide comfort to one less able to withstand *nada*. Surely he consciously misstates fact when, in an attempt to assuage Frazer's shame at lapsing into tears, he declares, " 'If I had a private room and a radio I would be crying and yelling all night long' " (482). Evidently this self-described "victim of illusions" (483) also possesses the old wait-er's ironic consciousness, for it is at the very heart of his dispassionate self-analysis, also delivered principally for Frazer's benefit: " 'If I live long enough the luck will change. I have bad luck now for fifteen years. If I ever get any good luck I will be rich' " (483). Although he fully realizes that "bad luck" will continue to predominate, like the other residents of the *metaphoric* clean, well-lighted place, the gambler is content to "continue, slowly, and wait for luck to change" (484). In the interim he will continue to try to instill in others some of the light and cleanness essential to the authentication of the self.

In their dealings with the various faces of *nada*, then, the old waiter figures represent the highest form of heroism in the Hemingway short story canon, a heroism matched in the novels perhaps only by the fisherman Santiago. Those who manage to adjust to life on the edge of the abyss do so because they see clearly the darkness that surrounds them yet create a personal sense of order, an identity, with which to maintain balance on this precarious perch. The failure either to see the significance of the encounter with *nada* or, if seen, to constitute an inner cleanness vitiates the lives not only of the young waiter and old man of "A Clean, Well-Lighted Place" but also of a host of similarly flawed figures through-out the canon.

Because of the frequency with which *nada* appears in the short fiction, we can only assume that the Void also played a major role in Heming-way's own life, whether as the shattering war wound or the countless subsequent experiences, both real and imagined, that threatened to make him a "nothing." Carlos Baker concluded as much in his biography: "'A Clean, Well-Lighted Place' was autobiographical . . . in the sense that it offered a brief look into the underside of Ernest's spiritual world, the nightmare of nothingness by which he was still occasionally haunted."[27] But if we are justified in seeing Hemingway's life in terms of his encoun-ters with *nada*, are we not equally justified in following Earl Rovit's lead and thereby treating his fiction as one of the by-products of these encounters—in fact, as a primary strategy for dealing with *nada*?[28]

Both the fiction itself and the author's comments on it seem to support us in this regard, for Hemingway's basic aesthetic suggests precisely the sort of perspective symbolized by the clean, well-lighted place. The need for clearsightedness, for instance, is the essence of the writer's celebrated remark on art in *Death in the Afternoon* (1932), a personal testament published just a year before "A Clean, Well-Lighted Place": "Let those who want to save the world if you can get to see it clear and as a whole. Then any part you make will represent the whole if it is made truly."[29] But unclouded vision alone, not uncommon among his fictional progeny, could guarantee neither a psychological nor an aesthetic clean, well-lighted place. A careful and conscious ordering of disparate material was also required in order to fill the Void of nothing (the blank page) with an enduring something. Thus, the characteristic Hemingway style: the clean, precise, scrupulously ordered prose that so often serves to illuminate shimmering individual objects against a dark background of chaos.[30] As for his old waiter figures, the actual places that inspired the author's descriptions pale against the deftly constructed "places" that *are* the descriptions; because the latter are no longer subject to the random, transitory world of fact but rather interiorized and subsequently transmuted into art itself, they are much more secure, and certainly more permanent, strongholds against nothingness.

In spite of the apparent disdain for utilitarian art in the passage from *Death in the Afternoon*, Hemingway also performed some of that function, albeit indirectly, by probing the sources of our well-documented modern malaise and offering at least tentative solutions to it in the form of resolute personal conduct. In this way he too displayed some of the Buberesque qualities of his short story heroes. It should come as no surprise, then, that Granville Hicks's summary of the author's artistic mission has a rather direct applicability to that of the old waiter as well. For in their potential impact on an attentive audience, Hemingway and his extraordinary character are virtually one and the same. Like the latter, "The artist makes his contribution to the salvation of the world by seeing it clearly himself and helping others to do the same."[31]

Perhaps nothing so effectively demonstrates the difficulty of maintaining the clean, well-lighted place than Hemingway's own failure to do so in the years immediately preceding his death. Like so many of his "old man" figures, he never lost sight of *nada* but did lose the essential inner cleanness, without which the light must eventually be overpowered by darkness. With his internal defenses in disarray, Hemingway turned to an old man's despairing act. In effect, in his suicide, he opted for the release from turmoil offered by the metaphorical "opiums" of Mr. Frazer: "He would have a little spot of the giant killer and play the radio, you could play the radio so that you could hardly hear it" (487).

"Only Let the Story End As Soon As Possible": Time-and-History in Ernest Hemingway's *In Our Time*

E. R. Hagemann

1914–1923

The sixteen italicized Chapters in *In Our Time* are in five states with some ninety variant readings and total 2552 words but only 759 different words.[1] Because Ernest Hemingway expended so much care in so few words, we should expend equal care (but not in so few words) to examine the interchapters as an artistic unit: time-and-history, hyphenated; time-and-history as record *and* imagination, for not every detail or event is verifiable. No less than fiction, history is in direct proportion of the writer, a rearrangement of reality and, above all, time. Time-and-history is a product of memory and desire and necessarily fragmented and *disar-ranged*.

These interchapters, drypoints (that is, intaglio) Edmund Wilson once astutely called them, haphazard as to time as printed in *In Our Time*, become an entity when rearranged chronologically (see Appendix at end of article); for what Hemingway has done is to reconstruct a decade, 1914–23. His choice is not random. The Great War and its aftermath were, collectively, *the* experience of his generation, the experience that dumped his peers and his elders into graves, shell-holes, hospitals, and onto gallows. These were "in our time," Hemingway is saying, and he remarks the significant and the insignificant.

And time, to quote the best definition I have ever read, is "the system of those relations which any event has to any other as past, present, or future. This relationship is realistically conceived as a sort of self-subsistent entity, or object of contemplation" (*The Century Dictionary and Cyclopedia* [1897]). Hemingway moves about in time and gives us sixteen vignettes for our "contemplation."

To iterate: the decade is from 1914 to 1923 inclusive. I will reconstruct it and present the what, the where, and the when so that the reader can conceive of the years as Hemingway does: "a stream flowing through the field of the present," to quote again from *Century*'s definition.

Time-and-history begin in *In Our Time* with Chapter IV ("It was a frightfully hot day") and Chapter III ("We were in a garden in Mons"). The terse narrator is Lieutenant Eric Edward Dorman-Smith, Royal Northumberland Fusiliers (Fifth Fusiliers), First Battalion, dedicatee of the 1924 edition, and a personal friend of Hemingway.

It is Sunday, August 23, 1914; the place is Mons, Belgium, where the British Expeditionary Force (BEF) has set up defense along a sixteen-mile stretch of the ruler-straight Mons-Condé Canal, spanned by eighteen bridges. (Hemingway errs when he calls it a "river" in Chapter III.) Dorman-Smith's battalion is responsible for the Mariette Bridge which he so jollily speaks of in Chapter IV. The German right wing under Alexander von Kluck went after the bridge early, despite the barricade, and sustained fearful losses as the Tommies "potted" them from "forty yards." The skirmish at the "absolutely perfect barricade" occurred prior to 5 P.M. at which time the English had to fall back and Dorman-Smith and his fellow Fusiliers were "frightfully put out."

The location of the garden, Chapter III, is unclear and unverifiable, nor is it known when the incident occurred during the battle. It is possible the garden was in Mons, but the city was not in the Fifth's sector. Unfortunately, it is not mentioned in official dispatches, but then neither is Dorman-Smith. What is important is that Hemingway introduces one of the controlling metaphors in the Chapters: the Wall. "The first German . . . climbed up over the garden wall. We waited till he got one leg over and then potted him."

Mons at once entered the realm of the Glorious in English history; to the BEF, however, it was to be but the first battle in four years of Pyrrhic warfare which drained England of her manhood.

The French were drained over and over again, and Chapter I ("Everybody was drunk") points to the Champagne. The identity of the kitchen corporal will never be known, but in 112 words this hapless *poilu* relates a desperately comical incident as he heads for slaughter. The Champagne was not a wine but a frontal assault against an intricate German defense. After a terrific artillery preparation on September 25, 1915, the French attacked and engaged the enemy until Christmas Day. In three months they lost 145,000 men, 120,000 in the first three weeks. The Germans suffered as heavily. A French tactical victory, military experts call it. This depends on one's viewpoint; plainly, the Champagne was mass execution.

"Everybody was drunk" and no one can blame them, while the insignificant kitchen corporal wrestles with his mess in the dark, and the drunken lieutenant tells him to put it out. It can be seen. "'It was funny going along that road,'" muses the corporal, the road that led to the Champagne.

From execution in battle Hemingway switches to execution in the streets of corrupt Kansas City, Missouri, in Chapter VIII ("At two o'clock in the morning two Hungarians got into a cigar store"). Maybe Hungarians did at some time but not on November 19, 1917, when two Italians, "Cap" Gargotta and Joe Musso, were killed by the cops as they fled after robbing the Parker-Gordon Cigar Company at 1028 Broadway. "They were shot on the seat of a covered wagon in which they had cigars valued at $3,000. . . . The men attempted to drive their team over the detectives ["Jack" Farrell and Carl Grantello] when ordered to stop," reported the *Kansas City Star* later the same day, not on page one but page three, so unimportant were the executions. Like Boyle says: "'They're crooks, ain't they? . . . They're wops, ain't they? Who the hell is going to make any trouble?'"[2]

Why Hemingway, who was in Kansas City working as a cub reporter on the evening *Star*, changed the ethnic origin of the robbers, although the cops in Chapter VIII do not, can be partially explained as a thematic tactic. The piece leads directly to the cryptic story, "The Revolutionist," which considers a Hungarian Red who is a political refugee from Regent-Admiral Miklós Horthy's arch-reactionary regime in Hungary. If this is so, this direct carry-over, then it is the only time that such occurs in *In Our Time*.[3]

Out there on our Western home front, Italians were dead on the pavement. Wops! Out there on the Italian war front thousands upon thousands of Italians—Wops! to connote the lowly victims and not to impart ethnic slurs—were dead on the ground defending the tawdry House of Savoy on the throne of Italy in the unimpressive person of Victor Emmanuel III, Prince of Naples.

In Chapter VII ("While the bombardment was knocking the trench to pieces") the final Austrian offensive of the war in Italy has just begun, June 15, 1918, and initial success brings them to Fossalta on the west bank of the Piave River on the 16th; their heavy mortars batter the Italians, and the narrator (*not*, I insist, Nick Adams) madly prays to "dear Jesus" to keep him "from getting killed." He has every reason to, for the Austrians were well equipped to reach their ultimate objective, the industrial heart of Italy. They failed. Perhaps the prayer helped. Whatever, the narrator never tells of Jesus when he is safe in Mestre and ascends the stairs with a whore in the Villa Róssa (Red Villa), the officers' brothel. "And he never told anybody."

The time is early July 1918 in Chapter VI ("Nick sat against the wall of the church"); the place is still the Piave, but now the Italians' counterattack is underway ("Things were getting forward in the town"). Nick

Adams is seriously wounded, and from his quasi-articulate words to his felled Italian comrade, Rinaldo Rinaldi, comes the germ of *A Farewell to Arms:* " 'You and me we've made a separate peace. We're not patriots.' " This is the sole appearance of the word "peace" in the Chapters. And this is the only time Hemingway permits one of his characters to speechify, if that is it, about The War. As he observed in his "Introduction" to *Men at War* (New York: Crown Publishers, 1942): "They [the various writers] had learned to tell the truth without screaming. Screaming, necessary though it may be to attract attention at the time, reads badly in later years" (xvi).

The incident is fictional; the battle is actual. The Austrians sustained, overall, 200,000 killed and wounded, 25,000 prisoners; the "victorious" Italians, 90,000 killed and wounded. In his brief combat duty in 1918, Hemingway served at Fossalta di Piave and was badly shot up during the night of July 8.

In Chapter VIII the Irish cops called the Hungarians Wops; in Chapter VI, Rinaldi, an Italian if not a Wop, is close to death, "breathing with difficulty"; and in Chapter XV ("They hanged Sam Cardinella at six o'clock in the morning") there is another Italian, doomed long before. "They" hanged him in Chicago not at six but shortly after nine in the morning on April 15, 1921, and it required eleven minutes for him to die of a broken neck. He died for the murder of one Andrew P. Bowman not quite two years previous. Cardinella was thirty-nine years old, the leader of a gang operating out of a pool room at 22nd and Clark Streets, and the father of six children. Hanged with him, but not members of his gang, were Giuseppe Costanzo and Salvatore Ferrara; a fourth victim, Antonio López, had been awarded a temporary reprieve. No Negroes died that day, Chapter XV to the contrary; rather, they died the following week. "They" hanged people in those days in Illinois, but not so many at one time since 1912 as "they" did on April 15.

"When the death march time arrived," said the *Chicago Tribune* on April 16, "[Cardinella] fought his guards like a maniac. . . . Finally he was carried to the scaffold in a chair, unable to stand erect, and gibbering insanely in Italian. . . . [S]till cringing in the chair, he was executed." So Hemingway does not exaggerate Cardinella's physical collapse.[4] The *Tribune* does not mention the two priests, and we can surmise that Sam's final prayers (the "gibbering"?) went unrecognized by a man of God, but there was no one to respond to the young *ufficiale's* prayers in the Fossalta trench, either.

In this episode Hemingway alludes to a procession and a wall—"they came out onto the gallows through a door in the wall"—and in Chapter II ("Minarets stuck up in the rain") he expands his processional metaphor.

Evacuation of Eastern Thrace began on October 15, 1922, pursuant to an armistice signed at Mudania between the Turks and the Greeks. Turks would occupy the district within forty-five days. Terrorized Greek Christians—*giaours* to the Muslim Turks—thousands of them, spilled onto the road through Adrianople and beyond to Karagatch, on the other side, the western side, of the Maritza River in Western Thrace, Greek territory.

Hemingway, on assignment for the *Toronto Star*, arrived in Constantinople on September 29. Some time subsequent to October 15, the 16th is a safe guess, he was in the melee on the Karagatch road: "twenty miles [thirty miles in the Chapter] of carts drawn by cows, bullocks and muddy-flanked water buffalo. . . . It is a silent procession," he wrote for the paper, October 20. Greek cavalry herded the Christians along like "cowpunchers driving steers," not dissimilar to the lieutenant herding his *poilus* in Chapter I. Hemingway walked in the rain for five miles, dodging camels. Under the bridge the Maritza was running "a brick-red [yellow in the Chapter] quarter-mile wide flood."[5] And behind them "minarets stuck up in the rain."

Greeks again appear in Chapter V ("They shot the six cabinet ministers at half-past six"), and Hemingway ingeminates the "wall" in the Cardinella vignette. As elsewhere in *In Our Time* what he recounts is true and less than true, an impression based on fact; fact, in turn, readjusted to respond to memory and time, "in our time." On November 22, 1922, at approximately 11 A.M., Demetrios Gounaris, Petros Protopapadakis, and Nicholas Stratos, former prime ministers; George Baltatzis, Nicholas Theotokis, former ministers; and George Hadjanestis, former military commander in chief in Ionia, were shot as they stood against a wall of the new Municipal Hospital in Athens, having been removed from the prison where they had heard the death verdict by a military court martial which adjudged them guilty of high treason and responsible for the debacle in Asia Minor.

Accounts differ and none agrees precisely with Hemingway, who was not a witness. Gounaris was stricken with typhoid and had to be supported to the wall, but he was not sitting in the rainwater with "his head on his knees." Hadjanestis, having been degraded, stood at attention. The six of them were slain from a distance of six meters, one infantry firing-squad per victim, and coups de grace were administered to all by pistol shots through their heads. They were hastily buried by their families that afternoon in an Athens cemetery. "They" shot people in those days in Greece like "they" hanged people in Cook County.

Chapters IX through XIV translates us from the hospital wall to the *barrera*, the red wood fence (wall) around the bull ring in Spain. Grouped together as they are, these six Chapters comprise a miniature *tauromaquia* derived ultimately from Francisco Goya's thirty-three etchings of 1816. There are three subgroups of two Chapters each: IX-X (the kid, the horse, and the bull; all perform but not brilliantly), XI-XII (the bad torero and the good torero), and XIII-XIV (the drunken torero and the "death" of Maera). Every one is tripartite. This structural device, not used any other place, is significant in that the bull ring is divided into three imaginary concentric circles and the fight itself into *tercios*, thirds. As Hemingway once wrote in the *Toronto Star*, October 20, 1923, "Bull fighting is not a sport. . . . It is a tragedy. A very great tragedy . . . played in three definite acts."[6]

Although new to *El Torero*, he knew what he was about here. He experiences the *afición* (passion) for it; he acknowledges the underside of it. He employs a modicum of technical language and analysis and foreshadows the Romero-Belmonte corrida in *The Sun Also Rises* three years later. By implication the season (*temporada*) is 1923.

Chapter IX ("The first matador got the horn") appeared in the Spring 1923 issue of *Little Review* before he had ever seen a *corrida de toros*. (His very first was that summer in Spain.) Therefore, I tentatively conclude (1) that he describes a fight that never took place and (2) that he describes the same mythical fight in his dispatch to the *Toronto Star Weekly*, dated October 27, 1923. There are those who would disagree, but nowhere in José María de Cossío's massive *Los Toros*: Tratado Técnico e Histórico (Madrid: Espasa-Calpe, 1960, 3 vols.) is such a corrida narrated, although Cossio does tell of the legendary Joselito (born José Gómez) killing six bulls on six different occasions in 1915 when he was just twenty years old.

It is reasonable to assume that Chapter X ("They whack-whacked the white horse") is a scene Hemingway witnessed with Hadley. Certainly the incident occurred long before the introduction in 1928 of the *peto*, the mattresslike covering to protect horses in the ring. It was an innovation Hemingway disapproved of and said so in *Death in the Afternoon*. Chapter XI ("The crowd shouted all the time") similarly is another bit of action from 1923 and a sad one, for the torero is self-admittedly bad: "'I am not really a good bull fighter!'"

"If it happened right down close in front of you" opens Chapter XII wherein Nícanor Villalta Sérres executes a flawless kill with the *estoque*. He was one of Hemingway's favorites that first summer in Spain. He nicknamed him "The Basque Telephone-Pole" and named his first son after him. The twenty-five-year-old Villalta was one of the best; in July he was awarded the coveted *Oreja de Oro* in Madrid, the supreme achievement in *Los Toros*. His unsurpassed killing ("the bull charged and Villalta charged [*a un tiempo*] and just for a moment they became one") was to gain him thirty-two ear-trophies by 1931.[7] Strange to report, though, that some of the details in XII seem to come from a *corrida* in which Chicuelo (born Manuel Jiménez Moreno) fought.

Chapter XIII ("I heard the drums coming down the street") and Chapter XIV ("Maera lay still, his head on his arms") have as protagonist the then famous *matador de toros* Manuel García López known as Maera. In 1923 he was twenty-seven and was to have fifty corridas; many aficionados regarded him as the potential champion of them all, now that Joselito was dead, killed in the ring on May 16, 1920, and that Juan Belmonte had retired the year before. It is impossible to identify the soused Luis in XIII. His antics are indicative of the underside of *El Toreo*. But he was Mexican and therefore regarded contemptuously by Maera. A Mexican bullfighter had many obstacles to overcome in Spain. Much more to the point is the fact that not only is Luis drunk but "Everybody was drunk" going to the Champagne.

That Chapter XIV is fiction is common knowledge. Maera did not die of a *cornada* (horn wound), did not die as Hemingway tells it. He died of tuberculosis on December 11, 1924.[8] However, artistry triumphs. The bullfighting Chapters begin with a *cornada* and end with one, and Maera, inert in the sand awaiting the coups de grace of the horns, is no different from the Greek politicos, fallen before the wall of the hospital, or the bull after the kill.

L'Envoi, Chapter XVI ("The king was working in the garden"), is the postscript. Hemingway never saw King George II who had ascended the throne of the Hellenes a year previous, nor did he ever see his queen, Elizabeth of Romania, great-granddaughter of Victoria. But his friend, Shorty Wornall, a movie-news cameraman, had, and he told about his audience with the royal pair in the palace garden ("She was clipping a rose bush"); and Hemingway expropriated the gossip for the *Star Weekly*, September 15, 1923. His picture of an affable, cynical, inept king, nice enough but no *king*, even though he considered himself to be "divinely annointed," is not excessive.

Colonel Nicholas Plastiras and his Revolutionary Committee, now in control of the government and distrusting the royal personages, had made virtual prisoners of them, confining them to the palace grounds. On December 18, 1923, at Plastiras's "request," George and Elizabeth went into exile, not to return for twelve years. "Like all Greeks he wanted to go to America." This is true. George wanted to go to California and observe agricultural methods in a climate and terrain very similar to Greece.

It was planned for 1924.

He never made it; the political climate was unseasonable.

Time-and-history in these sixteen Chapters begins in a garden in Mons and terminates artistically in a garden in Athens; begins with the Tommies shooting Germans and ends with George II saying that Plastiras "did right . . . shooting those chaps," that is, the six Greeks in Chapter V. The decade begins with death and ends with death, but as George so cheerfully puts it, " 'The great thing in this sort of an affair is not to be shot oneself.' " He was "frightfully" accurate and "frightfully" lucky. Luckier by far than the bulls, the horses, the Greeks, the Hungarians, the Germans, the bullfighters, the Italians. "Geue peace in oure time, O Lorde"; so goes the beseechment in Edward VI's First Prayer Book. The only problem is that there is no peace *In Our Time*, nor is there a "separate peace" unilaterally declared by Nick Adams as he sat against the wall of the church. " 'Only, let the story end as soon as possible,' " pleaded Demetrios Gounaris before he was shot down. The only problem is that story as time-and-history never ends; for, indeed, time as defined in the commencement of this article is "the system of those relations which any event has to any other as past, present, or future," and Ernest Miller Hemingway knew it, young as he was.

Appendix

Interchapters:

IV, III: August 23, 1914; Mons, Belgium

I: Late September–early October 1915; Champagne, France

VIII: November 19, 1917; Kansas City, Missouri

VII: June 16, 1918; Fossalta di Piave, Italy

VI: Early July, 1918; Fossalta

XV: April 15, 1921; Chicago, Illinois

II: October 16, 1922; Eastern Theatre

V: November 22, 1922; Athens, Greece

IX–XIV: Summer 1923; Spain

L'Envoi: August 1923; Athens

"Long Time Ago Good, Now No Good":
Hemingway's Indian Stories

Robert W. Lewis

●

Primitive simply means first, earliest, original, basic. Historically it refers to a way
of life prior to civilization—that is, the city-state—but to evoke it now is . . . to
temporalize the essence . . . the fuller human nature, the first nature, to which
we aspire.—Sherman Paul, *In Search of the Primitive: Rereading David Antin, Jerome
Rothenberg, and Gary Snyder*

Ever since Ernest Hemingway's childhood contact with neighboring
Ojibway and Ottawa Indians at the family summer home in northern
Michigan, Indians played a role, often small but sometimes significant, in
his life and writing. Two of his first stories, written in high school, were
about Indians: "Sepi Jingan" is about two Ojibways, and "The Judgment
of Manitou" is about two trappers, one white, and one Cree. Melodramatic and youthfully morbid, they nonetheless marked the beginning of his
career in fiction and his lifelong interest in Indians.[1] This interest
stemmed from both the Anglo-American fascination with the Noble
Savage and other "primitive" people and his own father's "white Indian"
ways. As a young man Clarence Edmonds Hemingway had spent some
months (Leicester Hemingway says three, Peter Griffin two) at "a mission
school for the Dakota Sioux" (Griffin, 6), "absorbing nature lore and
gaining a great admiration for Indian ways" (Leicester Hemingway, 20), a
feeling that he passed on to Ernest as he took him on visits to his Indian
patients in Michigan and as he taught him his highly developed hunting,
fishing, and other outdoorsman skills.[2] In 1916 Ernest also claimed Billy
Gilbert as his "old Ojibway Pal and woodcraft teacher" (Griffin, 10, 15,
23). Other influences in these formative years were at hand in domestic
Oak Park, such as the impact on the young Hemingway of Theodore
Roosevelt's widely publicized African safari, the new Field Museum of
Natural History in Chicago with its Hall of African Mammals, and the
"African passion" that swept Oak Park because of its churches' interest in
African missions and its role in helping present the African section of the

Chicago Exposition of 1913 (Reynolds, 1986, 228–32). If wild America were vanishing, there was yet another continent about which the boy could dream and in which the man could later adventure.

Indians were important characters in a number of the Nick Adams stories like the early "Indian Camp" (1925) and the later "Fathers and Sons" (1933), stories which also depict chronological opposites, the youth and the maturity of Nick Adams himself. In the neglected but successful satire *The Torrents of Spring* (1926), Indians are important foils to the white characters Yogi Johnson and Scripps O'Neil. But because Hemingway set no other novel of his in Indian country,[3] as characters Indians are absent from his long fictions and his nonfiction books except as recollections or as allusions. Such memories and references are still frequent enough to keep the connection of his Indian-consciousness constant: for instance, in *Death in the Afternoon*, a bullfighter is described as looking like an Indian; El Sordo in *For Whom the Bell Tolls* looks Indian but fights a last stand reminiscent of that of George Armstrong Custer (a historical battle elsewhere often alluded to by Hemingway); and in a later, unpublished story set in World War II, "Indian Country and the White Army," Hemingway (along with other U.S. personnel) perceived the fighting in the hedgerows and woods near the Siegfried Line as similar to Indian warfare in the early years of the American colonies and republic.

Furthermore, Hemingway at times seemed to want to perceive himself as "Indian." As an infant, "His first doll was a rubber papoose . . . and his second a white Eskimo" (Baker, 3). Growing up, "he was constantly aware of [the Indians'] presence, like atavistic shadows moving along the edges of his consciousness" (Baker, 13). Without any basis other than his own sometimes comic imagination and wishful thinking, he would claim to strangers and friends that he was one-eighth Indian (tribe often unnoted).[4] Even his much younger brother Leicester admiringly reported the disinformation as the truth in his biography *My Brother, Ernest Hemingway* (277). At times Hemingway would jokingly adopt a kind of stage-Indian dialect, making himself into a white Indian, to the embarrassment of some admirers and to the delight of some critics. Lillian Ross transcribed this dialect in her *New Yorker* "profile," and neither she nor Hemingway thought it was done maliciously. He continued on occasion to use what he termed his "Choctaw lingo." Similarly, he affected the lingo among his friends in Sun Valley, Idaho, referring to them as "a fine tribe," following or wishing to follow Indian custom when hunting or burying a friend, and calling his mistress "squaw" and himself an "old Indian" and identifying himself with the Shoshone of the region.[5]

More serious and more significant in establishing this persistent cross-cultural orientation and affinity are the references and allusions to Indian culture in his work; even in works not set in Indian country or featuring Indian characters, their culture was alive and at hand for Hemingway. For example, when Robert Jordan is alone in his sleeping bag recalling the smells he loves, one of them is the "Sweet grass the Indians used in their baskets" (*FWBT*, 260). The thought is coincidental, but it is part of a pattern in which Hemingway's characters and his own personas recognized their formation as being based partly but importantly on Indian culture. Another small note from the same novel alludes to the tribalism that is the dominant social organization of Indians. Wondering about the strangeness of Gypsies, Robert Jordan thinks, "Nobody knows what tribes we came from nor what our tribal inheritance is nor what the mysteries were in the woods where the people lived that we came from" (*FWBT*, 175).[6]

But in his fiction, and notably in some of the Nick Adams stories and the satire *The Torrents of Spring*, he most directly wrote about Indians. "Indian Camp," one of Hemingway's first stories, and "Fathers and Sons," one of his last, provide interesting ground for examination of his use of Indians and the theme of primitivism. In the former story Nick Adams as a boy accompanies his father (a medical doctor), his uncle George, and two Indians to an Indian logging camp where a woman is suffering greatly in childbirth while her husband, badly wounded by an ax, lies in the bunk over hers and helplessly listens to her screams. Working with only a jackknife and using fishing-line leaders as thread, the doctor successfully delivers the baby by Caesarian section assisted by the uncle and witnessed by the boy in the bad-smelling shanty. Then the doctor turns his attention to the wounded father: "'Ought to have a look at the proud father. They're usually the worst sufferers in these little affairs,'" he adds in another cliché that ironically proves prophetic (*Stories*, 94). The desperate father is found to have slit his throat from ear to ear during the operation. The boy witnesses this discovery too, and then the whites reverse their Stygian journey and leave the camp.

In this tale of initiation to the elemental acts of birth and death, Hemingway plays with and presents both stereotypes and individuation. On the one hand, the doctor repeatedly refers to the mother as an Indian "lady" while the narrator always uses "woman." When in her pain she bites the restraining Uncle George on his arm, he cries out, "'Damn squaw bitch!' and the young Indian who had rowed Uncle George over laughed at him" (*Stories*, 93). The all-business doctor contrasts with Uncle George who earlier had patronized the Indians (*Stories*, 91). Far from being noble exemplars of courage and endurance living in pristine nature, real Indians are men and women much like all others, and individuals among them can scream and laugh and die desperately. In the series of stories in which he figures, it is Nick's first lesson.

Yet apart from that conventional understanding of "Indian Camp," the boy is not learned enough to see the irony in the facts that his father is, like the Indians, a good woodsman, but unlike them he comes, the new "medicine man," from a wholly different culture, one that plays at being primitive but that is in fact sophisticated. In another ironic allusion the gift of tobacco in early Indian-white parleying and trading is echoed in skeptical Uncle George's giving cigars to the two Indians who accompany the whites to the camp. Perhaps one final allusion is again reversed and ironical: Indian youths sought their initiations through a vision, while Nick resists an understanding of life and death in what, for the reader at least, is a waking nightmare.

Other stories importantly involving Indians include "The Doctor and the Doctor's Wife," in which an Indian teases Dr. Adams into a rage and thus can forego sawing some logs he had agreed to saw in payment, the doctor says, "'for pulling his squaw through pneumonia and I guess he wanted a row so he wouldn't have to take it out in work'" (*Stories*, 102). The Indian is not a guileless child of nature but instead is "a half-breed and many of the farmers around the lake believed he was a white man" even though he lives with the Indians, is married to one, and speaks Ojibway. Is it because he is both "very lazy but a great worker once he was started" and he is clever that makes the stereotyping farmers believe him to be white? (*Stories*, 100). In fact, in a letter from Dr. Hemingway to Ernest, Carlos Baker found confirmation of such an actual event as the confrontation described in the story and identification of the real Dick Boulton as a mixed-blood Indian (Montgomery, 66). Although other details in the story were imagined, the ethnography was apparently drawn accurately from life.

In "Ten Indians" Nick Adams appears again, returning to the northern Michigan summer home from a Fourth of July celebration. He and his friends pass nine drunken Indians along the road, and when he reaches home, his father tells him about a tenth Indian he had seen that day, Prudence Mitchell, a girl whom the adolescent Nick has been courting. He is grieved to learn that she was making love in the woods with another man, and he goes to bed thinking his heart is broken. But "after a while he forgot to think about Prudence and finally he went to sleep. . . . In the morning there was a big wind blowing and the waves were running high up on the beach and he was awake a long time before he remembered that his heart was broken" (*Stories*, 336). Thus another phase of initiation for

Nick ends with a bittersweet joke about another cliché, that of romantic love. The association is significant in that Nick's disillusionment is related to both the errors of stereotyping erotic behavior and racial identity.

In "Now I Lay Me" we learn that Nick's father had a treasured collection of Indian axes, knives, arrowheads, and pottery that his mother thoughtlessly destroyed. The implication is that the son like the father valued the culture from which the artifacts came. Similarly, in "The Last Good Country" the idyllic flight from authority of Nick and his younger sister is to an Indian lair in Michigan. They are guided to it by Indian signs, they live off the land like Indians, and they have acquired the Indians' intimate knowledge of the last good country, which is primitive, Edenic, and Indian. Nick even says that he should have been an Indian, a wish sometimes reflected in Hemingway's letters and conversations (*NAS*, 111).

Close reading of another Nick Adams story, "The Light of the World," elevates the Indians in the barroom from wooden, unspeaking background details to figures who underscore an important theme. Furthermore, there is external biographical information indicating that Nick's young companion Tommy is an Indian.[7] Elsewhere (notably in *A Farewell to Arms* and "The Snows of Kilimanjaro") Hemingway had established patterns of imagery in which coldness is associated with goodness. Light-dark imagery (as in "A Clean, Well-Lighted Place" and this story) is less clearly associated with the conventional symbolic pattern in which light is knowledge or goodness. The "Clean, Well-Lighted Place" is an artificial refuge, and, in the stories of his wounding and his subsequent fear of the dark ("Now I Lay Me" and "A Way You'll Never Be"), Nick knows that the need to have a light on at night is unnatural. This pattern is repeated in "Big Two-Hearted River" where Nick is at once afraid of, yet drawn to, the darkness of the swamp. The traumatic wounding has temporarily reversed the natural pattern. When he is recovered, he will again be able to go to the dark as to the primordial.

In "The Light of the World" then, the minor Indian characters may be significant as people of darkness and cold who oppose the ironic white-light-warm imagery associated with knowledge and power but also conversely with confusion and the loss of spirituality. "Outside it was good and dark" whereas inside it is "crowded and hot . . . and full of stale smoke" (*Stories*, 385). The homosexual cook is repeatedly referred to as white in face and hands. The two "ordinary" whores, one of whom tells an outrageous lie, are peroxide blondes, whereas the three fat whores, including Alice who wins Nick's sympathy, are all clad in "silk dresses that change colors" (*Stories*, 386), that is, shimmering, symbolically ambiguous, between light and dark. The lying peroxide whore tells a story full of blasphemies and repeated allusions to mythic gods with whom she associates the dead white boxer Stanley Ketchel who she claims was her lover. Ketchel was defeated unfairly, she says, by the black Jack Johnson—"'That big dinge . . . the big black bastard. That nigger beat him by a fluke. . . . He was like a god he was. So white and clean and beautiful and smooth and fast and like a tiger or like lightning'" (*Stories*, 389).

At this point with the fantasy at its highest, the Indians leave for the cold and dark outside, and then Alice accuses the blonde of lying and gives her version of Steve Ketchel whom *she* claims to have loved, swearing to Jesus and Mary it is true. Just as Nick is beginning to feel attracted to Alice, wondering what it would be like making love to a 350-pound woman, his friend Tom (possibly also Indian) sees him looking at her and says, "'Come on. Let's go'" (*Stories*, 391)—let's go out with the red Indians, leaving the warm, lighted, whited sepulcher for the cold and dark suggestive of a simpler, better alternative to the contradictions of that other world. It is a striking and typical contrast of decadence and the primitive.

"Fathers and Sons," the last story in his collected stories, is also a Nick Adams story, but in it there is a chronological leap forward so that Nick is neither a child nor youth but a mature thirty-eight, with a son of his own to initiate. Biographical parallels continue, no doubt, but once again Hemingway twisted inchoate real life into a meaningful fiction by writing that his sexual initiation was with an Indian, and it was in "the forest primeval." In language reminiscent of many other descriptions of a golden age or a sacred time and place, Nick remembers, "there was still much forest then, virgin forest where the trees grew high before there were any branches and you walked on the brown, clean, springy-needled ground with no undergrowth and it was cool on the hottest days and they three"—Nick and his Indian girlfriend and her kid brother—"lay against the trunk of a hemlock wider than two beds are long, with the breeze high in the tops and the cool light that came in patches, and Billy said":

> "You want Trudy again?"
> [Nick] "You want to?"
> [Trudy] "Un Huh." (*Stories*, 492–93)

But the idyll is evanescent; Nick remembers his hypocrisy when he flew into a rage at learning that Trudy's and Billy's older half-brother wanted to sleep with Nick's sister and Nick threatened to shoot and scalp him. The idyll and its recollection are also marred by other memories of his loved but foolish father—sentimental, betrayed, and at last a suicide. Nick's own son, as if reading his mind, then asks what the Indians of Nick's youth were like.

"'They were Ojibways,'" Nick said. "'And they were very nice.'" Nick then silently remembers how Trudy "did first what no one has ever done better" (*Stories*, 497).[8] He also remembers both good and bad images associated with the Ojibways and rejects as unimportant the derogatory jokes about Indians, "Nor what they did finally. It wasn't how they ended. They all ended the same. Long time ago good. Now no good" (*Stories*, 498).[9]

Nick does not want to be caught up in futile nostalgia. He wants to remember exactly how it was. It is another stage in his education. But at the same time he feels some good in the naive past which has been detrimentally lost. The ambivalence here could parallel the many other places where Hemingway bitterly recognized the evanescence of human affairs, especially love, or, if he knew of Trudy's real-life counterpart's suicide, a parallel to the suicide of his father, the other person most fully remembered and depicted in the story and also an actual suicide.

"Long time ago good. Now no good" echoes phrases he claimed to have heard from an old Indian and that elsewhere he rendered, "Long time ago good, now heap shit" (*Letters*, xii), a version that would have broken the elegaic tone of the passage in the story. Nick returns from his reveries to answer his son, "'You might not like them [the Indians]. . . . But I think you would,'" just as Nick's father had (*Stories*, 498). The story ends with the son persuading Nick to visit the grandfather's (Nick's father's) tomb, to reverence the dead and the past.

At the time he began writing these Nick Adams stories, Hemingway had also been exposed to the nonsense in romanticizing primitives, playing at being an Indian or a black or a gypsy or some other supposedly innocent creature unspoiled by a mechanical world. Hemingway's reaction to such romanticizing triggered the satirical attack on Sherwood Anderson's *Dark Laughter* in his *The Torrents of Spring: A Romantic Novel in Honor of the Passing of a Great Race* (1926).

For Hemingway it was one thing to cultivate instinct and suspect mind and quite another thing to generalize romantically, as he felt Anderson had done: "That terrible shit about the nobility of any gent belonging to another race than our own (whatever that is) was worth checking," he had replied to Wyndham Lewis' praise of *The Torrents of Spring* (*Letters*, 264). Later, Hemingway's own extensive treatment of blacks in *Green Hills of Africa* would confirm his refusal to stereotype them as either noble or ignoble savages. Like the portrait of Bugs in "The Battler," they would be individuated. In a satire like *The Torrents of Spring*, however, he stereotyped to the extreme in order to mock and correct the tendency to romanticize the primitive and, in the United States and Europe, ever since Columbus but especially since Rousseau, to romanticize American Indians. If, to Europeans and European-Americans, Indians were not "howling savages," they tended to become "noble"—primitive innocents living close to a gentle Nature and uncorrupted by "unnatural" institutions of church and state. Hemingway was certainly exposed to and tempted by this anthropologically naive view that periodically in this country seems to charm persons with little or no direct experience of actual Indians, the vastly different cultures, languages, histories, and orientations of many different peoples all being lumped together into a hazy "Indianness."

Hemingway's antidote partly lay at hand in the summers of his youth when he came to know not "Indians" but Ojibways and Ottawas and, even better, the real-life counterparts of them that he imagined as individuals into his short stories.[10] Furthermore, Hemingway's primitivism was part of his artistic self-consciousness, which he shared with his generation of artists, and part of his disillusionment with the Western "civilization," which had produced not only the bloodiest war in history but also technocracy, bureaucracy, and moral hypocrisy, all of which had a staggering impact on artists such as Hemingway whose values were in many ways conventional. As Malcolm Cowley perceived, Hemingway's primitivism had nothing to do with romance, but was instead concerned with the substitution of the inauthentic for the authentic. Cowley was among the first to unlock stories like "Big Two-Hearted River," reading it as "incantation" and "spell" and accompanied by other stories of animal and human sacrifice, sexual initiation and union, self-immolation, conversion, and symbolic death and rebirth. Cowley also saw that "Memories of the Indians he knew in his boyhood play an important part in Hemingway's work" (xx). Of course there were to be other primitive models, and Cowley cites the Spanish as preeminent among the successors to the Indians of Michigan, as later does Leslie Fiedler. But they were first and they endured, later complemented by the Gypsies and peasants of Spain and the natives of East Africa.

Since the work of A. O. Lovejoy and Franz Boas, primitivism has come to be regarded as of two sorts, cultural and chronological, and Hemingway variously, at different points in his career, evidenced both varieties.[11] Far from suggesting crudity and undevelopment, primitivism is a recurrent cultural phenomenon which places value on the simplicity of social forms and finds sophistication a companion of cultural degeneration and even evil. The cultural primitive then wishes to restructure society and all aspects of it, from art to family, along lines that are felt to be more natural and better suited for the capacities and desires of human beings. Industrialization and urbanization are developments judged to be, in varying degrees, inhuman and hostile to spirit and art. Chronological primitivism looks not forward to amelioration of the human condition but backward to some time in the past when the human condition was if not Edenic at least holistic and characterized by reverence for life, high moral purpose, humane dealings, and beauty. If cultural primitivism tended to be Utopian, chronological primitivism was Arcadian. *In illo tempore* there was a Golden Age once, never to be seen again. Camelots riddle our cultural landscapes.

Nick Adams's thoughts in the idiom of an Ojibway, "Long time ago good. Now no good" (*Stories*, 498), perfectly if oversimply epitomize chronological primitivism. But what was the "long time ago?" While Hemingway was sometimes nostalgic for particular persons and activities from his past, he did not sentimentalize them, distorting them beyond recollection and reality. Indeed, as at the end of "Ten Indians" when Nick awakens, Hemingway gently mocks the idea of romantic love, one of the most enduring ideals associated with chronological primitivism. There seemed to be a tension that alternately drew and repelled Hemingway, who was sufficiently anachronistic for Scott Fitzgerald to cast him as a heroic medieval knight in one of his last unfinished stories, "Phillipe, Count of Darkness."

One working title for his own *Across the River and into the Trees* had been *A New Slain Knight* (from the ballad "The Twa Corbies"). Throughout that novel the modern knight, U.S. Army Colonel Richard Cantwell, pictures himself, albeit often ironically, as a knight errant. His lady, Renata, he asks to run for Queen of Heaven, an allusion Hemingway used in other stories too as well as in letters to some of the women he admired. In an early story, "The Three-Day Blow," he revealed a familiarity with the archetypal Tristan-Iseult love story which he often drew upon thematically. The title for *A Farewell to Arms* derives from the George Peele poem on the retirement of one of Queen Elizabeth I's knights. Other such allusions and references to chivalry occur in his work, from *In Our Time* to *Across the River and into the Trees*.[12] Two books published recently (1981) index the seven thousand volumes in Hemingway's Cuban library and trace his extensive reading from 1910 to 1940 (Reynolds, *Hemingway's Reading*, and Brasch and Sigman). These works are signs of a thorough reassessment of Hemingway as neither a "Dumb Ox" nor a merely accidental cultural primitive, someone who has mindlessly adopted a fashionable cultural pose. Yet problems of definition continue: Jeffrey Meyers succumbs to Wyndham Lewis's "Dumb Ox" view of Hemingway and subscribes to a stereotype of persons drawn to the primitive: Hemingway "outwardly suppressed the sensitive side of his nature and chose to cultivate a virile image [writing] about the Indians and violence of Michigan, rather than the stuffy culture of Oak Park" (7). A more telling misobservation is hard to imagine, with its suggestion that a sensitive person would opt for the "stuffy" and that a primitive would not be sensitive; yet the stance is prototypical. Lewis's *Paleface* (1929), "blasting" primitivism and praising *The Torrents of Spring*, also seems a misunderstanding of Hemingway's orientation. The superficial so-called primitivism and the easy patronizing of Indians and blacks from a position of privilege were what Hemingway parodied. However misguided, Lewis seemed to have thought he reversed his opinion of Hemingway when he later (in 1934) called him a "white version" of the Noble Savage. Some of these reassessments would make him out (if they were considered in isolation from other critical interpretations) to be a chronological primitive rather than a cultural primitive, and they place him among a group of other twentieth-century American writers who romanticized the Middle Ages. The name Henry Adams, the father of recurring protagonist Nick Adams, is the same as the name of the greatest of our medieval admirers. Mark Twain, James Branch Cabell, Scott Fitzgerald, T. S. Eliot, and Edwin Arlington Robinson, among others, were drawn to the Middle Ages, as were lesser but more popular writers like Maurice Hewlett. Another contemporary, Willa Cather, found her golden age in spiritually rich but materially simple cultures like our pioneer past, the early days of French Canada, and the early Spanish-Indian culture of the Southwest—anything but the machine-driven, commercial, and tawdry world of the urban United States.

All of this suggests that if Hemingway was no Miniver Cheevy, he was writing at at time when the Middle Ages (for Henry Adams, notably the twelfth century) were much admired by many serious writers as an era of belief, value, beauty, and, above all, stability, whereas the twentieth century, especially since World War I for Hemingway's generation, was an era of culture in crisis. And neither church nor country, religious nor secular values, survived those crises unshaken.

But Hemingway's flirtation with chronological primitivism in his interest in medievalism and his tendency to idealize the frontier past of America seem to have emerged later than his cultural primitivism, which was less consciously sought out and more naturally learned. In the 1930s he began to see America as spoiled, and except for *The Torrents of Spring* he never finished a novel set in it. In the 1940s he began his intensive reading in the Middle Ages. And in these years his writing that reflected this interest in medievalism (notably *Across the River and into the Trees*) diminished in quality. Only when he returned to the theme of cultural primitivism in *The Old Man and the Sea* were (for many readers) his talents again well engaged.

For primitives, a basic question is What is nature and the natural? For nature is superior and intrinsic and provides the norm and health, whereas custom, law, and the rational are contrivances that lead to a *seeming* order in which luxury and decorum or morality (strange but frequent bedfellows) rule. Ironically for chronological primitives, medieval Christianity seemed to partake of cultural primitivism, being anti-intellectual and Utopian, accepting the rule of grace, not mind. The two kinds of primitivism inevitably and repeatedly drew Hemingway and many of his contemporaries. Musicians like Debussy, Stravinsky, and Villa-Lobos, painters like Picasso and Klee, and writers like D. H. Lawrence, Sherwood Anderson, Gertrude Stein, Alfred Jarry, and Antonin Artaud helped create a cultural context which provided part of Hemingway's education, partly and to an important degree, in Paris, that most sophisticated of cities and locus earlier for the Indian-lover Rousseau whose primitivism was merely intellectual.

Thus, on the other side of chronological primitivism, manifested periodically and generally not well, was Hemingway's cultural primitivism, part of the Zeitgeist but also (for Hemingway) reinforced by direct experience with primitives and rendered in realistic fiction. Unlike Robinson Crusoe or other "moderns" eager to escape nature and return to civilization, Hemingway and his other American predecessors like Huck Finn will "light out for the Territory"—Indian country—literally or figuratively.

One more particular example, the very short "Banal Story," is slight, facetious, and melodramatic by turn, but nonetheless it provides a remarkably frank insight to Hemingway's tough-minded disparagement of Romance (read "false primitivism") and his sardonic recognition that ours is not a golden age but merely a brass age that sings a small paean to his anachronistic hero, the dead bullfighter Manuel Garcia Maera, one of the last of the great matadors. His passing brings relief to the lesser still-living fighters who will no longer be shamed by comparison with Maera. The chronological divide between golden and brass has been crossed. In contrast to Maera's values, the first part of the story, as in *The Torrents of Spring*, describes and mocks the intellectual longing for the primitive. As with Robert Cohn in *The Sun Also Rises,* who thinks he will find happiness and perhaps "splendid imaginary amorous adventures . . . in an intensely romantic land" (9), the unnamed protagonist of the first part of the story seeks Romance vicariously through his writing and through reading *The Forum,* a popular magazine appealing to typical middle-class, middlebrow Americans, in turn flattering their pretentions and raising mindless questions about the future and the past.

Here again, as in Hemingway's 1956 letter about East Africa and his initiation into the Kamba tribe, we find the banal President Coolidge and other deracinated patrons, sportsmen, and authors. "Our civilization—is it inferior to older orders of things?" The answer to the rhetorical question is an implied "Yes." "And meanwhile, in the far-off dripping jungles of Yucatan, sounded the chopping of the axes of the gumchoppers": this is an ironic illustration of the incursion of the banal and the destructive even into a jungle (*Stories,* 360).

The single reference to an Indian is to Pocahontas whom John Smith had converted into a princess and a lover, the archetypal dream of the dusky maiden who would bring primal joy to the white man longing to escape the enervation of civilization. She epitomizes a mockery of the cultural primitive's beliefs converted into a red fantasy, and she also illustrates the foolishness of at least some chronological primitives' beliefs when they are grounded in false history (an oxymoron?) and distortions of the past, for Pocahontas as she has come down to us in legend is a fabrication of John Smith, who was eager to promote settlement and investment in the Virginia colony. She is fairy sister to Odysseus' sirens, Melville's Fayaway, and hosts of other images in the fine and popular arts of Western civilization. "Live the full life of the mind," Hemingway's narrator mocks, "exhilarated by new ideas, intoxicated by the Romance of the unusual" (*Stories,* 361).

Soldered on to this story of banality is the one-paragraph counterpoint describing the death of one of the greatest modern bullfighters, Manuel Garcia Maera, a modern-day primitive much admired by Hemingway for his "grace under pressure" and his skill in an art now turned into another popular pastime. Bullfighting had had its golden age. There were no heroes left. Progress was a myth. And perhaps Hemingway, like Fitzgerald's Gatsby, was borne back "ceaselessly into the past" even as he struggled on disillusioned, disenchanted, but with some degree of courage.

References and allusions to Indians run throughout the public fiction and nonfiction and the private letters, not as a major element, but perhaps as a trace element essential to psychic health. In the fiction the trace element of Indianness accompanies the theme of primitivism, a central and recurring idea of some complexity and of both personal and historical interest. We may understand both Hemingway and his time within the context of his writing about Indians and, more broadly, the primitivism of which they provided him both a paradigm and auto-biographical, experiential material.

Story

Interpretations

Hemingway's "Banal Story"

Wayne Kvam

●

"Banal Story" first appeared in the *Little Review*, the spring-summer issue of 1926,[1] and after slight changes and additions it was reprinted in *Men Without Women*, published by Scribner's in 1927.[2] Perhaps because of its brevity and lack of plot, the story has attracted little attention among Hemingway's critics. Those few who have discussed "Banal Story" have failed to penetrate its surface. Joseph Defalco, for example, states that Maera, as an archetypal Christ figure, is the focal point of the story: "The world will not accept true heroes for long, and when heroes die the danger to convention goes with them. In 'Banal Story' . . . the focus points to the addiction of people to unimportant tabloid romances while a singular event is taking place: the death of a hero."[3] According to Nicholas Joost, "Banal Story" is not a story, but a sketch which depicts "the banality and sterility of American life, as typified by the stories, editorials, and advertisements of the *Forum*. . . . Hemingway contrasts American life to life in Spain, as typified by his great Spanish culture-hero Manuel Garcia, the matador known professionally as Maera."[4] In his recent biography of Hemingway, Carlos Baker passes over the story, labeling it simply a "final tribute to the matador Maera."[5]

It is my contention that "Banal Story" is more than a tribute, a sketch, or a satirical attack on the *Forum*; rather, it is a carefully constructed parable that embodies an aesthetic theory, the same theory that Hemingway was to express in various forms throughout his career. A knowledge of the original version of the story and the subsequent alterations, which were made sometime between 1926 and the publication date of *Men Without Women* in 1927, aid one in piecing the apparently divergent parts together. (1) In paragraph three of the second version (214.15), "mused" was changed to "read," thereby removing the narration from a free-flowing stream of consciousness and linking it concretely with the *Forum*, a prominent American magazine of the 1920s. (2) The introductory sentence of paragraph six (215.2) was changed from "His thoughts raced on" to "He read on"; thus the preceding statement—"I must read them"—is to be understood as a brief pause in the actual reading rather than an interruption in a thought process. (3) The next significant change occurs after paragraph eleven (215.25), where "It was a splendid booklet" is added. This informs us that "he" is still reading from the *Forum*. The irony in this statement becomes evident at the end of the story. (4) A final addition occurs at the end of paragraph eighteen (216.17). The statement "He laid down the booklet" separates the *Forum* material from the subject of Maera's death which follows.

The above alterations and additions clarify the two major divisions of the story. The first consists of paragraphs 1, 2, 9, and 19 (beginning, middle, and end); and the second of paragraphs 3–8, and 10–18. Paragraphs one and two introduce the "He" of the story (either Hemingway writing about himself or a fictional consciousness serving as a Hemingway spokesman) and offer a definition of life, followed by a definition of Romance. Paragraph nine links the beginning and ending of the story, the definitions of life and Romance with the account of death. Intervening are paragraphs 3–8 and 10–18, which illustrate the responses of the Hemingway writer, "he," to the editorial policy and contents of the *Forum*. These two divisions establish the main conflict in the story—that between the true and false responses to life and death.

As is the case with Hemingway's topical satire in *The Torrents of Spring* and *The Sun Also Rises* (also written in the mid-1920s), the satire in "Banal Story" loses much of its impact if considered apart from its historical context. To a new generation of readers unfamiliar with the *Forum* of the 1920s, the middle section of the story must indeed appear puzzling. According to the autobiography of Henry G. Leach, who assumed the editorship of the *Forum* in 1923, "In five years from 1923 to 1928, the circulation of the *Forum* increased from 2,000 to 102,000, which was in those days deemed satisfactory for an 'intellectual periodical.'" Carl Sandburg, Leach proudly recalled, "was so generous as to call the *Forum* 'the barometer of American intelligence.'" Known as the "magazine of controversy" in the 1920s, the *Forum* directed its appeal to what editor Leach felt was the thinking minority in the American populace. The major portion of each monthly issue was devoted to philosophical debates on the most controversial topics of the decade: prohibition, science vs. religion, the race question, sexual freedom, revolutionary trends in the arts, the population explosion, immigration, and the war debt. "Our editorial policy," Leach stated, "was to keep the magazine objective and recognize that there are sometimes more than two sides to any problem. There is seldom a 'yes or no' and often a 'both-and' in public issues, and we usually presented more than just two facets of a contemporary issue. My personal formula for the *Forum* was that it should 'encourage technological habits of thinking.'"[6]

Although the *Forum* of the 1920s could be considered progressive, at least from an intellectual standpoint, its literary standards were decidedly conservative. In judging fiction for publication, "the *Forum* demanded," according to Leach, "the three unities of plot, characterization, and style prescribed for the short-story of Poe and Hawthorne." In addition, Leach required that each issue contain "some humor and some religion."[7] Since the *Forum* debates, advertised as "high adventures of the mind," were seldom written in a humorous vein, it was the fiction which was often intended to supply a lighter side to the magazine. It is this combination of intellectual pomposity and critical naiveté in the *Forum*'s editorial policy that Hemingway is parodying in paragraphs three and four of "Banal Story."

To stimulate interest in the controversies sponsored by the *Forum*, Leach frequently posed a series of rhetorical questions in his editorial introductions. The following excerpt from the introduction to the March 1925 issue is a typical example:

> What constitutes a good poem? Is it merely a matter of opinion, of individual taste? Or are there standards which must be adhered to? By whom were they established? . . . To-day poetry is being written which does not adhere to the standards of the past: is it, then, to be banned? Or if we accept free rhythms and an absence of those conventions which formerly constituted good poetry, do we thereby repudiate the old standards as obsolete and unnecessary?[8]

The questions in the middle section of "Banal Story" parody this stylistic mannerism, and nearly all of them have specific sources in the monthly issues of the *Forum* published during 1925.

Corresponding to paragraph six in "Banal Story," for example, are the following questions from Leach's introductions: (1) May 1925: "the *Forum* professes to discuss in the coming years not only the mechanical means proposed to check war, but the substitutes that must be discovered for war if it is to be eliminated as a perennial purger of the human race. . . . If the Japanese are not to be decimated by war, where will they find a place under the sun?"[9] (2) September 1925: "How shall war be abolished? *Can* war be abolished? Ever? in our time? How can wars be made safer—not for the individual, obviously—but for mankind?"[10]

The problem of shifting populations on an overcrowded globe, alluded to in paragraph seven of "Banal Story" by the question "Or will we all have to move to Canada?" was a familiar subject in the *Forum*. In the introduction to the May issue of 1925 Leach asked, "Can the waste places of central Australia and the Canadian arctic and the wet jungles of the Amazon be inhabited?" and "Will scientific agriculture and diet and housing make more room?"[11] The first sentence of paragraph eight ("Our deepest convictions—will Science upset them?") refers to another major concern of *Forum* contributors during 1925.[12] In introducing a series of articles under the heading "Evolution and Daily Living" in the February issue, Leach wrote, "Science has of late been going the way of the agnostic and mechanist, forgetful of the mind, let alone the soul. . . . Some theologians, on the other hand, have made an equally sorry mess of it by blindfolding their eyes to science. The time has come for a reconciliation.[13] Two months later (April 1925), Leach stated, "In bringing together the views of future-minded scientists and religious thinkers, the *Forum* is trying to plumb the depths of a spiritual reawakening that may help to fuse into effective meaning the chaotic mass of facts with which modern research has overwhelmed us."[14]

The second sentence of paragraph eight in "Banal Story" echoes Leach's introduction to a series of anthropology studies under the general heading "What is Civilization?" which the *Forum* initiated in January 1925: "The Editor is setting out upon the impossible adventure of discovering civilization. He has been told that twentieth-century America, for all its radio and its bull markets, is not the be-all, nor the end-all of human life. Is it possible that men have already known better ways of living in the past and that we their descendants have recklessly obliterated the highroads they have built to happiness?"[15]

Hemingway was not only parodying Leach's stylistic mannerisms and the technological habits of thought which he sought to promote, but also the format which the *Forum* debates followed. Leach outlined this format in his introduction to the April 1925 issue:

> The *Forum* believes that the best way of dispelling the ignorance and the bias that obscure these tremendous issues is to present in juxtaposition, the interpretations—no matter how divergent—of writers who have devoted to them the most earnest consideration. Steel and flint are hard and useful *per se*, but only when they come into sharp impact do they strike off the incendiary spark of truth.[16]

The parody of this formula in "Banal Story" is two-fold. As we have already noted, the structure of the story itself follows the *Forum* pattern. Divergent interpretations (those of the Hemingway writer as opposed to those of the *Forum*) of "tremendous issues" (life and death) are juxtaposed. More specifically, Hemingway is reducing the formula to the level of the absurd in such examples as the following. In paragraph ten of "Banal Story" he borrows the title of a *Forum* article, "Big Men—Or Cultured?"[17] and proposes to answer the question according to Leach's formula of juxtaposing opposites: "Take Joyce. Take President Coolidge." The remainder of the paragraph follows the same pattern. The author of the article "Big Men—Or Cultured?" was a Yale student voicing a protest against the spirit of "be a big man or bust," which he felt had invaded the Yale campus. Hemingway asks, "What star must our college students aim at?" and answers with another set of opposites. Doctor Henry Van Dyke, whom the *Forum* advertised as "philosopher, poet, essayist, spiritual teacher, and master teller of tales,"[18] is placed between two prominent American prize fighters of the 1920s, Jack Britton and Young Stribling.

The rhetorical question which introduces paragraph eleven refers to Arthur Hamilton Gibbs's novel *Soundings*, serialized in the *Forum* from October 1924 through April 1925. Nancy Hawthorne, the heroine, is an eighteen-year-old English girl whose mother died at her birth and whose father attempts to raise her alone in the small village of Brimble. One night Curly, a village boy, kisses Nancy and she becomes restless, bringing "both father and daughter to the tardy realization that she is grown up."[19] As a result, Nancy's father decides to send her off to the Continent alone, to make the "Soundings" of life for herself. The novel, as one might suspect, is mawkishly sentimental. Nancy's hero is a major in the United States Army, who after "strafing the Huns" returns to her to live happily ever after, and the virtuous, strong-minded girl is rewarded with marriage and children. *Soundings* is an example of the fiction which the *Forum* advertised as "bits of real life." Holding the heroine Nancy Hawthorne up as a model for young girls to follow, is as false, Hemingway is saying, as substituting "some humor and some religion" for a realistic depiction of death and tragedy. The next statement, "It was a splendid booklet," then, is to be understood as sarcasm on the part of the writer as he pages through the *Forum*. The paragraph which follows is a return to the parody of editor Leach's formula for problem-solving, illustrated in paragraph ten.

The attack on the *Forum*'s editorial policy continues in paragraph fourteen. "Think of these things in 1925," rather than "feel" or "experience" these things, corresponds to Leach's promise of the "high adventure of the mind."[20] The question, "Was there a risqué page in Puritan history?" possibly relates to an article "In the Wicked Old Puritan Days," published in the *Forum* American Series in April 1926.[21] The question,

"Were there two sides to Pocahontas?" is another playful treatment of the *Forum* debates. "Did she have a fourth dimension?" a question added after the first printing of the story, could refer to Leach's introductory statement in the August 1925 issue. Here the editor wrote "that civilization is a multiplication of so many factors that it will be differently defined by every mind that attempts an analysis. It belongs to the 'fourth dimension' terms that baffle the average understanding."[22]

The sources for paragraph fifteen of "Banal Story" ("Are modern paintings—and poetry—Art? Yes and No. Take Picasso.") can also be found in specific issues of the *Forum*. In June 1925 Leach wrote, "Music has long claimed the right to be abstract as well as to imitate nature; but can painting and sculpture also break away altogether from illustrating things as they are, and claim to be pure art?"[23] Following was a debate entitled "Is Cubism Pure Art?" Walter Pack contributed the first article, "Picasso's Achievement,"[24] and Alfred Churchill countered with "Picasso's Failure."[25] The topic was introduced again at the end of the July 1925 issue when Leach reprinted letters from the readers under the title, "Pure Art? Or 'Pure Nonsense'?"[26]

The first sentence of paragraph sixteen—"Have tramps codes of conduct?"—likely refers to the article "Tramps and Hoboes," by Towne Nylander, published in the *Forum* in August 1925.[27] "Send your mind adventuring," the next sentence of the paragraph, was one of Leach's favorite mottoes. In the December 1924 issue, for example, Leach wrote, "Send your mind adventuring! is the invitation of the December *Forum*." Introducing an article by Vilhjalmur Stefansson, he added, "Stefansson carries the mind adventuring to the Orient by short cuts through the air across the Arctic ice. And the adventure of the mind is continued in other articles."[28] In the following issue, January 1925, Leach announced: "Send your mind adventuring! is the invitation of the *Forum* for the new year, the fortieth of its life as a magazine."[29]

The two concluding paragraphs of the *Forum* section of the story imitate Leach's manner of editorial advertising and are intended to be read ironically. Paragraph seventeen parallels the introduction of a new serial to appear in the *Forum* of May 1925: "Readers of the *Forum* have learned to expect a serial of wit and charm, rich in situations, brilliant in character development, challenging in thought."[30] Paragraph eighteen echoes Leach's statement in the December 1924 issue: "Other journals may follow other high adventures—sex, success, travel—but for the *Forum* we modestly announce the high adventure of the mind."[31]

Serving as a deliberate contrast to the responses to life offered by editor Leach and the *Forum* are the writer's responses to life and death, arranged at the beginning, the middle, and the end of "Banal Story." With this contrast in mind, we can follow the shift in tone which occurs in the middle section. In the first two paragraphs the writer is responding to the immediate, the commonplace and physical; therefore, he is emphatic ("How good it felt!") and colloquial ("Mascart had knocked Danny Frush cuckoo"). Turning to the *Forum* in paragraph three, Hemingway imitates the formal diction, the logical, abstract approach to experience, and the Socratic method of debate which the *Forum* prided itself upon.

Life that concerns the Hemingway writer is demonstrated in paragraph one. Life, "he" proclaims after rising from his writing table, consists of that which one perceives with one's senses, whether it be in the *tasting* and *smelling* of an orange, *seeing* the snow turn to rain, or *feeling* the heat of the stove on one's bottom. The writer's definition of life also includes romance, but this is not "the Romance of the unusual," which the *Forum* promises will intoxicate the minds of its readers, but it is the romance of everyday struggle encountered by people of all countries and all educational levels. Not limited to the writer's immediate environment, it is the romance that one might find recorded in the daily newspaper: a boxing match "Far away in Paris," a heavy snowfall "Far off in Mesopotamia," or a cricket match "Across the world in distant Australia."

In paragraph nine the writer's mind suddenly jumps from the pages of the *Forum* as he hears in his imagination the sound of the axes of gum-choppers in "the far-off dripping jungles of Yucatan." Why does Hemingway allow for this particular shift? There are at least three sources in the *Forum* of August 1925. Leach explained that "The cover design of the *Forum*, in use for eight months, was drawn by Alfred C. Bossom from old Mayan Indian motifs." The August issue contained an explanation of the design by Herbert J. Spinden.[32] This same issue featured an introductory poem "To the Mayas" by H. Phelps Clawson[33] and an essay entitled "The Answer of Ancient America," which dealt with the Mayan civilization in the Yucatán.[34]

Unlike the scholars represented in the *Forum*, the Hemingway writer approaches the Indians of the Yucatán on the level of the immediate and the physical. The sensual experience of sound reminds us of his response to life in paragraph one, while the adjective "far-off" links the action of the gum-choppers with the sense of struggle that characterizes his definition of Romance in paragraph two. At the same time the introductory "And meanwhile" of paragraph nine links this thought with the one introduced by the parallel "And meanwhile" in the final paragraph of the story. In this paragraph the account of Maera's death completes the writer's response to life. As Hemingway was to write in *Death in the*

Afternoon, "all stories if continued far enough end in death; and he is no true story-teller who would keep that from you."[35] This is something which the *Forum* writers with their "warm homespun, American tales, bits of real life . . . all with a healthy undercurrent of humor," have omitted.

The writer's response to death has none of the jealousy of Maera's fellow bullfighters, who envied his skill and were secretly relieved at his death. As *Death in the Afternoon* was to make clear, the writer, or Hemingway in this case, was a great admirer of Maera for what he was as a bullfighter and as a man. He was aware of Maera's prolonged suffering and his tortuous battle with death, neither of which could be recorded in a special newspaper supplement.[36] The funeral mourners who sit out of the rain and lose "the picture they had of him [Maera] in their memories" by looking at colored pictures, are similar to the *Forum* writers, who substitute colored pictures of life for reality.

The Hemingway writer, however, does not allow the picture in his mind to be distorted; his task is to capture what a photograph cannot. Hemingway expresses a similar idea at the conclusion of *Green Hills of Africa*. After the safari, P. O. M. complains that she can no longer remember Mr. J. P.'s face: "'I think about him and think about him and I can't see him. It's terrible. He isn't the way he looks in a photograph. In a little while I won't be able to remember him at all. Already I can't see him.'" Hemingway in turn responds, "'I can remember him. . . . I'll write you a piece sometime and put him in.'"[37]

The one sentence of paragraph nine, then, carries a heavier burden in "Banal Story" than its length might suggest. Placed in the middle of the story, it serves to link beginning and end, the writer's reaction to life with his reaction to death. It also illustrates how the response of Hemingway's writer, occupied with what he can see, hear, feel, taste, and smell, differs from the intellectual abstractions in the pages of the *Forum*. The writer's definition of life in "Banal Story" is similar to the guerilla El Sordo's definition in *For Whom the Bell Tolls*: "living was a field of grain blowing in the wind on the side of a hill. Living was a hawk in the sky. Living was an earthen jar of water in the dust of the threshing with the grain flailed out and the chaff blowing. Living was a horse between your legs and a carbine under one leg and a hill and a valley and a stream with trees along it, and the far side of the valley and the hills beyond."[38] Talking about life in purely abstract terminology, as did the *Forum*, is "talking horseshit." As Hemingway explained to the Old Lady in *Death in the Afternoon*: "we apply the term now to describe unsoundness in an abstract conversation or, indeed, any over-metaphysical tendency in speech."[39]

According to Hemingway's aesthetic, the ability to deal directly with physical sensations in writing is what separates the good artist from the poor. To re-create Navarra, for example, one would have to "make clouds come fast in shadows moving over wheat and the small, careful stepping horses; the smell of olive oil; the feel of leather; rope-soled shoes; the loops of twisted garlics; earthen pots; saddle bags carried across the shoulder; wine skins; the pitchforks made of natural wood (the tines were branches); the early morning smells; the cold mountain nights and long hot days of summer, with always trees and shade under the trees."[40] The same holds true for the painter. The reason Hemingway prefers Goya to El Greco and Velasquez, as he writes in *Death in the Afternoon*, is that "Goya did not believe in costume, but he did believe in blacks and grays, in dust and in light, in high places rising from plains, in the country around Madrid, in movement, in his own cojones, in painting, in etching, and in what he had seen, felt, touched, handled, smelled, enjoyed, drunk, mounted, suffered, spewed-up, lain-with, suspected, observed, loved, hated, lusted, feared, detested, admired, loathed, and destroyed. Naturally no painter has been able to paint all that but he tried."[41]

In *The Apprenticeship of Ernest Hemingway* Charles Fenton records a statement which Hemingway made to a circle of friends in Chicago in 1921. Discussing the responsibilities of the writer, he stated, "'You've got to see it, feel it, smell it, hear it.'"[42] It is this dictum, developed in the form of a parable with a deceptively ironic title, that is at the core of "Banal Story."

"This Is My Pal Bugs":
Ernest Hemingway's "The Battler"

George Monteiro

●

The black traveling with the "battler"—Mr. Adolph "Ad" Francis, former champion prizefighter now very much down on his luck—is known only as "Bugs." He is an ex-con, as is Ad. Indeed, it was in prison, Bugs tells us, that he first met Ad, looking him up on the outside after his own later release. He took to the little man, the beat-up fighter, liking him well enough to take over his care by becoming his companion in a world of drifters and marginal males. As he says to the young boy visiting this odd twosome in their temporary camp, "right away I liked him and when I got out I looked him up. He likes to think I'm crazy and I don't mind. I like to be with him and I like seeing the country and I don't have to commit no larceny to do it. I like living like a gentleman."[1] Bugs has worked out what is a routine but mutually beneficial relationship with the brain-damaged ex-con.

What landed them in prison to begin with is of some importance. Ad was "busting people all the time" after his wife had left him, while Bugs was "in for cuttin' a man" (77). We learn nothing from Bugs about his reason for cutting the man, but we do learn from Bugs that Ad's marital problems might have had their source in certain bizarre circumstances stretching back to his time in the prize ring. The woman he married had been his manager, and it was always being "written up in the papers all about brothers and sisters and how she loved her brother and how he loved his sister," Bugs tells Nick, "and then they got married in New York and that made a lot of unpleasantness" (77). Nick remembers this much. But what Bugs goes on to say is unexpected: "Of course they wasn't brother and sister no more than a rabbit, but there was a lot of people didn't like it either way and they commenced to have disagreements, and one day she just went off and never come back" (77).

But then Bugs, who admits to having seen the woman a couple of times, slyly hints that there is a closeness in his relationship to Ad that might otherwise escape notice. "She was an awful good looking woman," he admits; then he adds: "Looked enough like him to be twins. He wouldn't be bad looking without his face all busted" (77). And a bit later, having enjoyed making this revelation, Bugs repeats it in different words: "She's a mighty fine woman. . . . She looks enough like him to be his own twin" (78). Besides revealing affection and personal feeling, perhaps, these observations suggest that there exists a strong physical attraction between the two partners in this home-making couple. To put Bug's views of Ad's good looks into perspective, we need only recall that the narrative tells us that he has a "mutilated face" (78), that in this "misshapen[ed]" face, the "nose was sunken," the "eyes were slits," and the lips were "queer shaped" (68). In fact, "Nick did not perceive all this at once, he only saw the man's face was queerly formed and mutilated. It was like putty in color. Dead looking in the firelight" (68). There is no indication given that Nick sees any beauty in Ad, but obviously, as we subsequently learn, Bugs does. Nor does Ad's behavior serve to enhance his attractiveness, for even when he takes off his cap, he does so to call attention to the fact that he has "only one ear. It was thickened and tight against the side of his head. Where the other ear should have been there was a stump" (69). It is a subtle stroke on Hemingway's part when later, as Bugs checks to see that he has not hurt him badly by "tapp[ing]" him with the blackjack, the narration tells us that Bugs "splashed water with his hand on the man's face and pulled his ears gently. The eyes closed" (75). Note that Nick had seen that Ad had only "one" ear, but Bugs, ministering to the unconscious Ad, pulls gently at his "ears." Bugs simply sees Ad differently and more attractively. Is it going too far to say that he sees him with a lover's eyes? After all, he has just "tapped" Ad "across the base of the skull" with a "cloth-wrapped blackjack" (75) that Bugs seems to carry with him for just this purpose, explaining his actions to Nick: "I didn't know how well you could take care yourself and, anyway, I didn't want you to hurt him or mark him up no more than he is" (76).

The received reading of "The Battler" views Nick as the key to the story's motivation and purpose.[2] Quite simply it is Nick's reaction to what happens to him that is of primary importance to the way the reader focuses on the narrative. In this sense, even though there is no direct description of the emotions that Nick feels or any statement as to how and what such an encounter finally means to Nick's emotional, psychological, or moral development, the reader is expected to acknowledge that some change has either occurred or, more likely, is occurring. Sent away from the warm fire in the clearing that belongs to Bugs and Ad, Nick climbs the embankment and starts up the tracks. That the whole experience has deeply impressed him we are to get from the simple statement that now follows—Nick "found he had a ham sandwich in his hand and put it in his pocket" (79). "Found," of course, is the key word here, springing the larger meaning that the author wanted his tale to convey still another stage in Nick's education.

In 1925, shortly after he had written "The Battler" to fill out his collection of stories for the publisher Horace Liveright, Hemingway boasted to John Dos Passos—employing the tough-guy parlance he so commonly affected—of his "swell new Nick story about a busted down pug and a coon."[3] He had invented the circumstances, he insisted. But the principals—Ad and Bugs—are based on real-life prototypes, argues Hemingway's biographer:

> The battler was a punch-drunk prize-fighter named Ad Francis, whose personality was based on two real-life fighters known to Ernest: Ad Wolgast and Bat Nelson. Ad Francis's fictional companion, a polite and patient Negro named Bugs, was modeled on an actual Negro trainer who had looked after Wolgast in the period of his decline.[4]

Perhaps Ad and Bugs were drawn from life, but I would look elsewhere for their prototypes. I would suggest the possibility that the principal sources of this powerful story are literary.

If we put aside for a moment our source of the exact sequence of incidents and attendant details in this story of the pathos and horror in a decidedly unorthodox relationship between two males and its emblematic meaning for a third male who, at story's end, has not yet brought to his consciousness the full implications of what he has just experienced, we can see the employment of a dramatic structure growing out of a triangular male relationship that is not without precedent in classic American literature. The withholding from the reader of the true nature of the relationship of two males—one white and the other black—played out before the eyes of a third male who is, either by age or temperament, an innocent, is the basic structure of that most trenchant American parable of white-black relations, Herman Melville's "Benito Cereno."[5] Recall that emblematic scene in which the great American naif, Amasa Delano, witnesses the black Babo's ministrations to his captain, Benito Cereno, as he shaves him with a straight razor.

> Setting down his basin, the negro searched among the razors, as for the sharpest, and having found it, gave it an additional edge by

expertly strapping it on the firm, smooth, oily skin of his open palm; he then made a gesture as if to begin, but midway stood suspended for an instant, one hand elevating the razor, the other professionally dabbling among the bubbling suds on the Spaniard's lank neck. Not unaffected by the close sight of the gleaming steel, Don Benito nervously shuddered; his usual ghastliness was heightened by the lather, which lather, again, was intensified in its hue by the contrasting sootiness of the negro's body.[6]

Moments later, Captain Delano notices that Benito Cereno is not completely in control of his emotions.

Here an involuntary expression came over the Spaniard, similar to that just before on the deck, and whether it was the start he gave, or a sudden gawky roll of the hull in the calm, or a momentary unsteadiness of the servant's hand, however it was, just then the razor drew blood, spots of which stained the creamy lather under the throat: immediately the black barber drew back his steel, and, remaining in his professional attitude, back to Captain Delano, and face to Don Benito, held up the trickling razor, saying, with a sort of half humorous sorrow, "See, master—you shook so—here's Babo's first blood." (39)

(Bugs, Mr. Francis' friend, it will be recalled, was also a "barber" of sorts, having gone to prison for "cuttin' a man," that is to say, for drawing blood.) Only later does the good Captain Delano discover what the reader already knows: that the razor in Babo's hand is a weapon, used in that situation to intimidate the imprisoned captain. In short, the relationship between the captain and his slave Babo is just the opposite of what it appears to be to the American innocent, who sees it even as Melville's narrator does, even as is the relationship of Bugs to Ad—the expected relationship of black to white in America in the nineteenth century and well into the twentieth, in which the white dominates.

Sometimes the negro gave his master his arm, or took his handkerchief out of his pocket for him; performing these and similar offices with that affectionate zeal which transmutes into something filial or fraternal acts in themselves but menial; and which has gained for the negro the repute of making the most pleasing body-servant in the world; one, too, whom a master need be on no stiffly superior terms with, but may treat with a familiar trust; less a servant than a devoted companion. (7)

Indeed, even if it can not be said that "Benito Cereno" displays the theme of male sexuality as directly and to the extent that some of Melville's other texts do, there is still something of the sort hinted at in this story of sailors long at sea. Actually, it might well be that the apparent relationship of the young black Babo to his master Benito Cereno, if not the true relationship, owes as much to the traditional lore about sailors at sea as it does to the prevailing power relationships on the typical slaver. It would not be wise to make too much of this or to try to explicate the matter in fulsome detail. But that something of Melville's familiar theme of male sexuality—sometimes between a black and a white—characterizes Hemingway's story seems to me to be totally admissible.

In conclusion let me return to Hemingway's narration at the point just after Bugs has assured himself that he has not hurt his friend, Mr. Francis, by once again striking him across the base of the skull. " 'He's all right,' he said. 'There's nothing to worry about. I'm sorry, Mr. Adams.' 'It's all right' "(75). Of course, the reader already knows, as Nick is just beginning to discover that there is something to worry about. That things are not all right. Then Nick looks down, sees the blackjack and picks it up. "It had a flexible handle and was limber in his hand," he notices. "Worn black leather with a handkerchief wrapped around the heavy end. 'That's a whalebone handle,' the negro smiled. 'They don't make them any more' " (75-76).

That smile, I would venture, is Melvillean. It is the smile of a black who, too, would be seen as "less a servant than a devoted companion."

Preparing for the End:
Hemingway's Revisions of
"A Canary for One"

Scott Donaldson

●

Old lady: And is that all of the story? Is there not to be what we called in my youth a wow at the end?
Ah, Madame, it is years since I added the wow to the end of the story.—Ernest Hemingway, *Death in the Afternoon* (1932)

The trouble with "A Canary for One," for many readers,[1] is that it has a surprise ending, and while surprise endings may be all right for O. Henry, they seem all wrong for Ernest Hemingway. Indeed, if Hemingway *ever* wrote a story with a "wow" at the end, it is this poignant tale of a broken marriage whose final one-sentence paragraph, "We were returning to Paris to set up separate residences," strikes with the force of a revelation. Yet if one rereads the story immediately, as Julian Smith has suggested,[2] he will begin to see the groundwork the author has laid for this revelation. Furthermore, now that Hemingway's working manuscripts are available for inspection, it is possible to demonstrate in some detail what he did during textual revisions to cushion the shock of his finish.

There are three drafts of the story in the Kennedy library.[3] Each ends with the sentence about "separate residences," but Hemingway made substantial alterations elsewhere as he moved from pencil manuscript through typed manuscript to the final typescript which corresponds almost exactly with "A Canary for One" (rejected alternate title: "Give Her a Canary") as it was published in *Scribner's Magazine* for April 1927 and *Men Without Women* later that year. To omit that last sentence entirely,[4] the author apparently decided, would strip the story of significance, but at least he could prepare his readers for the surprise that lay in wait.

Like "Cat in the Rain," "Hills Like White Elephants," and other Hemingway stories of love and marriage in disrepair, not much happens on the surface of "A Canary for One." Three passengers share a *lit salon* compartment during an overnight train journey on a *rapide* from the

Riviera to Paris. One, referred to throughout as the American lady, is an unaware, insensitive, overly cautious person who has succeeded in breaking off her daughter's engagement to a Swiss engineer of good family. She talks a great deal, especially as contrasted to her fellow travelers, the husband and wife, also American, who are about to separate. The American lady thinks in absolutes. One of her settled convictions (twice insisted upon) is that "American men make the best husbands"; another is that "no foreigner can make an American girl a good husband." Acting on these axioms, she has destroyed her daughter's chance of happiness. The girl reacted badly; she would not eat or sleep after her mother took her away from her fiancé. By way of consolation the American lady has bought her a canary, not because the girl likes canaries but because her mother has "always loved birds."

Through most of its five printed pages, the story focuses on the American lady and her daughter's frustrated romance. But eventually the impersonal narrative voice of the husband switches to the first person, intruding himself and his wife on the reader's consciousness, and in retrospect almost everything the American lady has said or done stands in ironic counterpoint to the other domestic tragedy that is taking place before her imperceptive eyes and ears. The American lady is rather deaf, a clue to her general lack of awareness. When the train stops at Marseilles, she gets off to buy a *Daily Mail* and a half bottle of Evian water and then stays near the steps of the car because she is afraid "signals of departure" are given that she does not hear. The journey abounds in such signals, none more deafening than the sound of silence: at no time in the story do the husband and wife address each other, a foreshadowing of their impending departure the one from the other that the American lady seems to notice not at all. Other signals are provided by the desolateness of the urban wasteland, the burning farmhouse, and the train wreck the *rapide* passes in the course of its journey to Paris. The American lady misses much of this. The careful reader, trying to be one of those on whom nothing is lost and mindful of Hemingway's injunction that in his fiction "there is much more there than will be read at any first reading,"[5] catches most of it, on second reading, at least.

The single most important change Hemingway made in revision was to remove a large red herring from the roadbed. Both in the first (Ms-1) and second (Ms-2) drafts, the narrator observes, following the American lady's chitchat about the canary's morning song, that "My wife and I are not characters in this story. It was just that the American lady was talking to my wife." That piece of deliberate misinformation he wisely deleted from the final typescript (Ms-3). Hemingway's task was not to mislead his audience but to guide it toward understanding without erecting obvious signposts. This he aimed to achieve in other ways: through the flatness of the narrator's voice; through manipulation of the color palette; through ironic emphasis on the gap between reality and the American lady's perception of the real; through suggestions about the unreliability and impermanence of human relationships; and finally through the story's penultimate paragraph.

Only in the first of these categories did Hemingway find his original draft satisfactory. In all three versions of the story the narrator relates his tale in a flat monotone. The opening paragraphs overuse the inert verb "to be" to an extent unusual even for Hemingway. "A Canary for One" begins: "The train passed very quickly a long, red stone house with a garden and four thick palm-trees with tables under them in the shade. On the other side was the sea. Then there was a cutting through red stone and clay, and the sea was only occasionally and far below against rocks." The view from the compartment window is quite pleasant, but it recedes rapidly and the virtually ungrammatical "the sea was" suggests that the Mediterranean will cease to exist for the narrator once it passes from view. Contrasted with the blue Mediterranean is the stifling atmosphere of the train, again communicated through a series of "it was" and "there was" clauses:

> It was very hot in the train and it was very hot in the *lit salon* compartment. There was no breeze came through the open window. The American lady pulled the window-blind down and there was no more sea, even occasionally. On the other side there was glass, then the corridor, then an open window, and outside the window were dusty trees and an oiled road and flat fields of grapes, with gray-stone hills behind them.

This beginning underscores what the narrator-husband will be doing throughout the trip. He listens, or fails to listen, to the chatter of the American lady. He speaks only three times: to make a feeble joke that the lady does not hear, to change a painful subject, and to say goodbye. Though the train is a *rapide*, the journey goes slowly for him in the overheated compartment. He consults his watch or a timetable to discover how long the train will stop at Cannes (twelve minutes) and Marseilles (twenty-five minutes). He does not even read to pass the time. He merely sits, gazing first at the dusty roads and flat fields, later at the industrial detritus alongside the railroad tracks. The dullness of the narrator's prose and his selective perception of dreary land and cityscapes indicate that something is troubling him, a point further emphasized by two oddly unidiomatic phrases he uses. When the train stops in Avignon, he sees Negro soldiers on the platform. "Their faces were very black," he reports, "and they were too tall to stare." Too tall to stare? Why should they stare, unless possibly to stare back at the stranger on the train staring at them? He is the starer, seeking to shut off internal feelings through concentration on the world without. The other curious passage has to do with breakfast. Though the American lady sleeps badly, she rises and goes to the restaurant-car for breakfast the next morning. But to the narrator, "all that the train passed through looked as though it were before breakfast." The point is reinforced as the *rapide* reaches Paris: "Nothing had eaten any breakfast." Nothing? *Néant? Nada?* Since it would be awkward for them to go separately and there is no question of their going together, the narrator-husband and his wife have not had breakfast. Neither, it seems to him in his mood of negation, has anything or anyone other than the wholesome, middle-aged, and quite intolerable American lady.

Hemingway also uses chiaroscuro to communicate mood, with the cheerfulness of the sunlight outdoors opposed to the darker psychological mood of the narrator, a man who, like Robert Frost's persona in "Tree at My Window," is more concerned with "inner weather." This contrast is established early in the story. It is hot and sunny outside (the tables of the first paragraph are placed in the shade), but the narrator notes principally the coming of nightfall. As the train leaves Marseilles, he catches a glimpse of "the last of the sun on the water." "As it was getting dark," he sees the farmhouse burning in the field, with the bedding spread in the field and people watching the house burn. Then: "After it was dark the train was in Avignon." It is there that he sees the black troops, dressed in brown uniforms, under command (as Hemingway wrote, for the first time, in Ms-3) of "a short white sergeant."

This contrast between lights and darks, external brightness and internal darkness, is picked up and developed the next morning when the sun shines cheerfully, and incongruously, into the compartment. (The narrator or his wife have presumably raised the blind and opened the window while the American lady had her breakfast.) The sunshine prompts the canary to chirp briefly, but does not brighten the day for the narrator. Instead, as Hemingway made clear through several additions to the final draft of his story, his vision is concentrated on a sterile world of muted colors. Here, italicized, are those additions:

> The train was now coming into Paris. The fortifications were
> levelled *but grass had not grown*. There were many cars standing on

tracks—*brown* wooden restaurant-cars and *brown* wooden sleeping cars . . . and passing were the white walls and many windows of houses.

Then the train was *in the dark of* the Gare de Lyons . . . and we were on the *dim* longness of the platform.

In revising the story Hemingway made a number of changes designed to lay stress on the American lady's unreliability. Missing in both the first and second draft, for example, is the husband's joke about wearing "braces" instead of "suspenders," inasmuch as the American lady has thought him and his wife, probably because of their reticence, to be English rather than American. She does not hear the joke, because in her deafness she relies on reading lips and the husband had not looked toward her. As usual, he "had looked out of the window." Nor does the original draft include another piece of dialogue which calls attention to the American lady's deafness. The wife has begun to tell her about her honeymoon in Vevey: "We had a very fine room and in the fall the country was lovely." To which the American lady blankly responds, "Were you there in the fall?" Her tendency is to talk without listening, a point Hemingway called attention to by altering the beginning of the American lady's discussion of her couturier in Paris. Ms-1 reads, "My wife admired the dress the American lady was wearing," but this is out of character for the wife, and in later drafts it is the American lady who admires the wife's apparel and then rambles on without encouragement.

Actually, the wife initiates conversation but twice, once to ask pointedly, after hearing of the daughter's broken engagement, "Did she get over it?" and again to bring up the subject of her own honeymoon. This reminiscence about happier times and marital solidarity ("We" spent our honeymoon in Vevey. "We" stayed at the Trois Couronnes. "We" liked our room and enjoyed the good weather.) apparently distresses the husband. At any rate he interrupts to call attention to a train wreck involving three cars, of which the American lady, another touch missing in first draft, sees only the last car.

The wreck itself is the subject of an elaborate conceit in the original pencil manuscript: "Outside the window were three cars that had been in a wreck. They were splintered and opened up as boats are cross sectioned in a steamship advertisement showing the different decks or as houses are opened up by a bombardment." In working toward final copy Hemingway must have concluded that neither the holiday suggestions of the boat cruise nor the military connotations of the bombardment properly belonged in his story of marital separation. So the final draft reads, simply, "We were passing three cars that had been in a wreck. They were splintered open and the roofs sagged in."

With typical wrong-headedness, the American lady remarks of that part of the wreck she has seen, that she had been afraid of just such a thing all night, and congratulates herself on having "terrific presentiments." She will never travel on a *rapide* again, she says. "There must be *other comfortable* trains that don't go so fast." The adjectival qualification, "other comfortable," was omitted in the first draft and added later to flesh out the American lady's character. She is a woman who wants and expects life to be smooth and comfortable, as permanent as her own dress measurements or those of her daughter now that she is "grown up and there was not much chance of their changing" through pregnancy or other unsettling events.

She fails to realize that in taking her daughter away from the Swiss she was "simply madly in love" with she has repudiated a singularly eligible suitor. Hemingway makes two changes to emphasize his reliability. The first is to have the lovers take long walks together, rather than the more adventurous alternative of going skiing (as they had in the first and second draft). The other is to provide the suitor, in Ms-3, with the presumably methodical and trustworthy occupation of engineer. But letting her daughter marry any foreigner would have meant taking a risk, according to the American lady's prejudices, and she is afraid of all risks. It is with relief that she "put[s] herself in charge" of the emissaries from Thomas Cook at the Gare de Lyons in Paris (originally, Hemingway had written that she "was taken in charge of" by the men from Cook's).

But the world will not stand still for the American lady or anyone else, as Hemingway attempted to suggest through several additions to the first draft of his story. In telling the story of her daughter and the Swiss, for example, the American lady acquires a certain hesitancy in the third draft that was not in evidence earlier. These are the italicized additions: "'My daughter fell in love with a man in Vevey.' *She stopped.* 'They were simply madly in love.' *She stopped again.* 'I took her away, of course.'" Then she goes on to explain her "of course": "'I couldn't have her marrying a foreigner.' *She paused.* 'Some one, a very good friend, told me once, "No foreigner can make an American girl a good husband."'" American men make the best husbands, she soon reiterates, just as the husband is playing the useful soon-to-be-abandoned husbandly role of *"getting down the bags."*

Other important additions (again italicized) involve the narrator-husband's awareness that previous arrangements may have been altered in his absence. The *rapide* comes into the Gare de Lyons, and he duly observes the train "that would go to Italy at five o'clock, *if that train still left at five,*" and the cars that would go to the suburbs that evening with "people in all the seats and on the roofs, *if that were the way it were still done.*" The American lady, a great explainer, betrays at least a slight uncertainty. The husband can no longer be certain of anything.

Obviously aware of the hazard he ran with his ending, Hemingway tried five different versions of the passage that led up to it:

> We found a porter with a truck and he piled on the baggage and we said goodbye to the American lady whose name had been found by the man from Cook's on a typewritten page in a sheaf of typewritten sheets he carried which he replaced in his pocket. We were returning to Paris to set up separate residences (Ms-1).

> The porter brought a truck and piled on the baggage and my wife said goodbye and I said goodbye to the American lady [the passage about the man from Cook's repeated]. We followed the baggage truck along beside the train. It was a long train. At the end was a fence and a man at the gate took the tickets of people coming to Paris. We ourselves were returning to Paris to set up separate residences (Ms-2).

The most significant revision is the change from "we said goodbye to the American lady" to "my wife said goodbye and I said goodbye to the American lady." The husband and wife do not speak in unison; their status as a collective body of one is about to end. In addition Ms-2 adds several sentences to make the climax seem less abrupt.

Still not satisfied, in Ms-3 Hemingway tried again, twice. First, he eliminated the intermediate sentences about following the baggage truck, the length of the train, and the man taking the tickets: "The porter brought a truck and piled on the baggage and my wife said goodbye and I said goodbye to the American lady [passage about man from Cook's]. We were returning to Paris to set up separate residences." Then he restored and rewrote the intermediate sentences, this time in handwriting, though the rest of the draft is typed:

> The porter brought a truck and piled on the baggage and my wife said goodbye and I said goodbye to the American lady [passage about man from Cook's].

> We followed the porter with the truck down the long platform beside the train. At the gate a man took the tickets. We were returning to Paris to set up separate residences.

The husband and wife make the long walk together behind their luggage and pass through the gate toward separation. The extraneous comment about other people coming to Paris is crossed out in pencil, along with the repetitive "length" of the platform. Missing from the Ms-2 draft is the "fence" in front of which the ticket-taker mans his gate. As Julian Smith has shown, "A Canary for One" is a story full of traps and cages: that of the canary itself, that of the daughter shut off from her life by her dominating mother, that of the husband and wife in the hot compartment at the mercy of the mindless but painful talk of the American lady.[6] The fence would surely reinforce this motif, but Hemingway apparently decided that it was one thing he could do without.

Yet he was not quite through tinkering with his conclusion. Somewhere, perhaps in galleys, the concluding sentence was given greater emphasis by being set apart, as a paragraph of its own. Finally, Hemingway added one word to connote the hard, cold reality of the impending separation. The "long platform" of Ms-3 becomes the "long *cement* platform" of the printed story.

Considering its provenance, it is remarkable that Hemingway was able to tell that story at all as soon as he did. "A Canary for One" almost exactly recreates the journey that he and his first wife, Hadley, took from Antibes in August 1926, on their way to find separate residences in Paris.[7] Ernest had broken off with Hadley, by all accounts a wonderful person and a loving wife and mother, in order to marry Pauline Pfeiffer. It was a decision that troubled him for the rest of his life. Much later, he took to blaming others as well as himself for permitting his first marriage to fail.[8] But at the time he indulged in an orgy of self-disparagement. The separation was entirely his fault, he kept insisting in letters; he was a son of a bitch, and he felt miserable about the whole thing. Yet he put this story in the mail to *Scribner's Magazine* on October 25, 1926: it must have been written, and rewritten, within the two months following the actual separation. Hemingway may have sensed that he was too close to his material. In any case he imposed a kind of distance both by keeping the major characters anonymous (only the dressmakers have names) and by delaying until the last sentence the extent of the narrator's involvement in the proceedings.

One may regard with skepticism Hemingway's repeated proclamations of self-disgust about the breakup, inasmuch as he was able so rapidly, in Carlos Baker's phrase, "to siphon off his sorrow" in the form of this story.[9] But it is Hemingway the artist and not Hemingway the man who must finally stand judgment, and on that basis he emerges in "A Canary for One" as a skillful craftsman in command of difficult and sensitive subject matter. What is more, he ended his story at the right time and in the right way. To reveal the separation earlier would have deprived the reader of the retroactive enjoyment that derives from the sense of discovery—discovery of the American lady's persistently obtuse remarks, of the emotional deadness of the husband's reactions to his surroundings, of the wife's patient listening and pointed questions. Hemingway has done everything possible to lay a sound foundation for his "surprise ending." His textual revisions, which may after all be "as important as those of Keats,"[10] contribute brilliantly to that foundation.

El Pueblo Español: "The Capital of the World"

Bernard Oldsey

●

I don't like writing like God. It is only because you never do it, though, that the critics think you can't do it.—Ernest Hemingway in a letter to Maxwell Perkins, August 25, 1960

Ernest Hemingway's "The Capital of the World" is a relatively neglected piece of work. A quick check in Audre Hanneman's bibliography and its supplement on Hemingway shows four to five times the amount of critical commentary on "The Snows of Kilimanjaro" and "The Short Happy Life of Francis Macomber" as there is on "The Capital of the World."[1] Whether this is an appropriate ratio of response is a moot point, but it would appear that Hemingway's story about Madrid has been strangely neglected and that it begs for further analysis, especially along the interconnected lines of theme, technique, and social commentary. In this story, in less than a dozen pages of print, Hemingway managed to compress the material of an ordinary novel into a restricted but brilliant picture of Spanish society, *el pueblo español*, right on the eve of the Civil War.[2]

The story first appeared, under the undistinguished title of "The Horns of the Bull," in the June 1936 issue of *Esquire*. It thus stands in much the same relationship to the Spanish matter of *Death in the Afternoon* (1932) as "The Snows of Kilimanjaro" (August 1936, *Esquire*) and "The Short Happy Life of Francis Macomber" (September 1936, *Cosmopolitan*) do to the African matter of *Green Hills of Africa* (1935). These three stories make fictive use of materials Hemingway developed in, respectively, his encyclopedic commentary on tauromachy and his early-day nonfictional novel on hunting in Africa. These also happen to be the last three short stories Hemingway ever wrote, unless one considers a few odd pieces like "The Old Man at the Bridge." Moreover, they differ considerably from the author's previous short stories, especially those done in the *tranche de vie* mode, like most of the Nick Adams pieces or, for example, "Hills Like White Elephants."

One might make a claim for "The Short Happy Life" as an advanced form of narrative, since it contains more plot, more "mystery," than the earlier stories. But at the same time it marked a return to what Hemingway had derided as the "wow ending." From a technical standpoint "The Snows of Kilimanjaro" and "The Capital of the World" are the two stories that emerge as distinguished capstones to Hemingway's career in this area of composition. Both of these works are compressed, or condensed, novels.3 "The Snows of Kilimanjaro" achieves its compression through the temporal shifts associated with Ford Madox Ford's "time organ." But "The Capital of the World" gets its compression by crosscutting from character to character, scene to scene, much as the movies do. "Crosscutting" is in fact a cinematographic term, although the technique itself seems to have stemmed from literary sources: pioneer movie-maker D. W. Griffith confessed to learning the method from reading the novels of Charles Dickens.4 Eventually, of course, the influence of literary works on film reversed itself, so that it became reciprocal, with novels like James Joyce's *Ulysses*, John Dos Passos's *U.S.A.* trilogy (with its camera eye), and Katherine Anne Porter's *Ship of Fools* standing as prime examples of the reverse swing.

The interaction between movies and print-fiction is clearly shown in Hemingway's "The Capital of the World." The story reads like an adaptation script for a film, and with a few directive phrases added, lining up photographic angles and distances, it could very easily be made into a shooting script. The following brief paragraph indicates the extent to which this is true:

[Shot 1] Upstairs the matador who was ill was lying face down on his bed alone. [Shot 2] The matador who was no longer a novelty was sitting looking out of his window preparatory to walking out to the cafe. [Shot 3] The matador who was a coward had the older sister of Paco in his room with him and was trying to get her to do something which she was laughingly refusing to do.5

And this second paragraph is even more fully illustrative of the method:

[Shot 1] The auctioneer stood on the street corner talking with friends. [Shot 2] The tall waiter was at the Anarcho-Syndicalist meeting waiting for an opportunity to speak. [Shot 3] The middle-aged waiter was seated on the terrace of the Café Alvarez drinking a small beer. [Shot 4] The woman who owned the Luarca was already asleep in her bed, where she lay on her back with the bolster between her legs, big, fat, honest, clean, easy-going, very religious and never having ceased to miss or pray for her husband, dead, now, twenty years. [Shot 5] In his room, alone, the matador who was ill lay face down on his bed with his mouth against his handkerchief. (48)

The swift compression of these "camera shots" is immediately appreciable. And the way in which the writer presents the entire story of the woman who owns the Pension Luarca in one sentence, focusing on the "bolster" between her legs, is breathtakingly dramatic and satisfying.

Passages like these make one wonder whether Hemingway might not have outstripped fellow novelists F. Scott Fitzgerald and William Faulkner in writing for the movies had he the need or will to work for Hollywood as they did. Just a few years before writing "The Capital of the World" Hemingway did become involved with the movie industry, to the extent that the first in a long line of his works was made into a movie, *A Farewell to Arms*, produced by Paramount in 1932 and starring Gary Cooper and Helen Hayes.[6] Just after "The Capital of the World," Hemingway became as fully involved in movie-making as he ever would. Working with producer Joris Ivers, and scriptwriters Archibald MacLeish and Lillian Hellman, he wrote and delivered the voice-over commentary for *The Spanish Earth*, that clarion call for help which preceded *For Whom the Bell Tolls* and played to sympathetic audiences in Carnegie Hall and the White House.[7]

The movie that exerted the most important influence on "The Capital of the World," however, was not one that Hemingway himself had a hand in but one that he learned from and reacted to. In retrospect this particular film can be seen as the very prototype of the kind of formula film that is constantly being produced, the sort of thing one has grown used to in movies like *Airport, The Poseidon Adventure* and Porter's *Ship of Fools*, many of which are made from novels that have the formula built into their pages. The formula starts with the introduction of a series of characters as they enter a hotel, board a ship or airplane, or come together in some such fashion as to represent a microcosm of society, or a section of a given society. All of their stories and backgrounds are revealed in snippets, all intermingling eventually, until finally the ship lands, or the guests leave the hotel, and disbanding becomes denouement. Actually, the forgathering aspect of the formula reaches all the way back to Boccacio's *Decameron* and Chaucer's *The Canterbury Tales*.[8]

The prototype for this kind of formula film is the classic *Grand Hotel*. Vicki Baum's popular novel about Berlin was published in 1929, translated into English in 1930, and made into a movie the same year as *A Farewell to Arms*, 1932. An international success, it starred not only John and Lionel Barrymore, Joan Crawford, Wallace Beery, Lewis Stone, and Jean Hersholt, but more importantly Greta Garbo. (It was Garbo's second talking film, the one in which she first said "I want to be alone.") Garbo—who is mentioned three times in "The Capital of the World," and with special thematic emphasis in the final sentence of the story—represents more than a gratuitous link with what might be called Hemingway's "Not So Grand Hotel." The two sisters of Paco, the omniscient narrator says, have gone to a movie palace in the Gran Via to see Garbo in the movie adaptation of Eugene O'Neill's *Anna Christie*. Crosscutting from their brother, who lies dying back at the pension, Hemingway indicates how they, like the rest of the audience, "were intensely disappointed in the Garbo film, which showed the great star in miserable low surroundings when they had been accustomed to see her surrounded by great luxury and brilliance," as in *Grand Hotel*, where she plays the Russian prima ballerina, Grusinskaya.[9]

It is not hard to imagine how Hemingway used these contemporaneous materials. He obviously saw a way to use the *Grand Hotel* method in short form. In using Garbo so pointedly, he even drew attention to the work and technique he was improving on. Garbo was the epitome of glamour and illusion, a star starring as a star in *Grand Hotel*, a movie of high fashion and sophistication for its day. But Hemingway also saw Garbo's value as an emblem of degradation and *dis*illusion—'tis pity she's a whore in *Anna Christie*, a movie of the working class.[10] Hemingway understood the emphasis placed on the concepts of virginity and whoredom in a country like Spain, a center of Mariolatry where women have often been placed into two categories: the good mother, sister, wife; and then all the rest—serving girls, foreign women. This latter category includes "las suecas" (Swedes, or, by extension, all leggy blondes) and "las putas." It is "una puta," or whore, that the cowardly matador would make of a serving girl, one of Paco's sisters. "Not through you," she defiantly answers, reminding him that "a whore is also a woman" (a fact she seems to forget when she sees *Anna Christie* later).

Two real whores are introduced into the story toward the conclusion, and the hawk-faced picador emerges from a café with one of them eventually, even though the cowardly matador (having a bad day all around) had been buying her drinks all evening. According to Stephen A. Reid—who discerns an Oedipal pattern in "The Capital of the World"—even Paco's mother is something of a whore. "Paco's mother had no husband," Reid declares, "and there was, presumably, no individual man among his mother's lovers who stood strongly enough as a rival of him for his mother's love."[11] Hence the bull becomes a surrogate father, and so forth, and Paco, according to this presumptive reading, becomes one of the most scorned objects in Spain, "un hijo de puta," or whoreson.

If movies and women can be used to represent forms of illusion and disillusion, so can other elements in the story, which Hemingway once considered calling "The Capitol [sic] of Illusion."[12] Religion and bullfighting might be added to the long list of things that are considered the opium of the people. According to the Anarcho-Syndicalist waiter in the story, it is precisely these last two forms of beguiling illusion that are killing Spain, and so it is "necessary to kill the individual bull" and (shades of the war to come) the "individual priest" to get rid of "the two curses" (42). However, according to the two priests staying at the Luarca, it is the city of Madrid—as a center of bureaucratic power, the implication is—which is killing Spain. One of the priests sums up much of the theme of the story in this pithy complaint: "Madrid is where one learns to understand. Madrid kills" (45). The priests are bitterly disappointed about the amount of help they can get for their poor territory of Galicia (Pablo and his sisters are from the equally poor territory of Extremadura). If Hemingway's early title had been slightly changed to "The Capital of *Dis*illusion" it would have perfectly suited the condition of these priests. The little illusion they can summon up comes from the generous portions of unconsecrated wine they imbibe at the Pension Luarca.

What all of this makes clear is that "The Capital of the World" is a fictive anatomy of illusion-disillusion. It has a cast of twenty characters (if Garbo is counted), and with few exceptions they are graded on a basis of how much illusion or disillusion they represent, like the priests and the Anarcho-Syndicalist waiter. The three matadors at the Luarca, for example, stand among the thoroughly disillusioned: the sick one is coughing away his life with tuberculosis; the short one knows that his day as a novelty is over; and the cowardly one, who was once brave, has lost his courage through a particularly "atrocious" wounding. These toreros stay at the Luarca because it is a "good address" and because "decorum and dignity rank above courage as the virtues most highly prized in Spain" (39). At the same time they know their place in Spanish society, as second-rate bullfighters; along with the narrator they must know that "there is never any record of any bull fighter having left the Luarca for a better or more expensive hotel" (39).

Enrique—the dishwasher who is partially responsible for Paco's death—is only "three years older than Paco," but he has already taken his place among the disillusioned. In the priest's phrase Enrique has "learned in Madrid," and what he has learned is fear. "Miedo," as he says to Paco. "The same fear you would have in the ring with a bull" (46). Paco's own state of virginal illusion, and courage, is revealed in his thoughts: "No, he would not be afraid. Others, yes. Not he. He knew that he would not be afraid. Even if he ever was afraid he knew that he could do it anyway. He had confidence"(47).

Hemingway did not change the title of the story to "The Capital of the World" until the Spanish Civil War had broken out. The story first appeared under the new title with the publication of *The Fifth Column and the First Forty-nine Stories* in 1938. By that time Madrid had become something of a capital of the world: all eyes were focused on it as the center of conflict between fascist and antifascist forces. Then, too, provincial youths like Paco always see the capitals of their countries as the grand omphalos of the universe. There is a kind of universal naiveté and provincialism that makes youths think that Paris, Rome, Berlin, Tokyo, Moscow, Warsaw—each in its own right—is truly the capital of the world. A young American antecedent of Paco's—Hawthorne's Robin Molineux—thinks Boston is the hub of the universe, and in his concept of himself as a "shrewd youth" matches Paco for simplicity and innocence.

Several commentators have talked about the theme of "The Capital of the World" in a rather simplistic way. As one puts it, "this story advances the mordant conclusion that to be brave, good, and innocent is to be unfit for life."[13] As another says, in complementary manner, "the theme is the necessity for disillusion."[14] Hemingway himself, however, is not far from suggesting in the story that Paco is a "smart lad, to slip betimes away." This is his athlete dying young, one who will not know the suffering and frustration of the other characters in the story: "The boy Paco had never known about any of this [what has gone on about him in the pension] nor about what all these people would be doing on the next day or on the other days to come. He had no idea how they really lived nor how they ended. . . . He died, as the Spanish phrase has it, full of illusions"(51).

The very last sentence of the story brings theme and technique into mutual focus: "He had not even had time to be disappointed in the Garbo picture which disappointed all Madrid for a week." The Spanish translator of this story, in a 1960 edition of Hemingway's "Relatos," brings the word *disappointed* under the rubric of illusion-disillusion. As he translates the final sentence it comes out with a peculiarly Spanish emphasis: "Tampoco tuvo tiempo para *desilusionarse* por la pelicula de Greta Garbo, que defraudo a todo Madrid durante una semana" [Nor did he have time to disillusion himself with the movie of Greta Garbo, which defrauded all Madrid for a week].[15]

It has become a cliché that the thing left out is what characterizes a

Hemingway short story, which may be true for most of his stories but not "The Capital of the World" (nor for that matter "The Snows of Kilimanjaro").[16] Nor is "The Capital of the World" a typical Hemingway story in the sense of being fully rendered, with little or no auctorial commentary and exposition. Quite the opposite—here Hemingway wrote omnisciently, from the beginning anecdote, or "chiste," to the final editorial commentary of the last sentence. His "writing like God," which he would carry through in *For Whom the Bell Tolls* (the last half of which is dominated by the movielike crosscutting),[17] produced one of those fictive examples of "sabiduría," or folk wisdom, typical of Spain. "La vida es una lucha," Spanish folk say [Life is a battle]. Or, simply, "La vida es sueno" [Life is a dream]. What Hemingway says thematically in "The Capital of the World" is equally simple, but balanced, bivalent: "La vida es ilusión—y desilusión." The trick is to find a good balance between the two (as does the woman who runs the Luarca and, to a lesser extent, the middle-aged waiter).[18] Otherwise you find that the world has very suddenly severed your femoral artery, or you yourself reach for a shotgun.

The Poor Kitty and the Padrone and the Tortoise-shell Cat in "Cat in the Rain"

Warren Bennett

●

Ernest Hemingway's short story "Cat in the Rain," first published as an integral part of Hemingway's *In Our Time*, is a story that has never been given much critical acclaim. Scholarship has generally approached it as a story of "marital dissatisfaction" (Hovey, 10) and Philip Young groups it with four other stories about "couples under the spell of disenchantment": "Out of Season," "Hills Like White Elephants," "A Canary for One," and "The Sea Change" (Young, 178). Other commentators reduce the artistic value of the story by assigning it a biographical function. Carlos Baker says that "Cat in the Rain" is "derived from a rainy day [Ernest] spent with Hadley [in] February at the Hotel Splendide in Rapallo" (133), and the characters in the story are derived from "[Hemingway] and Hadley and the manager and chambermaid" (107). Jeffrey Meyers says that the story is based on "the disintegration of [Ernest's] marriage to Hadley" (144). "Cat in the Rain," however, is more than a story of marital dissatisfaction, and it is more than a disguised autobiography.[1] It may be one of Hemingway's best stories, subtly executed and powerfully suggestive in its characterization and imagery. This interpretation will consider three facets of the story: the function of the padrone in relation to the function of the husband, the function of the "poor kitty" (93) as an image in relation to the wife, and the significance of the tortoise-shell cat as an ironic image crucial to the story's resolution.

However, present critical opinion has produced two disputes which need to be considered before proceeding. One is the question of whether there is one cat or two cats in the story, and the second is the question of whether the wife *wants* to have a baby or whether she is already pregnant.

Carlos Baker calls "Cat in the Rain" a story about "the normal married state"(*Writer as Artist*, 141) and concludes that the story has a happy ending: "[the cat that the wife has seen in the rain] is finally sent up to her by the kindly old inn-keeper" (*Writer as Artist*, 136).

John V. Hagopian sees the story as a marriage crisis "involving the lack of fertility, which is symbolically foreshadowed by the public garden (fertility) dominated by the war monument (death)" (230). He suggests that the wife's feelings, "'very small and tight inside . . . really important . . . of supreme importance,' [are] all phrases that might appropriately be used to describe a woman who is pregnant. The conscious thought of pregnancy never enters her mind, but the feelings associated with it sweep through her" (Hagopian 231–32). Hagopian sees the resolution of the story as a "final, ironic coda. The girl's symbolic wish [for a cat] is grotesquely fulfilled" (Hagopian, 232) by a cat that "will most certainly not do" (232). Hagopian suggests, in contrast to Baker, that the "tortoise-shell" (94) is "probably not" (Hagopian, 232) the same cat as the one the wife saw in the rain, but he gives neither reason nor evidence for his conclusion.

David Lodge sides with Hagopian against Baker that there are two cats in the story, but he does so on the weak basis of a negative argument: "Hemingway would have described the kitty as 'tortoise-shell'" (198). He also agrees with Hagopian that the "cat as a child-surrogate is certainly a possible interpretation" (Lodge, 30), but he disagrees with Hagopian's interpretation of the girl's feelings.

> [Hemingway's phrases do] not, surely, . . . describe a woman who merely *wants* to be pregnant. Indeed, if we must have a gynaecological reading of the story it is much more plausible to suppose that the wife's whimsical craving for the cat, and for other things like new clothes and long hair, is the result of her *being* pregnant. (Lodge 30)

Lodge enlists biography in support of his thesis about pregnancy: the "Hemingways had left the chilly thaw of Switzerland and gone to Rapallo because Hadley had announced that she was pregnant" (Lodge, 30).

The number of cats in the story and the wife's condition are crucial elements in the story's meaning, and the disputes about them need to be reexamined in terms of all the textual and extratextual evidence.

Textual evidence in regard to the number of cats suggests that the "kitty" (91) the wife has seen and the "tortoise-shell" (94) the padrone sends to the room are two different cats. In the story, when the wife goes to look for the cat, which she describes as a "kitty," the wife is the only person who has seen it, and the maid expresses both surprise and disbelief: "'A cat?' the maid laughed. 'A cat in the rain?'" (92). The "kitty" is obviously an unknown stray animal, and the fact that the cat so quickly disappears, before the wife can get downstairs, reinforces its stray nature. The weather is "brutto tempo" (92), "raining harder" (92), and only one man, protected by a "rubber cape" (92), has ventured out in it. The padrone has an umbrella, which he sends via the maid, but the umbrella is insufficient protection: despite the umbrella the maid insists that "'We must get back inside. You will be wet'" (92). Since the padrone does not go out in this "bad weather" (92) but sends the maid, who is also unwilling to remain outside, it is highly improbable that either the padrone or the maid would leave the hotel later to look in the rain for a cat. And if they did, it would be impossible for either the padrone or the maid to find and capture a particular stray, wet cat which neither of them has ever seen. It is much more likely that the padrone has a cat of his own in the hotel, probably for protection against rats and mice, a "big tortoise-shell" (94), and that he sends his own cat to the girl in order to please her.

Extratextual evidence supports the view that there are two different cats. According to Baker, when Hemingway visited Ezra Pound in Rapallo, Pound gave Hemingway a copy of T. S. Eliot's *The Waste Land*. "Ernest was unable to take it seriously, though he echoed it once after watching the antics of a pair of cats on a green table in the hotel garden. 'The big cat gets on the small cat' he wrote. 'Sweeney gets on Mrs. Porter'" (Baker, 107). Since both the garden and the green table appear in the published story, it is reasonable to conclude that the "pair of cats" also appears. The "small cat" in Hemingway's note becomes the female "kitty" (91) the wife sees, and the "big" male cat becomes the "big tortoise-shell" (94) which the padrone sends to the room.

In regard to the question of pregnancy, Hagopian's interpretation that the wife "wants" to be pregnant is more valid than Lodge's counterinterpretation that the wife *is* pregnant. Lodge's thesis about the pregnancy seems to be derived from his assumption that the wife's desires for a "cat, and for other things like new clothes and long hair" (Lodge, 30) are merely "whimsical craving[s]" (30) which "result from her *being* pregnant" (30). The words, "whimsical craving," seem to refer to an old wives' tale that a woman who is pregnant may develop cravings for particular foods. The tale is scientifically sound; the cravings result from the foetus's need for particular nutrients. But Lodge's use of the tale is in error. Pregnancy cravings are biologically determined, not "whimsical," and consequently such cravings cannot be construed to include cats, clothes, candles, silver, or long hair. Textually, the relevant portion of the story to which Hagopian alludes in his interpretation, and about which Lodge assumes greater gynecological expertise, reads in full:

> As the American girl passed the office, the padrone bowed from his desk. Something felt very small and tight inside the girl. The padrone made her feel very small and at the same time really important. She had a momentary feeling of being of supreme impor- tance. She went on up the stairs. (*IOT*, 93)

In this passage the girl's sensations occur suddenly in relation to the padrone bowing from his desk, and they are "momentary" (93). There are no such sudden and momentary sensations of pregnancy. And the words "small" and "tight" do no gynecologically describe a condition of preg- nancy. The girl would not feel "small" because she would, in fact, be getting larger; neither would she feel "tight inside" because she would, in fact, be expanding. Furthermore, the text clearly states that it is the "padrone [who] made her feel very small and at the same time really important." If the girl were pregnant it would have to be the child in her to which her sensations are attributed, not the padrone, and if she were pregnant, it would be the child in her which would be "really important" and of "supreme importance," not herself in the presence of the padrone.

Lodge's citation of "extratextual support" (30) from Baker that the story was about Hemingway and Hadley and that they had come to Rapallo because "Hadley had announced that she was pregnant" (Lodge, 30) is misleading. Baker admits that his "identification of EH and Hadley with the persons of the story is my surmise. EH denied [it]" (Baker, 580). Baker refers here to a letter from Hemingway to F. Scott Fitzgerald, dated December 24, 1925.

> Cat in the Rain wasnt about Hadley. I know that you and Zelda always thought it was. When I wrote that we were at Rapallo but Hadley was 4 months pregnant with Bumby. The Inn Keeper was the one at Cortina D'Ampezzo and the man and the girl were a harvard kid and his wife that I'd met at Genoa. Hadley never made a speech in her life about wanting a baby because she had been told various things by her doctor and I'd—no use going into all that.
>
> The only story in which Hadley figures is Out of Season . . . I reported [the drunk of a guide] to the hotel owner—the one who appears in Cat in the Rain. (*Letters*, 180).

The relevant point for the purpose here is not that Hemingway denied the story was about Hadley, but that he disassociates Hadley from the wife in the story on the grounds that Hadley was already pregnant, which negates any assumption that Hemingway intended the wife in the story to also be pregnant. Contrary to Lodge's interpretation, both the textual evidence and the extratextual evidence confirm that the wife is *not* pregnant.

The most probable explanation for what Hemingway is rendering, whether accurately or inaccurately, in his description of the girl's sensations is female sexual arousal in conjunction with the masculine qualities which may initiate them. That Hemingway was much interested in sexual roles and female sexual desire is documented by Michael Reynolds.

> During [Hemingway's] Toronto winter [1920], he bought and read the Havelock Ellis book, *Erotic Symbolism.* . . . Ellis confirmed what Ernest suspected: women enjoyed sex as much as he did. In *Erotic Symbolism* he found detailed explanations of the female orgasm as well as copious analysis and examples of the Krafft-Ebing fetishes, including the erotic nature of hair. (120)

In January 1921 Hemingway sent a copy of *Psychology of Sex* to Hadley, and "two weeks later she and Ernest were exchanging 'essays' on male and female roles" (Reynolds, 185). In Hemingway's description in the story, the girl's feelings pass through three stages, tight inside, important, and of momentary supreme importance, and these stages reflect a correspondence to the sensations of desire, intercourse, and orgasm. An artistic purpose for Hemingway's description of the girl's feelings is necessary, and this seems to be the most sound way to interpret them.

When Hemingway made a note for a story which became "Cat in the Rain" and identified two copulating cats with Sweeney and Mrs. Porter, he was directly alluding to Eliot's *The Waste Land*. Hagopian appears to be picking up echoes in the story itself when he sees the public garden as symbolic of fertility, the war monument as symbolic of death, and the crisis in the marriage as a crisis involving the "lack of fertility" (Hagopian, 230). "What seems . . . likely," as Jackson J. Benson has suggested, "considering Hemingway's antagonism toward Eliot, is that both [men] were subject to the same influences, and among these was certainly Ezra Pound" (40). Both men were, of course, also looking at the same world, a world unheroically devastated by modern trench warfare and a disillusioned generation that had largely lost its way in the war's aftermath. Eliot's eventual response to this world was to turn to Christianity, both personally and poetically. Hemingway's response to this world was to try in his fiction to find a way to "live in it" (*SAR*, 148), and in that effort he sometimes created a role model or "code hero" figure. The role model is a man who is usually old and a foreigner, but more importantly, he is a man with dignity, will, and commitment (or endurance). Against this model others can be measured. Recognized role models, or "code heroes," in Hemingway's fiction are Pedro Romero in *The Sun Also Rises* (only nineteen, but with the "old thing" [*SAR*, 168]), and Santiago in *The Old Man and the Sea*.

The role of the padrone in "Cat in the Rain" has been seen as that of a "father" (Hagopian, 231), or a "father figure" (White, 243), who "seems to conform to [the wife's] notion of what a benevolent and protective father ought to be, not what a father is likely to be" (DeFalco, 159). The difficulty with this thesis is that the padrone does not treat the wife as he would treat a daughter. A father does not stand and bow to a daughter. Nor does the wife respond to the padrone as she would respond to a father. A daughter does not feel small and tight inside when she passes her father. The wife likes the padrone because of the particular qualities which he possesses, and these qualities are manifested through his profession as a hotel keeper. The qualities which the wife likes are delineated in the text in just four sentences: "She liked the deadly serious way he received any complaints. She liked his dignity. She liked the way he wanted to serve her. She liked the way he felt about being a hotel keeper." The padrone is an admirable man, and although briefly sketched, he is Hemingway's earliest role model. Each of the padrone's qualities corresponds to the qualities of the role model as he later appears in Hemingway's fiction: a man of dignity, will, and commitment. The padrone has dignity, and he lends dignity to his profession: he likes "being a hotel keeper" (92). His "will" is demonstrated in the "deadly serious way" (92) in which he "receives any complaints" (92), and his "commitment" to his profession as a hotel keeper is shown in his efforts to "serve" (92) the wife who is a guest in his hotel. The balance and strength in the padrone's character is elaborated in a manuscript fragment. Though on one hand he is described as "never servile nor obsequious" (JFK item 319), on the other hand he is shown not to be arrogant: the wife "like[s] the respect he had for her" (item 319). The padrone's age is also important in terms of the role model figure. Age is related to values that have been proven by experience over time, and in the presence of age the values which the young have lost are made apparent. This relationship between age and values can also be more clearly seen in the manuscript fragments where the padrone is described as "nice and old and polite" (item 319), and he is "nice" and "polite" because he "belong[s] to the older generation of polite Italians" (item 321). In addition to the padrone's age, even his tallness can be seen as a reflection of the stature of his character. The padrone has the "old thing" (*SAR*, 168) of an older generation.

The wife's recognition of the padrone's extraordinary character suggests that her husband, George, lacks the qualities which the wife finds so attractive in the padrone. George has neither dignity nor will nor commitment. He is a "kid" (*Letters*, 180) who throughout the story remains in the undignified position of "lying propped up" (91) on the bed. He makes a pretense of having the will to get up and take action, but in reality there is no such will in him. When his wife says, "I'm going down and get the kitty" (91), George says, "I'll do it" (91), but he makes no physical move to do so. He doesn't even look up from his book. His activity throughout the story is limited to "putting the book down" (93), "resting his eyes" (93), and, on one occasion, "shift[ing] his position in the bed" (93). George's lack of commitment is shown in the contrast between the way the padrone treats the guests in his hotel and the way George treats his wife. The padrone sends a maid with an umbrella to help the girl when he realizes that the girl is going outside. George, in contrast, makes a flippant, mean-spirited remark: "Don't get wet" (92). He does not have enough commitment to his wife to care that she is leaving the room with neither umbrella nor rainwear to go out in the rain. Later, when she returns without the cat, George asks, without looking up from his book, "Did you get the cat?" (93). If he were seriously interested, he would look up and see that she doesn't have a cat. And since he does not look up, he has no concern that his wife might be wet. His wife says, "It was gone" (93), to which he replies, "Wonder where it went to" (93), "resting his eyes from reading" (93). One would expect a response that would express concern for his wife, such as, "That's too bad," but the cat's new location is of greater interest to him than his wife who is before him. When his wife complains, "I want to eat at a table with my own silver and I want candles" (94)—which is a cry for recognition, a place, and a purpose— George orders her to "shut up and get something to read" (94). Rather than respect her, as the padrone does, George disdains her. His egocentricity is so concentrated that he expects his wife to deny her own desires, model herself on her husband, and do as *he* does.

The difference between the old padrone and George establishes a dichotomy throughout the story in which George functions as the padrone's antithesis, and it is the wife's situation in this dichotomy which creates the story's meaning. The wife quite clearly recognizes the qualities of the padrone, and she quite clearly feels the effect of George's lack of character, his indifference, and his rejection of her rightful place in the relationship. The effect is a sense of homelessness, similar to the condition of a homeless cat in the rain, and the authorial voice identifies the cat "crouched under one of the dripping green tables" (91) as a female, "trying to make herself so compact that she would not be dripped on" (91). When the wife sees the cat in the rain she has no way of knowing that it is female, yet she immediately makes a subconscious transference of her own sense of homelessness to the cat, and she wants to do for the cat what George will not do for her, provide a place of acceptance and comfort. Her identification with the cat remains subconscious: "I don't know why I wanted it so much" (93), but the identification is made explicit to the reader when the wife says, "'It isn't any fun to be a poor kitty out in the rain'" (93), and it is reinforced when she says that she wants a female kitty that will "'purr when I stroke her'" (93). The "poor kitty" (91) in the story is ironically the wife herself, an interpretation supported by the manuscript fragments. The fact that the original title of the story was "The Poor Kitty" (item 320), and the fact that in another fragment the husband calls his wife "Kitty" (item 321) indicates that Hemingway's original intention was to portray the wife as the "poor kitty" and the actual cat in the rain as symbolic of the wife.

The wife as a "poor kitty," whose circumstance is comparable to the fugitive circumstance of the cat in the rain, clarifies why Hemingway changes the way by which he identifies the wife in the course of the action. Early in the story, when she is in the room looking out of the window, she is called the "American wife" (91), and when she speaks to George about the cat, she is again called the "American wife" (91). Then when she leaves George to get the cat, she is called "the wife" (92), and when she passes the padrone on her way out of the hotel, speaking to him in Italian, "'Il piove'" (92), she is again called just "the wife" (92). The change here has to do with the couple's homelessness and isolation. They are the only "two Americans" (91) at the hotel, and they do not "know any of the people" (91) staying in the hotel. Their isolation is presented as resulting from a nationality barrier, but when the wife decides to act on her own, independent of the husband—"'No, I'll get it'"—she is no longer identified as "American," nor is she identified as "American" when she speaks Italian to the padrone. Outside, however, when the maid brings the umbrella, the nationality and language barrier is reintroduced in relation to the maid: "'There was a cat,' said the American girl" (92), and the maid's face "tightened" (92) when she "talked English" (92). At the same time, in relation to the maid, the wife is no longer identified as a "wife," but as a "girl." The implications here have to do with the wife's troubled marriage in relation to the padrone and the role of the maid in the story, but this will be considered later. Returning to the hotel, the wife is still the "American girl" (93), not "the wife." When she "passes the office" (93) of the padrone the second time and the padrone "bow[s] from his desk" (93), her identity is changed again. At this point Hemingway uses only the unmodified noun, "girl," in describing her sensations: "Something felt very small and tight inside the girl" (93). Figuratively, she has been a "poor kitty out in the rain," protected from the downpour, not by her husband, but by the padrone and his umbrella, which explains the girl's unusual responsiveness to the padrone. Neither her nationality nor her marriage are relevant at this moment with the padrone.

When the girl returns to "their room" (91), her sexual feelings are transferred to George. She goes over to George and tries to express her desire for closeness by sitting down "on the bed" (93). The following scene dramatizes how antithetical George's character is to the padrone's character and what it is about George that prevents the girl from having a satisfying relationship with him. George remains perversely propped "at the foot of the bed" (91), and he is using "the two pillows" (91)—hers as well as his—for himself. There is no place for her. When she says, "It isn't any fun to be a poor kitty out in the rain" (93), she is trying to tell him how unfulfilled and displaced his "kitty" is. But "George [is] reading again" (93). Rejected, she gets up from the bed and goes to the mirror. Again she tries to draw George's attention to her sexuality by suggesting that she let her "hair grow out" (93). This time she gets his attention: "George looked up and saw the back of her neck, clipped close like a boy's" (93). His response, "'I like it the way it is'" (93), is not what she wants to hear. George's preference, that she be "like a boy" (93), reflects his self-centeredness.[2] He wants and expects her to suppress her female sexuality and create the appearance of being like him, a male. But she is female and wants him to see her as such. She tells him, "'I get so tired of looking like a boy'" (93). Her insistence agitates him, so much so that he finally "shift[s] his position." He hasn't "looked away from her since she started to speak" (93) and he becomes equally insistent: "'You look pretty darn nice'" (93), that is, as a boy. The girl goes to the window. It is "getting dark" (93), symbolically as well as literally. The growing darkness, her sexual frustration, and George's rejection of her individuality all launch her into a desperate listing of things she "wants."

> "I want to pull my hair back tight and smooth and make a big knot at the back that I can feel," she said. "I want to have a kitty to sit on my lap and purr when I stroke her."
> "And I want to eat at a table with my own silver and I want candles. And I want it to be spring and I want to brush my hair out in

front of a mirror and I want a kitty and I want some new clothes."
(93–94)

George hears what she is saying, and he doesn't like it. He prefers her as a "boy," and he responds with both intolerance, "Oh, shut up" (94), and a self-centered prescription, "get something to read" (94), that is, like me. The authorial voice then identifies the girl by the possessive, "His wife" (94).

For both the cat which the girl has seen in the rain and for the girl as a "poor kitty," it is bad weather. It is "quite dark and now still raining in the palm trees" (94). Good weather would be "spring" (94), and the girl's garden would have an "artist with his easel" (91). The girl would "eat at a table with [her] own silver" (94), she would have someone to "stroke her" (93), and she would "purr" (93). But it is not good weather and her life with George is as empty as the square outside. She stands at the window, her back to the emptiness in the room, and stares out at the empty square, just as the "waiter" (91) earlier in the story stood in his door, his back to the emptiness of his cafe, and stared at the empty square. Now, however, the square is not only empty, it is shrouded in darkness, a symbol of existential nothingness, the loss of meaning and the loss of hope. In a final act of desperation and defeated defiance, the girl refuses to give up one thing: "I can have a cat" (94). If she cannot be her husband's kitty, she wants a kitty with which she can identify, and there is a strong sense of urgency in her. "I want a cat now" (94). "George [is] not listening. He [is] reading" (94). As she continues to look away from him and out of the window, she is again called "His wife" (94).

A "light [comes on] in the square" (94), which is an image that suggests hope, but artificial light is only a substitute for daylight, and the hope which this light foreshadows will be only a temporary substitute for what the girl really wants. There is a knock at the door, as if the padrone has heard the girl's complaint and is again trying to come to her rescue in response to her urgent "now." George, however, asserts his authority by calling, "Avanti" (94). He looks up from his book.

> In the doorway stood the maid. She held a big tortoise-shell cat pressed tight against her and swung down against her body.
> "Excuse me," she said, "the padrone asked me to bring this for the Signora." (94)

The maid's function in the story is significant because her attitude toward the girl introduces a factor that restrains the girl's search for meaning outside her marriage. In the earlier scene in the garden, the maid initially "smiled, speaking Italian" (92), but her smile is more professional than personal. When the girl "talked English the maid's face tightened" (92). The girl is an outsider. The padrone may like her and may want to "serve her" (92), but the maid does not like her, perhaps partly because the padrone does like her. When the maid is again dispatched by the padrone to "serve" the girl by giving her a cat, the maid's role acquires renewed significance by the strange way the maid is holding the padrone's cat. If the cat itself were the only important factor in the scene, the action could be simply stated: In the doorway stood the maid. She held a big tortoise-shell cat. "Excuse me," she said, "the padrone asked me to bring this for the Signora." But it is not simply stated. Instead, the maid is given a kind of precedence over the cat in the highly unusual way she holds it, "pressed tight against her and swung down against her body" (94). Since the cat is the padrone's and he has sent it to the girl, the cat personifies to the maid the padrone himself, in which case she is symbolically giving the padrone away to the girl. Holding the cat "pressed tight against her" (94) suggests possessiveness, not of the cat, but of the padrone. And holding the cat's body "down against her body" (94) is an implicitly sexual image. The description strongly implies feelings on the part of the maid toward the padrone which parallel the girl's feelings toward the padrone. The fact that the maid calls the cat a "this" (94) implies the maid's resentment of what the padrone has asked her to do for *this* "American girl." The maid's earlier hostility toward the girl as an outsider is now extended to an acted-out sexual possessiveness.

The tortoise-shell which the padrone has sent to the girl is a unique variety of tricolor cat. For a cat to be a tortoise-shell, it must have certain hues: black, light red, and dark red. A tortoise-shell is a handsome cat, gentle, affectionate, companionable, and especially good in a family situation. The tortoise-shell however, is a variety of cat whose occurrence is both accidental and extraordinary. Tortoise-shells do not naturally reproduce: that is, a female tortoise-shell will not reproduce tortoise-shell kittens and male tortoise-shells are sterile.[3]

Hemingway could have chosen any description of a cat, including just "a big cat," as in his notes, but he did not. The "tortoise-shell," therefore, must have a significance as an image beyond its literalness as a cat, and that significance must be related to the padrone who sends the cat, and to what is most notable about a tortoise-shell, which is that it cannot be naturally reproduced. That the "tortoise-shell" is figurative of the padrone is suggested by the language Hemingway uses in regard to each of them. The word "big" occurs only twice in the story, once to describe the padrone's "big hands" (92), which indicate a big man, and again to describe the "big tortoise-shell" (94), and the way the maid carries the cat suggests that it is not only big, but long, as the padrone is big and tall. The tortoise-shell is both extraordinary and unique, as the padrone is both extraordinary and unique, and the tortoise-shell is attractive, and the padrone is attractive to the girl—and to the maid. Most importantly, a tortoise-shell may occasionally appear, but a tortoise-shell cannot be naturally reproduced, and a man like the padrone, with dignity, will, and commitment, may occasionally appear, but a man like the padrone is too exemplary to be found elsewhere.

The tragic figure in "Cat in the Rain" is the girl, the wife. She is cut off from meaning and fulfillment both inside her marriage and outside. An exceptional person like the padrone will like her, respond to her, and give her protection, but others, like the maid, will resent her when she speaks English and will see her as an outsider. There is no place for her in another country, speaking another language. She is herself a kitty in bad weather, inside the room and outside, desperately searching for a place and for companionship. Ironically, what the girl wants is not really a "kitty . . . and some new clothes" (94); what the "poor kitty" wants is a loving place with a "padrone" incarnated in a man of her own generation. But this is impossible. A man like the padrone is unique. The feelings and desires which the padrone has inspired in her will be denied and will bear her no fruit. They have been aroused only to have her husband, the antithesis of the padrone, reject them and her; he will allow her no expression of her true identity and no true place in their marriage. Such betrayed feelings and lost hopes will turn into more loneliness and more despair. "April [will be] the cruellest month" (Eliot, 61) because her imagined "spring" (94) will never come. The poor kitty's destiny is that of a barren, wandering soul with no place and no purpose in the futility of the wasteland *In Our Time*.

Hemingway's "The Denunciation": The Aloof American

Kenneth G. Johnston

●

The American experience, broadly speaking, is not faithfully reflected in Ernest Hemingway's *For Whom the Bell Tolls*. Robert Jordan represents only the handful of American volunteers, fewer than three thousand idealists and adventurers, who were willing to risk their lives in the fight against fascism on the battlefields of Spain.[1] Actually, as historian Gabriel Jackson observes, the attitude of the United States toward the Spanish Civil War "was dominated by the twin desires for isolation and neutrality."[2] The policy of "moral aloofness," enunciated by the American Secretary of State, Cordell Hull,[3] was widely supported by both the American public and Congress. A joint resolution banning shipment of arms to either side in the Spanish conflict swiftly passed the Senate by a vote of 81 to 0 and the House by 406 to 1. In May 1937—the month and year in which Robert Jordan carried out his mission in Hemingway's novel—passage of a revised Neutrality Act gave further evidence that the nation was determined to stand aloof. Although there was widespread sympathy in the United States for the Loyalist cause, an official policy of neutrality was maintained throughout the war, a policy which, in the opinion of many, including Hemingway, doomed the legitimate government of Spain.[4]

To discover Ernest Hemingway's fictional response to the aloof American, one must turn to his neglected and underrated short story "The Denunciation." Though written in 1938 while the war was still in progress, it is not a propaganda piece. Ever the artist, Hemingway, in relating his tale of conflicting loyalties, raises the question of one's ultimate responsibility to self and to others. "If you get as much intensity and as much meaning in a story as some one can get in a novel," declared Hemingway, "that story will last as long as it is any good. A true work of art endures forever; no matter what its politics."[5]

In the final analysis "The Denunciation" is a story of self-denunciation, for it is sharply critical of the narrator for his failure, his refusal, to assume the responsibilities which come with commitment. His policy of moral aloofness, which helps neither friend nor foe, provides the rationale for his evasion of duty as a professed and loyal supporter of the Loyalist cause. Moreover, there is strong evidence in the story to suggest that Hemingway was aiming his criticism at America, as well as at his American, at the U.S. policy of nonintervention, as well as at the narrator's stand of self-righteous "impartiality."

"The Denunciation" takes place in Madrid one winter evening in 1937, the second year of the war. Fascist batteries are sporadically shelling the Loyalist capital, which has been under seige for a year now. The narrator, an American writer named Henry Emmunds, stops by Chicote's bar to wait out the bombardment. He has a special fondness for the place. Before the war Chicote's had an enviable reputation; it was where "the good guys" went. The service and the liquor there were the best in Spain; the atmosphere and the waiters were invariably pleasant. It was "like a club," declares the narrator: "It was the best bar in Spain, certainly, and I think one of the best bars in the world, and all of us that used to hang out there had a great affection for it."[6]

The story appears to center on an old waiter who is agonizing over whether or not to denounce a fascist, Luis Delgado, who sits in the bar enjoying a gin and tonic. The question is not an easy one. In the old days Delgado was a good client; furthermore, Chicote's has an apolitical tradition: that is, "you did not talk politics there" (89). The old waiter, with his "very old-fashioned manners which the war had not changed" (92), is part of that tradition, and thus he is tempted to a course of silence. Perhaps one of the other waiters will denounce Delgado, says the narrator. "No," replies the old waiter. "Only the old waiters know him and the old waiters do not denounce" (93). That should settle the matter.

Still, the old waiter feels strongly that it is his duty, his obligation, to denounce this fascist in their midst. "'I have nothing against him,' the waiter said. 'But it is the *Causa*. Certainly such a man is dangerous to our cause'" (93). It is a cause for which one of his sons has already given his life and another is serving at the front.

The old waiter wavers in his dilemma. At first he says the presence of the fascist in the bar is none of his business. But he cannot let it rest there. He tries to share the responsibility with Henry Emmunds. But the narrator will have none of it.

"It is thy problem."
"And you? Already I have told you."
"I came in here to have a drink before eating."

"And I work here. But tell me."

"It is thy problem," I said. "I am not a politician." (92)

When the waiter returns to the table for the third time, he concedes that the responsibility is his, and he writes down the phone number, which the narrator has offered to give him, of the security police. But still he is very reluctant to denounce the old client. "Perhaps then he is on our side now, too," he says. "No," the narrator tells him. "I know he is not" (93). The waiter leaves but soon returns, still wrestling with his problem.

"What do you think?" he asked.

"I would never denounce him myself," I said, now trying to undo for myself what I had done with the number. "But I am a foreigner and it is your war and your problem."

"But you are with us."

"Absolutely and always. But it does not include denouncing old friends."

"But for me?"

"For you it is different." (97)

With those last words the narrator has signed Luis Delgado's death warrant. The old waiter now makes the phone call because, as he tells the narrator, "it was my duty" (98). He is proud to have done this extremely difficult task, but his spirits are dashed when the narrator, by word and action, quickly disassociates himself from the denunciation. "I did not denounce for pleasure," the old man reminds him. Shamed by the mild rebuke, the narrator suggests that Delgado be told that he, Henry Emmunds, denounced him to the police. "No," the old man replies with quiet dignity. "Each man must take his responsibility" (98). Clearly, the old man is the touchstone by which we are to take the measure of the Hemingway hero, Henry Emmunds.

The Hemingway hero, too, is caught in a dilemma, the poles of which are his loyalty to the *causa* and his personal admiration for Luis Delgado's courage and style. His clumsy attempt at impartiality is simply an evasion of his larger responsibility if we take him at his word that he is "absolutely and always" loyal to the cause of the Republic. He admits as much when he accuses himself of "Pontius Pilatry" (97). His "neutrality" condemns the waiter to intense emotional and moral agony, and his old friend from the past to denunciation and death. It is quite clear that Henry Emmunds is a man of influence and could have spared his old friend's life if he had but urged the waiter to remain silent. Four times the waiter appeals to him for advice, and four times Emmunds denies him forthright counsel.

Instead, under the pretense of impartiality, he prolongs the agony and, word by contradictory word, sentences his old friend to death. (The scene in Chicote's is not unlike that in a courtroom. The narrator is at the "bar" [90]; he sits on a "bench" [91]; he listens to the accusations and appeals of the old waiter; he observes the accused, who is also at the bar; and by his judicial attempt at "impartiality," he helps to condemn this man to death. "You're the judge of that," he had said to Luis in the old days at San Sebastian, a remark prompted by Luis's judgment that they did not know one another well enough for him to accept a personal loan [96]. Now, four years later, the narrator must judge whether or not his past friendship for Delgado is such that he can come to his aid.)

The narrator's reluctance to denounce his old friend is understandable. Delgado exhibits traits which the Hemingway hero, wherever we find him, has unfailingly admired and/or aspired to: courage, zest, cheerfulness, a willingness to take risks and, when the gamble fails, to pay the piper uncomplainingly. The purpose of the flashback is to establish these qualities of character. At a pigeon shoot in the resort town of San Sebastian in 1933, Delgado, who "had shot beautifully but drawn almost impossible birds," graciously pays a heavy gambling debt, "a good deal more than he could afford to lose that year." "I remembered how pleasant he was and how he made it seem a great privilege to pay" (95). Then on the spur of the moment Delgado proposes they wager eight thousand pesetas, nearly a thousand dollars, on the flip of a coin. Again he loses, and again he pays without complaint, without bitterness. He politely turns down the narrator's offer of a personal loan—"'Don't be silly, Enrique,' he said. 'We've been gambling, haven't we?'" (96)—but accepts his offer of a drink. "So we had a gin and tonic and I felt very badly to have broken him and I felt awfully good to have won the money, and a gin and tonic never tasted better to me in all my life. There is no use to lie about these things or pretend you do not enjoy winning; but this boy Luis Delgado was a very pretty gambler" (96). Now, sitting at different tables, separated by the politics of war, they are both in Chicote's drinking gin and tonic. And once again Delgado is gambling for very high stakes, this time truly for more than he can afford to lose.

Although the narrator repeatedly refers to Delgado as a fool, "The utter bloody fool" (91), it is quite clear that he admires the dashing courage of this enemy, although in the end he will betray him.

I would have given plenty not to have seen him in there.

Still, if he wanted to do an absolutely damned fool thing like that it was his own business. But as I looked at the table and remembered the old days I felt badly about him and I felt very badly too that I had given the waiter the number of the counter-espionage bureau in Seguridad headquarters. . . . I had given him the shortest cut to having Delgado arrested in one of those excesses of impartiality, righteousness and Pontius Pilatry." (96–97)

For thirty pieces of silver Judas betrayed his Master to the chief priests and elders, who accused and denounced Jesus before Pontius Pilate, the Roman governor of Judea. For expediency's sake Pilate betrayed Jesus to the multitude. Denying responsibility for the death of Jesus, Pilate "washed his hands before the multitude, saying, I am innocent of the blood of this just person: see ye to it" (Matt. 27:24). The narrator, too, believes he is innocent of the blood of the accused, guilty only of having expedited the arrest; but, by washing his hands of the affair, he has betrayed Delgado to the embattled Madrilenos, who shows no mercy to fifth columnists, traitors, and spies.

The reference to the pieces of silver used in the gambling at San Sebastian enriches the imagery of the betrayal. They were "heavy silver five-peseta pieces," "big silver" coins "with the profile of Alfonso XIII as a baby showing" on one side (95). This king did indeed betray Spanish hopes for peaceful evolution toward parliamentary democracy when he gave his support and blessing to the military dictatorship of General Miguel Primo de Rivera in 1923. With the rise to power of Primo de Rivera, declares Jackson, "Spain lost the considerable intellectual and slight parliamentary liberty she had achieved since 1875,"[7] But the allusion to Alfonso's babyhood suggests that the betrayal of Spain's democratic hopes, which set the stage for the Spanish Civil War, began many years earlier. And the historians agree. During the regency of his mother Maria Christina, while Alfonso was a child, the conservative and liberal leaders made a mockery of the election process by agreeing in advance to a policy (*turno politico*) of alternating the two parties in power. "A two-party system involving fixed elections," Jackson believes, "ultimately undermined rather than developed the sense of political responsibility in Spain."[8] The arrangement insured "the minimum amount of friction," observes Theo Aronson, but "it was a policy of peace at any price, and sooner or later the price would have to be paid."[9]

Alfonso, "always a man for risks,"[10] serves as a counterpart to Luis Delgado. Like Delgado, he was a crack shot and spent many long summers in San Sebastian. He adored shooting, high-speed motoring, polo, any sport requiring speed and daring. "No amount of anxiety," writes Aronson, "seemed capable of subduing his high spirits."[11] On his wedding day he narrowly missed death in his royal carriage when a bombing attempt was made on his life. Twelve persons were killed in the procession and crowd and over a hundred wounded, and one of the horses which drew the royal coach lay dead in the street. The king calmly switched to "the carriage of respect—the empty coach preceding the royal carriage"—put his arm around his bride-queen, kissed her, and then "in a loud, clear, deliberate voice, for all that stunned crowd to hear, he ordered: 'Slowly, very slowly, to the palace.'" Remarked a British Colonel who had witnessed the assassination attempt, "I never saw such pluck."[12]

Alfonso, moreover, at the time of his abdication in 1931, enunciated a policy of neutrality not unlike that pursued by the narrator in Hemingway's story. "I could find ample means," the king declared in his farewell manifesto to the Spanish people, "to maintain my Royal Prerogatives in effective resistance to those who assail them: but I prefer to stand resolutely aside rather than provoke a conflict which might array my fellow-countrymen against one another in civil and patricidal strife."[13]

The betrayal motif, which surfaces rather late in the story, has a ripplelike effect which carries back to earlier sections. One now begins to understand why Hemingway identified his narrator as an American and why, at the beginning, he has him stop by the American Embassy. Through his denunciation of the aloof American, Hemingway is also denouncing the U.S. State Department policy of nonintervention. Henry Emmunds is seen implementing that policy, evading his rightful responsibilities, not on the international stage, but in a small Madrid bar. His visit to the Embassy is a reminder that the United States has also evaded its responsibilities to the duly elected government of Spain. At least that was Hemingway's view, one shared at the time by many other Americans, including Henry L. Stimson, former U.S. Secretary of State. In a now historic letter written to the *New York Times*, Stimson urged the lifting of the arms embargo, pointing out that the act violated "longstanding principles of American international conduct." The Loyalist government, Stimson reminded the American people, was recognized as "the true government of Spain" by the United States. "One of the most important rights which a state like Spain is entitled to expect from another government, which has recognized it as a friendly neighbor in the family of nations," argued the former Secretary, "is the right of self-defense against any future rebellions which may challenge its authority."[14] Herbert Matthews, the *New York Times* correspondent who covered the Spanish conflict, often in the company of Hemingway, puts America's evasion of responsibility into historical perspective: "The United States had never before denied to a legitimate government, with whom, incidentally, it had a 'Treaty of Friendship and General Relations,' the right to buy arms."[15]

The "ten pounds of fresh meat" which the narrator picked up at the Embassy provides the basis for further, albeit very subtle, criticism of U.S. policy. The narrator is spared the hardship of hunger in the besieged, food-scarce Spanish capital, and in the bar he claims exemption from the moral hardships. He is a well-fed American who enjoys a privileged position in the midst of the war. The fact that the meat is "wrapped in two envelopes which had brought copies of the *Spur*" (98) to the American Embassy supports this claim of privilege. The *Spur*, now defunct, was an American magazine of limited circulation exuding "an aura of wealth," according to Henry F. Pringle, whose article on class magazines, entitled "High Hat," appeared in *Scribner's Magazine* in July 1938, just four months before the publication of "The Denunciation." The pages of the *Spur*, Pringle said, were "littered with photographs of expensive ladies and gentlemen in riding clothes, articles on polo, tennis, golf, and yachting." It advised the "well-dressed man" that his proper wardrobe would cost $7500—"and this without such plebian accessories as underwear, shoes, or hose."[16] The *Spur*'s appeal, quite obviously, was to persons of wealth and privilege, and in Spain most of them were supporting the Franco side. This "high hat" magazine and, Hemingway implies, the Embassy which subscribed to it were completely out of touch with the democratic People's Army fighting for its very survival on the outskirts of Madrid.

The narrator's encounters with the minor characters in "The Denunciation" keep alive the question of responsibility and duty. In a relatively minor episode early in the story, the narrator buys three Communist party tracts from an old woman and tips her generously. "She said God would bless me. I doubted this but read the three leaflets and drank the gin and tonic" (91). With swift strokes and a minimum of words, Hemingway conveys, seemingly without effort, a cluster of ideas. One quickly notes the irony of the situation, a religious believer selling the tracts of the party of atheism, infamous for its attacks upon the church. The old woman's duty to God apparently takes precedence over her complete loyalty to the Communist *causa*. But Hemingway enriches the irony by making Emmunds purchase three tracts, probably to evoke the idea of the Father, the Son, and the Holy Ghost. The "doubt" which the narrator expresses may very well extend beyond the old woman's blessing to the very existence of God. Sitting beside a package of freshly butchered meat, reading his trinity of Communist leaflets, he is the very picture of the modern materialist. Marx claimed that religion was the opiate of the people but, as the Hemingway hero in "The Gambler, the Nun, and the Radio" acknowledges, "drink was a sovereign opium of the people, oh, an excellent opium."[17] Thus, the gin and tonic in Henry Emmunds's hand is the final deft touch in this brief but telling comment on the spiritual condition of a man who no longer serves his God. Nor does he say "adios," which means literally "to God (I commend you)," when he says goodbye on the phone to Pepe. Rather, as was the Loyalist custom throughout the war, he employs the word "salud," meaning "salute" or "health" (100).[18]

The Greek soldier who joins the narrator at his table in Chicote's serves both as a contrast and as a parallel to the American writer. John is a volunteer, a company commander in the XVth International Brigade; thus he has fully committed himself to the Loyalist cause, and as a commander he has undertaken very serious military responsibilities. Yet he has on two occasions acted irresponsibly. He must be held at least partly responsible for the death of four of his men; he had given them the all-clear signal when the enemy planes flew over: "Is pass the other three and I say to the company, 'Now is hokay. Now is all right. Now is nothing more to worry.' That the last thing I remember for two weeks" (93). The explosion of an aerial bomb killed his four men and buried him alive. John also recalls the time when he hired out at very high wages to dive in a harbor on the southern tip of South America, but he refused to carry on with his duties because of an encounter with an octopus. "So when I get up out of water they take off the helmet and so I say I don't go down there any more" (95).

But that was long ago and far away. Here in Chicote's harbor the narrator finds himself out of his moral depth, deeply troubled by the tentacles of responsibility which loom before him. The old waiter beckons him toward social responsibility; Delgado, toward private considerations. He is given a choice between two code heroes: the new socially conscious hero who places public interests above private ones, or the old individualistic hero who adheres to a private code of courage, pride, and honor. By his indecision he betrays them both. But he is uncomfortable in his "neutral" role, and twice—before he leaves Chicote's and again at the end—he tries, too late, with an empty theatrical gesture to share responsibility with the waiter. One should view as suspect the reason he gives, that he "did not wish him [Delgado] to be disillusioned or bitter about the waiters" at Chicote's before he died (100). His gesture, like all his earlier actions and statements, falls between the two codes; it satisfies neither. But it does reveal a vague sense of guilt for having sat by while an old man manfully shoulders an onerous duty, one which rightfully belonged to them both.

Hemingway is being *muy delgado* ("very subtle") at the story's end. The Spanish word *delgado* means "thin," "delicate," "tenuous"; the phrase *hilar delgado* means, colloquially, "to hew close to the line," "to split hairs." And that is what the narrator is doing at the conclusion of "The Denunciation"—splitting hairs. He tries to still his conscience by having Pepe tell the condemned man that he, Henry Emmunds, denounced him to the police. "Why when it will make no difference?" asks Pepe. "He is a spy. He will be shot. There is no choice in the matter" (99). But Henry Emmunds did have a choice, and the fact remains that he shirked his responsibility.

The Hemingway hero had announced a "separate peace" in 1918 in *A Farewell to Arms*,[19] and Hemingway the man reaffirmed that private pact in 1935 in *Green Hills of Africa*: "If you serve time for society, democracy, and the other things quite young," he wrote, "and declining any further enlistment make yourself responsible only to yourself, you exchange the pleasant, comforting stench of comrades for something you can never feel in any other way than by yourself."[20] The outbreak of the Spanish Civil War in 1936, however, led to the reenlistment of both. But Hemingway and his hero, ever the individualists, continued to wrestle with the question of responsibility to self and to others.[21] The attempt to resolve this question is at the thematic center of "The Denunciation."

To Embrace or Kill: *Fathers and Sons*

Richard McCann

●

Fathers ought to avoid utter nakedness before their sons. I did not want to know—not, anyway, from his mouth—that his flesh was as unregenerate as my own . . . I did not want to think that my life would be like his, or that my mind would ever grow so pale, so without hard places and sharp, sheer drops . . . I wanted the merciful distances of father and son, which would have permitted me to love him.—James Baldwin, *Giovanni's Room*

The speaker of Joseph Lobdell's "A Letter" begins, "I wanted to write a friend / who also has a father who is dead." The implied possession—of having a dead father as opposed to having no father at all—might also fit Hemingway's "Fathers and Sons." As Nick Adams travels back into his father's country he is claimed by the past, a past which, like the father, will neither wholly die nor nourish him. In "Fathers and Sons" the past is as dark as the "black murk of the swamp" Nick crosses, an image which repeats in "Big Two-Hearted River," yet it is also close and sensual, its very darkness presenting itself as an appeal. The story moves back through memory *as* darkness (the evening Nick drives through, the heavy trees of the small town, the swamp) but also suggests how memory might inevitably open into clarity and light. By traveling through darkness, Nick finally arrives into the deepest past, the past he would recover, a lit tableau in the woods. Though Nick does not live in the past, we discover how deeply it lives within him as he moves through the submerged layers of his own consciousness.

The landscape of "Fathers and Sons," the northern Michigan of Nick's youth, is heavy with the past. Everywhere it reflects Nick's ambivalence. Though Nick feels that after fifteen "he shared nothing" with his father, his encounters with the "natural" world yield forth the father out of the past Nick yearns for:

His father came back to him . . . when he saw shocks of corn, or
when he saw a lake, or if he ever saw a horse and buggy, or when he
saw, or heard, wild geese. . . . His father was with him, suddenly,
in deserted or in new-plowed fields, in thickets, on small hills, or
when going through dead grass, whenever splitting wood or hauling
water, by grist mills, cider mills and dams and always with open
fires.

"Fathers and Sons" rises from such ambivalence, as do Nick's memories.
Nick reveals his deep love for "the last good country," yet is an exile. He
strives to create a distance between his old and new selves, his past and
present, his father and himself, yet also strives to break that distance
down. Twice he decides to think no more of his father, yet he cannot stop
himself.

Though in one sense Nick "admits" the past in "Fathers and Sons," it
is perhaps more accurate to say he falls into it, falling into himself.
"Fathers and Sons" begins with a detour *not* taken, an image which
suggests that this story will lead into a center usually driven by. In this
landscape Nick finds the road he assumed had been repaired is still
incomplete; likewise, so are Nick's relationships with his father and his
past, relationships which even death—if not death especially—has left
undone. Nick's entrance into town at the beginning of the story signals
his entry into the interior of memory and self, just as Hemingway's
recurring use of the second-person singular and long heavy sentences
creates for Nick an interior voice, contemplative.

Because this movement into the past is not always characteristic of
either Nick or Hemingway, because "Fathers and Sons" may be read as a
semi-autobiographical story, it assumes added importance and dimension, suggesting that the story also operates as a metaphor for the creative
process. Here Nick does not only "fish" the cool shallows, avoiding all
but an absolute present, as he does in "Big Two-Hearted River," he also
searches within memory where "the waters pile up on you."

Traveling through the father's country, himself a father now, Nick
begins to make connections between the past and present, the father and
self. He also fears connection, however, not knowing if his image of his
father, and the part of the father which lives within him, should be
embraced or killed. On one hand he is moved by a great love for the
father; on the other the memory of the father is utterly spoiled, "no good
now." "On the other hand," a phrase Nick uses in thinking of his father,
best describes the structure of Nick's thought. Almost every paragraph
describing the father and the past is equally torn between love and guilt.

On one hand Nick loves his father's ability to hunt and see; on the other he is disgusted by his smell. He views his father heroically, the way his child-self might; from a distance, however, he knows his father's beard hides a weak chin.

This ambivalence is mirrored in Nick's uncertainty over how he should best approach his memories of his father. In the first third of the story Nick holds himself at some distance from the scenes he remembers and, in a sense, creates. Looking out from the car window, he imagines his father and himself back in the past. He becomes both "Nicholas" and "Nick." His vision is doubled, sometimes intimate, sometimes distant. Entering town he sees it as both a citizen and as a stranger might: "[He drove] under the heavy trees of the small town that are a part of your heart if it is your town and you have walked under them, but that are only too heavy, that shut out the sun and dampen the houses for a stranger." For Nick the trees function in both ways. They are "part of his heart," yet they also burden him, a fantastic weight.

Nick's conflict is, in part, in deciding which perspective to assume. The distance he holds from his father—a distance enforced by departure, geography, time, and finally death—may make him an exile, yet does provide the seemingly necessary emotional distance between his father and himself, the distance necessary for freedom from the weaknesses of the father which have disappointed the son. It also provides the aesthetic distance which Nick as writer (and Hemingway persona) requires in order to approach the past. Nick fears a past which might overwhelm him in an onslaught of immediate sensations he cannot control. The dangers of standing inside such a past are revealed through the metaphor of hunting quail. As Nick hunts "the country in his mind" (a pun which reinforces the sense of the landscape as mental), he simultaneously remembers his father and recites to himself how one must assume a distance from one's prey:

> In shooting quail you must not get between them and their habitual cover, once the dogs have found them, or when they flush they will come pouring out at you, some rising steep, some skimming by your ears, whirring into a size you have never seen them in the air as they pass, the only way being to turn and take them over your shoulder as they go, before they set their wings and angle down into the thicket.

The hunting metaphor also functions as it does in other Hemingway stories: as a test. How much can be captured? Can the hunter exercise the needed control? In "Fathers and Sons" the memory of the dead father becomes the object of the hunt. Repeatedly Nick likens the father to a bird. Hunting, Nick remembers the father's "hawk nose," the eyes which can see "as an eagle sees, literally." Later, he remembers his father as an eagle whose talons have caught in a canvas decoy, an image which recalls his father "trapped." Nick remembers his father when he sees "a thicket." No matter what the needed method, Nick will flush the memory out.

Yet if the father is the object of the hunt, Nick also becomes both hunter and hunted within his own search. Because the story takes place in memory the hunt for the father also becomes a hunt for the father within the self—the father internalized in Nick. Though Nick cannot find the distance he feels he needs to write about his father—"It was still too early for that"—"Fathers and Sons" gives us Nick's *rehearsal* of the story he will one day write, the story Hemingway writes through him. Thus "Fathers and Sons" becomes the search for the means of writing the story. The search for the father becomes a search within the self.

As the story progresses Nick splits into two characters, two selves which overlap. One is the writer, Nicholas Adams, who seeks to order an experience which resists resolution; he plays it over and over in his mind. The other is his child-self, the self "Nicholas" looks back upon. Likewise, if Nick's son represents the third generation of parenting in "Fathers and Sons," so he also represents Nick's own child-self, a self which sleeps beside him as he travels through memory, a self which finally wakes. The title, "Fathers and Sons," refers not only to the actual generations but also to the way Nick becomes a father to his younger self. The relationship of the older Nick to the younger is the same relationship the autobiographer has to the protagonist he creates.

This autobiographical structure of "Fathers and Sons," a man looking back at himself, reflects Nick's ambivalence. It simultaneously allows him the distance achieved by the creation of an intermediary and the closeness achieved by making contact with his younger self, the self which has never died. Likewise, if there are two Nicks, there are also two pasts. One is the spoiled past, the past which Nick feels he must "get rid of"—his father's weakness and sentimentality. The other is the past Nick hopes will yet nourish him—hunting with his father, his relationship with Trudy, the American past of the "virgin forest," a past in which masculinity has not been, in Nick's eyes, corrupted.

In embracing Trudy, and in embracing the whole scene in memory, Nick strives to overcome his distance from the past he yearns for—the past of wholeness and union, the past which might redeem the father's weakness. "Now if he could still feel of [the trail to the Indian camp] with bare feet," Nick imagines to himself and doing so descends into a past alive with rich sensual detail:

> First there was the pine-needle loam through the hemlock woods behind the cottage where the fallen logs crumbled into wood dust and long splintered pieces of wood hung javelins in the tree that had been struck by lightning. You crossed the creek on a log and if you stepped off there was the black muck of the swamp. You climbed a fence out of the woods and the trail was hard in the sun across the field with cropped grass and sheep sorrel and mullen growing and to the left the quaky bog of the creek bottom where the killdeer plover fed.

The sense of the two pasts is reinforced by the contrasting imagery used to describe the place. Half the view consists of that which is sharp, dark, burned, cut away, dead; the other half is clear in light and green. Yet Nick appears to overcome the dangers of his passage.

As he turns off the "main road" (which recalls the image of his driving through the detour), Nick travels back into the deepest self. He arrives in the "virgin forest where the trees grew higher before there were any branches and you walked on the brown, clean, springy-needled ground with no undergrowth." The deeper into the past he travels, the less spoiled the place: he returns to the past as a source. The scene in the woods becomes the emotional center for both Nick and the auto-biographical story he cannot yet write. This is the scene which rests inside all the other layers of time. The longest and most complete memory Nick searches out, it exists in the past like a tableau.

As Nick achieves union with Trudy (union with memory for the older Nick, union as experience for the child-self), so he makes contact with a self not yet separate from the "virgin forest." Nick Adams enters the garden, the instinctual life uncorrupted by the father's sentimentality. In doing so Nick goes beyond his father's life: the split. Whereas his father is as "unsound" on the subject of sex as he is sound about hunting, Nick unites hunting and sex within a single context and experience. He has discovered in Trudy a sexuality without inhibition or shame. "You think we make a baby?" she asks Nick, and then answers herself, "Make plenty baby what the hell." Nick embraces the world his father warned against: "His father had summed up the whole matter by stating that masturbation produced blindness, insanity and death, while a man who went with prostitutes would contract hideous venereal diseases and that the thing to do was keep your hands off of people." By recreating Trudy in his memory Nick not only breaks the distance of time but also breaks the emotional distance his father accepts. Nick does not keep his hands "off of people" but has instead entered a world untainted by the father's Puritanism.

Yet if the scene gives us Nick Adams in the garden, it also gives us his fall. Unlike the Indians, Nick does not have a natural ease with sex. Though he yearns to belong to the place, his father's blood betrays his "true heritage."

When Nick hears that Eddie, Trudy and Billy's half-brother, wants to have sex with his sister, he is outraged. He imagines himself killing Eddie, scalping him and throwing him to the dogs. Nick is pleased with the picture of himself he has created—a picture drawn from dime novels:

> . . . Having scalped that half-breed renegade and standing, watching the dogs tear him, his face unchanging, [Nick] fell backward against the tree, held tight around the neck, Trudy holding, choking him, and crying. "No kill him! No kill him! No kill him! No. No. No. Nickie. Nickie!"
>
> "What's the matter with you?"
>
> "No kill him."
>
> "He just a big bluff."
>
> "All right," Nickie said. "I won't kill him unless he comes around the house. Let go of me."
>
> "That's good," Trudy said. "You want to do anything now? I feel good now."
>
> "If Billy goes away." Nick had killed Eddie Gilby, then pardoned him his life, and he was a man now.

Trudy quickly recovers from the intrusion of Nick's violence. Nick does not: he silently continues the fantasy; he sends Billy away. Into the "Eden" he carries his rage, shame, and romanticism; into the scene which was to assure him of the masculinity his father could not provide, Nick carries the childish romance of conquering the foe and being transformed suddenly into "a man now." Nick shatters his own relationship to the forest's ease and innocence; in casting for himself the role of white man defending the pure maid from the "half-breed renegade," Nick suffers the same split as his father. He sentimentalizes. After Nick has sex with Trudy again, he is not vitalized, as is she, but feels instead that "something inside . . . had gone a long way away." He is no longer "hollow and happy," but emptied instead. He turns back toward his father's home.

And he turns again toward the present. The memory of Trudy remains for him something no one can take—a memory of his life in a more whole and innocent world—yet the memory fails to function in the present. "Long time ago good," Nick remembers. "Now no good." Even the mythical past has begun to disappear. The Indians now contribute to the wreckage of the forest; Nick recalls how each year "there was less forest and more open, hot, shadeless, weed-grown slashing." Nick finds what he shares with his father—that they are both citizens of the incomplete and fallen world—just when he'd begun to leave him.

When he turns back into the present Nick finds his own son awake beside him on the car seat. Nick's relationship to his father, and to his younger self, is underscored by the fact that he wakes into the present to find himself the father now. His son stresses both the distance and connection between Nick and his father when he tells Nick, "I hope we won't live somewhere so that I can never go to pray at your tomb when you're dead." He raises for Nick the question and fear of whether his son will have to assume the same distance, making for himself a life in a foreign place, far from the father.

The unquestioned love of Nick's son for his grandfather also reminds Nick of one's need for the past, a past which defines the present self, as Nick's does. The son is even more an exile than Nick; he has no sense of place. He does not understand the difference between being buried in America or France; he can't remember the grandfather except for having given him "an air rifle" and "an American flag," the dead symbols of Nick's past.

Yet the son, if an exile, also asks that his past be given him. In agreeing that they will visit the grandfather's tomb, Nick seems to agree to some acceptance of his father and of that past. Yet he also seems to agree to pass on to his son a past stripped of ambivalence. Of the Indians Nick says only, "they were very nice"; he cannot, he feels, speak to his son about Trudy. Likewise, he supports the heroic view of his own father, telling his son, "He was a great hunter and fisherman and he had wonderful eyes."

But if Nick wants to spare his son his own ambivalence, he also spares his son a full knowledge of the world—his father's limits, his own. In doing so he continues the cycle in which the son will grow, as did Nick, into disappointment with the father, grow to be betrayed and to betray. In this sense "Fathers and Sons" refers to a cycle without release. The father is doomed to fall from the son's heroic vision of him; the son is doomed to embrace and kill. In giving to his son the masculine world he himself yearned for—the world of hunting, fishing, of Fathers—Nick passes on both the *need* to prove oneself within that world and the resultant split. Nick himself does not resolve the split within the story; it seems in fact irresolvable. One can just "get rid of it" or move in close. But Nick does seem to begin to see more intimately, to create the past in detail, more the citizen of the small town than the stranger. He has begun, by rehearsal, to write the story we have read. But the ambivalence lasts even here. Nick agrees to "visit" the tomb of the father, not to "pray."

I mentioned earlier that "Fathers and Sons" may be read as a semi-autobiographical story; in doing so it is interesting to consider for a moment these images of distance in relationship to Hemingway's own creative process. For Hemingway, as for Nick, distance seems to have been a necessary stance in approaching his materials. Just as Nicholas has his younger self stand between himself and the experience he seeks to describe, Hemingway's terse and tense prose style serves to create the pace and intimacy of memory, gives us some idea of at least one thing that chaos came to mean—the past. "Fathers and Sons" is, in many ways, the obverse of "A Clean, Well-Lighted Place." It suggests how ambivalence and fear lie within the darkness which a "well-lighted place" staves off. To stay within the light becomes a way out of those traps—perhaps also "the trap" his father "helped create" and fell victim to, certainly the trap of darkness which will not allow the clarity Hemingway seeks.

Even that clarity, however, is not without ambiguity. Through a focus on the present moment it may provide grace, as do the fish in "Big Two-Hearted River," "keeping themselves steady in the current with wavering fins," yet it is also created by the same force which holds the fish: a great tension. "Fathers and Sons" reveals the way in which Hemingway's personal and stylistic ambiguity may rise from a deep ambivalence toward the past and self. As Jackson Benson has noted in *Hemingway: The Writer's Art of Self-Defense*, "Hemingway was the American in the middle, whose conflict was never resolved, and whose pain was relieved only temporarily by the use of a portable Corona." Hemingway's journey into the past, like Nick's, is not only an attempt to recover, it is also a testing of the self, to survive.

"Fathers and Sons" also points to an ambivalence over the masculine role. Though Hemingway never questions the role—it appears as a given—it is a source of the fantastic burden Nick feels. His shame over his father's weakness appears stultifying; Nick must constantly battle to redeem what the father lost. In thinking of Hemingway as a writer of boy's stories, it is interesting to recall how in "Fathers and Sons" the male is condemned repeatedly to suffer the loss of the boy's world, yet remain unable to create a wholly new one, a world that might be equally valued. Nick becomes the father, passing the conflict on to his son—inevitable.

If "Fathers and Sons" makes a peace with this, and with the father, it is perhaps made in the way in which Nick becomes a father also to himself. He seeks to become the father he lost. This motion necessarily recalls the way in which Hemingway himself came to create the role of "Papa," the American Father. One can only wonder if Hemingway's suicide was a desperate attempt to embrace the father, or if it was an admission of what he shared with the father and the possible distance he failed to create. Such a question is necessarily speculative, perhaps even unfair, yet it is interesting that becoming the father appears as the only way out in "Fathers and Sons." In this way Nick both possesses a dead father and at the same time tries to give birth to a new one: himself. It is perhaps useful here to create another full circle, as "Fathers and Sons" does, and quote the Lobdell poem with which we began:

> I wanted to write a friend
> who also has a father who is dead.
> Perhaps there were things we could do for each other.
> But perhaps he had already forgotten his father.
> I go back to the time
> my father used to check my body
> for ticks, a job I still recoil from
> though it is necessary to do.

Wise-Guy Narrator and Trickster Out-Tricked in Hemingway's "Fifty Grand"

Robert P. Weeks

●

Although "Fifty Grand" is generally considered one of Hemingway's finest short stories, the relatively small amount of critical and scholarly attention it has received sets it apart from other Hemingway stories of the first rank. Stories like "The Short, Happy Life of Francis Macomber," "The Snows of Kilimanjaro," "A Clean, Well-Lighted Place," and "The Killers" have been studied with remarkable thoroughness.[1] In contrast, not only has there been less published criticism of "Fifty Grand," but much of it focuses on extrinsic matters. The problem that most effectively sidetracks scholarly attention from the story itself is the long-standing effort to link the boxing match in the story to a specific championship fight. The efforts to solve that problem make it clear that the story was probably based not on one fight but at least two.[2] But this finding throws little or no light on the story itself or the process by which Hemingway wrote it. In contrast, two aspects of "Fifty Grand" that contribute substantially to the story's effectiveness as a work of narrative art have been virtually ignored: its innovative use of point of view and its rich comedy. Perhaps they have been for the most part ignored because no one has shown the remarkably interesting process through which "Fifty Grand" evolved. When this process is examined, one gets a revealing look at Hemingway's growing skill, particularly in his handling of narrative point of view and the motif of the trickster out-tricked. And, most important, "Fifty Grand" is revealed, as a consequence, to be far more than a grim account of the sordid world of professional boxing. It stands, instead, as a minor comic masterpiece.

When Hemingway was sixteen years old, he wrote what is in effect the first version of "Fifty Grand." It is a humorous story of a fixed prize fight entitled "A Matter of Colour."[3] From his high school years until his early twenties, Hemingway thought of himself as primarily a humorist. Much of what he wrote during this period has a comic intent: fiction, journalism, and occasional writing. His column in the school newspaper, for example, was an undisguised imitation of the humorist he most admired, Ring Lardner. "A Matter of Colour" resembles Lardner's work in several ways: it focuses on the seamy side of professional sport, uses a vernacular narrator, relies on dialogue, and exploits the stupidity of athletes for comic effect.4 "A Matter of Colour" appeared in the April 1916 issue of the Oak Park (Illinois) High School literary magazine, *Tabula*.5 Its first-person narrator is not the protagonist but a "character" in the story. It is not without significance that "A Matter of Colour" and "Fifty Grand" are the only two pieces of fiction by Hemingway narrated in this way, a fact that has hitherto escaped notice. The link between the two is strengthened in two additional ways: the narrators in the two stories are nearly identical; each is a prize fighter's handler with the outlook and speech of a tough, seasoned professional, a wise guy; the central episode in each story involves a trickster being amusingly out-tricked.

The narrator of "A Matter of Colour," Bob Armstrong, a handler, tells of a scheme to fix a fight. The boxer he handles, Danny, is not in shape to win because of an injury incurred in training, yet he has bet heavily on himself. To make his money safe Danny and the handler devise a ridiculous but seemingly foolproof way of fixing the fight. The ring in which the fight will take place is on a stage at the back of which is a curtain just behind the ropes. They place a Swede with a baseball bat behind the curtain and instruct him to watch through a peephole until Danny's black opponent is against the ropes, then to swing on the black man's head with the bat from behind the curtain. When the fight begins, Danny rushes his opponent to the ropes at the rear of the ring, but nothing happens behind the curtain. The handler motions wildly to the Swede looking out through the peephole, but by the time the Swede gets the bat in motion, it is Danny who is up against the ropes, and the Swede knocks him out with the bat. The trickster has been out-tricked. Back in the dressing room the handler asks the Swede over Danny's unconscious body, "Why in the name of the Prophet did you hit the white man instead of the black man?" The Swede replies, "I bane color blind." It is a contrived O'Henry ending, but that should not be allowed to obscure an important fact: even as a novice Hemingway was exploring the comic possibilities of showing that things are different from what they are like in story books or on sports pages. And at the same time he was developing a prose style suitable to that fresh view of the world, one motivated, in Daniel Fuchs' admirable phrase, "by a comic contempt of standard English . . . [and its] respectability, gentility, polite euphemism."6 His first-person narrator, the handler, encourages Hemingway's use of this prose style.

Once *The Sun Also Rises* was sent off to the publisher, Hemingway wrote in his notebook in early 1926 that he wanted to write short stories "for four or five months."[7] The most memorable of these was one in which he fully exploited the comic possibilities that he had explored in "A Matter of Colour." Following the example of the earlier story, he made his comic intent clear at the outset through the use of a first-person, wise-guy narrator. Like Old Bob Armstrong, the cocksure narrator offers an insider's vivid picture of the seamy details of the world of professional boxing, but because of the way it is narrated the reader is not shocked but amused. The story of a fixed fight whose comic potential he had crudely exploited in high school is now finally realized. The story is, of course, "Fifty Grand."

"Fifty Grand" is the story of Jack Brennan, skillful, quick-witted, stoical, aging welterweight champion of the world. It is narrated by his long-time trainer and friend, Jerry Doyle, a wise guy of limited sensibility but vast ring experience. The insider's view of the tough, tawdry world of the training camp and Madison Square Garden that Jerry provides is realistic yet edged with comedy. When it is comic, it is so in part because of the narrative angle from which this world is presented. Jerry's limited view, as against the reader's broader perceptions, frames and colors the sordid details and gives them a comic cast, a point perceptively made by Sheridan Baker.[8] Another source of humor is Jack himself. He is a worrying cheapskate. The aging champion is having great difficulty getting into shape to defend his title. He cannot work up a sweat; he cannot sleep; he worries about his property in Florida, his stocks, his kids. And he misses his wife but is too cheap to telephone her. The sports writers predict the challenger, Walcott, will tear him in two. The day before the fight, two underworld sharpshooters visit Jack at the training camp and make a deal with him to throw the fight. Jack, convinced he cannot win, bets fifty grand on Walcott at two to one odds. "I got to take a beating," he tells Jerry, then asks, "Why shouldn't I make money on it?" What Jack does not know is that the sharpshooters' gambling syndicate has arranged for Walcott to throw the fight. So, while Jack's fifty grand will be bet on Walcott, the gamblers' money will be bet, at more favorable odds, on Jack.

During the first eleven rounds Jack boxes doggedly, mechanically; as Jerry says, "he don't move around much and that left hand is just automatic. It's just like it was connected with Walcott's face and Jack just had to wish it in every time." Jerry also sees Walcott as a mechanism, but of a lower order; he says he's "a socking machine." Before the eleventh round begins, Jerry acknowledges that despite Jack's skill, the old champion is taking a whipping. He says to Jack of Walcott, "It's his fight," but Jack insists on standing up to him: "'I think I can last,' Jack says. 'I don't want this bohunk to stop me.'" To bet on his opponent does not, under the circumstances, violate his code, but to fight badly does. During the twelfth round Walcott's handler signals him to foul Jack, which he does "as hard as he could sock, just as low as he could get it." Jack is seriously hurt, but he is also instantly aware that he has been double-crossed and must act fast and effectively if he is to save the fifty grand he has bet on his opponent. It is a farcical situation, for now it is a contest to see who can *lose*. No longer a machine, Jack is alert, analytical, shrewd. He dumbfounds the dull-witted Walcott by saying to him, "it wasn't low. It was an accident. . . . Come on and fight." Walcott remains a machine: he's been signaled to deliver a low blow; he's done it; now he stands there baffled as the man he has fouled insists upon fighting on. When the referee orders the fight resumed, Jack is equal to the ludicrous situation. He swings wildly at Walcott's head, Walcott "covers up," and Jack drives his left into Walcott's groin and follows it through with a right. Walcott is now the winner because he has been unmistakably, decisively fouled: he has been beaten into the championship. Back in his dressing room, waiting for a doctor, Jack observes, "it's funny how fast you can think when it means that much money." When his manager responds, "you're some boy, Jack," Jerry reports Jack's rejoinder, which is the last line of the story: "No, it was nothing."[9] Despite his disclaimers, Jack has done much more than protect his fifty grand; he has, through his quickwittedness and stoicism, prevailed without loss of his self-respect.

In placing "Fifty Grand" in its developmental context as the final version of an earlier effort to tell a humorous story about a fixed prize fight, two important things about "Fifty Grand" became clear. First, because the earlier version of the story, despite the relative feebleness of its power to provoke laughter, is unmistakably humorous in intent, one is alerted to the possible presence of humor in "Fifty Grand," and given the fact that of all literary modes comedy is probably more powerfully affected than any other by the context in which it appears, such an alert should not be ignored. Second, and considerably more important, one recognizes two narrative elements in "Fifty Grand" that served comic purposes in the earlier version as they do in the final one. The two are the first-person narrator who is not the protagonist and the trickster out-tricked plot. The first of these, the first-person narrator, is not, of course, inherently comic, but it is used for comic purposes by casting as narrator a wise guy, a savvy insider whose vivid but limited view is incongruously at odds with the reader's broader perceptions. He sets up the humorous situation much as the humorless first-person narrator does who tells "The Celebrated Jumping Frog of Calaveras County."

Of the story's two chief comic elements, the humor of the trickster out-tricked plot is both easier and more difficult to account for. It is easier to the extent that it involves a clear case of the doubling of the double-cross with the familiar pleasures of observing the triumph of the underdog being provided by Jack's outsmarting of the big-time gamblers and their dull accomplice, Walcott. But a close examination of Walcott's behavior makes it clear that he is funny not merely because he is dull but because at the climax of the story when the demands on his resources are the greatest his behavior is ridiculously mechanical.

Bergson's claims that the *essence* of comedy is the mechanical are unconvincing; certainly no such claim is being made here. Mechanical behavior, however, can serve in a comic situation as a reinforcing device. For example, in the best-known version of the trickster out-tricked in American literature, "The Celebrated Jumping Frog of Calaveras County," a mechanical motif heightens the comic effect. Jim Smiley is the consummate trickster: shrewd, greedy, ruthless, contemptuous. And his bull-pup, Andrew Jackson, is sheer mechanical artifice: a fighting machine. Andrew would wait for Smiley to set up the bet, "but as soon as the money was up on him he was a different dog; his under-jaw'd begin to stick out like the fo'castle of a steamboat, and his teeth would uncover and shine like the furnaces." Andrew Jackson won every fight with the same mechanical tactic: he would make "a snatch for his pet holt," the hind leg of his opponent, then he would "freeze to it, not chaw, you understand, but only just grip" like a vise. Confronted, finally, by an opponent without any hind legs, Andrew Jackson "'peared surprised, and then he looked sorter discouraged-like, and didn't try no more to win the fight."[10] The machine stops. As fighters, Andrew Jackson and Walcott have more than a little in common. Each of them traces the comic rhythm of the trickster out-tricked plot, and at the crucial moment the trickster's victory is snatched from him because of his stupidly inflexible, mechanical behavior. The parallel between the two stories does not end there. In each story the mechanical ineptitude of the trickster is humorously contrasted to the quick-witted adaptability of his opponent. This occurs most pointedly at the climax of each story. Jim Smiley's frog sinks into defeat with a "double-handful of shot" that "planted [him] solid as a anvil." He becomes a cast-iron device through the quick-wittedness of the stranger in the same way that Walcott is shown to be less a man than a machine manipulated by the syndicate in contrast to quick-thinking, adaptable Jack Brennan.

For this important contrast between the two boxers to be communicated clearly and reliably to the reader, everything depends on the narrator. He must discern Walcott's mechanical behavior and Jack's lightning-quick response and report these to the reader if the contrast—and the accompanying comic effect—is to be produced. When one sees how markedly Hemingway's narrator has been misapprehended, it is not surprising that most critics have failed to identify or account for the comedy in "Fifty Grand." One critic describes Jerry as a "non-committed first-person narrator (tyro)," and another calls him "naive and innocent." Virtually no evidence is or can be cited in the story in support of such views, whereas the story abounds with evidence of Jerry's commitment to Jack and, more importantly, of his being not a tyro but a seasoned veteran.[11]

Building on Old Bob Anderson, the handler-narrator of "A Matter of Colour," Hemingway endows the narrator of "Fifty Grand" with the wise guy's limited yet knowing view of the world of boxing. It is thanks to Jerry's perceptive account that during the first eleven rounds of the match Jack and Walcott engage in a kind of Bergsonian *ballet mechanique*. And the way in which Hemingway establishes this comic element is through a masterful fusion of his two chief comic resources: the unfolding of the trickster plot as observed by the wise-guy narrator. It is savvy, perceptive Jerry Doyle who describes Jack's left hand as "automatic" and who sums up Walcott's boxing style in a vivid, pithy comment: "He certainly was a socking machine." When Jack tries to tie up Walcott in the twelfth round, Jerry makes use of another graphic machine image, commenting, "it was just like trying to hold on to a buzz saw."[12] The climactic machine image appears when Walcott, on cue, fouls Jack, then stands there "planted solid as a anvil," as incapable of action as an untended machine when Jack fails to collapse. That Jack is less machinelike than Walcott should not obscure the fact that during the first eleven rounds and up to the instant in the twelfth round when Walcott fouls Jack, the fight, as vividly described by Jerry, is a comic duel between two machines. Moreover, to emphasize how remarkable it is that Jack has summoned the human resources to respond to Walcott's low-blow swiftly, intelligently, and decisively, Hemingway has Jerry observe that immediately following his quick-witted response to Walcott's programmed betrayal, Jack slips back into his mechanical mode. Jerry describes him returning to his corner "walking that funny jerky way," and later quotes Jack's apt description of his injury: "I'm all busted inside."[13] But when it was necessary to transcend his mechanical behavior, Jack was able to, and that transcendent moment is the measure of his resolve and strength as an athlete, just as it is the source of the rich comedy at the expense of the dull, mechanical Walcott who, like the bull-pup, Andrew Jackson or the frog Dan'l, ends the fight a baffled automaton.

The wise guy narrator is, of course, present throughout the story as Jerry Doyle's "tight lips give us the wisdom of the ring as if it were the wisdom of the world,"[14] in Sheridan Baker's fine phrase. But none of the comic strategies in "Fifty Grand" is dominant; they are skillfully combined. The plot of the trickster out-tricked rises in a curve of what Susanne Langer, writing of comedy in general, refers to as "the upset and recovery of the protagonist's equilibrium in his contest with the world and his triumph by wit, luck and personal power."[15] Its comic nature stands by itself but is enhanced by Jerry's telling. Another source of humor as well as an underpinning for the trickster plot is Jack's stinginess. It is ridiculous but not vicious, hence what Aristotle called a comic deformity. Finally, there is the comedy provided by Jack's and Walcott's mechanized boxing and Walcott's stupid persistence in that mode.

In talking with students of the University of Mississippi in 1947, William Faulkner was asked to rank modern American writers. In a list of five, he placed Hemingway last because "he lacked the courage to get out on a limb of experimentation."[16] Nearly half a century later, Faulkner's characterization of Hemingway's achievement is for the most part accurate. For it is one of the commonplaces of Hemingway criticism that Hemingway's virtuosity is narrow. But it is this tendency to see a sameness, however excellent, in Hemingway's fiction that is largely responsible for depriving "Fifty Grand" of the critical attention that it deserves. Whether it possesses as much merit as "A Clean, Well-Lighted Place" or "The Short Happy Life of Francis Macomber" is not the point. What needs to be recognized, first of all, is that it is for Hemingway a successful experiment in narrating a story by means of a first-person narrator other than the protagonist. Moreover, its success results in large measure from the skillful use of Jerry Doyle as the wise-guy narrator whose vision is both reliable and comic. Similarly, although storytellers since Chaucer—and probably before him—have used the trickster out-tricked formula for comic purposes, Hemingway makes fresh use of it, artfully adapting it to comment humorously yet realistically on the world of professional athletics as well as on the larger world in which it is often not easy to satisfy the rival claims of self-respect and pecuniary gain.

A Reading of Hemingway's "The Gambler, the Nun, and the Radio"

Amberys R. Whittle

●

In looking through Louis MacNeice's *Varieties of Parable*, first presented as Clark Lectures at Cambridge shortly before the author's death, one finds a typical reluctance to admit the allegorical nature of some modern American literature. MacNeice is willing to say that "one very valuable kind of parable, and particularly so today, is the kind which on the surface may not look like a parable at all. This is a kind of double-level writing, or, if you prefer it, sleight-of-hand."[1] Length has nothing to do with the definition of parable, as MacNeice uses the term (there is a lengthy discussion as to why it was chosen). It is rather a matter of technique and intention, and "the writer of parable literature, whether it is novel, short story, poem or play, is, by contrast with other types of writer, engaged in projecting a special world."[2]

Being more specific, MacNeice considers each of Golding's first three novels "a parable of the human situation today. *The Lord of the Flies* approaches Kafka, in that its island run by little boys is a frightening parody of modern society."[3] He is willing to accept *Moby-Dick* as a parable but wishes to "exclude the bulls and big game of Hemingway, even though a case could quite well be made for their inclusion."[4] With this judgment, as stated here, I would agree—though if *Moby-Dick* is accepted, why should *The Old Man and the Sea* not be included? It is, however, with Hemingway's short stories that I am primarily concerned, and these are not even considered by MacNeice, even though they are among the best in the language, and a significant number of them cannot be fully understood except as modern forms of parable.

I wish to concentrate primarily, but not exclusively, upon one story to prove the point, that is, that under any reasonable definition of the term, Hemingway did in fact write parables. "The Gambler, the Nun, and the Radio" (1933) has, I think, not been accepted entirely for what it is, though certain aspects of the story have been adequately discussed. Philip Young of course points out the contrasts between the way Mr. Frazer faces his situation and the stoicism of the gambler with his "code." Young also contends that "it is in this story that rock bottom in Hemingway's pessimism is reached in the familiar passage: 'Religion is the opium of the people . . . and music . . . and sexual intercourse . . . and bread is the opium of the people.'"[5] In like vein, Maxwell Geismar writes of "a nihilistic spiritual world that reached its own perfection in such of his 'first forty-nine' stories as 'The Gambler, the Nun, and the Radio.'"[6]

It will be noticed that both Young and Geismar, like most critics, assume a close connection between the attitudes of Mr. Frazer and that of his creator. There is some reason for this. In 1930 Hemingway was involved in an automobile accident with John Dos Passos near Billings, Montana. Hemingway's right arm was badly broken, and the recovery was quite painful and slow. Many of the people Hemingway met in the hospital later went into the creation of the characters in the story.[7] In "The Gambler, the Nun, and the Radio" Mr. Frazer uses his radio as a kind of "opium," as had Hemingway, and like his creator he is able to "get rid" of things (the phrase is used by Nick Adams in "Fathers and Sons") by writing about them, under more favorable circumstances. However, it is his leg that is broken by a fall from a horse, and by this change, as minor as it may be, Hemingway suggests that Mr. Frazer is not just a mirror image of himself.

What, then, is the story "about," if it is not merely autobiographical material interestingly presented? An answer to that question might be suggested by an episode in which the doctor, "who was a most excellent doctor," pulled Mr. Frazer's bed toward the window so that he could see pheasants in the snow but forgot about the reading light on the bedstead: "Mr. Frazer was knocked out by the leaded base of the lamp hitting the top of his head. It seemed the antithesis of healing or whatever people were in the hospital for, and every one thought it was very funny, as a joke on Mr. Frazer and on the doctor. Everything is much simpler in a hospital, including the jokes."[8]

First, the jokes. While the story is ultimately disturbingly serious, there is enough humor in it to make one question whether it represents the bottom of Hemingway's own "pessimism." There is humor not only in the passage just quoted but in the opening altercation between the detective, the interpreter, and Cayetano; this perhaps reaches its climax when the interpreter insists that "he don't know who shot him. They shot him in the back."

"Yes," said the detective. "I understand that, but why did the bullets all go in the front?"

"Maybe he is spinning around," said the interpreter.

Humor is implied in comparing the actions of characters with those in movies and comic strips, in Sister Cecilia's readiness to pray for things great and small and in her discovery that becoming a saint is difficult in this world, in the complaint of the citizens that the hospital's "X-ray machine" "ruined" the morning reception of their radios, in having Cayetano serenaded by friends of the man who wounded him, and in the description of the carpenter "who had fallen with a scaffolding and broken both ankles and both wrists. He had lit like a cat but without a cat's resiliency." There are other examples, but for some reason readers are slow to respond to Hemingway's jokes, perhaps because they are often associated with violence. In this story the jokes help to create a sense of completeness. As Horace Walpole once said, "life is a comedy to the man who thinks and a tragedy to the man who feels." Comedy implies a logical response to life, tragedy an emotional one. Both responses are found in the story and are centered in Mr. Frazer. It will be observed that this kind of humor, given the setting and situation, approaches that of the theater of the absurd, a type of drama which often attempts to present an image, however distorted it may appear to be, of life in general, of life which is held to be philosophically absurd.

"Everything is much simpler in a hospital, including the jokes." That statement suggests that Hemingway is using the setting as a microcosm for a parable, "the kind which on the surface may not look like a parable at all," to use MacNeice's language. Beginning with jokes, turning to a contrast of characters and their responses to their situations in life, including the various kinds of "opiums" all men use to support themselves against the darkest realities, the story at its end describes the plight of all mankind as it is threatened by world revolution and tyranny.

John Killinger argues that the opiums, "a means of escape from the self," represent "bad faith, . . . a concept common to the thinking of all the major existentialists, . . . [which] means generally any acceptance of a way of living incognito, or of losing one's self in a larger entity, so as to slough off all personal responsibility for one's choices and actions."9 This seems to me an extreme view, based upon a failure to understand Mr. Frazer. It is Mr. Frazer's *thinking* (the idea is insisted upon; the word repeated) about his own suffering after his nerves have gone bad and about the suffering of mankind in the early 1930s that so tortures him. Cayetano is much more seriously ill, but he is, though a small-town gambler who will cheat to win, "a poor idealist. I am the victim of illusions." His hope is that his luck will change; his has been bad so long that if it ever changes (and should remain good as long) he will get rich. Another victim of illusions is the thin Mexican, who was an acolyte when a boy but who has rejected religion as the opium of the poor: "Now I believe in nothing. Neither do I go to mass." He does, however, believe in revolution, *without thinking.* His lack of logic is represented by the sentence just quoted, and near the end of the story he has to confess several times that he cannot follow Mr. Frazer's line of thought, when Mr. Frazer is trying to make him realize the consequences of his naive faith in revolution.

We should recall the history of the period, what was happening in the lives of people in the outside world, to which the radio in the story is a channel of communication. Hemingway's own accident took place in 1930; the story was published in 1933. In 1931 the Japanese invaded Manchuria. In reaction to a Chinese boycott of goods, the Japanese militarists bombed Shaghai in 1932, killing and injuring many civilians. Japan left the League of Nations in this same year, when her aggression in Manchuria was condemned. In January 1933 the National Socialist German Labor party led by Hitler was firmly in control of Germany. Italian fascism was becoming increasingly aggressive. The United States itself was in the midst of a dreadful depression and elected Roosevelt to the presidency in 1932, though he would not take office until March 1933. In 1927 President Coolidge had sent troops to Nicaragua, and in that same year a temporary compromise was worked out between the United States and Mexico concerning the properties of American petroleum companies in Mexico. Many in Latin America still denounced *Yanqui* imperialism and would continue to do so. Briefly, this was the state of affairs with which most knowledgeable citizens would have been familiar. It was a rather grim picture.

Lying awake in the hospital, Mr. Frazer recalls the Mexican revolutionary's hatred of religion as the opium of the people: "He believed that, that dyspeptic little joint-keeper." Notice that Mr. Frazer's tone is one of *anger*, not of approval. Mr. Frazer continues thinking, with relentless logic stripping away all possible forms of *illusion*, and not with pleasure. Music is another opium, and economics, "along with patriotism the opium of the people in Italy and Germany." Then there is sex, drink, and his own radio, gambling (including Cayetano's), ambition, "along with a belief in any new form of government." How can it all be reduced to "the real, the actual, opium of the people"? His conclusion, given with self-mockery, is that "Bread is the opium of the people." This conclusion startles Mr.

Frazer so much that he asks to have the revolutionary sent to him right away. Why? Because bread is not only the opium of the people. It is, according to the aphorism, the staff of life. In other words life cannot exist without some form of support. The Mexican, who reenters speaking of "the tune of the real revolution," would take cruelly from the people these supports of "opiums." "'Listen,' said Mr. Frazer. 'Why should the people be operated on without an anaesthetic?'" Mr. Frazer, having forced himself to strip away all illusions to understand the consequences, would not have the people of the world operated upon without an anesthetic; he would not have them face worldwide revolution without something to believe in. "Revolution, Mr. Frazer thought, is no opium. Revolution is a catharsis; an ecstasy which can only be prolonged by tyranny. The opiums are for before and for after. He was thinking well, a little too well."

In the midst of this situation, and despite what others have said of him, Mr. Frazer's frame of mind is basically that of the modern humanitarian consciousness. The original title of the story, "Give Us a Prescription, Doctor," is a kind of secular prayer for all that the story encompasses, a plea for the plight of modern man. Mr. Frazer neither likes nor accepts all that he *knows*. The opiums are slow to act for him, and, we might assume, once he is able to write again, he can put distance between himself and the world or "get rid" of it by putting it into proper form and pattern.

There is a passage in Emerson so like the scene of this story that I cannot help wondering if Hemingway knew of it. It appears in his essay, "Illusions," philosophically and psychologically one of the most profound of all of Emerson's essays: "When we break the laws [the moral laws of the universe], we lose our hold on the central reality. Like sick men in hospitals, we change only from bed to bed, from one folly to another; and it cannot signify much what becomes of such castaways, wailing, stupid, comatose creatures, lifted from bed to bed, from the nothing of life to the nothing of death."

"In this kingdom of illusions we grope eagerly for stays and foundations." This is an image of the loss of faith that one might more readily expect of Dostoevsky than of the almost constitutionally optimistic Emerson. It mirrors the world in which we live even more, and "The Gambler, the Nun, and the Radio" is its modern analogue.

Nevertheless, I am not arguing that Mr. Frazer has lost all faith; he has been appalled by his self-enforced attempt to see what his world looks like without any form of hope. He has compassion for those whom the revolution would operate on without an anesthetic. The prayer is "Give Us a Prescription, Doctor." In our era of multiple crises and almost instantaneous communication, who has not at times thrown up his hands in frustration? If Mr. Frazer is finally forced to do this, at the end of the story, he is no different. The parable still describes our time.

There are, of course, other of Hemingway's stories that are parables or parablelike to some degree. "The Killers" is an initiation into an awareness of the impersonal nature of violent death in the modern world and of the inhumanity of the times. "The Battler" presents a young man with the vision of a fallen hero mercilessly destroyed in the struggle that is life. "A Way You'll Never Be" gives a vivid picture of the horror and illogic of modern war. "The Capital of the World" in the form of Madrid, center of the bullfight, is the capital of death, even when death is mocked; illusion and reality may be one and the same. The older waiter in "A Clean, Well-Lighted Place," with his belief in an existential Nothingness, is intended to be representative (the café itself is a kind of secular temple, and he is its priest): "He would lie in bed and finally, with daylight, he would go to sleep. After all, he said to himself, it is probably only insomnia. Many must have it."

One could mention other stories or go on to the novels, especially *The Old Man and the Sea* and *A Farewell to Arms*, one basically positive, the other negative in its view of the struggle that is life. The point, however, is that a good deal of Hemingway's fiction is cast in the form of modern allegory. (Traditional wooden allegory, with the strings on the puppets showing, has for the most part dropped to the level of children's stories.) Failure to admit this has caused some strange (and partial) readings, especially of some of the short stories, which because of their representative nature and brevity should be called parables. There is no reason why one should be embarrassed to consider Hemingway a writer of parables or allegory because in its disguised forms, or as MacNeice calls it "sleight-of-hand," it is a form of narrative very much alive today, and it will continue to flourish so long as man tries to comprehend his world in terms of broad but important concepts and "representative" situations.

Gender-Linked Miscommunication in "Hills Like White Elephants"

Pamela Smiley

●

Like a Gregorian chant in which simple musical phrases elucidate intricate poetic lyrics, so does the simple, straightforward plot of "Hills Like White Elephants" frame its subtle and dramatic dialogue. The dialogue contains the essence of the story's power; for to read Jig's and the American's conversation is to recognize the powerless frustration of parallel interchanges—in different words, in different places, and on different topics, but all somehow the same. It is to recognize both the circular noncommunication of strong gender-linked language differences and the consequent existential limitations and creative power of language.

The notion that men and women have difficulty communicating is not new. What is new is research, much of it from the 1970s, which indicates that men and women miscommunicate because they speak different languages (Key, 124). If Hemingway's male and female characters are each clearly gender-marked—speaking as traditional American men and women would be expected to speak—then there are four distinct characters in the dyad of Jig and the American: Jig and the American as evaluated through the standard of traditional female gender-linked language patterns and Jig and the American as evaluated through the standard of traditional male gender-linked language patterns.

What is gender-marked language? Robin Lakoff has drawn a sketch of the typical male and female speaker. The male speaker's

> contribution is precise and to the point—utterly straightforward—
> and tells us as little as possible about the speaker's state of mind and
> his attitude toward the addressee. We expect . . . a low pitch, flat
> intonation, declarative sentence structure, no hedging or impreci-
> sion, and lexical items chosen for their pure cognitive content, not
> their emotional coloration. ("Stylistic," 66)

The female speaker's language is

> profoundly imprecise. There is a sense that the audience does not really know what she is talking about (nor does she), but that she is very concerned with whom she is talking to, concerned with whether he is interested in her and whether his needs are being met. . . . She uses interjections and hedges freely and her dialog is sprinkled with "I guess" and "kinda." ("Stylistic," 67)

When broken down into a more generalized paradigm, research indicates that there are three major areas of gender-linked differences in language: how, about what, and why men and women talk. This may seem all-encompassing, but as Tannen notes: "male-female conversation is cross-cultural communication. Culture, after all, is simply a network of habits and patterns based on past experience—and women and men have very different past experiences." (22)

Conversational patterns differ and miscommunication results because of intolerance for the opposite gender-marked language. The tendency is for speakers to tenaciously hold on to the irrefutable logic of their own language and refuse to entertain the possibility that alternative translations exist. "[T]rouble develops when there is really no difference of opinion, when everyone is sincerely trying to get along . . . this is the type of miscommunication that drives people crazy. It is usually caused by differences in conversational styles" (Tannen, 21). Lakoff has pointed out that many of the descriptive differences between male and female language become evaluative judgments since men are the dominant cultural group and women are "other" (Miller, 4–12), everything that man is not: emotional rather than logical, yin rather than yang, passive rather than active, body rather than intellect. The effect of this otherness is that many feminine characteristics—language included—are devalued in comparison to their male counterparts. Because women's language in general, and Jig's in particular, focuses on emotions rather than facts and objects, it is judged more ambiguous, less direct, and more trivial than masculine speech. If Jig is flighty, trivial, and deferential, then it must be remembered that all of those terms are judgments which depend on a foreign standard of maleness.

The qualification should be made that these gender-linked patterns are polarities, paradigms which are becoming less and less accurate as women attain positions of power and people become more sensitive to language patterns. Still, if such gender-marked traits in the dialogue are isolated and evaluated, first under the standards of the traditional male language patterns, then under the traditional female, four very different characters will emerge. Specific details from the story will make my hypothesis clearer.

The first conflict between Jig and the American is over the hills which she lightly compares to white elephants. Several characteristics of gender-marked speech are obvious from this interchange. The first is the content of language approriate for each sex; the second is the implicit conversational objective of each.

White Elephants

The man insists on the "facts" and "proof," while Jig talks of fantasies, emotions, and impressions. Adelaide Haas writes: "[Men] frequently refer to time, space, quantity, destructive action, perceptual attributes, physical movement and objects. [Women] use more words implying feeling, evaluation, interpretation and psychological state" (616). Feminine language tends to be relationship-oriented while masculine is goal-oriented.

Jig's conversational objective is to establish intimacy through shared emotions and joke-telling. Tannen notes that intimacy for women is shared words, intimacy for men is shared actions (22). In this context Jig's initial remark becomes an invitation to join in the intimacy of shared banter. The American's reply, "I've never seen one," effectively ends that conversational tactic.

Humor is often described as a means of decreasing social distance. Cohesion is also a result in situations in which a witty remark is ostensibly directed against a target, but actually is intended to reaffirm the collectivity and the values held in common (Neitz, 215). Therefore, refusal to laugh at someone's joke is a strong form of distancing and power (Neitz, 222).

The American gives several very important gender-linked conversational clues. Shutting down Jig's attempt at intimacy with terse phrases and insistence on facts reveals the American's attempts to control the conversation and, by extension, the relationship. Since the topic itself is too innocuous for such negativity, the American must be rejecting Jig for some reason other than her quip about the hills like white elephants. At the end of round one Jig looks at the beaded curtain and changes the subject. Her response to his rejection is, to use Lakoff's phrase, "classic female deference" ("Stylistic," 67).

All of the conclusions above evaluate the American through traditional female gender-linked language, however. If evaluated within a traditional male standard, speeches about hills like white elephants become irrelevant fluff and Jig's lightness and humor inappropriate in the context of a train ride to the Barcelona abortion clinic. The American, feeling victimized by Jig's pregnancy and mocked by her levity, insists on facts which protect him against her and reassert his control of his unstable world.

The differences in these translations of the American and Jig are important. Jig's superficiality and manipulativeness, for example, are judgmental labels linked to her language and contingent on an evaluation of her according to the foreign standard of a traditional male language. The American's sincerity in his love of Jig or his emotional manipulation of her depends on whether his rejection of Jig's attempts at intimacy is without justification or because of gender-linked presumptions. If the latter, then he makes a language, not a character, judgment which focuses and modifies his otherwise disproportionate cruelty.

Jig attempts reconciliation with her next question about the advertisement on the beaded curtain. Because the American can speak and read Spanish and Jig cannot, translation of her world is one of many things for which she is dependent upon him—permission to try new drinks, an audience to laugh at her jokes, entertainment, support, love are others. Such dependence can have several possible effects. One is that the man is flattered; ever since she could pick up *Seventeen,* a woman has been told to interest and soothe the ego of a man by asking lots of questions and allowing him to parade his knowledge. Jig's pattern of dependency on the American suggests that this tactic has proven successful before in their relationship. But this time, when Jig asks about the taste of Anis del Toro, the American answers politely but distantly, avoids even the most trivial personal disclosure—whether Anis del Toro tastes good with water—and follows Lakoff's paradigm of masculine language, to tell "as little as possible about the speaker's state of mind."

Another possible effect of dependence is that the man will sense entrapment and withdraw. At this awkward point in their relationship, Jig's dependency is probably not one of her most endearing qualities. Her questions remind him of his responsibility for her—a point he would rather forget.

Within the evaluative standard of traditional female speech patterns, the American's lack of disclosure is emotional withholding; he is not playing according to the rules. Within the evaluative standards of traditional male speech patterns, it is not the American's reaction, but Jig's action, which is at fault. Jig's dependence is smothering; because she is unable to make even the smallest decision on her own, the American's terseness becomes a kindness, giving her vital information to enable her to make her own decisions.

The conflict becomes more explicit in the next exchange, in which Jig voices her disappointment with the licorice taste of Anis del Toro and compares it to absinthe. Her reply, "like absinthe," must be an allusion to some disappointment in their shared past, which, since absinthe is an aphrodisiac, Johnston suggests is sexual. "Now he wished to be rid of the unwanted by-product of that passion. He is not amused by such ironic references" (237). Whatever the allusion, her remark hits a nerve, and she presses her advantage:

> "You started it," the girl said. "I was being amused. I was having a fine time."
>
> "Well, let's try and have a fine time."
>
> "All right. I was trying. I said the mountains look like white elephants. Wasn't that bright?"
>
> "That was bright."
>
> "I wanted to try this new drink. That's all we do, isn't it—look at things and try new drinks?"
>
> "I guess so."

Jig's series of questions are strongly gender-marked. She uses a proportionately large number of tag-end questions: "wasn't it?," "isn't it?" (Dietrich). She also uses circular and vaguely generalized evaluations of their activities rather than direct statements—"that's all we do"—the goal of her conversation being consensus.

Tag-end questions are words tacked on to the end of a statement which turn it into a question. Women's language uses more tag-end questions than does men's. The advantages of tag-end questions are that a speaker can invite contributions, avoid commitment, and effect consensus. The disadvantage is that the speaker seems to lack self-confidence and authority (Dietrich). Robin Lakoff writes "but the tag appears anyway as an apology for making an assertion at all . . . women do it more [than men] . . . hedges, like question intonation, give the impression that the speaker lacks authority or doesn't know what he's talking about" (*Language*, 54).

Her use of vague generalizations and circular patterns is the opposite of the traditional male pattern of direct and objective statements. According to Lakoff, "a woman's discourse is necessarily indirect, repetitious, meandering, unclear, exaggerated . . . while of course a man's speech is clear, direct, precise and to the point" (*Language*, 23), because, as Scott states, these qualities "are effective ones for affiliative interactions in which warmth, co-operation, and self-expression are valued" (206). His discourse achieves goals, hers facilitates consensus and builds relationships.

Evaluating Jig from the standard of women's language, it is clear that she is trying to do just those things: to lead the American into an admission that he is committed to her and desires a fuller life than they now lead. Evaluating Jig from the standard of male language, she is indirect and coercive and therefore superficial and manipulative.

The American's perfunctory replies are evasive. Since "to many women the relationship is working as long as they can talk things out," the traditional female standard would evaluate the American's weak replies as a warning sign of his insincerity (Tannen, 23), while the traditional male standard might see the evasion as discomfort with emotional disclosure since "men, on the other hand, expect to do things together and don't feel anything is missing if they don't have heart-to-heart talks all the time" (Tannen, 23).

There is no conversational intimacy in the American's echoes of her statements. Instead of effecting consensus, Jig's questions increase the distance between them.

If shared activities equal intimacy for a man, then Jig's reduction of their life-style to "trying new drinks" is a rejection of the American. That he resists retaliation is, therefore, at worst a gesture of apathy, but at best a gesture of affection. His reticence, instead of the withholding evaluated from the standard of feminine language, might be the kindest way of being gentle with Jig without compromising his own integrity.

His transition into the next conversational topic—that of the temperature of the beer—seems to support this softer view of the American. The American initiates small talk in which both he and Jig describe the beer, each remaining consistent in his or her use of gender-linked language. The American uses what Dietrich calls "neutral adjectives"—"nice and cool"; Jig uses an "empty adjective"—"lovely." Empty adjectives, characteristic of feminine speech, are words like "pretty," "adorable," "precious." Dietrich suggests women use these words to add impact linguistically they do not possess socially. Lakoff feels that their use dulls strong feeling and commitment (*Language*, 11).

Their agreement on the beer is a momentary lull, a lead-in to direct conflict: the abortion.

"It's really an awfully simple operation, Jig," the man said. "It's really not an operation at all."

The girl looked at the ground the table legs rested on.

"I know you wouldn't mind it, Jig. It's really not anything. It's just to let the air in."

The girl did not say anything.

"I'll go with you and I'll stay with you all the time. They just let the
air in and then it's all perfectly natural."

With goal-oriented, objective, and precise language, the American distances the abortion by reducing it to an operation which lets the air in. If
shared activity equals intimacy, then his offer to stay with Jig during the
abortion is a gesture of love.

Unfortunately this does not translate well into feminine language.
Since the American's facts do not fully describe Jig's experience, the
abortion being "not anything," for example, she projects that neither
could they fully describe his. Whether the distance between his language
and his experience is due to self-deception, dishonesty, or cowardice
hardly seems important. Both his reduction of the abortion to an operation and his offer to stay with Jig ignore the issue at the core of the conflict:
emotional commitment and self-actualizing growth.

Ignoring the issue of the simplicity of the operation, Jig follows his
appeal with a series of questions which keep bringing him back to the core
issues: their relationship and their attitudes toward life. She asks him
directly for the emotional commitment for which she previously only
hinted. Jig's direct attack is uncharacteristic of feminine speech, and
therefore very threatening (Lakoff, *Language*, 41).

As the argument continues, Jig asks him whether he "wants" her to
have the abortion; he translates his reply into what he "thinks," thereby
denying his emotions. Directly contradicting his desire for the abortion,
he twice repeats that he does not want Jig to do anything she doesn't want
to do. Making several obviously impossible promises—to always be
happy, to always love her, to never worry—he demonstrates flagrant bad
faith. From the standard of male language these contradictions are the
inevitable results of her unreasonable questions: abstract emotional responses to abstract emotional questions. From the standard of female
language, they are inauthentic answers and betray trust. The differences
stem from the genderlike premises that language does/does not deal with
emotion and is/is not the basis of intimacy.

Jig's series of questions exposes both the American's and Jig's conversational double binds. The double bind, as described by Bateson, is a
conversation with two objectives. To be true to one conversational
objective a speaker must be untrue to another (208).

Jig's direct insistence on the American's emotional commitment forces
him into a double bind. The American has two conversational objectives.
The first, as Tannen phrases it, is to "maintain camaraderie, avoid

imposing and give (or at least appear to give) the other person some choice in the matter" (22). For this reason he repeats six times within the forty-minute conversation: "I don't want you to [do anything you don't want to]." The American's other objective is the abortion. Unfortunately it is impossible to maintain easy camaraderie while insisting on the abortion. Instead of choosing one or the other, he chooses both and ignores the contradiction. While a traditional masculine standard of language might recognize the sincerity of the American's concern for Jig, the traditional feminine standard translates his contradiction as hypocrisy.

Jig is also caught in a double bind. She wants both the American and the baby. Her series of questions establishes that she can accomplish at least one of her objectives, so she releases the other with her self-sacrificing statement "I don't care about me." While Jig may be totally sincere, not caring about herself and having only the American's interests at heart, such total devotion is highly unlikely; it is more likely that she is well-taught in the skills of social deference. But in this situation, where the American's interests equal lack of growth, eternal adolescence, and sterility, her deference is self-destructive.

Of course, the unnaturalness of Jig's self-sacrifice and the artifice of her insincerity leave her vulnerable to the stereotype of "women as fickle, distrustworthy, and illogical" (Lakoff, "Stylistic," 71). Judged by traditional male language patterns, Jig is capricious and manipulative. Judged by traditional female language patterns, particularly within the context of the double bind, the progression of Jig's conversation is logical and inevitable.

The American's reaction to Jig's acquiescence is immediate emotional withdrawal and disavowal of responsibility for her decision or for her problem. His distance contradicts all of the protestations of love he made minutes before. It also contains a thinly veiled threat of permanent withdrawal. His knee-jerk response shows that his desire for noninvolvement and nonresponsibility is much stronger than his desire to maintain a relationship with Jig. Of course, objectively, the abortion is Jig's problem: it is her body, and the American has no right to interfere. However, the objective facts do not take into account the emotional dimension of their shared reality: the body is hers; the relationship and baby is theirs.

Even though Jig agrees to the abortion, it is obvious that she is not emotionally reconciled to it. She moves away from the table and him and, while staring at the fertile valley, continues the argument. Unwilling to give up her dream, she finds it impossible to believe he has deliberately chosen stagnation, sterility, and death. The American goes into shell-shock in this segment of the conflict. While she reveals her most intimate desires, he seems to be scarcely listening.

"And we could have all this," she said [gesturing to the landscape]. "And we could have everything and every day we make it more impossible." In traditional feminine language patterns, the goal of social facilitation leads to emphasis on politeness which, in turn, tends toward metaphors and indirect sentence patterns. Consistent with her gender-linked language, Jig speaks of the baby metaphorically, in terms of the land. This, Jig's most powerful argument, links the American's fertility to the obviously symbolic landscape. As Mary Dell Fletcher writes: "The life-giving landscape ("everything") is now associated in Jig's mind with . . . a fruitful life where natural relations culminate in new life and spiritual fulfillment, not barrenness and sterility, as represented by the dry hills" (17).

The possibility of change and self-actualization, the fertility of the land, and the continuation of life affirmed through Jig's pregnancy are evidence that sterility and stagnation are the American's choice, not his fate. As she stands next to the tracks, the crossroad of their choice, Jig turns her back on the sterile, burnt hills and the American and looks out onto the fertile fields. He calls her back into the shadows with him where there is both the anesthesia and sterility of his choice: "'Come on back in the shade,' he said. 'You mustn't feel that way.'"

The American distances himself further by paying so little attention to Jig's words that he must ask her to repeat herself. Assuming the truth of Tannen's argument that for a woman intimacy is shared emotion and conversation, the American's "what did you say?" sets him apart from and above her (22). Because she bases her argument on a series of factors which he does not recognize as being important or true, the more she reveals her deepest desires, the more he denies her reality and retreats from her. Feminist theorists argue that since women derive their language from a standard which is men's, women's language is inadequate to express her experiential world. Jig's stuttering and vague description of the world she sees slipping away from her seems to illustrate this inadequacy; her slippery language describing "forces" must frustrate his literal mindset which does not deal in such intangibles and insists on facts. The more she tries to establish intimacy, the less the concord between them. As Tannen observes, the more problems she exposes, the more incompetent and neurotic she knows she must appear in his eyes: the more they both see her as problem-ridden (22). They end this section of the conflict with this exchange:

"Doesn't it mean anything to you? We could get along."

"Of course it does. But I don't want anyone but you. I don't want anyone else. And I know it's perfectly simple."

Note how the American responds to the plural pronoun "we" with the singular pronouns "I" and "you." Tannen notes that the use of the singular pronoun is the standard in male speech, the use of the plural pronoun in female. Women often feel hurt when their partners use "I" or "me" in a situation in which they would use "we" or "us" (23). In traditional female speech patterns, plural pronoun use indicates that the speaker feels he/she is half of a couple, singular pronouns an independent person. Jig, who is feeling vulnerable and looking for reassurance, would recognize the American's singular pronoun as a direct signal that no relationship existed. The American, for whom the singular pronoun is traditionally standard, would not find this switch meaningful. As Dietrich has noted, because women are relationship-oriented, they have higher social I.Q.'s than men and are more sensitive to subtleties of words. This sensitivity can backfire, as this example of miscommunication pointedly illustrates.

In the next stage of the conflict there is simply more of the same. The repetition of key words and phrases and the circularity of issues has a tired predictability. As frustration from their miscommunication becomes more intense, each exhibits "more and more extreme forms of the behaviors which trigger in the other increasing manifestations of an incongruent behavior in an ever-worsening spiral." George Bateson calls this "conversational disorder" "complementary schismogenesis" (Stone, 88).

The final conflict in the story leaves the issue of abortion unresolved; the American states his intention of moving their bags to the other side of the track and Jig smiles. Politeness is a distinctive characteristic of women's speech, a facet of their role of making others feel at ease by decreasing distance and showing a lack of hostility. Unfortunately, Jig smiles at the American at a point when common sense indicates that she should have the most hostility toward him, leaving her again vulnerable to the charge of inauthenticity and manipulation.

In Jig's defense it should be noted that she has used a variety of language skills in her confrontation with the American: she has been metaphorical, amusing, self-sacrificing, sarcastic, direct—and none has worked. No matter which tack she chooses, the American comes back at her with the same two sentences: "I think you should do it" and "I don't want you to do anything you don't want to do." According to Dietrich, even though traditional female language is generally more skillful and creative than traditional male language, because his is more authoritative, and powerful, the male's best effects submission. Since our society values authority and power, the inevitable result of the American's repetition is Jig's silent smile.

The final exchange between Jig and the American shows how far they are from understanding one another. When the American drinks a solitary anise at the bar, he exposes the strain that this argument has had on his facade of reason and detachment. Johnston evaluates this gesture as the prelude to many other activities the American will do without Jig, since he is tired of her emotions and dependence (237).

The American's final question is the most powerful gender-linked language in the story. "Do you feel better?" assumes that Jig's pregnancy, her emotions, her desire to grow and change all are aberrations from which she must recover. As Lakoff writes, "women do not make the assumption that their ways are healthy and good ones, or the only ones; . . . women do not, on the basis of their misunderstanding, construct stereotypes of men as irrational, untrustworthy or silly" ("Stylistics," 71). As the more powerful, the American is able to define what is healthy, even when that definition condemns him, Jig, and the land to stagnation and sterility.

In spite of the sparse details of plot, the subtle and dramatic dialogue in "Hills Like White Elephants" reveals a clear, sensitive portrait of two strong personalities caught in a pattern of miscommunication due to gender-linked language patterns. Jig's language covers a wide range of moods, but whether she is light, sarcastic, emotional, or deferential, her language is traditionally feminine. The American uses few words, speaks in direct sentences, effectively translates the world and achieves his goals, and is therefore traditionally masculine.

In short Hemingway's accurate ear for speech patterns duplicates the gender-linked miscommunications which exist between men and women in the real world. As a result of these differences, there are two Jigs: the nurturing, creative, and affectionate Jig of female language, and the manipulative, shallow, and hysterical Jig of male language. There are also two Americans: in the female language he is a cold, hypocritical, and powerful oppressor; in the male language he is a stoic, sensitive, and intelligent victim.

Recognizing the existence of four characters in the dyad of Jig and the American in "Hills Like White Elephants" shifts emphasis from affixing blame for conflicts of noncommunication to understanding the causes—a foregrounding of the function of language in the Modernist world. For example, nowhere is gender-linked language's inadequacy to express the range of experience more poignantly revealed than in the American's solitary drink of anise; through the chinks in his language of power and stoicism, the American's underlying emotion and sensitivity are betrayed. It is not that the American perversely or stupidly chooses sterility and death, it is that he cannot imagine any escape. Jig's pregnancy, Family, Fatherhood, Love—all traditional solutions to his existential angst—are inadequate. What he does not recognize is that Jig does not represent tradition; she is "all this." Does this make him a victim of reality or a victim of his own definition of reality? The logical result of his definition of the world is his own victimization.

Even though the American's language is the language of power, it is also the language of limitation. The American is proof of Miller and Swift's thesis that masculine language's "inflexible demands . . . allow for neither variation nor for human frailty" (Lakoff, "Stylistics," 68). In contrast, one of the strengths of women's language, Irigaray argues, is that it is outside of traditional dualism and may creatively discover alternatives. Language does more than describe an objective reality; the relationship between the signifier and the signified is highly subjective—language does not describe as much as create reality.

Recognizing the subjective and creative potential of traditional gender-linked patterns at the comfortable distance afforded by "Hills Like White Elephants" verifies language's profound imaginative power to define and shape what has always been defined as objective reality, but what is, in fact, closer to the protean fluidity of Jig's "all this." It is only through an understanding of such linguistic functions that there is a possibility of harmonizing its frustrating circularity and actualizing its creative potential of breaking through the confining limitations of a language in which "all [is] so simple," so sterile, and so hopeless.

Hemingway's Primitivism and "Indian Camp"

Jeffrey Meyers

●

Hemingway's "Indian Camp" (1924)—the first story in his first trade book and always one of his favorites[1]—has been subjected to a wide variety of interpretations, ranging from the obvious to the absurd, by critics who have recognized its power and struggled with its meaning. The story contains two shocking incidents: the doctor performs a Caesarean operation with a jackknife but without anesthetic, and the husband silently commits suicide. At least one critic has sensed that the suicide seems gratuitous—"in the context of the situation as given, it is too extreme an action"[2]—but did not attempt to explain the Indian's behavior. My own interpretation, based on Hemingway's attitude to primitive people and on his knowledge of anthropology, explains the most difficult aspects of the story: why the husband remains in the bunk of the shanty during the two days his wife has been screaming, and why he does not leave the room if he cannot bear her agonizing pain and shrieks. Despite his badly cut foot, he could have limped or been carried out of range of the screams, if he had wished to, and joined the other men. "Indian Camp" reflects Hemingway's ambiguous attitude to primitivism and shows his notable success in portraying the primitive.

The interpretations of the story reveal the limitations of New Critical readings and of Hemingway criticism during the last thirty-five years. The obvious explanation of the Indian's suicide is provided by the doctor in the story—"He couldn't stand things, I guess"[3]—and has been dutifully repeated by more than twenty critics from 1951 to 1983.[4] Other students of the story, bored with the manifest simplicity of this interpretation, have strained for variant readings but offered little more than subjective opinions. George Hemphill (1949) tersely blames the breech-birth: "The cause of his trouble is accidental."[5] Thomas Tanselle (1962), whose short but influential note opened a can of worms by mentioning and then dismissing the theory that Uncle George is the father of the baby, stresses the guilt the Indian feels for engendering the child (men, paradoxically, get pleasure from sex; women, pain): "His small part in the plot is itself indicative of his plight as he finds himself superfluous. . . . The Indian father not only feels *de trop* but also guilty for causing so much pain in one he loves. . . . [Hemingway is concerned with] a man's helplessness and feeling of guilt during his wife's labor."[6]

Kenneth Bernard (1965)—like Peter Hays (1971), Larry Grimes (1975), and Gerry Brenner (1983)—pounces on the theory rejected by Tanselle and claims the Indian kills himself because Uncle George is the real father of his putative son: "The new, bastard, way of life is not one that the Indian husband can tolerate; hence another reason [apart from the obvious one] for his suicide."[7] A decade later, Grimes repeats the notion that Bernard got from Tanselle:

> He has been unsuccessful as a husband and an Indian. His wife has made him a cuckold and he must witness the terrible breech-end birth. . . . The unnaturally born child could then be seen as the bastard product of the white man's "rape" of the Indian. The Indian, unable to bear either his cuckoldry or the challenge of the white man's ways (medical intervention in the patterns of birth and death, particularly) slits his throat.[8]

This passage contains several disturbing distortions. Grimes states, but does not show, that "he has been unsuccessful as . . . an Indian." He mistakenly asserts that the breech-birth is "unnatural." He transforms the theoretical paternity of Uncle George into a white man's "'rape.'" He erroneously states the white man intervenes "in the patterns of . . . death." And he does not explain why the Indian "must witness" the terrible birth.

None of the critics explains why the violent Indian—who, if cuckolded, would be more likely to kill George than himself—has waited all this time to act. In "The Doctor and the Doctor's Wife" (also 1924), the next story in *In Our Time*, an Indian defies and humiliates Dr. Adams; and in "Indian Camp" there is nothing to prevent the Indian, if sufficiently motivated, to take his revenge. Indian girls are described as sexually promiscuous in "Ten Indians" (1927) and in "Fathers and Sons" (1933), where Nick sleeps with Trudy (while threatening to kill any Indian who even speaks to *his* sister) as Trudy's brother encourages and watches their sexual act. But married Indian women are quite a different matter, and there is no evidence in the story that George ever slept with the squaw.

George Monteiro (1973) offers a sociopathological explication: "It is the combination of his debilitating (even embarrassing) injury and the susceptibility (both physical and psychological) which always accompanies the sick role, I would submit, that causes his suicide."⁹ The feminists—who predictably impose rather than extract a meaning—present a far-fetched variant of Tanselle's guilt theme. Linda Wagner (1975) mentions the "husband's outspoken act of contrition" and condemns the well-meaning and helpful doctor for both his callousness and his cleanliness.¹⁰ Judith Fetterley (1978) carries Wagner's views to an absurd extreme and twists the meaning into precisely the opposite of what Hemingway intended. Lady Fetterley's lover is also guilt-ridden: "The lesson [for feminists] reflected in the double mirror of the two fathers [the doctor and the Indian] is one of guilt—guilt for the attitudes men have toward women and guilt for the consequences to women of male sexuality."¹¹ Fetterley's exposition deliberately ignores female sexuality (the Indian did not mate with himself) and diminishes rather than enhances the significance of the story.

Joseph Flora (1982), who has the longest elucidation of the story, twice repeats the standard interpretation and adds (but does not explain) a vicarious element: "His suicide suggests that he was dying in his wife's place." Flora, vaguely aware of the primitive aspect, states Nick Adams discovers that "the life of the more primitive people can teach him a great deal, for the primitive contains values [which?] that the doctor's son needs [why?] to discover." Instead of pursuing this fruitful line of inquiry, Flora offers a sentimental "apologies to the Iroquois" explanation: "'Indian Camp' conveys a great sense of their humanity, of their suffering and ability to love, and of their solidarity:"¹² We might expect to find these elements in the story, but in fact Hemingway disappoints our expectations by revealing the opposite—there is no evidence of humanity, love, or solidarity. The Indians are strikingly affectless and isolated. The men moved out of range of the screams, the husband rolled over against the wall, and the only direct contact with the squaw is made by three Indians who, with Uncle George, held her down.

Gerry Brenner (1983) adopts Bernard's George-as-father theory and exaggerates Flora's views into post-*Wounded Knee* cant. He maintains, against all reason, that the Indian's death is positive: "His suicide aims to inflict a strong sense of guilt on Uncle George, becomes a dignified act that affirms the need to live with dignity or not at all, and lays at the feet of another treacherous white man the death of yet one more of the countless, dispossessed native Americans."¹³

Kenneth Lynn's Freudian autobiographical interpretation (1987) relates the story to the circumstances surrounding the trouble-free birth of Hemingway's first son in 1923. He reiterates the Indian's demoralized apathy—"he cannot bring himself to help her in any way, or even watch the birth of his son"—and unconvincingly concludes: "when the Indian slits his throat, he acts out the thoughts of suicide to which Hemingway made reference in his letter to Gertrude Stein and Alice Toklas after Hadley and the baby had come home from the hospital."[14] Philip Young (1965), exasperated by the earlier bizarre interpretations, wittily claimed that *he* (not Uncle George) was the father and concluded: "The reason the husband cut his throat was that George had passed out all the cigars he had on him *before* he got to the camp."[15]

Hemingway's attitude toward primitivism was ambiguous. In *Torrents of Spring* (1926) he satirized the native primitivism of Sherwood Anderson but continued to write, with infinitely more sophistication and skill, in the Lawrencean mode. When Wyndham Lewis's *Paleface* (first published in his magazine the *Enemy* in September 1927) blasted the exaltation of Indian and Negro primitivism in Anderson's *Dark Laughter* (1925), linked it with D.H. Lawrence's *Mornings in Mexico* (1927), and praised Hemingway's satiric parody, Hemingway responded enthusiastically to Lewis's work:

I am very glad you liked *The Torrents of Spring* and thought you destroyed the Red and Black Enthusiasm very finely in *Paleface*. That terrible————about the nobility of any gent belonging to another race than our own (whatever it is) was worth checking. Lawrence you know was Anderson's God in the old days—and you can trace his effect all through [Anderson's] stuff. . . . In fact *The Torrents of Spring* was, in fiction form, performing the same purgative function as *Paleface*.[16]

At the time of *Porgy, All God's Chillun, The Emperor Jones, Nigger Heaven*, and the cult of jazz, Hemingway rejected the fashionable assumption that the emotional and sensual life of the dark races was superior to that of the white.

Lewis observed that *The Torrents of Spring* "amusingly pursues Mr. Sherwood Anderson through all the phases of his stupidity, especially stressing the 'he-man' foolishness, the 'bursting Spring' side of it."[17] But when Hemingway continued to portray instinctive and inarticulate characters, his former acquaintance and ally unleashed the most damaging attack ever made on his work. In "The Dumb Ox," published in *Men Without Art* (1934)—a title probably derived from *Men Without Women* (1927)—Lewis shot barbs into Hemingway's most vulnerable spots. Lewis emphasized his debt to Gertrude Stein, his lack of political awareness and his mindlessness, and wittily insisted: "Hemingway invariably invokes a dull-witted, bovine, monosyllabic simpleton . . . [a] lethargic and stuttering dummy . . . a super-innocent queerly-sensitive, village-idiot of a few words and fewer ideas."[18] Yet Lewis' reductive satire, which exalted reason over instinct, ignored Hemingway's conscious and complex use of primitivism. He had direct knowledge of the material in "Indian Camp"—it belonged to his childhood experience and was a source of his art—and had made it his legitimate subject.

Rousseau's belief in man's natural goodness and in the inevitable corruptions of civilization as well as the modern concern "with the subconscious mind and anti-rational modes of understanding"[19] inspired a kind of writing that emphasizes nature and freedom and that views instinctive and intuitive consciousness as a key to the deepest emotions. Artists who concentrate on the most crucial situations in life, writes Robert Goldwater, the author of the classic study of *Primitivism in Modern Art*, assume that "the further one goes back—historically, psychologically, or aesthetically—the simpler things become; and that because they are simpler they are more profound, more important, and more valuable."[20] Hemingway simplifies his early stories by presenting the events and omitting the explanation.

Hemingway expressed his lifelong attraction to primitive people—for the values of northern Michigan over those of Oak Park—in stories about Indians and Negroes, boxers and bullfighters, Africans and Spaniards, and tough, stoical heroes like Harry Morgan and Santiago. This literary mode also influenced his speech and behavior and found expression in his public as well as his fictional persona. He boasted of Indian blood, Indian mistresses, Indian daughters, and liked to imitate Indian speech. Though his youngest sister exclaimed: "Prudence Boulton was a most unattractive little girl. I knew her and that Indian camp there smelled terribly,"[21] Hemingway, in a rapturous passage that expressed his yearning for pure experience with instinctive people, claimed "she did first what no one has ever done better."[22] (In fact, his youthful sex life was severely restricted by his religious training, timidity, and fear of venereal disease; and it was the waitress, described in "Up in Michigan," who did first what other women did better—after he had experienced more sexual experience.)[23]

Hemingway had fifty-seven books on Indians in his library and was well read in anthropology. He owned Sir James Frazer's *The Golden Bough* (1890–1915) and Sigmund Freud's *Basic Writings*, which included *Totem and Taboo* (1913).[24] We do not know precisely when Hemingway first read Frazer. But, as John Vickery explains in *The Literary Impact of "The Golden Bough*,*"* "following its first edition [in 1890], Frazer's ideas made themselves felt in nearly every area of the humanities and social sciences, including literary history and criticism. . . . Even before the artist actually picked up Frazer's book, he could easily have had some idea of its basic concepts. . . . Throughout Frazer's career reviews, summaries, and critiques of his work occupied extended space in numerous periodicals" like the *Athenaeum*, the *Dial*, and the *Nation*.[25] During Hemingway's teens, for example, the *Chicago Evening Post* printed a substantial essay on *The Golden Bough*.[26] Eliot declared that *The Golden Bough* had influenced his generation profoundly,[27] and Frazer's book became intellectually fashionable and familiar after the publication of *The Waste Land* in 1922. Both Pound and MacLeish—whom Hemingway met in 1922 and 1924— read Frazer. And in *The Cantos* and "The Pot of Earth" (1925) they used his "anthropological vision of the primitive past to crystallize the enduring dilemmas of the cultural present."[28]

Hemingway was also receptive to Frazer's motifs and imagery and to his concepts of sex, superstition, and survival. Like Frazer, Hemingway believed that the primitive past influenced the psychology of the present, and Frazer confirmed what Hemingway already knew about Indians from observation and intuition. The anthropological material in "Indian Camp" is as well integrated and stylized as is Shakespeare's reading of Montaigne's "On Cannibals" in *The Tempest*.

Captain James Cook first used the word taboo—which is concerned "with specific and restrictive behaviour in dangerous situations"[29]—in his account of the Polynesians. Frazer beleives that taboos are "nothing but rules intended to ensure either the continued presence or the return of the soul. In short they are life preservers or lifeguards."[30] His ancient peoples, writes Vickery, "seek to endure by invoking myths of divine assistance and rites in which perfect performance assures divine conquest over enemies and hence human survival."[31]

In the section on "Tabooed Places" in *Taboo and the Perils of the Soul*, the part of *The Golden Bough* that clarifies the significance of Hemingway's story, Frazer states that in primitive society the rules of ceremonial purity observed by sacred kings, chiefs, and priests agree in many respects with the rules observed by "girls at their first menstruation, women after childbirth, homicides, mourners, and all persons who have come into contact with the dead." During childbirth "women are supposed to be in a dangerous condition which would infect any person or thing they might touch; hence they are put into quarantine until, with the recovery of their health and strength, the imaginary danger has passed away." Frazer offers massive and far-ranging documentation—from tribes in Australia, Tahiti, and Manaluki in the South Pacific, as well as from the Sinaugolos of New Guinea, the Kodiak Eskimos of Alaska, and the Ba-Pedi and Ba-

Thonga of South Africa—to illustrate the woman's uncleanliness, vulnerability, and danger during her ritual confinement at childbirth. Frazer also explains that after their wives give birth, the warrior-husbands, who now have a greater reason for living, become more cautious and absorb the wives' weakness: "The men become cowardly [and] weapons lose their force."[32]

Later anthropologists have developed and refined (instead of merely repeating, as literary critics tend to do) the ideas of Frazer. Lucien Lévy-Bruhl relates that the husband's behavior is compounded by fear for his wife and the desire to protect others "from the evil influence which will emanate from her, especially from her blood." He states that the husband associates the blood from his wife in childbed with the blood flowing from his own death-wound.[33]

Charles Winnick's explication of the concept of couvade—in which a man ritualistically imitates the symptoms of pregnancy and the moans during delivery—is crucial to an understanding of "Indian Camp" and explains why the husband joins his wife in ritualistic seclusion: "The imitation by the father of many of the concomitants of childbirth [takes place] around the time of the wife's parturition. . . . The father may retire to bed . . . and observe some taboos and restrictions in order to help the child." The father practices couvade, Winnick explains, in order to affirm his fatherhood, protect the child, and deflect potential evil from his wife: "The father asserts his paternity through appearing to share in the delivery. . . . The father simulates the wife's activities in order to get all the evil spirits to focus on him rather than her."[34]

In *Purity and Danger: An Analysis of the Concepts of Pollution and Taboo*, Mary Douglas follows Frazer and emphasizes the primitive belief in "horrible disasters which overtake those who inadvertently cross some forbidden line or develop some impure condition."[35] In the anthropological literature, as in "Indian Camp," the pregnant wife is considered unclean, vulnerable, and in danger; the husband absorbs her weakness and associates her blood with his own death, practices couvade to protect his wife and child, and resents the intrusion of those who assist at the birth.

In one of the Nick Adams stories Hemingway discusses the relation between imagination and reality and suggests that he knew enough about his father and the Indians to portray what he had never seen: "Everything good he's ever written he'd made up. . . . Of course he'd never seen an Indian woman having a baby. That was what made it good. Nobody knew that."[36] "Work in Progress," the original title of the story that first appeared in Ford's *Transatlantic Review*, not only imitates Joyce's title for the serialization of *Finnegans Wake* but also ironically alludes to the woman's pregnancy and labor. The story is carefully structured. The white men move from the idyllic to the brutal—the two dominant characteristics of the primitive world. They are ferried through the darkness and mist by their Charon-like rowers and conveyed to the smelly, secluded, and morbid world of the Indians. The Indian men and women are separated (with the exception of the husband and wife) before the intrusion of the white men. The three whites are balanced by the three Indians who help hold down the woman. The husband, who had cut himself with an ax three days earlier, is matched by the wife who is enduring her third day of labor. The husband's second mutilation intensifies his first, the gash on his throat repeats the one on her belly. His straight razor (which would have been useful in the Caesarean operation) corresponds to the doctor's jackknife. Neither George nor the husband has any real function, though both are implicated in the wife's pain by her bite and her screams. And both deflate the doctor—one by mockery, one by suicide—after his successful delivery has physically deflated the woman. The inarticulate screams, laughs, smiles, gestures, and mute acts of the nameless Indians (none of whom speaks) provide a contrast to the ironic words of the doctor ("the screams are not important") and of his son ("[It's] all right"). After the birth Dr. Adams realizes it was a mistake to bring Nick, who had watched the delivery, but turned away from the afterbirth and the sutures.

The red men in the story are not idealized and the husband, who kills himself—ironically—after his wife has survived the ordeal and given birth to a son, does not exhibit the stoicism one expects from a young Indian. In *A Farewell to Arms*, by contrast, after the death of Frederic Henry's baby and his wife in childbirth (based on the actual, rather than the imagined, Caesarean birth of Hemingway's second son in 1928), Henry represses his feelings and shows no outward emotion. He orders the attendants out of Catherine's room, shuts the door, and turns off the light. But "it was like saying good-bye to a statue. After a while I went out and left the hospital and walked back to the hotel in the rain."[37]

Hemingway portrays, in the double climax of gory birth and savage death, in pure action without conscious thought, the husband's fatal reaction to his wife's agony, but not the wife's reaction to the husband's suicide. The passive tense of "His throat has been cut" suggests the passivity of the Indian.[38] And Nick's delusive intimations of immortality after his confrontation with death and return to the idyllic lake (the certainty and absolutism of "he felt quite sure that he would never die" reveal Nick's naiveté) provide an ironic contrast to the soldier (an older

Nick) in the bombarded trench at Fossalta, who fears and expects death and prays: "If you'll only keep me from getting killed I'll do anything you say."[39]

The crossing of forbidden lines in dangerous situations exposes men and women to contamination and evil that cause sickness and death. The Indian husband has remained in the room to affirm his fatherhood, to share his wife's pain, and to protect his child. But the couvade (the hidden part of Hemingway's iceberg) is not effective and the wife remains vulnerable. The white men, summoned by the desperate Indians but ignorant of their customs, not only violate the sacred confinement of the woman in childbed, but are forced to treat her brutally and to use a hook (as if she were a squirming fish) to sew up her stomach. The contrast between the squalid and the clinical shows that the Indians need the white man's skill, but are also destroyed by it. The husband cannot bear this defilement of his wife's purity, which is far worse than her screams. In an act of elemental nobility, he focuses the evil spirits on himself, associates his wife's blood with his own death wound, and punishes himself for the violation of taboo. "Indian Camp" reveals that Hemingway—far from being the Dumb Ox—did not simply glorify the Indians, but based his story on profound understanding, gained from experience and from books, of their behavior, customs, and religion.

Hemingway's "The Killers": The Map and the Territory

Robert E. Fleming

●

Ernest Hemingway's "The Killers," first published in *Scribner's Magazine* in 1927, has interested numerous critics over the years chiefly because Hemingway seems to have been developing a pattern with certain key details within the story, but the figure in the carpet has not been traced fully by any explication of the story. If it is read as the story of Ole Andreson, "The Killers" appears to be a pointless exercise in slice-of-life realism, for nothing really happens: two killers stalk Ole, set up an elaborate ambush in a lunchroom which he frequents, and then, when he does not appear at his usual time, they just go away. Furthermore, Ole does not even appear in the eleven-page story until the bottom of the eighth page. When he does appear, he assures Nick Adams that nothing can be done to save him and turns his face to the wall. As Cleanth Brooks and Robert Penn Warren were the first to note, only if the story is correctly understood to focus on Nick Adams and his reaction to these events does it have a meaning: it is then "about the discovery of evil."[1] However, there remain a number of perplexing mysteries within the story even when its theme and protagonist have been agreed upon.

In spite of the life and death situation that develops in "The Killers," a good bit of the story is taken up with a number of petty details, as Edward C. Sampson noticed almost thirty years ago. The first scene takes place in Henry's lunchroom, but the counter man is named George, and no Henry appears in the story. The lunchroom looks more like a bar, and indeed, "Henry's had been made over from a saloon into a lunch-counter" (*SS*, 282). The second scene takes place in Hirsch's rooming house, but when Nick addresses the lady who answers the door as Mrs. Hirsch, she tells him, "I'm not Mrs. Hirsch. . . . She owns the place. I just look after it for her. I'm Mrs. Bell" (288).

At the very beginning of the first scene, the killers enter the lunchroom and attempt to order from the menu. Al orders a pork tenderloin dinner, but George tells him that "it isn't ready yet" (279). He then orders a second item on the menu, and George again tells him it isn't available. Dinners listed on the menu, he explains, are available only after six o'clock. When he looks at the clock, George reads the time as five o'clock, even though the clock reads five twenty. "It's twenty minutes fast," he explains (279). By this time the reader may feel that the story is akin to an absurdist drama, and in a sense this is what Hemingway presents.

Misunderstandings and false impressions continue to appear throughout the story. Al orders ham and eggs; Max, the second killer, orders bacon and eggs. When the orders come, and George is unsure which man ordered which meal, Max reaches for the ham and eggs to make George think he has made a mistake. The two men ask George if they can get anything to drink, and when he offers a list of soft drinks, Al replies, "I mean you got anything to *drink*?" (280), indicating that he means something alcoholic. As in the case of the menu and the clock, communication has broken down. Hemingway's authorial description of the two killers extends the series of false impressions. The two men, dressed alike in derbies and tight overcoats, look like "a vaudeville team" (285) as they leave the restaurant, even though the reader now knows they are hired killers whose stylish coats conceal weapons. The banter that the two killers engage in as they set up the ambush furthers the vaudeville image: the mixture of insults and bad jokes sounds a good deal like the "patter" that might be expected of a third-rate team of burlesque comedians. Other details contribute to the sense that Hemingway is emphasizing false impressions. Al, positioning Max and George at the lunch counter to allow the most efficient field of fire for his sawed-off shotgun, is described as being "like a photographer arranging for a group picture" (283).

Sampson's article correctly lists most of these "mix-ups" in the story, but asserts that their purpose is to convey the fact that "individuality has been lost, people have accepted their positions as agents of other people, . . . and even murder has become like everything else, mechanized, routine, efficient."[2] While this conclusion would embrace several of the discrepancies in the story, it would leave more than half of them, including the incorrect clock and menu and the ironic description of the killers, unaccounted for. However, when the story is placed in the context of the Nick Adams series of stories, the discrepancies and confusing details take on a more specific and purposeful meaning than any critic has suggested.

Read in terms of Nick's background, events of the story teach Nick that a great disparity exists between the normal signposts in life and the features of the real world to which those guides refer. S. I. Hayakawa has used the metaphor of a map versus the territory it describes in discussing the difference between the world one experiences at firsthand, or the "extensional world," and the world as one learns of it from peers, teachers, history, folklore, and literature, or the "verbal world":

Now this verbal world ought to stand in relation to the extensional world as a *map* does to the *territory* it is supposed to represent. If a child grows to adulthood with a verbal world in his head which corresponds fairly closely to the extensional world that he finds around him in his widening experience, he is in relatively small danger of being shocked or hurt by what he finds, because his verbal world has told him what, more or less, to expect. He is prepared for life. If, however, he grows up with a false map in his head—that is, with a head crammed with false knowledge and superstition—he will constantly be running into trouble, wasting his efforts, and acting like a fool. He will not be adjusted to the world as it is; he may, if the lack of adjustment is serious, end up in a mental hospital.[3]

The stories in which Nick Adams had appeared by the time Hemingway wrote "The Killers" had shown Nick in the process of shedding whole volumes of false knowledge. "Indian Camp" proves that neither medical science nor Nick's father holds all the answers about life and death. "The Doctor and the Doctor's Wife" again undercuts the power of Nick's father, denies the Victorian notion of family structure in which the father was the head of the family, and, as a minor point, notes the difference between Dr. Adams's implicit acceptance of the commandment "Thou shalt not steal" and his willingness to appropriate logs that have been lost by a lumber company. "The Battler" stresses the difference between the stories written about a major sports hero and the real man he has become. In "Ten Indians," the story that Hemingway finished on the same day he finished "The Killers," a younger Nick labels the way he feels about the loss of his Indian girl friend by using a characteristically romantic term: "My heart's broken. . . . If I feel this way my heart must be broken" (*SS,* 336). "The End of Something" and "The Three-Day Blow" show Nick's own failure to love the way a romantic hero might: his love (or something) for Marjorie seems composed of nine-tenths inertia and one-tenth physical attraction. Finally, "Chapter 7" of *in our time* depicts the gritty reality of modern war, as opposed to the glory of war in fiction. It is interesting that, as Hayakawa suggested might happen, Nick does temporarily lose his sanity in two later war stories, "Now I Lay Me" (1927) and "A Way You'll Never Be" (1933).

When he wrote "The Killers" in May 1926, Hemingway summed up one of the main points he had been making in the Nick Adams stories: life refuses to play fair. "The Killers" exaggerates the disparity between the map and the territory almost to an absurd extent. The real issue that is at stake, the impending death of Ole, is nearly obscured by a series of arguments and misunderstandings brought about by faulty clocks and menus that fail to tell the whole truth. Yet none of the parts of the story can be separated from the others, for what "The Killers" illustrates is that life does not operate as Nick, and perhaps the reader as well, has been taught. Life sets traps for honest, straightforward people who believe what they hear and what they read. For a time the individual may survive even though he follows the false map, as Ole has survived by running or as Nick has survived by following false and artificial codes of behavior, but in the end, reality must be faced. It is no easy task to confront the truth, which is, as Hemingway was to suggest by the title of his 1933 volume of short stories, that even the winners in life take nothing as a prize. Ole Andreson is a loser, not a winner, and he will soon die no matter what he does. His choice is as limited as the choices offered to the killers in the lunchroom, and Nick's suggestions about going to the police or running away correspond to the false choices on the menu. Ole's only real choice is how he will face death when it comes for him. Through his brief comments to Nick, he reveals a world gone mad, a world in which none of the truths passed down by previous generations are of any use, just as in the earlier scene of the story some of man's most trusted symbols—the printed word and the clock—have been proved false. The verbal world has become completely divorced from the world of experience.

"The Killers" is more self-conscious in its use of symbolism than the previous Nick Adams stories, and its pattern of faulty signs or incorrect maps evolved over a period of time. Examination of the different manuscript versions of "The Killers" shows just how Hemingway's thematic design evolved as he worked on the story. Three separate states of the story are present in the Hemingway collection at the Kennedy Library: a fragmentary beginning draft, a second draft with an extensive addition appended to it, and a clean carbon of the typescript apparently used as setting copy for the first publication of the story in *Scribner's Magazine*.[4] Few readers would recognize the genesis of the story in the seven-page fragment, the first page in corrected typescript, and the remainder in holograph. Nick Adams walks down the street in Petoskey, Michigan, stops at the Parker House restaurant, and orders a sandwich from the counter man, George O'Neal, from whom he accepts free shots of whiskey while the two engage in aimless conversation. At that point two men walk in, and the story begins much as in its published form with the killers trying unsuccessfully to order from the menu and noting the incorrect clock. But Hemingway apparently had no clear concept of the ultimate theme of the story, and this fragment ends when Max reaches for the ham and eggs ordered by Al.[5]

The second manuscript version of the story is undoubtedly the one Hemingway said he wrote, along with "Today is Friday" and "Ten Indians," in a single day while staying in a Madrid hotel. This manuscript, originally entitled "The Matadors," begins as the published story does, with two men entering the lunchroom. Petoskey is canceled out, and the setting has been changed to Summit. The story proceeds along the lines of the published story, with the various deliberate discrepancies already noted: Henry's lunchroom, run by George; the mix-ups over the clock and the menu; and the images of the killers as photographers and a vaudeville team. However, the corrected typescript ends inconclusively with Nick, George, and the cook all displaying their nervousness after the killers have left the lunchroom. A nine-page holograph addition to this version of the story results in its completion. A slug-line at the top of the first page reads "add the Killers," and the second scene, which takes place at Hirsch's rooming house, is appended to the lunchroom scene.[6] The only significant detail that does not appear in the holograph addition is the confusion about Mrs. Hirsch and Mrs. Bell. This further discrepancy between the verbal world and the extensional world was added only in the third version of the story, the corrected typescript.[7] By the time Hemingway was preparing the typescript for the *Scribner's Magazine* publication of the story, he had his effect firmly in mind.

Throughout the Nick Adams stories Hemingway had been making the point that Nick was growing up into a world in which the old values that guided his father's generation no longer applied. In "The Killers" Hemingway restated this thesis, compressing his perception of the changes his generation faced into a symbolic parable: just as menus, clocks, signs, and names mislead the trusting people who accept them and rely upon them, so too the moral and spiritual code passed down from previous generations will prove an inadequate and deceptive guide to Nick's troubled twentieth-century generation. The old maps no longer correspond to the territory, and the young man of Nick's generation who is to keep his sanity will have to find a new system of finding his way.

"The Last Good Country": Again the End of Something

David R. Johnson

●

As the fragment now appears in *The Nick Adams Stories*, "The Last Good Country" is over sixty pages in length—just three times that of "Big Two-Hearted River," otherwise the longest Nick Adams story. Manuscript sheets bear dates of 1952, 1953, and 1954, indicating that in Hemingway's mind this last story about his first fictional hero was no afternoon's false start, begun in recollection of other times, other tales. Moreover, the story introduced in these sixty pages indicates that there was another sixty and perhaps considerably more yet to come. Is seems clear that Hemingway was attempting the Michigan novel he had talked about, a portrait of the young Nick Adams at least as long as his immediately preceding success, *The Old Man and the Sea*. What is now available to readers is a promising beginning. There are slips, occasional bits of dialogue and several scenes where, as Philip Young has commented, Hemingway's characteristic brinksmanship does not keep him from slipping over into sentimentality,[1] but basically the tale reads too well to have been carelessly dropped and certainly well enough to spur speculation about why such a start did not lead to a completed manuscript.

Perhaps in part the reasons Hemingway did not complete "The Last Good Country" are to be found in the impulses that led him back to Nick Adams, impulses strong enough for sixty pages but insufficient to carry him through a novel. Certainly there must have been some feelings of nostalgia involved in the decision to attempt the Michigan novel, returning to his own boyhood and young manhood and at the same time to the world of his first fictional creation, Nick Adams. Of interest here is the work for which he suspended "The Last Good Country." *A Moveable Feast*, written concurrently with pieces of "The Last Good Country," is itself—regardless of what else it may be—a moving and perceptive recollection of the good, early days in Paris. In other words a work of nostalgia. To admit nostalgia as one impulse for Hemingway's return to Nick, however, is not to suggest it to be sufficient to sustain the job of writing through a substantial portion of a novel. As a collection of autobiographical essays, *A Moveable Feast* might well have been sustained by the pleasure of evoking with fondness a good life of the past. A work of fiction, presumably, requires stauncher stuff.[2] Perhaps adding to whatever nostalgia Hemingway brought to Nick and Michigan's waters and woods was the recent critical triumph of *The Old Man and the Sea*: it seems credible that the writer, "knowing all the tricks" and cheered by the success of his latest work, would attempt to repeat it with an old subject, an old theme, extending and perhaps revising the vision he had brought as a younger, fresher, but less wily writer to the earlier Nick Adams stories. If Hemingway could not send Nick off in a fishing skiff with kid sister, Littless, he could pack them both off for an idyllic sojourn in an unspoiled meadow, as cut off from the rest of the world as Santiago had been when "too far out" after his big fish. But of course Hemingway could just as easily, following *The Old Man and the Sea*'s success, have turned to new materials as to old—unless the critics were right in what they said before that book: that he was running out of stuff. At least by implication Hemingway admits the problem in *The Old Man and the Sea*: Santiago has lost his luck; he catches no fish. The parallel to Hemingway is clear enough, and the return to Nick and Michigan and to the early years in Paris draws on his past when there may have been nothing else to write about. And even some of that would not hold out, as abortive attempts to return to Spain and Africa for two books testify. So too does the fragment Mary Hemingway has entitled "The Last Good Country."

There are other possible explanations for Hemingway's failure to complete the Nick Adams novel. Viewing the fragment within the context of the collected Nick Adams stories, the tale becomes another stage in Nick's initiation into the world. Hemingway seems not to have decided just how old Nick is in this particular episode; he is young enough not to understand Mr. Packard's joke about his having original sin, yet old enough to have gotten Trudy pregnant (a detail excised before publication) and already writing stories that are too morbid. But if there is some confusion about Nick's age, it seems clear that Hemingway had in mind for this particular portrait the representation of a much more active Nick than is to be found in the other stories. Indeed, this Nick is impulsive, even willful. He has beaten the Evans boy in fights twice, and Nick contemplates killing him if he does not leave Nick alone. Fearing Nick will carry out his threat, Littless refuses to let him go out to hide without her, and here is a central conflict unique in the Nick stories. In the others Nick is essentially passive; things happen to him or to those around him, and the reader infers Nick's response. In "The Last Good Country" Nick

considers an irrevocable act, striking out for personal freedom by destroying that which intrudes upon it. But he must also consider Littless.

The reader can guess from the first sixty pages what the decision will be
and why Nick decides he must not kill the Evans boy. The telling factor is
Littless; once Nick agrees to take his sister with him, he assumes a duty he
evidently has not acknowledged before. Repeatedly he worries over her
comfort and safety, taking care that she rests well, eats well, and is warm
enough at night. It is Nick's love for Littless and his growing awareness of
responsibility for her that will lead him to admit responsibility not only for
himself but for the well-being of others. Packard explains just this to
Suzie:

> "Didn't you ever want to kill anybody, Mr. John?"
> "Yes. But it's wrong and it doesn't work out."
> "My father killed a man."
> "It didn't do him any good."
> "He couldn't help it."
> "You have to learn to help it."[3]

Just how Nick learns to "help it" the reader does not know; that is what,
in this case, Hemingway has left out. But sixty pages is enough of the
novel to see that Nick, by caring for Littless, is maturing into an understanding of what it is that he must always do. "I have to think about
things now the rest of my life," Nick says to Littless toward the end of the
fragment. His comment is his admission that he is neither as free nor as
separate from others as he wants to be. Just as the younger Nick of
"Indian Camp" is going to grow up to learn that he will indeed die, and
the older Nick of "Summer People" is going to have to face up, eventually, to the superficiality of his own sense of difference from others, Nick
in this story comes up against the reality that human relationships are
inextricably tangled, and that, as things will work themselves out, there is
no chance for the survival of the isolated meadow, a special sibling love,
or even a self held separate from an encroaching world. Having said all
this, Hemingway may have turned from the story because he found that,
in sixty pages, he had said all that he wanted to say in this particular
portrait of Nick.

Or perhaps Hemingway found his story headed in a direction he did
not want to go. Perceptive readers have not missed an aspect of this
fragment rare in the Hemingway canon, an aspect indicated by Mary
Hemingway's choice of a title. "The Last Good Country" is just that, a
virgin place unknown and unspoiled by those who have raped the land
around it, a land protected by a bad-tempered farmer and his worse-

tempered bull, an impassable cedar swamp, and hemlock slashings miles wide. It is a perfect spot for Nick and Littless to hide, but it is more than that as well. It is truly pastoral, a bucolic land where trout hide beneath the banks of the fast, clear stream, where partridge sit unwarily in the trees, and where berries ripen at the far end of the meadow. If the reader overlooks the mildly preposterous business of Nick's choosing twenty-two shorts in case he cannot get head shots at the partridge, he will find himself caught up in an idyll unmatched in Hemingway—and a communion surpassing those brief moments in *For Whom the Bell Tolls* when Robert Jordan and Maria find ways to isolate themselves from the rest of the strife-torn world.[4]

If the moments are not so brief in "The Last Good Country," nevertheless it is clear that they cannot last. Pressures begin building almost with the arrival of Nick and Littless at Camp Number One. The outside may find a way to get in, Nick fears, and of course (though the fragment ends before the event) all the internal signs suggest the world will come calling in the form of the Evans boy, the warden's son who cares only for trailing Nick and who will ruin everything. Spoiling it all, however, may have been a bit more than Hemingway could bring himself to do. It is easy to conjecture that the fragment ends with Nick and Littless in Camp Number One because Hemingway, after creating the pastoral, did not want to destroy it—and there was no way to continue the idyllic sojourn. His readers do not know the precise course Hemingway charted for the remainder of the novel, but the introduction of Splayzey, who in an obvious foreshadowing is warned not to use his gun against Nick, and Packard's recollection of Splayzey under a name other than Henry J. Porter (a plot device for extricating Nick later from a tough spot), and the use of Camp Number One, which implies there will be Camp Number Two and perhaps Camp Number Three, each presumably representing the stages of deteriorating security, all these suggest things will get much worse before getting better. There are too many references to murder, to Nick's desire to murder the Evans boy, to Littless's fear Nick will do it, to Splayzey's suspicious past, not to suggest an ugly predicament for Nick and Littless, a predicament perhaps in which Nick, by having chosen not to murder the Evans boy, places himself and Littless in clear danger of being murdered themselves, or brutalized. In addition, there are more than enough references to the love between Nick and Littless and to Littless's incipient sexuality ("Gee, I hope I won't start to be a girl while we're on the trip," Littless says) to suggest that Littless's whimsical imaginings of humble whores and whores' assistants may be a deliberate preparation for the threat of brutal rape, the paradigm for what man has done to the rest of the good country and what he will inevitably do to whatever he finds that is good and pure and innocent.

Evans and Splayzey are incapable of tracking Nick, but Packard and Suzie both fear the Evans boy might be able to find him. The easy way for Evans and Splayzey to get to Nick is to turn the boy loose to uncover Nick and his sister, hold Littless captive—a situation found in all three of the novels Littless carries with her—and try what they had earlier, making Nick come to them. Nick remarks of the three novels Littless carries that two are too old for her. Only *Kidnapped* is suitable, the story of a boy whose abduction leads mostly to a series of exciting adventures and finally to his rightful property and place. *Wuthering Heights* is too much a drama of sex and passion for Littless and too filled with incidents like the captivity of Cathy, held by Heathcliffe to force her marriage to Edgar Linton. It is *Lorna Doone* that Nick decides they will read together, certainly more appropriate for Littless than *Wuthering Heights*. But even *Lorna Doone* focuses in its central actions upon John Ridd's fears for the safety of Lorna, held against her will and starved until she will agree to marry Carver Doone. Indeed, Ridd arrives to free Lorna just as the two drunken Doone clansmen are attempting to force themselves upon her. Neither Evans nor Splayzey seems a likely candidate to molest a child, but the Evans boy might be another matter. It is he who, by trailing Nick, spoils things, and it is he who has been damned ambiguously by Suzie as "no good" and "terrible."

There are other incidents of rape in Hemingway, most notably that of Maria in *For Whom the Bell Tolls*. That occurs before the action of the novel, and the reader discovers it only as part of Maria's past. Her union with Robert Jordan is the best man can achieve in a corrupted world, and it is of course temporary. It comes close to the pastoral of "The Last Good Country," falling just short of the perfect union, the sibling love of Littless and Nick that Littless's sexual banterings assure us is asexual. But too good a thing is itself ominous. That union must suffer in the unwritten half of "The Last Good Country" the ruination that the outside world always serves up to innocence. "I guess those things straighten out," Nick thinks of his sister's too-strong attachment to him. And the reader knows just how these things straighten out in Hemingway's world. Viewing the first sixty pages of the novel in this manner, some attempted assault on Littless seems more and more likely, and the rest of the novel harder and harder to write.

A parallel speculation may shed some light. In the summer immediately following completion of *Adventures of Huckleberry Finn* Mark Twain lost considerable time attempting the sequel Huck promises, a fragment

Life magazine published in 1968 as "Huck and Tom Among the Indians."[5] Huck in that fragment finds himself being instructed as usual by the romantic notions of Tom, this time about Indians. Tom's opinions are shared as well by a luckless band of travelers the two fall in with, and the notions lead to the murder by Indians of all the travelers except the inevitable blond girl, who is carried off. The remainder of the fragment recounts the attempts of Huck, Tom, and the blond girl's fiancé, a frontiersman wise in the ways of Indians, to catch the fleeing band. Tension mounts between the naive musings of Huck and Tom, who think only of freeing the girl, and the studied silence of the frontiersman, who knows quite well what Indians do to white women. With the trio close upon the band the excerpt ends. Apparently Twain never attempted to complete the manuscript.

Writing of the fragment, Walter Blair speculates, "Almost in spite of itself, the story was moving toward a head-on collision with a deep personal taboo. . . . recounting such an atrocity [rape] was unthinkable."[6] Hemingway is not, of course, Mark Twain. But while Hemingway would have no special difficulty confronting another of the many instances in American literature of rapes by Indians, confronting the rape of Littless may be something very different. "The Last Good Country" is almost entirely fiction. The biographical incident upon which it is based is a slight one involving a warden, his son, and a blue heron the young Ernest had shot. It was straightened out quickly with a fine. But if Nick's escape into the woods with Littless is wholly fiction, the character of Littless is certainly not. She is clearly a representation of Madelaine (nicknamed Sunny by Hemingway), Ernest's younger sister with whom he did have a special relationship. It is just possible that the nostalgic Hemingway, remembering his kid sister, kept getting in the way of the artist Hemingway, who knew just exactly where the story was to go.

When in February 1953 *Ernest Hemingway* was finally published, Philip Young sent Hemingway the first available copy. Hemingway just as quickly returned it, but later comments make it clear that Hemingway did indeed read the book ("How would you like it if someone said that everything you've done in your life was because of some trauma?"[7] he asked one reporter), and surely he knew the gist of it long before that. Is it not at least conceivable that Hemingway, on returning to Nick and Michigan, chose (partly in response to Young) to make Nick, this time, an active, untraumatized character? If so, the failure to continue the work may have been due to the direction the story has turned—more of a substantiation of Young's thesis than a refutation. Disregarding the possibility of an assault on Littless, the reader still must confront the inevitability that something is going to happen to her, and that something spells yet another injury for Nick. "I ain't agoing to tell all that happened—it would make me sick again if I was to do that," Huck says at the end of the Shepherdson-Grangerford section of *Huck Finn*. One wonders if Hemingway quit "The Last Good Country" because to continue would be to place Nick again in the same position as Huck, and he himself in the position of contemplating, once again, an end of something—this one not so easy to write about.

Nick Adams and the Search for Light

Howard L. Hannum

●

Despite Hemingway's ranking of "The Light of the World" as one of his personal favorites, the full story has seldom been studied in the context of Nick Adams' adolescence. First of all, critical attention has too often focused on the dialogue between the whores Alice and Peroxide and the love which each claims to have enjoyed with the famous middleweight boxer Stanley Ketchel. Several critics have followed Matthew Bruccoli into analysis of this dialogue and the fascinating Ketchel-Jack Johnson prizefight which underlies it, then have fallen into the trap of trying to decide the argument between the two women.[1] But this has usually involved some loss of perspective, and the impact of the whole story on Nick has been minimized. A second tendency in the criticism has been the effort to relate the "light" of the title to one specific biblical text and to see this light chiefly in Christian terms in the exchange between Peroxide and Alice, again losing sight of the overall effect upon Nick. Oddly enough, after all the critical effort expended to show that "The Killers" was centered on Nick Adams and that it depended upon his response, the importance of the narrator in this story (assumed here to be Nick) has often been obscured.

The verbal battle between the whores is the most exciting part of "The Light of the World," but only a part of the whole shocking experience for Nick. Some of the other parts, especially entrances and exits, not only characterize Nick in this story, but also relate to complementary incidents or scenes in stories treating the same period of his life. "The Light of the World" (1933) shares many striking similarities with "The Battler" (1924) and "The Killers" (1927). Despite their different composition dates, all three are initiation stories, as Bruccoli observed,[2] in which Nick (or a central consciousness very much like him) learns by indirection. Further, the stark, brutal experiences of these stories are unlike anything else in the Nick Adams stories, even the war stories. Each of these three stories shows the transient Nick walking along tracks (streetcar tracks, in "The

Killers'') through autumn darkness and ends with Nick walking (or about to walk) out into that same darkness.

The experience really seems to begin in "The End of Something" and "The Three-Day Blow," as Nick breaks off his late-adolescent love affair with Marjorie and breaks out of the whole context of his boyhood and youth.³ The trip by which he accomplishes this takes him through northern Michigan in "The Light of the World" and "The Battler," with a stay in Summit, Illinois, in "The Killers," though we know now that Hemingway's manuscript originally showed the town as "Petoskey" (Michigan). These five stories carry Nick up to the time of his military service. Where the slightly older Bill had seemed the architect of Nick's conduct back at Hortons Bay, the slightly older Tom is his guide in "The Light of the World." In "The Battler" he is completely on his own, and in "The Killers" he disregards the advice of George by warning Ole Andreson. His personal involvement and response show a gradual increase with the stories in this sequence. Still, the lesson learned in each story is more apt to be stored and ruminated upon than to issue soon in direct action. This seems particularly true for the entranced Nick at the end of "The Light of the World."

The "light" of Hemingway's title certainly contrasts with the prevailing darkness of the story. Tom and Nick find no "light," physical or spiritual, in their entrance to the bar at the outset. Their youth works against them here. Hostile and suspicious, the bartender denies them free lunch, even beer, until he sees their money, then insults them by placing the bottle of rye whiskey out on the bar for his regular customer. Here Nick controls the angry Tom well enough to avoid a brawl but submissively shows his money and suggests departure just before being ordered out. Uncharacteristically, Hemingway offers scant description or visualization of scene. Only the bar and the hands playing across it come into focus: guardedly serving beer, serving rye, reaching for free lunch, reaching for the unrevealed pistol, placing coins on the wood. The dialogue is monosyllabic, curt. This is a place where men drink in catatonic silence. If "light" involves such qualities as love and hope and truth, this bar is properly dark.

At the railroad station the boys' entrance is met by apparent indifference from everyone but the homosexual cook. The group includes five other white men, apparently all lumberjacks, five whores (the three-hundred-and-fifty-pound Alice, two two-hundred-and-fifty-pounders, and two peroxide blondes, "just ordinary-looking"), and four Indians, who diminish to three (40, 43). The bartender's use of the word "punks" for the boys has been oddly prophetic, for its Elizabethan meaning anticipates the whores in the station. The boys' youth ironically works "for" them with the cook, and their reactions to him show their levels of experience. Angry and disgusted, Tom turns him aside with a crudity about "sixty-nine" when he asks their ages, but Nick naively tells the truth and talks to him "decently," an unintentional encouragement. Tom chides Nick for this, but himself naively asks the whores their names. Hemingway does visualize the scene this time, though he restricts it to the bench near the stove. The whores, like the iridescent dresses three of them wear, attract what light there is in the room, turning the bench into a stage. The cook's evident interest in the boys sets off some automatic antagonisms: of the heterosexual men toward the cook, of the whores toward the cook (their "natural rival" for men), and of the whores toward "mossbacks" (men who don't spend money on whores). Hemingway's dialogue here, and in much of the story, has the quality of counterpunching in boxing, with a brash assertion met by a brash response. This is a place where men and women badger each other; the potential violence implicit in the bar is vented here. Again, "hands" are in focus, as Alice and the lumberjacks turn the cook's white and delicate hands into a humorous symbol of his effeminacy. Alice has begun to shake with laughter at the attacks on the cook and on the mossbacks (the lumberjacks and the boys). Ridicule of the cook is in high gear when the shy lumberjack mentions "Steve Ketchel" and touches off the dialogue between Peroxide and Alice. Then for a time a false "light" plays over the scene, as each of the two argues the love of her life.

In the course of this exchange both whores will claim to have known Ketchel as "Steve," though the boxer Peroxide refers to clearly was Stanley Ketchel, the fabled "Michigan Assassin," middleweight boxing champion from 1908–10.[4] However, identification of Ketchel in the story is complicated by two elements: Stanley Ketchel apparently did in real life like to be called "Steve" by close friends,[5] and a boxer using the name "Steve" Ketchel did fight Ad Wolgast in 1915,[6] five years after Stanley Ketchel's death, but before the time of Hemingway's story. Thus, it is possible that Alice is referring to the second "Ketchel." Peroxide turns aside the suggestion that her Steve's name was Stanley and calls him "the finest and most beautiful man that ever lived," "the only man I ever loved." Her pipe dream and perhaps the only romantic "light" of her pathetic life is that he knew and loved her but that she nobly passed up marriage rather than "hurt his career." She climaxes her performance with the claim: "'We were married in the eyes of God and I belong to him right now and always will and all of me is his. I don't care about my body. They can take my body. My soul belongs to Steve Ketchel'" (45). For the moment Peroxide has affected everyone in the room (except the Indians, who have bought their tickets and gone outside to the platform!). Nick is so deeply involved in the scene that he does not perceive any satire. Alice is shaking now with tears, not laughter. But just as suddenly as Peroxide had seized the floor, Alice strikes back at her, "You're a dirty liar. . . . You never laid Steve Ketchel in your life and you know it." Alice, now calm, bores forward like a boxer and, despite a quick exchange of insults, controls the floor, which Peroxide seems to abandon in favor of her "true, wonderful memories." Alice, whose moods are now changing like the colors of her iridescent dress, signals her triumph with a smile at the boys.

Critics have felt compelled to take sides in this argument, generally finding the ring of truth in Alice's words. Carlos Baker set a pattern by declaring for the common sense of Alice, against the sentimental love of Peroxide.[7] Sheridan Baker thought Nick saw the light of truth in Alice's face.[8] James F. Barbour found Alice drawing on the strengths of truth, because she was a realist who had paid for her memories, where Peroxide was a romantic who had only imagined things.[9] Joseph M. Flora saw "heart's truth" in Alice's words, as opposed to Peroxide's "bilge."[10] And so the analysis of the dialogue has gone.

Despite her initial hold on the audience, Peroxide is objectively caught in a lie about being in California with Ketchel:

"Were you out on the coast with him?"
"No. I knew him *before that*." (44, italics added)

but then

"I thought you said you weren't on the coast," someone said.
"I went out just for that fight." (44)

and she is wrong about Ketchel's being shot by his father, but she does know the vital details of his fight with Johnson:

"Steve knocked him down," Peroxide said. . . .
"Steve turned to smile at me and that black son of a bitch from hell jumped up and hit him by surprise." (44–45)

She might indeed have gotten this (except her invention of the smile) from newspaper accounts, as Alice charges. But her words seem to have their own ring of truth when she challenges Alice's oft-repeated compliment from Ketchel ("You're a lovely piece, Alice") with the statement,

"Steve couldn't have said that. It wasn't the way he talked." Alice, for her part, shows no verifiable knowledge of Ketchel's life and career, and there is no objective evidence that she is telling the truth, only her determined manner. Nevertheless, she does hold sway; Alice levels several charges (including venereal disease and drug use) at Peroxide, who seems simply to drop the argument, as much as to lose it. There is no clear winner in logical terms.

The real point of the dialogue is that Nick is being taken in by Alice, is in fact beginning to respond to her personally, even sexually, and will have to be rescued from the situation by Tom, reversing the roles in the bar earlier. Both whores are lying, either inventing whole cloth or at best exaggerating what was a casual encounter to Stan (or Steve) Ketchel (possibly both) into a major love affair, which of course never took place. What "love" has always come down to for Peroxide and Alice is sex, bought and sold. Both now pathetically glorify a supposed relationship that gives dignity and self-respect to their lives.

The Indians in the station have rendered the actual "decision" in the dialogue between Peroxide and Alice by walking out on it: it was not worth listening to, it was a fake, as in all probability was the prizefight it was partly based upon. At Colma, California, on October 16, 1909, middleweight Stanley Ketchel fought the heavyweight champion, Jack Johnson, for the latter's title, in what has long been regarded as a "fixed" fight—in an era when boxing was generally illegal and unregulated and many fights were fixed. Ketchel was one of a series of boxers billed as The Great White Hope, to regain the heavyweight title for white America, from the black Johnson. At least four inches taller and at least forty pounds heavier, Johnson was supposed to "carry" Ketchel (not really attack him) for the benefit of the newsreel cameras and the white fans. In an apparent deception Ketchel suddenly charged Johnson in the twelfth round and knocked him down with a vicious punch, but Johnson rose and knocked the charging Ketchel out with three punches.[11] Even the weights recorded for the bout have been suspect: Ketchel's normal 154 pounds was given as 170$\frac{1}{4}$, and Johnson's "official" 205$\frac{1}{2}$ was regarded by many as deflated.[12]

Hemingway's fight between Peroxide and Alice is also being staged. Clearly, both women are performing for the group in the station, Peroxide in "a high stagey way" (44). But more than that, Hemingway has the two whores reenacting the Ketchel-Johnson fight here. As at Colma, the lighter, blonde Peroxide (Ketchel) is being sent up against the much heavier foe, Alice (Johnson), in a fight that is determined by one flurry from each antagonist, with the mountainous Alice definitely winning. Her hammering prose, with its Anglo-Saxon monosyllables, finally dominates:

"This is true, true, true, and you know it. . . ." (45)

"No, its true, true, true to Jesus and Mary true." (45)

". . . I'm clean and you know it and men like me, even though I'm big, and you know it, and I never lie and you know it." (46)

Alice's "and you know it" marked her first attack upon Peroxide and is like a boxer's one-two punch as she applies it. Peroxide's complete withdrawal into her memories suggests Ketchel's condition at the end of the fight: Johnson knocked him completely "out" for several minutes, so that he had to be carried back to his corner. Further, Ketchel soon began to drift off into his memories, for his career waned sharply after the Johnson fight. Often dissipated, he had only three fights and was in temporary retirement for his health when shot to death. Peroxide's embellishment that Ketchel was distracted and smiling at her when Johnson hit him is contrary to the facts of the fight, as the film shows, but Hemingway may well have borrowed it from the account of Ketchel's fatal shooting almost a year later: Goldie (Peroxide?) Smith, the cook whom Ketchel had just "insulted" the day before, switched his usual seat at the breakfast table, from one that faced the door, to one that put his back to it, so that her paramour, Walter Dipley, could take him by surprise.[13]

There is a precedent for thinking that Peroxide and Alice are putting on a show. Hemingway identified part of his imaginative source for "The Light of the World" as Guy de Maupassant's "La Maison Tellier," a story about five whores and their excursion to Madame Tellier's native village in Normandy to attend the Confirmation of her niece. In the process they unsuspiciously make a spectacle of themselves and dissolve in emotional memories of their own Confirmation days. Hemingway's whores, likewise on some sort of excursion, perhaps to Alice's Mancelona, look back to the one sexual encounter for each that had spiritual, meaningful quality, and they too make a spectacle of themselves. Many specific parallels between Maupassant's story and Hemingway's have been brought out by Martine, Peter Thomas, and Flora.[14] However, Madame Tellier's experience was essentially comic, Nick's is not.[15]

As the dialogue on boxing develops, the earlier stress upon "hands," in the bar and during the ridicule of the cook, becomes relevant. One way or another, hands, gloved and ungloved, play important parts in "The Battler," with the brakeman and Ad Francis, and in "The Killers," with Al and Max and Ole Andreson. Most often boxing is involved. Hemingway, as a lifelong boxing fan, who "taught" boxing to his literary friends in Paris and fought spontaneous bouts right into middle age, knew the sport and knew the legend of Stanley Ketchel. Gregory Green has cited Hemingway's use of the famous "sandbag trick" or "gimmick" in his high school story "A Matter of Color."[16] In this trick one boxer, with an accomplice hidden behind a curtain, would maneuver his opponent against the ropes in that direction so that the accomplice could hit him on the head from behind. As George Plimpton points out, Ketchel was associated with the use of this trick in one of the best known of boxing anecdotes.[17] Furthermore, Ketchel was most probably something of a hero to the younger Hemingway, for Ketchel, at sixteen, set off on a tour very much like that of Nick Adams in "The Light of the World" and "The Battler." Like Nick, and Hemingway himself, Ketchel started from Chicago and went north. Though he went across Canada to the Pacific Coast, Ketchel then "rode the rails" from Seattle to Butte, Montana, where he became the bouncer in a bordello. He, of course, got the look at life that Hemingway tried to give Nick.

"Christian" interpretations of "The Light of the World" have followed some familiar patterns. Bruccoli saw in Ketchel elements of a Christ-figure: his godlike appeal to Peroxide, his role as "saviour" to the two women, his being shot by his father in Peroxide's account (sacrificed for his father).[18] Thomas cited the "Christ-analogue" and saw Ketchel's loss to Johnson as Christ's "defeat" by the dark forces of human evil.[19] Several of Peroxide's remarks do of course reinforce the notion of deity in Ketchel: "There never was a man like that," "I loved him like you love God," "he was like a god." Both Thomas and Barbour saw a nun's spiritual marriage to Christ in Peroxide's love for Ketchel.[20] But the Christ symbolism does not seem broad enough to include all the implications of the story. Ketchel's brief fame as the Great White Hope of boxing carried an almost religious appeal to both whores, especially to Peroxide, who stressed his whiteness:

> "I never saw a man as clean and as *white* and as beautiful as Steve. . . ." (44)
> "He was the greatest, finest *whitest*, most beautiful man that ever lived. . . ." (44)
> "He was like a god, he was, so *white* and clean and beautiful and smooth and fast like a tiger or like lightning." (45)

This combination of whiteness and godliness suggests still another deity in Ketchel, the one depicted in Madame Tellier's "salon of Jupiter," the lounge of her establishment, with its drawing of "Leda stretched out under the swan."[21] Ketchel is thus the Swan, the whitest of the gods (Zeus, Jupiter). More like Swinburne's pagan deities than Christ, however, Ketchel has "visited" these mortals, or so they claim.

The "light" of Hemingway's title has of course been the target of every explication of the story. The most obvious biblical source is Christ's comment in John 8:12, "I am the light of the world: he that followeth me shall not walk in darkness, but shall have the light of life." Yet this applies to Nick only in the negative sense. He has found no Christian light in the bar, none in the station, and he will literally and figuratively walk forth into the cold Michigan darkness at the end. Furthermore, in the full context of John 8:2–12, Christ offers the woman taken in adultery her only option for salvation—to "follow" Him, an option that Nick is rejecting. Christ's comment in the Sermon on the Mount (Matthew 5:14), "You are the light of the world" applies, but only with telling irony, to everyone in the station—there is no one worth emulating. Hemingway might have intended a pun upon Alice, who is addressed by the cook as, "You big disgusting *mountain* of flesh," by Peroxide as "You big *mountain* of pus," and likened by the lumberjack to "a hay *mow*" (italics added, 41, 46, 42). But Alice hardly sheds Christian light upon her fellows, as the evangelist urges; critics have struggled to see Christian quality in her.[22]

Hemingway surely was, among other things, deploring the betrayal of Christian love in our culture, as William B. Stein has argued persuasively,[23] but as Hemingway himself said of this story, "It is about many things and you would be ill-advised to think it is a simple tale."[24] Efforts to relate either P.P. Bliss's gospel hymn or Holman Hunt's painting of Jesus with a lantern—both also entitled "The Light of the World"—to the story seem oversimplified. Hemingway, as his mother's son, was aware of the Christian suggestions in his title, but also as his mother's son, he very much realized that his views of life and art had moved beyond them, as Nick's had begun to do. Michael S. Reynolds shows that Hunt's painting had considerable satiric value for Hemingway (his mother's vanity in presenting a copy of it to her church in memory of *her* father), in addition to whatever religious values it held for him.[25] Beyond this, the prevalence of irony in the religious imagery undercuts the Christian intention of the story. In fact it is chiefly in inverted or ironic sense that "light" has meaning, for there is very little Christian value or sentiment to be found in the surface of the story. Critics who have looked for meaning in a specific biblical text have failed to recognize the extent of Nick's revolt and the secular character of the world Hemingway is sending him into. If anything, "The Light of the World" shows the failure of Christianity for Nick at this time, just as it is failing (and being failed by) the whores and lumberjacks who call on Christ so often.

The world Nick walks through is anything but Christian. The brutality of the bar and the stale carnality of the railroad station bespeak a world without hope or honesty or even meaning. This is a place of illusion and contradiction: Stan Ketchel is "Steve," four Indians become three, the man in the stagged trousers is at first the cook, but later the man who calls him "sister." And there is no promise of release from this world, where the five heterosexual white men retreat before the five grotesque whores, who live in memory (if at all), and the two groups join only in the derision of the cook. Sex has become a sick joke, and love a lie, here. As Sheridan Baker observed, the story makes masculine sexuality "the light of the world,"[26] and that is the false limelight that plays alternately upon Peroxide and Alice. It is Nick's growing excitement over Alice, as well. Martine identifies this light with the red light, "the archetypal light in the archetypal houses of the oldest profession in the world."[27] Still, it is the only force that rouses this crew from its lethargy.

Nick's journey in this story may well be the trip into town Saturday night that he talked of in "The Three-Day Blow" (216), his consolation that he might still see Marjorie again, [28] but what he finds instead is the realization of his earlier comment to Marge, "everything was gone to hell inside of me" (184). He is in Hell. The lumberjacks, cook, and whores suggest The Carnal, who have betrayed reason to their appetites, in Dante's *Inferno.* With its pervading darkness, and the bar and station its only features, the whole landscape suggests the underworld. A many-sided metaphor, the station shades back through the Walpurgis Night of Hawthorne's Major Molineux to merely sordid reality. Indeed, the story carries echoes of many literary works. The bar is like one in Jack London's *On the Road,*[29] and Nick and Tom's forced departure is like Robin's from the dark tavern in old Boston. Nick's fascination with Alice recalls Robin's with "the silvery sound of a woman's voice," and the giant whore's alternate sobbing and laughing suggest the "murmur" and "laughter" in the background of Hawthorne's story. Alice, as Carlos Baker noted,[30] is much like her near-namesake Alisoun, Chaucer's Wife of Bath. The argument that Nick and Tom provoke in the station recalls the one touched off by Christian and Faithful in Bunyan's Vanity Fair. Barbara Maloy has suggested a number of parallels between the story and Lewis Carroll's Wonderland-Looking Glass world.[31] More significantly here, the town and the railroad station are an Alice-in-Wonderland reversal of the life Nick knew at Hortons Bay. The shifting characters and identifications suggest Carroll's work, and Hemingway's Alice also "shrinks" to a sexually attactive size for Nick, a disturbing new measure of his sensuality. But Nick is the protagonist of this tale, and for him there will be no waking from a dream, safely back at home. More like Hawthorne's Robin, Nick has left home and will not return to it until after the war.

Pulled away while still under Alice's spell, Nick should find the cold night air salutary. He has come a long way from Marjorie and her castles on the shore at Hortons Bay, but, learning by indirection, he needs time to realize this. "Light" still eludes him. It might be up the track with Ad and Bugs or outside Ole Andreson's boarding house or on beyond that. Nick has made more progress than he knows, but he still walks through darkness.

"Nobody Ever Dies!": Hemingway's *Fifth* Story of the Spanish Civil War

Larry Edgerton

●

Composed in 1938, "Nobody Ever Dies!" appeared in the March 1939 *Cosmopolitan* and, except for two translations and a "timely" April 1959 reprint by *Cosmopolitan* editors responding to the new Cuban government (the text arrives with photographs of Castro and his revolution), has not been published elsewhere, unlike the four other Civil War stories written in 1938 and 1939 on the heels of *The Fifth Column and the First Forty-Nine Stories*.[1] These other war stories Scribner's appended in 1969 to a new printing of *The Fifth Column*.[2] Save for a paragraph in Baker's biography on Hemingway,[3] as Benson notes in his bibliography, the story has generated no criticism. Among the published Hemingway canon, even including the two uncollected *Atlantic* stories[4] and the fables,[5] "Nobody Ever Dies!" has been singularly ignored. Apparently it is the last unturned stone in the broad field of Hemingway short-story commentary. Although the story periodically surfaces as an entry in bibliographies and footnotes, it remains unknown and buried in *Cosmopolitan*'s pages, where in 1939 it served as a companion piece to fiction, similarly illustrated, by Faith Baldwin, Paul Gallico, A. J. Cronin, and Dorothy Kilgallen.

The plot is this: Enrique, a soldier fighting Spanish Fascists, returns to Cuba after fifteen months' absence and is secreted in a house which contains a weapons cache and which officials have had under surveillance. Through part of the day that the story covers, Enrique listens for intruders and observes a straw-hatted Negro who is standing under laurels near the house. At last comes a sympathizer, Maria, bringing food. She and Enrique are lovers. She learns, through him, that her brother has been killed in the war. Embittered, she challenges Enrique to tell her why her brother's death has meaning: why one should fight and die in what seems meaningless war. To prove that war deaths have meaning, Enrique first provides philosophy ("Where you die does not matter, if you die for liberty"), then shows his battle wound. Though the maxim does not move her, the wound does; she asks to be forgiven.

Enrique and Maria embrace, and, as they do, sirens go off: officials are coming to the house. The lovers' escape into an adjacent lot is unsuccessful. Submachine guns kill Enrique, and Maria is taken prisoner. She appeals to the dead (her brother, the war dead, Enrique) for help. Because nobody ever dies, the oxymoronic living dead can rescue her, filling her with a new, peaceful confidence, not unlike the confidence that animated Jeanne d'Arc. The police drive Maria away. The Negro informer who has been watching the house and turned them in is unnerved by her calm confidence. He fingers his voodoo beads but finds no peace. His magic has no primacy over her "older magic," which is to say, Maria's knowledge that her death will have meaning, just as Jeanne d'Arc (Hemingway says) understood that her death would become meaningful.

The story's scene-building calls to mind many Hemingway openings:

> The house was built of rose-colored plaster that had peeled and faded with the dampness and from its porch you could see the sea, very blue, at the end of the street. There were laurel trees along the sidewalk that grew high enough to shade the upper porch and in the shade it was cool. A mockingbird hung in a wicker cage at a corner of the porch, and it was not singing now, nor even chirping, because a young man of twenty-eight, thin, dark, with bluish circles under his eyes and a stubble of beard, had just taken off a sweater that he wore and spread it over the cage. The young man was standing now, his mouth slightly open, listening. Someone was trying the locked and bolted front door.

The beginning characteristically uses sentences that are compound ("The house . . . and . . . you could see the sea"), packed with information (colors, sounds), and that introduce leitmotivs (the mockingbird, "in the shade it was cool"). It tells who and where and demands answers to why: *why* is somebody trying a locked and bolted door, *why* is the door locked and bolted? *Why* has Enrique, the young man with "bluish circles under his eyes," covered the mockingbird's cage? The bird, we notice, is caged, like Enrique, and when he releases the bird, his own captivity is mocked. Later, when he tries to convince Maria of his sensitivity, he tells her about releasing the bird, and she, too, mocks him: "Aren't you kind!" We are also told, at about this point in the narrative, that "The wind was fresh now in the trees and it was cold on the porch." The cool winds in the story parallel Enrique's dry heart, the heart which war has deadened, which Maria calls a book ("You talk like a book," she says. "Not like a human being"), yet which can still be touched, "hurt deeply." Though Maria justifiably doubts Enrique's sensitivity of heart, his physical senses have not been dulled. The second paragraph escorts the reader through a catalog of the sounds to which Enrique pays attention—the wind in the laurels, a taxi's horn, children playing, the turn of a key in the bolted door, and the smack of a bat against a baseball. Enrique must examine each noise, just as he must carefully watch the street, in order to stay alive. War has sharpened his external senses while blunting his spiritual. When a siren on the radio falsely alerts him to danger, his reaction is a wave that crawls over his scalp "like prickly heat" and then disappears "as quickly as it came." What he experiences is not fear, but the physical vestiges of old fears long overcome. He behaves courageously, committed to a war he believes in.

The catalog of sounds functions in the story, then, and is not Hemingway's idle demonstration of technique nor a hollow recital to plug space before beginning the story proper. It tells something about Enrique's character through describing what he hears and sees. Description sets the stage and thematically suggests what is to follow. The statement "in the shade it was cool" points out a coolness that will be woven into the entire story, from the cool laurel shade to Enrique's cool heart to the Negro's cool treachery.

Similarly, the Negro, an ominous figure literally in the shadows in the beginning of the story and not fully seen until the last three paragraphs, is associated with the laurel trees described in the second sentence of the initial paragraph. The laurel trees begin innocently but pick up malevolent hues as they are attached to the cool wind and the Negro. The freed mockingbird flies into the laurels—the laurels now associated with the Negro; the mockingbird, an emblem for Enrique, by landing in the laurels links Enrique to the evil trees—the trees from which the Negro will later emerge to effect Enrique's death. The Negro is Chekhov's gun that, if mentioned in a story's first lines, must be fired by its last. Hemingway draws the story to a close around the Negro, who must consider, as engineer of this tragedy, the significance of his actions. What the Negro sets into motion, he witnesses and evaluates. He will contemplate Maria's confidence, wonder about the meaning of her death. The story thus begins and ends with the Negro, for all intents and purposes. It has the circular organization Hemingway often employed: the reappearance of opening material, reviewed from a new perspective, ripe with fresh nuance. From the point of view of form there seem to be no loose ends in "Nobody Ever Dies!" Elements introduced early are not forgotten and crop up later in the story. There are no superfluous actions or characters. Through the progression of sentences, pregnant words or phrases ("it was cool") are manipulated. Much of the dialogue is written with Hemingway's wonted skill. The famous style, evident in the lovely first paragraph, is at work on every page, usually as tuned as ever to modifiers, rhythms, and cadences. The normal prose is limpid and musical.

Superficially, then, "Nobody Ever Dies!" is a quick, dramatic narrative about lovers who argue, finally reach an understanding (physical and psychic), yet have their agreement fractured—here by gunfire and death. Yet, despite the resemblance of any Hemingway story to conventional patterns—pulp stories about bullfighting, boxing, and fishing—his imagination ordinarily travels past surfaces, so that rugged, dramatic, and even conventionally violent actions often have "larger meaning." Given, then, Hemingway's ability to invest common plots with philosophical depth, the reader should peer past *Cosmopolitan*'s frowzy graphics and the examples Miss Baldwin and Dr. Cronin have set, beyond the gangster machinery and clichés of romantic love in the story, for a retrievable ideology which may force this piece to be more serious than standard *Cosmopolitan* fare.

Yet Baker calls the story "one . . . in his worst vein of tough sentimentalism," and says Hemingway's plot choices are "inept."[6] Perhaps harsher than Baker's voiced judgment is the forty-four-year critical silence. However tidy its crafting, the story has not provoked commentary. It is ignored, and no doubt for good reasons. I agree with Baker's charge of sentimentalism and should like now to identify those aspects which justify that charge and also explain the story's lack of interest for scholars as anything but an entry in bibliographies.

The story is roughly at its midpoint when it disintegrates. Maria has been granted entrance into the house upon completing a pass phrase. She has learned from Enrique of her brother's death, expressed her inability to understand war's vindications, and challenged Enrique to answer why the deaths of her brother and other young men, in an unsuccessful operation in a foreign country, have purpose.

Up to now the story has been a straightforward tale of intrigue and love. We have learned that Enrique's life is endangered, that he has enhanced physical senses, that a Negro is spying on him, that he has an alarming war wound, that Maria loves him, that her brother has been killed, and that Enrique believes all men are brothers: "Some are dead and others still live." The information presented up to now is largely a survey of narrative essentials—who, what, where, when, why—set into motion; these are increasingly augmented by anguished speculation concerning the nature of war, the demands it makes upon the living, whether "war is worth it," as Enrique claims it is. So far Hemingway has not directly stated a philosophical position; what the reader knows he must gather through nuance. However, Hemingway at last grounds the story on a position when he has Enrique respond to Maria's troubled questioning:

> "There are no foreign countries, Maria, where people speak Spanish. Where you die does not matter, if you die for liberty. Anyway, the thing to do is to live and not to die."
> "But think of who have died—away from here—and in failures."
> "They did not go to die. They went to fight. The dying is an accident."

And a few lines later Enrique continues: "'Some things we had to do were impossible. Many that looked impossible we did. But sometimes the people on your flank would not attack. . . . But in the end, it was not a failure.'"

Enrique's claim, a claim that directs the plot's outcome, is that a life given in the defense of liberty is not without design. Though Maria's brother and other men like him are the "flower of the party," cut in bloom, they do not really die: nobody ever dies. That is why war is not a failure, why her brother's death is not pointless. Maria does not answer him; a wind in the trees rises, "and it was cold on the porch." The cold may be in Enrique's heart as well, but he can summon sufficient compassion to put his arms around Maria, who has begun to cry. He tells her that they must "check all romanticism. . . . We must proceed so that we will never again fall into revolutionary adventurism." Maria is not convinced. Breaking her silence, she accuses Enrique of talking like a book. "Your heart is a book," she says further. To counter her accusation, to prove his humanity (she rejects the uncaged mockingbird as proof), Enrique invites Maria to touch his war wound. Its size and effect ("not out of any book") cause her to scrap her antiwar beliefs and to accept Enrique's proposition of a meaningful death realized by defending liberty. She asks to be forgiven. Enrique says that there is "nothing to forgive," and they make love until real sirens, not a radio's imitation, interrupt them.

Enrique's proposition, which Maria is persuaded to accept, seems set upon the story from outside. What Enrique says comes like a sampler motto suddenly introduced into the story. I do not question the veracity of his preachings, only the manner in which Hemingway presents them and their consequences upon the story. Despite the wound, the reader is not, I think, as convinced as Maria. The war wound, however horrendous and pathetic, does not invalidate her protests. It may even reinforce them. The wound provokes her compassion but certainly is not a cogent reply to her argument. "We must check all romanticism," Enrique warns us, but Hemingway's move is to offer a romantic cliché: the power of the ghastly wound to sway Maria and to pull Hemingway out of an artistic corner—namely, how to conclude the story. Because Maria accepts the death-in-war position, the plot, however well it forges a shape suitable for *Cosmopolitan*, nevertheless commits itself to an inevitability of clichéd form. Stale art possesses its own inevitability. Now that Maria has agreed with Enrique, the story predictably gives a demonstration of his thesis. The sirens come as no surprise to lovers or readers, nor do the actions that follow—the slaughter of Enrique, Maria's capture and new confidence (her sentimental likening to Jeanne d'Arc), the Negro's uneasiness. There are, of course, stories whose familiar order of elements gives pleasure, and some of Hemingway's stories produce this pleasure—the deaths in "The Snows of Kilimanjaro" and "The Short Happy Life of Francis Macomber," to name works chronologically near "Nobody Ever Dies!" What is different with the latter fiction is the insistent propagandizing so blatantly introduced as part of the plot. An imposed credo, not an internal logic, dictates what will happen from the moment Enrique tells Maria that "Where you die does not matter, if you die for liberty." We know now who will die next and why. The questions now become *when* will Maria and Enrique die and in what fashion? The reader must now accompany Hemingway through expected plot steps (the escape, the death, and the capture), symbolism (Jeanne d'Arc and Maria), and the mystical ending out of Hollywood (the nature of Maria's "older magic").

This "internal logic" would ask for a different course of action, another ending. Though Hemingway apparently wants the reader to agree with Enrique, given the story's symbolic ending, he bizarrely loads the case in the other direction. When Maria claims that Enrique's heart is a book, her observation comes as no surprise because, with what has been told of Enrique, the claim is legitimate. We have no continuing evidence to the contrary. He is a man of physical sensitivity (his senses, the wound's pain) and of some spiritual sensitivity (lets the bird free, is hurt by Maria), but likened to cool winds, and as he admits, he is without gaiety. A soldier becomes desensitized; that is in the nature of the job. Enrique does in practice talk like a book. Maria's disillusion with war is met with bookish mottoes: one should discuss the living, not the dead. All men, dead or living, are brothers. "Where you die does not matter, if you die for liberty. The thing to do is live and not to die."

There is also a larger, subtler curiosity, another of the story's elements that seems opposed to Enrique's postulate. War is no longer absurd, a "failure," as Maria says, when liberty is defended (so goes Enrique's argument). It has aim. But we are told that a stupid decision has caused

Enrique to be placed in a house that is not directly surveyed because of him; rather, it is watched for the weapons cache. "I should not be put in a house that is being watched for other reasons. It is very Cuban," Enrique says. Presumably the Negro watched the house before Enrique's arrival. Cruelly, then, Enrique's death comes as an accident, a joke which reinforces Maria's claim that war *is* without meaning. It would be possible to read the story ironically as Hemingway's adroit suggestion that war is indeed meaningless. Other Hemingway stories certainly would support an ironic reading. As the story stands, however, nothing happens to prove irony; in fact, the contrary belief, war's meaningfulness, is shown by Enrique's death, which war ennobles, and Maria is given self-understanding and confidence as she approaches her own death.

The inconsistency is that the plot up to the philosophical revelation seems antiwar in tone. It "seems" so because nowhere is an avowed position declared contrarily; one learns by what the story suggests, that is, the stupidity which has placed Enrique in a watched house. Post-revelation (which Enrique has avowedly declared and which Hemingway then supports by the plotting), the story embraces a clichéd and illogical war stance. The writer's imagination has thus failed to appreciate the implications of his material; Hemingway has grafted a convenient shape onto what he had brought to life in the story's first half.

The consequences show up first with the story's grosser aspects, the imaginative failure that has allowed a prefabricated ending for the plot complete with hackneyed symbolism (Maria's "face shining in the arc light"). They show up second in the story's style and tone, a failure that has allowed style and tone to be ineptly wedded to the war philosophy. In short, style, tone, and philosophy have no organic connection.

Hemingway's stories routinely go about their business by working from nuances in style. His style has reason for being selectively tight-lipped: to provide possibilities for unspoken meanings that are partly the reader's job to flesh out. Hemingway will drop hints, but much of what is meant falls on the reader's shoulders. A story like "Nobody Ever Dies!" has the famous style as well as an outspoken meaning, a meaning which seems self-contradictory and redundant. If the style is to cause the reader to fill in gaps, come to conclusions, then why has it been allowed to introduce naked, unequivocal meaning? Is it not the style's duty to handle what the plot proposes, as though placed on a billboard? The story is clearly at artistic cross-purposes.

One result of this corruption of style and tone is a swing toward parody, such as we find in a paragraph of passion that follows the lovers' new mutual understanding:

Then, in the dark on the bed, holding himself carefully, his eyes closed, their lips against each other, the happiness there with no pain, the being home suddenly there with no pain, the being alive returning and no pain, the comfort of being loved and still no pain; so there was a hollowness of loving, now no longer hollow, and the two sets of lips in the dark, pressing so that they were happily and kindly, darkly and warmly at home and without pain in the darkness, there came the siren cutting, suddenly, to rise like all the pain in the world. It was the real siren, not the one of the radio. It was not one siren. It was two. They were coming both ways up the street.

The main sentence is the longest in the story. It falls into two parts. The first gathers Enrique's sensations and tells us that this bout of lovemaking, the wound notwithstanding, delivers happiness; whereas the second tells us that before—with Maria?—there had been a "hollowness of loving." That is, Enrique, a man with a cool heart, felt nothing before this moment. Now something has broken through, just as the wound broke through to Maria, and he can kiss her as she kisses him, "happily and kindly, darkly and warmly." The sentence, with its accumulated impressions, its singsong and repetitive syntax, tries to suggest the lovers' ecstasy. As their emotions wash over them, feeling washes through the sentence.

We could break the sentence up as a poem to show this locomotion, as well as the characteristics of the language:

> the happiness there with no pain
> the being home suddenly there with no pain,
> the being alive returning and no pain
>
> . . .
>
> there was a hollowness of loving,
> now no longer hollow

and so on. Pet words skip through the sentence: no pain, no pain, no pain, without pain, like all the pain; being alive, being loved; hollowness, hollow; in the dark, in the dark. Some words are then joined, as in: without pain in the darkness. This flight of poetic prose is to be a correlative of their lovemaking. As the words rise into poetry, so do Enrique and Maria. The breathy, panting sentence, the story's lone occasion of expansive prose, rather than gracefully apostrophizing these lovers, blasphemes them. Who can take them, lost in a froth of doggerel, seriously now? One can partly blame the sentence's elements for the description's defeat, too many repetitions, but the dialogue that prepares for the bliss has also been corrupted and thus gives the long sentence an unhappy, bathetic prelude that colors the reading of the sentence. Of the wound we are told:

"Does it hurt always?"
"Only when I am touched or jarred."

.   .   .

"Enrique, please forgive me."
"There is nothing to forgive. But it is not nice that I cannot make love and I am sorry that I am not gay."

.   .   .

"And I will take care of you."
"No. I will take care of you. I do not mind this thing at all. Only the pain of touching or jarring. It does not bother me. Now we must work."

Enrique's courage, far from earning our admiration, brings about giggles. He is too stoic, too blithe about his wound ("that grotesque scar from the wound the surgeon had pushed his rubber-gloved fist through in cleaning, which had run from one side of the small of his back through to the other"). His admission of lacking gaiety is funny for its stiff-upper-lip gawkiness, the humorless and somehow vaguely self-pitying delivery. These lovers seem to be in the process of translating from another language, of being cued from the wings as they speak their lines.

My claim is not that the dialogue, word for word, is badly written. Following, for example, Maria's entry into the house, it moves easily and with logic. What weakens the later dialogue is not Hemingway's ability to record human speech as it is spoken, but the assembly of words and the task that it is asked to discharge. The use of words to service ideas taints their honesty. We cannot believe how the lovers talk because we cannot believe what they say. As soon as the dialogue rehearses bald philosophy, it begins to sound like parody. Style coupled with a premade, often incongruous set of ideas moves writing toward parody. A mock-up of Dr. Johnson's sentences without direction may be entertaining but not parody. Join it with Marxist declarations or suppository advertising and the inclination for parody becomes irresistible.

What we have with "Nobody Ever Dies!" is a queer entity whose parts fit slickly together to make a handbook's schematic whole whose gears mesh; yet a whole that is disappointing and not true. The disastrous crippling may be that the story advances by formula and not the spontaneously selective inspiration that produced "Big Two-Hearted River." Hemingway's decision to push the story in the direction it follows is, as

Baker says, to choose a sentimental ending, one that is easily located and snapped into place. The cool wind, the mockingbird, the Negro, the wound, the martyr's death—have we not seen these elements before in other Hemingway? Placed at the disposal of mottoes, they carry no weight and could have been chosen from a parodist's wicked catalog of what you need to do Hemingway. There may be a line which great writers occasionally, unintentionally, cross—a line which separates sublime from ludicrous, which divides original from parody. The slightest miscalculation can shove a writer, unawares, over the line. Beerbohm's genius was to recognize where to place this marker, and then to sketch in, from the other side, his perverse and witty mirrors. "Nobody Ever Dies!" is the occasional example of Hemingway's stumbling—the wobbling across the border into parody, so that the result, seemingly ordered as well as any other Hemingway story, nevertheless is a parodist's naughty dream, a perverse mirror of the real thing.

Hemingway's "Out of Season": The End of the Line

William Adair

●

In *A Moveable Feast* Hemingway said that the first story he wrote after "losing everything"—that is, after most of his story manuscripts had been stolen—was "Out of Season" and that the "real end" of the story (based on his new theory of omission) was that "the old man hanged himself" after the story's conclusion.[1] But the statement hasn't met with universal belief; it's been argued instead that Hemingway is creating a fictionalized version of his past.[2] To some extent he probably was, but I want to suggest that he was telling the truth when he said that the real end, the omitted part, of the story was that the old fishing guide hanged himself.

In a December 1925 letter to F. Scott Fitzgerald, written almost two years after the completion of "Out of Season"—a story composed during a holiday in Cortina, Italy—Hemingway said,

> When I came in from the unproductive fishing trip I wrote that story right off on the typewriter without punctuation. I meant it to be a tragic [sic] about the drunk of the guide because I reported him to the hotel owner—the one who appears in Cat in the Rain—and he fired him and as that was the last job he had in town and he was quite drunk and very desperate, hanged himself in the stable. At that time I was writing the In Our Time chapters and I wanted to write a tragic story *without* violence. So I didn't put in the hanging. Maybe that sounds silly. I didn't think the story needed it.[3]

It seems incredible of course that Hemingway wrote a story and that during the writing, or immediately afterward, his fishing guide of that afternoon hanged himself and, further, that this became what the story was "about." But even if we assume that a hanging didn't take place (then, and as a consequence of Hemingway's complaint to the hotel owner), this isn't enough to invalidate his statement that the Peduzzi *of the story* hangs himself or that the story is "about" Peduzzi and is an early attempt at the omission style of composition.

Perhaps Hemingway had *heard* a story about a village drunk losing his job and hanging himself. (Other of his short stories and many of his vignettes were based on stories heard.) Or he might have *imagined* the hanging after reporting the old man. So if he considered it part of the story—and I see no good reason to doubt that he did—then it's something he must have known or imagined before writing the story, not something that happened *then*.

Nor does Hemingway's remark to Fitzgerald that the story doesn't need the hanging suggest that it was a dramatic afterthought and not originally in the story. The comment implies instead that the hanging is something that can be omitted yet felt by the reader. (Indeed, we may think that a story like "A Canary for One" might have been better if its punch-line ending had been omitted. And if the war had been mentioned in "Big Two-Hearted River," it would have reduced that story to a kind of clinical illustration of war trauma.) So it's omitted—but it's a rare reader who "feels" it.

Also of interest is Hemingway's comment to Fitzgerald that he was trying to write a tragic (he uses the word loosely) story without violence. Hemingway had written to Gertrude Stein about this time telling her that he was following her advice about writing and asking for more help.[4] And it's likely that she discouraged him from writing stories violent and shocking—pictures *inaccrochable* or unhangable, as we hear in *A Moveable Feast* (15). Also, Hemingway had recently been visiting Ezra Pound, and as a Pound critic puts it, Pound often "scolded that part of Hemingway that seemed eager for violence."[5] So that Hemingway was trying to write a tragic story with no violent, dramatic action in it—the marital tension and its omitted source hardly seems enough for a story, unless the omission was of something major—makes good sense.[6]

Perhaps Stein also suggested to Hemingway that he try for a kind of autobiographical realism in his writing; and the cantos (viii–xi) that Pound was then working on include not only that "factive personality," Sigismundo Malatesta, but also fragments of speeches and of a letter once stolen from Malatesta's mail. If Hemingway were writing from life, then it may be fruitful to consider the background, because both "Out of Season" and "Cat in the Rain"—for which he had taken notes shortly before writing "Out of Season"—seem to a great extent to be autobiographical stories; they both seem painterly arrangements, so to speak, of current experiences in Hemingway's life.

After spending Christmas and the early part of the following year

(1923) in Chamby, Switzerland, Hemingway and his wife went to Rapallo, Italy, to visit Pound and Mike Strater.[7] Again, in Rapallo Hemingway made notes for what was later to be "Cat in the Rain." And the story seems close to life. For instance, Strater was then painting seascapes, and in the story's opening paragraph we hear about painters working in Rapallo. And the short, blunt sentences of most of the opening paragraph seem comparable to the rough, textured brush strokes of a Cézanne painting. (Stein had made attempts to model fiction on modern painting, by the way, and Hemingway told her that in "Big Two-Hearted River" that he was trying to do the country like Cézanne.)[8] The story itself has a painterly quality. "Cat in the Rain" is largely a matter of composition or arrangement, balance and repetition: a trip down and up the stairs, the story ending as it begins, two cats, two pairs of characters, etc. Physical posture is also important: we have six vertical figures (if we include the statue of the soldier on the war memorial) and a seventh figure reclining, the young husband. Also, in Rapallo Hemingway got his first look at T. S. Eliot's new poem, "The Waste Land," and we find in "Cat in the Rain" a restless, unhappy lady sitting at her mirror, as we do in the "Game of Chess" section of Eliot's poem. In fact, the entire story seems to have a wasteland mood and theme.[9] Carlos Baker says that Hemingway saw two cats playing on a green table in the hotel garden and wrote a poem about them which mocked Eliot's poem and that the cats and table get into "Cat in the Rain." The tall hotel owner seems drawn from life—he's in the background of "Out of Season," Hemingway told Fitzgerald. Hemingway also told Fitzgerald that the young man in "Cat in the Rain" was a "Harvard kid" that he had met at a conference the year before in Genoa— that is, the young husband (except for the college degree) in the story is like Hemingway, a newspaper correspondent.[10]

From Rapallo Hemingway and his wife went with the Pounds on a walking tour of Piombino and Orbetello, where Malatesta (again, Pound was then working on the Malatesta cantos) had defeated Alphonse of Aragon in 1448. Hemingway showed Pound how Malatesta probably had fought there. And no doubt Pound filled him in on this remarkable Italian Renaissance figure, a soldier and patron of the arts.

Then Hemingway and his wife went to Cortina. And there, as he said, after an unproductive day of fishing, he came in and quickly wrote "Out of Season," which was "an almost literal transcription of what happened." Like "Cat in the Rain," it too is drawn from life (with the likely exception of the suicide).

And "Out of Season" is, we notice, a story much like "Cat in the Rain." In both stories we have a young couple not communicating very well (a lack of communication and mixed signals is general in both stories). Each story presents an unsuccessful quest, for fish, for a cat. Each story has, in addition to the young couple, an old man (the fishing guide in one, the hotel owner in the other) and a second girl (the girl at the Concordia who serves the marsalas and the maid with the umbrella). "Cat in the Rain" ends with the hotel owner sending a cat up to the young couple's room; "Out of Season" ends with the young man about to leave word with the "same" hotel owner. It rains in one story and sprinkles in the other. Both stories take place on holiday at an "out of season" place.[11] They both seem "Waste Land" stories (Peduzzi is a kind of aging, unsuccessful fisher king, a digger of frozen manure), with the hint of World War I hovering in the background (the war memorial, Peduzzi's claim of having been a soldier and his military jacket). Also, the "young gentleman"— perhaps he too is a Harvard grad—of "Out of Season" may be a newspaper correspondent, like the young man of "Cat in the Rain" (the Harvard man Hemingway had met at the Genoa conference): he thinks about Max Beerbohm drinking Marsala, a fact that Hemingway had picked up at the Genoa conference a year before. In fact it may be the same young man (and young couple) in both stories, and the same quarrel being carried on. The similarity of the two stories again suggests that Hemingway was writing from life.

And if both these stories are taken from the writer's life, then Hemingway's visit to Piombino (which came between his stays in Rapallo and Cortina) and perhaps the example of Malatesta may have some interpretive bearing on "Out of Season."

Malatesta, one-time captain of Venice, *condottiere* (not unlike the modern Arditi young Hemingway so admired), lover, and well-known patron of the arts, may have fired Hemingway's imagination; indeed, he is a "romantic" and finally defeated figure somewhat like General Ney, another Hemingway hero.[12] Perhaps Hemingway associated Peduzzi with Malatesta. Peduzzi, a former soldier, is now, like Malatesta, a man who has seen the final ruin of all his hopes; he is a man at the end of his luck, humiliated at the end of his life. (Hemingway's penchant for silently evoking the reader's pity also implies that the story is essentially "about" Peduzzi, not the young man and wife.)

More important I think is the word "Piombino." The word means plummet, plumb line.[13] Perhaps lead, *piombo*, was got from the earth at Piombino. Be that as it may, landscape was always significant to Hemingway, in and out of his fiction; it's easy to imagine him asking the learned Pound the meaning of "piombino" and "piombo" and getting in reply a long list of meanings (some of which are given below). As it turns out, the word *piombo* is associated not only with Malatesta (and the terrain of his battle) but with old Peduzzi too.

As "cat" (and "kitty") is repeated often in "Cat in the Rain," so toward the end of "Out of Season" "piombo" (and "lead") is used in rapid repetition: it appears nine times in less than half a page. It is likely that this repetition means something in addition to Peduzzi's disappointment and excitement.

The word has various meanings that may have some relation to the story: *piombare nella miseria* means to sink into poverty; a *piombone* is a lazy man; a *piombonatore* is a cesspool emptier (Peduzzi spades frozen manure); *cadere di piombonatore* means to fall suddenly, violently; *piombo* is a dressmaking term meaning to hang or fall; *i Piombi* (the Leads) is a prison in the Doges' palace in Venice (the young wife mentions jail); *piombo* can mean both bullet and kingfisher.

In the story, of course, it means the lead used to hang at the end of a fishing line (a small sinker). And it seems likely that the repetition of the word—like a splash of red paint on a gray canvas or a Stein-like repetition that calls for readerly attention—implies the hanging: Peduzzi ("ped" may imply "at the foot of") hanging from a rope, as a lead sinker hangs from the end of a fishing line.

Also, just before this repetition of the word "piombo," the young wife mentions "the game police," and the young man fears that a gamekeeper or a "posse" (a hanging posse?) of citizens may suddenly come after them. We hear about a high campanile (which would have a rope hanging from the bell) seen over the edge of a hill. We even get a sudden close-up shot of Peduzzi's neck (after he finds that they have no *piombo*): "The gray hairs in the folds of his neck oscillated as he drank." Seven lines later come the words "stretched out." Perhaps we should also notice that at the story's beginning Peduzzi is twice called "mysterious."[14] "Mystery" is a word Hemingway sometimes associated with his omission theory.

So it's a matter of words: "mysterious," "posse," "neck," "stretched out," and the suddenly and oft repeated "piombo," a weight to hang at the end of a line.

Apparently this is why Hemingway thought that the story didn't need the hanging (*in* the story). He thought it well enough implied that the "quite drunk and very desperate" and humiliated old man, whose mood quickly goes down, then up, and then down again near the story's end (and down to rock bottom later when he is fired) hangs himself.

And the story's final words ("I will leave word with the padrone at the hotel office," the young gentleman tells Peduzzi), words that lead to the suicide, give us an ironic ending, for the word left with the hotel owner has quite a different effect than the young gentleman imagines—as the cat sent up to the room by the "same" hotel owner in "Cat in the Rain" has a different effect than he supposed it would.[15]

Perversion and the Writer in "The Sea Change"

Robert E. Fleming

●

Ernest Hemingway's "The Sea Change," first published in 1931, has been one of his least popular stories among critics. Carlos Baker accorded only half a paragraph to the story in *The Writer as Artist* and referred to it in *Ernest Hemingway: A Life Story* as a "curious story, a lesser twin to 'Hills Like White Elephants.'"[1] While Philip Young made several perceptive points in his book-length study of Hemingway, among them discussions of the two literary allusions in the story, he did so primarily in footnotes, as if "The Sea Change" did not merit extensive treatment.[2] But "The Sea Change" is considerably more important in the Hemingway canon than has heretofore been recognized. A coherent reading of the story requires the correct interpretation of the two literary allusions; an understanding of the interaction, even tension, between the allusions makes it clear that Phil, the male protagonist of "The Sea Change," is a writer and that his perversion is more degrading than the lesbian tendencies of his former lover. Phil wants her to come back and tell him "all about" her sexual experiences not just to satisfy his morbid curiosity but to furnish the material he needs for his writing. Hemingway is dealing with meanings of "perversion" in a way that recalls a key idea of Hawthorne: "The Unpardonable Sin might consist in a want of love and reverence for the Human Soul; in consequence of which, the investigator pried into its dark depths, not with a hope or purpose of making it better, but from a cold philosophical curiosity,—content that it should be wicked in what ever kind or degree, and only desiring to study it out. Would not this, in other words, be the separation of the intellect from the heart?"[3]

Several prevalent misreadings of "The Sea Change" arise from critics' emphasis of the passage Phil attempts to quote from Alexander Pope's *An Essay on Man*: it reads

> Vice is a monster of so frightful mien,
> As, to be hated, needs but to be seen;

> Yet seen too oft, familiar with her face,
> We first endure, then pity, then embrace.
> But where th' Extreme of Vice, was ne'er agreed.[4]

Following Philip Young's lead, Joseph DeFalco centers his interpretation on this passage, arguing that Phil is in effect stating his willingness to embrace the vice that he has previously hated. DeFalco suggests that the relationship between Phil and the young woman "has been unrecognized vice,"[5] based on her remarks to Phil: " 'We're made up of all sorts of things. You've known that. You've used it well enough.' "[6] DeFalco takes this statement to mean that "the woman has appealed to [Phil] on the grounds that he too has perverse tendencies."[7] However, if Phil is a writer, as suggested by other elements in the story, her comment makes much more sense: He has used "all sorts of things" in human nature to enrich his writing.

But the sexual motif has found continued favor with critics. J. F. Kobler is willing to go further along DeFalco's line of reasoning to state that Hemingway is sympathetic to homosexuality in the story. The change that takes place in Phil during the course of the discussion seems to Kobler to be the result of capitulation to homosexual tendencies in himself: "There can be no question that he is moving toward a homosexual affair. He is about to embrace that which he earlier categorized as a vice."[8] Yet even Kobler finds it hard to believe that his single experience with lesbianism should have unleashed homosexual tendencies in Phil. Sheldon Grebstein seems on far safer ground when he observes that the ending of the story "implies a general perversion of character, a deduction supported by the story's conclusion which hints at the man's degradation. By permitting the girl's adventure, he is more culpable than she in living it."[9]

That homosexuality should be viewed not as Phil's own vice but as an effective metaphor for a writer's perverse willingness to use others for the sake of his art is suggested in an alternate ending for the story Hemingway discarded in favor of the existing conclusion. Among the manuscript versions of the story is a fragment in which Phil moves to the bar after his female companion has left the cafe; in view of his own recent conversion, Phil asks the bartender for the kind of drink that a "punk" might order.[10] As in the beginning of "The Light of the World," Hemingway uses the slang term "punk" to mean homosexual. This discarded ending might seem to support Kobler's contention that Phil has indeed been converted to homosexuality, and it is probably for that very reason that Hemingway omitted it; another explicit link between Phil and homosexuality might mislead the reader into taking literally an allusion intended to be a metaphor for what Phil has discovered himself to be, an exemplar of the "Extreme of Vice." Thus, Hemingway does not so much condone the lesbian affair of the woman as imply that the man's vice is a worse evil; the ending he chose emphasizes Phil's feelings of guilt rather than his sin. The specific nature of that sin is most clearly suggested by the title.

The "sea change" of the title, as Philip Young pointed out so long ago, alludes to "Ariel's Song" in Shakespeare's *The Tempest*:

> Full fathom five thy father lies;
> Of his bones are coral made;
> Those are pearls that were his eyes:
> Nothing of him that doth fade
> But doth suffer a sea-change
> Into something rich and strange.[11]

The sea change of "Ariel's Song" is a transformation of decaying human materials into bright coral and rich pearls. Surely if Phil is undergoing a change from heterosexual to homosexual, Hemingway could have used such a title only to underscore the most bitter irony, for his attitude toward homosexuality is, from first to last, anything but understanding. Even Kobler briefly notes Jake Barnes' attitude toward the male homosexuals who are with Brett Ashley when she makes her first appearance in *The Sun Also Rises*. Jake says, "somehow they always made me angry. I know they are supposed to be amusing, and you should be tolerant, but I wanted to swing on one, any one, anything to shatter that superior, simpering composure."[12] Other unsympathetic depictions of homosexuals appear in "A Simple Enquiry" (1927), *Death in the Afternoon* (1932), "The Mother of a Queen" (1933), and *A Moveable Feast* (1964). It seems unlikely that a writer who otherwise presents such a monolithic viewpoint should alter it in one short story.

Since the change from heterosexual to homosexual is unlikely to be considered positively, and since the title is unlikely to be applied only with such distorted irony, Hemingway must mean that something "rich and strange," something of value, was to grow from the perversion of Phil's former lover as well as from the ruins of their blighted relationship. The explanation of how this change is possible is not readily apparent in the text of the story; the key to the connection between the title and Phil's ultimate recognition of his own perversion is, in fact, "the thing left out" of the story in accordance with Hemingway's theory of constructing his stories on what he termed "the principle of the iceberg."[13] The importance of the omission was emphasized by Hemingway himself in an essay written in 1959: "In a story called 'A Sea Change,' [sic] everything is left out. . . . I knew the story too too well. . . . So I left the story out. But it is all there. It is not visible but it is there."[14] The omission that provides a logical connection between the title of the story and its ending—as well as explains the puzzling details—is Phil's occupation.

Identifying Phil as a writer of fiction causes the details of the story to fall into place. First of all, if Phil is a writer, "Ariel's Song" reads perfectly as a description of the creative process of transforming life or reality into something more enduring, more beautiful—art. An author takes the materials of life, which he may obtain through a sort of heartless observation of fellow human beings and even of himself, and transmutes them, if he is lucky, into something that is indeed "rich and strange." Morley Callaghan reports that Hemingway told him during their apprenticeship on the Toronto *Star*, "even if your father is dying and you are there at his side and heartbroken you have to be noting every little thing going on, no matter how much it hurts"; at about this same time, Hemingway also told Callaghan, "a writer is like a priest. He has to have the same feeling about his work."[15]

A second reason why it is logical to assume that Phil is a writer is that Hemingway so frequently uses writers as characters in his fiction, which contains a whole gallery of authors treated rather unsympathetically. In *The Sun Also Rises* Jake Barnes is an unpretentious journalist who is contrasted with writers such as Robert Prentiss, Braddocks (Cohn's "literary friend"), and Robert Cohn himself, who may be capable of using his "affair with a lady of title" in some future book.[16] Hubert Elliot writes about a life he is too timid to experience in "Mr. and Mrs. Elliot," and the ruined writer Harry, of "The Snows of Kilimanjaro," has made a living by prostituting his own vitality, first for readers and then for a succession of wealthy wives. Mr. Frazer of "The Gambler, the Nun, and the Radio" is an ineffectual observer who is contrasted with the Mexican gambler who lives by a code, as the phrase-maker apparently cannot. Although there are some positive examples of writers as well, from Bill Gorton of *The Sun Also Rises* to Robert Jordan of *For Whom the Bell Tolls*, Hemingway more often than not depicts authors unfavorably or at least ambiguously.

Hemingway recognized that it was possible for the writer to go even further in his abandonment of his humanity in favor of art if he manipulated other people so that he could use them as sources for his fiction. Richard Gordon of *To Have and Have Not* is such a writer. In a lengthy argument with Gordon, his wife Helen suggests that his sexual affair with the wealthy and exotic Helène Bradley is motivated by his curiosity: basically he is searching for new material. The ultimate insult that Helen can think of in her fight with Gordon is simply, "you writer."[17] Grebstein is correct when he asserts that Phil is "more culpable" than the woman in "The Sea Change" because Phil is motivated not by emotional attachment or something within his own sexual nature that he cannot resist but by a cool and detached intellectual certainty that he has more to gain if he lets his mistress go than if he convinces her to give up her lover and stay with him. Phil is overcome by the Faustian desire to barter his personal and human relationship with the woman in exchange for the chance to use her possibly tragic experience as material for his fiction. Little wonder that his voice changes to such a degree that he cannot recognize it as his own when he sends her away; he is aware of the depth to which he has fallen, the temptation to which he has succumbed, by sacrificing the relationship they share for his art. Underscoring his self-realization and the internal change which has taken place, Hemingway states that Phil "was not the same-looking man as he had been before he had told her to go" (400–401) and Phil says to the barman, "'I'm a different man James. . . . You see in me quite a different man'" (401). Like Hawthorne's Roger Chilling-worth, Phil feels that his external appearance should reflect his inner corruption. While Phil feels perverted and dirty and comments that "'vice . . . is a very strange thing,'" the barman, in a characteristic touch of Hemingway irony, sees only externals and assures him he looks "'very well'" (401).

Both literary allusions thus have a logical organic relationship to the story when the reader realizes that Phil is a writer. In fact the allusions work together, producing a tension that reflects the writer's dilemma. Phil's desire to embalm his mistress as a character in a literary work of art becomes so strong that his roles as man and lover are secondary to his role as an artist; in spite of his realization of what he is doing, at the end of the story he embraces the "monster of Vice," perhaps even the "Extreme of Vice." He has been seduced by the possibility that the product of the writer's unprincipled violation of confidence can be something as "rich and strange" as the pearls and coral of Shakespeare's own somewhat macabre sea change. The negative aspects of Pope's words and the positive connotations of Shakespeare's provide symbolic poles for the conflict and the nature of the artist. Both allusions are implicit in the words of Phil's mistress: "'We're made up of all sorts of things. You've known that. You've used it well enough'" (400).

Like Hawthorne characters such as Ethan Brand and Dr. Rappaccini, Phil is risking his integrity to achieve something he believes in totally. The story is open-ended: the reader cannot know whether the creative work of art will justify Phil's sacrifice, whether Phil the human being will survive the ruthlessness of Phil the artist. But the implication of the title, with its suggestion of a miraculous transformation of corrupt materials, may be indicative of Hemingway's own point of view on the nature of art and the function of the artist. Aside from possible autobiographical implications, "The Sea Change," read as a writer's moment of self-recognition, at the very least offers yet another aspect of Hemingway's exploration of the writer and the demands of his art.

Coming of Age in Hortons Bay:
Hemingway's "Up in Michigan"

Alice Hall Petry

●

In sharp contrast to the pantheon of Ernest Hemingway's "bitch goddesses"—those women, tough of mind, body, and spirit, who compromise or destroy the lives of those around them—there exists a small company of female characters of a more tender sort: Catherine Barkley of *A Farewell to Arms*, Maria of *For Whom the Bell Tolls*, and the patient and thoughtful Helen of "The Snows of Kilimanjaro." But perhaps Hemingway's most touching portrait of a female character appears in one of his earliest tales: she is Liz Coates of "Up in Michigan," written in December 1921, and printed in Paris in *Three Stories and Ten Poems* during the summer of 1923. What remarkably little critical attention "Up in Michigan" has received has tended to be of an oddly tangential nature. Historically, it is noted for being one of the few survivors of the infamous "lost suitcase" disaster of December 1922. Stylistically, it has usually been cited for its indebtedness to Sherwood Anderson and Gertrude Stein,[1] rather than for its intrinsic merits. But "Up in Michigan" is more carefully wrought than the rather pejorative label of "apprentice work" might lead one to believe. The primary sources of the story's excellence are Hemingway's sympathetic etching of Liz, the gentle, ingenuous kitchen maid whose sexual initiation he so graphically records, and his powerful depiction of the glaring disparity between male and female attitudes toward love and sex.

Unusually for Hemingway, the story is told essentially from Liz's point of view rather than from that of the main male character, Jim Gilmore. Although this is Liz's story, it begins—surprisingly but appropriately—with a description not of Liz but of Jim, the object of her infatuation and the agent of her downfall: "Jim Gilmore came to Hortons Bay from Canada. He bought the blacksmith shop from old man Horton. Jim was short and dark with big mustaches and big hands. He was a good horseshoer and did not look much like a blacksmith even with his leather apron on. He lived upstairs above the blacksmith shop and took his meals at D.J. Smith's" (SS 81).[2] The description deals entirely with simple facts of the sort which anyone in Hortons Bay might know about Jim, plus elements of his physical appearance. In short, all that is revealed about Jim are externals which tell absolutely nothing about Jim's personality, values, or intelligence, those comparative abstractions upon which love, in the mature sense of the word, is to be based. What little more that we learn of Jim in the course of the story—that he reads the area newspapers, likes to fish and hunt, and drinks whiskey—still are external elements which do not flesh Jim into a man. By virtue of the paucity of information about Jim, then, Hemingway conveys the fact that we have no sense of Jim's being worthy of the love of Liz or of anyone else, for that matter. In E. M. Forster's phraseology, Jim is a "flat" character, and an entirely physical one at that.

But it is precisely her limited and superficial knowledge of a man which would tend to generate infatuation in an inexperienced young girl, and in fact, in a passage redolent of the technique of Gertrude Stein in *Three Lives* and *The Making of Americans*,[3] we learn that Liz Coates' interest in Jim is indeed based upon such limited knowledge:

> Liz liked Jim very much. She liked it the way he walked over from the shop and often went to the kitchen door to watch for him to start down the road. She liked it about his mustache. She liked it about how white his teeth were when he smiled. She liked it very much that he didn't look like a blacksmith. She liked it how much D.J. Smith and Mrs. Smith liked Jim. One day she found that she liked it the way the hair was black on his arms and how white they were above the tanned line when he washed up in the washbasin outside the house. Liking that made her feel funny. (81)

The compact little catalog nicely conveys the flimsy basis of Liz's infatuation. Beginning with the general remark that "Liz liked Jim very much," Hemingway elaborates the qualities which she finds so intriguing, often using the nongrammatical syntax associated with "puppy love": "She liked it about his mustache." Further, as Sheldon Norman Grebstein points out, the repetition of "She liked" conveys the obsessive nature of her passion,[4] while at the same time suggesting the noncommittal quality of her interest: she "liked" aspects of him, but there is no indication at this stage that she feels her interest would, should, or even could develop into anything more than a rather distant infatuation. It is also significant that at this point in her life Liz still looks to others for justification of her feelings: her liking Jim is condoned, as it were, by the approval of him by the people for whom she works (and whom she evidently perceives as parental figures), the Smiths. As the catalog draws to a close, we learn that Liz "feel[s] funny" about liking the hair on Jim's arms and the whiteness of his upper arms—a part of his body not usually exposed. Hemingway is clearly indicating that her interest in Jim has a strong sexual dimension, but that she is not conscious of this; and, being unable to grasp the concept of sexual attraction, Liz also cannot articulate it: she "felt funny."

The rather pathetic way in which Liz attempts to deal with her erotic awakening is made comprehensible by the information Hemingway provides about her. The reader has it on good authority from Mrs. Smith, "who was a very large clean woman," that Liz was "the neatest girl she'd ever seen" (81). Liz "always wore clean gingham aprons," and even Jim notices that "her hair was always neat behind" (81). The emphasis on Liz's cleanliness and neatness serves, of course, to intensify the crudity of her seduction, but it also conveys the purity, the noncarnal nature of her impulses toward Jim. She is sufficiently young and inexperienced to perceive men in an entirely romanticized light—a tendency strikingly conveyed by her favorite preseduction activity: "From Smith's back door Liz could see ore barges way out in the lake going toward Boyne City. When she looked at them they didn't seem to be moving at all but if she went in and dried some more dishes and then came out again they would be out of sight beyond the point" (82). As the dish-drying suggests, Liz leads a decidedly prosaic life, but it is overlaid by a yearning for something beyond the village of Hortons Bay. The ore barges appeal to her inarticulate romantic nature, but of course they are as inappropriate a repository of her dreams as is Jim, who, by virtue of his occupation, is readily associated with ores. The ore barges also graphically suggest both the fact that she is maturing (like the movement of the barges, her sexual development is a continually on-going process which she barely perceives) and that her horizons are decidedly limited; and in fact Hortons Bay is as much a character in the story as is the heath in Thomas Hardy's *The Return of the Native*. The village consists of "only five houses on the main road between Boyne City and Charlevoix," plus a general store, a post office "with a high false front and maybe a wagon hitched out in front," a Methodist church, the township school, and Jim's blacksmith shop (81–82). Hemingway's quick sketch of tiny Hortons Bay does much to explain Liz's ignorance of male/female relationships—an ignorance so extensive that she does not recognize sexual urges when she feels them. In contrast, Jim comes "from Canada" (81), and by not mentioning a specific Canadian town, Hemingway imbues him with experience (after all, he at least has traveled) and a superficially attractive aura (technically he is a foreigner). The description of Hortons Bay also conveys the sad fact that Liz's seduction probably will become known in such a small town, an insult to be endured with her injury.

Part of what makes her seduction so insulting is that it literally is not what she had in mind. Her sexual urges, neither examined nor articulated, rather pathetically assume a domestic cast. As Jim and some friends prepare to hunt deer in the fall, Liz and Mrs. Smith cook food for them for four days, and Liz "wanted to make something special for Jim to take" (82). She does not do so, however—not because Mrs. Smith would disapprove, but because "Liz was afraid" (82). Both the reader and the effaced narrator share knowledge to which Liz is not privy: that what she fears is her own sexual being. As that being becomes more insistent, Hemingway begins to striate his text with highly sexual situations, diction, and symbols. Consider Hemingway's description of her reaction to Jim's absence on his hunting trip: "She couldn't sleep well from thinking about him but she discovered it was fun to think about him too. If she let herself go it was better" (82). Hemingway has provided what is, in effect, a bedroom scene, which contrasts stridently with her seduction on the warehouse dock. Even the diction is the sort usually applied to coitus: "If she let herself go. . . ." Not surprisingly, "the night before they were to come back she didn't sleep at all, that is she didn't think she slept because it was all mixed up in a dream about not sleeping and really not sleeping" (82–83). Sleeping—that most innocent and most sexual of activities, depending upon context—is mentioned four times in one sentence, and as such beautifully conveys that peculiar limbo of an innocent person experiencing erotic impulses. Similarly, the jumbled quality of the sentence readily suggests Liz's emotional turmoil. Her confused emotions lead, understandably, to vague expectations: "Liz hadn't known just what would happen when Jim got back [from the hunting trip] but she was sure it would be something. [But] Nothing had happened" (83). As a virtual self-fulfilling prophecy, "something" certainly does happen later that day: the seduction. In fine her sense that something "would happen" is accurate; but her lack of experience with sexual matters has precluded the development of a sense of sexual timing. That coitus is in the offing is clear from Hemingway's insistently sexual adjectives and even (taken out of context) his adverbs. Jim has killed "a *big* buck. It was *stiff* and *hard* to lift out of the wagon" (83, my emphasis). Likewise blatantly sexual is the fact that Jim has shot "a beauty" of a deer (83): "to die" is, of course, a traditional euphemism for an orgasm and guns are phallic symbols; and indeed Jim is destined to kill something "beautiful" in Liz. Hemingway's use of sexual diction and puns is so blatant that it seems clear that the very title of the story is an obscenity.[5]

As the very terminology of the story becomes coarsely sexual, Jim himself rapidly loses even the physical attractiveness which Liz finds so fascinating, although, significantly, she evidently does not perceive the loss. Even though Hemingway notes that "the men washed up" before dinner at the Smiths' the night they returned from the deer hunt, it is doubtful that Jim has bathed for days, and it is mentioned that "all the men had beards" (83). Moreover, Jim has been drinking whiskey, some of which has run down his shirt front (83). At this point, his essentially hedonistic character begins to emerge under the influence of alcohol: "Jim began to feel great. He loved the taste and the feel of whiskey. He was glad to be back to a comfortable bed and warm food and the shop" (84). Not surprising for a man whose very livelihood involves animals and brawn rather than humans and brains, Jim is totally oriented toward bodily comfort and pleasure; under the circumstances of inebriation, Jim would naturally regard coitus as the next element in his catalog of physical delights, and at this point he goes—eyes shining and hair rumpled (84)—to seduce the kitchen maid. That he lacks any personal interest in Liz is clearly conveyed. From the opening of the story we know that Jim "liked [Liz's] face because it was so jolly but he never thought about her" (81); likewise, whereas Liz found herself thinking about him "all the time," Jim "didn't seem to notice her much" (82) until, of course, he decided to engage in sexual intercourse. In effect Jim perceives Liz in exclusively sexual terms whereas Liz, due to her innocence, is conscious only of a nonsexual, romanticized attraction to him. The disparity between his fundamental disinterest in her as a person and Liz's romanticized obsession with his exterior is underscored by the fact that when he sought her out in the kitchen, she was waiting for him—but not because she expected a sexual encounter; rather, she had been hoping for a peek at him as he left after dinner "so she could take the way he looked up to bed with her" (84). This pathetic, jarring juxtaposition of the innocent and the erotic is further conveyed by her confused reaction to Jim's fondling her breasts. She was "terribly frightened" but thought "'He's come to me finally. He's really come'" (84). Given her innocence, her thoughts sound derived from a Prince Charming fairytale, and in fact it is doubtful that she comprehended what "it" was when "something clicked inside of her" and "she wanted it now" (84). The disparity between Jim's and Liz's sexual experience and attitudes toward one another renders the seduction scene all the more painful. Jim uses a traditional "make out" line— "'Come on for a walk'" (84)—to invite her outside to fornicate, and apparently Liz takes him at his word, for she grabs her coat (perhaps as the result of an instinctive—albeit ineffectual—impulse to protect and cover herself) and willingly accompanies him to the warehouse. Significantly, the moon—symbol of Diana, the protectress of chastity—is not out that night, and the physical environment through which Jim and Liz move (ankle-deep sand, cold, darkness) is stellar distances from what the romantic Liz would have wished for her first encounter with a man. That she does not resist Jim is attributable to her sexual ignorance: "no one had ever touched her" (84); she "was very frightened and didn't know how he was going to go about things" (85); but even so "she snuggled close to him" (85). Jim's lack of interest in Liz as anything but a sexual object—a fact transparent to both him and the reader, but not to Liz—is suggested by his being reduced to a "big hand" which pays no attention to her protests (85). It is his comparative sexual experience which makes plausible his failure to recognize that her statements—"'You mustn't,'" "'it isn't right'" (85)—are not stock phrases comparable to his "'come on for a walk,'" but rather genuine expressions of fear and doubt. As Liz is effectively immobilized by what Carlos Baker aptly characterizes as the attraction-repulsion phenomenon of sex,[6] Jim declares, "'You know we got to'" (85); and in fact Liz was, in effect, destined to copulate with him, in view of both her ignorance, vulnerability, confusion, and awakening sexuality, as well as Jim's comparative experience.

The enormous disparity between Jim's and Liz's attitudes toward each other and the sex act is also strikingly conveyed by the setting of the seduction and its aftermath. It occurs outside rather than in bed; that is, in a nonprivate, "natural" setting such as would be appropriate for animal copulation. Further, the dock itself is made of hemlock (symbolic of death) and the planks are "hard and splintery and cold and Jim was heavy on her and he had hurt her" (85). The coarse planks contribute to, and are symbolic of, the psychic and physical pain of the sex act, and the striking repetition of the word "and" conveys Liz's rush of negative emotions—emotions which are in no way mitigated by the fact that Jim falls asleep on top of her, "with his mouth a little open" (85). Liz "worked out from under him and sat up and straightened her skirt and coat and tried to do something with her hair" (85), a pathetic attempt to recreate the "neat," "clean" Liz of the opening of the story. But Liz's romantic illusions die hard, despite her brutal initiation into sex. Even though she is crying, cold, and miserable, and though "everything felt gone" (85), she kisses the sleeping drunk; and, as a gesture of her caring for him, tucks her coat "neatly and carefully" around him (86)—a last gasp of the maternal impulse which had previously surfaced as a desire to cook something

special for him.7 Appropriately, a cold mist ends the story as Liz Coates—
now coatless—returns home.

Hemingway tells us nothing of the aftermath of the seduction, and this
fade-out ending is singularly appropriate for this story. We are left with a
poignant sense of a girl caught in the Catch-22 of Western sexual mores:
the very elements which render Liz so attractive—her neatness, cleanliness, youth, innocence, and dawning sexuality—are precisely what set
her up for a disastrous deflowering on a warehouse dock. Small wonder
that Hemingway himself felt that "Up in Michigan" was more sad than
dirty.8

Crazy in Sheridan: Hemingway's "Wine of Wyoming" Reconsidered

Lawrence H. Martin, Jr.

●

On May 31, 1930, Ernest Hemingway wrote from Key West to Maxwell Perkins, his editor at Scribner's, enclosing the typescript of a new story that Perkins had requested for the August 1930 *Scribner's Magazine*. "I think you'll like it," Hemingway promised, adding, "this is a 1st flight story I promise you" (*Letters*, 323).[1] He mentioned that the story was long—6,000 words—and that the dialogue was partly in French. "Don't let anyone tell you it's not a good story or has too much French in it," Hemingway defensively ordered Perkins. "Everybody that reads Scribner's knows some French or knows somebody that knows some French" (*Letters*, 323).[2]

The story was "Wine of Wyoming." Perkins replied by return mail that the story was not only accepted but already in galleys, and *Scribner's Magazine* editor Robert Bridges sent a check for the handsome amount of $600 (Baker, *Life Story*, 270).[3] "Wine of Wyoming" appeared as promised in the August 1930 issue of *Scribner's*, by which date Hemingway had left Key West for his annual working, fishing, and shooting vacation in northern Wyoming, near the locale of the story.

In the early spring of 1932, experiencing what he called "a big revival of belief in the short story" (Baker, *Life Story*, 291, 797), Hemingway began plans for a third collection of stories, some new and some previously published. Writing to Perkins about his plans, Hemingway reported finishing "three fine stories," a number soon increased to seven, with two more in progress (Baker, *Life Story*, 797). Even though Hemingway had not yet finished *Death in the Afternoon* (it would be published in September 1932), he was looking ahead to the 1933 short-story collection *Winner Take Nothing*, which was—save for the anthologies *The Fifth Column and the First Forty-nine Stories* and eventually *The Collected Stories*—his third and last volume of short fiction.

When *Winner Take Nothing* appeared in October 1933, it contained fourteen stories, of which six were new and eight were republished magazine pieces. The new work included some important stories, nota-bly "The Light of the World," "A Way You'll Never Be," and "Fathers and Sons"; other new pieces, for example "A Day's Wait," were of minor merit, and one new "story," if it can be called that, was embarrassingly inferior: "One Reader Writes." The former magazine publications showed a similar range of artistic significance. The virtually definitive Hemingway story "A Clean, Well-Lighted Place," originally published in the March 1933 *Scribner's Magazine,* was included, and "The Gambler, The Nun, and The Radio," also a *Scribner's* piece, was reprinted (it had appeared as "Give Us a Prescription, Doctor" in May 1933). Recapitulat-ing a brilliant three-month run of appearances by Hemingway in *Scribner's* was the April 1933 "Homage to Switzerland." From other perodicals came "God Rest You Merry, Gentlemen" (*House of Books,* April 1933) and "The Sea Change" (*This Quarter,* December 1931). From Hem-ingway's own *Death in the Afternoon* came a modified version of Chapter 12, "A Natural History of the Dead." The lead story of the collection, the signature motif tale of *Winner Take Nothing,* "After The Storm," came from the May 1932 *Cosmopolitan.* The volume's oldest story, in terms of its original date of publication, was "Wine of Wyoming."

The reviewers were not pleased by *Winner Take Nothing.* In fact, the reviews were the worst Hemingway had received in his relatively brief career, and they contributed to a growing abrasiveness between the author and his critics, a feeling that would be crystallized and sharpened in disparaging remarks about critics and criticism in *Green Hills of Africa* (1935) and especially in private opinions and correspondence for the rest of his life.[4] This was not the first time, though, that Hemingway had received bad reviews, merited or unmerited. By 1933 Hemingway had been in the American literary arena a relatively short time, only eight years since the 1925 New York publication of *In Our Time.* Those eight years had been a remarkably productive period, seeing the publication of *In Our Time* (1925), *Torrents of Spring* (1926), *The Sun Also Rises* (1926), *Men Without Women* (1927), *A Farewell to Arms* (1929), and *Death in the Afternoon* (1932), and in addition numerous magazine pieces and the early private-press releases in France.

And Hemingway had in this brief time created, or accumulated, a personal and literary reputation[5] against which his reviewers tended to read succeeding new works. After the laudatory and perceptive 1924 review by Edmund Wilson[6] of the early, experimental *Three Stories and Ten Poems* ("Mr. Hemingway's Dry-Points"), a vocabulary of critical terms epitomizing Hemingway's work began to arise and to become, in effect, one-word summaries of Hemingway's new and then-controversial style and outlook. Relating the style of the *In Our Time* stories to "cubist painting and *Le Sacré du Printemps*," The *New Republic*'s Paul Rosenfeld noted Hemingway's "brute, rapid, joyous jab of period upon period" and his selection of "harsh impersonal forces in the universe . . . blood and pain . . . and brutalities of existence" as subjects (22–23). By the time *The Sun Also Rises* appeared, words such as "futility" ("Study in Futility," 5), "tragedy" ("Marital Tragedy," 27), "detachment" (Aiken, 4), and "hard-boiled" (Tate, 642) were the reviewers' staples. *Men Without Women* elicited "callous" (Dodd, 322), "raw" ("Mr. Hemingway's Stories," 7F), and another "tragedy" (Wilson, "The Sportsman's Tragedy," 102). *A Farewell to Arms* brought Robert Herrick's "What is Dirt?": a comparison of Remarque's *All Quiet on the Western Front*, which in Herrick's opinion (and in censored form) was "literature," and Hemingway's *A Farewell to Arms*, which Herrick considered "mere dirt." However, no less a curmudgeon than H. L. Mencken found the same book a "brilliant evocation of the horrible squalor and confusion of war" (127). Mixed with these observations of the sensational and melodramatic were admiration and praise in varying degrees for Hemingway's mastery of dialogue, economy of language, and basic sense of humanity, though focus and emphasis fell on what one paper, reporting later on *Winner Take Nothing*, called "realism to the point of being grewsome" [sic] ("Hemingway Tales," 7E).

By the time *Winner Take Nothing* was published, certain expectations among reviewers and critics (and readers, it might be assumed) had taken fixed form: that Hemingway had a predictable content and style, specializing in the brutal and the cruel expressed in terse dialogue and unelaborated narration and description.

Having established in the twenties and early thirties an innovative style and narrative technique, chosen frequently shocking subjects, and created a distinctive view of the modern postwar world, Hemingway now found himself a victim of his own invention. What the critics expected, evidently, was "growth," by which they meant intellectual maturity superseding a decade of preoccupation with violence and alienation. One writer archly summarized Hemingway's fault as a fixation upon "eating and drinking, travel, sport [and] coition . . . an enthusiastic *delectatio morbosa*," and accused him of being "in danger of becoming as fin de siècle as his contemporary, William Faulkner" (Troy, 570). While the critics still admired (though less fervently than a decade before) Hemingway's "sharply etched strokes" ("Hemingway's First Book of Fiction in Four Years") and "unforgettable incisiveness" (Canby, 217), they damned in chorus what they now saw as his "monotonous repetition"

(Troy, 570), "strong echoes of earlier work" (Fadiman, 74), and "the same things" (Kronenberger, 6), asking, in the end, "Why bother to redemonstrate it?" (Fadiman, 75).

Against the background of general critical disapproval and even squeamishness, there were a few words of commendation for individual stories in *Winner Take Nothing*. "The Gambler, The Nun, and The Radio" was praised for its full characterization and its tragicomic observations about "the opium of the poor" (*SS*, 478) and "After The Storm" for its sinister atmosphere, though not for any possible political or social implications. "Homage to Switzerland" was cited solely (but correctly) as evidence that Hemingway was "a humorist of the first water" (Butcher, 16). The only story to be mentioned favorably several times was "Wine of Wyoming."

Of those who recognized the significance of "Wine of Wyoming," Horace Gregory, writing for the *New York Herald Tribune*, identified it as one of two stories ("Gambler" was the other) "that show a sudden expansion of Hemingway's range." It was, Gregory claimed, "one of the few instances in contemporary literature where the short story may be regarded as a superlative work of art." Its "emotional truth," Gregory said, "has its source in the most universal of human experiences," and the story was successful because, in Gregory's interpretation, "Hemingway is no longer content to present a situation and then let it answer for itself" (5). In this latter point Gregory was setting "Wine of Wyoming" apart from Hemingway stories to which critics objected on the grounds that the author was far too objective—that he merely "observed, overheard, impaled with his intelligence," as Louis Kronenberger complained in the *New York Times Book Review* (6).

What Gregory broadly called "universal human experience" was defined somewhat more specifically by the *Cincinnati Enquirer*'s reviewer J. R. who found that "an expression of human sympathy" was the dominant quality of "Wine of Wyoming," particularly in the contrast of "the sweet and generous natures of Madame Fontan and her husband" and "the rudeness and vulgarity of their American customers" (7). Perhaps the brevity of a newspaper review cut short further development of this idea; it deserved elaboration, for the contrast of immigrant European generosity and native American crudity is the heart of the story and a comment particularly on the American experience as well as upon "universal experience." Oddly, the European-American tension of the story also drew a negative reading: that Hemingway was indulging in "all the old nostalgias" (Troy, 570)—in this case, nostalgia for an idealized Europe, perceived as the home of a culture superior to the former expatriate author's own. This is a short view and a shallow one, for the French family, the Fontans, generous and sweet as they may be, are bootlegging *paysans* rejecting a strange protestant culture, not European aristocrats, and their clients would still be crude and insensitive regardless of nationality. The tone of the critic's observation is negative, but nostalgia, if that is what it is, for decency in the face of rudeness is neither pretentious nor wrong.

After the 1933 reviews of *Winner Take Nothing*, despite favorable mention, "Wine of Wyoming" went into eclipse. While other Hemingway stories took their place in cultural mythology and school anthologies—is there a student who has not read "The Killers" or "A Clean, Well-Lighted Place"?—"Wine of Wyoming" became a literary orphan. According to the Wagner (1977) and Hanneman (1967, 1975) bibliographies, "Wine of Wyoming" has never been separately reprinted or anthologized. (The odd exception to this bibliographical fact is its translation into many other languages for foreign editions; it can be found in Norwegian, Korean, and Czech, among others.)

The virtual disappearance of "Wine of Wyoming" might be attributed to shortcomings on some scale of artistic excellence, to the macaronic Anglo-French dialogue whose difficulty for readers Hemingway underestimated when he recommended the story to Perkins, or more probably to the fact that in subject and tone the story is not "typical" or "classic" in the received mode of Hemingway's hallmark fiction. It lacks the startling violence of "Indian Camp," the looming threat of "The Killers," the stark alienation of "A Clean, Well-Lighted Place," the enigmatic heroism and death of "The Short Happy Life of Francis Macomber." It is not about aberration ("God Rest You Merry, Gentlemen," "The Sea Change") nor about war. It is, if anything, quite domestic—hardly "Hemingwayesque" in theme and subject. Yet it is quintessentially in the Hemingway fashion in its rhetorical obliqueness, perhaps Hemingway's most distinctive literary trait.

Like almost all of Hemingway's fiction, "Wine of Wyoming" began with the artist's personal experience. After six years in Europe, Hemingway returned to the United States with his second wife Pauline Pfeiffer in the spring of 1928, via Havana to Key West. In the summer of that year, he left Key West for the Rocky Mountains, partly to go fishing but mainly to work on the draft of *A Farewell to Arms* away from the tropical heat and humidity of his new home. After staying at a dude ranch for a few days, Hemingway abruptly left and took up residence at another ranch less frequented by tourists near Sheridan, Wyoming. In Sheridan he took Pauline in late August to meet Charles and Alice Moncini, a French couple who operated a speakeasy at their house, where one could sit "on the vine-shaded back porch drinking cold home-brewed beer, with a view across the yellow grainfields towards the distant brown mountains," and where the Moncinis and the Hemingways "all spoke French together" (Baker, *Life Story*, 252). Because 1928 was a presidential election year, with the vote between the Roman Catholic Alfred E. Smith and the postwar reconstruction expert Herbert Hoover only a few months in the future, conversation turned naturally to politics, as well as to Prohibition; the noble experiment of the Eighteenth Amendment, which the Moncinis (and much of the country) were flouting, had been law since 1920 and would continue so until 1933.

The summer of 1928 was a time of consolidation and recommencing for Hemingway. He had a new marriage, a new son, a new book nearing completion, and, in effect, a new country to enjoy and understand. He had left the United States a newlywed, twenty-two-year-old, unknown "Canadian" newspaperman, and he returned as the established author of four books, one of them the successful and epoch-making *The Sun Also Rises*. He was regarded as an important voice of the new postwar literary generation, and another book solidly confirming his reputation was about to be published. In this interlude full of optimism and promise, it is not surprising that he resolved "whenever it suited him" to "put the Moncinis into a story, a character sketch full of cleanliness and order, a quiet account of simple people who made and drank the wine of Wyoming" (Baker, *Life Story*, 252).

Finishing *A Farewell to Arms* intervened between Hemingway's mention of "good wine and a nice French family" in an August 18, 1928, letter to Guy Hickock (*Letters*, 284) and his May 31, 1930, letter to Perkins accompanying the finished Wyoming story. In those two years a minor incident, doubtless a commonplace in Prohibition days, evolved from a fragmentary anecdote into an extended piece of fiction. Much later, on November 16, 1933, three years after "Wine of Wyoming" first appeared and a few weeks after the reviewers had savaged *Winner Take Nothing,* Hemingway wrote a long letter to Perkins in which he answered the criticism critic by critic and point by point. The letter is remarkable not for Hemingway's rebuttals (a tendency that would grow over the years) or even for the wounded, bitter, and quite personal outbursts against individual critics, but for an assertion of his writing techniques. The explanation is an oversimplification, but even in its *reductio* terms it sets forth a philosophy of artistic composition: "I write some stories absolutely as they happen i.e. Wine of Wyoming, . . . others I invent completely— Killers, Hills Like White Elephants, The Undefeated," Hemingway heatedly told Perkins. Emphatically he added, *"Nobody* can tell which ones I make up completely. . . . The point is I *want* them all to sound as though they really happened." As for the "poor dumb" critics who dismissed his success at this technique as "just skillful reporting," Hemingway retorted, "I'm a reporter *and an imaginative writer* and I can still imagine plenty and there will be stories to write *as they happened* as long as I live" (*Letters*, 400).

Hemingway is referring, of course, to his aesthetic principle of truthfulness, whether reported or created. While it is conceivable that Hemingway's own example "Wine of Wyoming" was recorded "absolutely" as it happened—his biographer Baker says on uncertain evidence that at the Moncinis "Ernest listened intently, watching the faces and trying to remember all that was said" (*Life Story*, 252)—it is evident that this story is more complex, and far more interpretive, than the "skillful reporting" of a *Toronto Star* dispatch.

Verisimilitude was the effect Hemingway had been striving for, and achieving, since the early-twenties vignettes published as the interchapers in *In Our Time*, or perhaps even since the "Paris 1922" manuscript (Baker, *Life Story*, 119–20) or the Michigan "Crossroads" characters of 1919 (Griffin, 124–27). Whether the source was personal experience or inventive imagination, the intended artistic results were the same: actuality, presence, truth. And whether the story was "made up" or "really happened" was unimportant; the important effect was the appearance or "sound" of reality. Hemingway claimed, in fact, that "95 percent of The Sun Also was pure imagination," a numerical analysis that will certainly amuse the historical or biographical reader of that notorious roman à clef. But Hemingway significantly modifies the sense of his claim: he continues, "I took real people in that one and I controlled what they did" (*Letters*, 400), colloquially but concisely defining his philosophy of composition. Although in virtually the same breath Hemingway says that "Wine of Wyoming" is one of the "absolutely" historical stories, historicity is not centrally important. The art of fiction, for Hemingway, was the creation or re-creation of experience, made so vivid and perceptible that the reader vicariously relived the event.

This technique of invented or transmuted actuality finds its most widely recognized expression in Frederic Henry's near-fatal wounding in the Italian trenches (*A Farewell to Arms*), Robert Jordan's last moments in the Spanish forest (*For Whom the Bell Tolls*), or Santiago's agony and endurance on the Gulf Stream (*The Old Man and the Sea*). The apparent tranquility of an afternoon with the Moncinis of Sheridan, Wyoming, differs in both subject and tone from those other dramatic moments of suffering and self-sacrifice, but the artistic goal is the same: to intensify representation into what Hemingway later enigmatically called "a fourth and fifth dimension" (*Green Hills of Africa*, 27).

In "Wine of Wyoming," the technique is applied to the domestic and business affairs of the Fontans—immigrants from the provinces of France—and their customers in the home-brewed beer and wine trade. The setting in the American West (which Hemingway was seeing for the first time in 1928)[7] is mildly unusual but not exotic; the Fontans are fairly common folk, and the narrator is rather noncommittal. The ingredients seem far less promising as literary material than desperate outsiders of Paris or the Gulf or bullfighters or soldiers. Yet the episode at the Moncinis is unpromising material somewhat in the way that a solo fishing trip to the Fox River in Upper Michigan was unpromising. The story that resulted from that trip, a simple, systematic catalog of hiking, making camp, and catching fish, was "a story in which nothing happened" and was therefore "lacking in human interest," according to the half-joking, half-serious 1925 opinion of Princeton University's Dean Gauss and F. Scott Fitzgerald (Baker, *Writer as Artist*, 125). The story, of course, is "Big Two-Hearted River," one of the most remarkable demonstrations of the relationship of surface and subtext in all of Hemingway's writing and one of his best works of fiction.

The primary narrative of "Wine of Wyoming," the surface story, offers charm, local color, and a boyish delight in the minor crime of drinking illegal alcohol. Read only on this level, the story is a deft character sketch mainly of the talkative Mme Fontan who rattles on from incident to opinion to home truth in a non sequitur torrent of anglicized French. The humor falls short of hilarity, but it does justify Carlos Baker's verdict that Hemingway has "unappreciated skills as a comic writer" (*Writer as Artist*, 141). But comedy is not Hemingway's métier (though he does it with skill here and elsewhere), and a character sketch, however deft, is not the story's only merit.

The reviewers of *Winner Take Nothing* in 1933 disapproved of Hemingway's "youthful Red Indian brutality" and demanded instead a "leap forward" or "triumphant advance" (Fadiman, 74–75). The few who diverted their attention from the volume's tough, harsh "The Light of the World" or the ironic, parodic "A Natural History of the Dead" and were independent or original enough to appreciate "Wine of Wyoming" found in it what seemed the antithesis of Hemingway's by then traditional approach. There is certainly the appearance of what Baker not inappropriately called "the championship of the normal and the natural which runs like a backbone through the substance of the tale he elects to tell" (*Writer as Artist*, 141). The Fontans are undeniably good and simple people trying to live a good and simple life in their new land. They make good beer and wine, and their illegal but ordinary business brings relaxation and pleasure to clients who value a good drink in good company. Nothing could be more "normal" than this. The generous, voluble Fontans in their cool and pleasant wine garden inhabit a world that seems completely different from the café of "A Clean, Well-Lighted Place."

But beneath the surface of the Fontans' "simple . . . cleanliness and order" is a world surprisingly discordant and ungovernable. Their world fortunately lacks the horror of *nada* and the infinite despair held at bay only by order and light and warmth, but it is nonetheless a world where things go wrong, where hopes and wishes fail, and where calm order is always under threat.

The opening episode is a thematic statement of the story's tension between order and disorder, satisfaction and disappointment, completeness and incompleteness. The unnamed narrator is relaxing in the shade of the Fontans' back porch, about to drink the cold beer that Mme Fontan has brought from the cellar. A car arrives, two men get out, and one abruptly demands, "Where's Sam?" When Mme Fontan replies, "He ain't here. He's at the mines," the visitor asks with equal abruptness, "You got some beer?" Mme Fontan retorts, "That's a last bottle. All gone." Protesting "You know me," the man asks again for some beer, but Mme Fontan maintains, "Ain't got any beer." The men leave, one of them walking unsteadily. Mme Fontan solicitously tells the narrator that he can drink his beer, which he had placed out of sight on the floor, and explains her actions: "They're drunk. That's what makes the trouble" (*SS*, 450). Later she confides to the narrator a shocking, amazing incident: "Americans came here and they put whiskey in the beer . . . Et aussi une femme qui a vomis sur la table! Et après elle a vomis dans ses shoes" (460). Her husband remembers the beer-and-whiskey drinkers and their girl-friends, and he sums them up: "'Cochon,' he said delicately, hesitating to use such a strong word. 'C'est un mot très fort, . . . mais vomir sur la table'—he shook his head sadly." The narrator, understated until now, agrees: "That's what they are—cochons. Salauds." Some of the customers who drink at the Fontans' may be "pigs" and "dirty bastards," but others are a better class of clientele. Mme Fontan is at pains to make the point that "Il y a des gens très gentils, très sensibles, qui viennent aussi." On one beer-drinker, an army officer, her husband agrees: "C'est un original . . . mais vraiment gentil. He's a nice fella" (461).

The friendly and agreeable Fontans, who provide good beer and wine and companionship in a puritanically "dry" country, can't comprehend the eagerness of drinkers who mix moonshine whiskey in well-made beer and thus intentionally make themselves so drunk that they vomit on the table and on their own shoes. "My God," says the incredulous Mme Fontan, "I don't understand *that!*" (460). What she doesn't understand is the drinkers' enthusiasm for extreme sensations and their unwillingness or inability to appreciate the moderate sociableness of drinking a product that she and her husband are proud of.

The Fontans are abused and insulted not only by their rougher customers but by the Volstead Act enforcers. Arrested and convicted three times for violation of the Prohibition law, M. Fontan has been imprisoned and fined seven hundred fifty-five dollars for the crime of making and selling good wine and beer, for what was legal back in Lens and St. Etienne is illegal in Sheridan. The money for the fines came from the husband's work in the mines and the wife's earnings by doing washing; wine at a dollar a liter and beer at ten cents a bottle produce profit more social than fiscal.

The discussion of the hazards of their trade leads the Fontans into conversation with the narrator about the upcoming 1928 presidential election. Naturally, the Fontans favor Alfred E. Smith—"Schmidt," they say—a Catholic who favored repeal of Prohibition.[8] Yet the Fontans can not fully believe that Smith, a candidate for the leadership of the country, is a Catholic, and they accept the fact only on the authority of the narrator. "On dit que Schmidt est catholique," M. Fontan says. Mme Fontan responds with telling uncertainty, "On dit, mais on ne sait jamais." And later: "Je ne crois pas que Schmidt est catholique. Did he ever live in France?" (457). Their doubt is not merely political naiveté or lack of factual information. It is something much deeper, an insight about America that is anything but naive: "En Amérique il ne faut pas être catholique. The Americans don't like you to be catholique," Mme Fontan says, adding by way of sharp illustration, "It's like the dry law" (457). The problem with America, as the Fontans had earlier said about their first impression of their new country, is that "Il y a trop de churches." Too many churches, like too many books, "c'est une maladie" (456).

The sickness of which the Fontans complain is intolerance, particularly, as Kenneth G. Johnston points out in an analysis of political commentary[9] in "Wine of Wyoming," intolerance for foreigners in America. The parallels between the Fontans' disappointments and indignities and the anti-Catholic, anti-immigrant, anti-alcohol prejudices against the Democratic presidential candidate are strong, as Johnston demonstrates in elaborating his thesis that the story is Hemingway's criticism of the parochial, intolerant country he had come home to. In fact, the narrator himself claims to be Catholic (457), and his appreciation for a good drink is self-evident, traits that connect him with Smith and the Fontans. But when asked directly if Smith will be elected—as if he, a "real" American, despite his religion and his residence abroad, could foresee the future— the narrator answers simply "No" (458). The narrator's monosyllabic wisdom, which indeed proved true, sets the prevailing tone of the story: failed hope, rejected optimism, alienation.

The doomed Smith candidacy is not the only illustration of the Fon- tans' problem. One of their sons is married to a lazy, two-hundred- twenty-five-pound wife, a native American "Indienne" who reads in bed all day, neither cooks nor works, and feeds him "beans en can," yet "il est crazy pour elle" (451–52). The younger son André, a teenager "on the way to becoming Americanized" (Flora, 227), cadges a quarter for the movies but plans to pay the child's fifteen-cent admission, not the full fee, thus saving a dime for himself.[10] André also tries to take a rifle and go on a water-rat shooting expedition, but his parents forbid it, thinking that the boy and his friends "veulent shooter les uns les autres"; as his mother explains to the guest, "il est crazy pour le shooting" (456). And finally Fontan, trying to show his best hospitality to the appreciative narrator, finds himself locked out of his son's house where the latest vintage is hidden. "Il est crazy pour le vin" (459), his wife says, but he suffers the embarrassment of not being a good host and the narrator is left without a taste of the wine of Wyoming—the wine that symbolically can't be drunk, and ironically can't even be got out of its secret hiding place, even though it can be seen through the window. Significantly, Fontan doesn't have the key, and the neighbor's key won't turn the lock.

The Fontans' defeat is complete. Mme Fontan, who earlier had "looked like Mrs. Santa Claus, clean and rosy-faced and white-haired" (458), now lost "all the happiness from her face" (464), and Fontan, "incoherent and crushed . . . sat down in a corner with his head in his hands" (465). Sensing that they had overstayed their time and were intruding on the Fontans' sad disgrace, the narrator and his companion leave, with a halfhearted promise to return two years later. Once away from the house, they realize that they "ought to have gone last night" (466), before the good times had turned bad. Wistfully, the companion says, "I hope they have a lot of good luck" (466). The narrator realistically responds, "They won't . . . and Schmidt won't be President either" (466).

Driving out of Sheridan and away from the "ruined" (466) Fontans, the visitors admire the country, yet their thoughts return to their hosts:

"It's a fine country for la chasse, Fontan says."
"And when the chasse is gone?"
"They'll be dead then."
"The boy won't."
"There's nothing to prove he won't be."
"We ought to have gone last night."
"Oh, yes," I said. "We ought to have gone." (467)

On this note of pessimism and regret, the story about "cleanliness and order" ends.

Though the story focuses on the Fontans and uses their misfortunes to express a mood of dissatisfaction with America, it also portrays a writer-narrator changing from a sympathetic friend who enjoys good wine to a pessimistic doubter who foresees a cold future in which the Fontans won't have good luck and Al Smith won't be elected president. What begins as a warmly comic character sketch ends with cool detachment. As Joseph M. Flora points out in an analysis of the story, its four distinct parts move progressively away from anecdotal description of the Fontans toward self-revelation by the nameless narrator himself. "Ultimately," says Flora, "Hemingway puts the emphasis not on America, or the Fontans, but on the narrator" (234). The storyteller, who "is immediately established as 'one of them'" (Flora, 224)—that is, he shares with the Fontans certain attitudes and values—has by the end of the story evaded his host's invitation and made a promise that he probably won't keep.

By the time the narrator and his companion leave, the "exuberant humor of the work's earlier sections" has become "the sadness of the concluding episode" (Grebstein, 67). The thematic focus and narrative point of view have shifted from an outward direction (the narrator describing the Fontans) to an inward reflection (the narrator revealing himself). "The story's irony," Sheldon Norman Grebstein says, "apprehended simultaneously by the narrator and the reader, is that a seemingly trivial decision (breaking a promise in a small social occasion) can cause irreparable damage to a fragile relationship and produce strong moral consequences" (64). In this sense the point of "Wine of Wyoming" is not—or not only—to demonstrate a theme similar to that of "Cross-Country Snow," an expatriate's unhappiness with his return to America. "Wine of Wyoming" may be "Hemingway's international short story . . . his most Jamesian" because it juxtaposes the values of two cultures (Flora, 224), but even more importantly it reiterates an established Hemingway theme, the dominant theme of *Winner Take Nothing*: the ironic, if not tragic, outcome.

If "Wine of Wyoming" is about the "sweet and generous natures" of its main characters the Fontans, as an early reviewer said, it is about sweetness and generosity undermined by failure and repaid in despair. And if it is about "cleanliness and order," those traits are only a momentary stay against chaos, as they are in the far more famous "A Clean, Well-Lighted Place," a story also from the early thirties, published under the same descriptive title *Winner Take Nothing*.

"Wine of Wyoming" differs superficially from other, more typical stories of Hemingway from the period 1925–33, but structurally and aesthetically it is consistent with his work of that time. Missing from it are the characters and events that offended critics whose tastes were formed, evidently, in a gentler era, and who peevishly asked Hemingway to abandon his "consummate reporting of a highly masculine and often brutal world" (Kronenberger, 6) in favor of a new departure into a less melodramatic, less violent world. "Wine of Wyoming" is in fact less overtly violent and dramatic than, for example, "Indian Camp," but like that early story, also set in an isolated American locale, "Wine" depends for its sense and force not on surface events but on a powerful undercurrent of unstated attitudes and unvoiced conclusions.

Even the early reviewers of *Winner Take Nothing* knew that "Wine of Wyoming" was different, but they seemed not to know why. If they praised it, they praised it perhaps for the wrong reasons: for the warmth of the Fontans, for the charm of local color, for the apparent absence of the author's most provocative traits. Later, the topical allusions to a presidential election and cultural criticism of American life drew some attention. But the consistency of vision went unnoticed. Although in this story the means of expression differ somewhat from those of earlier work, the dominant tone continues Hemingway's view of the postwar world: loss, alienation, regret, mortality. Even in the trivialities of life in Sheridan, Wyoming, the story reiterates the inevitability of suffering and destruction.

Hemingway promised Perkins a "1st flight story," and he was right. "Wine of Wyoming" exhibits all of the Hemingway structural and stylistic hallmarks—strength of characterization, lucidity of plot, realism of dialogue (even in Anglo-French)—and it confirms once again the central Hemingway credo that, as he said in 1929, while this story was evolving, "The world kills the very good and the very gentle and the very brave impartially" (*A Farewell to Arms*, 249). "Wine of Wyoming" is not then an oddity to be set apart from the mainstream of Hemingway's work. It is consistent with the art, the viewpoint, and the attitude of his best.

IV

An
Overview
of the
Criticism

A Partial Review: Critical Essays on the Short Stories, 1976–1989

Paul Smith

●

Any review of the criticism of Hemingway's short stories written in the last thirteen years must be partial, if only because it doubled the number of critical studies in the preceding baker's dozen. At times, of course, some of that criticism since 1975 has doubled the work done earlier simply by repeating it, and so this review will be partial in the second sense of limiting its consideration to that criticism which, to my mind, has advanced or reoriented the study of Hemingway's stories.

With an apology to those critics I may have missed or misconstrued, I think it obvious that Hemingway's short stories, both the familiar and the neglected, still call for new forays to their approaches and heights from every critically intrepid generation, if only because they are still there. And it seems just as obvious that relatively few of the present generation of scholars have been emboldened or simply curious enough to try new ascents to that fiction.

That neglect is all the more curious since those younger scholars have been so generously endowed with new resources—manuscripts, letters, memoirs—and challenged with a wealth of new biographies. It cannot be that those resources are too intimidating or that the several biographies have said it all. Can it?

Or was the work in the decade before 1975 itself overwhelming? Certainly it engendered erstwhile and engaging hypotheses (the "code hero" was one) and attuned us to the fiction's unspoken nuances with that singular "theory of omission" from Hemingway's late memoir, but by now we should have come to recognize how such concepts may imprison as much as liberate the reader of Hemingway's stories.

Or, more recently, was it the light thrown on the novels that left some of the stories in the dark? Bright studies of *A Farewell to Arms*—from Judith Fetterley's in *The Resisting Reader* (1978) to James Phelan's in *Reading People, Reading Plots* (1989)—can persuade us to see Catherine Barkley one way or another, but once so dazzled we may confuse her after-image in those studies with the quite different features of the women in the stories, like Liz Coates in Hortons Bay, Jig in a Spanish train station, or Margot Macomber in Africa.

Or all of this—the sometimes intimidating resources and biographies, the conventions of earlier criticism, and the priority given to the novels—may have been a matter of critical fashion. (I have it on good authority that the first Yale dissertation on Hemingway since Charles Fenton's in 1952 was submitted in 1986, and although that says much about Yale, Yale says much about criticism.) If, in the old days, an ironic critical mode selected and celebrated ironic writers, it is understandable that a new generation of meta-critics interested in self-reflexive writers would have passed by a writer who seemed so certain of himself, so unreflective, such a dumb ox and never, well hardly ever, an old possum. Still, it is unfortunate that the most versatile and challenging decade of criticism since the 1940s has—with the exceptions recognized in this collection and Susan Beegel's (1989)—largely overlooked the short stories of a writer whose fiction begged for that criticism from his inheritors.

Three events of the 1980s bid fair to reorient criticism of the stories in the next decade. At the outset was the opening of the rich and various Hemingway Collection at the John F. Kennedy Library. With the conference on that occasion and the organization of the Hemingway Society in 1980, the words—hundreds of thousands of them—were out for everyone. For a time, however, Mary Hemingway's munificent gift caught the more conventional Hemingway critics unawares, for few were experienced in the practical matters of manuscript and textual studies or sensitive to the theoretical issues that mine that beguiling field.

Then midway in the decade came the biographies: Peter Griffin's and Jeffrey Meyers' in 1985, Michael Reynolds' the next year, and Kenneth Lynn's the next. Each of them consulted the manuscripts, more or less; but only Reynolds, writing a *literary* biography, took the critic's caution to date and place the act of writing so to sense that part of its meaning that may rest in its occasion. Both Meyers and Lynn are more conventional biographers and had little time for the development of Hemingway's short story craft, and although Griffin included five unpublished stories from the early Chicago period, they were often misdated or misconstrued.

Finally, three books appeared in 1989 that complement—and, of course, compliment—one another. Reynolds' second volume of the biography drew on the extensive manuscripts of *The Paris Years* to argue persuasively that, for example, stories like "Cat in the Rain" and "Big

Two-Hearted River" are more precisely reflected in Hemingway's situation from March to July 1924 than the fishing trip of 1919 or Hadley's pregnancy in 1923. Susan Beegel's collection of new essays on *Hemingway's Neglected Short Fiction* included several that consider the manuscripts as well and others that focus contemporary critical theory on those overshadowed stories: for example, Gerry Brenner's semiotic analysis of "A Simple Enquiry" and Bruce Henricksen's Bakhtinean analysis of the bullfight vignettes. And it is that sort of literary biography and criticism that my *Reader's Guide to the Short Stories* intended to serve with its review of the manuscripts, its summary of the past criticism done well but sometimes overlooked, and its identification of some of the major issues that remain for the criticism to come, as come it must.

It would be helpful for those future critics to have an authoritative edition of the short stories—indeed, of *any* Hemingway work. With the manuscripts at hand for a decade now and the textual variants sometimes glaring, it is unfortunate that there is no scholarly, much less a trade, edition of the stories one can trust. "The Finca Vigia Edition" of *The Complete Short Stories of Ernest Hemingway* (1987) is more than complete, with sections of unfinished novels, the fables, and occasional pieces offered more as dubious relics than candidates for canonization. This edition faithfully recreates instances of faulty editing and, if the past is prologue, may have added some.

So, to review that criticism of the stories since 1975 that has tried, in the old phrase, to "make it new."

Critical Books

Five critical books published in the 1980s show varying degrees of promise for redirecting scholarship on the stories.

Wirt Williams' *The Tragic Art of Ernest Hemingway* (1981) is among them for its ranging study of the stories within various theories of tragedy—from Aristotle and Friedrich Hegel and A. C. Bradley to Karl Jaspers and Jean-Paul Sartre, with Northrop Frye an eminence among a variety of moderns like George Steiner and Murray Krieger. Williams considers all of the stories through the late 1930s and has read most of the earlier criticism with tact and diligence.

If he finds all but "The Undefeated" from the first three collections "sub-tragic," either for their "miniaturization" ("Banal Story"), their concern with the observer rather than the victim ("In Another Country"), or their shrouding of an invoked tragedy ("The Killers"), the stories are neither diminished nor dismissed for falling short of the classic notion. The representative moment occurs when Nick Adams defers the "tragic adventure" of fishing the swamp in "Big Two-Hearted River," of which Williams writes that Hemingway might be admitting his reluctance to accept his "own tragic vision [and] to assume his robes as priest of tragedy" (38). To that mild reproof there is always the answer that when Hemingway did put on the priestly robes of any critical denomination, his short fiction often suffered.

With the three stories of 1936—"The Capital of the World," "The Short Happy Life of Francis Macomber," and "The Snows of Kilimanjaro"— Hemingway "reaches the threshold of his final phase as a tragic writer" and crosses it into *For Whom the Bell Tolls* (124). All three stories approach the formal structure and emotional intensity of classic tragedy with characters who risk death in obedience to some primary drive and achieve something of a tragic transcendence.

Others have conceived of Hemingway as a tragedian, but none with the complex theoretical structure or the panoramic compass of this judicious book.

In the following year Joseph M. Flora gathered in *Hemingway's Nick Adams* (1982) all the stories in which Nick, or a character with his familiar features, appears. That took some courage after the controversy Philip Young had occasioned with a similar strategy some thirty years earlier. Questions have been raised over Flora's chronology for the stories or his missing the manuscripts, but none vitiates his interpretations of the individual stories, for the chronology is not essential and the book must have been near completion when the manuscript collection was formally opened.

His strategy mixes conventional literary history and some biography, and for the sequence of stories he engages archetypal patterns and some telling, if rather simple, psychological readings. His brief introduction sets the stories in their literary traditions, and his literary analogues are gathered from afar: most often informative, at times decorative, the citations range, as in the discussion of "Big Two-Hearted River," from Genesis through nine other works to Robert Frost's "Directive." But among them he finds James Joyce's "The Dead" and recognizes the challenge that story must have set for the one Hemingway needed to end *In Our Time*.

Two of his persuasive insights will serve to suggest the quality of his book. The fictional biography of Nick Adams places three of the late stories in an interesting collation: "A Day's Wait," "Wine of Wyoming," and "Fathers and Sons." To read these stories together is to recognize a late set of marriage tales informing each other as did the earlier set from "Out of Season" to "A Canary for One." And in his remarks on the memory of Hopkins in "Big Two-Hearted River," Flora writes that Nick views its bitter ending "with ironic amusement, seeing it as part of a story and himself as writer" (164). Nearly a throwaway line here, the insight informs some of the later stories—"An Alpine Idyll" for one—in which the real if unrealized story of Nick Adams is the portrayal of the narrator as writer. Others, like Robert Fleming, are elaborating on this suggestion and should return to Flora's book for confirmation. For such perceptions any discomfort with the chronology is a small price to pay.

Gerry Brenner's *Concealments in Hemingway's Works* (1983) is largely devoted to the novels and nonfiction but notes almost all the stories, sometimes in a passing sentence or long footnote that reads like an outline for an intriguing critical essay—indeed, some have become articles since then. Although his method is somewhat ecumenical—here and there formalist and generic—his best insights derive from Freudian psychology. His work is original in several ways: it challenges the received psychobiographical notion that only Hemingway's mother licked him into shape, with a persuasive consideration of the influence of both his father's imposing strength and his humiliating weakness. This work, too often passed by, is an exemplar that offers a hard lesson to other critics, especially the biographers, whose armchair analyses show so little familiarity with the classic texts of psychology. And its range is wide both in its review of earlier criticism and attention to the hitherto neglected fiction: the analysis of the omniscient perspective in "A Natural History of the Dead," for one, brushes aside all the misconceptions of that work to demonstrate its affirmation of Hemingway's fierce humanism.

It is no surprise that some critics have been discomfited by this book without denying its validity, for few have attended to the way Brenner, in something like a sleight of hand, turns psychological criticism away from the fiction and toward his scholarly audience to draw their attention to their own "defense mechanisms" and to the way this fiction overcomes them through its affirmation of life in the pursuit of its own "esthetic ecstasies" (93–106).

The fourth book is Susan Beegel's *Hemingway's Craft of Omission* (1988). Although the old saw in her title might have restricted her analysis of the manuscript examples of the three stories ("Fifty Grand," "A Natural History of the Dead," and "After the Storm"), these chapters illuminate them, trace their biographical and historical origins, and show with

critical acumen how the manuscripts may direct and correct their interpretations.

The manuscripts of "Fifty Grand" clarify Hemingway's turgid relationship with Scott Fitzgerald, and this chapter, read with Scott Donaldson's
"The Wooing of Ernest Hemingway" (1982), brings to the surface the
story's involuted origins. The chapter on "A Natural History of the Dead"
uses a discarded coda to demonstrate how this seeming mongrel of a
narrative illustrates Hemingway's close engagement with the issues of
his time. The chapter on "After the Storm" is a model for the study of
sources—who now has time to read Coast Guard dispatches or *Lloyd's
Register*? It considers the intricate revisions through several drafts of a
story for which there was an array of newspaper accounts and a Key West
version of Conrad's Marlow (Bra Saunders) at hand. These revisions
represent important evidence for the understanding of the midpoint in
Hemingway's development as a writer of short stories and his craft of
omission, addition, or whatever.

Joseph M. Flora's latest book, *Ernest Hemingway: A Study of the Short
Fiction* (1989), is something of a miscellany that surveys settled territory
rather than striking out in the directions his first book discovered. That
the book seems intended for students may or may not excuse this
backtrailing. The better part of it begins with the stories of the late 1930s
and approaches its author's earlier standard with the Spanish Civil War
stories. The review of the two African stories rests heavily on the Jeffrey
Meyers and Kenneth Lynn biographies and rather too lightly on the
essential work of Warren Beck, Mark Spilka, Robert Lewis, and Max
Westbrook. Flora's synoptic view of the Spanish Civil War stories returns
to those insights he first offered with the late marriage tales, and his
serious consideration of the late stories published in the Finca Vigia
collection again illuminates each story with its counterparts or contemporaries.

If the book's later chapters forward criticism of the stories, the last half
of the book is padded, first, with an excerpt from Hemingway's preface to
The First Forty-nine and a version of "The Art of the Short Story" from the
manuscripts, and, second, with four brief passages from familiar critical
works and one long passage that finds analogues and metaphors for
Hemingway's style in *Ethan Frome* and the values of the efficiency
movement in the history of engineering.

Two other books published after 1975 deserve mention, even though
both are in different ways reissues. Joseph DeFalco's *The Hero in Hemingway's Short Stories* (1963) was republished in 1983, and it rewards a second

reading if we recall that it was the first to appear in the decade after Philip Young's survey of the fiction (1952). DeFalco's employment of archetypal and psychological patterns in 1963 made Young's book seem tame, and for its daring alone it should be reconsidered.

The other is Kenneth Johnston's *The Tip of the Iceberg: Hemingway and the Short Story* (1987), which collects his earlier articles, most published since 1975 and somewhat revised in the light of more recent criticism. Johnson is a graceful writer, has consulted the manuscripts and the critical canon, and offers new perceptions of a variety of stories—his study of "The Denunciation" is a notable instance (1979; in this collection).

Critical Anthologies

Four collections of critical essays on Hemingway have been published since 1975, with diminishing returns for the short stories until the boom of 1989.

Michael Reynolds' edition of *Critical Essays on Ernest Hemingway's* In Our Time (1983) balanced a dozen articles from the 1960s and earlier against others written since the 1970s, of which three were written for the volume. Of the latter group three were bibliographical and textual studies that reaffirmed the need for scholarly editions of Hemingway's works (two by E. R. Hagemann and one by Kathryn Zabelle Derounian on *In Our Time* chapters); one extended the range of influence on Hemingway to Henry Fielding (Nicholas Gerogiannis on "The Battler"), and mine questioned the validity of the "theory of omission," given the evidence of the manuscript of "Out of Season." Reynolds's introductory essay, "Looking Backward," offered a valuable study of the popular models Hemingway imitated in the short fiction of his Chicago years.

James Nagel's edition of the papers from the Hemingway Society's 1982 conference included my study of the manuscripts of "Ten Indians" and Max Westbrook's restoration of the family portraits of Grace and "Ed" Hemingway. With the unpublished family correspondence, he offered a less scarified image of the couple than that in their son's stories—giving heed to the biographers to come.

Linda Wagner's *Ernest Hemingway: Six Decades of Criticism* (1987) reprinted Westbrook's essay and Bernard Oldsey's original study of the manuscripts of three stories, "Indian Camp," "Big Two-Hearted River," and "The Short Happy Life of Francis Macomber."

Although these last two collections were either limited to conference papers or committed to a wider prospect of the fiction, they seemed an omen of a dwindling interest in the stories. Then came the year of the stories, 1989.

Susan Beegel's latest book, a collection of original essays on *Hemingway's Neglected Short Fiction* (1989), offered a model anthology. A bright and original introduction surveys some of the reasons for the neglect of that fiction—some only recently collected, others edited with an Olympian insouciance, and all upstaged by the "The Killers' Clean, Two-Hearted Camp" and those big novels, all during a time when criticism with a pursed morality favored the "herioc pathos" of a man's struggle with a fish but was not amused by those stories so perfectly dubbed, in this feisty editor's phrase, as Hemingway's horny dwarves (15).

Once into the collection there are headnotes for each selection that not only prepare the reader for what is to follow but also place and tactfully modify each essay with a brief summary of its antecedents. Any collection seeking twenty-five original essays will have to settle for some fillers, but this one has fewer than most. Again, it includes Brenner's and Henrickson's essays at semiotic and dialogic analysis to unfold the complexities of some of the unsung stories and vignettes. Several of the essays do as well in the more conventional critical modes: Phillip Sipiora's rhetorical analysis of "My Old Man," Bickford Sylvester's exploration of the archetypal wasteland motifs in "Out of Season," H. R. Stoneback's study of "Wine of Wyoming," the latest in a persuasive series of articles arguing for the abiding influence of Catholic thought on the fiction, and Robert Gajdusek's sensitive reading of the metaphoric patterns in "An Alpine Idyll." Finally, a good number of these essays are, in the best sense, stylish. Michael Reynolds' on "Homage to Switzerland," for one, has a graceful wit that delights us as much as it persuades us to see the story as an absurdist fiction inspired by contemporary accounts of Einstein's theories of relativity.

A promising volume for the next decade.

Critical Articles

Winnowing out the articles since 1975 that have advanced criticism of the stories reveals that many of the best were those engaged in critical controversies over three crucial stories: "Big Two-Hearted River," "A Clean, Well-Lighted Place," and "The Short Happy Life of Francis Macomber." Nor is that surprising, for when good critics clash or even elbow one another, they usually have a firm critical stance, their arguments secure, and a keen eye for their worthiest opponent's next move.

After reviewing the progress of the controversies over these three stories toward some momentary resolution—or their partisans' exhaustion—I will survey, briefly, a miscellany of articles on stories that are perhaps less controversial or crucial, or seemed so until they elicited closer scrutiny from either traditional or contemporary critical disciplines.

"Big Two-Hearted River"

Most of the critical disagreements over "Big Two-Hearted River" may be traced back to Malcolm Cowley. He and Kenneth Lynn have argued for years over whether Nick is a veteran with a traumatic wound, as Hemingway proclaimed from the grave in *A Moveable Feast*, or a boy as badly wounded by family skirmishes. Lynn maintains that there is no overt reference to the war in the story, overlooking the story's military imagery to discover other, as covert, allusions to Hemingway's restive homelife (1987; in this collection).

But Cowley's more telling remark was that many of Hemingway's stories seemed like "nightmares at noonday," and since then critics have divided on two major issues: first whether the terrain of the story is primarily inward or outward, passive and imagined or active and perceived; and second, whether the narrative is more a trying nightmare than a fulfilling dream. With the evidence of the dreamt streams in "Now I Lay Me," some recent critics have claimed further that "the entire landscape of the story is a mental one" (Robert Gibb, 1979, 23), or that it is "essentially the same landscape [with] the same emotive and symbolic value" that is found in Hemingway's work, from a 1922 *Toronto Daily Star* article to *Across the River and into the Trees* in 1950 (William Adair, 1977, 144). Some thirty-five years ago Philip Young did say that the story gives us both a world and a point of view, but he did not mean, as Gibb reads him, that the story gives us "a world *as* a point of view."

As a rule, those critics more concerned with Nick's character, his "inward terrain," stress the concluding vision of the swamp and find Nick's mental journey a fearful denial and a failure; while those more interested in the story's narrative and the scenes of the day's fishing find Nick's decision not to fish the swamp a reasonable one and the trip to the river ending with some version of an achievement. This latter reading in part distinguishes the commentary on the story after 1975 from that before. These critics read the story, variously, as a culminating initiation predicted by Nick's experience in "The Battler" (Frank Kyle, 1979), as a study of euphoria (Keith Carabine, 1982), even as a story patterned after a Romantic ode to joy (Howard Hannum, 1984). But, again, the most perceptive interpretation is Joseph Flora's of Nick Adams as a young writer casting out for "the affirmation that an artist needs . . . to create work that will have a life beyond life" (1982, 175).

With the publication of the story's original ending, titled "On Writing" in *The Nick Adams Stories* (1972), critics returned to Cézanne's role as master to the apprentice writer and the analogies between the paintings Meyly Chin Hagemann identified in the rejected conclusion and this and other stories (1979). But, as Bernard Oldsey noted (1980, in Wagner 1987), it was precisely the example of Cézanne that persuaded Hemingway to reject the conclusion celebrating the master (1980). Whatever Hemingway learned from Cézanne, the evidence will always remain in the misty midregions of analogy. I still suspect that Hemingway knew that and in a repeated strategy portrayed himself at the feet of a master painter in order to deny his debt to other writers—even to literature itself—and it worked (1983).

"A Clean, Well-Lighted Place"

Of the two issues recently engaging critical commentary on "A Clean, Well-Lighted Place," one, largely thematic, was favored until the mid-1970s and then was overshadowed by the second, largely textual. To that time almost all the criticism focused on whether the older waiter's vision of *nada* entailed a desperate negation of meaning or a final but courageous affirmation in the face of chaos. Most critics took the latter view, and their position found persuasive support in Annette Benert's nice perception that the older waiter was smart enough to "go one step beyond Beckett's tramps," to become "neither a hero nor a saint, but, to borrow from Camus, that more ambitious being, a man" (1973, 184, 187). Steven Hoffman concurred and advanced her argument with evidence drawn from the earliest of the Nick Adams stories to the latest set in Africa (1979; in this collection).

But by the later 1970s the controversy—for some instances, a polite term—over the attribution of the two waiters' dialogue was about to become a critical field in itself. And deservedly so, for more than many specializations, it demanded of its candidates a familiarity with critical theory, biography, and textual studies, as well as a good share of common sense.

The story had been published in 1933 with the dialogue that attributes the statement that the old man's "niece cut him down"—first to the older waiter who then attributes it to the younger one. No one seemed to notice that confusion for twenty-four years; arguments persisted for another twenty; and finally in 1977, Hans-Joachim Kann looked at the story's surviving manuscript. Two years later Warren Bennett studied that manuscript in precise detail to conclude that the confusion originated in a series of revisions and was then preserved through two publications until Scribner's, on the advice of some scholars, revised the dialogue in 1965.

But by then, a critical to-do: some critics called for the restoration of the original dialogue, some simply for the revisionists' heads, and one discovered that Hemingway himself had told an inquisitive reader that the original dialogue seemed fine to him (George Monteiro, 1974).

For five years following Bennett's 1979 article his major opponent was David Kerner. Kerner challenged his reading of the manuscript and argued that the convention of metronomic dialogue (alternating speakers indicated only by paragraphs) was countered by another long tradition of antimetronomic dialogue in Hemingway and others; and in two articles he compiled an anthology of examples (1979, 1985).

George H. Thomson, in an admirably conciliatory essay, tried to resolve the dispute, concluding that the original text was not corrupt, that the conversation may violate convention, and that, although "it requires some ingenuity of reading," one can make sense of the 1933 dialogue (1983, 32–42). Kerner refused the overture with a reply in 1984, and Warren Bennett bided his time until 1990 with a long and persuasive counterstatement, that—is it too much to hope?—may settle the issue.

Although the controversy may finally rest on whether or not Hemingway nodded when he wrote and edited, it has raised more important biographical, critical, and textual issues than any other in the history of Hemingway criticism, and we are all indebted to those scholars who took a stand.

"The Short Happy Life of Francis Macomber"

In 1980 William White compiled a "'Macomber' Bibliography" that included thirty-seven entries since 1975, and from 1980 on there have been some twenty more. As with "A Clean, Well-Lighted Place," much of the critical interest in "The Short Happy Life of Francis Macomber" has arisen from a crucial ambiguity in the text. And that interest was largely inspired by two fine critics in a two-handed game that went on into the evening hours—Warren Beck (1955, 1975) and Mark Spilka (1960, 1976, 1984). Their initial articles, rejoinders, and later rebuttals were models of the best critical play, with most of the theoretical cards on the table. At stake was the character of Margot Macomber and the validity of Robert Wilson's sense of her motives. In brief, Warren Beck argued that Margot shot her husband accidentally and was stricken with grief, while Robert Wilson consistently misundertood her character and a good deal else. This revisionist reading challenged two stereotypes associated with Hemingway—the irredeemable bitch and the infallible white hunter (1955). Mark Spilka's response challenged this with a persuasive phrase—a "necessary style," the mark of an "author's working vision of experience [that] persists throughout [his] whole production"—to support the more traditional view of Margot with, at least, a subconscious motive for murder, one correctly perceived by Wilson (1960, 287).

Nearly every article since then has been drawn into that critical vortex—proving, of course, its centrality. Robert Stephens' review of the earlier accounts of African hunting in Stewart Edward White's *The Land of the Footprints* (1912) and the complex system of hunter and gunbearer codes supports the traditional view of the murderous Margot (1977). Joseph Harkey's research in Swahili reveals that the word *mkubwa*, phonetically close to *Macomber*, has both the honorific sense of " 'sir' with a high degree of respect," and also its sneering opposite (1980, 346–47). Then Bernard Oldsey's study of a variety of manuscripts concludes with an analysis of the story's early drafts and lists of titles to demonstrate that, from the first, Hemingway kept "the case moot—in between involuntary manslaughter and second-degree murder"—even though the suspect comment in "The Art of the Short Story" (then unpublished) upheld the latter verdict (1980, 131 in Wagner).

Mark Spilka's most recent essay on the Victorian sources open to Hemingway finds intriguing parallels between the story and Frederick Marryat's *Percival Keene* and *The King's Own;* and for this story it includes no less than three instances in the former citing the lines from Shakespeare—"By my troth, I care not; a man can die but once; we owe God a death"—a line so talismanic for Hemingway, Robert Wilson, and for many Hemingway scholars.

The line from Shakespeare nicely divides critics on their assumptions of relevant contexts. For the traditionalists the line is, as Wilson says, "damned fine." And so it is in the context of Hemingway's biography, for whether he learned it in school reading Marryat or in 1919 from Chink Dorman-Smith, he treasured it, and so it may confer authority on Robert Wilson's sense of life (John McKenna and Marvin Peterson, 1981, 82–85). But the revisionists, reading the reference in its literary context (*Henry IV*, 2, III, ii), are reminded by Virgil Hutton that the lines are spoken by

Francis Feeble (note the name) who is both a lady's tailor and a fool (1964, 253–63). Something of that conflict over the priority of those contexts has divided Macomber criticism since 1975, for which two studies will be representative.

In "Margot Macomber's Gimlet," Bert Bender uses the sexual allusions in the story's opening dialogue—the phallic gimlet against the lemon squash—to argue that Margot needs "to be dominated sexually, physically, psychically, and the quashed Francis" is not the man to do it. The "opening volley of off-color puns penetrates the story's heart, where the arts of hunting, story-telling, and love lie grotesquely intertwined"—note the metaphors in the critic's language—and it is necessary for Macomber to complete his education by recognizing "the primitive regenerative power in Hemingway's male world of blood, violence, and sex." Although Margot "might well have unconsciously shot at Francis, . . . it seems of little consequence," for he has at last seen what lies at the story's heart. Bender insists that his "purpose is not to defend Hemingway's primitive sexist values" but to demonstrate how, given "what we know of his style and vision," they are commingled at the center of this story (1981, 14–19). The question raised by this challenging essay is whether such a sense of Hemingway's vision constricts the story's meaning, or whether Hemingway, in a flash of creative insight perhaps as brief as Macomber's, recognized a regeneration that transcends those primitive, sexist, and puerile attitudes.

In "The Education of Robert Wilson," Barbara Lounsberry begins with Warren Beck's portrait of the white hunter as an uncertain and ambivalent witness and adds that he is also, at three crucial moments, dead wrong on three matters: "his first assessments of Macomber's courage, . . . the significance of his moment of cowardice, and . . . the nature of his relationship with his wife." The story, then, interweaves three narratives of education: Macomber's learning to face death with courage, Margot's awakening to her husband's moral transformation, and Wilson's discovering "the ways of American life and death, cowardice and heroism." For Lounsberry that last course requires the study of corruption and pretense, and that Wilson passed it in the essential last scene. Then, although he had "earlier scorned Macomber's pleas 'to pretend to ourselves [that the lion] hasn't been hit' . . . , [he] must now pretend that a lion of a man has not been murdered" (1980, 30–32). The burden of this essay rests on the assumption that Macomber was murdered and that by adopting the pretense of an accident Wilson is repeating Macomber's earlier pretense about the wounded lion. But it is Wilson's assumption that Macomber wished to pretend the lion had not

been hit, when in fact Macomber was innocently unaware of the consequences of leaving it in the bush. Once those consequences are explained,
he immediately understands. The two scenes are not morally equivalent,
and one is left to wonder whether Wilson could ever learn anything as
demanding as the short happy education of the Macombers.

Nina Baym confirms this revisionist reading of the story, and in an
anecdote that makes us wince, shows how the stereotypical roles of men
and women that perplex this story are at times acted out when we teach
our students (1990, in this collection).

Once again, an encounter between two master critics on a controversial story has directed others to a reconsideration of our critical assumptions about this man and his work and the living issues the story enfolds.

Other Stories—Other Articles

A survey of the best criticism of the other stories suggests that it began
in the late 1970s with some exemplary work in the traditonal modes, was
challenged in the early 1980s with the new textual studies, and in the
following years was informed by a variety of essays with contemporary
critical perspectives.

The term "traditional" is obviously not meant to slight earlier
criticism—one could do worse than join Brooks and Warren, Crane or
Spilka—but rather to identify those critics who draw on the best formalist
criticism, in the most tolerant sense of that misunderstood movement,
and demonstrate its continuing validity. I think of Paul Witherington's
brief but compelling study of the dramatic changes in the narrative voice
in an overlooked story, "On the Quai at Smyrna" (1978); of Paul Jackson's
meticulous analysis of the complex structures in "Out of Season" and
"The Short Happy Life of Francis Macomber" (1980, 1981); of Colin Cass's
original discovery of the act of perception as the controlling metaphor in
"In Another Country," a discovery nicely supported by the manuscripts
of that story and one that links the story with Hemingway's other self-
reflective tales of the narrator narrating his tale and recreating himself
(1981); and of Richard McCann's essay on "Fathers and Sons," deftly
weaving the appropriate archetypal and psychoanalytic theory into a
precise stylistic and rhetorical analysis of one of Hemingway's most
difficult stories (1985; in this collection). Then John Hollander's essay on
"Hills Like White Elephants" is another of those with winning eloquence;
it traces with a poet's hand Hemingway's own poetic process to recreate
the riddling image of those white hills, and it leaves us with a sense of
criticism as moving, in its own right, as the story itself (1985).

There are signs of a new critical interest in studies of the Spanish Civil War stories. From the publication of *The Fifth Column and Four Stories of the Spanish Civil War* (1969) until 1975, only three critics afforded the stories any serious attention: Julian Smith read them for their religious allusions and Martin Light for their narrator (both in 1969), and in 1972 Linda Wagner wrote on the narrative and thematic elements that mark them as exercises leading to *For Whom the Bell Tolls*. That the stories were otherwise neglected may be pardonable, for after Hemingway's achievement in a little more than a decade from 1924 to 1936, these stories are reminiscent of his Chicago fiction thirty years earlier.

But for the few fine moments in "The Denunciation," "The Butterfly and the Tank," and "Under the Ridge," and for the evidence of an unrealized experiment with a set of stories sharing a locale and a narrator, a writer divided by his politics and his art in this tragically divided country, these stories deserve their recent studies, and more. Jay Gertzman began with the counterclaims of art and morality in "The Denunciation," and Wayne Kvam found those claims complicated in the writer-narrator of "Under the Ridge" in 1979. Allen Josephs returned to the stories to demonstrate how closely they record Hemingway's own shifting loyalties and served not so much to prepare as to purge him for the writing of the Spanish novel (1989, in Beegel).

The new textual studies that drew on the stories' manuscripts and published variants began with Scott Donaldson's essay on "Canary for One" in 1978 (in this collection), a year before the "Clean, Well-Lighted Place" industry was established and raised the primary question of the relevance of manuscript or published versions to established notions of a final text, much less a final reading. But even then Donaldson's sense of the various manuscript endings illuminated the story and its sad occasion and set a standard for later critics. Robert Fleming used the variant endings of "The Sea Change" to argue for the complexities of the resolution of its drama (1986; in this collection); as Warren Bennett did for the conclusion of "Cat in the Rain" (1988; in this collection). Their work and that of their colleagues cited earlier has enlivened criticism of the stories, but it still faces the demanding theoretical questions raised by Hershel Parker (1984).

Finally, it is fitting that the present collection, in its first section and elsewhere, offers a sample of critical essays from the last five years or so representing contemporary literary theory. These essays—citing names like Lacan and Bakhtin, Todorov and Barthes, unfamiliar in Hemingway criticism a decade ago—are remarkable in their tolerance, offering theoretical models to be tested with the stories and then modestly suggesting that they more often confirm than contradict conclusions reached with more traditional models. Or simply with a careful reading: Pamela Smiley's essay employing recent research in linguistics may not tell sensitive readers much they did not know about Jig and her feckless fellow in "Hills Like White Elephants," but it will tell them *why* they know it—and, incidentally, how they can tell others they are wrong (1988; in this collection).

In 1980 David Lodge introduced concepts of narratology and narrative grammar, the poetics of fiction, and modern rhetorical analysis—no mean feat in itself—to determine whether it is possible, and then useful, to train a battery of structuralist theory on a single text ("Cat in the Rain"), and showed it was. Oddvar Holmesland has more recently reviewed and modified some of that early work (1986; in this collection). Freudian psychology supports Gerry Brenner's review of the epistemological cruxes in a wide array of stories, ending with an original reading of "The Mother of a Queen" (1990; in this collection); and Lacanian theory, reviewed with unusual clarity in Ben Stoltzfus's essay, serves to raise "After the Storm" close to the rank of a major story, or at least to suggest why stories like it both trouble and transfix our gaze (1990; in this collection).

I end with Robert Scholes' two books, *Semiotics and Interpretation* (1982) and *Textual Power* (1985), to make a teacherly point. His semiotic analyses of cultural codes, in "A Very Short Story" (1982; in this collection) and in "The Revolutionist" in the latter book, offer new entries into the drama of the two sketches and promise others into the longer stories. When his reading of the codes in "A Very Short Story" meets with the best work on its biographical origins and the manuscript record of its writing, the illumination is bright. But perhaps the last and best thing to say of this critic is that he is less concerned with yet another critical discovery, however bright, than he is with the ways we can teach the power of Hemingway's texts. *Textual Power* makes explicit the sort and sequence of questions we should be asking our students, the next critical generation, and the difference between these questions and those we ask too often to impress ourselves.

In the summer of 1980 some forty Hemingway readers and critics gathered on Thompson Island and formed the Hemingway Society. Through the decade they met at other conferences—in Madrid and Boston, in Traverse City and Lignano Sabbiadoro, in Schruns and Boise. Now they number some four hundred; their society, unique among its kind, has recently assumed the rights and responsibilities of the Hemingway

Foundation and has been entrusted with its legacy of the manuscript collection.

Ten years ago they gathered on that island first to convince themselves and then to encourage others to bring the best theory and practice to bear on what would become a new canon for the criticism and teaching of Hemingway. Their hopes may have been high then, but now, ten years later, they seem quite reasonable.

V

A
Comprehensive
Checklist of Hemingway
Short Fiction Criticism,
Explication, and
Commentary,
1975–1989

Preface to the Comprehensive Checklist

This checklist is a supplement to the one which appeared in *The Short Stories of Ernest Hemingway: Critical Essays*, which listed the criticism of the short stories into 1975. The current list covers from 1975 to February 1990. It differs from the earlier list in several ways. The section arrangement has been changed, combining categories and reducing the number from six to three: Section I contains a list of books on Hemingway's work containing discussion of the short stories; Section II contains a list of articles, parts of general books (those not devoted exclusively to Hemingway), parts of Hemingway books, and dissertations containing discussion of *several* Hemingway short stories; Section III is a listing of criticism, explication, and commentary on *individual* stories, listed by story—including specific articles, segments from books on Hemingway's works, and segments from general books.

For those books of Hemingway criticism listed in Section I, discussions of several stories or groups of stories have been listed separately, by page numbers, in Section II and discussions of individual stories have been listed separately, by page numbers, in Section III. In an effort to make the listings in Section II (items dealing with several stories) more useful, we have indicated which story collections and which individual stories are referred to in each listed item. The individual stories are noted by the listing numbers used in Section III, so that if one were interested in reading all the criticism published in English during the period covered in the checklist on the Hemingway story, "Cross Country Snow," one would first consult the listings under (29) in Section III and then look for any items in Section II which refer to (29). The numbers assigned to stories in the first volume have been kept for this volume.

Dissertations have not been listed separately this time because we were unable to read, as we did before, every dissertation. It was simply too expensive to buy all the microfilms and too time-consuming to read them even if we could afford them. So we have depended on *Dissertation Abstracts International*, which means that listings for the contents are incomplete—we could only list those stories mentioned by title in the abstract. Reviews of Hemingway story collections have not been listed separately, since most of those were included in the first volume. A few additional reviews of *In Our Time*, however, have been uncovered and reprinted in Michael Reynold's *Critical Essays on Ernest Hemingway's "In Our Time,"* and these have been listed in Section I.

An explanation of the contents and format of each section precedes each section. The credit for the difficult and complex job of locating, arranging, and formatting the checklist that follows belongs to Anne Hunsinger and JoAnne Zebroski. For their hard work Hemingway scholars everywhere should be grateful.

Section I: Books on Hemingway's Work Containing Discussion of the Short Stories

Note: Discussions of individual stories and story collections in the following books are listed separately in Sections II and III (short story collections, groups of stories, and individual stories referred to as a part of a discussion of several stories are in Section II; individual stories [beyond mere mention of the title] in Section III). This practice of listing book contents in Sections II and III applies also to critical collections. Original essays and reprinted essays (providing the essay was originally published after mid-1975) which deal with groups of stories or individual stories will be listed first, as contents, in this section and then as individual items in the following sections. However, if the essay reprinted in an anthology was originally published prior to mid-1975, it will be listed, as part of the contents of the collection, only in Section I.

Baker, Carlos. *Hemingway: The Writer as Artist*. Princeton, N.J.: Princeton University Press, 1980.
[References from chapters I and II only, which the author states are "new" to this edition]

Bakker, Jan. *Fiction as Survival Strategy: A Comparative Study of the Major Works of Ernest Hemingway and Saul Bellow*. Amsterdam: Rodopi, 1983.

Beegel, Susan F. *Hemingway's Craft of Omission: Four Manuscript Examples*. Ann Arbor: UMI Research Press, 1988.

Beegel, Susan F. *Hemingway's Neglected Short Fiction: New Perspectives*. Ann Arbor: UMI Research Press, 1989.

    Pp. 1–18: "Introduction," by Susan Beegel.

    Pp. 19–30: "'The Mercenaries': A Harbinger of Vintage Hemingway" by Mimi Reisel Gladstein.

    Pp. 31–42: "Uncle Charles in Michigan" by Susan Swartzlander.

    Pp. 43–60: "Ethical Narration in 'My Old Man'" by Phillip Sipiora.

    Pp. 61–74: "'Out of Season' and Hemingway's Neglected Discovery: Ordinary Actuality" by James Steinke.

    Pp. 75–98: "Hemingway's Italian *Waste Land*: The Complex Unity of 'Out of Season'" by Bickford Sylvester.

    Pp. 99–106: "'A Very Short Story' as Therapy" by Scott Donaldson.

    Pp. 107–22: "The Bullfight Story and Critical Theory" by Bruce Henricksen.

    Pp. 123–30: "From the Waste Land to the Garden with the Elliots" by Paul Smith.

    Pp. 131–40: "Hemingway's 'On Writing': A Portrait of the Artist as Nick Adams" by Lawrence Broer.

    Pp. 141–48: "The Writer on Vocation: Hemingway's 'Banal Story'" by George Monteiro.

    Pp. 163–84: "'An Alpine Idyll': The Sun-Struck Mountain Vision and the Necessary Valley Journey" by Robert E. Gajdusek.

    Pp. 185–94: "Waiting for the End in Hemingway's 'A Pursuit Race'" by Ann Putnam.

    Pp. 195–208: "A Semiotic Inquiry into Hemingway's 'A Simple Enquiry'" by Gerry Brenner.

    Pp. 209–24: "'Mais Je Reste Catholique': Communion, Betrayal, and Aridity in 'Wine of Wyoming'" by H. R. Stoneback.

    Pp. 225–46: "'That's Not Very Polite': Sexual Identity in Hemingway's 'The Sea Change'" by Warren Bennett.

    Pp. 247–54: "'A Natural History of the Dead' as Metafiction" by Charles Stetler and Gerald Locklin.

    Pp. 255–62: "'Homage to Switzerland': Einstein's Train Stops at Hemingway's Station" by Michael S. Reynolds.

    Pp. 263–82: "Repetition as Design and Intention: Hemingway's 'Homage to Switzerland'" by Erik Nakjavani.

    Pp. 283–90: "Myth or Reality: 'The Light of the World' as Initiation Story" by Robert E. Fleming.

Pp. 291–302: "Up and Down: Making Connections in 'A Day's Wait'" by Linda Gajdusek.

Pp. 303–12: "Illusion and Reality: 'The Capital of the World'" by Stephen Cooper.

Pp. 313–28: "Hemingway's Spanish Civil War Stories, or the Spanish Civil War as Reality" by Allen Josephs.

Pp. 339–50: "Hemingway's Tales of 'The Real Dark'" by Howard L. Hannum.

Bloom, Harold, ed. *Ernest Hemingway*. New York: Chelsea House, 1985.

Pp. 1–5: "Introduction" by Harold Bloom.

Pp. 7–15: "Hemingway and His Critics" by Lionel Trilling, reprinted from the *Partisan Review* 6 (Winter 1939): 52-60.

Pp. 17–33: "Hemingway: Gauge of Morale" by Edmund Wilson, reprinted from *The Wound and the Bow*. New York: Farrar, 1968: 214–42.

Pp. 35–62: "Ernest Hemingway" by Robert Penn Warren, reprinted from *Selected Essays*. New York: Random House, 1958: 80–118.

Pp. 63–84: "Observations on the Style of Ernest Hemingway" by Harry Levin, reprinted from *Kenyon Review* 13 (Autumn 1951): 581–608.

Pp. 85–106: "The Way It Was" by Carlos Baker, reprinted from *Hemingway: The Writer as Artist*. Princeton: Princeton UP, 1980: 48–74.

Pp. 107–18: "The Death of Love in *The Sun Also Rises*" by Mark Spilka, reprinted from Shapiro, Charles, ed. *Twelve Original Essays On Great American Novels*. Detroit: Wayne State University Press, 1958: 238–56.

Pp. 119–36: "An Interview with Ernest Hemingway" by George Plimpton, reprinted from *Writers at Work: The Paris Review Interviews (Second Series)*. New York: Viking, 1963: 213–39.

Pp. 137–60: "For Ernest Hemingway" by Reynolds Price, reprinted from *Things Themselves*. New York: Atheneum, 1972: 176–213.

Pp. 161–71: "Mr. Papa and the Parricides" by Malcolm Cowley, reprinted from *And I Worked at the Writer's Trade: Chapters of Literary History, 1918-1978*. New York: Viking Penguin, 1978: 21–34.

Pp. 173–92: "'Nada' and the Clean, Well-Lighted Place: The Unity of Hemingway's Short Fiction" by Steven K. Hoffman, reprinted from *Essays in Literature* 6 (1979): 91–110.

Pp. 193–209: "Hemingway the Painter" by Alfred Kazin, reprinted from *An American Procession*. New York: Knopf, 1984: 357–73.

Pp. 211–16: "Hemingway's Extraordinary Reality" by John Hollander.

Brenner, Gerry. *Concealments in Hemingway's Works*. Columbus: Ohio State University Press, 1984.

[See also Rovit]

Brian, Denis. *The True Gen: An Intimate Portrait of Ernest Hemingway by Those Who Knew Him*. New York: Grove, 1988.

Bruccoli, Matthew J. *Scott and Ernest: The Authority of Failure and the Authority of Success*. New York: Random House, 1978.

Burgess, Anthony. *Hemingway and His World*. New York: Scribner's, 1978.

Capellan, Angel. *Hemingway and the Hispanic World*. Ann Arbor: UMI Research Press, 1985.

Cappel (Montgomery), Constance. *Hemingway in Michigan*. Waitsfield: Vermont Crossroads, 1977.

Cooper, Stephen. *The Politics of Ernest Hemingway*. Ann Arbor: UMI Research Press, 1985.

Dahiya, Bhim S. *The Hero in Hemingway: A Study in Development*. New Delhi: Bahri, 1978.

Donaldson, Scott. *By Force of Will: The Life and Art of Ernest Hemingway*. New York: Viking; Toronto: Macmillan, 1977.

Flora, Joseph M. *Ernest Hemingway: A Study of the Short Fiction*. Boston: Twayne, 1989. [124 pages of text by Flora, plus the articles listed below]

Pp. 127–28: "Preface to *The First Forty-nine*" by Ernest Hemingway, reprinted from *The Fifth Column and the First Forty-nine Stories*. New York: Scribner's, 1938: vi–vii.

Pp. 129–44: "The Art of the Short Story" by Ernest Hemingway.

Pp. 147–53: "Ernest Hemingway's Unhurried Sensations" by Tony Tanner, reprinted from *The Reign of Wonder: Naivety and Reality in American Literature*. Cambridge: Cambridge University Press, 1965: 228–48.

Pp. 153–56: "'In Another Country'" by Earl Rovit and Gerry Brenner, reprinted from *Ernest Hemingway: Revised Edition*. Boston: Twayne, 1986: 45–48.

Pp. 157–71: "Opportunity: Imagination Ex-Machina II" by Cecilia Tichi, reprinted from *Shifting Gears: Technology, Literature, Culture in Modernist America*. Chapel Hill: University of North Carolina Press, 1987: 216–29.

Pp. 172–73: "The Young Hemingway" by Michael Reynolds, reprinted from *The Young Hemingway*. New York: Basil Blackwell, 1986: 48–50.

Pp. 174–78: "'The Undefeated': The Moment of Truth" by Kenneth G. Johnston, reprinted from *The Tip of the Iceberg: Hemingway and the Short Story*. Greenwood, Fla.: Penkevill, 1987: 85–89.

Flora, Joseph M. *Hemingway's Nick Adams*. Baton Rouge: Louisiana State University Press, 1982.

Friedrich, Otto. *Going Crazy: An Inquiry into Madness "in our time."* New York: Simon and Schuster, 1976.

Fuentes, Norberto. *Hemingway in Cuba*. Secaucus, N.J.: Stuart, 1984.

Gaggin, John. *Hemingway and Nineteenth-Century Aestheticism*. Ann Arbor, Mich.: UMI Research Press, 1987.

Giger, Romeo. *The Creative Void: Hemingway's Iceberg Theory*. Bern: Francke, 1977.

Gladstein, Mimi Reisel. *The Indestructible Woman in Faulkner, Hemingway, and Steinbeck*. Ann Arbor: UMI Research Press, 1986.

Griffin, Peter. *Along With Youth: Hemingway, The Early Years*. New York: Oxford University Press, 1985.

Grimes, Larry E. *The Religious Design of Hemingway's Early Fiction*. Ann Arbor: UMI Research Press, 1985.

Hardy, Richard E., and John G. Cull. *Hemingway: A Psychological Portrait*. Sherman Oaks, Calif.: Banner, 1977.

Johnston, Kenneth G. *The Tip of the Iceberg: Hemingway and the Short Story*. Greenwood, Fla.: Penkevill, 1987.

Kert, Bernice. *The Hemingway Women*. New York: Norton, 1983.

Kobler, J. F. *Ernest Hemingway: Journalist Artist*. Ann Arbor: UMI Research Press, 1985.

Lee, Robert A., ed. *Ernest Hemingway: New Critical Essays*. London: Vision; Totowa, N.J.: Barnes, 1983.

Pp. 13–35: "'The Picture of the Whole': *In Our Time*" by David Seed.

Pp. 36–48: "The Short Stories After *In Our Time*: A Profile" by Colin E. Nicholson.

Pp. 151–71: "Hemingway the Intellectual: A Version of Modernism" by Brian Way.

Pp. 172–92: "Hemingway and the Secret Language of Hate" by Faith Pullin.

Pp. 193–211: "Stalking Papa's Ghost: Hemingway's Presence in Contemporary American Writing" by Frank McConnell.

Lynn, Kenneth S. *Hemingway*. New York: Simon and Schuster, 1987.

Meyers, Jeffrey, ed. *Hemingway: The Critical Heritage*. London: Routledge, 1982.

Meyers, Jeffrey. *Hemingway: A Biography*. New York: Harper, 1985.

Nagel, James, ed. *Ernest Hemingway: The Writer in Context*. Madison: University of Wisconsin Press, 1984.

Pp. 19–27: "Reflections on Ernest Hemingway" by Tom Stoppard.

Pp. 53–74: "The Tenth Indian and the Thing Left Out" by Paul Smith.

Pp. 107–28: "*A Farewell to Arms:* Pseudoautobiography and Personal Metaphor" by Millicent Bell.

Pp. 129–44: "Women and the Loss of Eden in Hemingway's Mythology" by Carol H. Smith.

Pp. 165–78: "Ernest and Henry: Hemingway's Lover's Quarrel with James" by Adeline R. Tintner.

Pp. 179–200: "Ernest Hemingway and Ezra Pound" by Jacqueline Tavernier-Courbin.

Nelson, Raymond S. *Ernest Hemingway: Life, Work, and Criticism*. Fredericton, N.B., Canada: York Press, 1984.

Nelson, Raymond S. *Hemingway, Expressionist Artist*. Ames: Iowa State University Press, 1979.

Noble, Donald R. ed. *Hemingway: A Revaluation*. Troy, N.Y.: Whitson, 1983.

Pp. 17–47: "Hemingway Criticism: Getting at the Hard Questions" by Jackson J. Benson.

Pp. 49–65: "Hemingway, Painting, and the Search for Serenity" by Alfred Kazin.

Pp. 67–82: "Hemingway and the Magical Journey" by Leo Gurko.

Pp. 83–97: "Hemingway's British and American Reception: A Study in Values" by Robert O. Stephens.

Pp. 99–113: "'The Truest Sentence': Words as Equivalents of Time and Place *In Our Time*" by Charles G. Hoffman and A. C. Hoffman.

Pp. 225–39: "Hemingway: The Writer in Decline" by Philip Young.

Oldsey, Bernard, ed. *Ernest Hemingway: The Papers of a Writer*. New York: Garland, 1981.

Pp. 25–35: "'Dear Folks . . . Dear Ezra': Hemingway's Early Years and Correspondence, 1917–24" by E. R. Hagemann, reprinted from *College Literature* 7 (1980): 202–12.

Pp. 37–62: "Hemingway's Beginnings and Endings" by Bernard Oldsey, reprinted from *College Literature* 7 (1980): 213–38.

Pp. 63–71: "'Proud and Friendly and Gently': Women in Hemingway's Early Fiction" by Linda W. Wagner, reprinted from *College Literature* 7 (1980): 239–47.

Pp. 117–31: "The Mystery of the Ritz Hotel Papers" by Jacqueline Tavernier-Courbin, reprinted from *College Literature* 7 (1980): 289–303.

Pp. 133–38: "Initial Europe: 1918 as a Shaping Element in Hemingway's *Weltanschauung*" by Zvonimir Radeljkovic, reprinted from *College Literature* 7 (1980): 304–9.

Pp. 139–47: "Hemingway Papers, Occasional Remarks" by Philip Young.

Oliver, Charles M., ed. *A Moving Picture Feast: The Filmgoer's Hemingway*. New York: Praeger, 1989.

Pp. 3–11: "Hemingway's Cinematic Style" by Eugene Kanjo.

Pp. 12–18: "Novelist Versus Screenwriter: The Case for Casey Robinson's Adaptations of Hemingway's Fiction" by Gene D. Phillips.

Pp. 26–31: "Death in the Matinee: The Film Endings of Hemingway's Fiction" by Frank M. Lawrence.

Pp. 125–34: "Literary Adaptation: 'The Killers'—Hemingway's Film Noir, and the Terror of Daylight" by Stuart Kaminsky.

Pp. 135–40: "That Hemingway Kind of Love" by Robert E. Morsberger.

Pp. 141–47: "A Soldier's Home: A Space Between" by Marianne Knowlton.

Pp. 148–61: "Hemingway, Film, and U.S. Culture: *In Our Time* and *Birth of a Nation*" by Stanley Corkin.

Phillips, Gene D. *Hemingway and Film*. New York: Ungar, 1980.

Raeburn, John. *Fame Became of Him: Hemingway as Public Writer*. Bloomington: Indiana University Press, 1984.

Rao, E. Nageswara. *Ernest Hemingway: A Study of His Rhetoric*. Atlantic Highlands, N.J.: Humanities Press, 1983.

Rao, P. G. Rama. *Ernest Hemingway: A Study in Narrative Technique*. New Delhi: S. Chand, 1980.

Reynolds, Michael. *Hemingway: The Paris Years*. New York: Basil Blackwell, 1989.

Reynolds, Michael S., ed. *Critical Essays on Ernest Hemingway's "In Our Time."* Boston: Hall, 1983.

Pp. 15–16: "Review of *In Our Time*" by Herbert J. Seligman, reprinted from the *New York City Sun*, October 17, 1925.

P. 17: "A New Chicago Writer" by Mary Plum, reprinted from the *Chicago Post*, November 27, 1925.

Pp. 18–20: "Tough Earth" by Paul Rosenfield, reprinted from the *New Republic* (November 1925): 22–23.

P. 20: "*In Our Time*" (anonymous), reprinted from the *Plain Dealer* (Cleveland), December 6, 1925.

Pp. 20–21: "In Our Time" by J.H.R., reprinted from the *News* (Parkersbury, W. Va.), December 6, 1925.

Pp. 22–23: "Another American Discovers the Acid in Language" by Schyler Ashley, reprinted from the *Kansas City Star*, December 12, 1925.

Pp. 23–24: "Chiseled Prose Found in Fiction of Hemingway: Realistic Stories are Found *In Our Time*" by Warren Taylor, reprinted from the *Tennessean* (Nashville), January 10, 1926.

Pp. 24–25: "*In Our Time*" (anonymous), reprinted from the *World Herald* (Omaha), January 10, 1926.

P. 25: "Review: *In Our Time*" (anonymous), reprinted from the *Portland Oregonian*, May 2, 1926.

P. 26: "Short Stories of Distinction" by Ruth Suckow, reprinted from the *Register* (Des Moines), September 12, 1926.

Pp. 31–37: "Two Hemingway Sources for *in our time*" by Michael S. Reynolds, reprinted from *Studies in Short Fiction* (Winter 1972): 81–86.

Pp. 38–51: "A Collation, with Commentary, of the Five Texts of the Chapters in Hemingway's *In Our Time*, 1923–38" by E. R. Hagemann, reprinted from *Papers of the Bibliographical Society of America* 75 (1979): 443–58.

Pp. 52–60: "Only Let the Story End as Soon as Possible: Time-and-History in Ernest Hemingway's *In Our Time*" by E. R. Hagemann, reprinted from *Modern Fiction Studies* 26 (Summer 1980): 255–62.

Pp. 61–75: "An Examination of the Drafts of Hemingway's Chapter 'Nick sat against the wall of the church . . .'" by Kathryn Zabelle Derounian, reprinted from the *Papers of the Bibliographical Society of America* 77 (1983): 54–65.

Pp. 76–87: "The Structure of *In Our Time*" by Robert M. Slabey, reprinted from *South Dakota Review* (August 1965): 38–52.

Pp. 88–102: "The Complex Unity of *In Our Time*" by Clinton S. Burhans, Jr., reprinted from *Modern Fiction Studies* (1968): 313–28.

Pp. 103–19: "Patterns of Connection and Their Development in Hemingway's *In Our Time*" by Jackson J. Benson, reprinted from *Rendezvous* (Winter 1970): 37–52.

Pp. 120–29: "Juxtaposition in Hemingway's *In Our Time*" by Linda W. Wagner, reprinted from *Studies in Short Fiction* 12 (1975): 243–52.

Pp. 130–37: "*In Our Time*: The Interchapters as Structural Guides to Pattern" by David J. Leigh, S.J., reprinted from *Studies in Short Fiction* 12 (1975): 1–8.

Pp. 138–40: "Neutral Projections in Hemingway's 'On the Quai at Smyrna'" by Louis H. Leiter, reprinted from *Studies in Short Fiction* (Summer 1968): 384–86.

Pp. 141–43: "Hemingway's *In Our Time*" by J. M. Harrison, reprinted from *Explicator* (May 1960): 51.

Pp. 144–45: "Hemingway's 'Indian Camp'" by G. Thomas Tanselle, reprinted from *Explicator* (February 1962): 53.

Pp. 146–47: "Hemingway's 'The Doctor and the Doctor's Wife'" by Aerol Arnold, reprinted from *Explicator* (March 1960): item 36.

Pp. 148–49: "Hemingway's 'The Doctor and the Doctor's Wife'" by R. M. Davis, reprinted from *Explicator* (September 1966): item 1.

Pp. 150–54: "The Biographical Fallacy and 'The Doctor and the Doctor's Wife'" by Richard Fulkerson, reprinted from *Studies in Short Fiction* 16 (1979): 61–65.

Pp. 155–56: "Hemingway's 'The End of Something'" by Joseph Whitt, reprinted from *Explicator* (June 1951): item 58.

Pp. 157–58: "Hemingway's 'The End of Something'" by Alice Parker, reprinted from *Explicator* (March 1952): item 36.

Pp. 159–71: "Ernest Hemingway's 'The End of Something': Its Independence as a Short Story and Its Place in the 'Education of Nick Adams'" by Horst H. Kruse, reprinted from *Studies in Short Fiction* (Winter 1967): 152–66.

Pp. 172–75: "Dating the Events of 'The Three-Day Blow'" by George Monteiro, reprinted from *Fitzgerald-Hemingway Annual* (1977): 207–10.

Pp. 176–88: "Nick Adams on the Road: 'The Battler' as Hemingway's Man on the Hill" by Nicholas Gerogiannis.

Pp. 189–98: "Hemingway's Concept of Sport and 'Soldier's Home'" by Robert W. Lewis, reprinted from *Rendezvous* (Winter 1970): 19–27.

Pp. 199–202: "In Defense of Krebs" by John J. Roberts, reprinted from *Studies in Short Fiction* 13 (1976): 515–18.

Pp. 203–17: "Another Turn for Hemingway's 'The Revolutionist': Sources and Meanings" by Anthony Hunt, reprinted from *Fitzgerald-Hemingway Annual* (1977): 119–35.

Pp. 218–26: "The Two Shortest Stories of Hemingway's *In Our Time*" by Jim Steinke.

Pp. 227–34: "Hemingway's 'Out of Season' and the Psychology of Errors" by Kenneth G. Johnston, reprinted from *Literature and Psychology* (November 1971): 41–46.

Pp. 235–51: "Some Misconceptions of 'Out of Season'" by Paul Smith.

Pp. 252–53: "Hemingway's 'My Old Man'" by Sidney J. Krause, reprinted from *Explicator* (January 1962): item 39.

Pp. 254–59: "He Made Him Up: 'Big Two-Hearted River' as Doppelganger" by Robert Gibb, reprinted from *Hemingway Notes* (1975): 20–24.

Pp. 260–67: "Landscapes of the Mind: 'Big Two-Hearted River'" by William Adair, reprinted from *College Literature* 4 (1977): 144–51.

Reynolds, Michael S. *Hemingway's First War: The Making of "A Farewell to Arms."* Princeton, N.J.: Princeton University Press, 1976.

Reynolds, Michael S. *The Young Hemingway.* New York: Basil Blackwell, 1986.

Rovit, Earl, and Gerry Brenner. *Ernest Hemingway.* Revised Ed. Boston: Twayne, 1986.

Smith, Paul. *A Reader's Guide to the Short Stories of Ernest Hemingway.* Boston: G. K. Hall, 1989.

Sojka, Gregory S. *Ernest Hemingway: The Angler as Artist.* New York: Lang, 1985 (American University Studies Series IV, English Language and Literature, Vol. 26).

Stoltzfus, Ben. *Gide and Hemingway: Rebels Against God.* Port Washington, N.Y.: Kennikat, 1978.

Svoboda, Frederic Joseph. *Hemingway and "The Sun Also Rises": The Creating of a Style.* Lawrence: University Press of Kansas, 1983.

Unfried, Sarah P. *Man's Place in the Natural Order: A Study of Hemingway's Major Works.* New York: Gordon, 1976.

Villard, Henry S. and James Nagel, eds. *Hemingway in Love and War: The Lost Diary of Agnes von Kurowsky, Her Letters, and Correspondence of Ernest Hemingway.* Boston: Northeastern University Press, 1989.

Wagner, Linda W., ed. *Ernest Hemingway: Six Decades of Criticism.* East Lansing: Michigan State University Press, 1987.

Pp. 19–40: "Grace Under Pressure: Hemingway and the Summer of 1920" by Max

Westbrook, reprinted from Nagel, James, ed. *Ernest Hemingway: The Writer in Context*. Madison: University of Wisconsin Press, 1984: 77–106.

Pp. 61–63: "Tough Earth" by Paul Rosenfield, reprinted from the *New Republic* (November 1925): 22–23.

Pp. 65–76: "The Structure of *In Our Time*" by Robert M. Slabey, reprinted from *South Dakota Review* (August 1965): 38–52.

Pp. 113–38: "Hemingway's Beginnings and Endings" by Bernard Oldsey, reprinted from *College Literature* 7 (1980): 213–38, and published in Oldsey, Bernard, ed. *Ernest Hemingway: The Papers of a Writer*. New York: Garland, 1981: 37–62.

Pp. 147–54: "The Social Basis of Hemingway's Style" by Larzer Ziff, reprinted from *Poetics* 7 (1978): 417–23.

Pp. 155–62: "Semantics and Style—With the Example of Quintessential Hemingway" by Richard L. McLain, reprinted from *Language and Style* 12 (1979): 63–78.

Pp. 163–65: "Review of *Men Without Women*" by Dorothy Parker, reprinted from the *New Yorker*, October 29, 1927: 92–94.

Pp. 167–69: "On Hemingway" by Claude McKay, reprinted from *A Long Way From Home*. New York: Furman, 1937: 249–52.

Pp. 209–19: "Hemingway's Women's Movement" by Charles J. Nolan, Jr., reprinted from the *Hemingway Review* 3, no. 2 (Spring 1984): 14–22.

Wagner, Linda Welshimer. *Hemingway and Faulkner: Inventors/Masters*. Metuchen, N.J.: Scarecrow, 1975.

Whitlow, Roger. *Cassandra's Daughters: The Women in Hemingway*. Westport, Conn.: Greenwood Press, 1984.

Wilkinson, Myler. *Hemingway and Turgenev: Nature of Literary Influence*. Ann Arbor: UMI Research Press, 1986.

Williams, Wirt. *The Tragic Art of Ernest Hemingway*. Baton Rouge: Louisiana State University Press, 1981.

Workman, Brooke. *In Search of Ernest Hemingway: A Model for Teaching a Literature Seminar*. Urbana, Ill.: NCTE, 1979.

Section II: Articles, Books Devoted to Hemingway's Work, Books Not Exclusively Devoted to Hemingway, and Dissertations Containing Discussion of *Several* Hemingway Short Stories

Note: Books devoted to Hemingway's work are referred to by the last name of the author. The name is then followed by the title of a Hemingway collection (*Men Without Women*) and then the page numbers in the book that refer to the Hemingway collection. There may be several such entries for each book. (References in books to individual stories are listed in Section III.)

Entries for articles in journals or critical essays in anthologies are usually followed by brackets which may contain the titles of any Hemingway story collections referred to in the essay and the *story number* from Section III of any individual story referred to (by more than just mention of its title) in the essay. Thus, [*In Our Time*, 6, 10, 88] means that the article or essay contains a substantial reference to the story collection *In Our Time* and to "Big Two-Hearted River," "Cat in the Rain," and "The Snows of Kilimanjaro." The same kind of notation is used for dissertations where the contents have been indicated in *DAI*. Items that do not refer to a specific story collection and are not followed by information in brackets indicate a general discussion wherein no collection or story is discussed individually at length.

Adair, William. "Ernest Hemingway and the Poetics of Love." *College Literature* 5 (1978): 12–23.

Adair, William. "Ernest Hemingway and the Poetics of Loss." *College Literature* 10 (Fall 1983): 294–306.

Adair, William. "Lying Down in Hemingway's Fiction." *Notes on Contemporary Literature* 16, no. 4 (September 1986): 7–8.

Adams, Michael. "Hemingway Filmography." *Fitzgerald-Hemingway Annual* (1977): 219–32.

Allen, Mary. "The Integrity of Animals: Ernest Hemingway" in *Animals in American Literature*. Urbana: University of Illinois Press, 1983: 177–96.
[6, 8, 10, 36, 67, 72, 86, 88, 96]

Allen, William Rodney. "All the Names of Death: Walker Percy and Hemingway." *Mississippi Quarterly: The Journal of Southern Culture* 36 (1982): 3–19.

Anderson, David. "American Regionalism, the Midwest and the Study of Modern American Literature." *Society for the Study of Midwestern Literature Newsletter* 15, no. 3 (1985): 10–20.

Ardat, Ahmad Kahlil. "A Linguistic Analysis of the Prose Styles of Ernest Hemingway, Sherwood Anderson, and Gertrude Stein." *DAI* 39 (1979): 4915A–16A (University of Miami). (Reprinted in part as "The Prose Styles of Selected Works by Ernest Hemingway, Sherwood Anderson, and Gertrude Stein." *Style* 14 [1980]: 1–21.)
[*In Our Time*]

Asselineau, Roger. "Hemingway, or 'Sartor Resartus' Once More." *The Transcendentalist Constant in American Literature*. New York: New York University Press, 1980: 137–52.
[27, 41, 89]

August, Jo. "The Papers of a Writer: Ernest Hemingway." *College Literature* 7 (1980): v–vi.
[*In Our Time*]

Backman, Melvin. "Death and Birth in Hemingway." *The Stoic Strain in American Literature: Essays in Honor of Marston LaFrance*. Ed. Duane J. MacMillan. Toronto: University of Toronto Press, 1979: 115–33.
[*Nick Adams Stories, In Our Time*, 5, 6, 27, 52, 56, 72, 78, 96, 107]

Badve, V. V. "The 'Camera Eye' Technique in Hemingway's Short Stories." *Journal of Shivaji University* (India) 9 (1976): 81–86.
[46, 51, 56, 94]

Baker. *In Our Time*. Pp. 32, 34–37, 42.

Baker. *in our time*. Pp. 12–13, 17–18.

Baker. *Three Stories and Ten Poems*. Pp. 16–17, 24.

Bakker. *In Our Time*. P. 4.

Bakker. *Men Without Women*. P. 4.

Bakker. *Winner Take Nothing*. P. 4.

Baley, Barney. "Woolf and Hemingway." *Virginia Woolf Miscellany* 24 (Spring 1985): 2–3.
[*Men Without Women*]

Balza, Marcelino Abelardo. "The Spanish Hero in Hemingway's Fiction." *DAI* 40 (1979): 1464A (Texas Tech University).

Barbour, James. "Fugue State as a Literary Device in 'Cat in the Rain' and 'Hills Like White Elephants.'" *Arizona Quarterly* 44, no. 2 (Spring 1988): 98–106.

Barron, James. "Hemingway on Little Travers: 'No More Place More Beautiful.'" *Kalamazoo Gazette*, November 29, 1985: E8.
[*The Nick Adams Stories*]

Bauman, M. Garrett. "How Good was Hemingway?" *Search 6: A Journal of Scholarly Research at the State University of New York* 3 (Fall 1977): 16–28.
[Biographical summary]

Beegel, Susan F. "Introduction." *Hemingway's Neglected Short Fiction*. Ed. Susan F. Beegel. Ann Arbor: UMI Research Press, 1989: 1–18.

Bell, Millicent. "*A Farewell to Arms*: Pseudoautobiography and Personal Metaphor." *Ernest*

Hemingway: The Writer in Context. Ed. James Nagel. Madison: University of Wisconsin Press, 1984: 107–28.
[*Men Without Women*, 51, 72]

Benson, Jackson J. "Criticism of the Short Stories: The Neglected and the Oversaturated—An Editorial." Comments on Hemingway's Short Stories, MLA convention, San Francisco, 1987. (Reprinted in the *Hemingway Review* 8, no. 2 [Spring 1989]: 30–35.)

Benson, Jackson J. "Hemingway Criticism: Getting at the Hard Questions." *Hemingway: A Revaluation*. Ed. Donald R. Noble. Troy, N.Y.: Whitson, 1983: 17–47.
[Survey of criticism, including that of the short stories]

Benson, J. J. "Hemingway the Hunter and Steinbeck the Farmer." *Michigan Quarterly Review* 24 (Summer 1985): 441–60.

Bigsby, C. W. E. "Hemingway: The Recoil from History." *The Twenties: Fiction, Poetry, Drama*. Ed. Warren French. DeLand, Fla.: Everett, 1975: 203–13.
[6, 27]

Bloom, Harold. Introduction. *Ernest Hemingway*. Ed. Harold Bloom. New York: Chelsea House, 1985: 1–5.
[43, 68, 73]

Bordinat, Philip. "Anatomy of Fear in Tolstoy and Hemingway." *Lost Generation Journal* 3 (1975): 15–17.
[*In Our Time*]

Boutelle, Ann Edwards. "Hemingway and 'Papa': Killing of the Father in the Nick Adams Fiction." *Journal of Modern Literature* 9 (1981): 133–46.
[*The Nick Adams Stories*, 6]

Brasch, James D. "Invention From Knowledge: The Hemingway-Cowley Correspondence." *Ernest Hemingway: The Writer in Context*. Ed. James Nagel. Madison: University of Wisconsin Press, 1984: 201–36.

Bredahl, A. Carl. "Divided Narrative and Ernest Hemingway." *Literary Half-Yearly* 24, no.1 (January 1983): 15–21.
[*In Our Time*, 6, 52]

Breidlid, Anders. "Courage and Self-Affirmation in Ernest Hemingway's 'Lost Generation' Fiction." *Edda: Nordisk Tideskrift for Litteraturforskning* (1979): 279–99.
[*In Our Time*]

Brenner. *In Our Time*. Pp. 10, 72.

Brenner. *Men Without Women*. Pp. 21–22, 53.

Brenner. *The Nick Adams Stories*. Pp. 17–18.

Brenner. *Winner Take Nothing*. P. 53.

Brkic, Svetozar. "Ernest Hemingway." *Svetla Lovina* (1972): 203–23. (Translated by Natasha Kolchevska and reprinted in Thorson, James L., ed. *Yugoslav Perspective on American Literature: An Anthology*. Ann Arbor, Mich.: Ardis, 1980: 89–101.)
[*In Our Time*, 52, 88]

Browne, Phiefer. "Men and Women, Africa and Civilization: A Study of the African Stories of Hemingway and the African Novels of Haggard, Greene, and Bellow." *DAI* 40 (1979): 246A (Rutgers University).

Bruccoli. *In Our Time*. P. 26.

Bruccoli. *Men Without Women*. Pp. 58, 60.

Burgess. *In Our Time*. Pp. 32, 40.

Burgess. *in our time*. Pp. 32, 35, 36.

Burgess. *Men Without Women*. P. 50.

Burns, Stuart L. "Scrambling the Unscrambleable: *The Nick Adams Stories*." *Arizona Quarterly* 33 (1977): 133–40.

Butterfield, Herbie. "Ernest Hemingway." *American Fiction: New Readings*. Ed. Richard Gray. London: Vision; Totowa, N.J.: Barnes, 1983: 184–99.
[*In Our Time*, *Men Without Women*, *Winner Take Nothing*, 6, 27, 46, 51, 67, 88, 92]

Cagle, Charles Harmon. "'Cezanne Nearly Did': Stein, Cezanne, and Hemingway." *Midwest Quarterly: A Journal of Contemporary Thought* 23 (1982): 268–78.
[*The Nick Adams Stories*, 6]

Camati, Anna Stegh. "Ritual as Indicative of a Code of Values in Hemingway's *In Our Time*." *Revista Letras* (*Parana, Brazil*) 31 (1982): 11–25.
[*In Our Time*]

Capellan. *In Our Time*. Pp. 68, 72, 77, 84, 85, 155, 169–70, 213, 222.

Capellan. *in our time*. P. 222.

Cappel. *In Our Time*. P. 58.

Cappel. *in our time*. P. 57.

Cappel. *Three Stories and Ten Poems*. Pp. 120, 160.

Carabine, Keith. "'A Pretty Good Unity': A Study of Sherwood Anderson's *Winesburg, Ohio* and Ernest Hemingway's *In Our Time*." *DAI* 39 (1978): 2936A–37A (Yale).

Carabine, Keith. "Hemingway's *In Our Time*: An Appreciation." *Fitzgerald-Hemingway Annual* (1979): 301–26.
[*In Our Time, in our time*]

Clifford, John. "A Response from the Margin." *College English* 49 (1987): 692–706.
[*In Our Time*]

Comley, Nancy. "Hemingway: The Economics of Survival." *Novel: A Forum on Fiction* 12 (1979): 244–53.
[6, 52, 89]

Cooper. *In Our Time*. Pp. 4, 15, 22–24, 25, 26, 32.

Cooper. *Men Without Women*. Pp. 26, 28, 33.

Cooper. *Winner Take Nothing*. P. 62.

Corkin, Stanley. "Hemingway, Film, and U.S. Culture: *In Our Time* and *The Birth of a Nation*." *A Moving Picture Feast: The Filmgoer's Hemingway*. Ed. Charles M. Oliver. New York: Praeger, 1989: 148–61.

Corkin, Stanley. "Realism and Cultural Form: The Common Structures of American Cinema and Realistic Literature in the Late Nineteenth and Early Twentieth Century." *DAI* 46 (1985): 185A (New York University).
[*In Our Time*, 6, 106]

Cowley, Malcolm. "Mr. Papa and the Parricides." *And I Worked at the Writer's Trade*. New York: Viking Penguin, 1978: 21–34. (Reprinted in Bloom, Harold, ed. *Ernest Hemingway*. New York: Chelsea House, 1985: 1961–71.)
[25, 27, 88]

Cox, James M. "*In Our Time*: The Essential Hemingway." *Southern Humanities Review* 22, no. 4 (Fall 1988): 305–20.

Culver, Michael. "The Image of Woman in the Art of Ernest Hemingway, Edward Hopper, and Howard Hawks." Dissertation, University of Louisville, 1986. Ann Arbor: UMI Research Press, 1987. 8621444.
[*In Our Time*, 6, 10, 15, 52, 86]

Dahiya. *In Our Time*. Pp. 19, 20, 21, 22, 42, 52, 116.

Dahiya. *Men Without Women*. P. 19.

Dahiya. *The Nick Adams Stories*. Pp. 18, 19–48.

Dahiya. *Winner Take Nothing*. P.19.

Dangulov, Savva. "Hemingway as Illustrated by Orest Vareisky." Trans. A. Miller. *Soviet Literature* 9 (1976): 161–64.
[56, 86, 88]

DeFalco, Joseph. "Hemingway, Sport, and the Larger Metaphor." *Lost Generation Journal* 3 (1975): 18–20.
[*The Fifth Column and the First Forty-nine Stories*, 6, 56, 86, 88, 96]

Donaldson. *In Our Time*. Pp. 19–20, 38, 39, 40, 98, 135, 195, 200, 201, 205, 224, 273, 296.

Donaldson. *in our time*. Pp. 201, 292.

Donaldson, Scott. "Woolf vs. Hemingway." *Journal of Modern Literature* 10 (1983): 338–42.
[*Men Without Women*]

Durham, Philip. "Ernest Hemingway's Grace Under Pressure: The Western Code." *Pacific Historical Review* 45 (1976): 425–32.
[*The Nick Adams Stories*, 41]

Dupre, Roger. "Hemingway's *In Our Time:* A Contextual Explication." *DAI* 40 (1979): 2662A (St. John's University).

Elliot, Gary D. "The Hemingway's Hero's Quest for Faith." *McNeese Review* 24 (1977-78): 18–27.
[27, 60, 93]

Falbo, Ernest S. "Carlo Linati: Hemingway's First Italian Critic and Translator." *Fitzgerald-Hemingway Annual* (1975): 293–306.
[*In Our Time*, 6, 52, 56, 89]

Fishkin, Shelley Fisher. "Ernest Hemingway." *From Fact to Fiction: Journalism and Imaginative Writing in America.* Baltimore: John Hopkins University Press, 1985: 135–64.
[*In Our Time, in our time*, 6, 29, 89]

Fleming, Robert E. "American Nightmare: Hemingway and the West." *The Midwest Quarterly* 30 (Spring 1989): 361–71.
[41, 61, 88, 108]

Fleming, Robert E. "The Importance of Count Mippipopolous: Creating the Code Hero." *Arizona Quarterly* 44, no. 2 (Summer 1988): 69–75.
[Briefly mentions 40, 41, 51, 86, 96]

Fleming, Robert E. "Portrait of the Artist as a Bad Man: Hemingway's Career at the Crossroads." *North Dakota Quarterly* 55.1 (1987): 66–71.
[41, 65, 88]

Flora (*Study of Short Fiction*). *The Fifth Column and the First Forty-nine Stories.* Pp. 89–100.

Flora (*Nick Adams*). *In Our Time.* Pp. 1, 8, 10, 11, 13, 16, 21–22, 34, 36, 43, 46, 52–53, 58, 61, 63, 68, 69, 83, 87, 92, 105, 106, 107, 109–15, 129, 148–49, 157, 178–83, 190, 191, 213, 224.

Flora (*Study of Short Fiction*). *In Our Time.* Pp. 26–27, 30, 41, 54, 55, 56, 59, 61–62, 90, 95, 100, 102–4, 108.

Flora (*Nick Adams*). *in our time.* Pp. 105, 145, 213.

Flora (*Study of Short Fiction*). *Men Without Women.* Pp. 33, 34, 36, 55, 59, 61–62, 100, 108.

Flora (*Nick Adams*). *Men Without Women.* Pp. 1, 16, 46, 68, 69, 106, 113, 123, 139, 179, 199, 200, 211, 213, 224.

Flora (*Nick Adams*). *The Nick Adams Stories.* Pp. 10, 14, 16, 68, 110, 176, 188, 198, 199, 216.

Flora (*Nick Adams*). *Winner Take Nothing.* Pp. 1, 16, 68, 70, 109, 113, 123, 125, 126, 210, 215–16, 217, 218, 223, 224, 230, 234, 236, 249, 251, 252, 259, 279.

Flora (*Study of Short Fiction*). *Winner Take Nothing.* Pp. 61, 63, 65, 66.

Flora, Joseph M. "A Closer Look at the Young Nick Adams and His Father." *Studies in Short Fiction* 14 (1977): 75–78.

Friedrich, Otto. *In Our Time.* Pp. 112–13.

Gajdusek, Robert E. "Dubliners in Michigan: Joyce's Presence in Hemingway's *In Our Time.*" *Hemingway Review* 2 (1982): 48–61.

Gajdusek, Robert E. "Purgation/Debridement as Therapy/Aesthetics." *Hemingway Review* 4, no. 2 (Spring 1985): 12–17.
[*In Our Time*, 52, 88]

Garnica, Olga K. "Rules of Verbal Interaction and Literary Analysis." *Poetics: International Review for the Theory of Literature* 6 (1977): 155–67.
[*in our time*]

Gelderman, Carol. "Hemingway's Drinking Fixation." *Lost Generation Journal* 6 (1979): 12–14.
[29, 65, 67, 78, 92, 106]

Gerogiannis, Nicholas. "Nick Adams on the Road: 'The Battler' as Hemingway's Man on the Hill." *Critical Essays on Ernest Hemingway's "In Our Time."* Boston: Hall, 1983: 176–88. [5, 59]

Giger. *In Our Time.* Pp. 24–36.

Griffin, Peter. "Introduction" (to "The Young Hemingway: Three Unpublished Stories"). *New York Times Magazine,* August 18, 1985: 15. [2a, 29a, 62a]

Grimes. *In Our Time.* Pp. 6, 9, 12–13, 14, 28, 35–52.

Grimes. *in our time.* Pp. 6, 37–39.

Grimes, Larry. "Night Terror and Morning Calm: A Reading of Hemingway's 'Indian Camp' as Sequel to 'Three Shots.'" *Studies in Short Fiction* 12 (1975): 413–15.

Grimes. *Men Without Women.* Pp. 53, 97.

Grimes. *Winner Take Nothing.* P. 53.

Gullason, Thomas A. "The 'Lesser' Renaissance: The American Short Story in the 1920's." *The American Short Story, 1900–1945: A Critical History.* Ed. Philip Stevick. Boston: Twayne, 1984: 71–101. [*In Our Time, Men Without Women,* 6, 46, 51, 56, 67, 96]

Gurko, Leo. "Hemingway and the Magical Journey." *Hemingway: A Revaluation.* Ed. Donald R. Noble. Troy, N.Y.: Whitson, 1983: 67–82. [1, 6, 27]

Hagemann, E. R. "A Collation, with Commentary, of the Five Texts of the Chapters in Hemingway's *In Our Time." PBSA: Papers of the Bibliographical Society of America* 73 (1979): 443–58. (Reprinted in Reynolds, Michael S., ed. *Critical Essays on Ernest Hemingway's "In Our Time."* Boston: Hall, 1983: 38–51.)

Hagemann, E. R. "A Preliminary Report on the State of Ernest Hemingway's Correspondence." *Literary Research Newsletter* 3 (1978): 163–72. [*In Our Time*]

Hagemann, E. R. "'Dear Folks . . . Dear Ezra'; Hemingway's Early Years and Correspondence." *College Literature* 7 (1980): 202–12. (Reprinted in Oldsey, Bernard, ed. *Ernest Hemingway: The Papers of a Writer.* New York: Garland, 1981: 25–35.) [*in our time,* 51, 107]

Hagemann, E. R. "'Only Let the Story End as Soon as Possible': Time-and-History in Ernest Hemingway's *In Our Time." Modern Fiction Studies* 26 (1980): 255–62. (Reprinted in Reynolds, Michael S., ed. *Critical Essays on Ernest Hemingway's "In Our Time."* Boston: Hall, 1983: 52–60.) [*In Our Time*]

Hagemann, E. R. "Word-Count and Statistical Survey of the Chapters in Ernest Hemingway's *In Our Time." Literary Research Newsletter* 5 (1980): 21–30.

Hagemann, Meyly Chin. "Hemingway's Secret: Visual to Verbal Art." *Journal of Modern Literature* 7 (1979): 87–112. [52, 78]

Hagopian, John V. "Hemingway: Ultimate Exile." *Mosaic: A Journal for the Interdisciplinary Study of Literature* 8 (1975): 77–87. [*Hemingway Reader, In Our Time, Three Stories and Ten Poems*]

Hamid, Syed Ali. "'A Separate Peace': Nature of Alienation in Hemingway's Short Fiction." *Panjab University Research Bulletin (Arts)* 18, no. 1 (April 1987): 55–57.

Hannum, Howard L. "The Case of Doctor Henry Adams." *Arizona Quarterly* 44, no. 2 (Summer 1988): 39–57. [35, 39, 52, 72, 91, 92]

Hannum, Howard L. "Hemingway's Revenge and the Vulcan Myth." *Studies in Short Fiction* 25, no. 1 (Winter 1988): 73–76. [35, 52, 60, 61, 105]

Hannum, Howard L. "Hemingway's Tales of 'The Real Dark.'" *Hemingway's Neglected Short Fiction*. Ed. Susan F. Beegel. Ann Arbor: UMI Research Press, 1989: 339–50.
[42, 61]

Hannum, Howard L. "Nick Adams and the Search for Light." *Studies in Short Fiction* 23 (Winter 1986): 9–18.
[5, 36, 56, 60, 92]

Hardy and Cull. *In Our Time*. P. 27.

Hardy and Cull. *Men Without Women*. Pp. 37–38.

Hays, Peter. "Hemingway, Faulkner, and a Bicycle Built for Death." *NMAL: Notes on Modern American Literature* 5 (1981): item 28.
[46, 86, 88, 107]

Hays, Peter. "Hemingway, Nick Adams, and David Bourne: Sons and Writers." *Arizona Quarterly* 44, no. 2 (Summer 1988): 28–38.
[5, 29, 35, 39, 46, 52, 56, 60, 72, 92, 93]

Hedeen, Paul M. "Moving in the Picture: The Landscape Stylistics of *In Our Time*." *Language and Style: An International Journal* 18, no. 4 (Fall 1985): 363–76.

Hemingway, Ernest. "The Art of the Short Story." *Paris Review* 79 (1981): 85–102. (Reprinted in Joseph M. Flora, ed., *Ernest Hemingway: A Study of the Short Fiction*. Boston: Twayne, 1989: 127–44.)
[6, 40, 56, 60, 67, 84, 86, 88, 91, 94, 96, 107]

Henricksen, Bruce. "The Bullfight Story and Critical Theory." *Hemingway's Neglected Short Fiction: New Perspectives*. Ed. Susan F. Beegel. Ann Arbor: UMI Research Press, 1989: 107–22.
[*In Our Time*, 19, 20, 21, 22, 23, 24]

Higa, Miyoko. "An Approach to Hemingway's First Wife, Elizabeth Hadley Richardson." *Kyushu American Literature* 24 (1983): 15–30.
[47, 51, 88]

Hily-Mane, Genevieve. "Point of View in Hemingway's Novels and Short Stories: A Study of the Manuscripts." *Hemingway Review* 5, no. 2 (Spring 1986): 37–44.

Hoffer, Bates. "Hemingway's Religious Themes." *Linguistics in Literature* 4 (1979): 57–70.
[94, 107]

Hoffer, Bates. "Hemingway's Use of Stylistics." *Linguistics in Literature* 1 (1976): 89–121.
[27, 36, 46, 88]

Hoffman, Charles G., and A. C. Hoffman. "'The Truest Sentence': Words as Equivalents of Time and Place *In Our Time*." *Hemingway: A Revaluation*. Ed. Donald R. Noble. Troy, N.Y.: Whitson, 1983: 99–113.
[*In Our Time*, 5, 6, 10, 19, 23, 24, 25, 29, 36, 52, 65, 74, 89, 92, 106]

Hoffman, Steven K. "Nada and the Clean, Well-Lighted Place: The Unity of Hemingway's Short Fiction." *Essays in Literature* 6 (1979): 91–110. (Reprinted in Harold Bloom, ed. *Ernest Hemingway*. New York: Chelsea House, 1985: 173–92.)
[6, 9, 29, 41, 56, 72, 88, 96, 107]

Holder, Robert Conner, Jr. "The Tip of the Iceberg: The Naturalistic Pattern in the Fiction of Ernest Hemingway." *DAI* 36 (1976): 5298A (Indiana University).
[*In Our Time*]

Iacone, Salvatore J. "Alienation and the Hemingway Hero." *DAI* 41 (1980): 251A (St. John's University).
[*In Our Time*, *Nick Adams Stories*, 6, 10, 27, 35, 51, 65, 72, 86, 88, 89, 107]

Johnston, Kenneth G. "Hemingway and Cezanne: Doing the Country." *American Literature* 56, no. 1 (March 1984): 28–37. (Revised as "Hemingway and Cézanne: Patches of White," and reprinted in *The Tip of the Iceberg: Hemingway and the Short Story*. Greenwood, Fla.: Penkevill, 1987: 11–25.)
[6, 105]

Johnston, Kenneth G. "Hemingway's Search for Story Titles." *Hemingway Review* 6, no. 2 (Spring 1987): 34–37.
[86, 88, 108]

Johnston, Kenneth G. "The Bull and the Lion: Hemingway's Fables for Critics." *Fitzgerald-Hemingway Annual* (1977): 149–56. (Revised as "'The Faithful Bull' and 'The Good Lion,'" and reprinted in *The Tip of the Iceberg: Hemingway and the Short Story*. Greenwood, Fla.: Penkevill, 1987: 233–43.)
[38, 44]

Joost, Nicholas, and Alan Brown. "T. S. Eliot and Ernest Hemingway: A Literary Relationship." *Papers on Language and Literature: A Journal for Scholars and Critics of Language and Literature* 14 (1978): 424–25.

Josephs, Allen. "Hemingway's Spanish Civil War Stories, or the Spanish Civil War as Reality." *Hemingway's Neglected Short Fiction*. Ed. Susan F. Beegel. Ann Arbor: UMI Research Press, 1989: 313–28.
[7, 33, 58, 69, 97]

Junkins, Donald. "Hemingway's Contribution to American Poetry." *Hemingway Review* 4, no. 2 (Spring 1985): 18–23.
[*In Our Time*, 10, 36]

Justus, James H. "Hemingway and Faulkner: Vision and Repudiation." *Kenyon Review* ns 7, no. 4 (Fall 1985): 1–14.
[*In Our Time*]

Kanjo, Eugene. "Hemingway's Cinematic Style." *A Moving Picture Feast*. Ed. Charles M. Oliver. New York: Praeger, 1989: 3–11.
[*In Our Time*, 79, 89]

Kann, Hans-Joachim. "Ernest Hemingway and the Arts: A Necessary Addendeum." *Fitzgerald-Hemingway Annual* (1974): 145–54.
[*The Nick Adams Stories*]

Kapoor, S. D. "Ernest Hemingway: The Man and the Mask: The Biographies of Ernest Hemingway." *Rajasthan University Studies in English* 8 (1975): 36–53.
[*In Our Time*, 88]

Kazin, Alfred. "Hemingway the Painter." *An American Procession*. New York: Knopf, 1984. 357–73. (Reprinted in Harold Bloom, ed. *Ernest Hemingway*. New York: Chelsea House, 1985: 193–209.)
[*In Our Time*, 5, 6, 52]

Kazin, Alfred. "Hemingway, Painting, and the Search for Serenity." *Hemingway: A Revaluation*. Ed. Donald R. Noble. Troy, N.Y.: Whitson, 1983: 49–65.
[*In Our Time*, 6, 105]

Keever, Martha L. "The Narration of the Nick Adams Stories." *DAI* 42 (1982): 3596A (University of North Carolina, Chapel Hill).

Kerner, David. "Fitzgerald vs. Hemingway: The Origins of Anti-Metronomic Dialogue." *Modern Fiction Studies* 28 (1982): 247–50.
[27, 92]

Kert. *In Our Time*. Pp. 138, 143–44, 151, 154, 169, 190.

Kobler. *in our time*. Pp. 11, 13, 26, 28.

Kobler, J. F. "Hemingway's Four Dramatic Short Stories." *Fitzgerald-Hemingway* (1975): 247–57.
[27, 46, 56, 84, 94]

Kort, Wesley A. "Human Time in Hemingway's Fiction." *Modern Fiction Studies* 26 (1980): 579–96.
[*In Our Time*]

Kretzoi, Charlotte. "Hemingway on Bullfights and Aesthetics." *Studies in English and*

American. Vol II. Eds. Erzsebet Perenyi and Tibor Frank. Budapest: Department of English, L. Eotrus University, 1975: 277–96.

Kriegel, Leonard. "Hemingway's River of Manhood." *Partisan Review* 44 (1977): 418–30.
[5, 39]

Kyle, Frank B. "Parallel and Complementary Themes in Hemingway's 'Big Two-Hearted River' Stories and 'The Battler.'" *Studies in Short Fiction* 16 (1979): 295–300.

Lamb, Robert Paul. "Eternity's Artifice: Time and Transcendence in the Works of Ernest Hemingway." *Hemingway Review* 4, no. 2 (Spring 1985): 422–52.
[*The Nick Adams Stories,* 88, 89]

Lawrence, Frank M. "Death in the Matinee: The Film Endings of Hemingway's Fiction." *A Moving Picture Feast.* Ed. Charles M. Oliver. New York: Praeger, 1989: 26–31.
[67, 88]

Leigh, David J., S. J. "*In Our Time:* The Interchapters as Structural Guides to a Psychological Pattern." *Studies in Short Fiction* 12 (1975): 1–8. (Reprinted in Reynolds, Michael S., ed. *Critical Essays on Ernest Hemingway's "In Our Time."* Boston: Hall, 1983: 130–37.)

Leland, John. "'The Happiness of the Garden': Hemingway's Edenic Quest." *Hemingway Review* 3 (1983): 44–53.
[6, 36, 46, 59, 88]

Lewis, Robert W. "Hemingway in Italy: Making It Up." *Journal of Modern Literature* 9 (1982): 209–36.
[*Winner Take Nothing,* 26, 68, 89]

Lohani, Schreedhar Prasad. "The Narrator in Fiction: A Study of the Narrator's Presence in Joyce's *Dubliners* and Hemingway's *In Our Time.*" *DAI* 45.8 (February 1985): 2517A (University of Southern Illinois, Carbondale).

Lowry, E. D. "Chaos and Cosmos in *In Our Time.*" *Literature and Psychology* 26 (1976): 108–17.

Lynn. *In Our Time.* Pp. 265–67, 270–71, 302, 306–7, 314, 331, 360.

Lynn. *in our time.* Pp. 90–91.

Lynn, Kenneth S. "Hemingway's Private War." *Commentary* 72 (1981): 24–33.

Lynn. *Men Without Women.* Pp. 262, 309–10, 365–66, 369–70.

Lynn. *The Fifth Column and the First Forty-nine Stories.* P. 471.

Lynn. *Three Stories and Ten Poems.* Pp. 215, 224.

Lynn. *Winner Take Nothing.* Pp. 408–11.

Mann, Susan Garland. "A Bibliographic and Generic Study of the Short Story Cycle: Essay on *Dubliners, Winesburg Ohio, In Our Time, Pastures of Heaven, The Unvanquished,* and *Go Down Moses.*" *DAI* 45.6 (December 1984): 1748A (Miami University).

Marx, Paul. "Hemingway and Ethics." *Essays in Arts and Sciences* 8 (1979): 35–44. (Reprinted in Filler, Louis, ed. *Seasoned Authors for a New Season: The Search for Standards in Popular Writing.* Bowling Green, Ohio: Popular Press, 1980. 43–50.)
[56, 62, 89]

Mayer, Charles W. "The Triumph of Honor: James and Hemingway." *Arizona Quarterly* 35 (1979): 373–91.
[*In Our Time*]

McCartin, James T. "Ernest Hemingway: The Life and the Works." *Arizona Quarterly* 39 (1983): 122–34.
[46, 84, 86]

McConnell, Frank. "Stalking Papa's Ghost: Hemingway's Presence in Contemporary American Writing." *Ernest Hemingway: New Critical Essays.* Ed. Robert A. Lee. London: Vision; Totowa, N.J.: Barnes, 1983: 193–211.
[*In Our Time,* 6, 56]

Messenger, Christian. "Hemingway and the School Athletic Hero." *Lost Generation Journal* 3 (1975): 21–23.
[5, 40, 56, 96]

Meyer, B. Ruth. "The Old Men in Hemingway's Fiction." *DAI* 40 (1979): 258A (Kansas State University).

[2, 10, 27, 73, 96]

Meyers (*A Biography*). *In Our Time*. Pp. 26, 83, 127, 143–46, 167–69, 188, 228.

Meyers (*A Biography*). *in our time*. Pp. 98–102, 105–6, 141–43, 146, 185, 284, 391.

Meyers (*A Biography*). *Men Without Women*. Pp. 112, 198.

Meyers (*A Biography*). *Three Stories and Ten Poems*. Pp. 49, 89, 141, 146.

Meyers (*A Biography*). *Winner Take Nothing*. Pp. 257–59, 261.

Meyers, Jeffrey. Introduction. *Hemingway: The Critical Heritage*. Ed. Meyers. London: Routledge, 1982: 1–62.

[*In Our Time, in our time, The Fifth Column and the First Forty-nine Stories, The Nick Adams Stories, Three Stories and Ten Poems, Winner Take Nothing*]

Moddelmog, Debra A. "The Unifying Consciousness of a Divided Conscience: Nick Adams as Author of *In Our Time*." *American Literature* 60 (December 1988): 591–610.

[*In Our Time*, 5, 6, 10, 29, 36, 39, 52, 65, 67, 72, 78, 89, 92, 106]

Monk, Donald. "Hemingway's Territorial Imperative." *Yearbook of English Studies* 8 (1978): 125–40.

[*In Our Time*, 6, 27, 56, 60]

Monteiro, George. "Hemingway's Unnatural History of the Dying." *Fitzgerald-Hemingway Annual* (1978): 339–42.

[*Winner Take Nothing*]

Monteiro, George. "Innocence and Experience: The Adolescent Child in the Works of Mark Twain, Henry James, and Ernest Hemingway." *Estudos Anglo-Americanos (Sao Jose de Rio Preto)* 1 (1977): 39–57.

Mottran, Eric. "Essential History: Suicide and Nostalgia in Hemingway's Fictions." *Ernest Hemingway: New Critical Essays*. Ed. Robert A. Lee. London: Vision; Totowa, N.J.: Barnes, 1983: 122–50.

[27, 39, 43, 52, 86, 88, 94]

Muller, Gilbert H. "*In Our Time:* Hemingway and the Discontents of Civilization." *Renascence: Essays on Value in Literature* 29 (1977): 185–92.

[*In Our Time*]

Murray, Donald M. "Thoreau and Hemingway." *Thoreau Journal Quarterly* 11 (1979): 13–33.

Nagel, James. "Literary Impressionism and *In Our Time*." *Hemingway Review* 6, no. 2 (Spring 1987): 17–26.

Nakajima, Kenji. "Literary Bravery in Hemingway's 'Chapter III' and 'Chapter IV' of *In Our Time*." *Kyushu American Literature* 27 (1986): 47–56.

Nakjavani, Erik. "The Aesthetics of Meiosis: Hemingway's 'Theory of Omission.'" *DAI* 46.6 (December 1985): 1628A.

[*In Our Time, The Nick Adams Stories*]

Nakjavani, Erik. "The Aesthetics of the Visible and the Invisible: Hemingway and Cezanne." *Hemingway Review* 5, no. 2 (Spring 1986): 2–11.

[*In Our Time, The Nick Adams Stories*]

Nakjavani, Erik. "Hemingway on Nonthinking." *North Dakota Quarterly* 57.3 (Summer 1989): 173–98.

[6, 29, 40, 41]

Nelson. *In Our Time*. Pp. 1, 12, 13, 19.

Nelson. *in our time*. Pp. 6, 12.

Nelson. *Men Without Women*. P. 12.

Nelson. *The Nick Adams Stories*. Pp. 16, 19, 25, 36, 38, 39.

Nelson. *The Short Stories of EH*. Pp. 13, 14–15.

Nelson. *Winner Take Nothing*. Pp. 8, 13.

Nicholson, Colin E. "The Short Stories After *In Our Time*: A Profile." *Ernest Hemingway: New*

Critical Essays. Ed. Robert A. Lee. London: Vision; Totowa, N.J.: Barnes, 1983: 36–48.
[*In Our Time*, 8, 27, 40, 41, 46, 51, 56, 72, 73, 81, 84, 88, 94, 107, 108]

Nolan, Charles J., Jr. "Hemingway's Women's Movement." *Hemingway Review* 3, no. 2 (Spring 1984): 14–22. (Reprinted in Wagner, Linda W., ed. *Ernest Hemingway: Six Decades of Criticism*. East Lansing: Michigan State University Press, 1987: 209–19.)
[*In Our Time*, 10, 36, 46, 78, 86, 88, 105]

Oldsey, Bernard. "Hemingway's Beginnings and Endings." *College Literature* 7 (1980): 213–38. (Reprinted in Oldsey, Bernard, ed. *Ernest Hemingway: The Papers of a Writer*. New York: Garland, 1981: 37–62; and in Wagner, Linda W., ed. *Ernest Hemingway: Six Decades of Criticism*. East Lansing: Michigan State University Press, 1987: 113–38.)
[6, 52, 86]

Oldsey, Bernard. "The Genesis of *A Farewell to Arms*." *Studies in American Fiction* 5 (1977): 175–85.

Oppenheim, Rosa. "The Mathematical Analysis of Style: A Correlation Based Approach." *Computers and the Humanities* 22 (1988): 241–52.
[*In Our Time*, 6]

O'Sullivan, Sibbie. "Love and Friendship/Man and Woman in *The Sun Also Rises*." *Arizona Quarterly* 44, no. 2 (Summer 1988): 76–97.
[Briefly mentions 5, 36, 67]

O'Sullivan, Sylvia Geraldine. "Hemingway vs. Hemingway: Femininity and Masculinity in the Major Works." *DAI* 48 (1987): 127A (University of Maryland).

Phillips, Gene D. "Novelist Versus Screenwriter: The Case for Casey Robinson's Adaptations of Hemingway's Fiction." *A Moving Picture Feast*. Ed. Charles M. Oliver. New York: Praeger, 1989: 12–18.
[67, 86, 88]

Pickard, Linda Kay Haskovec. "A Stylo-Linguistic Analysis of Four American Writers." *DAI* 36 (1976): 6103A (Texas Woman's University).
[*The Nick Adams Stories*]

Pizer, Donald. "The Hemingway-Dos Passos Relationship." *Journal of Modern Literature* 13, no. 1 (March 1986): 111–28.
[*In Our Time*, 86, 88, 90]

Portch, Stephen Ralph. "Writing Without Words: A Nonverbal Approach to the Short Fiction of Hawthorne, Hemingway, and O'Connor." *DAI* 43 (1983): 2349A (Penn State University).
[46, 56]

Portch, Stephen R. "The Hemingway Touch." *Hemingway Review* 2 (1982): 43–47.
[46, 56]

Pullin, Faith. "Hemingway and the Secret Language of Hate." *Ernest Hemingway: New Critical Essays*. Ed. Robert A. Lee. London: Vision; Totowa, N.J.: Barnes, 1983: 172–92.
[*In Our Time*, 6, 8, 10, 36, 46, 52, 65, 84, 86, 88, 89, 92, 106]

Putnam, Ann Lenore. "Retreat, Advance, and Holding Steady: Vision and Form in the Short Stories of Ernest Hemingway." *DAI* 46.2 (August 1985): 425A–26A (University of Washington).

Radeljkovic, Zvonimir. "Initial Europe: 1918 as a Shaping Element in Hemingway's Weltanschauung." *College Literature* 7 (1980): 304–9. (Reprinted in Bernard Oldsey, ed. *Ernest Hemingway: The Papers of a Writer*. New York: Garland, 1981: 133–38.)
[29a, 62a, 843–44]

Raeburn, John. "Hemingway in the Twenties: 'The Artist's Reward.'" *Rocky Mountain Review of Language and Literature* 29 (1975): 118–46.
[*In Our Time, in our time, Men Without Women*]

Rao, E. Nageswara. "Syntax as Rhetoric: An Analysis of Ernest Hemingway's Early Syntax." *Indian Linguistics: Journal of the Linguistic Society of India* 36 (1975): 296–303.
[*in our time*, 13, 29, 36]

Rao, E. Nageswara. "The Motif of Luck in Hemingway." *Journal of American Studies* 13 (1979): 29–35.
[55, 62, 85]

Rao, P. G. Rama. *In Our Time.* Pp. 15, 26, 27, 28, 31, 33, 46, 52, 56, 75, 77, 93, 158–65, 176, 177.

Rao, P. G. Rama. *Men Without Women.* Pp. 45, 122, 123, 126.

Rao, P. G. Rama. *Winner Take Nothing.* Pp. 45, 123, 132, 154.

Reboli, Nicola L. "Death as a Vehicle to Life in the Works of Ernest Hemingway." *Studi dell: Istituto Linguistico* 7 (1984): 333–46.
[*In Our Time,* 5, 35, 51, 56, 96]

Reich, Kenneth E. "Sport in Literature: The Passion of Action." *Jack London Newsletter* 12 (1979): 50–62.
[5, 40, 67, 88]

Reynolds (*The Paris Years*). *In Our Time.* Pp. 232–35, 242, 271–72, 276, 328–31.

Reynolds (*The Paris Years*). *in our time.* Pp. 80–81, 114–17, 123–28, 138–42, 151–52, 181, 198–99, 233–34, 243.

Reynolds (*The Paris Years*). *Three Stories and Ten Poems.* Pp.122, 127–28, 138, 142, 151, 152–53, 164, 181.

Roeder, Gordon Karl Walter. "In Search of a Father: A Comparative Study of Melville and Hemingway." *DAI* 47 (1987): 3421A (University of Oregon).
[*In Our Time,* 27]

Robinson, Sharon. "Hemingway, Emerson, and Nick Adams." *Studies in the Humanities* 7 (1978): 5–9.
[*In Our Time,* 6, 35, 36]

Rodgers, Bernard F., Jr. "The Nick Adams Stories: Fiction or Fact?" *Fitzgerald-Hemingway Annual* (1974): 155–62.
[*The Nick Adams Stories*]

Rohrkemper, John. "The Great War, The Midwest, and Modernism: Cather, Dos Passos, and Hemingway." *Midwestern Miscellany* 16 (1988): 19–29.
[*In Our Time*]

Roseman, Mona G. "Five Hemingway Women." *The Glaflin College Review* 2 (1977): 9–15.
[10, 46, 84, 86, 105]

Rovit and Brenner. *in our time.* Pp. 29–32, 66, 110.

Rovit and Brenner. *Winner Take Nothing.* Pp. 5, 53.

Sangwan, Surender Singh. "Humor in Hemingway's Short Stories." *Panjab University Research Bulletin (Arts)* 18, no. 1 (April 1987): 55–57.

Scafella, Frank. "'I and the Abyss,' Emerson, Hemingway, and the Modern Vision of Death." *Hemingway Review* 4, no. 2 (Spring 1985): 2–6.
[6, 72]

Scafella, Frank. "Imagistic Landscape of a Psyche: Hemingway's Nick Adams." *Hemingway Review* 2 (1983): 2–10.
[*In Our Time, The Nick Adams Stories*]

Scheel, Mark. "Death and Dying: Hemingway's Predominant Theme." *Emporia State Research Studies* 28 (1979): 5–12.

Scholes, Robert. *Textual Power: Literary Theory and the Teaching of English.* New Haven: Yale University Press, 1985: 25–38, 42, 59, 62–73.
[*In Our Time*]

Schwartz, Roberta. "Hemingway Haunts: The Famous Novelist's Roots are Planted Firmly in the Woods of Northern Michigan." *Heritage: A Journal of Grosse Pointe Life* 3 (December 1986): 41–45, 79.
[*The Nick Adams Stories*]

Seed, David. "'The Picture of the Whole': *In Our Time.*" *Ernest Hemingway: New Critical Essays.* Ed. Robert A. Lee. London: Vision; Totowa, N.J.: Barnes, 1983: 13–35.
[*In Our Time, in our time,* 15, 16, 17, 19, 25, 29, 52, 67, 82, 106]

Shaw, Patrick W. "How Earnest is the Image: Hemingway's Animals." *CEA Critic: An Official Journal of the College English Association* 37 (1975): 5–8.
[6, 86, 88]

Smith, Carol H. "Women and the Loss of Eden in Hemingway's Mythology." *Ernest Hemingway: The Writer in Context.* Ed. James Nagel. Madison: University of Wisconsin Press, 1984: 129–44.
[*In Our Time*, 89, 106]

Smith, Leverett T., Jr. "How to Live in it." *The American Dream and the National Game.* Bowling Green, Ohio: Bowling Green Popular University Press, 1975: 51–103.
[5, 6, 27, 40, 41, 56, 86]

Smith. *The Fifth Column and the First Forty-nine Stories.* Pp. 319–65.

Smith. *The Fifth Column and Four Stories.* Pp. 367–88.

Smith. *The Finca Vigia Edition.* Pp. 389–94.

Smith. *In Our Time.* Pp. 23–121.

Smith. *Men Without Women.* Pp. 123–213.

Smith. *Three Stories and Ten Poems.* Pp. 1–22.

Smith. *Winner Take Nothing.* Pp. 215–317.

Smith, Paul. "Hemingway's Apprentice Fiction: 1919–1921." *American Literature* 58, no. 4 (December 1986): 574–88.
[*In Our Time*, 2a, 29a, 31a, 56, 62, 62a, 80b, 105, 445, 532, 670, 604, 843–44]

Smith, Paul. "Hemingway's Early Manuscripts: The Theory and Practice of Omission." *Journal of Modern Literature* 10 (1983): 268–88.
[*In Our Time*, 6, 52, 93]

Smith, Paul. "Hemingway's Luck." *Hemingway Review* 7, no. 1 (1988): 38–42.
[*The Nick Adams Stories*, 29, 39, 59]

Smith, Paul. "Impressions of Ernest Hemingway." *Hemingway Review* 6, no. 2 (Spring 1987): 2–10.
[*In Our Time*, 6]

Smith, Peter A. "Hemingway's 'On the Quai at Smyrna' and the Universe of *In Our Time*." *Studies in Short Fiction* 24 (1987): 159–62.

Sojka, Gregory S. "Hemingway as Angler-Artist." *Lost Generation Journal* 3 (1975): 12–13.
[6, 72, 107]

Sojka, Gregory Stanley. "The 'Aesthetic of Contest' in Ernest Hemingway's Life and Writing." *DAI* 37 (1977): 5128A–29A (Indiana University).
[*The Nick Adams Stories*, 6, 51, 72, 107]

Spilka, Mark. "Hemingway and Fauntleroy: An Androgynous Pursuit." *American Novelists Revisited: Essays in Feminist Criticism.* Ed. Fritz Fleischmann. Boston: Hall, 1982: 339–70.
[86, 88]

Spilka, Mark. "Victorian Key to the Early Hemingway: Part I—John Halifax, Gentleman; Part II—Fauntleroy and Finn." *Journal of Modern Literature* (March and June 1983): 125–50, 289–310.
[*Men Without Women*]

Steinke, James. "Hemingway's 'In Another Country' and 'Now I Lay Me.'" *Hemingway Review* 5, no. 1 (Fall 1985): 32–39.

Steinke, James. "The Art of Hemingway's Early Fiction." *DAI* 44 (1983): 1455A–56A (University of California, Santa Barbara).
[*The Nick Adams Stories*, 6]

Steinke, James. "The Two Shortest Stories of Hemingway's *In Our Time*." *Critical Essays on Ernest Hemingway's "In Our Time."* Ed. Michael S. Reynolds. Boston: Hall, 1983: 218–26.
[*In Our Time, in our time*, 82, 108]

Stephens, Robert O. "Hemingway's British and American Reception: A Study in Values." *Hemingway: A Revaluation*. Ed. Donald Noble. Troy, N.Y.: Whitson, 1983: 83–97.
[*In Our Time, in our time, Men Without Women*]

Stephens, Robert O. Introduction. *Ernest Hemingway: The Critical Reception*. Ed. Robert O. Stephens. New York: Franklin, 1977: ix-xxxv.
[*In Our Time, in our time, The Fifth Column and the First Forty-nine Stories, Men Without Women, The Nick Adams Stories, Winner Take Nothing*]

Stetler, Charles, and Gerald Locklin. "De-Coding the Hero in Hemingway's Fiction." *Hemingway Notes* 5 (1979): 2–10.
[*In Our Time, 6*]

Stetler, Charles, and Gerald Locklin. "Hemingway and the Adult Sports Story." *McNeese Review* 30 (1983–84): 29–37.
[40, 67, 96]

Stevick, Philip. Introduction. *The American Short Story, 1900–1945*. Ed. Philip Stevick. Boston: Twayne, 1984: 1–31.
[15, 46, 92]

Stine, Peter. "Ernest Hemingway and the Great War." *Fitzgerald-Hemingway Annual* (1979): 327–54.
[5, 72, 74, 89]

Stoppard, Tom. "Reflections on Ernest Hemingway." *Ernest Hemingway: The Writer in Context*. Ed. James Nagel. Madison: University of Wisconsin Press, 1984: 19–27.
[*In Our Time, 6, 56*]

Strychacz, Thomas. "Dramatizations of Manhood in Hemingway's *In Our Time* and *The Sun Also Rises*." *American Literature* 61, no. 2 (1989): 245–60.

Svoboda. *In Our Time*. Pp. 1, 14–15, 33, 35, 114.

Svoboda. *in our time*. Pp. 114.

Svoboda. *The Nick Adams Stories*. P. 18.

Sylvester, Bickford. "*Winner Take Nothing*: Development as Dilemma for the Hemingway Heroine." *Pacific Coast Philology* 21, no. 1–2 (November 1986): 73–80.

Tavernier-Courbin, Jacqueline. "The Mystery of the Ritz-Hotel Papers." *College Literature* 7 (1980): 289–303. (Reprinted in Bernard Oldsey, ed. *Ernest Hemingway: The Papers of a Writer*. New York: Garland, 1981: 117–31.)
[40, 56, 96]

Tichi, Cecelia. "Opportunity: Imagination Ex Machina II." *Shifting Gears: Technology, Literature, Culture in Modernist America*. Chapel Hill: North Carolina University Press, 1987: 216–29. (Reprinted in Flora, Joseph M. *Ernest Hemingway: A Study of the Short Fiction*. Boston: Twayne, 1989: 157–71)
[6, 36]

Unrue, John. "Hemingway: The Vital Principal." *The Origins and Originality of American Culture*. Ed. Tibor Frank. Budapest: Akademiai Kiado, 1984: 261–67.
[27, 41, 47, 68, 107, 108]

Vaidyanathan, T. G. "The Nick Adams Stories and the Myth of Initiation." *Indian Studies in American Fiction*. Eds. M. K. Naik, S. K. Desai, and S. Mokashi-Punekar. Dharwar: Karnatak University; India: Macmillan, 1974: 203–18.
[5, 6, 29, 35, 36, 52, 56, 92, 107]

Verduin, Kathleen. "The Lord of Heroes: Hemingway and the Crucified Christ." *Religion and Literature* 19, no. 1 (1988): 21–44.
[*In Our Time, 60, 94*]

Wagner, Linda W. "Juxtaposition in Hemingway's *In Our Time*." *Studies in Short Fiction* 12 (1975): 243–52. (Reprinted in Reynolds, Michael S., ed. *Critical Essays on Ernest Hemingway's "In Our Time."* Boston: Hall, 1983: 120–29.)

Wagner, Linda W. "'Proud and Friendly and Gently': Women in Hemingway's Early

Fiction." *College Literature* 7 (1980): 239–47. (Reprinted in Bernard Oldsey, ed. *Ernest Hemingway: The Papers of a Writer*. New York: Garland, 1981: 63–71.)
[*In Our Time, Men Without Women*, 10, 29, 36, 46, 52, 59, 92, 105]

Wagner, Linda W. "The Poetry in American Fiction." *Prospects: Annual of American Cultural Studies* 2 (1976): 513–26.
[*Three Stories and Ten Poems*, 6, 29, 36, 52, 89]

Waldmeier, Joseph J. "And the Wench is Faith and Value." *Studies in Short Fiction* 24 (Fall 1987): 393–98.
[*In Our Time*, 51, 72]

Watson, James G. "The American Short Story: 1930–45." *The American Short Story, 1900–1945: A Critical History*. Ed. Philip Stevick. Boston: Twayne, 1984: 103–46.
[*In Our Time, The Fifth Column and First Forty-nine Stories, Winner Take Nothing*, 39, 88]

Way, Brian. "Hemingway the Intellectual: A Version of Modernism." *Ernest Hemingway: New Critical Essays*. Ed. Robert A. Lee. London: Vision; Totowa, N.J.: Barnes, 1983: 151–71.
[6, 36, 40, 88, 89, 96]

Wells, David J. "Hemingway in French." *Fitzgerald-Hemingway Annual* (1974): 235–38.
[6, 27, 56, 86, 88]

Westbrook, Max. "Grace Under Pressure: Hemingway and the Summer of 1920." *Ernest Hemingway: The Writer in Context*. Ed. James Nagel. Madison: University of Wisconsin Press, 1984: 77–106. (Reprinted in Linda W. Wagner, ed. *Ernest Hemingway: Six Decades of Criticism*. East Lansing: Michigan State University Press, 1987: 19–40.)

White, William. "Addenda to Hanneman: Hemingway's *Selected Stories*." *Papers of the Bibliographical Society of America* 73, no. 1 (1979): 121–23.
[*The Fifth Column and the First Forty-nine Stories*]

White, William. "A Misprint in Hemingway's *Winner Take Nothing*." *Papers of the Bibliographical Society of America* 72, no. 3 (1978): 360–61.

Whitlow, Roger. "The Destruction/Prevention of the Family Relationship in Hemingway's Fiction." *Literary Review: An International Journal of Contemporary Writing* 20 (1976): 5–16.
[*The Nick Adams Stories*, 35, 52, 86]

Widmayer, Jayne A. "Hemingway's Hemingway Parodies: The Hypocritical Griffon and the Dumb Ox." *Studies in Short Fiction* 18 (1981): 433–38.
[38, 44]

Wilkinson. *In Our Time*. Pp. 12, 33–34, 87.

Wilkinson. *Men Without Women*. P. 87.

Williams. *In Our Time*. Pp. 10, 31–32, 33–34, 35, 52, 89, 90, 93, 97, 143, 192, 229.

Williams. *Men Without Women*. Pp. 11, 89–97.

Williams. *The Nick Adams Stories*. Pp. 90, 100, 105–6.

Williams. *Winner Take Nothing*. Pp. 11, 89, 90, 97–106.

Wilson, Edmund. Introduction. *In Our Time*. By Ernest Hemingway. Volume 1. Scribner, 1925. (Reprinted in Lyle, Guy R., ed. *Praise From Famous Men: An Anthology of Introductions*. Metuchen, N.J.: Scarecrow, 1977: 169–74.)

Wilson, Mark. "Ernest Hemingway as Funnyman." *Thalia: Studies in Literary Humor* 3 (1980): 29–34.

Winchell, Mark Royden. "Fishing the Swamp: 'Big Two-Hearted River' and the Unity of *In Our Time*." *South Carolina Review* 18 (Spring 1986): 18–29.

Winn, Harlan Harbour, III. "Short Story Cycles of Hemingway, Steinbeck, Faulkner, and O'Connor. *DAI* 36 (1976): 4500A (University of Oregon).
[*In Our Time*].

Winn, Harbour. "Hemingway's African Stories and Tolstoy's 'Illich.'" *Studies in Short Fiction* 18 (1981): 451–53.
[86, 88]

Wyatt, David M. "Hemingway's Uncanny Beginnings." *Georgia Review* 31 (1977): 476–501. (Reprinted in *Prodigal Sons: A Study in Authorship and Authority*. Baltimore: John Hopkins University Press, 1980: 52–71.)
[*In Our Time*, 6, 25, 52, 106]

Young, Philip. "Hemingway Papers, Occasional Thoughts." *College Literature* 7 (1980): 310–18. (Reprinted in Oldsey, Bernard, ed. *Ernest Hemingway: The Papers of a Writer*. New York: Garland, 1981: 139–47.)
[Brief mention of *The Nick Adams Stories*, 6, 27, 29, 36, 90, 92]

Young, Philip. "Hemingway: The Writer in Decline." *Hemingway: A Revaluation*. Ed. Donald R. Noble. Troy, N.Y.: Whitson, 1983: 225–39.
[6, 39, 52, 59, 90]

Young, Robert D. "Hemingway's Suicide in His Works." *Hemingway Review* 4, no. 2 (Spring 1985): 24–30.
[6, 27]

Zapf, Hubert. "Reflections vs. Daydream: Two Types of Implied Reader in Hemingway's Fiction." *College Literature* 15, no. 3 (1988): 290–307.
[6, 86, 88]

III   Criticism, Explication, and Commentary on *Individual* Stories, Listed by Story—Including Specific Articles, Segments from Books on Hemingway's Work, and Segments from General Books

Note: Each title for an item of short fiction in the list below is followed by parentheses containing the following information:

(date of composition / date of first publication / place of first publication / abbreviations of Hemingway story collections in which the item has been reprinted).

The Hemingway story collections have been abbreviated as follows:

TSTP	*Three Stories and Ten Poems* (1923)
iot	*in our time* (1924)
IOT	*In Our Time* (1925)
MWW	*Men Without Women* (1927)
WTN	*Winner Take Nothing* (1933)
CS	(Collected Stories) *The Fifth Column and the First Forty-nine Stories* (1938); *The Short Stories of Ernest Hemingway* (1954)
FUS	*The Fifth Column and Four Unpublished Stories of the Spanish Civil War* (1969)
NA	*The Nick Adams Stories* (1972) [Preface by Philip Young]
EHA	*Ernest Hemingway's Apprenticeship: Oak Park, 1916–1917* (1971)
FV	Finca Vigía edition of *The Complete Short Stories of Ernest Hemingway* (1987)

This section is divided into three parts: (A) an alphabetical listing of stories published in Hemingway's lifetime, (B) an alphabetical listing of posthumously published apprenticeship fiction, fragments, parts of longer manuscripts published as short stories, and (C) a tentative list of unpublished sketches and stories. Since in the first volume of this series, parts A and B were listed together by number, the numbers in this new divided list are not sequential, although the story titles are, in each part, listed alphabetically. In part C, a tentative list of unpublished sketches and stories, the numbers given are the Kennedy Library item numbers.

Items listed under a story title which consist of last names followed by page numbers refer to books solely devoted to a discussion of Hemingway's works. Complete publication information for such books is given in Section I of this checklist. The page numbers which are incorporated in these entries differ from the pages listed for particular stories in the book indexes, in that pages listed here refer to something more than mention of the story title, a brief quotation from the story without comment, or brief summary of the story's subject or plot.

Remember also to check for items referring to a particular story, by story number, in Section II (items referring to more than one story). If you have a particular essay in mind, but cannot find it in this section, it will probably be listed in Section II (and can be located by the name of the author or by story number). In a few instances a single story may be mentioned in an essay title while the essay in fact may deal substantially with more than one story.

I am grateful to Paul Smith for reviewing the publication information given in the headings for each story in this section and for his help in putting together information on the unpublished materials. However, any errors in these items should be assigned to me.

A. Published Short Stories (during Hemingway's lifetime)

(1)   **After the Storm**
         (1932/May 1932/*Cosmopolitan*/WTN, CS, FV)
         Beegel (*Craft of Omission*), pp. 6–12, 69–88, 91–92.
         Busch, Frederick. "Icebergs, Islands, Ships Beneath the Sea." *A John Hawkes Symposium: Design and Debris*. Eds. Anthony C. Santore and Michael Pocalyko. New York: New Directions, 1977: 50–63.
         Flora (*Study of Short Fiction*), p. 46.
         Fuentes, p. 133.
         Kert, p. 246.
         Nelson (*H. Expressionist Artist*), p. 36.
         Rao, P. G. Rama, pp. 4, 122, 133–37.
         Smith, pp. 340–45.
         Walker, Robert. "Irony and Allusion in Hemingway's 'After the Storm.'" *Studies in Short Fiction* 13 (1976): 374–76.
         Williams, pp. 97–98, 120.

(2)   **An Alpine Idyll**
         (1926/September 1927/*American Caravan* [anthology]/ MWW, CS, NA, FV)
         Armistead, Myra. "Hemingway's 'An Alpine Idyll.'" *Studies in Short Fiction* 14 (1977): 255–58.
         Brenner, p. 20.
         Dahiya, p. 43.
         Donaldson, p. 284.
         Flora (*Nick Adams*), pp. 198–216.
         Gajdusek, Robert E. "'An Alpine Idyll': The Sunstruck Mountain Vision and the Necessary Valley Journey." *Hemingway's Neglected Short Fiction*. Ed. Susan F. Beegel. Ann Arbor: UMI Research Press, 1989: 163–84.
         Grimes, pp. 71, 73–74.
         Nelson (*H. Expressionist Artist*), p. 30.
         Oinas, Felix J. "The Transformation of Folklore into Literature." *American Contributions to the Eighth International Congress of Slavists, Zagreb and Ljubljana, Sept. 3–9, 1978*. Ed. Victor Terras. 2 vols. Columbus: Slavica, 1978. 1: 570–603.
         Putnam, Ann. "Dissemblings and Disclosure in Hemingway's 'An Alpine Idyll.'" *Hemingway Review* 6, no. 2 (Spring 1987): 27–33.
         Rovit and Brenner, pp. 66, 67.
         Smith, pp. 132–37.

Svobada, p. 17.

Tavernier-Courbin, Jacqueline. "Ernest Hemingway and Ezra Pound." *Ernest Hemingway: The Writer in Context.* Ed. James Nagel. Madison: University of Wisconsin Press, 1984: 179–200.

Unfried, pp. 41–42.

Wagner (*Inventors/Masters*), p. 67.

Williams, pp. 95–96.

(4) **Banal Story**

(1925/Spring–Summer 1926/*Little Review*/MWW, CS, FV)

Brenner, p. 22.

Kvam, Wayne. "Hemingway's 'Banal Story.'" *Fitzgerald-Hemingway Annual* (1974): 181–91.

Monteiro, George. "The Writer on Vocation: Hemingway's 'Banal Story'" *Hemingway's Neglected Short Fiction.* Ed. Susan F. Beegel. Ann Arbor: UMI Research Press, 1989: 141–48.

Nelson (*H. Expressionist Artist*), p. 36.

Rao, P. G. Rama, p. 123.

Reynolds (*The Paris Years*), pp. 266–67, 294.

Smith, pp. 110–14.

Williams, pp. 93–94.

Yannella, Philip R. "Notes on the Manuscript, Date, and Sources of Hemingway's 'Banal Story.'" *Fitzgerald-Hemingway Annual* (1974): 175–79.

(5) **The Battler**

(1925/October 5, 1925/*In Our Time*/ CS, NA, FV)

Baker, pp. 5n, 11n, 24, 35–36.

Bakker, pp. 4, 5–6.

Brenner, pp. 18, 20.

Capellan, pp. 79, 216.

Cappel, pp. 89–91, 168.

Cooper, p. 22.

Dahiya, pp. 21, 22, 41, 42, 43.

Donaldson, p. 136.

Dyer, Joyce. "Hemingway's Use of the Pejorative Term 'Nigger' in 'The Battler.'" *Notes on Contemporary Literature* 16, no. 5 (November 1986): 5–10.

Fitts, Bill D. "'The Battler': Lexical Foregrounding in Hemingway." *Language and Literature* 7 (1982): 81–92.

Flora (*Nick Adams*), pp. 20, 83–109, 115, 148, 157, 161, 162, 210, 256.

Gaggin, pp. 25, 96.

Grimes, pp. 42, 60.

Kobler, pp. 101–2, 118.

Krigel, Leonard. "Hemingway's Rites of Manhood." *Partisan Review* 44 (1977): 415–30.

Lynn, pp. 271–72, 551, 582.

Monteiro, George. "Dating the Events of the 'Three-Day Blow.'" *Fitzgerald-Hemingway Annual* (1977): 207–10. (Reprinted in Michael S. Reynolds, ed. *Critical Essays on Ernest Hemingway's "In Our Time."* Boston: Hall, 1983: 172–75.)

Monteiro, George. "'This is My Pal Bugs': Ernest Hemingway's 'The Battler.'" *Studies in Short Fiction* 23 (Summer 1986): 324–26.

Nakajima, Kenji. "Nick as 'The Battler.'" *Kyushu American Literature* 19 (1978): 45–48.

Nelson (*H. Expressionist Artist*), pp. 56–57.

Phillips, pp. 79–84.

Rao, E. Nageswara, pp. 68–69.

Rao, P. G. Rama, pp. 40, 44, 75, 84, 162.

Reynolds (*The Paris Years*), pp. 279–80.

Rovit and Brenner, pp. 27, 66, 79, 98.

Singer, Glen W. "Huck, Ad, Jim, and Bugs: A Reconsideration: Huckleberry Finn and Hemingway's 'The Battler.'" *NMAL: Notes on Modern American Literature* 3 (1978): item 9.

Smith, pp. 115–21.

Sojka, pp. 74, 77.

Unfried, pp. 18–20.

Wagner (*Inventors/Masters*), pp. 58, 63.

Willis, Mary Kay. "Structural Analysis of 'The Battler.'" *Linguistics in Literature* 1 (1976): 61–67.

(6)   **Big Two-Hearted River**
        (1924/Spring 1925/*This Quarter*/IOT, CS, NA, FV)

Adair, William. "Landscapes of the Mind: 'Big Two-Hearted River.'" *College Literature* 4 (1977): 144–51. (Reprinted in Michael S. Reynolds, ed. *Critical Essays on Ernest Hemingway's "In Our Time."* Boston: Hall, 1983: 260–67.)

Asselineau, Roger. *The Transcendentalist Constant in American Literature.* New York: New York University Press, 1980: 7, 141, 144.

Bakker, pp. 6, 7–8, 28.

Benoit, Raymond. "Again with Fair Creation: Holy Places in American Literature." *Prospects: An Annual Journal of American Cultural Studies* 5 (1980): 315–30.

Brenner, pp. 11, 53, 219.

Bruccoli, pp. 26–27, 57.

Burgess, p. 41.

Capellan, pp. 84, 85, 214.

Cappel, pp. 20, 141–44, 153–58, 170.

Carabine, Keith. "'Big Two-Hearted River': A Reinterpretation." *Hemingway Review* 1 (1982): 39–44.

Cooley, John R. "Nick Adams and 'The Good Place.'" *Southern Humanities Review* 14 (1980): 57–68.

Cooper, pp. 24, 31–32.

Cowley, Malcom. "Hemingway's Wound—and Its Consequences for American Literature." *Georgia Review* 38, no. 2 (Summer 1984): 223–39.

Dahiya, pp. 20, 21.

Donaldson, pp. 79, 176, 191, 234, 240, 245.

Flora (*Nick Adams*), pp. 8, 13, 58, 69, 112, 113, 117, 122, 133, 145–85, 188, 198, 203, 212, 222, 225, 237, 239, 248, 266, 270–78.

Flora (*Study of the Short Fiction*), pp. 51–60.

Fuentes, p. 210.

Gaggin, pp. 25–26, 65–66.

Gibb, Robert. "He Made Him Up: 'Big Two-Hearted River' as Doppelganger." *Hemingway Notes* 5 (1979): 20–24. (Reprinted in Michael S. Reynolds, ed. *Critical Essays on Ernest Hemingway's "In Our Time."* Boston: Hall, 1983: 254–59.)

Giger, pp. 14, 73.

Griffin, p. 222.

Grimes, pp. 21, 35, 49–52, 53, 55, 59, 66–67, 72, 121–22.

Guetti, James. *Word-Music: The Aesthetic Aspect of Narrative Fiction.* New Brunswick, N.J.: Rutgers University Press, 1980: 12–13, 141–43.

Gutwinski, Waldemar. "Cohesion in Hemingway." *Cohesion in Literary Texts: A Study of Some Grammatical and Lexical Features of English Discourse*. The Hague: Mouton, 1976: 127–66.

Hannum, Howard L. "Soldier's Home: Immersion Therapy and Lyric Pattern in 'Big Two-Hearted River.'" *Hemingway Review* 3, no. 2 (Spring 1984): 2–13.

Hardy and Cull, p. 47.

Helfand, Michael. "A Champ Can't Retire Like Anyone Else." *Lost Generation Journal* 3 (1975): 9–10.

Iwasa, Masazumi. "Beauty and Ugliness in Hemingway." *Chu-Shikoku Studies in American Literature* 13 (1977): 1–12.

Johnston, Kenneth G. "Hemingway and Cézanne: Doing the Country." *American Literature* 56, no. 1 (March 1984): 28–37.

Kert, p. 151.

Kobler, pp. 45–47, 60, 118–19, 143.

Lynn, pp. 102–8, 227n.

McLain, Richard L. "Semantics and Style—With the Example of Quintessential Hemingway." *Language and Style: An International Journal* 12 (1979): 63–78. (Reprinted in Linda W. Wagner, ed. *Ernest Hemingway: Six Decades of Criticism*. East Lansing: Michigan State University Press, 1987: 155–62.)

Meyers (*A Biography*), pp. 52, 98, 114, 145, 296, 488.

Nakajima, Kenji. "'Big Two-Hearted River' as the Extreme of Hemingway's Nihilism." Monthly meeting, *Kyushu American Literature Society*. Fukuoka City, June 24, 1978. (Revised and published with the same title in Tokyo: Eichosha, 1979.)

Nelson (*H. Expressionist Artist*), pp. 7, 43, 58, 68.

Phillips, p. 158.

Raeburn, pp. 196–97.

Rao, E. Nageswara, p. 55.

Rao, P. G. Rama, pp. 40, 45, 56, 57, 76, 94, 131, 160, 164.

Reynolds (*H's First War*), pp. 9, 172.

Reynolds (*The Paris Years*), pp. 201–5, 209, 220–21, 247–48, 263, 292.

Reynolds (*Young H*), pp. 40–41.

Rovit and Brenner, pp. 9, 63, 64–67, 98.

Schnitzer, Deborah. *The Pictorial in Modernist Fiction: From Stephen Crane to Ernest Hemingway*. Ann Arbor: UMI Research Press, 1988: 118–38.

Smith, B. J. "'Big Two-Hearted River': The Artist and the Art." *Studies in Short Fiction* 20 (1983): 129–32.

Smith, pp. 85–101.

Sojka, pp. 85–103.

Splake, T. Kilgore. "A Northern Monument to the Young Ernest Hemingway." *Midwestern Miscellany* 13 (1985): 7–9.

Stewart, Jack F. "Christian Allusions in 'Big Two-Hearted River.'" *Studies in Short Fiction* 15 (1978): 194–96.

Svoboda, pp. 18–19, 111–12.

Tintner, Adeline R. "Ernest and Henry: Hemingway's Lover's Quarrel with James." *Ernest Hemingway: The Writer in Context*. Ed. James Nagel. Madison: University of Wisconsin Press, 1984: 165–78.

Unfried, pp. 33–36.

Vijgen, Theo. "A Change of Point of View in Hemingway's 'Big Two-Hearted River.'" *NMAL: Notes on Modern American Literature* 6 (Spring–Summer 1982): 5–6.

Wagner (*Inventors/Masters*), pp. 56–59, 60, 65.

Weeks, Lewis E., Jr. "Two Types of Tension: Art vs. Campcraft in Hemingway's 'Big Two-Hearted River.'" *Studies in Short Fiction* 11 (1974): 433–34.

Whitlow, p. 19.

Wilkinson, pp. 37, 38–39, 45–46.

Williams, pp. 33, 37–38, 39.

(7) **The Butterfly and the Tank**
     (1938/December 1938/*Esquire*/FUS, FV)

Capellan, p. 249.

Donaldson, pp. 113–14.

Flora (*Study of the Short Fiction*), pp. 92–93.

Smith, pp. 375–77.

Wagner (*Inventors/Masters*), pp. 89–90.

(8) **A Canary for One**
     (1926/April 1927/*Scribner's Magazine*/MWW, CS, FV)

Donaldson, pp. 151, 189.

Donaldson, Scott. "Preparing for the End: Hemingway's Revisions of 'A Canary for One.'" *Studies in American Fiction* 6 (1978): 203–11.

Flora (*Nick Adams*), pp. 200, 210, 213–14, 261.

Flora (*Short Fiction*), pp. 36–39.

Hardy and Cull, p. 34.

Ingman, Trisha. "Symbolic Motifs in 'A Canary for One.'" *Linguistics in Literature* 1 (1976): 35–41.

Kert, pp. 183, 185.

Lynn, p. 347.

Martin, W. R., and Warren U. Ober. "Hemingway and James: 'A Canary for One' and 'Daisy Miller.'" *Studies in Short Fiction* 22, no. 4 (Fall 1985): 469–71.

Meyers (*A Biography*), pp. 153, 154.

Nelson (*H. Expressionist Artist*), pp. 34, 45.

Rao, P. G. Rama, p. 122.

Reynolds (*Young H*), p. 201.

Rudnick, Lois P. "Daisy Miller Revisited: Ernest Hemingway's 'A Canary for One.'" *Massachusetts Studies in English* 7 (1978): 12–19.

Smith, pp. 159–63.

Wagner (*Inventors/Masters*), p. 67.

Williams, pp. 92–93.

(9) **The Capital of the World**
     (1936/June 1936/*Esquire*, as "The Horns of the Bull"/CS, FV)

Capellan, pp. 6, 21, 36, 52, 57, 126, 174.

Cooper, Stephen. "Illusion and Reality: 'The Capital of the World.'" *Hemingway's Neglected Short Fiction*. Ed. Susan F. Beegel. Ann Arbor: UMI Research Press, 1989: 303–12.

Dahiya, p. 10.

Flora (*Nick Adams*), p. 253.

Grebstein, Sheldon Norman. "Hemingway's Dark and Bloody Capital." *The Thirties: Fiction, Poetry, Drama*. Ed. Warren French. Revised ed. Deland, Fla.: Everett, 1975: 21–30.

Kobler, p. 28.

Meyers (*A Biography*), pp. 228, 322.

Oldsey, Bernard. "El Pueblo Espanol: 'The Capital of the World.'" *Studies in American Fiction* 13, no. 1 (Spring 1985): 103–10.

Rao, P. G. Rama, p. 140.
Rovit and Brenner, pp. 55–56.
Smith, pp. 321–26.
Williams, pp. 11–12, 124.

(10)   **Cat in the Rain**
(1923–24/October 5, 1925/*In Our Time*/CS, NA, FV)
Bennett, Warren. "The Poor Kitty and the Padrone and the Tortoise-shell Cat in
'Cat in the Rain.'" *Hemingway Review* 8, no. 1 (Fall 1988): 26–36.
Bruccoli, p. 35.
Capellan, p. 72.
Carter, Ronald. "Style and Interpretation in Hemingway's 'Cat in the Rain.'"
Language and Literature: An Introductory Reader in Stylistics. Ed. Ronald Carter.
London: Allen, 1982: 65–80.
Cowley, Malcolm. *And I Worked at the Writer's Trade: Chapters of Literary History,*
1918–1978. New York: Viking, 1978: 208.
Dahiya, p. 186.
Donaldson, pp. 150–51, 242–44.
Flora (*Nick Adams*), p. 191.
Friberg, Ingegerd. "The Reflection in the Mirror: An Interpretation of Heming-
way's Short Story 'Cat in the Rain.'" *Modern Sprak* 76 (1982): 329–38.
Giger, p. 14.
Grimes, pp. 28, 36, 48.
Holmesland, Oddvar. "Structuralism and Interpretation: Ernest Hemingway's
'Cat in the Rain.'" *English Studies* 67 (June 1986): 221–33.
Kennedy, J. Gerald. "What Hemingway Omitted from 'Cat in the Rain.'" *Les*
Cahiers de la Nouvelle: Journal of the Short Story in English 1 (1983): 75–81.
Kert, pp. 133–34.
Lodge, David. "Analysis and Interpretation of the Realist Text: A Pluralistic
Approach to Ernest Hemingway's 'Cat in the Rain.'" *Poetics Today: Theory and*
Analysis of Literature and Communication 1 (1980): 5–19.
Lynn, pp. 199, 251–53, 265.
Meyers (*A Biography*), pp. 49, 119, 177.
Miall, David S. "Affect and Narrative: A Model of Response to Stories." *Poetics*
17.3 (1988): 259–72.
Miller, Leslie. "'Cat in the Rain.'" *Linguistics in Literature* 1 (1976): 29–34.
Rao, E. Nageswara, p. 65.
Rao, P. G. Rama, pp. 44, 77–79, 123, 163.
Reynolds (*The Paris Years*), pp. 113, 175–76, 211.
Smith, pp. 43–49.
Steinke, Jim. "Hemingway's 'Cat in the Rain.'" *Spectrum* 25, no. 1–2 (1983): 36–
44.
Stubbs, Michael. "Stir Until the Plot Thickens." *Literary Text and Language*
Study. Ed. Ronald Carter and Deirdre Burton. London: Arnold, 1982: 57–
85.
Toolan, Michael. "Analyzing Fictional Dialogue." *Language and Communication*
5, no. 3 (1985): 193–206.
Wagner (*Inventors/Masters*), pp. 58–59, 61, 63, 65–66.
Watts, Cedric. "Hemingway's 'Cat in the Rain': A Preter-Structuralist View."
Studi dell' Istituto Linguistico 6 (1983): 310–23.
White, Gertrude M. "We're All 'Cats in the Rain.'" *Fitzgerald-Hemingway*
Annual (1978): 241–46.
Williams, pp. 32, 33, 36.

(11)   **Chapter I** (Vignette: "Everybody was drunk")
            (1923/Spring 1923/*Little Review*/iot, IOT, CS, FV)
            Meyers (*A Biography*), pp. 143–44.

(12)   **Chapter II** (Vignette: "Minarets stuck up in the rain")
            (1923/Spring 1923/3rd vignette in *Little Review* and iot/IOT, CS, FV)
            Baker, pp. 13–14.
            Capellan, pp. 155–56.
            Cooper, p. 22.
            Meyers (*A Biography*), pp. 143–44.
            Nakajima, Kenji. "To Discipline Eyes Against Misery: 'Chapter II,' *In Our
            Time*." *Kyushu American Literature* 26 (October 1985): 11–19.

(13)   **Chapter III** (Vignette: "We Were in a Garden at Mons")
            (1923/Spring 1923/4th vignette in *Little Review* and iot/IOT, CS, FV)
            Griffin, p. 95.
            Meyers (*A Biography*), pp. 143–44.

(14)   **Chapter IV** (Vignette: "It was a frightfully hot day")
            (1923/Spring 1923/5th vignette in *Little Review* and iot/IOT, CS, FV)
            Baker, p. 12.
            Meyers (*A Biography*), pp. 143–44.
            Nelson (*H. Expressionist Artist*), p. 24.

(15)   **Chapter V** (Vignette: "They shot the six cabinet ministers")
            (1923/Spring 1923/6th vignette in *Little Review* and iot/IOT, CS, FV)
            Baker, p. 13.
            Capellan, p. 156.
            Meyers (*A Biography*), pp. 105–6, 143–44.
            Reynolds (*The Paris Years*), pp. 115–16.

(16)   **Chapter VI** (Vignette: "Nick sat against the wall")
            (1923/Spring 1923/*in our time* as "Chapter VII"/IOT, CS, NA, FV)
            Capellan, pp. 69, 80.
            Cooper, pp. 22, 24, 25.
            Derounian, Kathryn Zabelle. "An Examination of the Drafts of Hemingway's
            Chapter 'Nick sat against the wall. . . .'" *Papers of the Bibliographical Society of
            America* 77 (1983): 54–65. (Reprinted in Michael S. Reynolds, ed. *Critical Essays
            on Ernest Hemingway's "In Our Time."* Boston: Hall, 1983: 61–75.)
            Flora (*Nick Adams*), pp. 61, 106–7, 115, 156.
            Meyers (*A Biography*), pp. 143–44.
            Nakajima, Kenji. "Shot, Alive, and Was Glad: On Hemingway's 'Chapter VI,'
            In Our Time. *Kyushu American Literature* 21 (1980): 13–17.

(17)   **Chapter VII** (Vignette: "While the bombardment was knocking the trench to
            pieces")
            (1923/Spring 1924/*in our time* as "Chapter VIII"/IOT, CS, FV)
            Meyers (*A Biography*), pp. 143–44.
            Reynolds (*The Paris Years*), pp. 124–25.

(18)   **Chapter VIII** (Vignette: "At two o'clock in the morning two Hungarians")
            (1923/Spring 1924/*in our time* as "Chapter VIII"/IOT, CS, FV)
            Capellan, p. 49.

Meyers (*A Biography*), pp. 26, 143–44.
Reynolds (*The Paris Years*), p. 123.
Scholes, Robert. *Textual Power: Literary Theory and the Teaching of English.* New Haven: Yale University Press, 1985: 26–38.

(19)　**Chapter IX** (Vignette: "The first matador got the horn")
　　　(1923/Spring 1923/2nd vignette in *Little Review* and iot/IOT, CS, FV)
　　Meyers (*A Biography*), pp. 143–44, 228.
　　Nakajima, Kenji. "The Bullfight, a Test of Manhood: On Hemingway's 'Chapter IX,' *In Our Time.*" *Kyushu American Literature* 28 (October 1987): 19–27.
　　Scholes, Robert. *Textual Power: Literary Theory and the Teaching of English.* New Haven: Yale University Press 1985: 63, 64, 65, 67.

(20)　**Chapter X** (Vignette: "They whack-whacked the white horse")
　　　(1923/Spring 1924//*in our time* as "Chapter XII"/IOT, CS, FV)
　　Lynn, pp. 211–12.
　　Meyers (*A Biography*), pp. 143–44, 228.
　　Reynolds (*The Paris Years*), pp. 138–39.
　　Scholes, Robert. *Textual Power: Literary Theory and the Teaching of English.* New Haven: Yale University Press, 1985: 63, 64, 65, 67.

(21)　**Chapter XI** (Vignette: "The crowd shouted all the time")
　　　(1923/Spring 1924/*in our time* as "Chapter VIII"/IOT, CS, FV)
　　Meyers (*A Biography*), pp. 143–44, 228.
　　Nakajima, Kenji. "The Role of the Bullfight Spectators in 'Chapter XI' of Hemingway's *In Our Time.*" *Kyushu American Literature* 29 (1988): 13–22.
　　Scholes, Robert. *Textual Power: Literary Theory and the Teaching of English.* New Haven: Yale University Press, 1985: 63, 64, 65, 67.

(22)　**Chapter XII** (Vignette: "If it happened right down close in front of you")
　　　(1923/Spring 1924/*in our time* as "Chapter XIV"/IOT, CS, FV)
　　Meyers (*A Biography*), pp. 143–44, 228.
　　Scholes, Robert. *Textual Power: Literary Theory and the Teaching of English.* New Haven: Yale University Press, 1985: 63, 64, 65, 66, 68–69.

(23)　**Chapter XIII** (Vignette: "I heard the drums coming down the street")
　　　(1923/Spring 1924/*in our time* as "Chapter XV"/IOT, CS, FV)
　　Capellan, p. 56.
　　Meyers (*A Biography*), pp. 143–44, 228.
　　Scholes, Robert. *Textual Power: Literary Theory and the Teaching of English.* New Haven: Yale University Press, 1985: 63, 64, 65, 69, 70.

(24)　**Chapter XIV** (Vignette: "Maera lay still")
　　　(1923/Spring 1924/*in our time* as "Chapter XVI"/IOT, CS, FV)
　　Flora (*Nick Adams*), p. 54.
　　Meyers (*A Biography*), pp. 143–44, 228.
　　Reynolds (*The Paris Years*), pp. 139–40.

(25)　**Chapter XV** (Vignette: "They hanged Sam Cardinella")
　　　(1923/Spring 1924/*in our time* as "Chapter VII"/IOT, CS, FV)
　　Capellan, p. 49.
　　Flora (*Nick Adams*), p. 54.

Meyers (*A Biography*), pp. 52–53, 145–44.
Reynolds (*The Paris Years*), pp. 141–42.

(26) **Che Ti Dice la Patria?**
  (1927/May 18, 1927/*New Republic* as "Italy—1927"/MWW, CS, FV)
  Brenner, pp. 20, 22.
  Cooper, pp. 28, 29.
  Donaldson, p. 94.
  Flora (*Nick Adams*), pp. 214–15.
  Kobler, p. 83.
  Meyers (*A Biography*), p. 84.
  Nelson (*H, Expressionist Artist*), p. 30.
  Rao, E. Nageswara, p. 49.
  Smith, pp. 193–96.
  Wagner (*Inventors/Masters*), p. 67.
  Williams, p. 96.

(26a) **Christmas in Paris** (article published as a story)
  (1923/December 1923/*Toronto Star Weekly*/reprinted privately as part of *Two Christmas Tales*, 1959)
  Smith, pp. 277–88.

(27) **"A Clean, Well-Lighted Place"**
  (1932/March 1933/*Scribner's Magazine*/WTN, CS, FV)
  Bakker, pp. 126, 127–29.
  Beegel (*Craft of Omission*), pp. 91–92.
  Bender, Bert A. "Let There be (Electric) Light! The Image of Electricity in American Writing." *Arizona Quarterly* 34 (Spring 1978): 55–70.
  Bennett, Warren. "The Manuscript and the Dialogue of 'A Clean, Well-Lighted Place.'" *American Literature* 50 (1979): 613–24.
  Berryman, John. "Hemingway's 'A Clean, Well-Lighted Place.'" *The Freedom of the Poet.* New York: Farrar, Straus & Giroux, 1976: 217–21.
  Bier, Jesse. "Don't Nobody Move—This is a Stichomythia (Or: An Unfinal Word on Typography in Hemingway)." *Hemingway Review* 3 (1983): 61–63.
  Brenner, pp. 19, 53.
  Broer, Lawrence. "The Iceberg in 'A Clean, Well-Lighted Place.'" *Lost Generation Journal* 4 (1976): 14–15, 21.
  Burgess, pp. 61, 112.
  Capellan, pp. 6, 57, 87, 95, 109, 166, 175, 181.
  Donaldson, pp. 233–34, 284.
  Flora (*Nick Adams*), p. 160.
  Flora (*Short Fiction*), pp. 19–25.
  Giger, p. 14.
  Grimes, pp. 53, 71, 74–75.
  Hardy and Cull, p. 33.
  Hoffman, Steven K. "Nada and the Clean, Well-Lighted Place: The Unity of Hemingway's Short Fiction." *Essays in Literature* 6 (1979): 91–110. (Reprinted in Harold Bloom, ed. *Ernest Hemingway.* New York: Chelsea House, 1985: 173–92.)
  Hurley, C. Harold. "The Attribution of the Waiters' Second Speech in Hemingway's 'A Clean, Well-Lighted Place.'" *Studies in Short Fiction* 13 (1976): 81–85.
  Hurley, C. Harold. "The Manuscript and the Dialogue of 'A Clean, Well-Lighted Place': A Response to Warren Bennett." *Hemingway Review* 2 (1982): 17–20.

Johnston, Kenneth G. "'A Clean, Well-Lighted Place': Black on Black." *The Tip of the Iceberg: Hemingway and the Short Story.* Greenwood, Fla.: Penkevill, 1987: 161–67.

Kann, Hans-Joachim. "Perpetual Confusion in 'A Clean, Well-Lighted Place': The Manuscript Evidence." *Fitzgerald-Hemingway Annual* (1977): 115–18.

Kerner, David. "Counterfeit Hemingway: A Small Scandal in Quotation Marks." *Journal of Modern Literature* 12, no. 1 (March 1985): 91–108.

Kerner, David. "The Foundation of the True Text of 'A Clean, Well-Lighted Place.'" *Fitzgerald-Hemingway Annual* (1979): 279–300.

Kerner, David. "The Manuscripts Establishing Hemingway's Anti-Metronomic Dialogue." *American Literature* 54 (1982): 385–96.

Kerner, David. "The Thomson Alternative." *Hemingway Review* 4, no. 1 (Fall 1984): 37–39.

Kert, p. 251.

Lynn, pp. 191, 265.

Meyers (*A Biography*), pp. 186, 198, 258–59.

Meyer, William E., Jr. "The Artist's American: Hemingway's 'A Clean, Well-Lighted Place.'" *Arizona Quarterly* 39 (1983): 156–63.

Monteiro, George. "Ernest Hemingway, Psalmist." *Journal of Modern Literature* 14, no. 1 (Summer 1987): 83–95.

Monteiro, George. "Hemingway on Dialogue in 'A Clean, Well-Lighted Place.'" *Fitzgerald-Hemingway Annual* (1974): 243.

Nitsaisook, Malee. "An Analysis of Certain Stylistic Features of Selected Literary Works and Their Relationship to Readability." *DAI* 40 (1980): 4453A (Southern Illinois University at Carbondale).

Rao, E. Nageswara, pp. 15, 82, 104.

Rao, P. G. Rama, pp. 41, 103.

Rovit and Brenner, pp. 93, 94, 97–98, 117, 124–25.

Smith, Paul. "A Note on a New Manuscript of 'A Clean, Well-Lighted Place.'" *Hemingway Review* 8, no. 2 (Spring 1989): 36–39.

Sojka, pp. 5, 72, 75.

Stoltzfus, p. 42.

Svoboda, p. 82.

Thomson, George H. "'A Clean, Well-Lighted Place': Interpreting the Original Text." *Hemingway Review* 2 (1983): 32–43.

Wagner (*Inventors/Masters*), pp. 69–71.

Wilkinson, pp. 34–35.

Williams, p. 102.

(29)   **Cross Country Snow**

(1924/January 1925/*Transatlantic Review*/IOT, CS, NA, FV)

Brenner, p. 20.

Capellan, p. 85.

Cooper, p. 25.

Donaldson, p. 151.

Flora (*Nick Adams*), pp. 63, 115, 179, 180, 191–202, 209, 210, 212, 218, 224, 234, 237.

Flora (*Short Fiction*), pp. 41–43.

Gaggin, p. 88.

Grimes, pp. 48, 121.

Johnston, Kenneth G. "Nick/Mike Adams? The Hero's Name in 'Cross Country

Snow.'" *American Notes and Queries* 20 (1982): 16–18. (Revised as "'Cross-Country Snow': Freedom and Responsibility," reprinted in *The Tip of the Iceberg: Hemingway and the Short Story*. Greenwood, Fla.: Penkevill, 1987: 63–71.)

Kert, p. 132.

Lynn, pp. 191, 265.

Meyers (*A Biography*), p. 120.

Rao, P. G. Rama, p. 164.

Reynolds (*The Paris Years*), pp. 188–89.

Reynolds (*Young H*), p. 201.

Sanders, Barbara. "Linguistic Analysis of 'Cross Country Snow.'" *Linguistics in Literature* 1 (1976): 43–52.

Smith, pp. 81–84.

Wagner (*Inventors/Masters*), pp. 58, 62–63.

Whitlow, pp. 91–92.

Williams, pp. 33, 36.

(32) **A Day's Wait**
       (ca. 1933/October 27, 1933/*Winner Take Nothing*/CS, FV)

Brenner, p. 53.

Flora (*Nick Adams*), pp. 13, 14, 16, 215–24, 234, 235, 236, 248, 249.

Flora (*Short Fiction*), pp. 44–46.

Gajdusek, Linda. "Up and Down: Making Connections in 'A Day's Wait.'" *Hemingway's Neglected Short Fiction*. Ed. Susan F. Beegel. Ann Arbor: UMI Research Press, 1989: 291–302.

Hays, Peter L. "Self-Reflexive Laughter in 'A Day's Wait.'" *Hemingway Notes* 6 (1980): 25.

Hemingway, Patrick. "*Islands in the Stream*: A Son Remembers." *Ernest Hemingway: The Writer in Context*. Ed. James Nagel. Madison: University of Wisconsin Press, 1984: 13–18.

Smith, pp. 302–6.

Williams, p. 104.

(33) **The Denunciation**
       (1938/November 1938/*Esquire*/FUS, FV)

Capellan, pp. 249, 250.

Cooper, pp. 96, 97–98.

Donaldson, p. 113.

Gertzman, Jay A. "Hemingway's Writer-Narrator in 'The Denunciation.'" *Research Studies* 47 (1979): 244–52.

Johnston, Kenneth G. "Hemingway's 'The Denunciation': The Aloof American." *Fitzgerald-Hemingway Annual* (1979): 371–82. (Revised as "'The Denunciation': The Aloof American," and reprinted in *The Tip of the Iceberg: Hemingway and the Short Story*. Greenwood, Fla.: Penkevill, 1987: 217–29.)

Wagner (*Inventors/Masters*), pp. 88–89.

(34) **A Divine Gesture** (Allegory)
       (1921/May 1922/*Double Dealer*/. . .)

Baker, p. 10.

Donaldson, p. 237.

Kert, pp. 97, 117.

Reynolds (*Young H*), pp. 241–42.

(35) **The Doctor and the Doctor's Wife**
       (1924/December 1924/*Transatlantic Review*/IOT, CS, NA, FV)

Brenner, pp. 17–18, 99.

Capellan, pp. 2, 78.

Cappel, pp. 29, 53, 65–70, 100–101.

Dahiya, pp. 28, 29, 30, 33, 45, 103.

Donaldson, pp. 191, 296.

Flora (*Nick Adams*), pp. 34–51, 67, 69, 96, 118, 130, 210, 234, 262, 266, 267.

Flora (*Short Fiction*), pp. 18–19.

Friedrich, p. 113.

Fulkerson, Richard. "The Biographical Fallacy and 'The Doctor and the Doctor's Wife.'" *Studies in Short Fiction* 16 (1979): 61–65. (Reprinted in Michael S. Reynolds, ed. *Critical Essays on Ernest Hemingway's "In Our Time."* Boston: Hall, 1983. 150–54.)

Gaggin, pp. 88, 96.

Griffin, p. 222.

Grimes, pp. 42, 57, 59, 119.

Guetti, James. *Word-Music: The Aesthetic of Narrative Fiction.* New Brunswick, N.J.: Rutgers University Press, 1980: 11.

Kert, pp. 150–51.

Kobler, p. 42.

Phillips, p. 82.

Rao, P. G. Rama, p. 75.

Reynolds (*The Paris Years*), pp. 186–88, 249–50, 277–78, 296.

Reynolds (*Young H*), p. 132.

Smith, pp. 61–67.

Sojka, p. 73.

Unfried, pp. 14–15.

Wagner (*Inventors/Masters*), p. 58.

Whitlow, pp. 96–99.

Wilhelm, Albert E. "Dick Boulton's Name in 'The Doctor and the Doctor's Wife.'" *Names* 34 (December 1986): 423–25.

Williams, pp. 32, 33, 36.

(36) **The End of Something**
(1924/October 5, 1925/*In Our Time*/CS, NA, FV)

Brenner, p. 20.

Cappel, pp. 14, 128–34, 184, 190.

Cooper, p. 25.

Dahiya, pp. 19, 20, 21, 22, 37, 38, 39, 42.

Donaldson, pp. 145, 169.

Flora (*Nick Adams*), pp. 13, 53, 54–67, 92, 97, 161, 211.

Flora (*Short Fiction*), pp. 28–30, 32–33.

Florick, Janet L., and David M. Raabe. "Longfellow and Hemingway: The Start of Something." *Studies in Short Fiction* 23 (Summer 1986): 324–26.

Grimes, pp. 42–43, 55.

Gunn, Jessie C. "Structural Matrix: A Stylistic Analysis of 'The End of Something.'" *Linguistics in Literature* 1 (1976): 53–60.

Meyers (*A Biography*), pp. 49, 153, 244.

Nelson (*H, Expressionist Artist*), p. 63.

Phillips, p. 109.

Rao, E. Nageswara, p. 49.

Rao, P. G. Rama, pp. 75, 76, 162.

Reynolds (*Young H*), p. 148.

Smith, pp. 50–55.

Unfried, pp. 36–38.
Wagner (*Inventors/Masters*), pp. 58, 63–64.
Welland, Dennis. "Idiom in Hemingway: A Footnote." *Journal of American Studies* 18, no. 3 (December 1984): 449–51.
Whitlow, pp. 86–88, 92.
Wilkinson, p. 78.
Williams, pp. 33, 36, 93.

(37) **L'Envoi** (Vignette: "The king was working in the garden")
    (1923/Spring 1924/*in our time* as "Chapter XVIII"/IOT, CS, FV)
    Flora (*Nick Adams*), p. 108.
    Wagner (*Inventors/Masters*), pp. 59–60, 69.

(38) **The Faithful Bull** (Fable)
    (1950/March 1951/*Holiday*/FV)
    Flora (*Short Fiction*), pp. 111–12.
    Rao, P. G. Rama, p. 61.

(39) **Fathers and Sons**
    (1933/October 27, 1933/*Winner Take Nothing*/CS, NA, FV)
    Baker, Carlos. "The Champion and the Challenger: Hemingway and O'Hara." *John O'Hara Journal* 3 (1980): 22–30.
    Bakker, pp. 8, 116.
    Brenner, p. 142.
    Brian, p. 87.
    Cappel, pp. 65, 67, 82–84, 86–88, 101, 102–6.
    Dahiya, p. 116.
    Donaldson, pp. 178, 179–80, 297–98.
    Fleming, Robert E. "Hemingway's Treatment of Suicide: 'Fathers and Sons' and *For Whom the Bell Tolls.*" *Arizona Quarterly* 33 (1977): 121–32.
    Flora (*Nick Adams*), pp. 34, 198, 216–20, 234–71, 277, 279.
    Flora (*Short Fiction*), pp. 46–51.
    Gaggin, p. 88.
    Griffin, p. 10.
    Grimes, pp. 59, 69–71, 120.
    Johnston, Kenneth G. "'Fathers and Sons': The Past Revisited." *The Tip of the Iceberg: Hemingway and the Short Story.* Greenwood, Fla.: Penkevill, 1987: 183–92.
    Kert, pp. 43–44, 230–31, 251.
    Kobler, p. 42.
    McCann, Richard. "To Embrace or Kill: 'Fathers and Sons.'" *Iowa Journal of Literary Studies* 3, no. 1–2 (1981): 11–18.
    Meyers (*A Biography*), pp. 10, 16, 133, 234, 249, 259, 314.
    Phillips, pp. 85, 186.
    Rao, E. Nageswara, pp. 27, 41.
    Rao, P. G. Rama, pp. 44, 45, 56, 91, 123.
    Smith, pp. 307–17.
    Sojka, pp. 94, 95, 100, 106, 115.
    Strong, Paul. "Gathering Pieces and Filling in the Gaps: Hemingway's 'Fathers and Sons.'" *Studies in Short Fiction* 26, no. 1 (1989): 49–58.
    Unfried, pp. 43–44.
    Wagner (*Inventors/Masters*), p. 71.

Whitlow, pp. 101–5.
Williams, pp. 97, 104–5.

(40)   **Fifty Grand**
(1924/July 1927/*Atlantic*/MWW, CS, FV)
Beegel (*Craft of Omission*), pp. 6–12, 13–30, 91–92.
Brenner, pp. 18, 22, 115.
Bruccoli, pp. 39–40.
Capellan, pp. 83, 118.
Dahiya, p. 43.
Donaldson, pp. 198–99, 270.
Donaldson, Scott. "The Wooing of Ernest Hemingway." *American Literature* 53
(1982): 691–710.
Grimes, pp. 53, 71, 77–78.
Meyers (*A Biography*), pp. 116, 165.
Reynolds (*The Paris Years*), pp. 331–32, 339–40.
Rovit and Brenner, pp. 44–45, 98.
Smith, pp. 125–31.
Sojka, pp. 2, 147.
Wagner, p. 67.
Weeks, Robert P. "Wise-Guy Narrator and Trickster Out-Tricked in Heming-
way's 'Fifty-Grand.'" *Studies in American Fiction* 10 (1982): 83–91.
Williams, pp. 96–97.

(41)   **The Gambler, the Nun, and the Radio**
(1931–32/April 1933/*Scribner's Magazine*, as "Give Us a Prescription, Doc-
tor"/WTN [revised], CS, FV)
Bakker, pp. 126–27.
Brenner, p. 19.
Capellan, pp. 95, 96, 193.
Cooper, p. 62.
Donaldson, pp. 189, 236, 277.
Flora (*Nick Adams*), p. 223.
Flora (*Short Fiction*), pp. 69–74.
Kobler, p. 57.
Monteiro, George. "Hemingway's Nun's Tale." *Research Studies* 46 (1978): 50–53.
Morton, Bruce. "Music and Distorted View in Hemingway's 'The Gambler, the
Nun, and the Radio.'" *Studies in Short Fiction* 20 (1983): 79–85.
Murolo, Frederick L. "Another Look at the Nun and Her Prayers." *Hemingway
Review* 4, no. 1 (Fall 1984): 52–53.
Nelson (*H, Expressionist Artist*), p. 21.
Pearson, Donna. "'The Gambler, the Nun, and the Radio.'" *Linguistics in
Literature* 1 (1976): 21–28.
Rovit and Brenner, pp. 53, 90, 97.
Smith, pp. 289–96.
Sojka, pp. 75, 83.
Whittle, Amberys R. "A Reading of Hemingway's 'The Gambler, the Nun, and
the Radio.'" *Arizona Quarterly* 33 (1977): 173–80.
Williams, pp. 100–101.

(42)   **Get a Seeing-Eye Dog**
(1956/November 1957/*Atlantic*/FV)

Flora (*Nick Adams*), p. 261.
Flora (*Short Fiction*), pp. 113–16.
Lynn, p. 575.
Rao, P. G. Rama, p. 91.
Rovit and Brenner, pp. 39–40.
Smith, pp. 391–94.

(43)   **God Rest You Merry, Gentlemen**
          (1932/April 1933/*God Rest You Merry, Gentlemen* [pamphlet]/WTN, CS, FV)
Brenner, p. 53.
Burgess, p. 19.
Capellan, p. 49.
Donaldson, pp. 237–38.
Flora (*Nick Adams*), p. 215.
Kert, p. 251.
Lynn, pp. 53, 71–72, 180, 408.
Rao, E. Nageswara, p. 20.
Rao, P. G. Rama, p. 19.
Smith, pp. 246–51.
Williams, pp. 100–101.

(44)   **The Good Lion** (Fable)
          (1950/March 1951/*Holiday*/([*Hemingway Reader*], FV)
Flora (*Short Fiction*), pp. 109–12.
Meyers (*A Biography*), pp. 425, 441, 452.

(46)   **Hills Like White Elephants**
          (1927/August 1927/*Transition*/MWW, CS, FV)
Brenner, pp. 12, 53.
Brown, Nancy Hemond. "Aspects of the Short Story: A Comparison of Jean
     Rhys's 'The Sound of the River' with Ernest Hemingway's 'Hills Like White
     Elephants.'" *Jean Rhys Review* 1 (Fall 1986): 2–13.
Bruccoli, p. 62.
Capellan, pp. 33, 56.
Chatman, Seymour. "Towards a Theory of Narrative." *New Literary Theory* 6
     (1975): 295–318.
Donaldson, pp. 151, 220.
Elliott, Gary D. "Hemingway's 'Hills Like White Elephants.'" *Explicator* 35
     (1977): 22–23.
Fleming, Robert E. "An Early Manuscript of Hemingway's 'Hills Like White
     Elephants.'" *NMAL: Notes on Modern American Literature* 7 (1983): item 3.
Fletcher, Mary Dell. "Hemingway's 'Hills Like White Elephants.'" *Explicator* 38
     (1980): 16–18.
Flora (*Nick Adams*), pp. 210, 213.
Flora (*Short Fiction*), pp. 33–35, 38–39.
Giger, pp. 13, 14, 37–50, 52.
Gilligan, Thomas Maher. "Topography in Hemingway's 'Hills Like White
     Elephants.'" *NMAL: Notes on Modern American Literature* 8, no. 1 (Spring–
     Summer 1984): item 2.
Gilmour, David R. "Hemingway's 'Hills Like White Elephants.'" *Explicator* 41
     (1983): 47–49.
Grimes, pp. 53, 71–73.
Hardy and Cull, p. 47.

Hollander, John. "Hemingway's Extraordinary Reality." *Ernest Hemingway.* Ed. Harold Bloom. New York: Chelsea House, 1985. 211–16.

Johnston, Kenneth G. "'Hills Like White Elephants': Lean, Vintage Hemingway." *Studies in American Fiction* 10 (1982): 233–38. (Revised as "'Hills Like White Elephants': A Matter of Life and Death," and reprinted in *The Tip of the Iceberg: Hemingway and the Short Story.* Greenwood, Fla.: Penkevill, 1987: 125–34.

Kert, pp. 205–6, 235.

Kobler, J. F. "Hemingway's 'Hills Like White Elephants.'" *Explicator* 38 (1980): 6–7.

Lynn, pp. 363–64, 408.

Meyers (*A Biography*), pp. 196–97, 295.

Nelson (*H, Expressionist Artist*), pp. 35, 44.

Organ, Dennis. "Hemingway's 'Hills Like White Elephants.'" *Explicator* 37 (1979): 11.

Passey, Laurie. "Hemingway's 'Hills Like White Elephants.'" *Explicator* 46, no. 4 (Summer 1988): 32–33.

Rao, E. Nageswara, pp. 55, 58, 65.

Rao, P. G. Rama, pp. 44, 75, 91, 102–4, 123.

Sipiora, Phillip. "Hemingway's 'Hills Like White Elephants.'" *Explicator* 42, no. 3 (Spring 1984): 50.

Smiley, Pamela. "Gender-Linked Miscommunication in 'Hills Like White Elephants.'" *Hemingway Review* 8, no. 1 (Fall 1988): 2–12.

Smith, pp. 204–13.

Trilling, Lionel. Commentary on "Hills Like White Elephants." *Prefaces to "The Experience of Literature."* Ed. Trilling. New York: Harcourt Brace and Jovanovich, 1979: 145–49.

Urgo, Joseph R. "Hemingway's 'Hills Like White Elephants.'" *Explicator* 46, no. 3 (1988): 35–37.

Wagner (*Inventors/Masters*), pp. 66–67.

Weeks, Lewis E., Jr. "Hemingway Hills: Symbolism in 'Hills Like White Elephants.'" *Studies in Short Fiction* 17 (1980): 75–77.

Whitlow, pp. 93–96.

Williams, p. 93.

(47)   **Homage to Switzerland**
(1932/April 1933/*Scribner's Magazine*/WTN, CS, FV)

Brenner, p. 151.

Donaldson, p. 151.

Flora (*Nick Adams*), pp. 210, 217, 259.

Flora (*Short Fiction*), pp. 64–66.

Kert, p. 251.

Nakjavani, Erik. "Repetition as Design and Intention: Hemingway's 'Homage to Switzerland.'" *Hemingway's Neglected Short Fiction.* Ed. Susan F. Beegel. Ann Arbor: UMI Research Press, 1989: 263–82.

Reynolds, Michael S. "'Homage to Switzerland': Einstein's Train Stops at Hemingway's Station." *Hemingway's Neglected Short Fiction.* Ann Arbor, Mich.: UMI Research Press, 1989: 255–62.

Smith, pp. 252–56.

Williams, pp. 77, 99–100.

(51)   **In Another Country**
(1926/April 1927/*Scribner's Magazine*/MWW, CS, NA, FV)

Bakker, pp. 6–7.

Brenner, pp. 18, 22, 34.

Capellan, pp. 80, 81.

Cass, Colin S. "The Look of Hemingway's 'In Another Country.'" *Studies in Short Fiction* 18 (1981): 309–13.

Cooper, pp. 33, 45.

Dahiya, p. 50.

Flora (*Nick Adams*), pp. 113, 114, 124, 135–44, 178, 204, 220, 275.

Fowler, Doreen. "'In Another Country': Faulkner's *A Fable.*" *Studies in American Fiction* 15 (1987): 43–54.

Giger, pp. 14, 15–16, 74, 79–80.

Hardy and Cull, p. 34.

Johnston, Kenneth G. "'In Another Country': The Strategy of Survival." *The Tip of the Iceberg: Hemingway and the Short Story.* Greenwood, Fla.: Penkevill, 1987. 115–22.

Kert, pp. 185, 198.

Kobler, p. 55.

Lynn, pp. 84–85, 353–55.

Meyers (*A Biography*), pp. 36, 115, 116, 198.

Nelson (*H, Expressionist Artist*), p. 36.

Phillips, pp. 67, 85.

Rao, P. G. Rama, pp. 41, 72, 131.

Reynolds (*H's First War*), p. 23.

Robinson, Forrest. "Hemingway's Invisible Hero of 'In Another Country.'" *Essays in Literature* 15, no. 2 (Fall 1988): 237–44.

Rovit and Brenner, pp. 44, 45–48, 78, 79–81, 89, 98, 110–12, 123.

Smith, pp. 164–71.

Sojka, pp. 82, 86, 99, 154.

Unfried, pp. 31–33.

Villard and Nagel, pp. 266–67.

Wagner (*Inventors/Masters*), p. 66.

Williams, p. 94.

(52)   **Indian Camp**

(1924/April 1924/"Work in Progress," *Transatlantic Review*/IOT, CS, NA, FV)

Baker, p. 24.

Bakker, pp. 4, 5.

Brasch, James D. "Hemingway's Doctor: José Luis Herrera Sotolongo Remembers Ernest Hemingway." *Journal of Modern Literature* 13, no. 2 (July 1986): 185–210.

Brenner, pp. 11, 99.

Bruccoli, p. 10.

Capellan, pp. 72, 155, 221, 222.

Cappel, pp. 57–64, 82.

Cooper, p. 22.

Dahiya, pp. 22, 27, 28, 33, 34, 47.

Donaldson, pp. 135–36, 296–97.

Flora (*Nick Adams*), pp. 14, 21, 22–35, 36, 37, 40, 41, 43, 51, 57, 59, 96, 103, 112, 115, 118, 137, 145, 222, 238, 240.

Flora (*Short Fiction*), p. 54.

Friedrich, p. 113.

Gladstein, p. 56.

Griffin, p. 222.

Grimes, pp. 42, 49, 55–58, 118–20, 137–38.

Johnston, Kenneth G. "In the Beginning: Hemingway's 'Indian Camp.'" *Studies in Short Fiction* 15 (1978): 102–4. (Revised as "'Indian Camp': In the Beginning," and reprinted in *The Tip of the Iceberg: Hemingway and the Short Story*. Greenwood, Fla.: Penkevill, 1987: 49–60.)

Kert, p. 145.

Kobler, p. 75.

Lynn, pp. 46, 227–29.

Meyers (*A Biography*), pp. 15-16, 83, 214, 556.

Meyers, Jeffrey. "Hemingway's Primitivism and 'Indian Camp.'" *Twentieth Century Literature* 34, no. 2 (Summer 1988): 117–20.

Nichols, Olivia Murray. "An Example of Folklore in Hemingway's 'Indian Camp.'" *Kentucky Folklore Record* 27 (1981): 33–35.

Penner, Dick. "The First Nick Adams Story." *Fitzgerald-Hemingway* (1977): 195–202.

Phillips, pp. 80–81, 82–83, 86, 138.

Rao, E. Nageswara, pp. 32, 52.

Rao, P. G. Rama, pp. 39, 45, 56, 57, 61, 84, 160, 161.

Reynolds (*The Paris Years*), pp. 165–67.

Rovit and Brenner, p. 161.

Smith, pp. 34–42.

Sojka, p. 73.

Unfried, pp. 13–14.

Wagner (*Inventors/Masters*), pp. 58, 60–61, 63–64.

Wainwright, J. Andrew. "The Far Shore: Gender Complexities in Hemingway's 'Indian Camp.'" *Dalhousie Review* 66 (1986): 181–87.

Wilkinson, pp. 40–41, 42.

Williams, pp. 31–32, 33, 36.

Workman, pp. 11–18.

(55)   **The Judgment at Manitou** (Juvenilia)
    (ca. 1916/1916/*Tabula*/EHA)

Brian, p. 258.

Cappel, pp. 43–47, 54.

Donaldson, p. 285.

Griffin, pp. 26–27.

Meyers (*A Biography*), p. 19.

Reynolds (*Young H*), p. 73.

(56)   **The Killers**
    (1926/March 1927/*Scribner's Magazine*/MWW, CS, NA, FV)

Brenner, p. 18.

Bruccoli, pp. 53, 57, 62.

Capellan, pp. 79, 80.

Dahiya, pp. 22, 35, 37, 41, 43, 47.

Davis, William V. "'The Fall of Dark': The Loss of Time in Hemingway's 'The Killers.'" *Studies in Short Fiction* 15 (1978): 319–20.

Donaldson, pp. 137, 199, 202–3, 270, 284.

Fleming, Robert E. "Hemingway's 'The Killers': The Map and the Territory." *Hemingway Review* 4, no. 1 (Fall 1984): 40–43.

Flora, Joseph M. "The Device of Conspicuous Silence in the Modern Short Story." *Proceedings of the Comparative Literature Symposium* (*Texas Tech Press, Lubbock*) 13 (1982): 27–45.

Flora (*Nick Adams*), pp. 1, 14, 17, 88, 93–104, 107, 108, 113, 115, 161, 176, 210, 222, 257.

Gaggin, p. 25.

Grimes, pp. 60–61.

Hays, Peter L., and Stephanie Tucker. "No Sanctuary: Hemingway's 'The Killers' and Pinter's *The Birthday Party*." *Papers on Language and Literature* 21, no. 4 (Fall 1985): 417–24.

Johnston, Kenneth G. "'The Killers': The Background and the Manuscripts." *Studies in Short Fiction* 19 (1982): 247–51. (Revised as "'The Killers': The Shaping of a Classic," and reprinted in *The Tip of the Iceberg: Hemingway and The Short Story*. Greenwood, Fla.: Penkevill, 1987: 105–11.)

Kaminsky, Stuart. "Literary Adaptation: 'The Killers'—Hemingway, Film Noir, and the Terror of Daylight." *A Moving Picture Feast*. Ed. Charles M. Oliver. New York: Praeger, 1989: 125–341.

Kert, pp. 179, 186, 202, 428.

Kobler, p. 59.

Lafontaine, Cecile Aurore. "Waiting in Hemingway's 'The Killers' and Borges' 'La espera.'" *Revue de Litterature Comparee* 57 (1983): 67–80.

Lynn, p. 112.

Meyers (*A Biography*), p 133.

Monteiro, George. "The Hit in the Summit: Ernest Hemingway's 'The Killers.'" *Hemingway Review* 8, no. 2 (Spring 1989): 40–45.

Phillips, pp. 8, 14, 65, 66–70, 71, 72, 74, 75, 78, 98, 105, 161.

Rao, E. Nageswara, pp. 55–56.

Rao, P. G. Rama, pp. 45, 102, 122, 124–31, 136, 145, 154, 155.

Reynolds (*The Paris Years*), p. 332.

Rovit and Brenner, pp. 66, 79, 98.

Schlepper, Wolfgang. "Hemingway's 'The Killers': An Absurd Happening." *Literatur in Wissenschaft und Unterricht* 10 (1977): 104–14.

Smith, pp. 138–53.

Sojka, p. 73.

Stark de Valverde, Dorothy. "An Analysis of 'The Killers' and the Work of Ernest Hemingway." *Revista de la Universidad de Costa Rica* 39 (1974): 129–37.

Stuckey, W. J. "'The Killers' as Experience." *Journal of Narrative Technique* 5 (1975): 128–35.

Unfried, p. 20.

Wagner (*Inventors/Masters*), pp. 66–67.

Williams, pp. 94–95.

(60)   **The Light of the World**
(1932/October 27, 1933/*Winner Take Nothing*/CS, NA, FV)

Barbour, James F. "'The Light of the World': The Real Ketchel and the Real Light." *Studies in Short Fiction* 13 (1976): 17–23.

Barbour, James. "'The Light of the World': Hemingway's Comedy of Errors." *Notes on Contemporary Literature* 7 (1977): 5–8.

Brenner, pp. 18, 53.

Bruccoli, Matthew J. "Stan Ketchel and Steve Ketchel: A Further Note on the 'Light of the World.'" *Fitzgerald-Hemingway Annual* (1975): 325–26.

Capellan, p. 215.

Cappel, pp. 27, 53–54, 89, 91–95.

Collins, William J. "Taking on the Champion: Alice as Liar in 'The Light of the World.'" *Studies in American Fiction* 14, no. 2 (Autumn 1986): 225–32.

Dahiya, pp. 22, 34, 41, 43.

Donaldson, pp. 136, 175, 188, 237–38.

Elliot, Gary D. "Hemingway's 'The Light of the World.'" *Explicator* 40 (1981): 48–50.

Fleming, Robert E. "Myth or Reality: 'The Light of the World' as Initiation Story." *Hemingway's Neglected Fiction* Ed. Susan F. Beegel. Ann Arbor: UMI Research Press, 1989: 283–90.

Flora (*Nick Adams*), pp. 11, 68–104, 115, 138, 161, 217, 252, 256.

Flora (*Short Fiction*), pp. 66–69.

Gaggin, pp. 25, 94, 96.

Grimes, p. 3.

Kert, p. 251.

Lynn, pp. 408–9.

Maloy, Barbara. "The Light of Alice's World." *Linguistics in Literature* 1 (1976): 69–86.

Meyers (*A Biography*), pp. 135, 186.

Petry, Alice Hall. "Hemingway's 'The Light of the World.'" *Explicator* 40 (1982): 46.

Rao, P. G. Rama, pp. 44, 73, 123.

Reynolds, Michael S. "Holman Hunt and 'The Light of the World'" *Studies in Short Fiction* 20 (1983): 317–19.

Reynolds (*H's First War*), p. 44n.

Reynolds (*Young H*), p. 105.

Smith, pp. 257–63.

Sojka, p. 75.

Unfried, pp. 17–18.

Wagner (*Inventors/Masters*), pp. 64, 69–70.

Williams, p. 100.

(61)   **A Man of the World**
(1957/November 1957/*Atlantic*/FV)

Ferguson, J. M. "Hemingway's Man of the World." *Arizona Quarterly* 3 (1977): 116–20.

Flora (*Short Fiction*), pp. 112–13.

Lynn, p. 575.

Smith, pp. 391–94.

Williams, pp. 197–98.

(62)   **A Matter of Colour** (Juvenilia)
(1916/1916/*Tabula*/EHA)

Cappel, pp. 43, 47–50, 54.

Donaldson, p. 270.

Meyers (*A Biography*), pp. 19–20.

Rao, P. G. Rama, p. 6.

(64)   **The Mother of a Queen**
(ca. 1931–32/October 27, 1933/*Winner Take Nothing*/CS, FV)

Brenner, pp. 11–12, 20.

Dahiya, p. 43.

Donaldson, p. 183.

Gaggin, pp. 96, 97.

Smith, pp. 264–67.

Stetler, Charles, and Gerald Locklin. "Beneath the Tip of the Iceberg in Hemingway's 'The Mother of a Queen.'" *Hemingway Review* 2 (1982): 68–69.
William, pp. 103–4.

(65) **Mr. and Mrs. Elliot**
(1924/Autumn–Winter 1924–25/*Little Review*/IOT,CS, FV)
Baker, p. 27.
Brenner, p. 20.
Capellan, p. 72.
Donaldson, pp. 38, 66, 181.
Flora (*Nick Adams*), p. 191.
Flora (*Short Fiction*), p. 16.
Grimes, p. 48.
Hoetker, James. "Hemingway's 'Mr. and Mrs. Elliot' and Its Readers." *Kyushu American Literature* 24 (1983): 11–14.
Lynn, pp. 244–46.
Meyers (*A Biography*), pp. 144, 153, 200, 346.
Nelson (*H, Expressionist Artist*), pp. 31, 64.
Rao, P. G. Rama, pp. 44, 123, 163, 165.
Reynolds (*The Paris Years*), pp. 192–94, 292–93.
Scholes, Robert. *Textual Power: Literary Theory and the Teaching of English*. New Haven: Yale University Press, 1985: 60–61.
Smith, pp. 75–80.
Smith, Paul. "From the Waste Land to the Garden with the Elliots." *Hemingway's Neglected Short Stories*. Ed. Susan F. Beegel. Ann Arbor: UMI Research Press, 1989: 123–30.
Wagner (*Inventors/Masters*), p. 58.
Williams, pp. 33, 38.

(67) **My Old Man**
(1922/Summer 1923/*Three Stories and Ten Poems*/IOT, CS, FV)
Baker, p. 12.
Brenner, pp. 8–9, 11, 17, 222.
Brian, pp. 43–44.
Bruccoli, pp. 9–10, 27, 29.
Capellan, pp. 2, 82, 222.
Cooper, p. 22.
Donaldson, pp. 195–96, 198, 270.
Flora (*Nick Adams*), pp. 52, 68, 69, 146.
Grimes, pp. 1, 28–33, 36, 46, 49, 69–70.
Kert, pp. 128, 133, 138, 169.
Lanford, Ray. "Hemingway's 'My Old Man.'" *Linguistics in Literature* 1 (1976): 11–19.
Lynn, pp. 199, 208, 222.
Meyers (*A Biography*), p. 144.
Nelson (*H, Expressionist Artist*), p. 31.
Phillips, pp. 97–105, 161.
Rao, P. G. Rama, pp. 97, 123, 164, 165.
Reynolds (*The Paris Years*), pp. 4, 58–61, 78, 103, 128, 151, 208.
Sipiora, Phillip. "Ethical Narration in 'My Old Man.'" *Hemingway's Neglected Short Fiction*. Ed. Susan F. Beegel. Ann Arbor: UMI Research Press, 1989: 43–60.
Slattery, William C. "The Mountain, the Plain, and San Siro." *Papers on Language*

and Literature: A Journal for Scholars and Critics of Language and Literature 16 (1980): 439–42.

Smith, pp. 10–15.

Svoboda, pp. 34–35.

Wagner (*Inventors/Masters*), pp. 65, 83.

Williams, pp. 33, 37, 38–39.

(68)   **A Natural History of the Dead**
    (1929–31/September 23, 1932/as part of Chapter XII of *Death in the After-noon*/WTN [revised], CS, FV)

Beegel (*Craft of Omission*), pp. 6–12, 31–49, 91–92.

Brenner, pp. 74–75, 151.

Donaldson, pp. 232–33, 283.

Flora (*Nick Adams*), pp. 126–27, 128.

Griffin, p. 66.

Grimes, p. 35.

Kobler, p. 70.

Lewis, Robert W. "The Making of *Death in the Afternoon*." *Ernest Hemingway: The Writer in Context*. Ed. James Nagel. Madison: University of Wisconsin Press, 1984: 31–52.

Meyers (*A Biography*), p. 229.

Nelson (*H, Expressionist Artist*), p. 26.

Raeburn, p. 34.

Reynolds, (*The Paris Years*), p. 131.

Reynolds (*Young H*), p. 30.

Smith, pp. 231–39.

Sojka, p. 154.

Stetler, Charles, and Gerald Locklin. "'A Natural History' as Metafiction." *Hemingway's Neglected Short Fiction*. Ed. Susan F. Beegel. Ann Arbor: UMI Research Press, 1989: 247–55.

Wagner (*Inventors/Masters*), p. 70.

Wilkinson, pp. 34, 82.

Williams, pp. 102–3.

(69)   **Night Before Battle**
    (1938/February 1939/*Esquire*/FUS, FV)

Cooper, pp. 86, 95.

Donaldson, p. 113.

Flora (*Short Fiction*), pp. 93–95.

Johnston, Kenneth G. "Hemingway's 'Night Before Battle': Don Quixote, 1937." *Hemingway Notes* 6 (1980): 26–28.

Smith, pp. 278–81.

(71)   **Nobody Ever Dies** ("Flower of the Party")
    (1938/March 1939/*Cosmopolitan*/FV)

Capellan, p. 250.

Cooper, pp. 91–92, 98.

Cooper, Stephen. "Politics Over Art: Hemingway's 'Nobody Ever Dies.'" *Studies in Short Fiction* 15, no. 2 (Autumn 1985): 163–77.

Edgerton, Larry. "'Nobody Ever Dies!': Hemingway's *Fifth* Story of the Spanish Civil War." *Arizona Quarterly* 39 (1983): 35–47.

Flora (*Short Fiction*), pp. 99–100.

Fuentes, pp. 131–32.

Johnston, Kenneth G. "'Nobody Ever Dies': Hemingway's Neglected Story of Freedom Fighters." *Kansas Quarterly* 9 (1977): 53–58.

Smith, pp. 382–84.

Wagner (*Inventors/Masters*), pp. 93–95.

(71a) **A North of Italy Christmas** (article published as a story)

(1923/December 1923/*Toronto Star Weekly*/reprinted privately as part of *Two Christmas Tales*, 1959)

(72) **Now I Lay Me**

(1926/October 14, 1927/*Men Without Women*/CS, NA, FV)

Bakker, p. 6.

Beegel (*Craft of Omission*), p. 45.

Brenner, pp. 17, 22, 33–34, 53, 99.

Bruccoli, pp. 62–65.

Capellan, pp, 80, 166, 229.

Cappel, pp. 28–29, 109.

Cooper, pp. 3, 24, 33, 37.

Dahiya, pp. 21, 94.

Donaldson, pp. 126, 169, 171.

Eby, Cecil D. "The Soul in Ernest Hemingway." *Studies in American Fiction* 12 (Autumn 1984): 223–26.

Flora (*Nick Adams*), pp. 33, 113, 114–36, 139–43, 156, 157, 163, 166, 168, 176, 178, 179, 220, 222, 256, 262.

Griffin, p. 12.

Grimes, pp. 21, 35, 63–64, 120–21, 122, 126.

Kert, p. 205.

Lynn, pp. 46–48, 105, 368.

Meyers (*A Biography*), pp. 21, 36.

Rao, E. Nageswara, pp. 38, 57.

Rao, P. G. Rama, pp. 41, 72, 76, 131.

Reynolds (*H's First War*), p. 31.

Rovit and Brenner, pp. 63, 161–62.

Smith, pp. 172–79.

Sojka, pp. 34, 78, 80, 86.

Unfried, pp. 26–29.

Villard and Nagel, p. 266.

Wagner (*Inventors/Masters*), pp. 68–69, 71.

Whitlow, pp. 99–101.

Williams, pp. 93, 97.

(73) **Old Man at the Bridge**

(1938/May 19, 1938/*Ken*, as "The . . ."/CS, FV)

Brenner, pp. 19, 53, 151.

Capellan, pp. 6, 58, 95, 248, 249, 266.

Cooper, pp. 87, 96, 98.

Donaldson, p. 102.

Flora (*Nick Adams*), pp. 251, 253.

Flora (*Short Fiction*), pp. 90–92.

Fuentes, p. 157.

Meyers (*A Biography*), pp. 98, 322.

Rao, P. G. Rama, p. 123.
Rovit and Brenner, p. 67.
Smith, pp. 362–65.
Wagner (*Inventors/Masters*), p. 93.
Walker, Anna. "The Old Man and Jesus: Uses of Biblical Matrix." *Linguistics in Literature* 4 (1979): 77–82.
Watson, William Braasch. "'Old Man at the Bridge': The Making of a Short Story." *Hemingway Review* 7, no. 2 (1988): 152–65.
Wilkinson, pp. 42–43.

(74)   **On the Quai at Smyrna** (Vignette)
   (1926–27/October 24, 1930/*In Our Time*/CS)
Cooper, p. 22.
Flora (*Short Stories*), p. 148.
Grimes, p. 36.
Meyers (*A Biography*), pp. 98, 100–2.
Nelson (*H, Expressionist Artist*), pp. 22, 24, 63, 71.
Phillips, p. 98.
Smith, pp. 189–92.
Wagner (*Inventors/Masters*), pp. 57, 59.
Williams, p. 30, 33, 35–36, 38.
Witherington, Paul. "Word and Flesh in Hemingway's 'On the Quai at Smyrna.'" *NMAL: Notes on Modern American Literature* 2 (1978): item 18.

(76)   **One Reader Writes**
   (1932–33/October 27, 1933/*Winner Take Nothing*/CS, FV)
Brenner, p. 151.
Flora (*Short Fiction*), pp. 61–62, 63.
Smith, pp. 297–301.
Smith, Paul. "The Doctor and the Doctor's Friend: Logan Clendening and Ernest Hemingway." *Hemingway Review* 8, no. 1 (Fall 1988): 37–39.
Wagner (*Inventors/Masters*), p. 70.
Williams, p. 100.

(77)   **One Trip Across**
   (ca. 1933/April 1934/*Cosmopolitan* [became Part I of *To Have and Have Not*]/FV)
Cooper, p. 66.
Fuentes, p. 121.
Kert, p. 276.
Lynn, p. 454.
Phillips, pp. 49, 50.

(78)   **Out of Season**
   (1923/Summer 1923/*Three Stories and Ten Poems*/IOT, CS, FV)
Baker, p. 15.
Beegel (*Craft of Omission*), p. 12.
Bruccoli, p. 10.
Capellan, p. 72.
Flora (*Nick Adams*), pp. 191, 213.
Flora (*Short Fiction*), pp. 30–33.
Ganzel, Dewey. "A Geometry of His Own: Hemingway's 'Out of Season.'" *Modern Fiction Studies* 34, no. 2 (Summer 1988): 171–83.
Giger, pp. 14, 91, 93.

Grimes, pp. 48, 72.

Jackson, Paul R. "Hemingway's 'Out of Season.'" *Hemingway Review* 1 (1981): 11–17.

Kert, pp. 136, 138.

Lynn, p. 454.

McComes, Dix. "The Geography of Ernest Hemingway's 'Out of Season.'" *Hemingway Review* 3, no. 2 (Spring 1984): 46–49.

Meyers (*A Biography*), pp. 139, 154, 346.

Rao, P. G. Rama, pp. 30, 123, 163.

Reynolds (*The Paris Years*), p. 122.

Smith, pp. 16–21.

Smith, Paul. "Some Misconceptions of 'Out of Season.'" *Critical Essays on Ernest Hemingway's "In Our Time."* Ed. Michael S. Reynolds. Boston: Hall, 1983: 235–51.

Steinke, James. "'Out of Season' and Hemingway's Neglected Discovery: Ordinary Actuality." *Hemingway's Neglected Short Fiction.* Ed. Susan F. Beegel. Ann Arbor: UMI Research Press, 1989: 61–74.

Sylvester, Bickford. "Hemingway's Italian *Waste Land:* The Complex Unity of 'Out of Season.'" *Hemingway's Neglected Short Fiction.* Ed. Susan F. Beegel. Ann Arbor: UMI Research Press, 1989: 75–98.

Wagner (*Inventors/Masters*), p. 58.

Williams, pp. 32, 33, 36, 106.

(79) **Paris, 1922** (sentence-length sketches)
(1922/1969/*Ernest Hemingway: A Life Story*/ . . .)

Baker, p. 13n.

Kanjo, Eugene. "Hemingway's Cinematic Style." *A Moving Picture Feast.* Ed. Charles M. Oliver. New York: Praeger, 1989: 3–11.

Reynolds (*The Paris Years*), pp. 95–97, 114.

(81) **A Pursuit Race**
(1926–27/October 4, 1927/*Men Without Women*/CS, FV)

Brenner, p. 22.

Bungert, Hans. "Functions of Character Names in American Fiction." *The Origins and Originality of American Culture: Papers Presented at the International Conference in American Studies: Budapest, 9–11 April 1980.* Ed. Tibor Frank. Budapest: Akademiai Kiado, 1984: 165–75.

Fontana, Ernest. "Hemingway's 'A Pursuit Race.'" *Explicator* 42, no. 4 (Summer 1984): 43–45.

Grimes, pp. 71, 75–77, 78.

Putnam, Ann. "Waiting for the End in Hemingway's 'A Pursuit Race.'" *Hemingway's Neglected Short Fiction.* Ed. Susan F. Beegel. Ann Arbor: UMI Research Press, 1989: 185–94.

Rao, P. G. Rama, p. 121.

Smith, pp. 180–84.

Williams, p. 94.

(82) **The Revolutionist** ("Chapter XI" from *in our time:* "In 1919 he was traveling on railroads in Italy")
(1923/Spring 1924/*in our time*/IOT, CS, FV)

Capellan, p. 6.

Cooper, pp. 26–28, 91.

Donaldson, p. 98.

Flora (*Nick Adams*), p. 213.

Grimes, pp. 42, 45.

Hunt, Anthony. "Another Turn for Hemingway's 'The Revolutionist': Sources and Meanings." *Fitzgerald-Hemingway Annual* (1977): 119–35. (Reprinted in Michael S. Reynolds, ed. *Critical Essays on Ernest Hemingway's "In Our Time."* Boston: Hall, 1983: 203–17.)

Rao, E. Nageswara, p. 49.

Scholes, Robert. *Textual Power: Literary Theory and the Teaching of English.* New Haven: Yale University Press, 1985: 41–45, 47, 50, 52, 54–57, 69.

Smith, pp. 30–33.

Wagner (*Inventors/Masters*), p. 63.

Williams, pp. 30, 33, 38.

(84) **The Sea Change**

(1930–31/December 1931/*This Quarter*/WTN, CS, FV)

Atherton, Robin. "'The Sea Change': The Pull of Moral Tides." *Linguistics in Literature* 4 (1979): 71–75.

Bennett, Warren. "'That's Not Very Polite': Sexual Identity in Hemingway's 'The Sea Change.'" *Hemingway's Neglected Short Fiction.* Ed. Susan F. Beegel. Ann Arbor: UMI Research Press, 1989: 225–46.

Brenner, pp. 12, 20, 53.

Brian, pp. 189, 190.

Donaldson, p. 181.

Fleming, Robert E. "Perversion and the Writer in 'The Sea Change.'" *Studies in American Fiction* 14, no. 2 (1986): 215–20.

Flora (*Nick Adams*), pp. 210, 217, 261.

Flora (*Short Fiction*), p. 66.

Gaggin, p. 97.

Hough, Julie. "Hemingway's 'The Sea Change': An Embracing of Reality." *Odyssey: A Journal of the Humanities* 2 (1978): 16–18.

Kert, p. 251.

Meyers (*A Biography*), pp. 78, 200, 346.

Rao, P. G. Rama, pp. 44, 73, 91, 122.

Smith, pp. 223–30.

Williams, p. 99.

(85) **Sepi Jingan** (Juvenilia)

(1916/1916/*Tabula*/EHA)

Cappel, pp. 43, 49–55, 67.

Meyers (*A Biography*), p. 20.

Rao, P. G. Rama, p. 7.

Reynolds (*Young H*), p. 74.

(86) **The Short Happy Life of Francis Macomber**

(1934–36/September 1936/*Cosmopolitan*/CS, FV)

Bakker, pp. 49, 56–59, 60, 61, 80, 114.

Beck, Warren. "Mr. Spilka's Problem: A Reply." *Modern Fiction Studies* 22 (1976): 256–69.

Beck, Warren. "The Shorter Happy Life of Mrs. Macomber: 1955." *Modern Fiction Studies* 21 (1975): 363–76.

Bender, Bert. "Margot Macomber's Gimlet." *College Literature* 8 (1981): 12–20.

Bocaz, Sergio H. "Senecan Stoicism in Hemingway's 'The Short Happy Life of Francis Macomber.'" *Studies in Language and Literature: The Proceedings of the*

23rd Mountain Interstate Foreign Language Conference. Ed. Charles L. Nelson. Richmond: Eastern Kentucky University Press, 1976: 81–85.

Brenner, p. 147.

Brian, pp. 84–85.

Burgess, pp. 68–70.

Capellan, p. 97.

Coleman, Arthur. "Francis Macomber and Sir Gawain." *American Notes and Queries* 29 (1981): 70.

Cooper, p. 66.

Cunliffe, Marcus. "A Source for Hemingway's Macomber?" *Journal of American Studies* 21 (1987): 103.

Dietze, R. F. "Crainway and Son: Ralph Ellison's *Invisible Man* as Seen Through the Perspective of Twain, Crane, and Hemingway." *Delta: Revue du Centre d'Etudes* 18 (April 1984): 25–46.

Donaldson, pp. 34–35, 80–81, 135, 163, 171, 284.

Fleming, Robert E. "When Hemingway Nodded: A Note on Firearms in 'The Short Happy Life.'" *NMAL: Notes on Modern American Literature* 5 (1981): item 17.

Flora (*Nick Adams*), pp. 190, 234, 252, 253, 261.

Flora (*Short Fiction*), pp. 74–81.

Fleissner, Robert F. "Hemingway's 'The Short Happy Life of Francis Macomber.'" *Explicator* 41 (1983): 45–47.

Gibson, Andrew. "Hemingway on the British." *Hemingway Review* 2 (1982): 62–75.

Giger, p. 21.

Gladstein, pp. 62–64.

Harkey, Joseph H. "The Africans and Francis Macomber." *Studies in Short Fiction* 17 (1980): 345–48.

Hellenga, Robert R. "Macomber Redivivus." *NMAL: Notes on Modern American Literature* 3 (1979): item 10.

Herndon, Jerry A. "'Macomber' and the 'Fifth Dimension.'" *NMAL: Notes on Modern American Literature* 5 (1981): item 24.

Herndon, Jerry A. "No 'Maggies' Drawers' for Margot Macomber." *Fitzgerald-Hemingway Annual* (1975): 289–91.

Howell, John M. "McCaslin and Macomber: From *Green Hills* to *Big Woods.*" *Faulkner Journal* 2 (Fall 1986): 29–36.

Hurley, C. Harold. "Hemingway's 'The Short Happy Life of Francis Macomber.'" *Explicator* 38 (1980): 9.

Jackson, Paul R. "Point of View, Distancing, and Hemingway's 'Short Happy Life.'" *Hemingway Notes* 5 (1980): 2–16.

Johnston, Kenneth G. "In Defense of the Unhappy Margot Macomber." *Hemingway Review* 2 (1983): 44–47. (Revised as "'The Short Happy Life of Francis Macomber': Charge and Countercharge," and reprinted in *The Tip of the Iceberg: Hemingway and the Short Story.* Greenwood, Fla.: Penkevill, 1987: 207–13.)

Kaplan, E. Ann. "Hemingway, Hollywood and Female Representation: *The Macomber Affair.*" *Literature and Film Quarterly* 13, no. 1 (1985): 22–28.

Kert, pp. 275–76, 277–78, 347, 489.

Kobler, J. F. "The Short Happy Illusion of Francis Macomber." *Quartet* (*Texas A&M*) 45–46 (1974): 62–66.

Kobler, pp. 38–42, 56, 60, 105–6, 123.

Lefcourt, Charles R. "The Macomber Case." *Revue des Langues Vivantes* 43 (1977): 341–47.

Leger, Brosnahan. "A Lost Passage From Hemingway's 'Macomber.'" *Studies in Bibliography: Papers of the Bibliographical Society of the University of Virginia* 38: 328–30.

Lounsberry, Barbara. "The Education of Robert Wilson." *Hemingway Notes* 5 (1980): 29–32.

Lynn, pp. 431–36.

McKenna, John J. "Macomber: The 'Nice Jerk.'" *American Notes and Queries* 17 (1979): 73–74.

McKenna, John J., and Marvin Peterson, V. "More Muddy Water: Wilson's Shakespeare in 'The Short Happy Life of Francis Macomber.'" *Studies in Short Fiction* 18 (1981): 82–85.

Meyers (*A Biography*), pp. 253, 267–75, 391, 501.

Meyers, Jeffrey. "Wallace Stevens and 'The Short Happy Life of Francis Macomber.'" *American Notes and Queries* 21 (1982): 47–48.

Moorhead, Michael. "Hemingway's 'The Short Happy Life of Francis Macomber' and Shaw's 'The Deputy Sheriff.'" *Explicator* 44 (Winter 1986): 42–43.

Morsberger, Robert E. "'That Hemingway Kind of Love': Macomber in the Movies." *Literature/Film Quarterly* 4 (1976): 54–59. (Reprinted in *A Moving Picture Feast*. Ed. Charles M. Oliver. New York: Praeger, 1989: 135–40.)

Morton, Bruce. "Hemingway's 'The Short Happy Life of Francis Macomber.'" *Explicator* 41 (1982): 48–49.

Morton, Bruce. "Macomber and Fitzgerald: Hemingway Gets Even in 'The Short Happy Life of Francis Macomber.'" *Zeitschrift fur Anglistik und Amerikanistik* 30 (1982): 157–60.

Nelson (*H, Expressionist Artist*), p. 62.

Phillips, pp. 89–97, 102, 110, 112.

Raeburn, p. 56.

Rao, P. G. Rama, pp. 4, 74, 137, 146–54.

Reynolds, Michael S. "Macomber: An Old Oak Park Name." *Hemingway Review* 3 (1983): 28–29.

Reynolds (*Young H*), pp. 52, 72–73.

Rovit and Brenner, pp. 56–57.

Seydow, John J. "Francis Macomber's Spurious Masculinity." *Hemingway Review* 1 (1981): 33–41.

Smith, pp. 327–48.

Smith, Wallace. "On Hemingway's 'The Short Happy Life of Francis Macomber.'" *Bulletin of the Faculty of Humanities, Seikel University (Tokyo)* 13 (1977): 1–14.

Spilka, Mark. "A Source for the Macomber 'Accident': Marryat's *Percival Keene*." *Hemingway Review* 3, no. 2 (Spring 1984): 46–49.

Spilka, Mark. "Warren Beck Revisited." *Modern Fiction Studies* 22 (1976): 245–55.

Stephens, Robert O. "Macomber and that Somali Proverb: The Matrix of Knowledge." *Fitzgerald-Hemingway Annual* (1977): 137–47.

Wagner (*Inventors/Masters*), pp. 72–73, 77–78.

Watson, James Gray. "'A Sound Basis of Union': Structural and Thematic Balance in 'The Short Happy Life of Francis Macomber.'" *Fitzgerald-Hemingway Annual* (1974): 215–28.

Whitlow, pp. 12, 59–68, 70, 88.

Williams, pp. 11, 126–29.

Yamamoto, Shoh. "Hemingway's Macomber Story: Its Structure and Meaning." *Poetica: An International Journal of Linguistic-Literary Studies (Tokyo)* 23 (1986): 98–115.

(87)   **A Simple Enquiry**
        (1926–27/October 14, 1927/*Men Without Women*/cs, FV)
        Brenner, pp. 18, 20, 22.
        Brenner, Gerry. "A Semiotic Inquiry into Hemingway's 'A Simple Inquiry.'"
            Hemingway's Short Fiction. Ed. Susan F. Beegel. Ann Arbor: UMI Research
            Press, 1989: 195–208.
        Cooper, p. 33.
        Donaldson, p. 183.
        Flora (*Nick Adams*), p. 113.
        Meyers (*A Biography*), pp. 200–201.
        Rao, P. G. Rama, pp. 44, 91.
        Smith, pp. 185–88.
        Wagner (*Inventors/Masters*), p. 67.
        Williams, p. 97.

(88)   **The Snows of Kilimanjaro**
        (1935/August 1936/*Esquire*/cs, FV)
        Bakker, pp. 49, 56, 59–61, 80, 87, 154.
        Brenner, p. 147.
        Blumenthal, Jay Allan. "Ernest Hemingway's Aesthetic Theory: An Analysis of
            His Concepts of Literary Truth and Literary Knowledge." *DAI* 38 (1977):
            2738A (Drew University).
        Bruccoli, pp. 130–33, 139–41.
        Burgess, p. 67.
        Capellan, pp. 97, 98, 99, 100, 231, 233.
        Cheng, Young-Hsiao T. "Fact and Fiction in Hemingway's 'The Snows of
            Kilimanjaro.'" *American Studies* (Taiwan) 7, no. 3 (September 1977): 41–55.
        Cooper, p. 66.
        Dahiya, pp. 18, 92, 93–113, 116, 119, 141.
        Donaldson, pp. 34–35, 53, 163, 212, 269, 284.
        Elia, Richard L. "Three Symbols in Hemingway's 'The Snows of Kilimanjaro.'"
            Revue des Langues Vivantes 41 (1975): 282–85.
        Flora (*Nick Adams*), pp. 190, 234, 252, 253, 261.
        Flora (*Short Fiction*), pp. 81–88, 114–15.
        Fuentes, p. 98.
        Gaggin, pp. 35–36.
        Gladstein, pp. 49, 64–65.
        Hardy and Cull, pp. 26–27, 44.
        Herndon, Jerry A. "'The Snows of Kilimanjaro': Another Look at Theme and
            Point of View." *South Atlantic Quarterly* 85 (Autumn 1986): 351–59.
        Johnston, Kenneth G. "The Silly Wasters: Tzara and the Poet in 'The Snows of
            Kilimanjaro.'" *Hemingway Review* 8, no. 1 (Fall 1988): 50–57.
        Johnston, Kenneth G. "'The Snows of Kilimanjaro': An African Purge." *Studies
            in Short Fiction* 21, no. 3 (Summer 1984): 223–27. (Reprinted in *The Tip of the
            Iceberg: Hemingway and the Short Story*. Greenwood, Fla.: Penkevill, 1987: 195–
            204.)
        Johnston, Kenneth G. "The Songs in Hemingway's 'The Snows of Kiliman-
            jaro.'" *American Notes and Queries* 23 (November–December 1984): 46–49.
        Kert, pp. 70, 124–25, 277–79, 281.
        Kobler, pp. 39, 50, 51, 123.
        Kolb, Alfred. "Symbolic Structure in Hemingway's 'The Snows of Kiliman-
            jaro.'" *NMAL: Notes on Modern American Literature* 1 (1976): item 4.

Lynn, pp. 180–81, 189–90, 214–15, 429–31, 437–38.

Madison, Robert D. "Hemingway and Selous: A Source for 'Snows'?" *Hemingway Review* 8, no. 1 (Fall 1988): 62–63.

Meyers (*A Biography*), pp. 41, 98, 106–7, 195, 263, 265, 275–79, 294, 317, 326, 352, 488, 535–36.

Meyers, Jeffrey. Introduction. *Disease and the Novel, 1880-1960.* London: Macmillan, 1985: 1–18.

Meyers, Jeffrey. "Tolstoy and Hemingway: 'The Death of Ivan Ilych' and 'The Snows of Kilimanjaro.'" *Disease and the Novel, 1880-1960.* London: Macmillan, 1985: 19–29.

Monteiro, George. "Hemingway's Samson Agonistes." *Fitzgerald-Hemingway Annual* (1979): 411–16.

Morsberger, Robert E. "ED on Kilimanjaro." *Dickinson Studies: Emily Dickinson (1830–86)* 30 (1976): 105–6.

Nelson (*H, Expressionist Artist*), p. 21.

Nicholson, Colin. "Signatures of Time." *Canadian Literature* 107 (1985): 90–101.

Petry, Alice Hall. "Voice Out of Africa: A Possible Oral Source for Hemingway's 'The Snows of Kilimanjaro.'" *Hemingway Review* 4, no. 2 (Spring 1985): 7–11.

Phillips, pp. 8, 80, 90, 106, 123, 159.

Raeburn, pp. 174–75, 204–7.

Rao, P. G. Rama, pp. 4, 54, 74, 79, 123, 137–46, 197, 207, 208.

Reynolds (*H's First War*), pp. 216–17.

Rovit and Brenner, pp. 19–22, 56, 57, 62, 63, 98.

Shuster, Marilyn R. "Reading and Writing as a Woman: The Retold Tales of Marguerite Duras." *French Review* 58, no. 1 (October 1984): 48–57.

Smith, pp. 349–61.

Titner, Adeline R. "Wharton's Forgotten Preface to Vivienne de Watteville's *Speak to the Earth:* A Link with Hemingway's 'The Snows of Kilimanjaro.'" *NMAL: Notes on Modern American Literature* 8, no. 2 (Autumn 1984): item 10.

Villard and Nagel, p. 265.

Wagner (*Inventors/Masters*), pp. 72–73, 77–78.

Whitlow, pp. 68–74, 88.

Whitlow, Roger. "Critical Misinterpretation of Hemingway's Helen." *Frontiers: A Journal of Women Studies* 3 (1978): 52–54.

Williams, pp. 129–35.

(89)   **Soldier's Home**

(1924/June 1925/*Contact Collection of Contemporary Writers* [anthology]/IOT, CS, FV)

Barron, Cynthia M. "The Catcher and the Soldier: Hemingway's 'Soldier's Home' and Salinger's *The Catcher in the Rye.*" *Hemingway Review* 2 (1982): 70–73.

Boyd, John D. "Hemingway's 'Soldier's Home.'" *Explicator* 40 (1981): 51–53.

Broer, Lawrence. "Soldier's Home." *Lost Generation Journal* 3 (1975): 32.

Capellan, pp. 4, 72, 81, 166.

Cooper, pp. 4, 23, 32, 90.

Donaldson, pp. 189, 224–25.

Elder, Harris James. "From Literature to Cinema: The American Short Story Series." *DAI* 40 (1980): 4279A (Oklahoma State University).

Flora (*Nick Adams*), pp. 43–44, 48, 98, 106, 107, 112, 194, 262, 268–69, 270.

Giger, p. 20.

Grimes, pp. 35, 42, 45.

Johnston, Kenneth G. "'Soldier's Home': Conflict on the Home Front." *The Tip of the Iceberg: Hemingway and the Short Story*. Greenwood, Fla.: Penkevill, 1987: 75–82.

Jones, Horace P. "Hemingway's 'Soldier's Home.'" *Explicator* 37 (1979): 17.

Kert, pp. 70–71.

Knowlton, Marianne H. "'Soldier's Home': A Space Between." *A Moving Picture Feast*. Ed. Charles M. Oliver. New York: Praeger, 1989: 141–47.

Kobler, pp. 58, 112.

Lynn, pp. 85, 258–60.

Meyers (*A Biography*), pp. 10, 47, 55, 83, 115.

Monteiro, George. "Hemingway's 'Soldier's Home.'" *Explicator* 40 (1981): 50–51.

Nakajima, Kenji. "Hemingway's View of Alienation in 'Soldier's Home.'" *Kyushu American Literature* 20 (1979): 21–28.

Phillips, p. 160.

Rao, E. Nageswara, pp. 20, 52, 66.

Rao, P. G. Rama, pp. 40, 131, 162.

Reynolds (*H's First War*), p. B7.

Reynolds (*The Paris Years*), pp. 189–91.

Reynolds (*Young H*), p. 52.

Roberts, John J. "In Defense of Krebs." *Studies in Short Fiction* 13 (1976): 515–18. (Reprinted in Michael S. Reynolds, ed. *Critical Essays on Ernest Hemingway's "In Our Time."* Boston: Hall, 1983: 199–202.)

Rovit, Earl. "On Ernest Hemingway and 'Soldier's Home.'" *The American Short Story*. Ed. Calvin L. Skaggs. 2 vols. New York: Dell, 1977. 1: 251–56.

Sarason, Bertram D. "Krebs in Kodiak." *Fitzgerald-Hemingway Annual* (1975): 209–15.

Skaggs, Calvin L. Introduction. *The American Short Story*. Ed. Skaggs. 2 vols. New York: Dell, 1977. 1: 14.

Smith, pp. 68–74.

Villard and Nagel, p. 257.

Wagner (*Inventors/Masters*), pp. 58–59, 60, 63.

Williams, pp. 32, 33, 36.

Ziff, Larzer. "The Social Basis of Hemingway's Style." *Poetics: International Review for the Theory of Literature* 7 (1978): 417–23. (Reprinted in Wagner, Linda W., ed. *Ernest Hemingway: Six Decades of Criticism*. Boston: Hall, 1987: 147–54.)

(91) **Ten Indians**

(1925-27/October 14, 1927/*Men Without Women*/CS, NA, FV)

Bakker, pp. 4, 5.

Brenner, p. 18.

Capellan, pp. 78–79.

Cappel, pp. 13, 26, 61, 96–105.

Dahiya, pp. 31, 32, 33, 34, 40, 41.

Fleming, Robert E. "Hemingway's Dr. Adams: Saint or Sinner." *Arizona Quarterly* 39 (1983): 101–10.

Flora (*Nick Adams*), pp. 44–57, 67, 71, 93, 94, 96, 104, 113, 161, 183, 216, 240, 265, 267.

Griffin, p. 222.

Hardy and Cull, p. 47.

Kert, p. 179.

Meyers (*A Biography*), pp. 16, 133.

Rao, P. G. Rama, pp. 44, 45, 123.

Reynolds (*The Paris Years*), p. 332.
Rovit and Brenner, p. 161.
Smith, pp. 197–203.
Smith, Paul. "The Tenth Indian and the Thing Left Out." *Ernest Hemingway: The Writer in Context*. Ed. James Nagel. Madison: University of Wisconsin Press, 1984: 53–74.
Unfried, pp. 15–16.
Wagner (*Inventors/Masters*), p. 67.
Whitlow, pp. 101–2.
Williams, p. 93.

(92)   **The Three-Day Blow**
(1924/October 5, 1925/*In Our Time*/CS, NA, FV)
Brenner, pp. 20, 37, 222.
Cappel, pp. 14, 128, 134–40, 190.
Cooper, p. 25.
Dahiya, pp. 19, 20, 22, 33, 38, 42, 45.
Donaldson, pp. 191, 248–49.
Flora (*Nick Adams*), pp. 13, 53, 58–68, 69, 71, 73, 77, 83, 93, 97, 121, 122, 141, 161, 165, 177, 192, 195, 196, 197, 218, 233, 238, 248, 250, 272.
Grimes, pp. 42–43, 55.
Hannum, Howard L. "Dating Hemingway's 'The Three Day Blow' by External Evidence: The Baseball Dialogue." *Studies in Short Fiction* 21, no. 3 (Summer 1984): 267–68.
Johnston, Kenneth G. "'The Three-Day Blow': Tragicomic Aftermath of a Summer Romance." *Hemingway Review* 2 (1982): 21–25. (Reprinted in *The Tip of the Iceberg: Hemingway and the Short Story*. Greenwood, Fla.: Penkevill, 1987: 95–101.)
Kobler, pp. 42, 66–67, 100.
Lynn, pp. 121–22, 255.
Meyers (*A Biography*), p. 49.
Monteiro, George. "Dating the Events of 'The Three Day Blow.'" *Fitzgerald-Hemingway Annual* (1977): 207–10. (Reprinted in Michael S. Reynolds, ed. *Critical Essays on Ernest Hemingway's "In Our Time."* Boston: Hall, 1983: 172–75.)
O'Brien, Matthew. "Baseball in 'The Three-Day Blow.'" *American Notes and Queries* 16 (1977): 24–26.
Raeburn, p. 194.
Rao, E. Nageswara, p. 15.
Rao, P. G. Rama, pp. 101, 162, 164, 165.
Reynolds (*Young H*), pp. 201, 226.
Smith, pp. 56–60.
Wagner (*Inventors/Masters*), pp. 58, 63.
Whitlow, pp. 88–89.
Williams, pp. 33, 36, 93.

(94)   **Today is Friday**
(1926/Summer 1926/*Today is Friday* [pamphlet]/MWW, CS, FV)
Brackenridge, Lois. "Analysis of 'Today is Friday' by Ernest Hemingway." *Linguistics in Literature* 1 (1976): 1–10.
Brenner, pp. 19, 22.
Bruccoli, p. 53.
Donaldson, p. 237.
Flora (*Nick Adams*), p. 214.
Kert, p. 179.

Lynn, p. 343.
Meyers (*A Biography*), pp. 133, 185.
Rao, P. G. Rama, p. 42.
Rovit and Brenner, p. 47.
Smith, pp. 154-58.
Stolzfus, p. 43.
Williams, p. 96.

(95) **The Tradesman's Return**
(1935/February 1936/*Esquire*/[revised to become Part II of *To Have and Have Not*], FV)
Cooper, p. 66.
Fuentes, p. 121.
Kert, p. 276.
Lynn, pp. 454–56.
Meyers (*A Biography*), pp. 116, 228, 488.
Phillips, p. 49.

(96) **The Undefeated**
(1924/Summer 1925/*Querschnitt*, as "Steirkampf" in German/MWW, CS, FV)
Beegel, Susan. "The Death of El Espartero: An Historic Matador Links 'The Undefeated' and *Death in the Afternoon*." *Hemingway Review* 5, no. 2 (Spring 1986): 12–23.
Brenner, pp. 19, 21–22, 101, 219.
Capellan, pp. 6, 21, 87, 88, 125, 133, 146, 150, 153, 170, 203.
Cooper, pp. 79, 115.
Dahiya, p. 43.
Donaldson, pp. 53, 91, 189, 278.
Flora (*Nick Adams*), p. 113.
Gaggin, pp. 47–48.
Johnston, Kenneth G. "'The Undefeated': The Moment of Truth." *The Tip of the Iceberg: Hemingway and the Short Story*. Greenwood, Fla.: Penkevill, 1987: 85–92.
Kert, pp. 185, 202.
Kobler, pp. 25–26, 27, 28, 55.
Lynn, pp. 268–69.
Rao, E. Nageswara, p. 102.
Rao, P. G. Rama, p. 123.
Reynolds (*The Paris Years*), pp. 246–47, 263, 276–77.
Rovit and Brenner, pp. 43, 44, 62, 67, 98.
Smith, pp. 102–9.
Sojka, pp. 3, 125, 157.
Stoltzfus, pp. 49, 54–55, 62, 63–64, 73–74.
Wagner (*Inventors/Masters*), p. 66.

(97) **Under the Ridge**
(1939/October 1939/*Cosmopolitan*/FUS, FV)
Capellan, p. 250.
Cooper, pp. 96–97.
Donaldson, p. 113.
Flora (*Short Fiction*), p. 95.
Gaggin, pp. 63–64.
Knight, Christopher. "Ernest Hemingway's 'Under the Ridge': A Textual

Note." *NMAL: Notes on Modern American Literature* 7 (Winter 1983): item 15.

Kvam, Wayne. "Hemingway's 'Under the Ridge.'" *Fitzgerald-Hemingway Annual* (1978): 225–40.

Smith, pp. 385–88.

Wagner (*Inventors/Masters*), pp. 91–92.

(105)   **Up in Michigan**
          (1921/Summer 1923/*Three Stories and Ten Poems*/CS[revised])

Bruccoli, p. 10.

Capellan, p. 222.

Cappel, pp. 14, 119–27, 128, 184.

Donaldson, pp. 38, 145, 178.

Flora (*Short Fiction*), pp. 21–22, 54, 68, 182, 186.

Grimes, pp. 5, 25–27, 72.

Kert, pp. 74, 114, 128, 138, 143, 154.

Lynn, pp. 108–10, 170, 224–25.

Meyers (*A Biography*), pp. 49, 143, 147, 435.

Nelson (*H, Expressionist Artist*), p. 22.

Paul, Angus. "Hemingway Scholar [Paul Smith] Offers New Views on the Story 'Up in Michigan.'" *The Chronicle of Higher Education* 32 (March 5, 1986): 5, 10.

Petry, Alice Hall. "Coming of Age in Hortons Bay: Hemingway's 'Up in Michigan.'" *Hemingway Review* 3, no. 2 (Spring 1984): 23–28.

Rao, E. Nageswara, p. 58.

Rao, P. G. Rama, pp. 44, 97, 163.

Reynolds (*The Paris Years*), pp. 37, 98, 169.

Reynolds (*Young H*), pp. 95, 246–47.

Smith, pp. 3–7.

Smith, Paul. "Three Versions of 'Up in Michigan.'" *Resources for American Literary Study* 15, no. 2 (Autumn 1985): 163–77.

Spenka, James Leo. "A Long Look at Hemingway's 'Up in Michigan.'" *Arizona Quarterly* 39 (1983): 111–21.

Swartzlander, Susan. "Uncle Charles in Michigan." *Hemingway's Neglected Short Fiction: New Perspectives*. Ed. Susan F. Beegel. Ann Arbor: UMI Research Press, 1989: 31–42.

Wagner (*Inventors/Masters*), pp. 30, 63.

Whitlow, pp. 83–86, 93.

Wilkinson, p. 78.

(106)   **A Very Short Story** ("Chapter X" from *in our time*; "One hot evening in Milan")
          (1923/Spring 1924/*in our time*/IOT, CS)

Brian, p. 29.

Capellan, pp. 69, 80.

Cappel, p. 115.

Cooper, pp. 32–33.

Donaldson, p. 145.

Donaldson, Scott. "'A Very Short Story' as Therapy." *Hemingway's Neglected Short Fiction: New Perspectives*. Ed. Susan F. Beegel. Ann Arbor: UMI Research Press, 1989: 99–106.

Flora (*Nick Adams*), pp. 105, 132, 213.

Flora (*Short Fiction*), pp. 30, 61, 62.

Grimes, pp. 35, 42, 45.

Kert, p. 131.

Meyers (*A Biography*), pp. 40–41, 147, 199, 506.

Phillips, p. 84.

Rao, P. G. Rama, pp. 46, 123, 162, 165, 175–77.

Reynolds (*H's First War*), pp. 181, 216, 280.

Reynolds (*The Paris Years*), pp. 126, 270.

Smith, pp. 25–29.

Villard and Nagel, pp. 264–65.

Williams, pp. 30, 32, 33, 36, 65, 106.

(107)   **A Way You'll Never Be**

  (1932/October 27, 1933/*Winner Take Nothing*/CS, NA)

Bakker, p. 6.

Brenner, pp. 53, 75.

Brian, p. 200.

Capellan, p. 80.

Cappel, pp. 109, 200.

Cooper, pp. 3, 24, 25, 90.

Donaldson, pp. 126, 137.

Flora (*Nick Adams*), pp. 110, 111, 113, 123–40, 149, 154, 156, 216, 237, 252, 255.

Gaggin, pp. 65–66.

Grimes, pp. 35, 64–67, 68, 78, 120, 122.

Holcombe, Wayne C. "Philip Young or Youngerdunger?" *Hemingway Review* 5, no. 2 (Spring 1986): 24–33.

Johnston, Kenneth G. "'A Way You'll Never Be': A Mission of Morale." *Studies in Short Fiction* 23 (Fall 1986): 429–35. (Reprinted in *The Tip of the Iceberg: Hemingway and the Short Story*. Greenwood, Fla.: Penkevill, 1987: 171–79.)

Kert, p. 250.

Lynn, pp. 405, 408.

Meyers (*A Biography*), pp. 29–30, 229, 245, 258, 289.

Nelson (*H, Expressionist Artist*), pp. 23, 27, 34, 46, 68.

Rao, P. G. Rama, pp. 40, 45, 94.

Reynolds (*H's First War*), p. 172.

Reynolds (*The Paris Years*), p. 127.

Rovit and Brenner, pp. 63–64.

Smith, pp. 268–76.

Sojka, pp. 34, 80, 86, 96.

Unfried, pp. 29–31.

Villard and Nagel, p. 265.

Wagner (*Inventors/Masters*), pp. 69–71.

Williams, pp. 98–99.

(108)   **Wine of Wyoming**

  (1929–1930/August 1930/*Scribner's Magazine*/MTV, CS)

Brenner, pp. 20, 53.

Flora (*Nick Adams*), pp. 14, 16, 210, 218, 223–35, 236, 237, 241, 245, 248, 249, 260, 262.

Flora (*Short Fiction*), pp. 65–66.

Johnston, Kenneth G. "Hemingway's 'Wine of Wyoming': Disappointment in America." *Western American Literature* 11 (November 1974): 159–67. (Revised as "'Wine of Wyoming': Disappointment in America," and reprinted in *The Tip of the Iceberg: Hemingway and the Short Story*. Greenwood, Fla.: Penkevill, 1987: 147–58.)

Kobler, p. 42.

Martin, Lawrence H., Jr. "Crazy in Sheridan: Hemingway's 'Wine of Wyoming'

Reconsidered." *Hemingway Review* 8, no. 1 (Fall 1988): 13–25.

Nelson (*H, Expressionist Artist*), p. 45.

Putnam, Ann. "'Wine of Wyoming' and Hemingway's Hidden West." *Western American Literature* 22, no. 1 (May 1987): 17–32.

Smith, pp. 217–22.

Stoneback, H. R. "'Mais Je Reste Catholique': Communion, Betrayal, and Aridity in 'Wine of Wyoming.'" *Hemingway's Neglected Short Fiction.* Ann Arbor: UMI Research Press, 1989: 209–24.

Williams, pp. 101–2.

B. Posthumously Published: Apprenticeship Fiction, Fragments, Parts of Longer Manuscripts Published as Short Stories

(1a)   **An African Story** (part of unfinished novel)
    (. . . /1987/*Finca Vigía*/ . . .)

(2A)   **The Ash Heel's Tendon—A Story**
    (1930/August 1985/*New York Times Magazine*/ . . .)
    Griffin, pp. 174–80 (story plus brief comment).
    Reynolds (*Young H*), pp. 91–93, 218.

(6a)   **Black Ass at the Crossroads**
    (1956/1987/*Finca Vigía*/ . . .)
    Flora (*Short Fiction*), pp. 102–4.

(29a)   **Crossroads—An Anthology**
    (1919/August 1985/*New York Times Magazine*/ . . .)
    Griffin, pp. 124–27 (story plus brief comment).
    Reynolds (*The Paris Years*), p. 251.

(31)   **Crossing the Mississippi** (fragment)
    (. . . /1972/*The Nick Adams Stories*/ . . .)
    Capellan, p. 80.
    Dahiya, p. 46.
    Flora (*Nick Adams*), pp. 176–78, 266.
    Unfried, p. 24.

(31a)   **The Current—A Story**
    (1921/September 1985/*Along with Youth*/ . . .)
    Griffin, pp. 200–209 (story plus brief comment).

(45)   **Great News from the Mainland**
    (ca. 1955/1987/*Finca Vigía*/ . . .)
    Flora (*Short Fiction*), pp. 107–8.

(49)   **I Guess Everything Reminds You of Something**
    (ca. 1955/1987/*Family Circle*/FV)
    Flora (*Short Fiction*), pp. 105–7.
    Meyers (*A Biography*), pp. 291–92.

(54)   **The Indians Moved Away** (fragment)
    (. . . /1972/*The Nick Adams Stories*/ . . .)
    Capellan, p. 79.

Dahiya, p. 34.
Flora (*Nick Adams*), pp. 32–34, 35.
Unfried, p. 16.
Williams, p. 106.

(58)   **Landscape with Figures**
         (1938/1987/*Finca Vigía*/ . . .)

(59)   **The Last Good Country** (part of unfinished novel)
         (1952–58/1972/*The Nick Adams Stories*/FV)
Capellan, p. 112.
Dahiya, pp. 44, 45.
Donaldson, pp. 83, 291.
Flora (*Nick Adams*), pp. 15, 43, 53–54, 69, 253–79.
Gaggin, pp. 26, 88.
Grimes, pp. 59–60.
Johnson, David R. "'The Last Good Country': Again the End of Something."
     Fitzgerald-Hemingway Annual (1979): 363–70.
Lerfald, Robert Allan. "Hemingway's Search for the Sacred: A Study of the
     Primitive Rituals of a Twentieth-Century American Adam." *DAI* 37 (1977):
     7752A (University of Minnesota).
Lynn, pp. 56–58, 322.
Meyers (*A Biography*), pp. 10, 15, 435.
Reynolds (*Young H*), pp. 51, 72, 141.
Sojka, pp. 75, 76.
Spanier, Sandra Whipple. "Hemingway's 'The Last Good Country' and the
     Catcher in the Rye: More than a Family Resemblance." *Studies in Short Fiction* 19
     (1982): 35–43.
Spilka, Mark. "Original Sin in 'The Last Good Country': Or, The Return of
     Catherine Barkley." *The Modernists: Studies in a Literary Phenomenon.* Eds.
     Lawrence B. Gamache and Ian S. MacNiven. Rutherford, N.J.: Fairleigh
     Dickinson University Press, 1987: 210–33.
Unfried, pp. 20–24.
Williams, pp. 105–6.

(62a)   **The Mercenaries—A Story**
         (1919/August 1985/*New York Times Magazine*/ . . .)
Flora (*Short Fiction*), p. 101.
Gladstein, Mimi Reisel. "'The Mercenaries': A Harbinger of Vintage Heming-
     way." *Hemingway's Neglected Short Fiction.* Ed. Susan F. Beegel. Ann Arbor:
     UMI Research Press, 1989: 19–30.
Griffin, pp. 104 (story plus brief comment).
Lynn, pp. 111–12.
Reynolds (*Young H*), pp. 125–27.

(70)   **Night Before Landing** (fragment from unfinished novel, *Along with Youth: A
         Novel*)
         (1925/1972/*The Nick Adams Stories*/ . . .)
Capellan, p. 250.
Dahiya, pp. 45, 47, 51.
Donaldson, p. 137.
Flora (*Short Stories*), pp. 60, 110–13, 129, 131, 132.

Grimes, p. 61.
Meyers (*A Biography*), pp. 311, 372.
Unfried, pp. 24–25.
Wagner (*Inventors/Masters*), pp. 90–91, 96.

(75) **On Writing** (part of "Big Two-Hearted River" manuscript)
(1924/1972/*The Nick Adams Stories*/ . . .)
Broer, Lawrence. "Hemingway's 'On Writing': A Portrait of the Artist as Nick Adams." *Hemingway's Neglected Short Fiction*. Ed. Susan F. Beegel. Ann Arbor: UMI Research Press, 1989: 131–40.
Gaggin, p. 26.
Giger, p. 21.
Phillips, p. 98.
Reynolds (*The Paris Years*), p. 40.
Svoboda, p. 18.
Unfried, pp. 39–41.
Wagner (*Inventors/Masters*), p. 57.

(80a) **The Porter** (part of unfinished novel)
(. . . /1987/ . . . *Finca Vigía*/ . . .)

(80b) **Portrait of the Idealist in Love—A Story**
(1921/September 1985/*Along With Youth*/ . . .)
Griffin, pp. 161–64 (story plus brief comment).

(89a) **The Strange Country** (part of unfinished novel)
(ca. 1950/1987/*Finca Vigía*/ . . .)
Flora, Joseph M. "Hemingway's 'The Strange Country' in the Context of *The Complete Short Stories*." *Studies in Short Fiction* 25 (Fall 1988): 409–20.

(90) **Summer People**
(1924/1972/*The Nick Adams Stories*/FV)
Donaldson, pp. 145–46, 178.
Flora (*Nick Adams*), pp. 8, 53, 181–87, 188, 189, 191, 194, 211, 273.
Griffin, pp. 131–33.
Griffin, Peter M. "A Substantive Error in the Text of Ernest Hemingway's 'Summer People.'" *American Literature: A Journal of Literary History, Criticism, and Bibliography* 50 (1978): 471–73.
Kert, p. 46.
Lindholdt, Paul J. "Ernest Hemingway's 'Summer People': More Textual Errors and a Reply." *Studies in Short Fiction* 20 (1983): 319–20.
Lynn, pp. 128–29.
Meyers (*A Biography*), pp. 23, 217.
Reynolds (*The Paris Years*), pp. 229–31, 252.
Reynolds (*Young H*), pp. 123–24.
Unfried, pp. 38–39.
Williams, p. 106.

(93) **Three Shots** (part of "Indian Camp" manuscript)
(1924/1972/*The Nick Adams Stories*/ . . .)
Capellan, p. 97.
Dahiya, pp. 23, 25, 28, 29, 33, 48.

> Flora (*Short Fiction*), pp. 31–32, 117, 130.
> Grimes, pp. 2, 55–56, 57, 118, 121.
> Meyers (*A Biography*), p. 15.
> Sojka, pp. 74, 78.
> Unfried, pp. 11–12.

(95a)　　**A Train Trip** (part of unfinished novel)
　　　　　(. . . /1985/*Finca Vigía*/ . . .)

(107a)　　**A Wedding Day**
　　　　　(. ? . /1972/*The Nick Adams Stories*/ . . .)
　　　　　Flora (*Nick Adams*), pp. 188–89, 194, 212, 218.
　　　　　Kert, pp. 102–3.

C. Tentative List of Unpublished Sketches and Stories (with Kennedy Library item number)

(241a)　　**"An American citizen not yet thirty-five years old . . ."**
　　　　　ms, 12 pp., signed [sketch of life in Paris]

(252)　　**"As Alice came walking down the road . . ."**
　　　　　ts, 4 pp. [satiric sketch on New Deal]

(260)　　**"At one o'clock in the morning . . ."**
　　　　　ms, 8 pp. [unfinished sketch of World War I soldier dying of pneumonia in hospital]
　　　　　Griffin, pp. 95–96.

(265a)　　**The Autobiography of Alice B. Hemingway**
　　　　　ts, 6 pp. [seriocomic response to Stein's AABT]

(340–41)　**Crime and Punishment**
　　　　　ms, 11 pp. [experimental episodic story, after 1927]

(351)　　**Culture Hour at the Floridita**
　　　　　ms, 7 pp. [bar in Havana, cruise ships]

(356–56a)　**"The day we drove back from Nancy to Paris . . ."**
　　　　　ts, 12 pp. [WW II story]

(360–62a)　**Death of the Standard Oil Man**
　　　　　ms. fragments, see also 397, 518, 526, 847. [various drafts, sections, etc. for a story on characters in Constantinople, 1922]

(407a)　　**Fragments from Ernest von Hemingstein's Journal**
　　　　　ts, 5 pp. [humorous sketch of writers in Paris]

(435a)　　**The Great Black Horse**
　　　　　ms, ts, 11 pp. [fable, 1950s; part in Adriana Ivancich's hand]

(445)　　**"He had known he would not get up . . ."**
　　　　　ms, 17 pp.

Griffin, pp. 222–25.
Lynn, pp. 130–31.

(477.5) **The Home Front**
ts, 6 pp.
Meyers (*A Biography*), p. 256.

(496–96b) **Indian Country and the White Army**
ts, 19 pp. [World War II story]

(529a) **James Allen lived in a studio . . .**
ms, 45 pp. [the beginning of a novel manuscript about a writer in Paris at the time he is divorcing his wife]
Meyers, (*A Biography*), pp. 178, 557.

(532) **"John Wesley Marvin was hulked . . ."**
ms, 4 pp., see also 286a [high school fighting story]
Reynolds (*The Young H*), pp. 57–58.

(538–41) **A Lack of Passion**
Capellan, p. 203.
Meyers (*A Biography*), p. 230.
Reynolds (*The Paris Years*), p. 260.

(541b) **Landscape with Figures**
ts, 33 pp. [complete Civil War story]
Flora (*Short Fiction*), pp. 96–98.

(546a) **"Lawrence lived alone comfortably . . ."**
ts, 2 pp. [possibly incomplete sketch, Paris literary figure]

(575a) **The Mink Jacket**
[full sketch, dated January 12, 1951, not described in catalog]

(580-80a) **The Monument**
ts, 14 pp. [World War II story]
Meyers (*A Biography*), pp. 346, 401.

(604) **"Nick lay in bed in the hospital . . ."**
ms, 4 pp. [unfinished sketch, wounded World War I, with soldier and nurse]
Griffin, p. 95.
Reynolds (*The Young H*), pp. 33–34.

(634) **"One night Frankie and Johnnie Clinton . . ."**
ts, 11 pp. [in six installments, early story (1919–21) intended for magazine like *St. Nicholas*]

(648a) **Philip Haines was a writer . . .**
ms, 31 pp. [related to 529a, beginning of a novel about a married couple in Paris getting a divorce]
Meyers (*A Biography*), pp. 178–79.

(648b)   **Philip Haines was a writer** . . .
           ms, 29 pp. [gathering of disconnected fragments related to 529a and 648a]

(660)   **Portrait of Three or the Paella**
           ms, 10 pp. [sketch of picnic, ca. 1931, with Stanley Franklin and bullfighters]

(670a-b)   **"Red Smith lay on a cot . . ."** (The Visiting Team)
           ts, 17 pp. [Chicago story, 1919–21]

(673-74)   **A Room on the Garden Side**
           ts, 11 pp. [Ritz Hotel in Paris, World War II]

(692a-b)   **The Shot**
           ms, 9 pp. [hunting with children, Cuba]

(714)   **Spain**
           ms, 10 pp. [three sketches, each titled Spain; Pamplona with Hadley]

(828)   **"When I was a boy I answered advertisements . . ."**
           ms, 11 pp. ["framed letter" story (cp. One Reader Writes), including the letter
           from Mark Schorer/EH July 30, 1929]
           Griffin, pp. 123–24.
           Reynolds (*The Young H*), pp. 58–59.
           Svoboda, pp. 33, 35.

(843–44)   **The Woppian Way** (The Passing of Pickles McCarty)
           ts, 17 pp. [1919 story]
           Griffin, pp. 123–24.
           Meyers (*A Biography*), p. 50.
           Reynolds (*The Young H*), pp. 58–59, 89, 237, 254, 265.
           Svoboda, pp. 33, 35.

(859)   **"You think it is pretty hot playing football . . ."**
           ms. fragments, 10 pp. [high school story (1916)]

Notes and References

●

Debra A. Moddelmog, "The Unifying Consciousness of a Divided Conscience: Nick Adams as Author of *In Our Time*"

1 *The Nick Adams Stories* (New York: Scribner's, 1972). All references to this work are to the Bantam edition (1973) and are designated *NAS* in the text.

2 Philip Young, for instance, asserts that "the 'he,' the consciousness of the piece, shifts from Nick to Hemingway back to Nick again"—"'Big World Out There': The Nick Adams Stories," in *The Short Stories of Ernest Hemingway: Critical Essays*, ed. Jackson J. Benson (Durham, N.C.: Duke University Press, 1975), p. 31. Paul Smith also criticizes this passage, citing as its most incriminating sentence: "He, Nick, had wanted to write about country so it would be there like Cézanne had done it in painting" (*NAS*, 218). Smith maintains that the unnecessary appositive here emphasizes the "autobiographical character" of this ending: "it is as if [Hemingway] had to remind himself he was writing a work of fiction"—"Hemingway's Early Manuscripts: The Theory and Practice of Omission," *Journal of Modern Literature* 10 (1983): 282.

3 Consider, for example, Chaman Nahal's discussion of this ending in *The Narrative Pattern in Ernest Hemingway's Fiction* (Rutherford, N.J.: Fairleigh Dickinson University Press, 1971), pp. 193–94.

4 "He Made Him Up: 'Big Two-Hearted River' as Doppelganger," in *Critical Essays on Ernest Hemingway's "In Our Time,"* ed. Michael S. Reynolds (Boston: Hall, 1983), pp. 255, 256.

5 *Hemingway's Nick Adams* (Baton Rouge: Louisiana State University Press, 1982), p. 181.

6 In *Ernest Hemingway: Selected Letters 1917–1961*, ed. Carlos Baker (New York: Scribner's 1981), p. 133.

7 Possibly it was Gertrude Stein who alerted Hemingway to the problem with this ending. In *The Autobiography of Alice B. Toklas* she recalls that in the fall of 1924 Hemingway "had added to his stories a little story of meditations and in these he said that The Enormous Room was the greatest book he had ever read" [Nick actually says it was "one of the great books," *NAS*, 219]. It was then that Gertrude Stein had said, "Hemingway, remarks are not literature"—(New York: Random House, 1933), p. 219. Pointed out by Paul Smith, p. 284.

8 *Hemingway's Nick Adams*, p. 189.

9 *Ernest Hemingway: A Reconsideration* (University Park: Pennsylvania State University Press, 1966), p. 62.

10 *In Our Time* (New York: Scribner's 1930). All references are to this edition and are designated *IOT* in the text.

11 Carlos Baker notes that during the decade when Hemingway wrote his first forty-five stories, "he was unwilling to stray very far from the life he knew by direct personal contact, or to do any more guessing than was absolutely necessary"—*Hemingway: The Writer as Artist*, fourth ed. (Princeton, N.J.: Princeton University Press, 1972), p. 128.

12 Kenneth Lynn traces this reading to Edmund Wilson's "Ernest Hemingway: Bourdon Gauge of Morale" (1939) and Malcolm Cowley's introduction to the Viking *Portable Hemingway* (1944)—Lynn, *Hemingway* (New York: Simon and Schuster, 1987), pp.

104–5. The most influential version of the war trauma theory of "Big Two-Hearted River" has probably been Philip Young's interpretations; see especially his *Ernest Hemingway* (New York: Rinehart, 1952) and his *Ernest Hemingway: A Reconsideration*, pp. 43–48. However, not all scholars hold with this view. Lynn, for example, argues that critics could see Nick's troubles as war-related only by importing external evidence from Hemingway's life into the story. Ironically, Lynn also uses Hemingway's life to identify the nature of "the other needs" that Nick is escaping when he asserts that among those needs was Hemingway's desire to get away from his mother (pp. 103–4).

13　See the Preface to *The Nick Adams Stories*, p. v.

14　"'Big World Out There': The Nick Adams Stories," p. 13.

15　I am not the first to argue that "Big Two-Hearted River" is as much a marriage story as a war story. See, for example, Flora, pp. 179–80.

16　"Ernest Hemingway as Short Story Writer," in *The Short Stories of Ernest Hemingway*, ed. Benson, pp. 287–88.

17　*Ernest Hemingway: A Reconsideration*, p. 32.

18　Fitzgerald's exact words are that the book "takes on an almost autobiographical tint"— "How to Waste Material: A Note on My Generation," *Bookman* 63 (1926): 264.

19　Meyers states that "Hemingway's wound, far from being psychologically traumatic (as Philip Young has argued in an influential book), had an extraordinarily positive effect on his life," although he also proposes that after Agnes von Kurowsky jilted him, Hemingway probably "lost his perilous balance and began to suffer the delayed psychological effects of shell shock"—*Hemingway: A Biography* (New York: Harper & Row, 1985), pp. 35, 46. Lynn argues that Hemingway's anxiety about his wounding in World War I did not occur until after World War II, when he was suffering deep depression and thinking of suicide (p. 106).

20　*Hemingway*, p. 160. Meyers simply states that the sense of loss was one of Hemingway's great themes (p. 145).

21　*Hemingway: A Biography*, p. 182.

22　*Hemingway*, p. 10.

23　Nearly all of Hemingway's biographers have emphasized his tendency to lie about his life. For example, Carlos Baker notes that this inclination began early: "Since the age of four he had delighted in tall tales, usually with himself as hero. Now that he was nineteen, the content had merely become a little more worldly"—*Ernest Hemingway: A Life Story* (New York: Scribner's, 1969), p. 56. Michael Reynolds states simply that Hemingway found that writing allowed him to "create his life exactly as he wished it to be, and eventually come to believe it"—*The Young Hemingway* (Oxford: Basil Blackwell, 1986), p. 149.

24　"Punching Papa," *New York Review of Books* 1 (special issue, 1963): 13.

Ben Stolzfus, "Hemingway's 'After the Storm': A Lacanian Reading"

Beegel, Susan. "After the Storm." *Hemingway's Craft of Omission: Four Manuscript Examples* (Ann Arbor: University of Michigan Research Press, 1988), pp. 69–88.

Brenner, Gerry. *Concealments in Hemingway's Works* (Columbus: Ohio State University Press, 1983).

Davis, Robert Con. "Introduction: Lacan and Narration." *Lacan and Narration: The Psycho-*

analytic Difference in Narrative Theory. Ed. Robert Con Davis (Baltimore: Johns Hopkins University Press, 1983), pp. 849–59.

Freud, Sigmund. *The Standard Edition of the Complete Psychological Works.* Vols. I–XXIII. Trans. James Strachey (London: Hogarth, 1953).

Gallop, Jane. *Reading Lacan* (Ithaca: Cornell University Press, 1985).

Hemingway, Ernest. "After the Storm." *The Short Stories of Ernest Hemingway* (New York: Scribner's, 1953), pp. 372–78.

———. *Time* 64 (December 13, 1954): 72.

Lacan, Jacques. *Ecrits: A Selection.* Trans. Alan Sheridan (New York: Norton, 1977).

———. *Le séminaire: Livre II. Le moi dans la théorie de Freud et dans la technique de la psychanalyse.* Ed. Jacques-Alain Miller (Paris: Seuil, 1978). In the text references to this edition are listed as S-II.

Reynolds, Michael S. *Hemingway's Reading, 1910–1940: An Inventory* (Princeton, N.J.: Princeton University Press, 1981).

Oddvar Holmesland, "Structuralism and Interpretation: Ernest Hemingway's 'Cat in the Rain'"

1 David Lodge, "Analysis and Interpretation of the Realist Text: A Pluralistic Approach to Ernest Hemingway's 'Cat in the Rain,'" *Poetics Today* 1, no. 4 (Summer 1980): 5–22.

2 The terminology is discussed by Lodge, with references to relevant bibliography (p. 8).

3 Ernest Hemingway, *A Moveable Feast* (New York, 1964), p. 75.

4 Greimas's terminology is discussed by Lodge, with references to relevant bibliography (p. 6).

5 The terms are discussed by Jonathan Culler, *Structuralist Poetics: Structuralism, Linguistics, and the Study of Literature* (London, 1975), pp. 213–14.

6 Roman Jakobson, "Closing Statement: Linguistics and Poetics," in *Style in Language,* ed. Thomas A. Sebeok (Cambridge, Mass., 1960), p. 358.

7 Carlos Baker, *The Writer as Artist* (Princeton, N.J., 1972), pp. 135–36.

8 John V. Hagopian, "Symmetry in 'Cat in the Rain,'" in *The Short Stories of Ernest Hemingway: Critical Essays,* ed. Jackson J. Benson (Durham, N.C., 1975), pp. 230–32.

9 Lodge, p. 6.

10 Hagopian, p. 231.

11 Lodge, p. 16.

12 Jonathan Culler, "Defining Narrative Units," in *Style and Structure in Literature: Essays in the New Stylistics,* ed. Roger Fowler (Oxford, 1975), pp. 139–40.

13 Emily Brontë, *Wuthering Heights* (Harmondsworth, 1965), p. 163.

14 Northrop Frye, *Fables of Identity: Studies in Poetic Mythology* (London, 1963), pp. 18–20.

15 See *herm* and *Hermes* in *Encyclopacdia Britannica.*

Susan F. Beegel, "'That Always Absent Something Else': 'A Natural History of the Dead' and Its Discarded Coda"

1 "A Natural History of the Dead" is not present in the earliest extant manuscript of *Death in the Afternoon,* now at the University of Texas in Austin. For a description of the Texas manuscript, see Matthew Bruccoli and C. E. Frazer Clark, Jr., comps. *Hemingway at*

Auction: 1930–1973 (Detroit: Gale Research Press, 1973), p. 34, and Robert W. Lewis, "The Making of *Death in the Afternoon*," in *Ernest Hemingway: The Writer in Context*, ed. James Nagel (Madison: University of Wisconsin Press, 1984), pp. 31–52. I am indebted to Professor Lewis for sharing with me his firsthand knowledge of the Texas manuscript.

2   Folder 31, Ernest Hemingway Papers, John Fitzgerald Kennedy Library, Boston: I am indebted to Jo August Hill, former curator of the Hemingway Papers, for her assistance with this material.

3   The coda is present with the original typescript of "A Natural History" as an additional four pages typed on legal-sized paper and accompanied (as the rest of the story is not) by a pencil manuscript (Folder 31, Hemingway Papers, J.F.K. Library, Boston). Yet while "A Natural History of the Dead" is present in the *Death in the Afternoon* galleys (Folder 49, Hemingway Papers, J.F.K. Library, Boston), the coda is not. All of this evidence suggests that Hemingway composed the coda as an afterthought while *Death in the Afternoon* was being typed, then discarded the material before sending the typescript to Scribner's to be set in galleys. All citations from manuscripts of "A Natural History of the Dead" in this chapter have previously appeared in Susan F. Beegel, "Hemingway's Craft of Omission: Four Manuscript Examples" (Ph.D. diss., Yale University, 1987), pp. 84–132.

4   Hemingway to Perkins, February 11, 1940, *Ernest Hemingway: Selected Letters. 1917–1961*, ed. Carlos Baker (New York: Scribner's, 1981), p. 501.

5   See *MLA Bibliography* (1933 to 1985); Audre Hanneman, *Ernest Hemingway: A Comprehensive Bibliography* (Princeton: Princeton University Press, 1967) and *Supplement* (1975), and Jackson Benson, "A Comprehensive Checklist of Ernest Hemingway Short Fiction Criticism," in *The Short Stories of Ernest Hemingway: Critical Essays* (Durham, N.C.: Duke University Press, 1975), pp. 311–75.

6   John Portz, "Allusion and Structure in Hemingway's 'A Natural History of the Dead,'" *Tennessee Studies in Literature* 10 (1965): 27–44, and John A. Yunck, "The Natural History of a Dead Quarrel: Hemingway and the Humanists," *South Atlantic Quarterly* 62 (Winter 1963): 29–43.

7   Yunck, p. 33.

8   Hemingway merely omitted the intrusions of the Old Lady and added to his sentence on natural death from Spanish influenza. Writing to Arnold Gingrich about *Winner Take Nothing* on June 7, 1933, Hemingway announced that he would include "A Natural History of the Dead" in the volume "as it is a story and people might not have had $3.50 to read it in the other book [*Death in the Afternoon*]." *Selected Letters*, p. 393.

9   According to Michael S. Reynolds' *Hemingway's Reading: 1910–1940* (Princeton: Princeton University Press, 1981), Hemingway owned and/or read the following works by these natural historians: Gilbert White, *The Natural History and Antiquities of Selborne* (1789); Edward Stanley, Bishop of Norwich, *A Familiar History of the Birds* (1840); and W. H. Hudson, *Adventures among Birds* (1913), *Afoot in England* (1909), *Birds in London* (1898), *Birds in Town and Village* (1920), *The Book of a Naturalist* (1919), *Dead Man's Pack, An Old Thorn, and Poems* (1924), *Far Away and Long Ago* (1918), *Hampshire Days* (1903), *A Hind in Richmond Park* (1922), *The Land's End: A Naturalist's Impression in West Cornwall* (1908), *The Naturalist in La Plata* (1892), *Nature in Downland* (1906), *South American Sketches* (1909), and *A Traveler in Little Things* (1921). Although Reynolds does not cite Mungo Park, Hemingway's quotation in "A Natural History of the Dead" is from the English explorer's *Travels in the Interior Districts of Africa* (1799). For a complete discussion of

Hemingway's allusions to eighteenth- and nineteenth-century natural historians, see Portz, "Allusion and Structure."

10 Unless otherwise indicated, I have chosen to quote from the version of "A Natural History of the Dead" published in *Death in the Afternoon*. Variant readings in the *Death in the Afternoon* typescript and the *Winner Take Nothing* anthology will be described when relevant.

11 Marcelline Hemingway Sanford, *At the Hemingways: A Family Portrait* (London: Putnam, 1962), pp. 29–30.

12 Ibid., p. 32.

13 Ibid.

14 Ibid., pp. 38–39.

15 Ibid., pp. 32–33.

16 Sigmund Freud, "Reflections on War and Death," in *Character and Culture*, ed. Philip Rieff (New York: Collier Books, 1963), p. 124.

17 After his wounding, nineteen-year-old Ernest wrote to his parents that "Dying is a very simple thing. I've looked at death and I know." Hemingway to his Family, October 18, 1918, *Selected Letters*, p. 19. In *Across the River and into the Trees*, Colonel Cantwell recalls that "No one of his wounds had ever done to him what the first big one did. I suppose it is just the loss of immortality, he thought. Well, in a way, that is quite a lot to lose" (ARIT, 33).

18 In *Winner Take Nothing*, Hemingway revised this passage to amplify the grotesquerie of natural death: "In this you drown in mucus, choking, and how you know the patient's dead is: at the end he turns to be a little child again, though with all his manly force, and fills the sheets as full as any diaper with one vast, final, yellow cataract that flows and dribbles on after he's gone" (SS, 444–45). While recuperating from his war wounds in a Milan hospital, Hemingway tried to assist his nurse-lover, Agnes von Kurowsky, to intubate a critically ill influenza patient's lungs. The patient died before they could begin. The incident is the subject of an untitled, unpublished Hemingway short story on American Red Cross Hospital stationery. See Peter Griffin, *Along with Youth: Hemingway, the Early Years* (New York: Oxford University Press, 1985), pp. 94–96, 240.

19 The typescript of "A Natural History of the Dead" reads: "A persevering traveller like Mungo Park or me lives on and maybe yet will live to see the death of Irving Babbitt or Paul Elmer More or watch the noble exit Seward Collins makes." See Folder 31, Hemingway Papers, J.F.K. Library, Boston.

20 In the typescript of "A Natural History of the Dead," this passage contains an additional sentence: "It may be when you come to die the articles you've written in a magazine will not help you overmuch and controversy suddenly will seem of not such great importance and afterwards you'll stink the same as any mean inglorious Rousseau stinks unless they embalm you skillfully." See Folder 31, Hemingway Papers, J.F.K. Library, Boston.

21 See "Boston Police Bar *Scribner's Magazine:* Superintendent Acts on Objections to Ernest Hemingway's Serial, *Farewell to Arms*," *New York Times*, June 21, 1929, p. 2.

22 Robert Herrick, "What Is Dirt?," *Bookman* 70 (November 1929): 261.

23 Seward Collins, "Chronicle and Comment," *Bookman* 70 (February 1930): 645.

24 Ibid.

25 Paul Elmer More, b. 1864; Irving Babbitt, b. 1865; Clarence Hemingway, b. 1871; Grace Hall Hemingway, b. 1872.

26 Herrick, p. 259; Collins, p. 641.

27 Bernice Kert, *The Hemingway Women* (New York: Norton, 1983), pp. 143, 197.

28 Herrick, p. 259.

29 Paul Fussell, *The Great War and Modern Memory* (Oxford: Oxford University Press, 1975), p. 21.

30 An exploding figure also occurs in the famous passage on abstract words from *A Farewell to Arms;* "the sacrifices were like the stockyards at Chicago if nothing were done with the meat except to bury it" (FTA, 185).

31 Robert Coates, Rev. "*Death in the Afternoon,*" *New Yorker* (October 1, 1932), p. 62.

32 Baker, ed., *Selected Letters*, p. 381, fn. 1.

33 Hemingway to Perry, February 7, 1933, *Selected Letters*, p. 380.

34 Ibid., p. 381. Hemingway may be consciously or unconsciously paraphrasing Coates's review, which preceded this letter.

35 Hemingway's treatment of unrealistic war fiction is more extended in the typescript of "A Natural History of the Dead":

> I recall reading in either some contemporary war correspondence or in one of the books published at the time a description of the dead in which the allied dead were described as all having fallen with their faces pointing toward, I believe, Berlin while the German dead lay in a variety of attitudes. There was also mention of the clean white bodies of these particular allied soldiers in contrast to the general soiled appearance of the French and German dead. Such an observer, if he were not prejudiced, must have been remarkably fortunate in his opportunities for observation. I believe the passage occurred in a book called Living Bayonets but I may be mistaken. Folder 31, J.F.K. Library, Boston.

36 Hemingway, "Monologue to the Maestro: A High Seas Letter," *Esquire* (October 1935), rpt. in *By-Line: Ernest Hemingway*, ed. William White (New York: Scribner's, 1967), p. 219.

37 In *Psychiatry and Military Manpower Policy* (New York: King's Crown Press, 1953), pp. 28–29, Dr. Eli Ginzberg observes that there is "some undertone of suicide in a great many of the combat neuroses." Hemingway purportedly experienced his first suicidal impulse during World War I as he lay wounded in a dressing station under heavy shelling. Describing the experience in 1919, Hemingway said that he "was surrounded by so many dead and dying that to die seemed more natural than to go on living: for a time he even thought of shooting himself with his officer's pistol." Carlos Baker, *Ernest Hemingway: A Life Story* (New York: Scribner's, 1969), pp. 45, 571.

38 "Wherefore is light given to him that is in misery, and life unto the bitter in soul; which long for death, but it cometh not; and dig for it more than for hid treasures; which rejoice exceedingly when they can find the grave?" Job 3:20–22.

39 "Then the Lord answereth Job out of the whirlwind, and said, 'Who is this that darkeneth counsel by words without knowledge? Gird up now thy loins like a man; for I will demand of thee, and answer thou me.'" Job 38:1–3.

40 Hemingway has in mind Francisco Goya's series of lithographs—*Los Desastres de la Guerra*—depicting the horrors of Spain's Peninsular War. Indeed, the nightmarish subject matter and dramatic contrast of light and darkness in this scene from "A Natural History of the Dead" deliberately echo Goya's *Los Desastres*.

41 Herrick, p. 259.

42 Arthur Waldhorn, *A Reader's Guide to Ernest Hemingway* (New York: Farrar, Straus & Giroux, 1972), p. 134.

43 The coda's manuscript and typescript have been described previously in notes 1 and 3.

The following portions of the coda are transcribed in their entirety, copying verbatim Hemingway's idiosyncrasies of style, spelling, punctuation, and paragraphing. Where Hemingway's handwritten corrections to the manuscript are indecipherable, I have placed my best guess in brackets, and where his references are potentially obscure, I have provided footnotes.

44 "The uniformity of their sex" refers back to "Regarding the sex of the dead it is a fact that one becomes so accustomed to the sight of all the dead being men that the sight of a dead woman is quite shocking" (DIA, 135). "The seeming unwillingness of many of them to die, even though unconscious and fatally wounded" refers back to the plight of the cat in the coal bin and the dying soldier in the mountain cave. "The consequent nervous effect on the surviving members of their species" refers back to "the just related anecdote" about the Italian lieutenant's hysterical reaction to the dying soldier. Finally, "the matter of their progressive changes in appearance" refers back to "Until the dead are buried they change somewhat in appearance each day" (DIA, 137).

45 Northrop Frye, "The Mythos of Winter: Irony and Satire," in *Anatomy of Criticism: Four Essays* (Princeton, N.J.: Princeton University Press, 1973), p. 224.

46 Ecclesiastes 3:20.

47 "Late on a July afternoon in the summer of 1918": less than one week before Hemingway was wounded on July 8, 1918.

48 "Fossalta di Piave": the "low-lying heavily damaged village" situated near an L-shaped bend in the Piave River, at this time the site of a major Austrian offensive. Hemingway would be wounded at Fossalta di Piave. See Baker, *A Life Story,* p. 43.

49 "Back in the mountains" and "Schio": the mountains here are the foothills of the Dolomites, where Hemingway had been stationed at Schio, Section Four Headquarters of the American Red Cross. He doubtless still had friends at the Schio barracks, known affectionately to the corpsmen as the "Schio Country Club." Baker, *A Life Story,* pp. 41–42.

50 "The Lido": a fashionable beach resort outside Venice.

51 "The old outhouse": The outhouse, affectionately referred to as Hemlock Park, belonged to Hemingway's parents' summer cottage on Walloon Lake in Michigan. The outhouse's nickname not only refers to its situation beneath the hemlock trees, but also constitutes a jest about the propriety of Oak Park, Illinois, where the Hemingway family maintained their year-round home. Hemingway's sister Madelaine includes two photographs of the outhouse and the following information in her biography of Ernest: "This, our outhouse, had great distinction. It was decorated with deer antlers and had a fine assortment of magazines and catalogues. "Hemlock Park" was a fine retreat when undesirable jobs were to be done." See Madelaine Hemingway Miller, *Ernie* (New York: Crown, 1975), pp. 48–49.

52 "St. Nicholas Magazine": A Victorian children's publication subscribed to by Hemingway's parents. See Sanford, p. 135.

53 "I was an awful dope when I went to the last war. I can just remember thinking that we were the home team and the Austrians were the visiting team." Hemingway to Maxwell Perkins, May 30, 1942, on Baker, *A Life Story,* p. 38.

54 "The road between Grau and Valencia": Grau de Roi, France, where Hemingway honeymooned with Pauline Pfeiffer in 1927, and Valencia, Spain, where they toured later that summer. Perhaps Hemingway witnessed this incident in 1927. See Baker, *A Life Story,* pp. 185–86.

55 Charles Yale Harrison, author of *Generals Die in Bed,* seems to have taken such criticism to heart. He composed a piece called "Story for Mr. Hemingway," *Modern Monthly* 8

(February 1935), pp. 731–37 and prefaced with a headnote quoting "A Natural History of the Dead" on *Generals Die in Bed*.

56 For a medical discussion of the iodine's probable effect on the lieutenant's eyesight, see Susan F. Beegel, "Note in Answer to Query on 'A Natural History,'" *Hemingway Newsletter* 6 (July 1983), p. 3.

57 Philip Young, *Ernest Hemingway: A Reconsideration* (University Park: Pennsylvania State University Press, 1966).

58 Sigmund Freud, *Beyond the Pleasure Principle*, trans. James Strachey (New York: Norton, 1966), p. 11.

59 Ibid., p. 24.

60 Ibid., p. 11.

61 Ibid.

**Hubert Zapf, "Reflection vs. Daydream:
Two Types of the Implied Reader in Hemingway's Fiction"**

1 Earl Rovit, *Ernest Hemingway* (Boston, 1963), p. 31.

2 See especially Julian Smith, "Hemingway and the Thing Left Out," *Journal of Modern Literature* 1 (1970): 169–82. The connection between literary styles and certain kinds of reader-responses was investigated by Walter J. Ong in "The Writer's Audience Is Always a Fiction," *PMLA* 90 (1975): 9–21, where he comes close to the conception of an "implied reader" in that he discusses several writers, among them Hemingway, in the way they "fictionalize" the reader in their texts, that is, induce the real, historical reader to let himself become part of the fictional world, actively participating in its imaginative construction.

3 *Death in the Afternoon* (New York: Scribner's, 1932), p. 192.

4 See, for example, Raymond S. Nelson, *Hemingway: Expressionist Artist* (Ames, Iowa, 1979).

5 See Wolfgang Iser, *The Implied Reader: Patterns of Communication in Prose Fiction from Bunyan to Beckett* (Baltimore: Johns Hopkins University Press, 1978), and *The Act of Reading: A Theory of Aesthetic Response* (Baltimore: Johns Hopkins University Press, 1979). A useful introduction to Iser's theory is his article "The Reading Process: A Phenomenological Approach," *New Literary History* 3 (1971): 279–99.

6 This notion of "schematized views," as well as of the "indeterminacy" of literature, derives from Roman Ingarden's phenomenological theory of literature: *The Cognition of the Literary Work of Art* (Evanston, Ill.: Northwestern University Press, 1974).

7 Iser, "The Reading Process," 282ff.

8 Ibid., 292.

9 See, for example, Edmund Husserl, *Cartesianische Meditationen: Husserliana*, vol. 1 (The Hague, 1950), p. 73. Here the principle of reflection is formulated as the basic principle of human consciousness and knowledge. Engl. trans, *Cartesian Meditations* (Boston: Kluwer, 1977).

10 For this term see Hans-Georg Gadamer, *Truth and Method: Basics of a Philosophical Hermeneutics* (New York, 1975).

11 Walter Schulz. "Anmerkungen zur Hermeneutik Gadamers" ["Notes on Gadamer's Hermeneutics"] in *Hermeneutik und Dialektik I*, ed. R. Bubner, K. Kramer, R. Wiehl (Tübingen, 1970), pp. 305–16.

12 Sigmund Freud. "Der Dichter und das Phantasieren" ["The Poet and Fantasy"] *Sigmund Freud: Studienausgabe*, vol. 10, *Bildende Kunst und Literatur* [*Visual Art and Literature*] (Frankfurt, 1969), pp. 171–79.

13 Thus, for example, in Norman Holland's *5 Readers Reading* (New Haven, Conn., 1975), p. 127.

14 Thus when N. Holland has the reader project any fantasy into the text "that yields the pleasure he characteristically seeks": *Poems in Persons: An Introduction to the Psychoanalysis of Literature* (New York, 1973), p. 77, or in David Bleich's classroom experiments with his "subjective criticism," *Readings and Feelings: An Introduction to Subjective Criticism* (Urbana, Ill., 1975).

15 Ernest Hemingway, *The Sun Also Rises* (New York: Scribner's, 1970), p. 4. All subsequent references to the text are to this edition and are given in parentheses after the quotation.

16 Beoncheong Yu, "The Still Center of Hemingway's World" in *Ernest Hemingway: Five Decades of Criticism*, ed. Linda W. Wagner (East Lansing, Mich., 1974), pp. 109–31.

17 Paul Goodman, "The Sweet Style of Ernest Hemingway," in *Ernest Hemingway: Five Decades of Criticism*, pp. 153–60.

18 "Big Two-Hearted River," *The First Forty-nine Stories* (London: Jonathan Cape, 1944), pp. 165–85.

19 Ibid., p. 183.

20 This shows that while Freud defines literature in undialectic opposition to reality, Hemingway dramatizes the collision between daydream and reality *within* the literary work itself.

21 "The Short Happy Life of Francis Macomber," *The First Forty-nine Stories*, pp. 11–40.

22 These problematical implications, especially with regard to Mrs. Macomber's role in the story and to the male-chauvinist distortions created by Wilson's simplistic "code," were first pointed out by Warren Beck in his article "The Shorter Happy Life of Mrs. Macomber," *Modern Fiction Studies* 1–2 (1955): 28–37, where he argues for a much more positive view of Margot Macomber than most critics before him. The article set off a controversy with Mark Spilka which continued over more than twenty years.

23 *The Old Man and the Sea* (New York: Scribner's, 1952), p. 9.

24 On pp. 16, 18, 20, 23, 30 of *The Old Man and the Sea*, this hope of a great fish is explicitly expressed.

25 See the rebirth motif of Jake's bathing in the sea at the end of the novel and Nick's gradual, if slow, approximation of the deeper levels of reality in "Big Two-Hearted River."

Nina Baym, "'Actually, I Felt Sorry for the Lion'"

1 Among essays making this point over the years have been: Mona G. Rosenman, "Five Hemingway Women," *Claflin College Review* 2, no. 1 (1977): 9–13; Linda Wagner, "Proud and Friendly and Gently," *College Literature* 7 (1980): 239–47; Charles J. Nolan, "Hemingway's Women's Movement," *Hemingway Review* 3, no. 2 (1984): 14–22.

2 Mary Anne Ferguson, ed., *Images of Women in Literature* (Boston: Houghton Mifflin, 1973, 1977, 1981, 1985). "The Short Happy Life of Francis Macomber" is included in a section called "The Dominating Wife: The Bitch."

3 The argument was first made by Warren Beck in "The Shorter Happy Life of Mrs.

Macomber," *Modern Fiction Studies* 1 (1955): 28–37, but this essay was roundly attacked; reviewing the scholarship in 1968, William White concluded that the majority concurred that Margot Macomber "meant to kill her husband when she shot at the buffalo" (*American Literary Scholarship/1968* [Durham, N.C.: Duke University Press, 1970], p. 113). Nevertheless, the issue did not disappear; the argument was revived by John M. Howell and Charles A. Lawler, "From Abercrombie & Fitch to *The First Forty-nine Stories:* The Text of Hemingway's 'Francis Macomber'" *Proof* 2 (1972): 213–81; K. G. Johnston "In Defense of the Unhappy Margot Macomber," *Hemingway Review* 2, no. 11 (1983): 44–47; and Kenneth Lynn, *Hemingway* (New York: Simon & Schuster, 1987).

4 For the distinction between voice and focus, see Gerard Genette, *Narrative Discourse: An Essay in Method* (Ithaca, N.Y.: Cornell University Press, 1980); for the idea of fiction as a field of multiple and often competing voices, see M. M. Bakhtin, *The Dialogic Imagination* (Austin: University of Texas Press, 1981). For the identification of the five points of view (which, following Genette, I would call foci) in "The Short Happy Life of Francis Macomber," see James Nagel, "The Narrative Method of 'The Short Happy Life of Francis Macomber,'" *English Studies* 41 (1973): 18–27.

5 The importance of embedded stories in a larger narrative as a redaction and intensification of the action is brought home to us by Tvetzan Todorov in *The Poetics of Prose* (Ithaca, N.Y.: Cornell University Press, 1977).

6 Page citations are to *The Short Stories of Ernest Hemingway: The First Forty-nine Stories and the Play "The Fifth Column"* (New York: Random House, 1938).

7 Wilson and Hemingway are both quoted in Lynn: Wilson, p. 433; Hemingway, p. 432. For an excellent chronicle of Hemingway's orchestration of his public image in the latter half of his career, see John Raeburn, *Fame Became of Him: Hemingway as Public Writer* (Bloomington: Indiana University Press, 1984).

8 Howell and Lawler, p. 224.

9 Carlos Baker, *Hemingway: The Writer as Artist*, 3rd ed. (Princeton, N.J.: Princeton University Press, 1963), p. 187.

10 Baker, 189–90.

11 Surprisingly, however, Lynn writes that "Wilson instantly leaps to the conclusion that Margot has deliberately shot Macomber, and he thinks he understands why" (435–36). But the last pages of the story allow no entry into Wilson's thoughts—they only tell us what he does and says. At an earlier point in the narration, when Wilson perceives Macomber's new found bravery, he does *not*, in fact, imagine that Macomber will now leave his wife: what he thinks rather is that Macomber's change "probably meant the end of cuckoldry too. Well, that would be a damned good thing. Damned good thing" (132). Nor, for that matter, do his words to Margot, uttered in a "toneless" voice—"That was a pretty thing to do. . . . He *would* have left you too" (135)—imply anything about Wilson's sincerity or lack of it. I assume that we are meant to believe that Wilson knows perfectly well that the killing was accidental.

12 According to Lynn, the supposed real-life model for Wilson, Philip Percival, said that the rifle was so powerful that its use on safaris was unsportsmanlike and that therefore he never carried one (434).

13 Howell and Lawler, p. 227.

14 The paragraphs that follow are based on a transcript of a class hour on "The Short Happy Life of Francis Macomber" conducted by an apprentice teacher in an introductory fiction course.

**William Braasch Watson, "'Old Man at the Bridge':
The Making of a Short Story"**

I wish to thank the many friends and scholars who read this article at various stages along the way, but especially Carl Oglesby for a sensitive reading of an early draft and Tom Keily and Jim Hinkle for their encouragement.

1   EH to Maxwell Perkins, February 1, 1938, Princeton University Library (PUL): Scribner's Archive I (SA), Hemingway Correspondence, 3/18/311.

2   EH to Perkins, March 19, 1938, written from *Ile de France*. "I hope to have several more [stories] by the time the book must go to press. Will that be July or August? Please let me know." PUL: SA, 3/18/318.

3   Hemingway's decision to return to Spain appears to have been made almost as soon as the news from Spain reached him, for on March 9, the day the Rebel offensive began, he wired Perkins that it was "maybe necessary return Spain." (EH telegram to Perkins, March 9, 1938, PUL:SA, 3/18/315). On his feeling "like a blood shit" and on his efforts to wind up his affairs, see EH to Perkins, March 15, 1938, at PUL:SA, 3/18/316; and EH telegram to Rollin Dart, March 17, 1938, PUL:SA, 3/18/317. The sailing dates are from the *New York Times*, March 18 & 25, 1938. On Martha Gellhorn's return to Europe, see an unsigned cable to EH, March 21, 1938, announcing an arrival in Cherbourg on March 28. I believe the cable is from Gellhorn. If so, she must have sailed on the *Queen Mary*, which left New York on March 23 and arrived in Cherbourg on the 28th. Sailing dates from *The Times*, March 23 & 29, 1938. (Unsigned cable among unidentified incoming cables in the Hemingway Collection at the John F. Kennedy Library [JFK].) For his trip to the Spanish border, see Jeffrey Shulman's article in the *Hemingway Review*.

4   Whether Martha Gellhorn went into Spain with the others at this time is uncertain. The above mentioned cable indicates that a car was being shipped to France on April 1, but whether this is the car Hemingway took into Spain is not known. We know from other sources that Gellhorn was in Barcelona with Hemingway for much of this time, but Sheean, for understandable reasons of discretion, chose not to mention her presence in his book on these events. See Vincent Sheean, *Not Peace but a Sword* (New York: Doubleday, Doran, 1939): 235–42.

5   Sheean, *Not Peace*, 236–41, says they arrived in Barcelona on April 1, but Hemingway's authorization from the Spanish military to visit the Aragon front is dated March 31, 1938. (EH Spanish Civil War miscellaneous papers at JFK.) Sheean notes that Hemingway had a room waiting for him at the Hotel Majestic in Barcelona when they arrived that evening, something that a celebrity like Hemingway could have others arrange for him without difficulty. His departure for the front the next day with Herbert Matthews is inferred from a pencil notation of "Saturday April Second" on the second draft of his cable text for the dispatch of April 3 (ms 401, JFK). It had been a two day trip, and it is not likely he began the article before he and Matthews returned to Barcelona.

6   EH, Dispatch 19, "Flight of Refugees," *Hemingway Review* (Spring, 1988: 68–70).

7   For all the dispatches of the spring of 1938, see Dispatches 19–30, *Hemingway Review* (Spring 1988): 68–92.

8   Ms 716 is an autograph note (AN), JFK. These notes are not identified as the field notes for the short story, but the description of the old man with steel spectacles and other similarities with the story leave little doubt as to what they are. Many of the details in

these notes are confirmed by Herbert Matthews's dispatch, datelined Barcelona, April 17 (*New York Times*, April 18, 1938: 1 & 5).

9   See the field notes for Dispatch 19 in "A Variorum Edition of Dispatch 19," *Hemingway Review* (Spring 1988): 93.

10 Field notes for Dispatch 21 (ms 455, JFK).

11 Field notes for Dispatch 29 (ms 556, JFK).

12 The cable is time dated by the Catalan censor in Barcelona: "autoriza la transmisió d'aquesta informació. Barcelona, 17 de abril del 1938, a 23:10" (ms 627, JFK). According to Martha Gellhorn and confirmed by Herbert Matthews, they would leave Barcelona at 4:00 or so in the morning, drive six hours to the front, spend what time they needed, and return the same day after another six or so hours of driving. How long they spent at Amposta is not known, but the field notes suggest it was not much more than a couple of hours. Allowing for twelve hours of driving and two or three hours of looking around, Hemingway could have been back in Barcelona by six or seven o'clock that evening. The cable was sent out just after eleven that night, that is, four or five hours after they returned. Hemingway must have written the entire story in this brief interval.

13 These similarities between the story and the news dispatches led some critics to assume mistakenly that Hemingway originally sent out "Old Man at the Bridge" as a news dispatch, only later deciding that it was a short story. See William White, "Hemingway Needs No Introduction," in Ernest Hemingway, *By-line: Ernest Hemingway*, ed. William White (New York: Scribner's, 1967), p. xii. Carlos Baker, *Ernest Hemingway: A Life Story* (New York: Scribner's, 1969), pp. 327–28 & 625, perhaps following White's judgment. Carlos Pujol, ed., *Obras selectas de Ernest Hemingway* (Barcelona: Planeta, 1969), p. 103.

14 Hemingway's previous article for *Ken* was "The Cardinal Picks a Winner," published in *Ken* on May 5, 1938. Since *Ken* had a lead time of about one month, the piece was probably written in Paris just before Hemingway left for Spain on March 30. His contract with *Ken* called for an article every two weeks, for which he was sent a biweekly check of $200.

15 EH to Arnold Gingrich, October 22, 1938, in *Selected Letters of Ernest Hemingway*, ed. Carlos Baker (New York: Scribner's 1982), p. 472.

16 The story was first published in *Ken*, 1, 4 (May 19, 1938): 36, and later that year in *The Fifth Column and the First Forty-nine Stories* (New York: Scribner's, 1938), pp. 176–78. It is currently available in *The Short Stories of Ernest Hemingway* (New York: Scribner's, n.d.), pp. 78–80.

17 Cable of Arnold Gingrich to EH in Barcelona, April 18, 1938 (cable, JFK).

18 EH to Perkins, July 12, 1938, in *Selected Letters*, p. 469.

19 Edmund Wilson, "Hemingway and the Wars," *Nation* 147 (December 10, 1938): 628 & 630.

20 EH to Edmund Wilson, [December 1938] (JFK). The letter is unfinished and undated, but it was probably written soon after the Wilson review, which appeared in the *Nation* of December 10, 1938. Hemingway complained to Perkins about Wilson's review in a letter of December 24, repeating in almost identical words the attack he had made in his letter to Wilson as one of those who took no part in the defense of the Spanish Republic but stayed home and discredited those who did. (EH to Perkins, December 24, 1938, PUL:SA. A copy of this letter to Perkins was kindly sent to me by the late Professor Carlos Baker.)

21 For the complete text of the field notes see "A Variorum Edition of Dispatch 19," *Hemingway Review* (Spring 1988): 93.

22   EH to Wilson, [December 1938]. See above, note 21.
23   Although Hemingway's reports on the flight of Christian refugees from the advancing Turks in Thrace are similar to his account of the Spanish refugees, in the Spanish refugee piece he has a better sense of control over his material, has learned how to use details to represent larger themes, and has learned to restrain his own presence in the account even though he was more personally involved in the drama of the Spanish refugees than he was in the sufferings of the refugees in Thrace. See Ernest Hemingway, *Dateline: Toronto*, ed. William White (New York: Scribner's, 1985), pp. 232 & 249–52.
24   See the field notes for the story on p. 93.
25   Michael S. Reynolds, "The Hemingway Sources for in our time," *Critical Essays on Ernest Hemingway's In Our Time*, ed. Michael S. Reynolds (Boston: Hall, 1983), pp. 31–37. Reynolds shows how Hemingway changed the details of news accounts to achieve greater fictional clarity and dramatic effect.
26   San Carlos de la Rápita is a small town in the Ebro Delta about twelve kilometers, as Hemingway said it was, south of Amposta. It was about to be overtaken by the Rebels the day the old man fled it.
27   Anne Tyler, "Introduction," *The Best American Short Stories, 1983* (Boston: Houghton Mifflin, 1983), pp. xiv–xv, notes the importance of a point of stillness in a good short story.

Paul Smith, "Hemingway's Apprentice Fiction: 1919–1921"

1   *Death in the Afternoon* (New York: Scribner's, 1932), p. 53.
2   I gratefully acknowledge the permission granted to cite items 445, 550, 604, 670, 800, 801, 820, and 843, unpublished manuscripts in the Hemingway Collection of the John F. Kennedy Library, copyright 1986, Mary Hemingway, John Hemingway, Patrick Hemingway, and Gregory Hemingway. Those manuscripts will be identified by their item numbers in the *Catalog of the Ernest Hemingway Collection at the John F. Kennedy Library* (Boston: Hall, 1982).
3   Peter Griffin's *Along with Youth: Hemingway, the Early Years* (Oxford: Oxford University Press, 1985) and Michael Reynolds' *The Young Hemingway* (Oxford: Basil Blackwell, 1986) differ on what counts as a "Chicago" manuscript. Each cites eight of the thirteen considered here; Griffin adds another from the late 1920s (item 260), and Reynolds adds two that might be dated earlier (items 581, 634). Reynold's selection, dating, and interpretation are trustworthy. Griffin's dating is sometimes unsupported by manuscript evidence (see notes 13, 21). Jeffrey Meyers' *Hemingway: A Biography* (New York: Harper & Row, 1985) does not consider these manuscripts.
4   Griffin, *Along with Youth*, pp. 104, 112.
5   Griffin, *Along with Youth*, pp. 125, 126.
6   Carlos Baker, *Ernest Hemingway: A Life Story* (New York: Scribner's, 1969), p. 22.
7   Reynolds, *The Young Hemingway*, p. 62.
8   *A Farewell to Arms* (New York: Scribner's, 1929), p. 18.
9   Reynolds, *The Young Hemingway*, p. 58.
10   Baker, *Ernest Hemingway: A Life Story*, pp. 53, 55–56. Hemingway was immediately attracted to Edward Eric Dorman-Smith, a veteran of the war in France, when they met in early November 1918. He tried to match the true experiences of this veteran with

some of his own inventions. James Gamble, Hemingway's superior officer, entertained him during Christmas week at Taormina and later offered to support him for a year in Europe. Agnes von Kurowsky, the nurse Hemingway was in love with, scotched the offer by sending him home with the apparent promise to marry him. Jeffrey Meyers suggests she suspected that Gamble's attraction was homosexual (*Hemingway*, p. 40).

11 Griffin, *Along with Youth*, p. 203.

12 "The Current" has its antecedents in Hemingway's prewar fiction. Two sketches, "Bob Fitzpatrick . . ." (item 286A) and "John Wesley Marvin . . ." (item 532), share its style, Chicago setting, and story of a flawed hero uplifted (morally and from the mat) by some older adviser with the vision and experience of a Hanna Club speaker.

13 The typescript, with the title Griffin gave it crossed out, has several of the sort of errors of omission and repetition one makes in a quick copy of another text. Its style is like nothing else Hemingway wrote, nor is it a parody. I suspect it is a rough copy of another person's letter with Hemingway's frame to ridicule its author and his windy idealism.

14 *A Farewell to Arms*, pp. 18–19, 26–27, 30–31.

15 The fictional citation, incidentally, repeats the story Hemingway told Dorman-Smith of leading a platoon into battle. Its language, however, is close to that of Hemingway's own citation, reprinted in Robert W. Lewis, "Hemingway in Italy: Making it Up," *Journal of Modern Literature* 9 (1981–82): 22–24.

16 (New York: Scribner's, 1950), pp. 18–19.

17 *A Farewell to Arms*, p. 20.

18 There is an accidental mark of irony on the typescript of this story Hemingway circulated for comments. He added an autobiographical note describing himself as the "Late 1st Lieut. ARC with [the] Italian Army. Wounded in Action July 8, 1918. Fossalta de Piave." One reader who found "laughs all through [the story] and a tear at the end," wondered rightly whether the author was dead or alive. Hemingway, of course, meant *lately*, but one might read this slip as his most serious, albeit unintentional, jest. The undated letter in the Kennedy Library's Hemingway Collection is from "R McB" to Y. K. Smith, and the handwriting is very close to that in which corrections are made on item 445.

19 Hemingway's titles for other stories of this period, "The Woppian Way" and "The Ash Heels Tendon," for example, depend on ethnic or class slurs for their "humor." Here the title, at least in part, turns against both the characters and the narrator in the story.

20 Another sketch, "Jock leaned out . . ." (item 531), recounts the story of a Red Cross officer, Brackell, who goes from post to post each day and tells the Italian commanders it is his birthday. He reaps the benefits of wine, capes, and pistols as presents, until he is finally caught out. The sketch ends with a glimpse of him, a short, swarthy fellow, "with a wicked eye."

21 *Ernest Hemingway: 88 Poems*, ed. Nicholas Gerogiannis (New York: Harcourt Brace Jovanovich, 1979), p. 37. The poem marked the occasion of Hadley's gift of a Corona typewriter for Hemingway's twenty-second birthday on July 21, 1921. The similar images and the corrections on the typescript (item 445) in a hand close to that of the letter cited above (note 18) to Y. K. Smith argue for a 1921 date for this story while Hemingway was still on speaking terms with Y. K., probably sometime in the summer. Griffin, perhaps because of the fight at a bridge, dates this story sometime in the 1930s, anticipating *For Whom the Bell Tolls* (*Along with Youth*, p. 251).

22 Hemingway originally placed Washington's wound in the chest; someone else

(R McB?) lowered it to the groin, providing us with an unlikely avatar for Jake Barnes.

23 Michael Reynolds' "Introduction: Looking Backward," *Critical Essays on Ernest Hemingway's "In Our Time"* (Boston: Hall, 1983), documents with the correspondence Hemingway's deliberate imitation of Howe's sketches in the fall of 1919. Compare Peter Griffin's suggestion that the style of "Cross Roads" originated in the psychic wound Hemingway suffered when Agnes von Kurowsky jilted him six months earlier: "His sentences now were short and simple, the irony bitter and harsh, each word like his first steps without crutches or his cane." *Along with Youth,* p. 124.

24 Griffin, *Along with Youth,* p. 125.

25 The preceding four paragraphs summarize the argument in my "Three Versions of 'Up in Michigan': 1921–1930," *Resources for American Literary Study* (forthcoming).

26 *The Short Stories of Ernest Hemingway* (New York: Scribner's, 1954), p. 289.

Kenneth Lynn, "The Troubled Fisherman"

1 EH to Howell Jenkins, c. September 15, 1919, in *Ernest Hemingway: Selected Letters, 1917– 1961,* ed. Carlos Baker (New York: Scribner's, 1981), p. 29.

2 EH to Gertrude Stein and Alice B. Toklas, August 15, 1924, *Selected Letters,* p. 122.

3 Ernest Hemingway, *The Complete Short Stories of Ernest Hemingway: The Finca Vigía Edition* (New York: Scribner's,) p. 163.

4 *Short Stories,* p. 164.

5 *Short Stories,* pp. 163, 164.

6 *Short Stories,* p. 164.

7 *Short Stories,* p. 167.

8 *Short Stories,* p. 169.

9 *Short Stories,* p. 177.

10 *Short Stories,* p. 180.

11 *Short Stories,* p. 180.

12 *The Portable Edmund Wilson,* ed. Lewis M. Dabney (New York: Viking Press, 1983), p. 399.

13 EH to Harvey Breit, July 23, 1956, *Selected Letters,* p. 867.

14 Malcolm Cowley, ed., *The Viking Portable Hemingway* (New York: Viking Press, 1944), p. ix.

15 *Portable Hemingway,* p. x.

16 Philip Young, *Ernest Hemingway: A Reconsideration* (University Park: Pennsylvania State University Press, 1966), p. 5.

17 *A Reconsideration,* p. 47.

18 Mark Schorer, "Ernest Hemingway," in *Major Writers of America,* ed. Perry Miller (New York: Harcourt Brace & World, 1962), p. 675.

19 Ernest Hemingway, *A Moveable Feast* (New York: Scribner's, 1964), p. 76.

20 Malcolm Cowley, "Hemingway's Wound," *Georgia Review* 38 (Summer 1984): 229–30.

21 EH to Charles Poore, January 23, 1953, *Selected Letters,* p. 798.

22 Norman Mailer, "The Big Bite," *Esquire* 58 (November 1962), p. 134.

23 Norman Mailer, "Punching Papa," *New York Review of Books* 1 (August 1963): 13.

Gerry Brenner, "From 'Sepi Jingan' to 'The Mother of a Queen': Hemingway's Three, Epistemologic Formulas for Short Fiction"

1 Kenneth S. Lynn, *Hemingway* (New York: Simon and Schuster, 1987), p. 44.

2 Michael S. Reynolds, *The Young Hemingway* (New York: Basil Blackwell, 1987), pp. 82–86.

3 Reprinted in *Ernest Hemingway's Apprenticeship*, ed. Matthew J. Bruccoli (Washington, D.C.: NCR Microcard Editions, 1971), pp. 96–97; originally published in *Tabula* 22 (February 1916): 9–10.

4 The textual perplexities in the story partly explain the steady flow of criticism the story generates, some of it historical—to "solve" the Stanley vs. Steve Ketchel problem—more of it interpretive, to "solve" the matter of which whore to believe. See, most recently, William J. Collins, "Taking on the Champion: Alice as Liar in 'The Light of the World,'" *Studies in American Fiction* 14, no. 2 (1986): 225–32; and Howard L. Hannum, "Nick Adams and the Search for Light," *Studies in Short Fiction* 23, no. 1 (1986): 9–18.

5 I refer here, of course, to Hemingway's admission that he "had omitted the real end of [the story] which was that the old man hanged himself," *A Moveable Feast* (New York: Scribner's, 1962), p. 75. For a good discussion of how the doctor-daughter ambiguity informs the story's issues, see Kenneth G. Johnston, "Hemingway's 'Out of Season' and the Psychology of Errors," *Literature and Psychology* 21 (1971): 41–46, reprinted as "'Out of Season': The Tip of the Iceberg" in his *The Tip of the Iceberg: Hemingway and the Short Story* (Greenwood, Fla.: Penkevill, 1987), pp. 29–38.

6 For an insightful reading of this exercise in textual perplexity, see Michael Reynolds, "'Homage to Switzerland': Einstein's Train Stops at Hemingway's Station," in *Hemingway's Neglected Short Fiction: Current Perspectives* (Ann Arbor: University of Michigan Research Press, 1989) pp. 255–62.

7 For a brief discussion of this perplexity, see my *Concealments in Hemingway's Works* (Columbus: Ohio State University Press, 1983), p. 239.

8 A recent reading of the story is Kenneth G. Johnston's "'A Way You'll Never Be': A Mission of Morale," *Studies in Short Fiction* 23 (1986): 429–35; reprinted in his *The Tip of the Iceberg*, pp. 171–78.

9 The commentators who have advanced this view are legion, making it a critical commonplace. But it continues to get advanced as though it were a fresh insight. See, for example, Stephen R. Portch's "Silent Ernest," in his *Literature's Silent Language: Nonverbal Communication* (New York: Peter Lang, 1985), pp. 89–116; Roger Whitlow, *Cassandra's Daughters: The Women in Hemingway* (Westport, Conn.: Greenwood Press, 1984), pp. 93–96; and Kenneth G. Johnston, *The Tip of the Iceberg*, pp. 125–31.

10 Robert E. Fleming reads "Sea Change" as one of Hemingway's stories about the transformative power of the artist in "Perversion and the Writer in 'The Sea Change,'" *Studies in American Fiction* 14 (1986): 215–20.

11 See my "A Semiotic Inquiry into Hemingway's 'A Simple Enquiry,'" in Susan F. Beegel, ed., *Hemingway's Neglected Short Fiction*, pp. 195–207.

12 Lynn contentiously argues that psychological readings of Nick "trying to block out fear-ridden recollections of being wounded" are unprovable, that "Nick's state of mind [is] not to be found in the story," that all readings of the story that emphasize a "physically crippled" Nick derive from external information—other stories, Hemingway's reconstructions, and gullible critics, 104–7. But Lynn pays no attention to the obsessively

detailed account of Nick's trek and his excessively methodical routines, both of which speak to some measure of neurotic compulsiveness in Nick. And he insists that some mention of the war must be in the text to warrant the insights that Malcolm Cowley first brought to it, ignoring the khaki shirtpocket as sufficient synecdoche.

13   Peter J. Rabinowitz discusses this aspect of theories of reading in *Before Reading: Narrative Conventions and the Politics of Interpretation* (Ithaca, N.Y.: Cornell University Press, 1987).

14   Susan Beegel discusses the removal of the story's "thinking theme" in her "'Mutilated by Scott Fitzgerald?': The Revision of Hemingway's 'Fifty Grand,'" in her *Hemingway's Craft of Omission: Four Manuscript Examples* (Ann Arbor: University of Michigan Press, 1988), pp. 15–18.

15   Susan F. Beegel discusses the background and composition history of this story in "'Just Skillful Reporting?': Fact and Fiction in 'After the Storm,'" in her *Hemingway's Craft of Omission*, pp. 69–88.

16   Brenner, *Concealments*, pp. 8–9.

17   In his essay, "The Art of the Short Story," *Paris Review* 79 (1981): 93–94, Hemingway is unequivocal that "the woman, who [sic] I knew very well in real life but then invented out of, to make the woman for this story, is a bitch for the full course and doesn't change. . . . The woman called Margot Macomber is no good to anybody now except for trouble."

18   See William White, "'Macomber' Bibliography," *Hemingway Notes* 5 (1980): 35–38, and Earl Rovit and Gerry Brenner, *Ernest Hemingway*, rev. ed. (Boston: Twayne, 1986), p. 185.

19   *The Complete Short Stories of Ernest Hemingway* (New York: Scribner's, 1987), p. 317; subsequent quotations from the story are from this edition.

20   Charles Stetler and Gerald Locklin, "Beneath the Tip of the Iceberg in Hemingway's 'The Mother of a Queen,'" *Hemingway Review* 2 (1982): 68–69.

21   For Kenneth Lynn the mother of the story is Grace Hemingway, and in it "Hemingway updated his quarrel with Grace by dealing symbolically with their current financial relationship; unfortunately, its account of a young homosexual who stops paying the rent on his mother's grave and allows her remains to be dumped on a public bone-heap was nothing but a revolting expression of a famous man's resentment at having to send a woman he hated a monthly allowance," p. 408.

22   See, for example, his letter to Harvey Breit, July 23, 1956, which ridicules Charles A. Fenton, Carlos Baker, Philip Young, and Malcolm Cowley, in *Ernest Hemingway: Selected Letters, 1917–1961*, ed. Carlos Baker (New York: Scribner's, 1981), pp. 866–67.

23   Frederick L. Gwynn and Joseph L. Blotner, eds., *Faulkner in the University* (New York: Vintage Books, 1959), p. 149.

24   Lynn, *Hemingway*, p. 408.

Steven K. Hoffman, "*Nada* and the Clean, Well-Lighted Place: The Unity of Hemingway's Short Fiction"

1   Carlos Baker, *Hemingway: The Writer as Artist*, fourth ed. (Princeton, N.J.: Princeton University Press, 1972), p. 128.

2   Baker, p. 124.

3   Of course, "A Clean, Well-Lighted Place" is not the only story in *Winner Take Nothing*

(New York: Scribner's, 1933) that conveys the sense of desolation. "After the Storm," "The Light of the World," "A Natural History of the Dead," and "A Way You'll Never Be" are apt companion pieces, and Hemingway's epigraph firmly sets the tone for the entire collection:

> Unlike all other forms of lutte or combat the conditions are that the winner shall take nothing; neither his ease, nor his pleasure, nor any notions of glory; nor, if he win far enough, shall there be any reward within himself.

In addition to the commentary of the *nada* theme, at least a dozen articles have been written on the difficulty of attributing certain portions of dialogue in "A Clean Well-Lighted Place." In perhaps the most provocative of them, Joseph Gabriel argues that the speeches of the old and young waiter were intentionally confused so that the reader might not only witness but actually experience the uncertainty of nothingness in the very act of reading the tale. See "The Logic of Confusion in Hemingway's 'A Clean, Well-Lighted Place,'" *College English* 22 (May 1961): 539–47. For an overview of the dialogue controversy, see Charles May, "Is Hemingway's 'Well-Lighted Place' Really Clean Now?" *Studies in Short Fiction* 8 (1971): 326–30.

4   Annette Benert also stresses the response to *nada* in this particular tale, but only the old waiter's, in "Survival Through Irony: Hemingway's 'A Clean, Well-Lighted Place,'" *Studies in Short Fiction* 11 (1974): 181–89.

5   *The Short Stories of Ernest Hemingway* (New York: Scribner's, 1966), p. 383. All subsequent references to Hemingway's stories and all page references are to this volume. Dates provided for individual stories refer to their initial publication.

6   *Time of Need: Forms of Imagination in the Twentieth Century* (New York: Harper, 1972), pp. 83–92. for a useful, if overly systematic, study of Hemingway and existential thought, see John Killinger's *Hemingway and the Dead Gods: A Study in Existentialism* (Lexington: University of Kentucky Press, 1960). See also Richard Lehan's section of Hemingway, Sartre, and Camus in *A Dangerous Crossing: French Literary Existentialism and the Modern American Novel* (Carbondale: Southern Illinois University Press, 1973), pp. 46–56.

7   For more detailed theological and linguistic analyses of the old waiter's prayer, see John B. Hamilton, "Hemingway and the Christian Paradox," *Renascence* 24 (1972): 152–54; David Lodge, "Hemingway's Clean, Well-Lighted, Puzzling Place," *Essays in Criticism* 21 (1971): 33–34; and Earl Rovit, *Ernest Hemingway* (New York: Twayne, 1963), pp. 111–14.

8   Evidently leaning heavily on the old waiter's statement "and man was a nothing too," Joseph Gabriel sees *nada* from a Sartrian perspective. In *Being and Nothingness* Sartre posits that the human self ("pour soi") is by its very nature a "nothing" with only the possibility of becoming "something." Although I claim no direct influence, in most of his stories Hemingway seems to be operating under the Kierkegaardian and Heideggerian senses of *nada* as an external "force." He does appear to be more Sartrian, however, in "The Short Happy Life of Francis Macomber" and "The Snows of Kilimanjaro"; I will treat the consequences when discussing those tales.

9   "Ernest Hemingway: A Critical Essay," in *Ernest Hemingway: Five Decades of Criticism*, ed. Linda Wagner (East Lansing: Michigan State University Press, 1974), p. 214.

10 *Irrational Man* (Garden City, N.Y.: Doubleday, 1958), p. 284. Carlos Baker seems to come closest to my viewpoint in *Hemingway: The Writer as Artist*. He sees a rather explicit appearance of *nada* in "Now I Lay Me" and connects it generally with the idea of "not home," a significant image in the short stories and novels alike. See especially pp. 133ff.

11 See Frederick J. Hoffman, "No Beginning and No End: Hemingway and Death," *Essays in Criticism* 3 (January, 1953): 73–84, and Robert Penn Warren, "Ernest Hemingway," in *Ernest Hemingway: Five Decades of Criticism*, pp. 75–103.

12 Without dealing directly with *nada*, Young traces Nick's initiation and the frequent refusals of initiation in *Ernest Hemingway: A Reconsideration* (New York: Harcourt, 1966), pp. 29–55.

13 *Hemingway: The Writer's Art of Self-Defense* (Minneapolis: University of Minnesota Press, 1969), p. 130.

14 For more information on their versions of nothingness and the existential "authentication" of the self, see Kierkegaard's *Either/Or*, trans. D. Swenson and W. Lowrie (1843; reprint Princeton, N.J.: Princeton University Press, 1944), and Heidegger's *Being and Time*, trans. J. Macquarrie and E. Robinson (1927; rpt. London: SCM Press, 1962).

15 "The Logic of Confusion," p. 542. See also John Hagopian's discussion of the young waiter's limited sensitivity to the word *nothing* in "Tidying Up Hemingway's 'A Clean, Well-Lighted Place,'" *Studies in Short Fiction* 1 (1964): 141–47.

16 "Character, Irony, and Resolution in 'A Clean, Well-Lighted Place.'" *American Literature* 42 (1970): 78. Reacting to Hemingway's own claim that he often omitted the real ending of his stories, Bennett proceeds to speculate that the omitted ending here is the fact that the young waiter's wife has indeed left him, presumably for the soldier who passes by the window of the café.

17 Delmore Schwartz expanded on this idea in his discussion of "Cross-Country Snow" in "The Fiction of Ernest Hemingway":

> Skiing and activities like it give the self a sense of intense individuality, mastery and freedom. In contrast, those activities which link the self with other beings and are necessary to modern civilization not only fail to provide any such self-realization but very often hinder it. The individual feels trapped in the identity assigned him by birth, social convention, economic necessity; he feels that this identity conceals his real self; and the sense that he is often only an enormous part of the social mass makes him feel unreal.

See *Selected Essays of Delmore Schwartz*, ed. Donald Dike and David Zucker (Chicago: University of Chicago Press, 1970), p. 257.

18 Tillich distinguishes between the three forms of "existential" anxiety (of death, meaninglessness, and condemnation), which "belong to existence as such and not to an abnormal state of mind," and "pathological" anxiety, which represents an escape into neurosis, in *The Courage To Be* (New Haven, Conn.: Yale University Press, 1952), pp. 64–70.

19 In using this term Kaplan underscores the unintelligent natural violence, the concentrated destructiveness of the bull. See *The Passive Voice* (Athens: Ohio University Press, 1966), p. 106.

There are many who see Garcia, and the old man as well, as representations of the Hemingway "code hero" precisely because of their dignity in the face of potentially catastrophic external circumstances. These critics, and Kaplan is one, point to Garcia in particular because as a bullfighter he is in constant touch with danger yet maintains a certain grace by virtue of his role in the bullfight, a ritualistic form of order imposed upon the chaos of life.

Granted, both the old man and Garcia display admirable courage, but they lack the firm internal order I see necessary for the true Hemingway hero. As his desperate attempt at suicide and very unsteady balance suggest, the old man's place of refuge is now totally external. Garcia's form has also eroded to the point that he can hardly be considered an exemplar of dignity. There is a certain desperate foolhardiness in his stubborn insistence on making a comeback and his unrealistic hope for "an even break" after his recent disasters in the ring; as his friend Zurito admits, these are signs of empty pride. On the other hand, the picador himself, though aged, is still a thoroughly professional craftsman. Thus, I agree with Arthur Waldheim's view in *A Reader's Guide to Ernest Hemingway* (New York: Farrar, 1972) that Zurito, along with the old waiter, is much more fully representative of the "code hero."

20 Edward Stone, "Hemingway's Mr. Frazer: From Revolution to Radio," *Journal of Modern Literature* 1 (1971): 380.

21 *The Hidden God* (New Haven, Conn.: Yale University Press, 1963), p. 6.

22 See Malcolm Cowley, "Nightmare and Ritual in Hemingway," in *Ernest Hemingway: A Collection of Critical Essays*, ed. Robert Weeks (Englewood Cliffs, N.J.: Prentice-Hall, 1962), pp. 40–52; and Sheridan Baker, "Hemingway's 'Big Two-Hearted River,'" in *The Short Stories of Ernest Hemingway*, ed. Jackson Benson (Durham, N.C.: Duke University Press, 1975), pp. 150–59. In addition to the ritual series in the tale, Baker finds a suggestion of desperate defensiveness against a shadowy threat in the image of Nick's tent, "stretched as tightly as his own state of mind, equally protective in its static tension" (pp. 151–52).

23 "'The Snows of Kilimanjaro': Harry's Second Chance," *Studies in Short Fiction* 5 (1967): 58.

24 Buber's most detailed consideration of this ethics is in *I and Thou*, 2d ed. 1923, rpt. trans. R. Smith (New York: Scribner's, 1958).

  Randall Stewart has also noted the old waiter's proclivity for compassion and sees it as crucial both to the clean, well-lighted place and to the tale's quasi-Christian ritual:

  The cafe is a place where congenial souls may meet. The older waiter, particularly, has a sympathetic understanding of the elderly gentleman's problem. Living in a clean, well-lighted place does not mean solitary withdrawal so long as there are others who also prefer such a place. One can belong to a communion of saints, however small.

  See *American Literature and Christian Doctrine* (Baton Rouge: Louisiana State University Press, 1958), p. 135. See also Richard Hovey's discussion of the need for communion in *Hemingway: The Inward Terrain* (Seattle: University of Washington Press, 1968), p. 25.

25 Because of her faith in the transcendent forces "A Clean, Well-Lighted Place" negates and her naive ambition for sainthood, Sister Cecilia seems an apt equivalent for the unrealistic young waiter. Indeed, as Paul Rodgers has pointed out in "Levels of Irony in Hemingway's 'The Gambler, the Nun, and the Radio,'" *Studies in Short Fiction* 7 (1970): 446, her blindness–also the young waiter's defect–is suggested by the very etymology of her name (from the Latin *caecus*, or "blind").

  Upon closer examination, two other stories reveal a similar triad. "The Undefeated" has its own version of the old waiter (Zurito) and the old man (Garcia), but it also has a young waiter in the person of the young bullfight critic. He too neither empathizes nor sympathizes with the victim's plight and thus engages in facile criticism of him. Moreover, like the young waiter, he is far more interested in a midnight tryst; consequently, he too hurries away, leaving the old man figure to his fate. In "The Battler" (1925) the naive Nick Adams meets only confusion in his encounter with the despairing, jumbled Ad Francis (old man), and fails to fully appreciate the compassionate efforts on both his and Francis's behalf of the eternally watchful Bugs (old waiter).

26 *Time of Need*, p. 94.

27 *Ernest Hemingway: A Life Story* (New York: Scribner's, 1969), p. 305.

28 Rovit convincingly argues that *nada* was both a challenge to and a stimulus for Hemingway's art in *Ernest Hemingway*, pp. 168 ff. See also Jackson Benson, *Hemingway: The Writer's Art of Self-Defense* on this point.

29 *Death in the Afternoon* (New York: Scribner's 1932), p. 278.

30 See Ihab Hassan's illuminating discussion of Hemingway's literary pointillism in "Valor Against the Void," in *The Dismemberment of Orpheus: Toward a Postmodern Literature* (New York: Oxford, 1971), pp. 80–110.

Tony Tanner makes a similar point about the Hemingway style in *The Reign of Wonder* (New York: Cambridge University Press, 1956), pp. 241–50. In Tanner's terms Hemingway characteristically resisted disorder by erecting a verbal "cordon sanitaire" around each individual image, thus creating any number of miniature, aesthetic clean, well-lighted places.

31 *The Great Tradition: An Interpretation of American Literature Since the Civil War*, 3d ed. (Chicago: Quadrangle, 1969), p. 277.

E. R. Hagemann, "'Only Let the Story End As Soon As Possible': Time-and-History in Ernest Hemingway's *In Our Time*"

1 Without going into too much detail, the five states are "In Our Time," *Little Review* 9 (Spring 1923): 3–5, six chapters; *in our time* (Paris: Three Mountains Press, 1924), eighteen chapters; *In Our Time* (New York: Boni & Liveright, 1925), fifteen chapters and L'Envoi, First American Edition; *In Our Time* (New York: Charles Scribner's Sons, 1930), fifteen chapters, L'Envoi, and "Introduction by the Author," pp. 9–12, Second American Edition; and *The Short Stories of Ernest Hemingway* (New York: Modern Library, 1942). This text for this article is the 1925 edition.

2 Incidentally, the *Star* robbery story, "Death Breaks Up a Gang," was immediately followed by the regular column, "Gossip of Society," the first item of which read: "Mr. and Mrs. Ford will entertain with a dinner tonight in compliment to Mr. and Mrs. W. L. Velie of Moline, Ill."

3 Not only did Hemingway change the ethnicity, he also changed the Kansas City street geography. The police station was not on 15th Street but at 1420 Walnut; the cigarstore was not at 15th and Grand, although there are three stores elsewhere on Grand.

4 Oddly, Hemingway does not describe Cook County Jail but Jackson County Jail in Kansas City, and this may have led Fenton and others astray when they say that Cardinella was hanged there. In 1917 capital punishment was forbidden by law in Missouri.

5 William White, ed., *By-Line: Ernest Hemingway* (New York: Scribner's, 1967), pp. 51, 59; the dispatches are headlined "A Silent, Ghastly Procession," October 20, 1922, and "Refugees from Thrace," November 14, 1922.

6 White, *By-Line*, p. 96; "Bull Fighting a Tragedy," October 20, 1923.

7 Villalta was born on November 11, 1898. He received the *alternativa*, the ceremony in which a *matador de novillos* graduates to *matador de toros*, at San Sebastian on August 6, 1922. It was confirmed in Madrid a little over six weeks later. See Barnaby Conrad, *La Fiesta Brava* (Boston: Houghton Mifflin, 1953), p. 176, and throughout the book.

8 Maera was born in 1896. Before his success as a matador, he had worked as a *banderillero*

for Juan Belmonte. His *alternativa* came on August 28, 1921 at Puerto de Santa Maria; it was confirmed in Madrid on May 15, 1922. Bullfighting details have been derived from Cossio, cited above.

A Note to the Reader: Rather than inundate this article with footnotes, I have chosen to cite historical data only occasionally. One can be assured that the facts are as accurate as possible. They have been taken from both standard and specialized histories of the period as well as from contemporary accounts. Spellings of proper nouns are of the time.

Much more work is needed on the interchapters. At present I am engaged on a book-length rhetorical-thematic analysis, some elements of which are stressed herein, for example, the Wall and the Procession.

Then there are the bullfighting episodes. Perhaps someone with better research facilities at hand will be able to identify the events and the participants.

I wish to acknowledge the pioneering work by Michael S. Reynolds in his article, "Two Hemingway Sources for *In Our Time*," *Studies in Short Fiction* 9 (Winter 1972): 81–86.

Robert W. Lewis, "'Long Time Ago Good, Now No Good': Hemingway's Indian Stories"

1 Peter Griffin's biography reveals that in Hemingway's junior year in high school he worked on an "Indian Passion Play," "No Worst [sic] Than a Bad Cold" which is an unfinished satire of Indian clichés foreshadowing *The Torrents of Spring* (pp. 27–28, 233). Griffin also notes that Longfellow's *Hiawatha* was the young Hemingway's favorite poem (p. 233).

2 Clarence may have been honored with an Indian name, "Nec-tee-ta-la—Eagle Eye," but Griffin cites no source and "Eagle Eye" would not be "Nec-tee-ta-la" in any Sioux dialect (p. 6). Hemingway himself seems never to have acknowledged his father's stay among the Sioux. (I am grateful for my colleague John Crawford's help on the linguistic point.)

3 Nor indeed in the United States at all except for the Caribbean periphery in *To Have and to Have Not*.

4 For instance, in a letter to Robert M. Brown, from "The Finca," Hemingway described his initiation to an African tribe: "I was the first and only white man or 1/8 Indian who was ever a Kamba, and it is not like President Coolidge being given a war bonnet by a tame Blackfoot or Shoshone." Jeffrey Meyers goes so far as "Everyone believed that Hemingway had Indian blood" (p. 240). The usual one-eighth Indian blood that Hemingway claimed would have been only one-sixteenth if his arithmetic as well as his history were accurate, for in a letter to Charles Scribner he claimed "a Cheyenne great-great-grandmother" (*Letters*, p. 659). The tribe is further specified as Northern Cheyenne in a prideful letter in part about youngest son Gregory, "a real Indian boy (Northern Cheyenne) with the talents and the defects," both of which Hemingway associated with his own youth (*Letters*, p. 679).

5 Lloyd R. Arnold, *High on the Wild with Hemingway* (Caldwell, Idaho: Caxton, 1968), pp. 36, 37, 50, 53–54, 59, 67–68.

6 Curiously, in *The Sun Also Rises*, published four years after Hemingway's poem, "There Are Seasons: Translations from the Esquimaux," Jake thinks, "The English spoken

language—the upper classes anyway—must have fewer words than the Eskimo. Of course I didn't know anything about the Eskimo. Maybe the Eskimo was a fine language. Say the Cherokee. I didn't know anything about the Cherokee either'' (p. 149).

7 Montgomery, p. 93. The youths are seventeen and nineteen. Nick is actually not named in the story, but Montgomery and other Hemingway scholars identify him on the basis of parallels and circumstantial evidence.

8 Carlos Baker (*Life,* p. 26) suggests that Hemingway did not have his first sexual encounter with Trudy or any Indian counterpart. But according to Mary Hemingway, Hemingway perpetuated the myth with her (p. 102). For a careful analysis of the writing and revisions of ''Ten Little Indians,'' including information and speculation on the pregnancy and subsequent suicide of the Indian girl Prudence Boulton, the model for the girl in the story, see Paul Smith.

9 Twenty years later these last words were still on his mind. In a letter to Bernard Berenson, Hemingway writes that he has ''complicated blood. . . . One time when I was out at the Wind River reservation a very old Indian spoke to me and said, 'You Indian boy?' I said, 'Sure.' He said, 'Cheyenne?' I said, 'Sure.' He said, 'Long time ago good. Now no good''' (*Letters,* p. 815). He had virtually the same lines in a 1949 letter to Malcolm Cowley: ''Us old ex-Cheyennes have various things that we believe in but as an Indian said to me one time, 'Long time ago, good, now no good''' (*Letters,* p. 681).

10 Just as, he wrote to Maxwell Perkins about *For Whom the Bell Tolls,* the Gypsies ''in this book are not book gypsies anymore than my indians were ever book-indians'' (*Letters,* p. 513).

11 Instead of cultural and chronological, Stanley Diamond uses *prospective* and *retrospective* to name two types of primitivism. His study is an excellent synthesis of past work and thought as well as speculation for the future.

12 See my *Hemingway on Love* (Austin: University of Texas Press, 1965, rpt. New York: Haskell House, 1973), and (the most recent relevant essay) Kim Moreland, ''Hemingway's Medievalist Impulse: Its Effect on the Presentation of Women and War in *The Sun Also Rises,''* *Hemingway Review* 6, no. 1 (1986): 30–41.

Baker, Carlos. *Ernest Hemingway: A Life Story* (New York: Scribner's, 1969).

Brasch, James D., and Joseph Sigman. *Hemingway's Library: A Composite Record* (New York: Garland, 1981).

Cowley, Malcolm. ''Introduction.'' *Hemingway* (New York: Viking Press, 1944).

Diamond, Stanley. *In Search of the Primitive: A Critique of Civilization* (New Brunswick, N.J.: Transaction Books, 1974).

Fiedler, Leslie. *The Return of the Vanishing American* (New York: Stein and Day, 1968).

Griffin, Peter. *Along with Youth: Hemingway, The Early Years* (New York: Oxford University Press, 1985).

Hemingway, Ernest. *Death in the Afternoon* (New York: Scribner's, 1932).

———. *88 Poems,* ed. Nicholas Gerogiannis (New York: Harcourt Brace & Jovanovich, 1979).

———. *For Whom the Bell Tolls* (New York: Scribner's, 1940).

———. Letter to Robert M. Brown (July 22, 1956). Humanities Research Center, University of Texas, Austin.

———. *The Nick Adams Stories* (New York: Scribner's, 1972).

———. *Selected Letters, 1917–1961,* ed. Carlos Baker (New York: Scribner's, 1981).

———. *The Short Stories of Ernest Hemingway* (New York: Scribner's, 1938).

————. *The Sun Also Rises*. New York: Scribner's, 1926.

————. *The Torrents of Spring*. Harmondsworth: Penguin, 1966 and 1926; New York: Scribner's, 1972.

Hemingway, Leicester. *My Brother, Ernest Hemingway*. Cleveland: World, 1962.

Hemingway, Mary Welsh. *How it Was*. New York: Knopf, 1976.

Lewis, Robert W. *Hemingway on Love*. Austin: University of Texas Press, 1963; reprint New York: Haskell House, 1973.

Lewis, Wyndham. "Ernest Hemingway: The 'Dumb Ox.'" *Men Without Art*. London: Cassell, 1934.

————. *Paleface: The Philosophy of the "Melting Pot."* London: Chatto and Windus, 1929.

Meyers, Jeffrey. *Hemingway: A Biography*. New York: Harper & Row, 1985.

Montgomery, Constance Cappel. *Hemingway in Michigan*. New York: Fleet, 1966.

Moreland, Kim. "Hemingway's Medievalist Impulse: Its Effect on the Presentation of Women and War in *The Sun Also Rises*." *The Hemingway Review* 6, no. 1 (1986): 30–41.

Paul, Sherman. *In Search of the Primitive: Rereading David Antin, Jerome Rothenberg, and Gary Snyder*. Baton Rouge: Louisiana State University Press, 1986.

Plimpton, George, ed. "Hemingway." *Writers at Work: The "Paris Review" Interviews*. Second series. New York: Viking Press, 1965.

Reynolds, Michael. *Hemingway's Reading, 1910–1940: An Inventory*. Princeton, N.J.: Princeton University Press, 1981.

————. *The Young Hemingway*. Oxford: Blackwell, 1986.

Ross, Lillian. *Portrait of Hemingway*. New York: Simon and Schuster, 1961.

Smith, Paul. "The Tenth Indian and the Thing Left Out." *Ernest Hemingway: The Writer in Context*, ed. James Nagel. Madison: University of Wisconsin Press, 1984.

Some other works on Hemingway's Indians and primitivism include the following:

Burnham, Tom. "Primitivism and Masculinity in the Work of Ernest Hemingway." *Modern Fiction Studies* 1 (August 1955): 20–24.

Hassan, Ihab. *Radical Innocence: Studies in the Contemporary American Novel*. Princeton, N.J.: Princeton University Press, 1961.

Lewis, Robert W. "Hemingway." *The Indian Historian* 4 (Summer 1971): 56.

Love, Glen. "Hemingway's Indian Virtues: An Ecological Reconsideration." *Western American Literature* 22, no. 1 (1987): 201–13.

McClellan, David. "The Battle of the Little Big Horn in Hemingway's Later Fiction." *Fitzgerald/Hemingway Annual 1976*, ed. Matthew J. Bruccoli. Englewood, Colo.: Information Handling Services, 1978. Pp. 245–48.

St. John, Donald. "Hemingway and Prudence." *Connecticut Review* 5 (April 1972): 78–84.

Schulz, Franz. *Der nordamerikanische Indianer und seine Welt in den Werken von Ernest Hemingway und Oliver Lafarge*. Munich, Germany: Max Huber Verlag, 1964.

Schiers, Elaine. Untitled review. *The Indian Historian* 4 (Spring 1971): 54, 66.

Wayne Kvam, "Hemingway's 'Banal Story'"

1 Ernest Hemingway, "Banal Story," *The Little Review* 12, no. 1 (Spring-Summer 1926): 22–23.

2 Hemingway, "Banal Story," *Men Without Women* (New York: Scribner's, 1927), pp. 214–17.

3   Joseph Defalco, *The Hero in Hemingway's Short Stories* (Pittsburgh: University of Pittsburgh Press, 1963), p. 95.

4   Nicholas Joost, *Ernest Hemingway and the Little Magazines* (Barre, Mass.: Barre Publishers, 1968), pp. 150–51.

5   Carlos Baker, *Ernest Hemingway: A Life Story* (New York: Scribner's, 1969), p. 184.

6   Henry G. Leach, *My Last Seventy Years* (New York: Bookman Associates, 1956), pp. 175–77.

7   Ibid., p. 180.

8   Leach, "An Introduction by the Editor," *Forum* 73 (March 1925). The editor's introduction usually appeared on the inside of the unnumbered cover page for each issue.

9   *Forum* 73 (May 1925).

10 *Forum* 74 (September 1925). Henry P. Fairchild's "The Land-Hunger Urge to War," the first article in the series "War or Peace?" also appeared in this issue.

11 *Forum* 73 (May 1925). Canada and Canadians were favorite topics of the editor's, as the following statement from his autobiography illustrates: "Canada, dear Canada! My Canadian friends occupy a place in my affections beside the Scandinavian. The average Canadian is clear-headed, direct, objective, practical, and helpful." Turning to economic development, Leach added, "The Canadian dollar has a way of becoming more valuable than even the American dollar. Canada is today the Promised Land." *My Last Seventy Years*, p. 136.

12 See, for example, J. B. S. Haldane, "Biology Moulding the Future," *Forum* 73 (March 1925): 331–41; H. F. Osborn, "Credo of a Naturalist," *Forum* 73 (April 1925): 486; Francis Crookshank, "The Threefold Origin of Man," *Forum* 73 (May 1925): 690–97; Osborn, "The Earth Speaks to Bryan," *Forum* 73 (June 1925): 796–803; William J. Bryan, "Mr. Bryan Speaks to Darwin," *Forum* 74 (August 1925): 322–24; E. E. Free, "The Origin of Life," *Forum* 74 (October 1925): 552–60.

13 *Forum* 73 (February 1925).

14 *Forum* 73 (April 1925).

15 *Forum* 73 (January 1925).

16 *Forum* 73 (April 1925).

17 Laird S. Goldsborough, "Big Men—Or Cultured?" *Forum* 73 (February 1925): 209–14.

18 *Forum* 74 (October 1925): xiii.

19 Arthur H. Gibbs, "Soundings," *Forum* 72 (December 1924): 838.

20 *Forum* 72 (December 1924).

21 Roy Dibble, "In the Wicked Old Puritan Days," *Forum* 75 (April 1926): 518–24.

22 *Forum* 74 (August 1925).

23 *Forum* 73 (June 1925).

24 "Picasso's Achievement," *Forum* 73 (June 1925): 760–75.

25 "Picasso's Failure," *Forum* 73 (June 1925): 776–83.

26 "Pure Art? Or 'Pure Nonsense'?" *Forum* 74 (July 1925): 146.

27 "Tramps and Hoboes," *Forum* 74 (August 1925): 227–37.

28 *Forum* 72 (December 1924).

29 *Forum* 73 (January 1925).

30 *Forum* 73 (May 1925).

31 *Forum* 72 (December 1924).

32 *Forum* 74 (August 1925).

33 "To the Mayas," *Forum* 74 (August 1925): 161.

34 Herbert Spinden, "The Answer of Ancient America," *Forum* 74 (August 1925): 162–71.

35 Hemingway, *Death in the Afternoon* (New York: Scribner's, 1932), p. 122.

36 Ibid., pp. 77–83.

37 Hemingway, *Green Hills of Africa* (New York: Scribner's, 1935), p. 295.

38 Hemingway, *For Whom the Bell Tolls* (New York: Scribner's 1940), pp. 312–13.

39 Hemingway, *Death in the Afternoon*, p. 95.

40 Ibid., p. 275.

41 Ibid., p. 205.

42 Charles Fenton, *The Apprenticeship of Ernest Hemingway* (1954; reprint New York: Mentor, 1961), p. 88.

George Monteiro, "'This Is My Pal Bugs': Ernest Hemingway's 'The Battler'"

1 *In Our Time* (New York: Scribner's, n.d.), pp. 77–78. All subsequent quotations from "The Battler" are from this text and are so indicated by page references within the body of the paper.

2 See, particularly, Philip Young, *Ernest Hemingway* (New York: Rinehart, 1952), pp. 8–11, 205–7; William B. Bache, "Hemingway's 'The Battler,'" *Explicator* (October 1954): 13, item 4; Joseph DeFalco, *The Hero in Hemingway's Short Stories* (Pittsburgh: University of Pittsburgh Press, 1963), pp. 71–81; Richard B. Hovey, *Hemingway: The Inward Terrain* (Seattle: University of Washington Press, 1968), p. 20; Joseph M. Flora, *Hemingway's Nick Adams* (Baton Rouge: Louisiana State University Press, 1982), pp. 83–104; and Nicholas Gerogiannis, "Nick Adams on the Road: 'The Battler' as Hemingway's Man on the Hill," *Critical Essays on Ernest Hemingway's "In Our Time,"* ed. Michael S. Reynolds (Boston: Hall, 1983), pp. 176–88.

3 Ernest Hemingway, *Selected Letters 1917–1961*, ed. Carlos Baker (New York: Scribner's, 1981), p. 157.

4 Carlos Baker, *Ernest Hemingway: A Life Story* (New York: Scribner's, 1969), p. 141.

5 Philip Young argues for the relationship between Mark Twain's Huck and Jim as a precedent for Ad and Bugs, and in passing he mentions Ishmael and Queequeg as a second possibility (pp. 205–7). In both cases, however, there is a lack that makes the difference: there is no third person participant-observer, who, in Hemingway's story, is the young Nick Adams and, in Melville's, the "innocent" Benito Cereno.

6 Herman Melville, "Benito Cereno," *A Benito Cereno Handbook*, ed. Seymour L. Gross (Belmont, Calif.: Wadsworth, 1965), p. 38. All subsequent quotations from Melville's story are from this text and are so indicated by page references within the body of this essay.

Scott Donaldson, "Preparing for the End: Hemingway's Revisions of 'A Canary for One'"

1 This objection has been raised by a number of my students over the years, as well as by critics. Among the few extended discussions of "A Canary for One" are: Martin Dolch, John V. Hagopian, and W. Gordon Cunliffe, "A Canary for One," *Insight I: Analyses of American Literature*, ed. John V. Hagopian and Martin Dolch (Frankfurt-am-Main: Hirschgraben, 1962), pp. 96–99; Joseph DeFalco, *The Hero in Hemingway's Short Stories*

(Pittsburgh; University of Pittsburgh Press, 1963), pp. 174–76; and Julian Smith, "'A Canary for One'" Hemingway in the Wasteland," *Studies in Short Fiction* 5 (1968): 355–61.

2   Smith, "Canary," p. 355.

3   The three drafts are numbered Ms-307, Ms-308, and Ms.-309 in the finding aid to the Hemingway collection at the Kennedy Library. I am indebted to Jo August and William Johnson of the library for their assistance.

4   A possibility Smith proposed in yet another essay: "Hemingway and the Thing Left Out," *Journal of Modern Literature* 1 (1971): 169–82.

5   George Plimpton, interview of Ernest Hemingway, *Writers at Work,* second series (New York: Viking Press, 1965), p. 230.

6   Smith, "Canary," pp. 358–60.

7   Carlos Baker, *Ernest Hemingway: A Life Story* (New York: Scribner's, 1969), pp. 177, 592–93.

8   See, among others, the attack on "the rich" in the concluding chapter of *A Moveable Feast* and self-recriminations of Thomas Hudson in *Islands in the Stream.*

9   Baker, *Ernest Hemingway,* p. 177.

10   Michael S. Reynolds, *Hemingway's First War: The Making of A Farewell to Arms* (Princeton, N.J.: Princeton University Press, 1976), p. 283.

Bernard Oldsey, "*El Pueblo Español:* 'The Capital of the World'"

1   See Audre Hanneman's *Ernest Hemingway: A Comprehensive Bibliography* and its *Supplement.* Perhaps the most flagrant indication of critical neglect is afforded by Lawrence Broer's book-length study of Hemingway and Spain, *Hemingway's Spanish Tragedy* (1973), in which "The Capital of the World" is never even mentioned. Yet, the story was quickly translated into many languages, including German, Polish, Portuguese, Japanese, and Spanish (the first time as "Los cuernos del toro," in *Hoy,* November 4, 1937). And it was made into a fine ballet—score by George Antheil, choreography by Eugene Loring—produced by the Ford Foundation Television Workshop on *Omnibus,* December 6, 1953, and later that month by the Ballet Theatre at the Metropolitan Opera House, December 27, 1953.

2   The Spanish Civil War broke out on July 17, 1936, just a few weeks after "The Capital of the World" was published.

3   In that sometimes wise, sometimes gaga essay Hemingway wrote on "The Art of the Short Story," he indicates that he was aware of just how much material he was putting into a story like "The Snows of Kilimanjaro." "So I invent," he says confidingly, "and put into one short story things you would use for, say, four novels. . . . I throw everything I had been saving into the story and spend it all" (Item #251, Hemingway Collection, John F. Kennedy Library). With perhaps just a little less ebullience he could have said the same thing about the composition of "The Capital of the World," because he put into that story most of what he had learned about Spain and its people.

4   Gerald Mast, *Short History of the Movies* (New York: Bobbs Merrill, 1979), p. 68.

5   All references are to "The Capital of the World" as published in *The Stories of Ernest Hemingway* (New York: Scribner's, 1953); pagination is entered parenthetically in the text. (It should be noted that Frank L. Laurence, in *Hemingway and the Movies* [Jackson:

486 Notes and References

University Press of Mississippi, 1981] comments on Hemingway's crosscutting methods but with different emphases.)

6 Carlos Baker, *Ernest Hemingway: A Life Story* (New York: Scribner's, 1969), p. 235.

7 Baker, *Ernest Hemingway*, pp. 313–15.

8 Katherine Anne Porter's *Ship of Fools* has as progenitor the German classic *Das Narrenshiff* (1494). This satire helped prepare for the Protestant Reformation and was often imitated later, as in Alexander Barclay's *Ship of Fools* (1509).

9 See *The Oxford Companion to Film* (New York: Oxford University Press, 1976) and *World Encyclopedia of Film* (New York: Galahad Books, 1972).

10 Hemingway either did not know the facts or took liberties with them. In "The Capital of the World" he implies that the public knew Garbo solely through films with lavish backgrounds in which she plays sophisticated ladies—like *Queen Christina* (1934), *Anna Karenina* (1935), and the movie in question, *Grand Hotel* (1932). But the working-class *Anna Christie* (1930), which was her first talkie, preceded these luxurious films. So did one of her earliest silent films, *The Joyless Street* (1925), directed by G. W. Pabst. According to Gerald Mast, "Pabst's street is joyless because it is a dead end of prostitution and early death." See Mast, *Short History*, p. 182.

11 Stephen A. Reid, "The Oedipal Pattern in Hemingway's 'The Capital of the World,'" *Literature and Psychology* 13 (Spring, 1963): 37–43.

12 Baker, *Ernest Hemingway*, p. 617. Also see letter to Arnold Gingrich, April 4, 1936, in which Hemingway listed other possible titles for the story: "Outside the Ring," "The Start of the Season," "A Boy Named Paco," "To Empty Stands," "The Judgment of Distance," and " The Sub-Novice Class." The ironic purchase of a title like "The Capital of the World" shows that Hemingway here, as he had in so many other instances, eventually chose a title worthy of the fiction it designates.

13 Reid, "Oedipal Pattern," p. 37.

14 Sheldon Grebstein, "Hemingway's Dark and Bloody Capital," in *The Thirties: Fiction, Poetry, Drama*, ed. Warren French (Deland, Fla.: Everett Edwards, 1967), p. 25.

15 The translator is unnamed; the book is *Ernest Hemingway: Relatos* (Barcelona: Luis de Caralt, 1960), pp. 193–207. This edition, done under Franco's regime and heavy censorship, omits many things which the censors thought harmful to the purity and security of Spanish readers. There are, for example, no references to whores or whoring in this translation of "The Capital of the World"; all of that, including the cowardly matador's attempted seduction of Pablo's sister, was deleted. Even more bowdlerizing is the dropping of the parody forms of the Pater Noster and Ave Maria in this book's version of "A Clean, Well-Lighted Place."

16 Into these stories Hemingway put everything that he could, but in a compressed manner, and this compression—this microcosmic presentation of a world view in "The Capital of the World"—is one of the things that readers of the story seem not to have given just due, probably because the foregrounding of Paco's agony is so powerfully spotlighted.

17 Hemingway used crosscutting most extensively in *For Whom the Bell Tolls*, shifting from Robert Jordan to, among others, Anselmo, El Sordo, Andres, Karkov, and the fascist Lt. Berrendo. He even considered a conclusion for the novel which would cut away from the wounded Jordan to summarize what was happening away from the guerrilla action. As the epigraph for this essay indicates, Hemingway discussed this possible conclusion in a letter to Max Perkins. See *Ernest Hemingway: Selected Letters, 1917–1961*, ed. Carlos Baker (New York: Scribner's, 1981), pp. 514–15.

18 The hidden heroine of this story is the woman who owns the Pension Luarca. She may use a "bolster" to maintain a low-level illusion, but she is also a sympathetic and realistically decent personage. Much of her character is revealed in this auctorial comment: "The descent from the Luarca was swift since anyone could stay there who was making anything at all and a bill was never presented to a guest unasked until the woman who ran the place knew that the case was hopeless" (p. 39). The middle-aged waiter also maintains a kind of balance, or at least does not give way to either illusion or disillusion. When the Anarcho-Syndicalist waiter chides him, saying "You are a good comrade. . . . But you lack ideology," the middle-aged waiter (a literary relative of the older waiter in "A Clean, Well-Lighted Place") responds, "Mejor si me falta eso que el otro" [It is better that I lack the one, ideology, than the other, work] (p. 42). He has always worked: "To work," he declares, "is normal." This matter-of-factness contrasts markedly with the youthful all-inclusiveness of Paco, who says nothing during the discussion between the two older men, but who thinks "He himself would like to be a good catholic [sic], a revolutionary, and have a steady job like this, while, at the same time, being a bullfighter" (pp. 42–43). "Ah, youth," as Joseph Conrad says in a story with that key word in the title.

Warren Bennett, "The Poor Kitty and the Padrone and the Tortoise-shell Cat in 'Cat in the Rain'"

1 Gertrude M. White, "We're All 'Cats in the Rain,'" draws on Clinton S. Burhans, Jr.'s "The Complex Unity of *In Our Time*" and rightly attempts to locate her interpretation within the context of *In Our Time:*
> The story, in short, seems less like the drama of a particular crisis in a particular relationship than a paradigm of man's plight as Hemingway presents it again and again in his fiction: "the world as it actually is set against man's expectations and hopes; and his consequent problems and difficulties in trying to live in it with meaning and order." ([Burhans, p. 326] White, p. 244).

2 The fact that George prefers to have his wife look like a "boy" is the first time the subject of androgyny explicitly appears in Hemingway's fiction. It reaches its most complete exploration in the posthumously published *The Garden of Eden*.

3 I am indebted here to two of my seminar students, Linda Froshag and Teri Matravolgyi, who knew more about cats than I did. I also want to thank Professor Richard Davison, University of Delaware, for sharing with me the work one of his students did on the gene complement and chromosomes of tortoise-shell cats. Normal female cats have two X chromosomes; males have one, plus the Y chromosome that determines maleness. Male tortoise-shells, however, have an extra X chromosome. Thus their genetic constitution is XXY. The student concludes, "This animal, obviously, is genetically abnormal; hence, when it does occur, it is always sterile."

Baker, Carlos. *Ernest Hemingway: A Life Story* (New York: Scribner's, 1969).
———. *Ernest Hemingway: Selected Letters* (New York: Scribner's, 1981).
———. *Ernest Hemingway: The Writer as Artist* (Princeton, N.J.: Princeton University Press, 1952).
Benson, Jackson J. "Patterns of Connection and Their Development in Hemingway's *In Our Time.*" *Rendezvous* 5, no. 2 (1970): 37–52. Special Hemingway issue.

DeFalco, Joseph. *The Hero in Hemingway's Short Stories* (Pittsburgh: University of Pittsburgh Press, 1963).

Eliot, T. S. "The Burial of the Dead," *The Waste Land. The Complete Poems and Plays of T. S. Eliot* (London: Faber and Faber, 1969), pp. 59–75.

Hagopian, John V. "Symmetry in 'Cat in the Rain,'" *The Short Stories of Ernest Hemingway: Critical Essays,* ed. Jackson J. Benson (Durham, N.C.: Duke University Press, 1975).

Hemingway, Ernest. "Cat in the Rain." *In Our Time* (New York: Scribner's, 1953), pp. 91–94.

———. *The Sun Also Rises* (New York: Scribner's, 1954).

———. Cat in the Rain, ms. items 319, 320, and 321. The Hemingway Collection, John F. Kennedy Library, Boston. All quotations from the manuscripts are copyrighted in the name of the Ernest Hemingway Foundation.

Hovey, Richard. *The Inward Terrain* (Seattle: University of Washington Press, 1968).

Lodge, David. *Working with Structuralism* (Boston: Routledge and Kegan Paul, 1981).

Meyers, Jeffrey. *Hemingway: A Biography* (New York: Harper and Row, 1985).

Reynolds, Michael. *The Young Hemingway* (New York: Basil Blackwell, 1986).

White, Gertrude M. "We're All 'Cats in the Rain.'" *Fitzgerald-Hemingway Annual* (1978): 241–46.

Young, Philip. *Ernest Hemingway: A Reconsideration* (New York: Harcourt, 1966).

Kenneth G. Johnston, "Hemingway's 'The Denunciation': The Aloof American"

1 "The total number of foreigners who fought in the International Brigade was about 40,000. . . . The United States contributed about 2,800. Of these, about 900 were killed." (Hugh Thomas, *The Spanish Civil War* [New York: Harper, 1961], p. 637).

2 Gabriel Jackson, *The Spanish Republic and the Civil War, 1931–1939* (Princeton, N.J.: Princeton University Press, 1965), p. 255.

3 In a talk on October 10, 1936, in Washington with newly appointed Spanish Ambassador, Senor de los Rios, "Mr. Hull stated that the United States had proclaimed a policy of aloofness in the Spanish situation and was using its moral influence and its persuasion to maintain effective this point of view." (Richard Southgate, "Memorandum by the Chief of the Division of Protocol and Conferences," in *Foreign Relations of the United States: Diplomatic Papers 1936* [Washington, D.C.: U.S. Government Printing Office, 1954], 2:538.)

"Our policy," Hull later wrote, "had nothing to do with our views on the right or the wrong in the Spanish Civil War. We were not judging between the two sides. . . . Our peace and security required our keeping aloof from the struggle." (*The Memoirs of Cordell Hull* [New York: Macmillan, 1948], 1:483, 491).

4 "For the Republican government," declares Herbert L. Matthews, "the American embargo was a crushing blow, perhaps a decisive one." (*Half of Spain Died: A Reappraisal of the Spanish Civil War* [New York: Scribner's, 1973], p. 177).

"If this loyalist government is overthrown," former U.S. Secretary of State Henry L. Stimson wrote in 1939, "it is evident now that its defeat will be solely due to the fact that it has been deprived of its right to buy from us and other friendly nations the munitions necessary for its defense." (Henry L. Stimson, "Text of Letter to Sec. Hull," *New York Times,* January 24, 1939, p. 6.)

In an article in *Ken* magazine Hemingway denounced the State Department for having done its "disgusting efficient best" to end the Spanish conflict by "denying the Spanish government the right to buy arms to defend itself against the German and Italian aggression." ("H. M.'s Loyal State Department," *Ken*, 1 [June 16, 1938]: 36.)

5   Hemingway to Ivan Kashkeen, Soviet translator and critic, August 19, 1935, in "Letters of Ernest Hemingway to Soviet Writers," *Soviet Literature*, no. 11 (1962): 162.

6   Hemingway, "The Denunciation," in *The Fifth Column and Four Stories of the Spanish Civil War* (New York: Scribner's, 1969), p. 90. Subsequent references will be cited parenthetically in the text. The story first appeared in *Esquire* 10 (November 1938): 39, 111–14.

7   Jackson, p. 7.

8   Jackson, pp. 5–6.

9   Theo Aronson, *Royal Vendetta: The Crown of Spain 1829–1965* (Indianapolis: Bobbs-Merrill, 1966), p. 147.

10 Aronson, p. 183.

11 Aronson, p. 188.

12 Aronson, pp. 180–81.

13 Sir Charles Petrie, *King Alfonso XIII and His Age* (London: Chapman & Hall, 1963), p. 226.

14 Stimson, p. 6.

15 Matthews, p. 177.

16 Henry F. Pringle, "High Hat," *Scribner's Magazine* 104 (July 1938): 17, 18, 20. Pringle lists *The Spur's* circulation at 27,000, as compared to that of *Good Housekeeping* with 2,210,835.

17 Hemingway, "The Gambler, the Nun, and the Radio," in *Winner Take Nothing* (New York: Scribner's, 1933), pp. 218–19.

18 Reports Hugh Thomas (*The Spanish Civil War*, p. 175): "No one said 'adios' any more, but always 'salud.' A man named Fernandez de Dios even wrote to the Minister of Justice asking if he could change his surname to Bakunin, 'for he did not want to have anything to do with God.'"

19 "I was going to forget the war. I had made a separate peace," Frederic Henry told himself after his desertion. (Hemingway, *A Farewell to Arms* [New York: Scribner's, 1929] p. 252).

20 Hemingway, *Green Hills of Africa* (New York: Scribner's, 1935), p. 148.

21 The self-denunciation of Henry Emmunds was possibly intended as self-criticism by Ernest Hemingway. It does not escape the reader's notice that his choice for narrator is an American writer with the initials H. E. Hemingway was a fund raiser, a propagandist, and a spokesman for the Loyalist cause. But he did not commit himself to battle. He did not join the International Brigades, and in October 1938, according to Carlos Baker, he "turned down an offer of a staff captaincy in a French outfit which was then being organized to help the Loyalists" (*Ernest Hemingway: A Life Story* [New York: Scribner's, 1969], p. 334). Although he was occasionally under enemy fire while on assignment—he worked on the filming of *The Spanish Earth* and covered the war for the North American Newspaper Alliance—he was, for all practical purposes, a privileged spectator of the war. He knew people in high places—ambassadors, generals, politicians; he suffered no lack of food, liquor, money, vehicles, gasoline, chauffeurs, or companionship, male and female; and he was free to leave the war zone whenever he wished. He spent some eleven months in Spain covering the war, with interludes in Bimini, Key West, and Wyoming.

Henry Emmunds accuses himself of being motivated by "the always-dirty desire to see how people act under an emotional conflict, that makes writers such attractive friends" (p. 97). Hemingway, too, may have felt a sense of guilt for artistically exploiting the war. There is no question that as an artist he profited handsomely from the tragedy. The "Spoils of Spain" (Baker's term) included six short stories, one play, and one novel. When Madrid fell on 28 March 1939, Hemingway was in Key West and some 15,000 words into his novel *For Whom the Bell Tolls;* he had already written the scene in which Anselmo denounces Pablo for putting "thy foxhole before the interests of humanity" (*For Whom the Bell Tolls* [New York: Scribner's, 1940], p. 11).

Robert P. Weeks, "Wise-Guy Narrator and Trickster Out-Tricked in Hemingway's 'Fifty Grand'"

1 In the comprehensive checklist of "Criticism, Explication, and Commentary on Individual Stories" in Jackson J. Benson, ed., *The Short Stories of Ernest Hemingway: Critical Essays* (Durham, N.C.: Duke University Press, 1975), there are 229 entries for these four stories, each receiving approximately fifty entries. In contrast, "Fifty Grand" has only seventeen entries, of which only three are articles; the other fourteen consist of brief comments on the story in books on Hemingway's work.

2 The first article published on "Fifty Grand," Charles A. Fenton, "No Money for the Kingbird: Hemingway's Prize-fight Stories," *American Quarterly* 4 (1952): 342–47, approaches it primarily from a biographical point of view, placing it alongside Hemingway's other boxing stories to show young Hemingway's interest in the ring and, more important, his admiration for those boxers who combined courage and professionalism. P. G. and R. R. Davies, "Hemingway's 'Fifty Grand' and the Jack Britton-Mickey Walker Prize Fight," *American Literature* 37 (1965): 251–58, insists that central to an understanding of the story is the fact that Hemingway based it on "newspaper accounts of the welterweight championship fight between the champion, Jack Britton, and the challenger, Mickey Walker, at Madison Square Garden, November 1, 1922." Their assertion that the story is "only a slight reworking of existing materials" is greatly overstated, but the similarities in names, ages, and circumstances of the two contenders in the story and in the Britton-Walker fight make it highly likely that Hemingway did, indeed, make some use of that fight in the story.

Without mentioning the Davies' article, Carlos Baker in *Ernest Hemingway: A Life Story* (New York: Scribner's, 1969) asserts "Fifty Grand" is based on the Benny Leonard-Jack Britton welterweight championship bout at the New York Hippodrome, January 26, 1922 (Baker, p. 157). James J. Martine, "Hemingway's 'Fifty Grand': The Other Fight(s)," *Journal of Modern Literature* 2 (1971): 123–27, dismisses Baker's case by making use of the recently discovered first three pages of typescript of "Fifty Grand" that Hemingway deleted at the suggestion of F. Scott Fitzgerald. An apparent reference to the Leonard-Britton fight in the deleted pages makes it clear that that fight has already been fought. Martine concludes, "it is hard to imagine the Britton-Leonard fight as the source of 'Fifty Grand': a fighter does not go to camp to prepare for a bout he has already fought" (p. 124). Martine effectively scales down the Davies' claims, then offers as a possible source yet another fight, the Siki-Carpenter bout that Hemingway attended, September 24, 1924, in Paris. He reasonably concludes that because it was "the greatest doublecross in fight history," Hemingway probably made some use of it as well as of the Britton-Walker fight—and possibly other fights as well—in creating "Fifty Grand."

3   Fenton is first to link the high school story to "Fifty Grand," remarking merely that both dealt with boxing. Sheridan Baker goes somewhat further: "Hemingway has soaked up the lore, and some of the speech, of the boxing world, foreshadowing 'Fifty Grand' (1927) and, to some extent, 'The Battler' (1925)." See *Ernest Hemingway: An Introduction and Interpretation* (New York: Holt, Rinehart, & Winston, 1967), p. 8.

4   Charles A. Fenton, *The Apprenticeship of Ernest Hemingway: The Early Years* (New York: Farrar, Straus & Young, 1954) provides the earliest and fullest account of Hemingway as humorist, including his admiration of Lardner. See especially, pp. 26, 44, 81. Hemingway was referred to in the school paper, *The Trapeze*, as "our Ring Lardner, Jr." See *Ernest Hemingway's Apprenticeship*, ed. Matthew J. Bruccoli (Washington, D.C.: Microcard Editions, 1971), pp. 33, 41, 57, 79.

5   *Hemingway's Apprenticeship*, pp. 98–100.

6   "Ernest Hemingway, Literary Critic," *American Literature* 36 (1965): 433.

7   Baker, *Hemingway: A Life Story*, p. 166.

8   Baker, *Hemingway: An Introduction*, pp. 61–62.

9   "Fifty Grand," *The Short Stories of Ernest Hemingway* (New York: Scribner's, 1953), pp. 313, 322, 323, 324, 326.

10   *The Complete Short Stories of Mark Twain*, ed. Charles Neider (New York: Doubleday, 1957), p. 3.

11   Earl Rovit, *Ernest Hemingway* (New York: Twayne Publishers, 1963), p. 61; Joseph DeFalco, *The Hero in Hemingway's Short Stories* (Pittsburgh: University of Pittsburgh Press, 1963), p. 211. These misapprehensions of Jerry's character and role are corrected in Sheldon Norman Grebstein's careful analysis in *Hemingway's Craft* (Carbondale: Southern Illinois University Press, 1973). He concludes of Jerry, "The I-witness of 'Fifty Grand' can be named an 'almost-reliable' narrator, dependable enough for the reader to accept his account as substantially true, thus assuring the story of its basically 'realistic' and 'objective' quality" (p. 60). It assures the story, as well, of its comic dimension, although Grebstein does not go into that.

12   "Fifty Grand," p. 326. Hemingway's tendency to see boxers, especially second-rate ones, as machines is further evidenced in the original title, never used, of "The Battler: A Great Little Fighting Machine." See Baker, *Hemingway: A Life Story*, p. 141.

13   "Fifty Grand," p. 326.

14   Baker, *Hemingway: An Introduction*, p. 52.

15   *Feeling and Form* (New York: Scribner's, 1953), p. 331.

16   The language is not Faulkner's but Baker's; see Baker, *Hemingway: A Life Story*, p. 461.

Amberys R. Whittle, "A Reading of Hemingway's 'The Gambler, the Nun, and the Radio'"

1   *Varieties of Parable* (Cambridge: Cambridge University Press, 1965), pp. 2–3.

2   Ibid., p. 7.

3   Ibid., p. 6.

4   Ibid., p. 3.

5   *Ernest Hemingway: A Reconsideration* (University Park: Pennsylvania State University Press, 1966), pp. 66–67.

6   *Literary History of the United States*, ed. Robert E. Spiller et al., 4th ed. (New York: Macmillan, 1974), p. 1301.

7 These are described by Carlos Baker in *Ernest Hemingway: A Life Story* (New York: Charles Scribner's Sons, 1969), pp. 217–18.

8 *The Short Stories of Ernest Hemingway* (New York: Scribner's, 1953), p. 473. All further quotations are from this edition.

9 *Hemingway and the Dead Gods: A Study in Existentialism* (Lexington: University Press of Kentucky, 1960), p. 37.

Pamela Smiley, "Gender-Linked Miscommunication in 'Hills Like White Elephants'"

Bateson, George, *Steps to an Ecology of the Mind* (New York: Ballantine, 1972).

Dieterich, Dan. "Men, Women, and the Language of Power." Madison, Wis.: Women's Studies Program Lecture, March 7, 1986.

Fletcher, Mary Dell. "Hemingway's 'Hills Like White Elephants.'" *Explicator* 38, no. 4 (19): 16–18.

Goldsmith, Andrea. "Notes on the Tyranny of Language Usage." In *The Voices of Men and Women*, ed. Cheris Kramarae (Oxford: Pergamon Press, 1980), pp. 179–91.

Haas, Adelaide. "Male and Female Spoken Language Differences." *Psychological Bulletin* 86 no. 3 (1979): 616–26.

Hemingway, Ernest. "Hills Like White Elephants." *Men Without Women* (New York: Scribner's 1927).

Irigaray, Luce. *This Sex Which Is Not One* (Ithica: Cornell University Press, 1985).

Johnston, Kenneth G. "Hills Like White Elephants: Lean, Vintage Hemingway." *Studies in American Fiction* 10, no. 2 (1982): 233–38.

———. "Hemingway and Freud: The Tip of the Iceberg." *The Journal of Narrative Technique*, 14, no. 1 (1984): 68–71.

Jones, Deborah. "Gossip: Notes on Women's Oral Culture." *The Voices and Words of Men and Women*, ed. Cheris Kramarae (Oxford: Pergamon Press, 1980), pp. 193–97.

Kennedy, Carol Wylie. "Patterns of Verbal Interruptions Among Men and Women in Groups." *Dissertation Abstracts International*, 40, no. 10 (1980): 5425.

Kramarae, Cheris. "Sex-Related Differences in Address Systems." *Anthropological Linguistics* 17 (1975): 198–210.

Key, Mary Ritchie. "Male and Female Linguistic Behavior: Review of *Words and Men* by Casey Miller and Kate Swift." *American Speech : A Quarterly of Linguistic Usage*, 55, no. 2 (1980): 124–29.

Lakoff, Robin. *Language and Woman's Place* (New York: Harper and Row, 1975).

———. "Stylistic Strategies Within a Grammar of Style." *Language, Sex, and Gender: Does La Difference Make a Difference?* ed. Judith Grasanu, Mariam K. Slater, and Lenore Loeb Adler (New York: Annals of the New York Academy of Science, 1979). Vol. 327: 53–80.

Miller, Jean Baker. *Toward a New Psychology of Women* (Boston: Beacon Press, 1976).

Neitz, Mary Jo. "Humor, Hierarchy and the Changing Status of Women." *Psychiatry* 43 (1980): 211–22.

Organ, Dennis. "Hemingway's 'Hills Like White Elephants.'" *Explicator* 37, no. 4 (1979): 11.

Presley, John. "Hawks Never Share: Women and Tragedy in Hemingway." *Hemingway Notes* (Spring 1973): 10.

Salem, Christine. "On Naming the Oppressor: What Woolf Avoids Saying in A Room of

One's Own." In *The Voices and Words of Men and Women*, ed. Cheris Kramarae (Oxford: Pergamon Press, 1980). Pp. 209–17.

Scott, Kathryn P. "The Perceptions of Communication Competence: What's Good for the Goose is not Good for the Gander." *The Voices and Words of Men and Women*, ed. Cheris Kramarae (Oxford: Pergamon Press, 1980). Pp. 199–207.

Stein, Gertrude. *Autobiography of Alice B. Toklas* (New York: Harcourt Brace, 1933).

Stone, Elizabeth. "Are You a Talking Hog, a Shouter, or a Mumbler?" *McCall's* (1986): 24ff.

Tannen, Deborah. "Why Can't He Hear What I'm Saying?" *McCall's* (1986): 20–24ff.

Jeffrey Meyers, "Hemingway's Primitivism and 'Indian Camp'"

1 *Ernest Hemingway: Selected Letters, 1917–1961*, ed. Carlos Baker (New York: Scribner's, 1981), p. 180.

2 Samuel Shaw, *Ernest Hemingway* (New York: Ungar, 1973), p. 29.

3 "Indian Camp," *The Short Stories of Ernest Hemingway* (New York: Scribner's, 1953), p. 95.

4 See Harry Levin, "Observations on the Style of Ernest Hemingway," *Kenyon Review* 13 (Autumn 1951): 606; Philip Young, *Ernest Hemingway: A Reconsideration* (1952), rev. ed. (New York, 1966), p. 32; Delmore Schwartz, "The Fiction of Ernest Hemingway," *Perspectives USA* 13 (Autumn 1955): 84; John Killinger, *Hemingway and the Dead Gods: A Study in Existentialism* (Lexington: University Press of Kentucky, 1960) (New York, 1965), p. 17; S. F. Sanderson, *Ernest Hemingway* (New York: Grove Press, 1961), p. 30; Joseph DeFalco, *The Hero in Hemingway's Short Stories* (Pittsburgh: University of Pittsburgh Press, 1963), p. 30; Alan Holder, "The Other Hemingway," *Twentieth Century Literature* 9 (Oct. 1963): 157; Julian MacLaren-Ross, review of *A Moveable Feast*, *London Magazine* 4 (August 1964), in Jeffrey Meyers, *Hemingway: The Critical Heritage* (London: Routledge, 1983), p. 490; Constance Cappel Montgomery, *Hemingway in Michigan* (New York: Fleet, 1966), pp. 63–64; Richard Bennett Hovey, *Hemingway: The Inward Terrain* (Seattle, 1968), p. 15; Nicholas Joost, *Ernest Hemingway and the Little Magazines: The Paris Years* (Barre, Mass.: Barre Publishers, 1968), p. 85; Tony Tanner, review of *By-Line: Ernest Hemingway*, *London Magazine* 8 (May 1968), in Meyers, *Hemingway: The Critical Heritage*, p. 527; Carlos Baker, *Ernest Hemingway: A Life Story* (New York: Scribner's, 1969), p. 125; Peter Hays, *The Limping Hero* (New York: New York University Press, 1971), p. 71; Arthur Waldhorn, *A Reader's Guide to Ernest Hemingway* (New York: Farrar, 1972), p. 54; Louis Rubin, review of *The Nick Adams Stories*, *Washington Sunday Star*, April 23, 1972, in Meyers, *Hemingway: The Critical Heritage*, p. 586; Norman Grebstein, *Hemingway's Craft* (Carbondale, Ill.: Southern Illinois University Press, 1973), p. 17; Samuel Shaw, *Ernest Hemingway*, p. 29; Scott Donaldson, *By Force of Will: The Life and Art of Ernest Hemingway* (New York: Viking, 1977) (New York, 1978), p. 297; Wirt Williams, *The Tragic Art of Hemingway* (1977) (Baton Rouge: Louisiana State University Press, 1981), p. 36; David Seed, "The Picture of the Whole: *In Our Time*," *Ernest Hemingway: New Critical Essays*, ed. A. Robert Lee (London: Vision, 1983), p. 21.

5 George Hemphill, "Hemingway and James," *Kenyon Review* 11 (Winter 1949): 56.

6 Thomas Tanselle, "Hemingway's 'Indian Camp,'" *Explicator* 20 (February 1962), item 53.

7 Kenneth Bernard, "Hemingway's 'Indian Camp,'" *Studies in Short Fiction* 2 (Spring 1965): 291.

8 Larry Grimes, "Night Terror and Morning Calm: A Reading of Hemingway's 'Indian Camp' as Sequel to 'Three Shots,'" *Studies in Short Fiction* 12 (1975): 414.

9 George Monteiro, "The Limits of Professionalism: A Sociological Approach to Faulkner, Fitzgerald and Hemingway," *Criticism* 15 (Spring 1973): 153–54.

10 Linda Wagner, "Juxtaposition in *In Our Time*," *Studies in Short Fiction* 12 (Summer 1975): 245.

11 Judith Fetterley, *The Resisting Reader* (Bloomington: Indiana University Press, 1979), p. 46.

12 Joseph Flora, *Hemingway's Nick Adams* (Baton Rouge: Louisiana State University Press, 1982), pp. 31, 25, 30.

13 Gerry Brenner, *Concealments in Hemingway's Works* (Columbus: Ohio State University Press, 1983), p. 239, n15.

14 Kenneth Schuyler Lynn, *Hemingway* (New York: Simon & Schuster, 1987), p. 229.

15 Philip Young, reply to Kenneth Bernard, *Studies in Short Fiction* 3 (Fall 1965), ii.

16 Quoted in Wyndham Lewis, *Rude Assignment* (London, 1950), pp. 203–4.

17 Wyndham Lewis, *Paleface* (London: Chatto & Windus, 1929), p. 202.

18 Wyndham Lewis, "The Dumb Ox," *Men without Art* (London: Cassell, 1934), p. 29.

19 Michael Bell, *Primitivism* (London: Methuen, 1972), p. 71.

20 Robert Goldwater, *Primitivism in Modern Art*, rev. ed. (New York: Vintage Books, 1966), p. 251.

21 Carol Gardner, quoted in Denis Brian, *The True Gen: An Intimate Portrait of Ernest Hemingway by Those Who Knew Him Best* (New York: Grove Press, 1987), p. 183.

22 Ernest Hemingway, "Fathers and Sons," *The Short Stories of Hemingway*, p. 497.

23 In his 1950 interview with Lillian Ross, he dropped his articles and spoke a kind of humorous Indian language. But after her malicious piece had appeared, he insisted that he had not "talked like a half-breed chocktaw" (*Letters*, p. 744). On his second African safari in 1954 Hemingway moved from primitivism to primitive. Though going native was especially frowned upon during the Mau-Mau emergency, he shaved his head, hunted with a spear, dyed his clothes the rusty Masai color, and began an elaborate courtship of his African "fiancée." His white hunter described her as "an evil-smelling bit of camp trash," but Hemingway associated her with Prudy Boulton. See Jeffrey Meyers, *Hemingway: A Biography* (New York: Harper and Row, 1985), p. 502.

24 See James Brasch and Joseph Sigman, *Hemingway's Library: A Composite Record* (New York: Garland, 1981).

25 John B. Vickery, *The Literary Impact of "The Golden Bough"* (Princeton: Princeton University Press, 1973), pp. 81, 74–75.

26 Irving Howe, *Sherwood Anderson* (Stanford, Calif.: Stanford University Press, 1951), pp. 57–58.

27 T. S. Eliot, "A Prediction in Regard to Three English Authors," *Vanity Fair* 21 (February 1924): 29.

28 Vickery, *The Literary Impact of "The Golden Bough,"* p. 149.

29 E. E. Evans-Pritchard, Preface to Franz Steiner, *Taboo* (London, 1956), p. 20.

30 James Frazer, *The Golden Bough*, 3rd ed. (London, 1911), 3:29.

31 Vickery, *The Literary Impact of "The Golden Bough,"* pp. 72–73.

32 James Frazer, "Women Tabooed at Menstruation and Childbirth," *Taboo and the Perils of the Soul*, in *The Golden Bough*, 3:138, 147, 151.

33 Lucien Lévy-Bruhl, "Taboos Relating to Confinements," *Primitives and the Supernatural*, trans. Lilian Clare (New York: Dutton, 1935), p. 331.

34 Charles Winnick, *Dictionary of Anthropology* (New York: Philosophical Library, 1956), p. 137.

35 Mary Douglas, *Purity and Danger: An Analysis of the Concepts of Pollution and Taboo* (London: Routledge, 1966), p. 1.

36 Ernest Hemingway, "On Writing," *The Nick Adams Stories* (New York: Bantam, 1972), pp. 217–18.

37 Ernest Hemingway, *A Farewell to Arms* (New York: Scribner's, 1969), p. 332.

38 The Indian's suicide provides a striking contrast to Leopold Bloom's sympathetic and humane response to Mrs. Purefoy's screaming three-day labor in "The Oxen of the Sun" chapter in *Ulysses* (New York: Random House, 1922).

39 Interchapter 7, *The Short Stories of Hemingway*, p. 143.

Robert E. Fleming, "Hemingway's 'The Killers': The Map and the Territory"

1 Cleanth Brooks and Robert Penn Warren, *Understanding Fiction* (New York: Appleton-Century-Crofts, 1943), pp. 316–25. For a minority argument—that Ole is the true protagonist—see Oliver Evans, "The Protagonist of Hemingway's 'The Killers,'" *Modern Language Notes* 73 (December 1958): 589–91.

2 Edward C. Sampson, "Hemingway's 'The Killers,'" *The Explicator* 11, no. 2 (October 1952), item 2.

3 S. I. Hayakawa, *Language in Thought and Action* (New York: Harcourt, Brace, 1949), p. 32.

4 First publication of the story was in *Scribner's Magazine* 81, no. 3 (March 1927): 227–38.

5 Box 25, File 535, Hemingway Collection, John F. Kennedy Library.

6 Box 25, File 536, Hemingway Collection.

7 Box 25, File 536a, Hemingway Collection, contains a copy of the text. The original is in the Houghton Library, Harvard University.

David R. Johnson, "'The Last Good Country': Again the End of Something"

1 "'Big World Out There': *The Nick Adams Stories*," *Novel* 6 (1972): 5–19.

2 Conversely, Stephen L. Tanner argues in "Hemingway: The Function of Nostalgia" (*Fitzgerald/Hemingway Annual 1974* [Englewood, Colo.: Microcard Edition Books, 1974], p. 167) that "It is very possible that the basis of his motivation to write and the satisfaction he got from writing was this special tendency to retain and cherish memories of past experience."

3 Ernest Hemingway, *The Nick Adams Stories* (New York: Scribner's, 1972), p. 107.

4 See, for instance, *For Whom the Bell Tolls* (New York: Scribner's 1940), pp. 158–61.

5 *Life*, December 20, 1968, pp. 32–50a.

6 *Life*, p. 50a.

7 Quoted in Philip Young, *Three Bags Full* (New York: Harcourt Brace Jovanovich, 1972), p. 27.

Howard L. Hannum, "Nick Adams and the Search for Light"

1 Matthew J. Bruccoli, "'The Light of the World': Stan Ketchel as 'My Sweet Christ,'" *Fitzgerald/Hemingway Annual* 1 (1969): 125–30; James J. Martine, "A Little Light on Hemingway's 'The Light of the World,'" *Studies in Short Fiction* 7 (Summer 1970): 465–67; James F. Barbour, "'The Light of the World': The Real Ketchel and the Real Light," *Studies in Short Fiction* 13 (Winter 1976): 17–23.

2 Bruccoli, p. 129.

3 Ernest Hemingway, *The Nick Adams Stories* (New York: Scribner's, 1972), p. 41. Further references to the stories are to the same edition, in parentheses within the text.

4 See Nat(haniel) Fleischer, *The Ring Record Book and Boxing Encyclopedia, 1982* (New York: Ring Publishing/Atheneum, 1983), and "The Michigan Assassin" *The Saga of Stanley Ketchel* (New York: C. J. O'Brien, 1946); Alva Johnson, *The Legendary Mizeners* (New York: Farrar, Straus, & Young, 1952).

5 John Lardner, "Ketchel Was a Wild Man," *Boxing Annual* (Greenwich, Connecticut: Whitestone, 1964), p. 65. Ketchel's brother is supposed to have given him the nickname "Steve" as a boy; Stanley liked the name, and it stuck.

6 Fleischer, *The Ring Record Book and Boxing Encyclopedia, 1982*, p. 764. For more than a quarter-century after Ketchel's death, his surname was a drawing card in boxing arenas. In addition to the second Steve Ketchel cited here, Dan Ketchell fought Jack Dempsey in 1916 and 1918, Billy Ketchel fought Jersey Joe Walcott (Arnold R. Cream) four times in 1936, and a Stanley Ketchel fought Joe Louis, the Brown Bomber himself, in Buffalo in 1937. The name "Ketchel (1)" then became for a long time like the names taken by generations of black boxers, "Tiger Flowers" and "Joe Walcott"; Arnold Cream was only one of a succession of fighters to use that name, adding "Jersey."

7 Carlos Baker, *Hemingway, The Writer as Artist* (Princeton, N.J.: Princeton University Press, 1952), p. 140.

8 Sheridan Baker, *Ernest Hemingway: An Introduction and Interpretation* (New York: Holt, Rinehart & Winston, 1957), p. 30.

9 Barbour, pp. 20–21.

10 Joseph M. Flora, *Hemingway's Nick Adams* (Baton Rouge: Louisiana State University Press, 1982), p. 82.

11 Curt Gowdy-Floyd Patterson, *HBO (Home Box Office) Greatest Fights*, "Middleweights," Zarate-Pintur Video Cassette. Johnson rises quickly to one knee, then waits for a count of seven before standing. As Ketchel attempts to "finish" him, Johnson hits him with a left and a right, which stiffens him, and an unnecessary second right.

12 Fleischer, *The Ring Record Book and Boxing Encyclopedia, 1982*, p. 555.

13 *New York Times*, Sunday, October 16, 1910, 1 : 1, and Monday, October 17, 1910, 7 : 3. At the farm of Colonel R. P. Dickerson, in Conway, Missouri, Walter A. Dipley (alias Hurtz), a deserter from the U.S. Navy, had a rifle trained on Ketchel before the boxer could see him. Ketchel at first thought it was a joke; Dipley, knowing Ketchel always carried a pistol, grew nervous and shot him in "self-defense." Dickerson hired a special train to carry Ketchel to Springfield for medical treatment, but he died shortly after arrival.

14 Martine, pp. 465–66; Peter Thomas, "A Lost Leader: Hemingway's 'The Light of the World,'" *Humanities Association Bulletin* (Bulletin de L'Association canadienne des Humanities) 21 (Fall 1970): 14–19; Flora, pp. 70–78.

15 Carlos Baker saw Hemingway's story as comic, a view which subsequent readings have shared. In this reading the comedy seems a lesser element.

16 Gregory Green, "A Matter of Color: Hemingway's Criticism of Race Prejudice," *Hemingway Review* 1 (Fall 1981): 27–28.

17 George Plimpton, *Shadowbox* (New York: Berkley Medallion, 1977), p. 35.

18 Bruccoli, pp. 125–29.

19 Thomas, p. 17.

20 Thomas and Barbour.

21 Guy deMaupassant, *Short Stories of the Tragedy and Comedy of Life* (New York: W. Walter Dunne, 1903), 1: 140–41.

22 Bruccoli qualifies his introduction of the influence of Ketchel "as Christ"; so does Barbour, but Thomas, Sheridan Baker, and Flora seem to regard the Christian analogy as Hemingway's major intention in writing the story.

23 William B. Stein, "Love and Lust in Hemingway's Short Stories," *Texas Studies in Literature and Language* 3 (1961): 234–36.

24 Ernest Hemingway, "The Art of the Short Story," *Paris Review* 23 (Spring 1981): 92.

25 Reynolds, "Holman Hunt and 'The Light of the World,'" *Studies in Short Fiction* 20 (Winter 1983): 317–19.

26 Sheridan Baker, p. 30.

27 Martine, pp. 465–66.

28 Flora, pp. 71–72, offers this suggestion, but sees Nick playing a cowboy in a saloon in the American West.

29 Jack London, *The Road* (Santa Barbara, Calif.: Peregrine Smith, 1978), pp. 133–36.

30 Carlos Baker, *The Writer as Artist*, p. 140.

31 Barbara Maloy, "The Light of Alice's World," *Linguistics in Literature* 1 (Spring 1976): 74–86.

Larry Edgerton, "'Nobody Ever Dies!': Hemingway's *Fifth* Story of the Spanish Civil War"

1 "Nobody Ever Dies!" in *Cosmopolitan*, March 1939, pp. 28–31, 74–76; reprinted in *Cosmopolitan*, April 1959, pp. 78–83; trans. Gunnar Larsen into Norwegian, "Ingen dør forgjeves," *Vinduet* 6, no. 1 (1952): 63–71; trans. Pop Simion into Romanian, "Educaţia Revoluţionariă," *Secolul* 20, no. 2 (July 1962): 55–66.

2 Ernest Hemingway, *The Fifth Column and Four Stories of the Spanish Civil War* (New York: Scribner's, 1969). The stories are "The Denunciation," *Esquire*, November 1938; "The Butterfly and the Tank," *Esquire*, December 1938; "Night Before Battle," *Esquire*, February 1939; and "Under the Ridge," *Cosmopolitan*, October 1939. They have been treated most completely by Martin Light, "Of Wasteful Deaths: Hemingway's Stories About the Spanish Civil War," *Western Humanities Review* 23 (1969): 29–42; and Julian Smith, "Christ Times Four: Hemingway's Unknown Spanish Civil War Stories," *Arizona Quarterly* 25 (1969): 5–17.

3 Carlos Baker, *Ernest Hemingway: A Life Story* (New York: Scribner's, 1969), p. 338.

4 "Get a Seeing-Eye Dog," *The Atlantic Monthly*, November 1957, pp. 66–68, and "A Man of the World," *Atlantic Monthly*, November 1957, pp. 64–66.

5 "A Divine Gesture," *The Double Dealer* 3 (1922): 267–68; "The Faithful Bull," *Holiday*, March 1951, p. 51; and "The Good Lion," *Holiday*, March 1951, pp. 50–51.

6 Baker, p. 338.

William Adair, "Hemingway's 'Out of Season': The End of the Line"

1 *A Moveable Feast* (New York: Scribner's, 1964), p. 75. Further references will be to this edition and will be included in the text.

2 See Paul Smith's "Some Misconceptions of 'Out of Season,'" in *Critical Essays on Hemingway's 'In Our Time,'* ed. Michael S. Reynolds (Boston: Hall, 1983), pp. 235–51.

3 *Ernest Hemingway: Selected Letters, 1917–1961*, ed. Carlos Baker (New York: Scribner's, 1981), pp. 180–81.

4 *Selected Letters*, p. 79.

5 George Kearns, *Guide to Ezra Pound's 'Selected Cantos'* (New Brunswick, N.J.: Rutgers University Press, 1980), p. 75.

6 Kenneth G. Johnston's "Hemingway's 'Out of Season' and the Psychology of Errors" argues that the couple is quarreling over an abortion; this essay is collected in *Critical Essays on Hemingway's 'In Our Time'* (cited above), pp. 227–34; Smith's article provides a convincing reply. My suggestion is that the story is "about" Peduzzi, as Hemingway said in his letter to Fitzgerald; the topic of the couple's quarrel—perhaps it is about the young man's extended trips as a news correspondent, if he is one (Hemingway and wife quarreled on this subject some four months previous to the trip to Cortina, where "Out of Season" was written)—seems of no importance.

7 The background information in this paragraph, and the next four paragraphs, comes from Carlos Baker's *Ernest Hemingway: A Life Story* (New York: Scribner's, 1981), pp. 105–9.

8 Cézanne's "The House of the Hanged Man," which is simply a picture of a house by a road, was at the Louvre during the 1920s; it may have been an influence on "Out of Season."

9 The function of the statue of the soldier (assuming there is one) on the war memorial has always seemed to me comparable to the function of Michael Furey in James Joyce's "The Dead": a reminder in the wasteland of all the dead heroes, to be contrasted with the prone husband of "Cat in the Rain."

10 *Selected Letters*, p. 180.

11 Frederic and Catherine at Stresa and Col. Cantwell in Venice are staying at "out of season" hotels.

12 Hemingway refers to Malatesta twice in *Selected Letters*, pp. 375, 654: first in a 1932 letter, where he says that Malatesta's name in twenty years will sound more honest than Stalin's; second in a 1948 letter, where he recalls his walking trip with Pound.

13 This definition, and the ones two paragraphs below, come from *The Cambridge Italian Dictionary* (New York: Cambridge Press, 1962).

14 In the article cited in note 2 above, Paul Smith suggests (p. 239) that there must have been at least three stages in the story's composition: (1) the original typed version, along with its typed revisions; (2) the later penciled revisions, made on the original typescript; and (3) final revisions incorporated in the setting copy for publication.

In the original version "mysteriously" has been typed in as an interlinear addition. But the "mysterious" of the second paragraph does not appear in the story until the final version for publication.

In the original version "piombo" appears eight times. With the penciled revisions we find that the word has been added twice: in the sentences "We must have piombo" and "Your stuff is all clean and new but you haven't [*sic*] any piombo." In the final, for-publication version this second sentence replaces "piombo" with "lead": "Your stuff is all clean and new but you have no lead." Obviously, Hemingway is using these words with great care, which may suggest that they are intended to imply something below the story's surface.

See Hemingway's typescript (EH/ts. 644) and carbon for setting copy (EH/ts. 203) in the Kennedy Library's Hemingway collection.

15 If "Cat in the Rain" and "Out of Season" are really "twin" stories, then it may be worth noticing that at the end of the first one the big cat brought up to the room by the maid (sent by the hotel owner who is "in" both stories) is in a sense "hanging": the cat "pressed tight against her and swung down against her body." The drop on the scaffolding from which Sam Cardinelli is to be hung "swung" on ball bearings. Again it's a matter of words.

Robert E. Fleming, "Perversion and the Writer in 'The Sea Change'"

1 Carlos Baker, *Ernest Hemingway: A Life Story* (New York: Scribner's, 1969), p. 227.
2 Philip Young, *Ernest Hemingway: A Reconsideration* (New York: Harcourt, Brace & World, 1966), pp. 178–79.
3 Nathaniel Hawthorne, *The American Notebooks*, ed. Randall Stewart (New Haven, Conn.: Yale University Press, 1932), p. 106.
4 Alexander Pope, *An Essay on Man* in *The Poems of Alexander Pope*, ed. Maynard Mack (New Haven, Conn.: Yale University Press, 1964), 3:81-82.
5 Joseph DeFalco, *The Hero in Hemingway's Short Stories* (Pittsburgh: University of Pittsburgh Press, 1963), p. 177.
6 Ernest Hemingway, *The Short Stories of Ernest Hemingway* (New York: Scribner's, 1966), p. 400. Future references to "The Sea Change" are from this text and appear in parentheses.
7 DeFalco, p. 176.
8 J. F. Kobler, "Hemingway's 'The Sea Change': A Sympathetic View of Homosexuality," *Arizona Quarterly* 26 (1970): 322.
9 Sheldon Norman Grebstein, *Hemingway's Craft* (Carbondale: Southern Illinois University Press, 1973), p. 114.
10 Box 28, Item 681, Hemingway Collection, John F. Kennedy Library. This manuscript is catalogued as Item 80 D, under the title "What do the punks drink, James?" in Philip Young and Charles Mann, *The Hemingway Manuscripts: An Inventory* (University Park: Pennsylvania State University Press, 1969), p. 52.
11 William Shakespeare, *The Tempest* I, ii, 396–401. *The Complete Plays and Poems of William Shakespeare*, ed. William Allan Neilson and Charles Jarvis Hill (Boston: Houghton Mifflin, 1942), p. 546.
12 Ernest Hemingway, *The Sun Also Rises* (New York: Scribner's, 1970), p. 20.
13 George Plimpton, "An Interview with Ernest Hemingway," in *Hemingway and His Critics*, ed. Carlos Baker (New York: Hill and Wang, 1961), p. 34. The interview first appeared in *Paris Review* 5, no. 18 (1958): 60–89. On Hemingway's application of the iceberg principle, see Julian Smith, "Hemingway and the Thing Left Out," *Journal of Modern Literature* 1 (1970): 169–82.
14 Ernest Hemingway, "The Art of the Short Story," *Paris Review* 23, no. 79 (Spring 1981): 88.

15 Morley Callaghan, *That Summer in Paris* (Toronto: Macmillan, 1963), p. 30.

16 *The Sun Also Rises*, p. 178.

17 Ernest Hemingway, *To Have and Have Not* (New York: Scribner's, 1937), p. 186.

Alice Hall Petry, "Coming of Age in Hortons Bay: Hemingway's 'Up in Michigan'"

1 See Arthur Waldhorn, *A Reader's Guide to Ernest Hemingway* (New York: Farrar, Straus and Giroux, 1972), pp. 43–44, and Charles A. Fenton, *The Apprenticeship of Ernest Hemingway: The Early Years* (New York: Farrar, Straus & Young, 1954), pp. 152–54. It should be noted, however, that even in this early work Hemingway was no slavish imitator of either writer. Philip Young remarks that "Up in Michigan" is "too hardheaded" for Anderson and "cut off by its subject matter" from Stein (*Ernest Hemingway* [New York: Rinehart, 1952], p. 150). In fact, Stein contended that the tale was *inaccrochable*, which Young explains as "an invented and rather difficult term no one seems to want to translate. Literally, 'unhookable—or, since *accrocher* can mean among things 'to pawn,' 'unhockable'? Probably not; perhaps she meant that because of the sex you couldn't hook it up with an editor; hence, in effect, 'unprintable'" (*Ernest Hemingway: A Reconsideration* [University Park: Pennsylvania State University Press, 1966], p. 180n). In fact, Hemingway did encounter difficulty in attempting to publish "Up in Michigan." Neither Edmund Wilson nor Maxwell Perkins cared for the story, and publisher Horace Liveright declined to include it in *In Our Time* (Carlos Baker, *Ernest Hemingway: A Life Story* [New York: Bantam, 1970], pp. 174, 234, 423). It initially was privately printed in *Three Stories and Ten Poems* (1923) in a limited edition of 300 copies; it first became available to the general public in *The Fifth Column and the First Forty-nine Stories* (New York: Scribner's, 1938).

2 For information on the background and prototypes of "Up in Michigan," see Constance Cappel Montgomery, *Hemingway in Michigan* (New York: Fleet, 1966), pp. 119–27.

3 Fenton, pp. 152–54.

4 Sheldon Norman Grebstein, *Hemingway's Craft* (Carbondale and Edwardsville: Southern Illinois University Press, 1973), p. 80.

5 Young argues that the title is a "sardonic allusion" to "a popular song of the period which praised the bucolic virtues of life in that region" (*Ernest Hemingway*, p. 236, n. 5). This seems doubtful, especially in view of Hemingway's blatant use of sexual diction and symbols in this story. My belief that the title is an obscenity has been anticipated by Joseph M. Flora in "Hemingway's 'Up in Michigan,'" *Studies in Short Fiction* 6 (Summer 1969), pp. 465–66.

6 Carlos Baker, *Hemingway: The Writer as Artist* (Princeton, N.J.: Princeton University Press, 1963), p. 135.

7 I disagree with the contention of Robert W. Lewis, Jr., that Liz's "thoughts on love are only heightened by the act of sex" (*Hemingway on Love* [Austin: University of Texas Press, 1965], p. 4). Liz clearly is confused throughout the seduction, and "everything felt gone" when Jim was finished.

8 Baker, *Life*, p. 423.

Lawrence H. Martin, Jr., "Crazy in Sheridan: Hemingway's 'Wine of Wyoming' Reconsidered"

1 The May 31, 1930, Hemingway-Perkins letter is obviously about "Wine of Wyoming." There is a possibility—the dates are plausible—that the story may be the one referred to in an October 11, 1928, letter to Perkins as "3/4 done." JFK Library catalog lists item 837, a "typescript/manuscript," differing from other "sparsely corrected" typescripts of the story.

2 The dialogue is about half French and half English, sometimes each language alone and sometimes mixed. In the story the narrator notes of Mme. Fontan, "She spoke French, but it was only French occasionally, and there were many English words and some English constructions" (*SS*, p. 451). Hemingway knew French reasonably well, but his knowledge was colloquial, not literary. Doubting his own accuracy, Hemingway prevailed on Lewis Galantière in New York in June 1930 to check the galleys for idiom and accent. Galantière had helped Marguerite Gay translate Sherwood Anderson's books into French. In 1921 Anderson had written letters introducing Hemingway to Galantière (then in France), Gertrude Stein, Sylvia Beach, and others. See Baker, *Life Story*, pp. 270, 109–10.

3 The $600 fee for "Wine of Wyoming" was a considerable amount of money in 1930, but it was only a fraction of the $2700 Hemingway received from *Cosmopolitan* for the May 1932 publication of "After The Storm," which became the opening story in *Winner Take Nothing*. In a March 26, 1932, letter to John Dos Passos, Hemingway gleefully reports that he had "sold the After The Storm story for plenty" (*Letters*, p. 355).

4 At this time Hemingway was developing the notion that critics got their opinions from each other and that they formed a clique, particularly in New York. In *Green Hills of Africa* (p. 23) he advises writers to avoid reading critics, whose opinions might inflate the writer's self-image or make him lose confidence in good work, all without just cause. Nonetheless, Hemingway assiduously followed reviews of his own books.

5 For a provocative thesis about Hemingway's creating and cultivating a personal reputation and mystique, see John Raeburn, *Fame Became of Him: Hemingway as Public Writer* (Bloomington: Indiana University Press, 1984).

6 On October 18, 1924, Hemingway wrote from Paris to thank Wilson for the favorable review. In it he briefly explains the content and technique of *In Our Time*, which he was trying to sell in the United States. Hemingway gruffly flatters Wilson for his intelligence and authority (he had been wise enough to recognize Hemingway) and for his writing style (*Letters*, pp. 128–29). Later, critics who gave Hemingway unfavorable reviews were "dumb" and worse.

7 Hemingway's enthusiasm for the West emerged as an article, "The Clark's Fork Valley, Wyoming," in *Vogue* 93 (February 1939): 68, 157.

8 The 1928 Democratic party platform included a weak, pro forma endorsement of Prohibition, but both the party and its candidate were assumed to favor repeal.

9 It is an interesting measure of the story's obscurity or lack of appeal even to Hemingway specialists that Johnston's article, "Hemingway's 'Wine of Wyoming': Disappointment in America," *Western American Literature* 9 (1973): 159–67, is the only published essay on the subject. Johnston explains the political and social issues of the day, and he makes a convincing case that "Wine of Wyoming" is a strongly political statement about—as

Hemingway said in *To Have and Have Not* (1937)—"the American dream when it becomes a nightmare." Johnston concentrates on social and political questions; he does not consider the story in the context of Hemingway's aesthetics or broader philosophical themes.

The story's point of view and narrator are discussed by Sheldon Norman Grebstein, *Hemingway's Craft*, pp. 63–67. Grebstein focuses on ways in which the narrator resembles, and differs from, the Fontans, and he emphasizes the way that the narrator's identity contributes to the story's criticism of American cultural values.

Joseph M. Flora, in *Hemingway's Nick Adams*, pp. 223–35 gives essay-length treatment to "Wine of Wyoming," especially the story's progress—or descent—from comedy to irony.

10 Flora says that young André "entertain[s]" the narrator and "creates an aura of a normal family life" (p. 227). But there is an edge to the son's cleverness about cheating on the price of the movies and his badgering about the use of a rifle. He does read books ("a library book—*Frank on a Gunboat*"), but he seems to illustrate conduct less lovable than ordinary adolescent rambunctiousness.

Aiken, Conrad. "Expatriates." *New York Herald Tribune* (October 31, 1926): VII, 4.

Baker, Carlos, ed. *Ernest Hemingway: Selected Letters, 1917–1961* (New York: Scribner's, 1981).

———. *Ernest Hemingway: A Life Story* (New York: Scribner's, 1969).

———. *Hemingway: The Writer as Artist*. 3rd ed. (Princeton: Princeton University Press, 1963).

Butcher, Fanny. "Short Stories Still Live As Works of Art." *Chicago Daily Tribune* (October 28, 1933): 16.

Canby, Henry Seidel. "Farewell to the Nineties." *Saturday Review of Literature* 10 (October 28, 1933): 217.

Dodd, L. W. "Simple Annals of the Callous." *Saturday Review of Literature* 4 (November 19, 1927): 322–33.

Fadiman, Clifton. "A Letter to Mr. Hemingway." *New Yorker* 9 (October 28, 1933): 74–75.

Flora, Joseph M. *Hemingway's Nick Adams* (Baton Rouge: Louisiana State University Press, 1982).

Grebstein, Sheldon Norman. *Hemingway's Craft*. (Carbondale, Ill.: Southern Illinois University Press, 1973).

Gregory, Horace. "Ernest Hemingway Has Put On Maturity." *New York Herald Tribune* (October 29, 1933): VII, 5.

Griffin, Peter. *Along With Youth: Hemingway, The Early Years* (New York and Oxford: Oxford University Press, 1985).

Hanneman, Audre. *Ernest Hemingway: A Comprehensive Bibliography* (Princeton, N.J.: Princeton University Press, 1967).

———. *Supplement to Ernest Hemingway: A Comprehensive Bibliography* (Princeton, N.J.: Princeton University Press, 1975).

Hemingway, Ernest. *The Short Stories of Ernest Hemingway* (New York: Scribner's, 1938).

———. *Green Hills of Africa* (New York: Scribner's, 1935).

———. *A Farewell To Arms* (New York: Scribner's, 1929).

"Hemingway's First Book of Fiction in Four Years." *Kansas City Star*, November 4, 1933.

"Hemingway's Tales." *Springfield Republican* (November 26, 1933): 7E.

Herrick, Robert. "What Is Dirt?" *Bookman* 70 (November 1929): 258–62.

Johnston, Kenneth G. "Hemingway's 'Wine of Wyoming': Disappointment in America." *Western American Literature* 9 (1973): 159–67.

J. R. "Hemingway's Gamy Dishes." *Cincinnati Enquirer* (November 4, 1933): 7.

Kronenberger, Louis. "Hemingway's New Stories." *New York Times Book Review* (November 5, 1933): 6.

"Marital Tragedy." *New York Times Book Review* (October 31, 1926): 27.

Mencken, H. L. "Fiction By Adept Hands." *American Mercury* 19 (January 1930): 127.

"Mr. Hemingway's Stories of Life In The Raw." *Springfield Republican* (November 20, 1927): 7F.

Raeburn, John. *Fame Became of Him: Hemingway As Public Writer* (Bloomington: Indiana University Press, 1984).

Rosenfeld, Paul. "Tough Earth." *New Republic* 45 (November 1925): 22–23.

"Study in Futility." *Cincinnati Enquirer* (October 30, 1925): 5.

Tate, Allen. "Hard-Boiled." *Nation* 123 (December 15, 1926): 642.

Troy, William. "Mr. Hemingway's Opium." *Nation* 137 (November 15, 1933): 570.

Wagner, Linda Welshimer. *Ernest Hemingway: A Reference Guide* (Boston: Hall, 1977).

Wilson, Edmund. "Mr. Hemingway's Dry-Points." *Dial* 77 (October 1924): 340–41.

———. "The Sportsman's Tragedy." *New Republic* 53 (December 14, 1927): 102–3.

Paul Smith, "A Partial Review: Critical Essays on the Short Stories, 1976–1989"

Adair, William. "Landscapes of the Mind: 'Big Two-Hearted River.'" *College Literature* 4 (1977): 144–51.

Beck, Warren. "The Shorter Happy Life of Mrs. Macomber." *Modern Fiction Studies* 21 (November 1955): 28–37.

———. "Then and Now—Hemingway." *Modern Fiction Studies* 21 (Autumn 1975): 377–85.

Beegel, Susan. *Hemingway's Craft of Omission: Four Manuscript Examples* (Ann Arbor: University of Michigan Research Press, 1988).

———, ed. *Hemingway's Neglected Short Fiction: New Perspectives.* (Ann Arbor: University of Michigan Research Press, 1989). Includes:

Gerry Brenner, "A Semiotic Inquiry into Hemingway's 'A Simple Enquiry.'"

Robert E. Gajdusek, "'An Alpine Idyll': The Sun-Struck Mountain Vision and the Necessary Valley Journey."

Bruce Henricksen, "The Bullfight Story and Critical Theory."

Allen Josephs, "Hemingway's Spanish Civil War Stories, or the Spanish Civil War as Reality."

Michael Reynolds, "'Homage to Switzerland': Einstein's Train Stops at Hemingway's Station."

Phillip Sipiora, "Ethical Narration in 'My Old Man.'"

H. R. Stoneback, "'Mais Je Reste Catholique,' Communion, Betrayal, and Aridity in 'Wine of Wyoming.'"

Bickford Sylvester, "Hemingway's Italian *Waste Land*: The Complex Unity of 'Out of Season.'"

Bender, Bert. "Margot Macomber's Gimlet." *College Literature* 8 (1981): 12–20.

Benert, Annette. "Survival Through Irony: Hemingway's 'A Clean, Well-Lighted Place.'" *Studies in Short Fiction* 11 (1974): 181–87.

Bennett, Warren. "The Manuscript and the Dialogue of 'A Clean, Well-Lighted Place.'" *American Literature* 50 (1979): 613–24.

———. "The Characterization and the Problematic Dialogue in Hemingway's 'A Clean, Well-Lighted Place.'" *Hemingway Review* 9 (Spring 1990): 94–123.

Brenner, Gerry. *Concealments in Hemingway's Works* (Columbus: Ohio State University Press, 1983).

Carabine, Keith. "'Big Two-Hearted River': A Reinterpretation." *Hemingway Review* 1 (Spring 1982): 39–44.

Cass, Colin S. "The Look of Hemingway's 'In Another Country.'" *Studies in Short Fiction* 18 (1981): 309–13.

Cowley, Malcolm. Introduction. *The Portable Hemingway* (New York: Viking Press, 1945).

DeFalco, Joseph. *The Hero in Hemingway's Short Stories.* 1963 (Richard West, 1983).

Donaldson, Scott. "The Wooing of Ernest Hemingway." *American Literature* 53 (January 1982): 691–710.

Fetterley, Judith. *The Resisting Reader: A Feminist Approach to American Fiction* (Bloomington: Indiana University Press, 1978).

Flora, Joseph M. *Hemingway's Nick Adams* (Baton Rouge: Louisiana State University Press, 1982).

———. *Ernest Hemingway: A Study of the Short Fiction* (Boston: Twayne, 1989).

Gertzman, Jay A. "Hemingway's Writer-Narrator in 'The Denunciation.'" *Research Studies* 47 (December 1979) 244–52.

Gibb, Robert. "He Made Him Up: 'Big Two-Hearted River' as Doppelganger." *Hemingway Notes* 5 (Fall 1979): 20–24.

Griffin, Peter. *Along With Youth: Hemingway, The Early Years* (New York: Oxford University Press, 1985).

Hagemann, Meyly Chin. "Hemingway's Secret: From Visual to Verbal Art." *Journal of Modern Literature* 7 (February 1979): 87–112.

Hannum, Howard L. "Soldier's Home: Immersion Therapy and Lyric Pattern in 'Big Two-Hearted River.'" *Hemingway Review* 3 (Spring 1984): 2–13.

Harkey, Joseph H. "The Africans and Francis Macomber." *Studies in Short Fiction* 17 (Summer 1980): 345–48.

Hollander, John. "Hemingway's Extraordinary Reality." *Modern Critical Views: Ernest Hemingway.* Ed. Harold Bloom (New York: Chelsea Press, 1985).

Hutton, Virgil. "The Short Happy Life of Francis Macomber." *University Review* (Kansas City) 30 (Summer 1964): 253–63.

Jackson, Paul R. "Hemingway's 'Out of Season.'" *Hemingway Review* 1 (Fall 1981): 11–17.

———. "Point of View, Distancing, and Hemingway's 'Short Happy Life.'" *Hemingway Notes* 2 (Spring 1980): 2–16.

Johnston, Kenneth G. *The Tip of the Iceberg: Hemingway and the Short Story* (Greenwood, Fla.: Penkevill, 1987).

Kann, Hans-Joachim. "Perpetual Confusion in 'A Clean, Well-Lighted Place': The Manuscript Evidence." *Fitzgerald/Hemingway Annual* (1977): 115–18.

Kerner, David. "Counterfeit Hemingway: A Small Scandal in Quotation Marks." *Journal of Modern Literature* 12 (November 1985): 91–108.

———. "The Foundation of the True Text of 'A Clean, Well-Lighted Place.'" *Fitzgerald/Hemingway Annual* (1979): 279–300.

———. "The Thomson Alternative." *Hemingway Review* 4 (Fall 1984): 37–39.

Kvam, Wayne. "Hemingway's 'Under the Ridge.'" *Fitzgerald/Hemingway Annual* (1979): 225–40.

Kyle, Frank B. "Parallel and Complementary Themes in Hemingway's 'Big Two-Hearted River' and 'The Battler.'" *Studies in Short Fiction* 16 (1979): 295–300.

Lewis, Robert W., Jr., and Max Westbrook. "'The Snows of Kilimanjaro' Collated and Annotated." *Texas Quarterly* 13 (Summer 1970): 64–143.

Light, Martin. "Of Wasteful Deaths: Hemingway's Stories about the Spanish Civil War." *Western Humanities Review* 23 (Winter 1969): 29–42.

Lodge, David. "Analysis and Interpretation of the Realist Text: A Pluralistic Approach to Ernest Hemingway's 'Cat in the Rain.'" *Poetics Today* 1 (1980): 5–19.

Lounsberry, Barbara. "The Education of Robert Wilson." *Hemingway Notes* 2 (Spring 1980): 29–32.

Lynn, Kenneth S. *Hemingway* (New York: Simon & Schuster, 1987).

McKenna, John J., and Marvin V. Peterson. "More Muddy Water: Wilson's Shakespeare in 'The Short Happy Life of Francis Macomber.'" *Studies in Short Fiction* 18 (Winter 1981): 82–85.

Meyers, Jeffrey. *Hemingway: A Biography*. New York: Harper, 1985.

Monteiro, George. "Hemingway on Dialogue in 'A Clean, Well-Lighted Place.'" *Fitzgerald/ Hemingway Annual* (1974): 243.

Nagel, James, ed. *Ernest Hemingway: The Writer in Context* (Madison: University of Wisconsin Press, 1984). Includes:

Paul Smith, "The Tenth Indian and the Thing Left Out."

Max Westbrook, "Grace under Pressure: Hemingway and the Summer of 1920."

Parker, Hershel. *Flawed Texts and Verbal Icons* (Evanston, Ill.: Northwestern University Press, 1984).

Phelan, James. *Reading People, Reading Plots* (Chicago: University of Chicago Press, 1989).

Reynolds, Michael S., ed. *Critical Essays on Ernest Hemingway's In Our Time* (Boston: Hall, 1983). Includes:

Kathryn Zabelle Derounian, "An Examination of the Drafts of Hemingway's Chapters "Nick sat against the wall of the church. . . .'"

E. R. Hagemann, "A Collation, with Commentary, of the Five Texts of the Chapters in Hemingway's *In Our Time*."

———. "'Only Let the Story End as Soon as Possible': Time and History in Hemingway's *In Our Time*."

Nicholas Gerogiannis, "Nick Adams on the Road: 'The Battler' as Hemingway's Man on the Hill."

Michael Reynolds, "Introduction: Looking Backward."

Paul Smith, "Some Misconceptions of 'Out of Season.'"

———. *Hemingway: The Paris Years* (Oxford: Basil Blackwell, 1989).

———. *The Young Hemingway* (Oxford: Basil Blackwell, 1986).

Scholes, Robert. *Semiotics and Interpretation* (New Haven, Conn.: Yale University Press, 1982).

———. *Textual Power: Literary Theory and the Teaching of English* (New Haven, Conn.: Yale University Press, 1985).

Smith, Julian. "Christ Times Four: Hemingway's Unknown Spanish Civil War Stories." *Arizona Quarterly* 25 (Spring 1969): 5–17.

Smith, Paul. "Hemingway's Early Manuscripts: The Theory and Practice of Omission." *Journal of Modern Literature* 10 (July 1983): 268–88.

———. *A Reader's Guide to the Short Stories of Ernest Hemingway* (Boston: Hall, 1989).

Spilka, Mark. "The Necessary Stylist: A New Critical Revision." *Modern Fiction Studies* 6 (Winter 1960–61): 289–96.

———. "A Source for the Macomber 'Accident': Marryat's *Percival Keene*." *Hemingway Review* 3 (Spring 1984): 29–37.

———. "Warren Beck Revisited." *Modern Fiction Studies* 22 (Summer 1976): 245–69.

Stephens, Robert O. "Macomber and the Somali Proverb: The Matrix of Knowledge." *Fitzgerald/Hemingway Annual* (1977): 137–47.

Thomson, George H. "'A Clean, Well-Lighted Place': Interpreting the Original Text." *Hemingway Review* 2 (Spring 1983): 32–43.

Wagner, Linda W., ed. *Ernest Hemingway: Six Decades of Criticism* (East Lansing: Michigan State University Press, 1987). Includes:
Bernard Oldsey, "Hemingway's Beginnings and Endings."

———. "The Marinating of *For Whom the Bell Tolls.*" *Journal of Modern Literature* 2 (November 1972): 533–46.

White, William. "'Macomber' Bibliography." *Hemingway Notes* 5 (Spring 1980): 35–38.

Williams, Wirt. *The Tragic Art of Ernest Hemingway* (Baton Rouge: Louisiana State University Press, 1981).

Witherington, Paul. "Word and Flesh in Hemingway's 'On the Quai at Smyrna.'" *Notes on Modern American Literature* 2 (1978): Item 18.

Young, Philip. *Ernest Hemingway: A Reconsideration.* 1952 (New York: Harcourt, 1966).

About the Contributors

●

William Adair is an Instructor at San Joaquin Delta College, Stockton, California, and the author of a number of essays on Hemingway including *"A Farewell to Arms:* A Dream Book" and "Landscapes of the Mind: 'Big Two-Hearted River,'" both reprinted in critical collections.

Nina Baym is LAS Jubilee Professor of English at the University of Illinois. Among her publications are *Women's Fiction: A Guide to Novels by and About Women in America, 1820–1870* and *Novels, Readers, and Reviewers: Responses to Fiction in Antebellum America.*

Susan F. Beegel is an independent scholar living on Nantucket. She is the author of *Hemingway's Craft of Omission: Four Manuscript Examples,* and the editor of *Hemingway's Neglected Short Fiction: New Perspectives.*

Warren Bennett is professor of English at the University of Regina in Regina, Canada. Among Hemingway scholars Bennett is best known for his work on "A Clean, Well-Lighted Place"; his most recent article is "'That's not very polite': Sexual Identity in Hemingway's 'The Sea Change,'" which appeared in Susan Beegel's collection of essays on Hemingway's neglected stories.

Gerry Brenner is Professor of English at the University of Montana and the author of *Concealments in Hemingway's Works.* He co-authored (with Earl Rovit) the revised edition of *Ernest Hemingway,* and he is in addition the author of many essays on Hemingway's work.

Scott Donaldson, Louis G. T. Cooley Professor of English at the College of William and Mary, is the author of biographies of Winfield Townley Scott, Ernest Hemingway, F. Scott Fitzgerald, and John Cheever.

Larry Edgerton is Senior Writing Instructor in a minorities program at the University of Wisconsin—Madison; he has published fiction, poetry, and critical articles on Dickens, Milton, twentieth-century literature, and composition theory.

Robert E. Fleming is Professor of English at the University of New Mexico. His articles on Hemingway have appeared in *American Literature, Arizona Quarterly, Hemingway Review, Journal of Modern Literature, North Dakota Quarterly,* and *Studies in American Fiction.*

E. R. Hagemann, a retired Professor of English and Humanities, has published articles on Hemingway, Fitzgerald, James, and Crane, among others. He resides in Louisville, Kentucky, and is working on a Hemingway project.

Howard L. Hannum is Associate Professor of English at La Salle University and the author of several articles on Hemingway's work, including "Soldier's Home: Immersion Therapy and Lyric Pattern in 'Big Two-Hearted River'" and "The Case of Dr. Henry Adams."

Steven K. Hoffman taught English at Virginia Polytechnic Institute and State University and is now a lawyer in Washington, D.C. He is the author of several articles on modern American fiction and poetry.

Oddvar Holmesland is Associate Professor of English Literature at the University of Trondheim, Norway. He is the author of *A Critical Introduction to Henry Green's Novels: The Living Vision* and "Freedom and Community in Joyce Cary's Fiction: A Study of *The Horse's Mouth.*"

David R. Johnson is Associate Professor of English at Lafayette College. He is the author of articles on American literature and culture and is currently completing a biography of American novelist Conrad Richter.

Kenneth G. Johnston is Professor of English at Kansas State University and the author of *The Tip of the Iceberg: Hemingway and the Short Story;* "Hemingway's 'Night Before Battle': Don Quixote, 1937"; and "'The Butterfly and the Tank': Casualties of War."

Wayne Kvam is Professor of English at Kent State University and is the author of *Hemingway in Germany* and "Hemingway's 'Under the Ridge.'"

Robert W. Lewis is Professor of English at the University of North Dakota and Editor of *North Dakota Quarterly*. He is the author of *Hemingway on Love* and edited *Hemingway in Italy and Other Essays*.

Kenneth Lynn is Arthur O. Lovejoy Professor of History Emeritus at Johns Hopkins University. His books on American writers include *Mark Twain and Southwestern Humor; William Dean Howells: An American Life;* and *Hemingway*.

Richard McCann, co-director of the MFA program in creative writing at American University, has published fiction and poetry in such periodicals as *The Atlantic* and *Esquire* and a book of poems, *Dream of the Traveler*.

Lawrence H. Martin, Jr., is Professor of English at Hampden-Sydney College, Virginia, and the author of "Stories That Can't Be Hung: Miss Stein's Use of '*Inaccrochable*'"; "The Tenses of Nature in 'Big Two-Hearted River'"; and "Odd Exception or Mainstream Tradition: 'The Shot' in Context."

Jeffrey Meyers is Professor of English at the University of Colorado and is the editor and author of many books, including *Hemingway: The Critical Heritage* and *Hemingway: A Biography*.

Debra A. Moddelmog is Assistant Professor of English at Ohio State University. She is the author of "Narrative Irony and Hidden Motivations in Katherine Anne Porter's 'He'" and "The Oedipus Myth and the Reader Response in Thomas Pynchon's *The Crying of Lot 49*."

George Monteiro is Professor of English at Brown University. He is the author of *Robert Frost and the New England Renaissance* and *Double Weaver's Knot: Poems*, and the translator of *Self-Analysis and Thirty Other Poems* by Fernando Pessoa.

Bernard Oldsey is Professor of English at West Chester University and the editor of *College Literature*. Among the books he has published are *Ernest Hemingway: The Papers of a Writer; Hemingway's Hidden Craft;* and *The Art of William Golding*.

Alice Hall Petry is Associate Professor of English at the Rhode Island School of Design, Providence. Her books include *A Genius in His Way: The Art of Cable's Old Creole Days; Fitzgerald's Craft of Short Fiction;* and *Understanding Anne Tyler*.

Robert Scholes is Professor of English and Comparative Literature at Brown University. He is the author of many influential books, including *Textual Power: Literary Theory and the Teaching of English* and *Protocols of Reading*.

Pamela Smiley teaches at the University of Wisconsin—Madison and is currently working on an analysis of the effects of orthodoxy on Roman Catholic women authors.

Paul Smith, James J. Goodwin Professor of English at Trinity College, is the author of *A Reader's Guide to the Short Stories of Ernest Hemingway* and of a number of articles on Hemingway.

Ben Stoltzfus is Professor of French, Comparative Literature, and Creative Writing at the University of California, Riverside. He is a novelist and critic, as well as the author of *Postmodern Poetics* and "Hemingway's *The Garden of Eden:* A Post-Lacanian Reading."

William Braasch Watson, a Professor of Modern European History at M.I.T., has published widely on Spanish history and edited "Hemingway's Spanish Civil War Dispatches" for *The Hemingway Review*.

Robert P. Weeks was Professor of Humanities at the Residential College at the University of Michigan, Ann Arbor, and the editor of *Commonwealth vs. Sacco and Vanzetti* and *Hemingway: A Collection of Critical Essays*.

Amberys R. Whittle, Professor of English at Georgia Southern University, is the author of " 'The Dust of Seasons': Time in the Poetry of Trumbull Stickney" and "*Modern Chivalry:* The Frontier as Crucible," and editor of *The Poems of Trumbull Stickney*.

Hubert Zapf is Professor of English and American Literature at the University of Paderborn, West Germany, and the author of *Saul Bellow; Theory and Structure of Modern English Drama;* and other articles on English and American literature and literary theory.

Jackson J. Benson is Professor of American Literature at San Diego State University. He is the author of *Hemingway: The Writer's Art of Self-Defense* and *The True Adventures of John Steinbeck, Writer: A Biography*, and editor of *The Short Stories of Ernest Hemingway: Critical Essays* and *The Short Novels of John Steinbeck: Critical Essays*.

Permissions

●

"Hemingway's 'Banal Story'" by Wayne Kvam, reprinted from the *Fitzgerald-Hemingway Annual* (1974), copyright 1974 by Bruccoli Clark Layman.

"'This is My Pal Bugs': Ernest Hemingway's 'The Battler'" by George Monteiro, reprinted from *Studies in Short Fiction* 23 (Spring 1986), copyright 1986 by Newberry College.

"Preparing for the End: Hemingway's revisions of 'A Canary for One'" by Scott Donaldson, reprinted from *Studies in American Fiction* 6 (1978), copyright 1978 by Northeastern University.

"*El Pueblo Espanol:* 'The Capital of the World'" by Bernard Oldsey, reprinted from *Studies in American Fiction* 13 (Spring 1985), copyright 1985 by Northeastern University.

"The Poor Kitty and the Padrone and the Tortoise-shell Cat in 'Cat in the Rain'" by Warren Bennett, reprinted from *Hemingway Review* 8 (Fall 1988), copyright 1988 by Ohio Northern University.

"Hemingway's 'The Denunciation': The Aloof American" by Kenneth G. Johnston, reprinted from *Fitzgerald-Hemingway Annual* (1979), copyright 1979 by Bruccoli Clark Layman.

"To Embrace or Kill: 'Fathers and Sons'" by Richard McCann, reprinted from *Iowa Journal of Literary Studies* 3 (1981), copyright 1981 by the University of Iowa.

"Wise-Guy Narrator and Trickster Out-Tricked in Hemingway's 'Fifty Grand'" by Robert P. Weeks, reprinted from *Studies in American Fiction* 10 (1982), copyright 1982 by Northeastern University.

"A Reading of Hemingway's 'The Gambler, the Nun, and the Radio'" by Amberys R. Whittle, reprinted from *Arizona Quarterly* 33 (1977), copyright 1977 by the University of Arizona.

"Gender-Linked Miscommunication in 'Hills Like White Elephants'" by Pamela Smiley, reprinted from *Hemingway Review* 8 (Fall 1988), copyright 1988 by Ohio Northern University.

"Hemingway's Primitivism and 'Indian Camp'" by Jeffrey Meyers, reprinted from *Twentieth Century Literature* 34 (Summer 1988), copyright 1988 by Hofstra University.

"'The Killers': The Map and the Territory" by Robert E. Fleming, reprinted from *Hemingway Review* 4 (Fall 1984), copyright 1984 by Ohio Northern University.

"'The Last Good Country': Again the End of Something" by David R. Johnson, reprinted from *Fitzgerald-Hemingway Annual* (1979), copyright 1979 by Bruccoli Clark Layman.

"Nick Adams and the Search for Light" by Howard L. Hannum, reprinted from *Studies in Short Fiction* 23 (Winter 1986), copyright 1986 by Newberry College.

"'Nobody Ever Dies!': Hemingway's *Fifth* Story of the Spanish Civil War" by Larry Edgerton, reprinted from *Arizona Quarterly* 39 (Summer 83), copyright 1983 by the University of Arizona.

"Hemingway's 'Out of Season': The End of the Line" by William Adair, first printing in this volume.

"Perversion and the Writer in 'The Sea Change'" by Robert E. Fleming, reprinted from *Studies in American Fiction* 14 (1986), copyright 1986 by Northeastern University.

"Coming of Age in Hortons Bay: Hemingway's 'Up in Michigan'" by Alice Hall Petry, reprinted from *Hemingway Review* 3 (Spring 1984), copyright 1984 by Ohio Northern University.